T0191729

Lecture Notes in Computer Science　13312

More information about this series at https://link.springer.com/bookseries/558

Pei-Luen Patrick Rau (Ed.)

Cross-Cultural Design

Applications in Learning, Arts, Cultural Heritage, Creative Industries, and Virtual Reality

14th International Conference, CCD 2022
Held as Part of the 24th HCI International Conference, HCII 2022
Virtual Event, June 26 – July 1, 2022
Proceedings, Part II

 Springer

Editor
Pei-Luen Patrick Rau
Tsinghua University
Beijing, China

ISSN 0302-9743   ISSN 1611-3349 (electronic)
Lecture Notes in Computer Science
ISBN 978-3-031-06046-5   ISBN 978-3-031-06047-2 (eBook)
https://doi.org/10.1007/978-3-031-06047-2

This Springer imprint is published by the registered company Springer Nature Switzerland AG
The registered company address is: Gewerbestrasse 11, 6330 Cham, Switzerland

Foreword

Human-computer interaction (HCI) is acquiring an ever-increasing scientific and industrial importance, as well as having more impact on people's everyday life, as an ever-growing number of human activities are progressively moving from the physical to the digital world. This process, which has been ongoing for some time now, has been dramatically accelerated by the COVID-19 pandemic. The HCI International (HCII) conference series, held yearly, aims to respond to the compelling need to advance the exchange of knowledge and research and development efforts on the human aspects of design and use of computing systems.

The 24th International Conference on Human-Computer Interaction, HCI International 2022 (HCII 2022), was planned to be held at the Gothia Towers Hotel and Swedish Exhibition & Congress Centre, Göteborg, Sweden, during June 26 to July 1, 2022. Due to the COVID-19 pandemic and with everyone's health and safety in mind, HCII 2022 was organized and run as a virtual conference. It incorporated the 21 thematic areas and affiliated conferences listed on the following page.

A total of 5583 individuals from academia, research institutes, industry, and governmental agencies from 88 countries submitted contributions, and 1276 papers and 275 posters were included in the proceedings to appear just before the start of the conference. The contributions thoroughly cover the entire field of human-computer interaction, addressing major advances in knowledge and effective use of computers in a variety of application areas. These papers provide academics, researchers, engineers, scientists, practitioners, and students with state-of-the-art information on the most recent advances in HCI. The volumes constituting the set of proceedings to appear before the start of the conference are listed in the following pages.

The HCI International (HCII) conference also offers the option of 'Late Breaking Work' which applies both for papers and posters, and the corresponding volume(s) of the proceedings will appear after the conference. Full papers will be included in the 'HCII 2022 - Late Breaking Papers' volumes of the proceedings to be published in the Springer LNCS series, while 'Poster Extended Abstracts' will be included as short research papers in the 'HCII 2022 - Late Breaking Posters' volumes to be published in the Springer CCIS series.

I would like to thank the Program Board Chairs and the members of the Program Boards of all thematic areas and affiliated conferences for their contribution and support towards the highest scientific quality and overall success of the HCI International 2022 conference; they have helped in so many ways, including session organization, paper reviewing (single-blind review process, with a minimum of two reviews per submission) and, more generally, acting as goodwill ambassadors for the HCII conference.

This conference would not have been possible without the continuous and unwavering support and advice of Gavriel Salvendy, founder, General Chair Emeritus, and Scientific Advisor. For his outstanding efforts, I would like to express my appreciation to Abbas Moallem, Communications Chair and Editor of HCI International News.

June 2022   Constantine Stephanidis

HCI International 2022 Thematic Areas and Affiliated Conferences

Thematic Areas

- HCI: Human-Computer Interaction
- HIMI: Human Interface and the Management of Information

Affiliated Conferences

- EPCE: 19th International Conference on Engineering Psychology and Cognitive Ergonomics
- AC: 16th International Conference on Augmented Cognition
- UAHCI: 16th International Conference on Universal Access in Human-Computer Interaction
- CCD: 14th International Conference on Cross-Cultural Design
- SCSM: 14th International Conference on Social Computing and Social Media
- VAMR: 14th International Conference on Virtual, Augmented and Mixed Reality
- DHM: 13th International Conference on Digital Human Modeling and Applications in Health, Safety, Ergonomics and Risk Management
- DUXU: 11th International Conference on Design, User Experience and Usability
- C&C: 10th International Conference on Culture and Computing
- DAPI: 10th International Conference on Distributed, Ambient and Pervasive Interactions
- HCIBGO: 9th International Conference on HCI in Business, Government and Organizations
- LCT: 9th International Conference on Learning and Collaboration Technologies
- ITAP: 8th International Conference on Human Aspects of IT for the Aged Population
- AIS: 4th International Conference on Adaptive Instructional Systems
- HCI-CPT: 4th International Conference on HCI for Cybersecurity, Privacy and Trust
- HCI-Games: 4th International Conference on HCI in Games
- MobiTAS: 4th International Conference on HCI in Mobility, Transport and Automotive Systems
- AI-HCI: 3rd International Conference on Artificial Intelligence in HCI
- MOBILE: 3rd International Conference on Design, Operation and Evaluation of Mobile Communications

List of Conference Proceedings Volumes Appearing Before the Conference

18. LNCS 13319, Digital Human Modeling and Applications in Health, Safety, Ergonomics and Risk Management: Anthropometry, Human Behavior, and Communication (Part I), edited by Vincent G. Duffy
19. LNCS 13320, Digital Human Modeling and Applications in Health, Safety, Ergonomics and Risk Management: Health, Operations Management, and Design (Part II), edited by Vincent G. Duffy
20. LNCS 13321, Design, User Experience, and Usability: UX Research, Design, and Assessment (Part I), edited by Marcelo M. Soares, Elizabeth Rosenzweig and Aaron Marcus
21. LNCS 13322, Design, User Experience, and Usability: Design for Emotion, Well-being and Health, Learning, and Culture (Part II), edited by Marcelo M. Soares, Elizabeth Rosenzweig and Aaron Marcus
22. LNCS 13323, Design, User Experience, and Usability: Design Thinking and Practice in Contemporary and Emerging Technologies (Part III), edited by Marcelo M. Soares, Elizabeth Rosenzweig and Aaron Marcus
23. LNCS 13324, Culture and Computing, edited by Matthias Rauterberg
24. LNCS 13325, Distributed, Ambient and Pervasive Interactions: Smart Environments, Ecosystems, and Cities (Part I), edited by Norbert A. Streitz and Shin'ichi Konomi
25. LNCS 13326, Distributed, Ambient and Pervasive Interactions: Smart Living, Learning, Well-being and Health, Art and Creativity (Part II), edited by Norbert A. Streitz and Shin'ichi Konomi
26. LNCS 13327, HCI in Business, Government and Organizations, edited by Fiona Fui-Hoon Nah and Keng Siau
27. LNCS 13328, Learning and Collaboration Technologies: Designing the Learner and Teacher Experience (Part I), edited by Panayiotis Zaphiris and Andri Ioannou
28. LNCS 13329, Learning and Collaboration Technologies: Novel Technological Environments (Part II), edited by Panayiotis Zaphiris and Andri Ioannou
29. LNCS 13330, Human Aspects of IT for the Aged Population: Design, Interaction and Technology Acceptance (Part I), edited by Qin Gao and Jia Zhou
30. LNCS 13331, Human Aspects of IT for the Aged Population: Technology in Everyday Living (Part II), edited by Qin Gao and Jia Zhou
31. LNCS 13332, Adaptive Instructional Systems, edited by Robert A. Sottilare and Jessica Schwarz
32. LNCS 13333, HCI for Cybersecurity, Privacy and Trust, edited by Abbas Moallem
33. LNCS 13334, HCI in Games, edited by Xiaowen Fang
34. LNCS 13335, HCI in Mobility, Transport and Automotive Systems, edited by Heidi Krömker
35. LNAI 13336, Artificial Intelligence in HCI, edited by Helmut Degen and Stavroula Ntoa
36. LNCS 13337, Design, Operation and Evaluation of Mobile Communications, edited by Gavriel Salvendy and June Wei
37. CCIS 1580, HCI International 2022 Posters - Part I, edited by Constantine Stephanidis, Margherita Antona and Stavroula Ntoa
38. CCIS 1581, HCI International 2022 Posters - Part II, edited by Constantine Stephanidis, Margherita Antona and Stavroula Ntoa

http://2022.hci.international/proceedings

Preface

The increasing internationalization and globalization of communication, business and industry is leading to a wide cultural diversification of individuals and groups of users who access information, services and products. If interactive systems are to be usable, useful, and appealing to such a wide range of users, culture becomes an important HCI issue. Therefore, HCI practitioners and designers face the challenges of designing across different cultures, and need to elaborate and adopt design approaches which take into account cultural models, factors, expectations and preferences, and allow to develop cross-cultural user experiences that accommodate global users.

The 14th Cross-Cultural Design (CCD) Conference, an affiliated conference of the HCI International Conference, encouraged papers from academics, researchers, industry and professionals, on a broad range of theoretical and applied issues related to Cross-Cultural Design and its applications.

Cross-cultural design has come to be a lateral HCI subject that deals not only with the role of culture in HCI and across the amplitude of HCI application domains, but also in the context of the entire spectrum of HCI methods, processes, practices, and tools. In this respect, a considerable number of papers were accepted to this year's CCD Conference addressing diverse topics, which spanned a wide variety of domains. One of the most prominent topic categories was interaction design, as seen from a cross-cultural perspective, exploring cross-cultural differences and intercultural design. Application domains of social impact, such as learning, arts and cultural heritage have constituted popular topics this year, as well as work conducted in the context of creative industries and virtual reality. Health, well-being, and inclusiveness were emphasized, as was business and communication, which are fields that were all challenged during the ongoing pandemic. Furthermore, among the contributions, views on contemporary and near-future intelligent technologies were presented, including those addressing mobility and automotive design, as well as design in intelligent environments, cities, and urban areas.

Four volumes of the HCII2022 proceedings are dedicated to this year's edition of the CCD Conference:

- Cross-Cultural Design: Interaction Design Across Cultures (Part I), addressing topics related to cross-cultural interaction design, collaborative and participatory cross-cultural design, cross-cultural differences and HCI, as well as aspects of intercultural design.
- Cross-Cultural Design: Applications in Learning, Arts, Cultural Heritage, Creative Industries, and Virtual Reality (Part II), addressing topics related to cross-cultural learning, training, and education; cross-cultural design in arts and music; creative industries and Cultural Heritage under a cross-cultural perspective; and, cross-cultural virtual reality and games.
- Cross-Cultural Design: Applications in Business, Communication, Health, Well-being, and Inclusiveness (Part III), addressing topics related to intercultural business

communication, cross-cultural communication and collaboration, HCI and the global social change imposed by COVID-19, and intercultural design for well-being and inclusiveness.

- Cross-Cultural Design: Product and Service Design, Mobility and Automotive Design, Cities, Urban Areas, and Intelligent Environments Design (Part IV), addressing topics related to cross-cultural product and service design, cross-cultural mobility and automotive UX design, design and culture in social development and digital transformation of cities and urban areas, and cross-cultural design in intelligent environments.

Papers of these volumes are included for publication after a minimum of two single–blind reviews from the members of the CCD Program Board or, in some cases, from members of the Program Boards of other affiliated conferences. I would like to thank all of them for their invaluable contribution, support and efforts.

June 2022   Pei-Luen Patrick Rau

14th International Conference on Cross-Cultural Design (CCD 2022)

The full list with the Program Board Chairs and the members of the Program Boards of all thematic areas and affiliated conferences is available online at

http://www.hci.international/board-members-2022.php

HCI International 2023

The 25th International Conference on Human-Computer Interaction, HCI International 2023, will be held jointly with the affiliated conferences at the AC Bella Sky Hotel and Bella Center, Copenhagen, Denmark, 23–28 July 2023. It will cover a broad spectrum of themes related to human-computer interaction, including theoretical issues, methods, tools, processes, and case studies in HCI design, as well as novel interaction techniques, interfaces, and applications. The proceedings will be published by Springer. More information will be available on the conference website: http://2023.hci.international/.

General Chair
Constantine Stephanidis
University of Crete and ICS-FORTH
Heraklion, Crete, Greece
Email: general_chair@hcii2023.org

http://2023.hci.international/

Contents – Part II

Creative Industries and Cultural Heritage under a Cross-Cultural Perspective

Cross-Cultural Learning, Training, and Education

From Nature to Reality: The Approach of Transforming Chinese Characters into Product

Jing Cao[1,2(✉)], Po-Hsien Lin[2], and Rungtai Lin[2]

[1] School of Media and Design, Hangzhou Dianzi University,
Hangzhou, People's Republic of China
872027708@qq.com
[2] Graduate School of Creative Industry Design, National Taiwan University of Arts,
New Taipei City, Taiwan
{t0131,rtlin}@ntua.edu.tw

Abstract. Human beings explore the relationship between humans and nature for linking them and pursuing the unity of function and aesthetics. Based on this kind of thought, the creation of "learning from nature" appears. In the past, creators usually focused on the form and function of the product, ignoring the inspiration from nature. Yet, the shape, sound and meaning of Chinese characters coincide with the shape, color and sound in nature, which accurately reflect the notion of "learning from nature". Therefore, this study takes a basic design course as the research sample, which teaches students the methods of transforming Chinese characters into products. The design process was summarized into six types of transformation from Chinese characters to products. Through the course, this study found that: (1) The design process of the six categories of Chinese characters has an obvious effect on inspiring students' creative thinking and can be improved with more design connotation. (2) The approach of transforming Chinese Characters into products has inherent value.

Keywords: Learning from nature · Chinese characters transformation · Product design

1 Introduction

The development of human material civilization follows the rule of "learning from nature," such as "survival of the fittest" and "each is in his proper place" [1, 2]. The natural designs are amazing without artificial processing. Some of them have complete functions, some are beautiful and exquisite, some use reasonable materials that follow the economic principles of nature, and some are even formed according to the rules of mathematics. Chinese characters originated from nature, which embodies the principle of "learning from nature". The earliest Chinese characters were created based on the description of the creature appearance. They are a kind of natural symbols. Chinese characters reflect the process from complex to simple in its evolution. The similarity to real-life objects

P.-L. P. Rau (Ed.): HCII 2022, LNCS 13312, pp. 3–13, 2022.
https://doi.org/10.1007/978-3-031-06047-2_1

continues to decrease, which is a change process from concrete to abstract [3]. It is imperative to find a scientific mode of thinking and observation, help students majoring in design understand the principle and basis of natural modeling through the design teaching of Chinese characters, and train designers' abilities to analyze, understand, and create things.

At present, the international design trend has gradually shifted from design execution to design thinking. However, most design education still focuses on "perceptual" or "technical" teaching, lacking rational thinking and scientific teaching modes [4]. There are cognitive differences between rational thinking and design thinking. Design thinking often adopts irrational conjectures to think about problems and tends to infer rather than demonstrate, and it also includes design education [5–7]. This kind of educational environment will make students only copy rigid models and design methods after entering society, which is not beneficial to designers and the development of the design industry in future. Design is a comprehensive discipline that needs to integrate perceptual thinking and rational thinking. Simon pointed out in the theory of limited rationality that rationality is important but limited. Rationality and irrationality play irreplaceable roles in human activities and civilization progress, restricting, and promoting each other [8]. Innovative thinking requires free imagination, but reasonable design modes and methods can appropriately focus the scope of imagination and provide a reference for rational thinking of design. Based on this, this study takes Chinese characters as the study case and teaching as the carrier, introduces the design methods of cultural products, integrates the design principle and design process of "learning from nature" into design teaching through Chinese characters, evaluates the teaching effect with scientific methods, and discusses how to enhance the original creativity and integration ability of students majoring in design. The purposes and outstanding issues of this study are as follows:

Purposes of the Study:

1. To carry out design thinking cultivation and help students understand the relationship between nature and design and the key points of design through the principle of "learning from nature."
2. To carry out design education practice, take teaching of design methods as a basic skill, summarize the design process of the six categories of Chinese characters, and incorporate and improve design culture characteristics and innovative thinking.

2   Literature Discussion

2.1   Importance and Transformation Modes of "Learning from Nature"

Everything in nature has gone through natural selection and evolution for hundreds of millions of years, and the truths arising there serve as a basis for the generation of various types of designs. The essence of human and natural creation can be summarized as "survival design". The consciousness of nature worship and reverence for life is of practical significance to contemporary human survival and production modes [9]. For designers, nature is like an inexhaustible design database. Nature hides design inspiration and excellent design everywhere. Mastering the design principle of nature is an important part of design learning. First, human's cognition for object form starts from nature. Understanding nature helps designers learn about the essence of object shape. Second, product forms are used to express design ideas and to create information [10] to understand the reasons for the existence of forms. Third, understanding nature meets the experience needs of modern people for product pleasure [11] bringing the concept of coordinated development between humans and nature into design. Finally, understanding nature can stimulate designers' inspiration and creativity, and explore richer design language forms [12, 13]. Therefore, when practicing the design principle of "learning from nature," designers do not simply carry out imitation, but extract and summarize the organic forms of nature [13, 14].

There are countless cases of mastering the transformation of natural forms into the symbolic images. Simplification is an important way to extract and summarize natural images [15–17]. It is a process of reducing and summarizing the details and structure of objects, which can more clearly express their esthetic perception [18]. Graphic simplification method can be divided into two modes: overall shape extraction, and component feature extraction [19].

2.2 Significance of Integrating Chinese Character Transformation Design into Teaching

The formation of Chinese characters is the thinking expression of the ancients to understand the world. The esthetics and modeling of Chinese characters can be regarded as the unity of "standing image and doing everything". At the beginning of its formation, it contains the concept of a character plane object [20]. The thinking mode derived from Chinese characters affects the development of culture, literature, art, and other fields and profoundly impacts the design of cultural products [21]. The product modeling of Chinese character transformation often shows the meaning of pictographic symbols, which are deeply related to nature. Chinese characters are born from nature, and the products are indirect bionics of nature to some extent, which constitute the design esthetics of "learning from nature" [22]. Therefore, it is a meaningful and unique direction to start teaching cultural product design with Chinese characters, take materials from the three-dimensional modeling of natural objects, transform them into the plane image of Chinese characters, and then create a cultural product design from the plane image of Chinese characters. Studies have shown that the thinking mode of novice designers will go through the stages from representation to abstraction, from simple abstraction, simplifying shape, reorganizing structure, and adding personal imagination [23]. Chinese characters belong to the creation of processing shapes, and there are many common principles with the form of character formation. The method and composition of Chinese characters are the crystallization of the wisdom and ingenuity of our ancestors. Designers can use the characteristics of Chinese characters to develop creative laws, apply the shape and proportion structure of Chinese characters, and then stimulate the form and shape of innovative ideas [24].

2.3 Design Program and Application of Chinese Character Transformation Products

At present, the application of Chinese characters in the design of product modeling can be roughly planned in two ways: one is based on products, while the other is based on characters. However, no matter whether the designer is based on characters or products, several steps need to be followed in the process of applying Chinese characters to design. Because the abstraction of Chinese characters is a highly rational product of simplification [25]. Therefore, the designer first needs to understand the meaning represented by Chinese characters and to think about which products are more suitable for the meaning of Chinese characters. In Explaining Words and Analyzing Compound Characters by Shen Xu (a Chinese litterateur in the Eastern Han Dynasty), the characteristics of the structures of Chinese characters were summarized as "the six categories of Chinese characters," namely, self-explanatory characters, pictographic characters, associative compounds, pictophonetic characters, phonetic loan characters, and synonymous characters [26].

"The six categories of Chinese characters" are the basic features of Chinese character formation and the basic idea of the creative design of Chinese characters. The concise and abstract configuration of Chinese characters is the best embodiment of the characteristics of "abstract" and "freehand brushwork" [27], which have important reference value for the study of the modeling of Chinese characters and the creative design derived from Chinese characters. At present, there are few studies on the relationship between the six categories of Chinese characters and design or on how to convert Chinese characters into cultural products. The application of the six categories of Chinese characters in interpreting the meaning of product design echoes the use of nature to interpret the design intention.

In addition to modeling, the most important thing in the design of the cultural products of Chinese characters is how to express their meaning and esthetic principles in a reasonable way [27]. The design process of cultural products is the same as that of words, which is an innovation of complexity, simplification, and essence. Figure 1 is the procedure for the design of Chinese character transformation cultural products summarized according to the above thinking logic [27], reflecting the specific mode and steps of exploring Chinese characters featuring "artistic creation comes from learning from nature, but the beauty of nature cannot automatically become the beauty of art. For this transformation process, the artist's inner feelings and structure are indispensable." "The three Chinese characters "YI," "MING," and "CHEN" are the practice of analyzing the form and structure of Chinese characters and indicate the meaning of the six categories of Chinese characters. The two-dimensional pattern of "YI" is the transformation of pictographic characters and self-explanatory characters, representing the analysis of form feature. The two-dimensional pattern of "MING" is the transformation of associative compounds and pictophonetic characters, representing the analysis of function feature. The two-dimensional pattern of "CHEN" is the transformation of synonymous characters and phonetic loan characters, representing the analysis of impression feature. When transforming to three-dimensional product design, the designer triggers synesthesia imagination through two-dimensional patterns, integrates the semantics of two-dimensional graphics through the three characteristics of six categories of Chinese characters and product form, and visually extracts the factors of forms to construct product design. The supporter transformed by the character "LU" comes from the variation and deconstruction of the form features of Chinese characters. "JU" means dwelling and house in Chinese characters. As a supporter design, it is the embodiment of shape following function. The CD shelf transformed by the character "CE" is derived from the meaning of ancient bamboo books, which display impressions and cultural connotations.

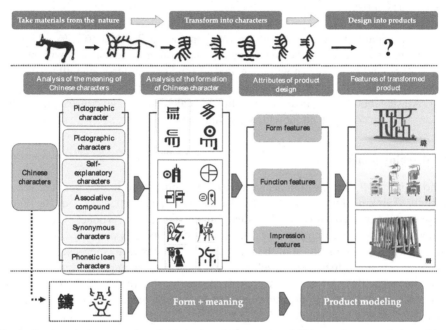

Fig. 1. Product design procedure for imitating six categories of Chinese characters (adopted from [27]).

3 Teaching Implementation

3.1 Teaching Input and Object

The scope and implementation of this study are as follows:

1. Teaching research is implemented in the freshman compulsory course of the Department of art and design. The course name is "basis of design", with a total of 48 class hours and completed in 6 weeks.
2. The course is a compulsory core course, which is divided into three stages and independent units. It is required to enable students to master the basic skills and related concepts of two-dimensional and three-dimensional design in teaching.
3. Evaluation of teaching results (students): after each stage of the course, teachers will issue a mutual evaluation form, and students are invited to observe and evaluate the

works. Please state your learning experience at each stage and record it. In order to timely grasp the implementation effect of the teaching design proposed in this study at the corresponding stage, and let students integrate into teaching activities.

4. Teaching result evaluation (teacher): the teacher will recycle the students' self-evaluation form and learning experience, and evaluate and score the three assignments in combination with the students' classroom performance. In addition to the teachers, three teachers and professors with rich teaching experience are invited to score the course.

The participants were 37 students in total, including 25 girls (67.5%), 12 boys (32.5%), and one teacher. At the end of the course, another three teachers with professional background in art design will be invited. A total of four teachers will participate in the scoring. All four teachers have many years of teaching experience and design creativity. All students have basic drawing ability and calculator model construction skills, and complete the course in an individual teaching unit.

3.2 Teaching Steps

As shown in Fig. 2, the teaching design divides the course into three steps: Pre-school Creativity, Thinking Inspiration, and Course Design. The vertical axis of the figure represents the expected progress of students' understanding of product type features, functional features, and impression features after the course is promoted, in order to increase the design connotation of the product. The transverse axis represents the core content corresponding to the three teaching steps, which aims to improve logical thinking skills. The course design formulates a feasible teaching plan for the theme of "Chinese characters". The objectives include transforming cultural products, setting a gradual course framework and content, analyzing, evaluating the excellent works produced by the teaching after the teaching process is finished, allowing students to understand the essence of "learning from nature" design, and revealing teaching results in order to reflect.

Step 1: Pre-school Creativity.
On the condition that the teacher does not teach basic design theory, students take their Chinese names as an example (choose three Chinese characters) and design creative products according to their understanding of design, so as to experience the cultural philosophy of "learning from nature" and "Chinese characters".

Step 2: Thinking Inspiration.
After the "learning from nature" phase, the universality and importance of "learning from nature" are conveyed to the students, and the relationship between Chinese characters and nature is emphasized. Afterwards, the origin and thought process of the natural transformation of Chinese characters from the six categories of Chinese characters are illustrated. After mastering the basic theoretical knowledge, the students are asked to simplify and abstract their Chinese names and design 2D visual transformations in order to apply the concept of element extraction and variant elements in the design of three-dimensional Chinese character transformation products.

Step 3: Course Design.

After the first two steps, comprehensive training is applied. Students are required to design cultural and creative products based on their Chinese names. According to the four steps of the situational story method, this study discusses the feasibility and possibility of Chinese character design of one's own name. This step is designed to test students' mastery of design thinking and design mode as well as evaluate students' mastery of design software and their ability to apply design effects.

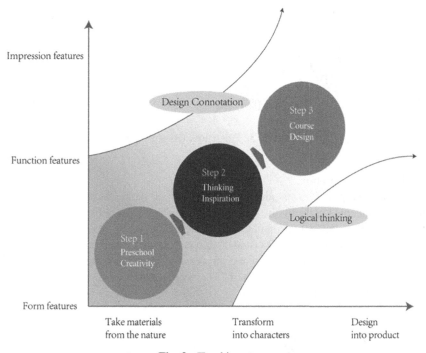

Fig. 2. Teaching steps

4   Teaching Cases and Discussion

Chinese characters contain various elements, including shape, sound and meaning. Because of this, it is difficult to correctly apply the relationship between the shape and meaning of Chinese characters to the shape of the products. The following are the results of the application of Chinese characters in product form design based on the three steps of teaching. These results indicate that the form of the product derived from the shape and meaning of the Chinese characters is imaginative and creative.

Step 1: Pre-school Creativity.

Figure 3 shows the work designed by students before systematic teaching of curriculum theory. Case A (Left side in Fig. 3) is a cabinet. The main concept is derived from the association of the Chinese character "Qiao". The author is a female student whose Chinese name contains the Chinese character "Qiao", which means lively and lovely in Chinese. Red and rounded lines are used to represent the meaning of the text. Case B (Right side in Fig. 3) is a pen holder designed according to the Chinese character of the number "Nine". The design of the two works echoes the pictographic features of characters. Special attention was given in expressing the appearance of the product, but there's still room for improvement in finding the balance between form and function.

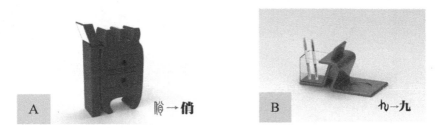

Fig. 3. Per-school cases

Step 2: Thinking Inspiration.
Figure 4 is an example of how students deconstruct their names based on the simplified and abstract concepts taught by the teacher. Case C (Left side in Fig. 4) is the analysis of the Chinese character "Chen", and Case D (Right side in Fig. 4) is the analysis of the Chinese character "Ming". The 2D visual design is designed based on the characteristics of Chinese character's form, function and impression. In the next step, we establish the basics on how to use the characteristics of "The six categories of Chinese characters" to transform product modeling.

Fig. 4. Thinking Inspiration cases

Step 3: Course Design.
Figure 5 shows the design of two lamps obtained as a result of a transformation from the Chinese character "Ming". Case E (Left side in Fig. 5) is transformed according to the morphological characteristics and functional characteristics of the Chinese character "Ming". The overall shape is similar to the appearance of the Chinese character "Ming", with a simple and neat sense of composition. Case F (Right side in Fig. 4) is based on the impression characteristics and functional characteristics of the Chinese character

"Ming". There is a Chinese idiom that goes, "moonlight and stars are rare", which means that when the moon is bright, all the stars appear and the earth becomes brighter. The two cases in Fig. 5 are inspired by Case D in Fig. 4, echoing the cultural connotation of the Chinese character "Ming".

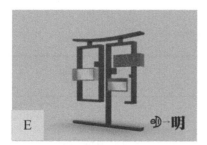 

Fig. 5. Course Design cases

5 Research Conclusion

After the course, a total of 13 works were used as research cases for questionnaire evaluation to evaluate the teaching effect. The following conclusions were obtained:

1. Effective Teaching. After the questionnaire was analyzed by statistical software, as shown in Table 1, the two works with the highest average score in creative evaluation were the CD rack transformed from Chinese character "CE" and the lamp transformed from Chinese character "MING". The lowest-scoring works were an umbrella stand trans-formed from Chinese character "YU" and a sheltering frame transformed from the Chinese character for "PEI". It can be seen that "CE" is the award-winning work and "MING" is the course design work, which was completed after the course theory and model were taught. "Yu" and "PEI" are pre-school creative works created by students' own understanding before the course. Therefore, it can be inferred that the teaching mode is effective.
2. Teaching significance. This teaching design can effectively stimulate students to transform plane elements into abstract and three-dimensional visual association, master systematic and comprehensive design skills, and stimulate students' innovative thinking. Through logical analysis of the teaching design and original "sensibility" abstract, the cultural elements and connotations are extracted. Furthermore, through the theoretical research method and the design process, we link the students' design practice and case studies and guide them towards the "rational" logical thinking direction in order to improve the students' creativity, imagination, and verify whether the teaching method can improve innovation ability.
3. Shorten the gap between theory and practice. By exploring the cultural connotation of "nature" borrow from Chinese characters in order to apply it to the product design program "theory" performed by the practical design case content, encouraging students to explore the essential connotation of Chinese culture, learn about the

connotation of the characters in the psychological awareness course, analyze different design concepts starting from "things" to "content", learn about the process of improving emotional experience and cultural connotation, as well as bridge the gap between design procedures and patterns and design practices.

Table 1. Creative evaluation results

Chinese characters	Chinese phonetic alphabet	5. Design cases	6. Main content
冊	CE		CD rack: "CE" represented many bamboo slips were connected in series to become "one volume". The design used a CD rack to interpret the understanding of "CE".
明	MING		Lamp: "MING" means light and brightness. The design interprets the understanding of "MING" with the morphological variation and literal meaning of Chinese characters.
雨	YU		Umbrella stand: "YU" means rain and rainy day. The design interprets the understanding of "YU" with an umbrella stand.
裴	PEI		Bookshelf: "PEI" is the last name of the creator. The design is based on the analysis of the two-dimensional form of Chinese characters.

References

1. Lin, R.: A study of nature form for basic design instruction. J. Technol. **2**(1), 17–24 (1987)
2. Liu, G.Z., Li, Y.C.: Wheels and design. New Art **27**(2), 96–102 (2006)
3. Lin, H.Y., Lin, R., Hsieh, H.Y.: Exploring the possibilities of transforming Chinese characters into product design. J. Design **10**(2), 77–88 (2005)

4. Why Design Education Must Change. https://www.core77.com/posts/17993/why-design-edu cation-must-change-17993. Accessed 26 Nov 2016
5. Dorst, K.: The core of 'design thinking' and its application. Des. Stud. **32**(6), 521–532 (2011)
6. Razzouk, R., Shute, V.: What is design thinking and why is it important? Rev. Educ. Res. **82**(3), 330–348 (2012)
7. Eke, A.S.M., Usta, G.: The first year of design education: abstract-concrete problem-centered model. Glob. J. Arts Educ. **6**(1), 11–19 (2016)
8. Simon, H.A.: Bounded rationality. In: Eatwell, J., Milgate, M. (eds.) Utility and Probability. Palgrave Macmillan, London (1990)
9. Yu, F.: The concept and trend of bionic design. ZhuangShi **37**(4), 25–27 (2013)
10. McHarg, I.L.: Design with Nature. American Museum of Natural History, New York (1969)
11. Roy, R., Goatman, M., Khangura, K.: User-centric design and Kansei engineering. CIRP J. Manuf. Sci. Technol. **1**(3), 172–178 (2009)
12. Bar-Cohen, Y.: Biomimetics—using nature to inspire human innovation. Bioinspir. Biomim. **1**(1), 1–12 (2006)
13. Luo, S.J., Zhang, Y.F., Bian, Z., Shan, P.: Research status and progress of bionic design of product shape. J. Mech. Eng. **54**(21), 138–155 (2018)
14. Tian, B.Z.: Analysis of bionic design methods. Art Design **3**(3), 169–171 (2009)
15. Coelho, D.A.: A comparative analysis of six bionic design methods. Int. J. Design Eng. **4**(2), 114–131 (2011)
16. Lu, J.N.: Analysis of biomorphic feature extraction in bionic design. ZhuangShi **32**(1), 136–138 (2009)
17. Rinaldi, A.: Naturally better: science and technology are looking to nature's successful designs for inspiration. EMBO Rep. **8**(11), 995–999 (2007)
18. Arnheim, R.: Visual Thinking. University of California Press, Oakland (1997)
19. Hsu, C.C., Wang, W.Y.: Categorization and features of simplification methods in visual design. Art Design Rev. **6**(1), 12–28 (2018)
20. Papanek, V., Fuller, R.B.: Design for the Real World. Thames & Hudson, London (1972)
21. Han, T.T.: The literary creation of imitation furniture – taking hieroglyphics as an example. J. Nanjing Acad. Arts: Art Design Edn. **39**(4), 191–193 (2016)
22. Lu, H.P., Lin, H.H.: From representation to abstraction: discussion on the thinking modes of novice designers. In: Education and Awareness of Sustainability: Proceedings of the 3rd Eurasian Conference on Educational Innovation 2020, Hanoi, Vietnam, pp. 437–441 (2020)
23. Fu, M.C., Sun, Q.W., Yang, Y.J.: An experimental study on promoting recognition of Chinese character shape. J. Art **2**(102), 41–63 (2018)
24. Li, G.W.: Research on the visual schema design of image Chinese characters inspired by the word formation method of "six categories of Chinese characters." Packag. Eng. (Art Edn.) **36**(18), 110–114 (2015)
25. Xu, S.: Explaining Words and Analyzing Compound Characters. Zhonghua Book Company, Beijing (2013)
26. Luo, D.Q.: Pictograph, pictorial meaning and ideographic expression – on the existence of aesthetic symbols of Chinese characters. J. Nanjing Norm. Univ. (Soc. Sci. Edn.) **3**(5), 141–147 (2014)
27. Lin, R.: Learn from the design of the six categories of Chinese characters. Art Appreciat. (2005)

Utilization of XR Technology in Distance Collaborative Learning: A Systematic Review

Jiadong Chen[1] and Shin'ichi Konomi[2(✉)]

[1] Graduate School of Information Science and Electrical Engineering,
Kyushu University, Fukuoka, Japan
`chen.jiadong.450@s.kyushu-u.ac.jp`
[2] Faculty of Arts and Science, Kyushu University, Fukuoka, Japan
`konomi@artsci.kyushu-u.ac.jp`

Abstract. Extended reality technology are raising high hopes among researchers for its use to overcome the difficulties associated with spatial separation in collaborative learning. In this work, a systematic review of the research literature was conducted on the use of extended reality (XR) technology to support distance collaborative learning. We searched Web of Science to collect relevant articles. The articles were manually screened using the inclusion and exclusion criteria which refer to PRISMA [23]. By examining the relevant articles closely, we show the advantages of using XR technology in collaborative learning, such as increasing engagement, increasing students' interest, and facilitating student interactions. We then analyse the challenges in the application of XR, such as skill requirements for teachers and students, lack of accessibility, and technical issues. Finally, we put forward suggestions for the future development of XR-supported distance collaborative learning environments.

Keywords: Collaborative learning · Virtual reality · Extended reality

1 Introduction

In the last two decades digital technology has been increasingly used for educational purposes. Networked computers have been used as tools for collaborative learning, and online digital learning became widespread in the last ten years [35]. People have explored the potential of various novel technologies including extended reality (XR) technology for supporting education. XR technology, as a general concept encompassing VR, AR, and MR technologies, is rapidly growing and being applied in wide range of application domains including education.

In 2020, COVID-19 broke out on a global scale. In order to curb the spread of the virus, people have to maintain social distancing. This situation has brought a huge impact on teaching activities, especially the teaching based on the collaborative learning mode. Collaborative learning as an educational approach presupposes that learners work in pairs or groups to solve problems, discuss concepts,

P.-L. P. Rau (Ed.): HCII 2022, LNCS 13312, pp. 14–29, 2022.
https://doi.org/10.1007/978-3-031-06047-2_2

complete tasks, or create products [18]. At a time when traditional education has almost completely shifted to a distance mode, how the intervention of XR technology will affect collaborative learning in the context of the viral pandemic becomes a valuable question to be explored.

There have been several studies reviewing the application of XR in educational setting [1,22,28], but they usually focus only on VR or AR alone, and do not specifically focus on distance collaborative learning. Therefore, in this review, we will focus on the applications of XR in distance collaborative learning. Under the guidance of PRISMA [23], we collect relevant articles from the digital databases on Web of Science. The content of the articles is analysed to reveal the advantages and challenges of applying XR. We then, discuss and provide our suggestions for the future developments of XR-supported distance collaborative learning environments.

2   Related Work

With the launch of consumer-grade XR products, such as HTC Vive and Samsung Gear VR, researchers have been interested in exploring the application of XR technology. In previous studies, several reviews have already explored the advantages and challenges of XR.

Suh et al. [31] focused on exploring the state of research on immersive technologies, and they set their research in the areas of education, marketing, business and healthcare. In their research, the authors categorise and integrate factors related to the use of immersive technologies through a literature review approach and propose a categorical theoretical framework for the use of immersive technologies. However, this work overview the research methods and theories applied in immersion technology research, but education issues have not been paid special attention.

Jensen and Konradsen [15] reviewed the use of head mounted display (HMD) in education and training of skills acquisition. They focused on the impact of immersion and presence factors on learning. The results confirmed that HMD can be used to acquire cognitive, psychomotor and affective skills. The research only investigated VR based on HMD devices and other technologies such as desktop-based VR applications were excluded. Radianti et al. [28] also focused on HMD in their review, but they included more types of learning in the analysis. The authors provide a perspective on previous research in terms of learning content, design elements and educational theory, revealing that the development of current VR applications is rarely based on educational theories and few articles describe in detail how to use VR-based systems in teaching. This makes the current VR application still in the experimental stage.

Akçayır et al. [1] argue for the need to fill the gap that no comprehensive explication of the educational effects and implications of AR exists [29]. They review the research on AR technology in education and summarise its advantages and challenges. The results show that AR's support for learning and teaching is significant, and that the biggest challenge at the moment is the usability of AR technology. The article also highlights the fact that when studying the usability of AR technology, particular care must be taken to exclude factors such as lack of technical experience or interface design errors from interfering with the results.

Camilleri et al. [6] discuss that the e-learning platforms need to shift from simplistic and monolithic frameworks dealing with the fundamentals of course management, design, and delivery, to more flexible paradigms involving active learners and the use of external stimuli that augment their motivation. Alzahrani et al. [2] set the exploration of the benefits and the challenges of using AR specifically in the context of e-learning. In the review, the authors mention that the use of AR technology can enhance kinesthetic and collaborative learning, realize high-risk real-time e-learning, and visualize interactive objects to support real-world simulations, and improve learners' motivation, satisfaction, attention and content retention. They pointed out that the learning, pedagogical, and technological issues are the current challenges to adopt and implement AR.

Barteit et al. [3] extended the techniques involved in the systematic review to XR. They discussed the effectiveness of VR, AR, and MR in medical education. Their results show that HMD-based VR and AR are most commonly used in training in the field of surgery and anatomy. Compared with traditional teaching and training, students have shown greater enthusiasm and fun when receiving training in the use of XR. Meanwhile, most of the HMD-based interventions are still small-scale, as short-term pilots and difficult to carry out on a large scale. But the value of XR as an additional tool for medical teaching is recognized. However, the value of XR as an additional tool for medical teaching is recognized.

Based on previous review studies, we found that few reviews have focused on examining the potential of XR technology as an interactive tool, and online usage scenarios have not been paid special attention. Therefore, driven by the current context, this review will focus on online collaborative learning and examine the application of various technologies in educational settings under the XR concept.

3   Methods

3.1   Search Strategy

A systematic search was carried out to collect articles relevant to the purpose of this study. The search was conducted on the Web of Science which is one of the world's largest online academic databases. In order to ensure the quality of the articles collected in this review, the scope of the indexes was restricted to the: Web of Science Core Collection (SCI-EXPANDED, SSCI, A&HCI, CPCI-S, CPCI-SSH, BKCI-S, BKCI-SSH, ESCI, CCR-EXPANDED, IC). There is no limit on the publication period of the documents in the search, but non-English articles was not included in this review.

To make the search more comprehensive and accurate. Based on the interest of this review, we attempted to select search terms from three aspects: technology, educational format, and scenario, respectively, as illustrated in Table 1. The XR concepts include Augmented Reality, Virtual Reality, Mixed Reality, but since we consider all technologies that fit the XR concepts, we have used

Boolean operators to link these keywords in order not to create omissions. It is worth noting that the abbreviations AR, MR, VR, were not used because the researchers found through their attempts that these abbreviations would be ambiguous with the abbreviations of concepts in other fields, which led to a large number of irrelevant studies being retrieved. XR has not been excluded because it is not a direct abbreviation of other phrases, and it has come to be regarded as a independent term. However, when referring to technologies such as VR and AR in articles, the full name is often used first. As for the educational forms, we wanted to cover more educational strategies that require rich interactions among students in our review. Therefore, in addition to collaborative learning, we added problem-based learning, team-based learning, and other educational forms as keywords. In addition, spatial segregation needs to be specifically emphasized, so keywords such as online, remote, etc. are linked in the search terms with the Boolean operator 'and' to avoid obtaining results in a face-to-face scenario.

Table 1. Query term

	"XR" OR "Extended Realty" OR "Virtual Reality" OR "Augmented Reality" OR "Mixed Reality"
AND	"online" OR "remote" OR "distant"
AND	"Collaborative Learning" OR "Cooperative learning" OR "CSCL" OR "Computer-Supported Collaborative Learning" OR "project-based learning" OR "pbl" OR "problem-based learning" OR "tbl" OR "team-based learning"

3.2 Inclusion and Exclusion Criteria

In order to set clear boundaries and scope for the inclusion of publications and articles, inclusion and exclusion criteria were developed. These criteria were set after the research questions and objectives had been identified. The use of these standards will be able to emphasize the focus of this research. The purpose of this research is to review previous work and provide insights for researchers to solve the interaction difficulties caused by spatial separation in collaborative under the current pandemic. Essentially, what we want to improve is the quality of education. To this end, the included research work should be carried out in the educational context. After that, the analyzsd XR applications should be able to be used by multiple users. This is due to the fact that we are concerned with how XR is used to handle interactions. The XR applications discussed or proposed in the articles should allow remote students to join, not only in offline or face-to-face scenarios because spatial separation is an indispensable factor. In particular, the objects studied in some articles include both face-to-face student groups and online student groups. If the focus of the research is on how to promote cross-group interaction, the article will be included [4]. The articles included in this study need to be published, which increases the credibility of the articles. Only articles in English were included in the review. Due to language barriers, there may be misunderstandings when reviewing non-English articles. In this review, duplicate articles will be removed. Some studies may have multiple versions of articles, we only keep the original articles for analysis. Finally, the article needs to be accessible, and it cannot be reviewed if the original text is not available.

The abstracts and titles of all retrieved articles are reviewed by the researcher to determine whether they are relevant. If deemed relevant and eligible, the full text will be searched and a full review will be conducted. The inclusion and exclusion criteria established above, as illustrated in Table 2, will be used to screen these articles when reading the full text.

Table 2. Inclusion and exclusion criteria.

Inclusion criteria	Exclusion criteria
Using XR in education setting	Using XR in other scenarios
Multi-user application	Single user application
Allow remote students to participate	All students need to be face to face
Written in English	Non-English publication
Published study	Unpublished study
Original publication	Duplicate
Accessible	Inaccessible

3.3   Data Extraction and Synthesis

As mentioned above, the researcher reviewed the full text of articles that met the criteria. With reference to [2], we adopted thematic synthesis method for article content analysis [32]. This method can be applied to the synthesis of qualitative and quantitative data, and can highlight patterns in the data by summarizing evidence. The thematic synthesis method includes three steps: the coding of text "line-by-line"; the development of "descriptive themes"; and the generation of "analytical themes". The first step will mainly involve coding. The researcher develops a code framework for the data, and all articles selected by the inclusion and exclusion criteria will be coded by the reviewer. In the second step of the analysis, the similarities between the codes will be compared. Similar codes will be further grouped into descriptive themes, and this allows patterns in cross-research data to be captured. The final step will involve the development of analytical topics. In this step, we will mainly synthesize the results of the research and explain their implications for the research question in order to obtain data-based insights. Furthermore, in this review, we also used a hybrid analysis method to analyse the articles content based on the code. The analysis results will be presented in the following chapters.

The coding of the data was conducted by using on the qualitative analysis software MAXQDA, which provided the functionality and qualitative and mixed methods of analysis to assist the reviewer in coding the articles. The descriptive summaries extracted from the data were summarized in a table developed by the researcher. The key items in the table include author and publication year, participant types, advantages, challenges, etc.

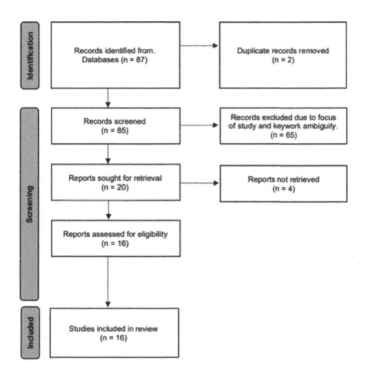

Fig. 1. PRISMA flow diagram.

4   Results

4.1   Search Results

According to the method described in the previous section, we searched the Web of Science database and initially obtained 87 articles. The titles and abstracts of these articles were further reviewed. Due to the ambiguity brought by the search terms, such as searched because the abbreviation author's name is XR, we have excluded 7 articles. Using the above inclusion and exclusion criteria, 58 articles were deemed inconsistent with the theme of this review, so only 22 articles finally entered the stage of full-text review. As there was no open access, the full-texts of the 4 articles were not available, so they were excluded. In the remaining articles we found cases where there were multiple articles describing the same work, for example [7,12], and we reserve the study for only those articles whose focus is more related with this review. In the end, 16 articles were screened and used to analyse the use of XR technology in distance collaborative learning. The entire screening process is shown in Fig. 1.

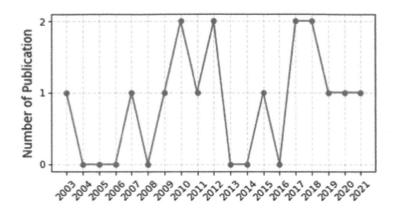

Fig. 2. Publication year of the selected papers

4.2 Results of the Mixed Analysis

The content of selected articles is coded according to qualitative analysis methods. Some of the code statistics are showed to help us discover patterns in the data. First, the publication year of the article is counted as a variable, as illustrated in Fig. 2.

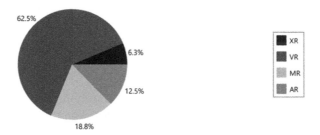

Fig. 3. Type of technology used

For the types of technology covered in the study, 10 of the 16 articles are VR, three are MR, two are AR, and one is XR, as illustrated in Fig. 3. The XR here stands for the article covers the multiple techniques.

In addition, the education level of the participants was also examined. Participants were divided according to education level, but there were also cases where the educational level of participants was not mentioned in the study, for these articles were coded as none noted. Of the results, eight researches had participants with university-level education or higher, one with high school level, two with primary level, four with their level unknown, one with no participants, and one where the participant were teachers, as illustrated in Fig. 4.

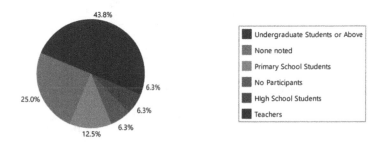

Fig. 4. Education level of participants

In particular, teachers are not here to participate in research as students who use XR technology for learning, but as managers who use XR for education.

4.3   Results of the Thematic Analysis

Through thematic analysis, we have summarised the content of the article in terms of descriptive themes, as illustrated in Table 3. The results show that XR has a variety of benefits in online collaborative learning which include the virtual environment can provid the sense of presence for students, XR can enhance learners interest and improving their learning experience, the use of avatars facilitates student interaction, etc. Also, some challenges in application of XR are also identified, such as the impact of network quality on online learning, issues regarding the equipment required to use XR, and whether teachers and students have sufficient skills for XR, etc.

Table 3. Summary of research methods, advantages and challenges.

Author/Date	Methods	Benefits	Challenges
Bower 2017 [4]	Interview, Questionnaire	Provide a sense of presence. Increased student participation and interaction	Technical performance affects the learning experience. There are requirements for teachers and students' skills
Han 2020 [11]	Interview	Three-dimensional representation and avatars enhance the sense of social presence. The novelty drives teamwork	None noted
Zhang 2017 [36]	Interview	Can facilitate learning for students with different learning styles	Lack of high speed internet
Thorsteinsson 2010 [33]	Observation	Can be useful in game based cooperative and collaborative activities	The interaction design of VR application affect the students' performance and response speed
Chen 2019 [7]	Questionnaire	Ability to engage students and enhance their learning experience	None noted
Coyne 2018 [8]	Questionnaire	Can provide a sense of engagement and a higher sense of responsibility for students	The VR equipment was uncomfortable to wear and some students felt vertigo
Forland 2021 [9]	Questionnaire	Provide a participatory and inclusive environment with a high level of social presence, and alleviate feelings of loneliness.	Complex set-up and sound issues affect collaboration. High cost of equipment
Gu 2011 [10]	Technology development	Ability to visualise abstract concepts. As a referential anchor for acilitating meaning negotiation in collaboration	None noted
Jong 2003 [16]	Questionnaire	Attracted the interest of teachers and students. The virtual environment can mirror the learner's interpersonal relationship in the real environment	None noted

(*continued*)

Table 3. (*continued*)

Author/Date	Methods	Benefits	Challenges
Kirner 2007 [17]	Case analysis	Ability to facilitate user perception, interaction and motivation. Very useful for stimulating learning and developing group skills	None noted
Le 2015 [19]	Interview, Questionnaire	Positive effect on the sensory, cognitive and emotional aspects of the user	Have additional skills requirements for students and teachers
McArdle 2012 [21]	Questionnaire	Maintaining the interest of participants and creating a sense of presence and social awareness	None noted
Nikolic 2018 [24]	Questionnaire	Provides a strong sense of presence and allows collaboration to occur	None noted
Peña-Ríos 2012 [25]	Technology development	Provides a sense of engagement and enhances the interaction and learning experience	None noted
Petrakou 2010 [26]	Ethnographic	Provides spatiality and increased opportunities for interaction	Students lack usage skills. The virtual environment is difficult to cope with a large number of learning activities
Schaf 2009 [30]	Case analysis	Provides a sense of presence and enhances student motivation. Reduced costs from real experimental materials	Communication quality is limited by network infrastructure

5   Discussion

In this section, the discussion of the study results will be provided. First, through the discussion we will try to answer the current advantages and challenges of XR in online collaborative learning. After that, we will discuss the design of the collected research reports to reveal the general form of current researches.

5.1   Advantages of XR

This systematic review revealed that in the context of distance collaboration learning, the availability of various XR technologies has been investigated. Through statistics on the types of technologies used in the research, we can find that VR is the most used. In these studies, the most recognized advantage of VR is that it can provide students with the sense of participation.

McArdle et al. [21] stated that one of the key attributes of the 3D VR multi-user environment is that can create the sense of both presence and social awareness, along with the ability to collaborate with others. Research by Bulu et al. [5] suggests that a sense of social presence is one of the most important factors influencing participants' positive perceptions of learning outcomes, and therefore an increased sense of presence can facilitate students' learning. Forland et al. [9] mentioned the added benefit that the presence of the VR environment can help alleviate the loneliness experienced during the lockdowns caused by viruses. In addition, interaction through avatars in a virtual environment also increases the presence of the participants to a great extent. Lee et al. [20] asserts that "social presence occurs when technology users successfully simulate other humans or nonhuman intelligences". The virtual space created by VR allows for an added dimension of interaction between students. Entering the virtual environment, students are placed in the spatial dimension, and the interaction between them in informal and non-specific tasks has been increased [26], such as the exchanges between students when they jointly explore the rich environmental information in the virtual space. In addition, having the spatial dimension, allowing researchers to study interpersonal relationships in the real world through the positional relationship of students in a virtual environment [16].

Regarding AR, study [10] mentioned that AR can visualize scientific phenomena, which offers interactively hands-on experiences for students to understand abstract knowledge of science subjects. For collaborative learning, the networked interactive visualization serves as a referential anchor for facilitating meaning negotiation in collaboration, which is beneficial for the construction of mutual understanding. The advantages of visualization capabilities have also been mentioned in some other educational scenarios [27,34], but the ability as an anchor for collaborators' meaning negotiation should be paid special attention in the online environment. The study [17] used AR-based collaboration environment in the education scene, and got the conclusion that such environment is very useful for stimulating learning and the development of ability in group.

MR is a technology between VR and AR, which combines the advantages of AR and VR. In [25,30], the MR Labs developed by the researchers brings a sense of immersion to the learners and enhances their learning experience. The cross-dimensional objects provided in the Labs link online and offline learners to facilitate their interactions. Including VR, AR, MR, these technologies are novel for students, and the freshness of using them will arouse great interest among students. Found by [11], students are driven by the novelty of VR at the beginning, and then quickly focus on the parts related to the learning goals. Compared with other online courses, the higher interest makes students willing to choose VR as a learning platform. Compared with face-to-face courses, students are less willing to drop out [8].

5.2 Challenges of XR

Through the review of the collected articles, we confirmed that the challenge mainly comes from three aspects, These are (1) accessibility (2) technical limitations, and (3) requirements for user skills. In the study [8], some participants reported that the weight of the HMD they were wearing while using VR was too heavy and made them feel uncomfortable to wear. Some students wearing glasses reported difficulty in wearing the HMD and others experienced vertigo during use. In [9], the problem about cost of equipment was pointed out. If the number of participants is too large, it is difficult to have enough equipment to provide for each participant. These mentioned factors restrict the application of XR technology in education on a large scale. However, these challenges mainly involve immersive VR. If display-based VR applications are used, the above problems can be avoided, but this comes at the cost of loss of immersion. Regarding the importance of immersion to learning, we need more research to explore. As for technical limitations, Studies [30] and [36] both mention the impact of the quality of the network on the delivery of the course, especially for some areas where the network is not well established. Study [9] reported complex set-up and sound issues with collaboration tools directly affect the collaboration process and even reduce the willingness of students to use them. When there are a large number of students in a virtual environment, the inability to distinguish the speaker will cause communication difficulties [26].

When using XR technology, the users need certain skills and extra effort, both for the teacher and the student. Teachers need to have technical knowledge of the XR application they are using, so that they can deal with the technical problems that students encounter in the classroom [4]. For the virtual environment and 3D model that will be used in the class, teachers need to prepare in advance [19]. Students' lack of skills will have a direct impact on their interactions. Reference [26], the student need to acquainted with the virtual world before it is possible for them to focus on the actual course content. In particular, one of the collected articles reported a negative result that primary school students did not collaborate effectively in the virtual environment, and the avatars did not play a role [33]. This may be due to the VR environment interaction design. The high cognitive load of using VR environment leads to difficulties for students to collaborate. In statistics on the educational level of the participants, the Fig. 4, we found that most of participants were college students or above. This fact suggests that researchers are more positive about using XR for distance collaborative learning with mature users.

5.3 Research Designs

The current research in this topic has generally adopted a qualitative research design. The methods used by the researchers include questionnaires, ethnography, and interviews. This makes the researcher's analysis mainly based on qualitative data, and the results of the research are more subjective. In these studies, studies that clearly indicate the learning theory on which their analysis is based are also relatively rare. The research is discussed more from the point of view of the usability of the application, and the satisfaction of the users. According to [13,14], students must make meaningful connections to their own lived experiences for authentic learning to take place. The novelty itself is more entertaining and meaningless. Therefore, the good experience reported by the students may be different from the achievement of the learning goals expected by the teacher. In addition, most of the work is similar to exploratory study, they do not focus on clear and specific research questions, but the potential of XR in distance collaborative learning has been confirmed.

6   Conclusions

In this work, we conducted a systematic review of papers focusing on the use of XR in online collaborative learning. By reviewing the collected articles, the advantages of XR are identified. Overall, the use of XR stimulates students' interest, keeps them motivated, and motivates them to persevere in order to achieve their learning goals.

Individually, VR provides students with a strong sense of presence and social awareness, which is regarded as the important factors in collaborative learning. VR also opens up a new dimension for the interaction among students. By being in a virtual environment with spatial attributes, the opportunities for student interaction are increased. Meanwhile, the spatial dimension provides the possibility for researchers to investigate the spatial relationships of students in the virtual space, and with a large number of methods used in the real world to be referenced, we think this is a very interesting direction for future research. AR can visualize complex concepts to help students understand, and in online context, the virtual objects it provides have more prominent advantages as a carrier for interaction between students. MR has the advantages of both. It provides online solutions for some collaborative experimental teaching that needs to interact with actual objects.

In addition, we also summarized three challenges from the review. The first is the lack of accessibility, the inability of the HMD design to accommodate the individual differences of students and the high cost of purchasing the device make the use of XR technology somewhat of a barrier. The second is the technical limitation, network delays and complicated settings can seriously interfere with the course. The third is the need for user skills, with teachers and students requiring training or extra effort before using XR technology. The lack of technical experience can make XR a disincentive to learn instead. The limitation of this study comes from the fact that we only identify relevant studies in the Web of Science database. Although it contains most of the high-impact journals and conference papers in the relevant field, there is still a possibility that some studies related to this topic are missed.

As for the current state of research, the research designs are mostly case studies or exploratory studies, qualitative methods are clearly dominant. At present, this field is still in its infancy, the problems discovered in previous researches need to be further explored under the guidance of educational theory.

Acknowledgement. This work was supported by JSPS KAKENHI Grant Numbers 20H00622 and 17KT0154.

References

1. Akçayır, M., Akçayır, G.: Advantages and challenges associated with augmented reality for education: a systematic review of the literature. Educ. Res. Rev. **20**, 1–11 (2017)
2. Alzahrani, N.M.: Augmented reality: a systematic review of its benefits and challenges in E-learning contexts. Appl. Sci. Basel **10**(16), 5660 (2020). https://doi. org/10.3390/app10165660
3. Barteit, S., Lanfermann, L., Bärnighausen, T., Neuhann, F., Beiersmann, C., et al.: Augmented, mixed, and virtual reality-based head-mounted devices for medical education: systematic review. JMIR Serious Games **9**(3), e29080 (2021)
4. Bower, M., Lee, M.J.W., Dalgarno, B.: Collaborative learning across physical and virtual worlds: factors supporting and constraining learners in a blended reality environment. Br. J. Educ. Technol. **48**(2), 407–430 (2017). https://doi.org/10. 1111/bjet.12435
5. Bulu, S.T.: Place presence, social presence, co-presence, and satisfaction in virtual worlds. Comput. Educ. **58**(1), 154–161 (2012)
6. Camilleri, V., Montebello, M.: Ariel: augmented reality in interactive e-learning (2008)
7. Chen, X., et al.: ImmerTai: immersive motion learning in VR environments. J. Visual Commun. Image Represent. **58**, 416–427 (2019). https://doi.org/10.1016/ j.jvcir.2018.11.039
8. Coyne, L., Takemoto, J.K., Parmentier, B.L., Merritt, T., Sharpton, R.A.: Exploring virtual reality as a platform for distance team-based learning. Currents Pharm Teach. Learn. **10**(10), 1384–1390 (2018). https://doi.org/10.1016/j.cptl.2018.07. 005
9. Forland, E.P., McCallum, S., Estrada, J.G.: Collaborative learning in VR for cross-disciplinary distributed student teams. In: 2021 IEEE Conference on Virtual Reality and 3D User Interfaces Abstracts And Workshops (VRW 2021), IEEE; IEEE Comp Soc; Virbela; Tecnico Lisboa; Immers Learning Res Network; Qualcomm; Vicon; HitLabNZ AIGI; Microsoft; Appen; Facebook Real Labs Res; XR Bootcamp; NSF; Fakespace Labs (2021), 28th IEEE Conference on Virtual Reality and 3D User Interfaces (IEEE VR), ELECTR NETWORK, pp. 320–325, 27 March–03 April (2021). https://doi.org/10.1109/VRW52623.2021.00064
10. Gu, J., Li, N., Duh, H.B.L.: A Remote Mobile Collaborative AR System for Learning in Physics. In: Hirose, M., Lok, B., Majumder, A., Schmalstieg, D. (eds.) 2011 IEEE Virtual Reality Conference (VR), Proceedings of the IEEE Virtual Reality Annual International Symposium, IEEE; IEEE Visualizat & Graph Tech Comm (VGTC); IEEE Comp Soc (2011), IEEE Virtual Reality Conference (VR), pp. 257+, Singapore, 19–23 March 2011

11. Han, S., Resta, P.E.: Virtually authentic: graduate students' perspective changes toward authentic learning while collaborating in a virtual world. Online Learn. **24**(4, SI), 5–27 (2020). https://doi.org/10.24059/olj.v24i4.2326
12. He, T., et al.: Immersive and collaborative Taichi motion learning in various VR environments. In: 2017 IEEE Virtual Reality (VR) Proceedings of the IEEE Virtual Reality Annual International Symposium, IEEE; IEEE Comp Soc; IEEE Comp Soc Visualizat & Graph Tech Comm (2017), 19th IEEE Virtual Reality Conference (VR), Los Angeles, CA, pp. 307–308, 18–22 March 2017
13. Heath, S.B., McLaughlin, M.W.: Learning for anything everyday. J. Curriculum Stud. **26**(5), 471–489 (1994). https://doi.org/10.1080/0022027940260501
14. Hiebert, J.: Problem solving as a basis for reform in curriculum and instruction: the case of mathematics. Educ. Res. **25**(4), 12–21 (1996)
15. Jensen, L., Konradsen, F.: A review of the use of virtual reality head-mounted displays in education and training. Educ. Inf. Technol. **23**(4), 1515–1529 (2017). https://doi.org/10.1007/s10639-017-9676-0
16. Jong, B., Lin, T., Chan, T., Wu, Y.: Using VR technology to support the formation of cooperative learning groups. In: Devedzic, V., Spector, J.M., Sampson, D.G. (eds.) 3rd IEEE International Conference On Advanced Learning Technologies, Proceedings, Informat & Telemat Inst, Ctr Res & Technol Hellas; IEEE Learning Technol Task Force; IEEE Comp Soc; Dais Cultural & Athlet Ctr (2003), 3rd IEEE International Conference on Advanced Learning Technologies, Athens, Greece, pp. 37–41, 09–11 July 2003. https://doi.org/10.1109/ICALT.2003.1215022,
17. Kirner, C., Santin, R., Kirner, T.G., Zorzal, E.R.: Collaborative augmented reality environment for educational applications. In: Cardoso, J., Cordeiro, J., Filipe, J. (eds.) ICEIS 2007: Proceedings of the Ninth International Conference On Enterprise Information Systems: Human-computer Interaction, INSTICC; Univ Madeira; FCT; ACM SIGMIS; Assoc Advancement Artificial Intelligence (2007), 9th International Conference on Enterprise Information Systems, ICEIS 2007, Funchal, Portugal, pp. 257+, 12–16 June 2007
18. Laal, M., Ghodsi, S.M.: Benefits of collaborative learning. Procedia. Soc. Behav. Sci. **31**, 486–490 (2012)
19. Le, Q.T., Pedro, A., Park, C.S.: A social virtual reality based construction safety education system for experiential learning. J. Intell. Robot. Syst. **79**(3–4, SI), 487–506, August 2015. https://doi.org/10.1007/s10846-014-0112-z
20. Lee, K.M.: Presence, explicated. Comm. Theory **14**(1), 27–50, January 2006. https://doi.org/10.1111/j.1468-2885.2004.tb00302.x
21. McArdle, G., Bertolotto, M.: Assessing the application of three-dimensional collaborative technologies within an e-learning environment. Interact. Learn. Environ. **20**(1), 57–75 (2012). https://doi.org/10.1080/10494821003714749
22. Merchant, Z., Goetz, E.T., Cifuentes, L., Keeney-Kennicutt, W., Davis, T.J.: Effectiveness of virtual reality-based instruction on students' learning outcomes in k-12 and higher education: a meta-analysis. Comput. Educ. **70**, 29–40 (2014)
23. Moher, D., Liberati, A., Tetzlaff, J., Altman, D.G., Group, P.: Preferred reporting items for systematic reviews and meta-analyses: the prisma statement. PLoS Med. **6**(7), e1000097 (2009)
24. Nikolic, S., Nicholls, B.: Exploring student interest of online peer assisted learning using mixed-reality technology. In: Auer, M.E., Guralnick, D., Simonics, I. (eds.) Teaching and Learning in a Digital World, vol. 1. Advances in Intelligent Systems and Computing, vol. 715, pp. 48–54 (2018), 20th International Conference on Interactive Collaborative Learning (ICL), Budapest, Hungary, 27–29 September 2017. https://doi.org/10.1007/978-3-319-73210-7_6

25. Pena-Rios, A., Callaghan, V., Gardner, M., Alhaddad, M.J.: Remote mixed reality collaborative laboratory activities: learning activities within the InterReality Portal. In: Li, Y., Zhang, Y., Zhong, N. (eds.) 2012 IEEE/WIC/ACM International Conference on Web Intelligence and Intelligent Agent Technology Workshops, WI-IAT Workshops 2012, vol. 3, IEEE; Assoc Comp Machinery; Web Intelligence Consortium; IEEE Comp Soc; Univ Macau; Hong Kong Baptist Univ; IEEE Comp Soc Tech Comm Intelligent Informat; ACM SIGART (2012). https://doi.org/10.1109/WI-IAT.2012.43,11th IEEE/WIC/ACM International Joint Conference on Web Intelligence and Intelligent Agent Technology (WI-IAT), Macau, Peoples Republic of China, pp. 362–366. 04–07 December 2012
26. Petrakou, A.: Interacting through avatars: virtual worlds as a context for online education. Comput. Educ. **54**(4), 1020–1027, May 2010. https://doi.org/10.1016/j.compedu.2009.10.007
27. Quintero, E., Salinas, P., González-Mendívil, E., Ramírez, H.: Augmented reality app for calculus: a proposal for the development of spatial visualization. Procedia Comput. Sci. **75**, 301–305 (2015)
28. Radianti, J., Majchrzak, T.A., Fromm, J., Wohlgenannt, I.: A systematic review of immersive virtual reality applications for higher education: design elements, lessons learned, and research agenda. Comput. Educ. **147**, 103778 (2020)
29. Radu, I.: Why should my students use AR? a comparative review of the educational impacts of augmented-reality. In: 2012 IEEE International Symposium on Mixed and Augmented Reality, ISMAR, pp. 313–314. IEEE (2012)
30. Schaf, F.M., Mueller, D., Bruns, F.W., Pereira, C.E., Erbe, H.H.: Collaborative learning and engineering workspaces. Ann. Rev. ControL **33**(2), 246–252 (2009). https://doi.org/10.1016/j.arcontrol.2009.05.002
31. Suh, A., Prophet, J.: The state of immersive technology research: a literature analysis. Comput. Hum. Behav. **86**, 77–90 (2018)
32. Thomas, J., Harden, A.: Methods for the thematic synthesis of qualitative research in systematic reviews. BMC Med. Res. Methodol. **8**(1), 1–10 (2008)
33. Thorsteinsson, G., Page, T., Niculescu, A.: Using virtual reality for developing design communication. Stud. Informat Control **19**(1), 93–106 (2010)
34. Virata, R.O., Castro, J.D.L.: Augmented reality in science classroom: perceived effects in education, visualization and information processing. In: Proceedings of the 10th International Conference on E-Education, E-Business, E-Management and E-Learning, pp. 85–92 (2019)
35. Zawacki-Richter, O., Latchem, C.: Exploring four decades of research in computers & education. Comput. Educ. **122**, 136–152 (2018)
36. Zhang, B., Robb, N., Goodman, L.: Emerging educational technologies for cross-cultural collaboration: current perspectives and future directions. In: Proceedings of the 10th EAI International Conference on Simulation Tools and Techniques, SIMUTOOLS 2017, pp. 98–102. Association for Computing Machinery, New York (2017). https://doi.org/10.1145/3173519.3173520

A Study on Research and Teaching Platform System of Doctoral Education in Design Program

Fan Chen[✉], Jingyi Yang, and Lin Li

Tongji University, Shanghai 200092, People's Republic of China
chenfantj@foxmail.com

Abstract. Research and Teaching Platform (RTP) can be considered as an essential occasion of doctoral education in design (DED), which provides students with opportunities for communication and reflection. However, varied RTP systems and training backgrounds lead to the cooperative barrier. Based on this condition, the researcher investigates 1,229 RTPs from 71 DED programs worldwide and attempts to find out a common foundation of academic communication. From this point, the researcher hopes to expand the cooperation among design research communities. Four findings emerge: Cross-discipline cooperation becomes more frequently, and the boundaries of design discipline have been expanded; Secondly, the naming of overseas RTPs is narrative, conducive to spreading and ideological consolidation; Thirdly, the linkage between RTPs and commerce helps to the raising funding and the transformation of research outputs; Lastly, some RTPs released their outputs only to their staff, which is contrary to the principle of Open Science and instructing the public. Based on the above findings, the research outputs will be expected to help RTPs and their DED programs in mainland China to improve and have more cooperation with ones overseas.

Keywords: Research and teaching platform · Doctoral education in design · Comparative research · Future of design education in mainland China

1 Introduction

General courses and mentoring are currently the main pedagogies for doctoral education in design (DED) programs. Among them, design labs are important occasions for doctoral students to conduct scientific research and teaching activities. Here, 'occasion' means a place where special thing(s) happen for some reasons at a certain time. With the increase in the flexibility of doctoral education, the signifier and signified of 'design lab' as scientific research and teaching occasions are constantly expanding. Different higher education institutions (HEI) have begun to regard labs, studios, offices, professional classrooms, comprehensive performance spaces, and even an abstract platform concept as an occasion for training doctoral students. For instance, there is no fixed place for activities of some research groups, so the members choose existing space or temporary construction according to actual needs. The blur and the ablation of the functional space

P.-L. P. Rau (Ed.): HCII 2022, LNCS 13312, pp. 30–43, 2022.
https://doi.org/10.1007/978-3-031-06047-2_3

boundary reflect the ambiguity of the discipline boundary: the connection between disciplines is becoming closer, and the trend of interdisciplinary is becoming more and more obvious. For the convenience of description, we temporarily call the above occasion 'Research and Teaching Platform (RTP)' which is a place where triggers related activities for the purpose of doctoral students training and communication. The reason for using this title is mainly to distinguish it from the phrase 'Teaching and Research Platform', because in the Chinese context, 'Teaching and Research' means education-related research, which refers to the occasions of education and teaching research for a certain subject.

On the other hand, the RTP system is a reflection of the HEI and its doctoral programs in the research direction setting, presenting the vision of the HEI. Since the beginning of this century, mainland China has started to build the DED program. So far, 23 DED programs have been established. Although there is a trend of accelerating growth in numbers, due to the long-term follow-up of the design education models in Europe and the United States, DED in mainland China has not formed its distinctive characteristics. Therefore, it is difficult to conduct large-scale refined researches in certain fields. This is also one of the main reasons leading to the homogeneity of DED nationally. Additionally, many DED programs in the West have formed a stable development route, due to fundamental differences in educational paradigms, there will inevitably be poor communication when conducting cross-regional and cross-discipline cooperation.

Based on the above conditions, the researcher tries to explore the construction of the RTP systems in the HEIs, which is to find out the connection between Chinese and foreign RTPs, and common background of dialogue for doctoral students with different training backgrounds. Finally, this study hopes to contribute knowledge to the development of DED in Mainland China.

2 Literature Review

Design as a discipline has been updated and expanded ever since the Bauhaus emerged in the 1920s [1]. As the scope of design expands, many design practitioners believe that more attention should be paid to the relationship between design and other disciplines [2]. Regarded as the very first modern design curriculum, Bauhaus's four-year course has five basic research directions: 1. Space, colour, composition; 2. Materials; 3. Characteristics; 4. Materials and tools; 5. Construction and expression [3]. After a century of development, cross-discipline cooperation provides a broader perspective, so many people think that comprehensive universities have advantages over specialized design schools [4]. Although the disciplinary nature of design is still controversial, interdisciplinary is regarded as an inherent attribute of design research. Different places emphasize different cultural backgrounds of graduate students. Recognizing these differences helps to find methods for DED in different places [5]. Although everyone agrees that interdisciplinary research is important, it is not clear to what extent it has been theorized [6]. Therefore, the exploration of interdisciplinary design research from different perspectives needs to be put on the agenda. When design becomes more embedded in society, new forms of practice are also emerging, and design becomes important to other disciplines. But apart from its importance, design practice and education still rarely touch the entire scientific field [7].

Design is a project-based studio teaching discipline [8]. The 'design studio' is considered to be the central mode of teaching art and design today. It is a place for students to share plans or development processes for individuals or groups [9]. There are three main characteristics of studio-based teaching, namely interaction, active learning, and social integration, which can be seen as the examining standards of efficiency during studio-based learning. In terms of online design studios, successful collaboration relies on a high degree of student participation, rapid feedback, ease of navigation, well-designed modules, and smooth operation of the technology platform [8]. However, according to Collins' Interactive Ritual Chain theory, compared with offline learning, online learning is more difficult to form high-density emotional energy, which affects the performance of group unity and ultimately affects the learning effect [10]. And the current situation of the global epidemic has put forward higher requirements on the online learning platform technology.

The above statements have pointed out the importance and essences of both offline and online RTPs, which would benefit the future improvement of RTP in mainland China in the near future. As mentioned in the Introduction session, an interdisciplinary and inclusive RTP system of design is growing in mainland China over the last 20 years. However, the existing research literatures on this field are mainly discussing single cases emerging in a certain HEI, and most of them lack an empirical research process. Hence, this situation leaves an opportunity for this study to conduct a wider-spectrum investigation on a global scale for the first time.

The comparative study of the RTPs in this study can be expected to discover the interdisciplinary trend of the DED to which they belong, and explore the new organizational form of RTP under the current situation, and provide research resources for the field.

3   Research Methodology

This study is part of the researcher's doctoral research and belongs to the Material Structure, which is one of the six DED systems. The purpose of establishing the Material Structure is to clarify the impact of material-related support on DED, like the available studios, laboratories, equipment, scholarships, study groups, external cooperation and political supports. There are 71 DED programs worldwide which have been regarded as the research objectives in this study, they are selected from the 219 HEIs in the QS World University Rankings which have the authority to grant the doctorate in the design field. The researcher sorted out 1,229 RTPs (including both online and offline ones) of the 71 DED programs through inductive reasoning and classified them into 28 categories according to their research attributes and the existing subject classification. 11 of the categories are listed in the Subject Catalogue of General Higher Education Institutions issued by the Chinese Ministry of Education in 2020 [11], and the rest 17 categories are found in the process of RTP investigation toward the 71 DED programs. In addition, 1,229 are the total number of existing RTPs in the 71 DED programs.

After the classification, the researcher compared mainland China and overseas from three dimensions: the number of RTPs of each DED and the number of RTPs of each category. The purpose is to explore the differences in RTP direction between DED programs and try to explain the situation.

Because the ranking of the amount of RTPs can reflect the popularity of the fields, thus the researcher uses D-value (Difference value) to represent the difference of the RTPs belonging to the same category between mainland China and overseas, then ranks D-value to get the trends of RTP setting between the two sides. The calculation method is to use the amount of a certain category of RTP in mainland China to minus the amount of same category overseas, then put the account of the result above the horizontal line if it is positive (i.e. 1, 2, etc.), otherwise under the line (i.e. -1, -2, etc.), such as shown in the Fig. 5.

4   Research Methodology

4.1   The Overall Status of DTP Settings

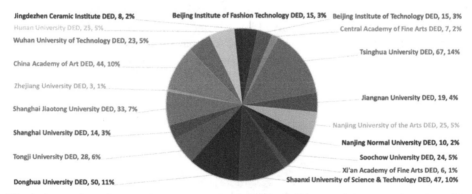

Fig. 1. Proportion of RTPs of DED programs in mainland China. Each item consists of the title of the HEI, the number of the RTP, and the proportion of the RTP (created by the author).

Figure 1 depicts the RTP proportion of the DED programs in mainland China. According to statistics, Tsinghua University (THU) DED program has the largest number of RTPs, and Zhejiang University (ZJU) has the least. On the other hand, the researcher noticed that due to the low degree of information disclosure in some HEIs, the information cannot effectively be disseminated.

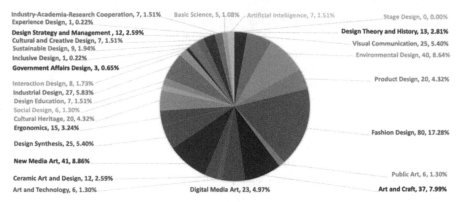

Fig. 2. Proportion of each RTP in mainland China. Each item consists of the title of the RTP, the number of the RTP, and the proportion of the RTP (created by the author).

The Fashion Design RTP occupies the largest proportion in the mainland, and the smallest proportion is experience design (Fig. 2). From the results, it can be found that the top nine RTPs belong to the Subject Catalogue. On the other hand, six universities, Beijing Institute of Technology (BIT), Central Academy of Fine Arts (CAFA), Tsinghua University (THU), Shaanxi University of Science and Technology (SUST), Tongji University (TJU), and China Academy of Art (CAA) have set Design Education RTPs. Nevertheless, these HEIs mainly focus on the research of teaching cases.

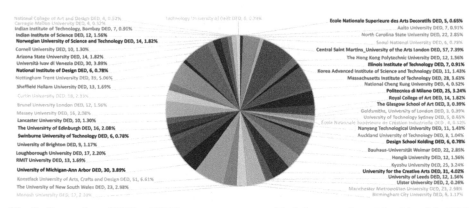

Fig. 3. Proportion of RTPs of DED programs overseas. Each item consists of the title of the HEI, the number of the RTP, and the proportion of the RTP (created by the author).

The researcher compared the RTPs of 52 overseas DED programs and found that Central Saint Martins (CSM) has the most RTPs, while Ulster University has the least (Fig. 3). The UK HEIs generally have more RTPs, reflecting its well-developed DED supports. However, incomplete information disclosure has also appeared in overseas DED programs. For example, the Queensland University of Technology DED program currently only discloses its faculty.

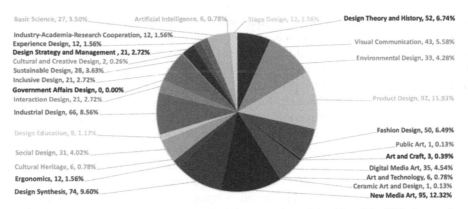

Basic Science, 27, 3.50%
Artificial Intelligence, 6, 0.78%
Stage Design, 12, 1.56%
Design Theory and History, 52, 6.74%

Industry-Academia-Research Cooperation, 12, 1.56%
Experience Design, 12, 1.56%
Design Strategy and Management , 21, 2.72%
Cultural and Creative Design, 2, 0.26%
Sustainable Design, 28, 3.63%
Inclusive Design, 21, 2.72%
Government Affairs Design, 0, 0.00%
Interaction Design, 21, 2.72%
Industrial Design, 66, 8.56%

Design Education, 9, 1.17%

Social Design, 31, 4.02%
Cultural Heritage, 6, 0.78%
Ergonomics, 12, 1.56%
Design Synthesis, 74, 9.60%

Visual Communication, 43, 5.58%
Environmental Design, 33, 4.28%

Product Design, 92, 11.93%

Fashion Design, 50, 6.49%
Public Art, 1, 0.13%
Art and Craft, 3, 0.39%
Digital Media Art, 35, 4.54%
Art and Technology, 6, 0.78%
Ceramic Art and Design, 1, 0.13%
New Media Art, 95, 12.32%

Fig. 4. Proportion of each RTP overseas. Each item consists of the title of the RTP, the number of the RTP, and the proportion of the RTP (created by the author).

The researcher found that New Media Art RTP accounted for the largest proportion, and Government Affairs Design RTP accounted for the smallest (Fig. 4).

4.2　Explanation of the Status Quo

Design Theory and History RTP mainly includes research on design history, design theory, and design ontology. Mainland China contains a total of 13 RTPs in this field. In addition, the researcher has incorporated thematic libraries or formal publishing platforms into the field, such as Jiangnan University (JNU)'s Daguan Collection [12] and TJU Sheji [13] publishing platform. CAA and Shanghai Jiaotong University (SJTU) have Oriental Design studios, which specialize in Asian cultural research. Besides, overseas RTPs of this catalogue also have collections for special objects or documents, which is equivalent to a thematic museum, such as the Materials and Products Collection of CSM. The RTP that integrates exhibitions and research narrows the distance between the subject and object of research, and improves the efficiency of teaching and research.

Visual Communication refers to the RTP that takes two-dimensional planes, colours, packaging, and information visualization as research objects. With the iteration of the professional connotation of visual communication design, the scope of its services has been transformed from two-dimensional to three-dimensional, and even some RTPs of this type have been entrusted with the task of enhancing the national image. For example, CAFA's Advanced Innovation Center for Visual Arts and CAA's Visual China Communication Collaborative Innovation Center. Both of them promote Chinese and Eastern culture through multiple communication channels, implement the national innovation-driven strategy through top-level design, and cultivate the active genes of Chinese culture [14]. A part of overseas RTPs emphasizes printing skills, reflecting the attention to the practice of visual communication.

Environmental Design refers to RTP involving three-dimensional spaces and their design technologies, like architecture, landscape architecture, urban planning, light environment, interior design, furniture design and other fields. THU and SJTU have the most such platforms. The environmental design subject evolved from the interior decoration department established by the Central Academy of Arts and Crafts (now THU Academy of Fine Arts) in 1957. After half a century of development, its connotation has developed unique characteristics in different HEIs [15]. The SJTU School of Design was formed after the integration of architecture, landscape, and design at the end of 2017, and the school counts the tutors' personal studios as RTPs, which expanded the learning channels for students [16]. Inter-institutional cooperation is also an important form of studio construction. For example, the TJU-MIT (Massachusetts Institute of Technology) Shanghai City Science Laboratory and the Fraunhofer Urban Ecological Development Center of SJTU have strengthened academic and teaching exchanges. CSM's Identity, In, and Through, the Built Environment RTP regards the environment as a projection of human needs and desires, and as a carrier for the formation, expression, and reconstruction of the user's identity [17]. This philosophical thinking extends the boundaries of environmental design teaching and research.

Product design and industrial design can be understood as different titles for the same thing by practitioners with engineering and art backgrounds. In this study, Product Design RTP holds prototyping, concept implementation, material research and other activities. The THU Intelligent Product Design Innovation Research Institute empowers product design with intelligent technology [18]. JNU's Creativitive and Cultural Products Research Center enable product design with culture, while the Academy of Fine Arts of Nanjing Normal University (NNU) sets up a special toy design research direction. The naming of overseas product design RTP is generally accurate to specific types of work, such as plastic, wood, and metal. Monash University provides a new classification method for various materials from the perspective of operating methods. For example, Hot Workshops classifies materials that need to be heated, including metals, glass, wax, clay and plastics [19]. Konstfack has established a product design RTP system containing 29 processes, with the most detailed classification [20]. The Center for Bamboo Initiatives of the National Institute of Design of India (NID) takes local materials and their processing methods as the research object, reflecting the characteristics of local product innovation design [21].

'Clothing and Apparel Design' and 'Fashion Design' are different titles in mainland China and overseas for the same profession. They are RTPs that both include research and teaching activities on apparel, clothing, material craftsmanship, and production technology. The latter's research scope is more extensive, and it also involves photography, marketing and other fields. Therefore, this study uses Fashion Design to represent this type of RTP. Due to historical accumulation, Beijing Institute of Fashion Technology (BIFT) and Donghua University (DHU) have developed more complete fashion design RTP systems, SUST also formed a fashion design laboratory group. Politecnico di Milano (Polimi)'s Fashion in Process is an interdisciplinary team that empowers the sustainable development of the fashion industry through design research, transforms traditional culture into a usable knowledge base, and provides strategic consulting for the industry [22]. In addition, the International Centre for Indian Crafts (ICIC) of NID also has such functions [23]. Università IUAV di Venezia (IUAV) integrates visual, performing arts and fashion research into one research direction, opening up the interdisciplinary nature of fashion design [24].

Public Art refers to RTP that creates and researches works of art in public spaces. The public art major was originally an art design discipline founded by Professor Wang Dawei at the Fine Arts College of Shanghai University in 1998 [25]. After that, the Fine Arts College established the Shanghai Public Art Coordination Center (PACC) to push the teaching and research to intensive development [26]. Overseas HEIs are less specialized in the concept of public art, the related practices and research are more closely related to environmental design.

Art and Craft refer to RTP that conducts research on products that are made by hand for decorative or practical function with Chinese characteristics. THU and Nanjing University of the Arts (NUA) have the most diverse RTPs of such field, including paper, wood, glass, lacquer, metal, clay sculpture, wood carving, printing and dyeing, etc. In addition, with the development of digital technology, the connotation of art and craft has spread outward, such as the digital handicraft studio of NUA [27] and the digital printing laboratory of Soochow University (SU). Art and crafts are cultural forms with Chinese characteristics. There are few such RTPs overseas, which can be corresponded with product design.

Digital Media Art refers to RTP for artistic creation and research through information. It is also a branch of new media art. Digital media art is an emerging research field in mainland China and is closely related to interactive design and virtual reality. The overseas Digital Media Art RTPs have more specific research objects. For example, Ecole Nationale Superieure des Arts Decoratifs's Spatial Media is a space-based RTP, and Digital Entertainment of The Hong Kong Polytechnic University (PolyU) based on video games, MIT's Opera of the Future based on music creation and performance.

The connotation of Art and Technology in mainland China is similar to that of overseas Entertainment Design, which refers to a field of artistic creation and research on the environment, games, and information through the use of computer technology. THU has more such RTPs.

Ceramic Art and Design refers to the RTP that specializes in the creation and research of ceramics, and is closely related to Art and Craft. Jingdezhen Ceramic University is the only HEI with ceramic characteristics in mainland China.

New Media Art is the largest RTP overseas and the second largest in mainland China, reflecting the current trend of global design. This RTP mainly includes the spaces of photography, videography, animation, sound, and computer rooms. Among them, SUST and Wuhan University of Technology have relatively complete RTP systems in this field. In addition, TJU Sound Lab is a typical RTP jointly built by the HEI and artist studio [28]. ICINEMA CENTRE of the University of New South Wales uses artificial intelligence technology to help monitor emergencies, such as forest fires, and improve the ability of humans to predict natural disasters [29]. This is an exploration of the RTP in a practical field.

Design Synthesis refers to RTP that is compatible with multiple disciplines and their works, such as comprehensive research centres, multidisciplinary research groups, and maker spaces. The researcher also incorporates galleries and multi-functional performance hall into this field, because occasions with multi-functional attributes can be given more flexibility of utility, and therefore have the potential to stimulate dialogues. TJU Sino-Finnish Center establishes a foundation for promoting cooperation between China and Finland. The Street is an indoor public corridor in CSM, and it is also a meeting point forward to other functional spaces. The information exchanges that occur here make this space an occasion with the highest accessibility, informal communication usually inspires research activities [30]. Official or self-organized forums, informal publications, and even broadcasts can also be regarded as the Design Synthesis RTPs. Different frequencies and in-depth exchanges complement formal research, such as Curtin FM and Online publications of Curtin University.

Ergonomics RTP includes ergonomics and human factors engineering research. This RTP is mainly set up in comprehensive and fashion-focused HEIs, the latter focuses on ergonomics research, such as BIFT, DHU, and Polimi's E4Sport-Engineering for Sport Laboratory.

Cultural Heritage refers to an RTP for cultural relics and traditional culture. In addition, this RTP also includes research on celebrity works, such as Zhang Ding, Wu Guanzhong, and Han Meilin Art Research Centre of THU, Xu Beihong Institute of NNU, etc. There are few such RTPs overseas. The more prominent ones are the five platforms of the IUAV in the field of ancient building materials, construction technology, and architectural culture [31].

Social Design refers to an RTP that uses an interdisciplinary approach to iterate the social system from the bottom up. It is worth noting that the SJTU Rural and Agricultural Design Institute projects the objects of social design on the countryside, in response the national call of rural revitalization policy. The proportion of such RTPs overseas is high, and they involve reducing crime rates, organic food, revitalizing the local traditional lifestyle, etc. DESIS Network is an important alliance in the field of social design. It uses DESIS Lab established in HEIs to create design knowledge and promote social innovation and sustainable activities. At present, more than 50 Labs have been established around the world [32].

The Design Education of this study includes three types of RTPs: aesthetic education, art education, and design education, most of which carry out research and teaching for the former two, such as Pedagogic Research in the Arts in Leeds University (LU). In terms of design education, most RTPs focus on sharing teaching cases, and seldom touch on HEI field. More involved in design education are the CCA National Institute of Art Education and the TJU Design Education and Teaching Center. The Transark of the Norwegian University of Science and Technology (NTNU) is a teaching development centre established in the Faculty of Architecture and Design. Its goal is to rely on design education experience to develop higher education pedagogy, focusing on education as a promotion responsibility for social change, self-learning ability, teaching ability, and transformable skills [33]. This is the only RTP that explores education and teaching from a design perspective.

Industrial Design refers to a 'Product Design' RTP that focuses on engineering, aesthetics, and economic factors. The researcher found that science and engineering HEIs emphasize engineering technology, while art HEIs tend to aesthetic perspective. For example, BIT's Defense Equipment Design and Research Centre, THU Health and Medical Industry Innovation Design Institute, Hunan University (HNU)'s State Key Laboratory of Advanced Design and Manufacturing for Vehicle Body, CAA Zhejiang Province Key Laboratory of Healthy and Smart Kitchen System. The University of Michigan (UM)'s industrial design RTPs are all related to engineering, involving navigation satellite systems, batteries, lasers, marine fluid mechanics, etc. [34].

Interaction Design refers to the RTP that uses digital technology to exchange content and structure between two or more interactive individuals. The THU-Alibaba Natural Interactive Experience Joint Laboratory has established a model of HEI-enterprise collaboration in mainland China.

Government Affairs Design mainly refers to a field that reflects national ideology through art or design means and improves the efficiency of government work. At present, two HEIs in mainland China have RTPs in this field. The CAFA National Thematic Art Creation Research Centre is mainly responsible for the creation of major national themes, reflecting the achievements of China's socialist construction and Reform and Open [35]. The vision of the CAA Government Application Design Institute is to assist government departments in promoting their digital transformation, innovation management, and the standardization of government application platforms [35].

The Inclusive Design RTP solves the obstacles that users encounter when interacting with the surrounding environment. It is typically designed for disadvantaged groups, such as the elderly, children, the disabled, and people with diseases. Mainland China has recently raised the issue of elderly care to a political level, which has gradually attracted attention from all walks of life. There have not been many such platforms in HEIs. The only two are the THU Health Service and Innovative Design Institute. There are many such RTPs overseas. Among them, Cornell University and the Royal College of Art (RCA) have formed relatively complete inclusive design RTP systems, such as the research on the minority, the inclusiveness on business and social impact.

Sustainable Design specifically refers to an RTP for sustainable research and education on the ecological environment and the built environment, the latter accounting for a large proportion in mainland China. Overseas HEIs conduct more sustainable teaching and research on lifestyle and ecological environment, such as Polimi LeNS lab, Kyushu University's BioFoodLab, LU Water@Leeds, KTH Royal Institute of Technology in Stockholm's WaterCentre@KTH, Rooftop Renewable Energy Lab in Nottingham Trent University. CSM Maison0 and RCA Burberry Material Futures Research Group are Industry-University-Research RTPs dedicated to the teaching and research of the sustainable fashion industry.

Cultural and Creative Design refers to the RTP that uses creative or technical means to market intellectual property rights. This field is also related to crafts and cultural heritage in mainland China. At present, there is only the PolyU Research Centre on Creative Culture Industries for Western China RTP overseas, and more only the concept of creative industries. THU Cultural and Tourism Industry Innovation Research Institute connects the ecology of cultural and creative industries with the tourism industry, expanding this field's application scenarios. In addition, the USC-SJTU Institute of Cultural and Creative Industry (ICCI) is an RTP based on the field of digital cultural and creative industries, it combines professional education, industrial education and general education [37].

Design Strategy and Management mainly refers to the RTP engaged in enterprise development and management research. In addition, the TJU Design Competitiveness Research Center and the CAA Urban-Rural Coordination Research Institute further enhance its connotation to the national strategic level. Similar to this are Polimi Design Policy, École Nationale Supérieure de Création Industrielle's Design and Politics, Hongik University's International Design Trend Center.

The Industry-Academia-Research Cooperation RTP mainly serves as an incubator, providing an environment for the industrialization of student projects. HEIs in mainland China provide consultation through joint platforms with off-campus enterprises, such as the SU Menglan Design Institute, and the SUST Northwest Research Center of the Zhuoya National Industrial Design Center, DHU Swarovski Creative Design Center, HNU DJI Innovation Lab. It is worth noting that Zhejiang Wenzhou Research Institute of Light Industry is a policy consulting platform jointly established by SUST and the Wenzhou Municipal Government, which provides a reference for the extension of the same type of RTP.

Basic Science is a type of RTP involving philosophy, literature, science, and engineering to support the development of design discipline. For example, the SJTU Aroma Plant Research Center, the CAA Art Philosophy and Cultural Innovation Institute, the CAA Urban Spatial Geography Digital Simulation Laboratory, the HNU Key Laboratory of Embedded and Network Computing. MIT and UM have established many basic research platforms with the help of a strong science and engineering foundation. The former is supported by computer science and the latter is supported by mechanical engineering science.

Artificial Intelligence (AI) is a type of RTP that uses AI-enabled design practices as the research object. HNU and TJU have more RTPs dedicated to this field. The Artificial Intelligence Design Laboratory (AIDL) jointly built by PolyU and RCA.

HEIs with Stage Design RTPs are generally among art colleges with design majors, such as CSM, University of Creative Arts, Edinburgh College of Art, Nottingham College of Art and Design, and Arizona State University Herberger Institute for Design and the Arts. In mainland China, such RTPs are set up in departments with majors in drama, film, and television, and seldom in design schools.

4.3 DTP Setting Trends

Figure 5 shows the trend of RTP settings among the 71 DED programs. The blue column represents the number of D-Value. The part above the horizontal line are RTPs which are more popular in mainland China, and the part below the horizontal line is the opposite. As can be seen from the figure, Art and Craft, Cultural Heritage, Ceramic Art and Design, Cultural and Creative Design are popular in mainland China, they are fields with Chinese cultural characteristics. 考工记 (The Artificers' Record), written in the Spring and Autumn Period (from 770 BC to 476 BC), is the earliest document to record Chinese handicraft technology, involving 30 categories in six categories, including woodworking, metalworking, leather, dyeing, scraping, and ceramics. These contents have an important position in the history of Chinese science and technology, the history of arts and crafts, and the history of culture. Therefore, related fields have become the research and teaching platform of many art colleges. More than two thousand years of cultural accumulation constitutes the main foundation of Chinese contemporary design. The Industrial Revolution and the Westernization Movement brought Western scientific and technological achievements to China, which constituted an important content of engineering design education.

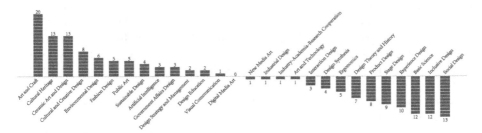

Fig. 5. D-Value ranking (created by the author).

The D-Value tends to zero in Visual Communication, Digital Media Art, New Media Art, Industrial Design, Industry-Academia-Research Cooperation, and Art and Technology, indicating that they have similar popularity worldwide. Among them, Visual Communication, Digital Media Art, New Media Art, and Industrial Design are at the forefront of the total amount, indicating that these fields are in a stage of rapid development globally. Taking Visual Communication as an example, there are endless cases of AI technology helping visual design, which basically liberates the hands of traditional graphic designers. The combination of computer technology and traditional art brings an interactive experience to the audience, and the constant pursuit of freshness is an inexhaustible driving force for the advancement of the media art field.

The world order after World War II is in urgent need of adjustment. Scholars in various fields have begun to think about complex social issues at a more macroscopic and inter-professional level. This is followed by the emergence of interdisciplinary cooperation and emerging research fields, like social design and inclusive design. Mainland China failed to join this wave of social transformation due to historical reasons. Instead, these new ideas were introduced after the Chinese Reform and Open in 1978. The high penetration rate of Basic Science RTPs overseas shows that these DED programs attach great importance to basic research.

5   Conclusion

The researcher summarized this study from four aspects: educational function, cross-professional trend, RTP sustainable development motivation, and discourse production.

Some RTP information is not open to the public, such as the MIT Center for Extreme Bionics, which is contrary to the principles of open science. Usually, there are four major challenges in professional education in universities: 1. Create new knowledge; 2. Protect existing knowledge; 3. Train professional practitioners; 4. Instruct and educate people [38]. The educational function is the final leap for the university to realize its ultimate value.

The trend of inter-professional cooperation between RTPs is becoming more and more obvious. This situation reminds us to consider thoroughly and enhance the ability of interdisciplinary cooperation. Only in this way can we overcome the increasingly complex social challenges.

The linkage between the RTP and the business is conducive to the raising of funds and the transformation of research outputs. Therefore, when RTP conducts academic research, it should also consider the linkage with the capital. This is an important motivation for achieving sustainable development and 'designing for the real world'.

In addition to disciplinary names, overseas RTPs also use titles with the quality of story-telling. This naming method improves the efficiency of discourse production based on knowledge production, thereby promoting the production of rights. Therefore, in the information age, output efficiency and communication efficiency play an equally important role in the sustainable development of RTP.

The researcher will continue to pay attention to the changing trends of the RTP system and provide scientific research materials for the DED field.

References

1. Murphy, E., Jacobs, N.: Designing a new design PhD? In: Bohemia, E., Rieple, A., Liedtka, J., Cooper, R. (eds.) Proceedings of the 19th DMI: AcademicDesign Management Conference, pp. 3063–3079. Design Management Institute (2014)
2. Margolin, V.: Doctoral education in design: problems and prospects. Des. Issues **26**(3), 70–78 (2010)
3. Meyer, M., Norman, D.: Changing design education for the 21st century. Sheji **6**(1), 13–49 (2020)
4. Davis, M.: Why do we need doctoral study in design? Int. J. Des. **2**(3), 71–79 (2008)
5. Melles, G.: Global perspectives on structured research training in doctorates of design—what do we value? Des. Stud. **30**(3), 255–271 (2009)
6. Melles, G., Wölfel, C.: Postgraduate design education in Germany: motivations, understandings and experiences of graduates and enrolled students in master's and doctoral programmes. Des. J. **17**(1), 115–135 (2014)
7. Broadbent, J., Cross, N.: Design education in the information age. J. Eng. Des. **14**(4), 439–446 (2003)
8. Fleischmann, K.: From studio practice to online design education: can we teach design online? Can. J. Learn. Technol. **45**(1), 1–19 (2019)
9. Park, J.: Design education online: learning delivery and evaluation. Int. J. Art Design Educ. **30**(2), 176–187 (2011)
10. Collins, R.: Interaction Ritual Chains. Princeton University Press, New Jersey (2005)
11. Ministry of Education of the People's Republic of China. https://www.ukri.org/councils/ahrc/career-and-skills-development/supporting-universities-and-consortia-to-develop-careers/. Accessed 2 Dec 2021
12. JNU School of Design. http://designlabs.jiangnan.edu.cn/gsys/dgzsg.htm. Accessed 2 Dec 2021
13. College of Design and Innovation. https://tjdi.tongji.edu.cn/about.do?ID=117&lang=. Accessed 2 Dec 2021
14. Central Academy of Fine Arts. https://www.cafa.edu.cn/sp/nljg/?j=305. Accessed 2 Dec 2021
15. THU Academy of Fine Arts. https://www.ad.tsinghua.edu.cn/xygk/xyjs_lsyg_.htm. Accessed 2 Dec 2021

16. SJTU School of Design. https://designschool.sjtu.edu.cn/summarize/introduction. Accessed 2 Dec 2021
17. Central Saint Martins. https://www.arts.ac.uk/colleges/central-saint-martins/research-at-csm/identity-in-and-through-the-built-environment. Accessed 2 Dec 2021
18. THU Academy of Fine Arts. https://www.ad.tsinghua.edu.cn/info/1057/43186.htm. Accessed 2 Dec 2021
19. Monash University. https://www.monash.edu/mada/current-students/facilities. Accessed 2 Dec 2021
20. Konstfack. https://www.konstfack.se/en/About-Konstfack/Workshops/. Accessed 2 Dec 2021
21. National Institute of Design. https://www.nid.edu/research_&_developments/center-for-bamboo-initiatives/detail. Accessed 2 Dec 2021
22. Fashion in Process. https://www.fashioninprocess.com/manifesto/. Accessed 2 Dec 2021
23. National Institute of Design. https://nid.edu/research_&_developments/international-centre-for-indian-crafts-icic/detail. Accessed 2 Dec 2021
24. IUAV.   http://www.iuav.it/INTERNATIO/ABOUT-IUAV/Iuav-profi/at-a-glanc/index.htm. Accessed 2 Dec 2021
25. Shanghai Academy of Fine Arts. https://safa.shu.edu.cn/mygk/xbjs/ggysjssyjxzx.htm. Accessed 2 Dec 2021
26. PACC. https://pacc.gssuit.com/about. Accessed 2 Dec 2021
27. Tencent. https://mp.weixin.qq.com/s/9j6cIARKN-wdn5tf8vA3iQ. Accessed 2 Dec 2021
28. College of Design and Innovation. https://tjdi.tongji.edu.cn/about.do?ID=70&lang=. Accessed 2 Dec 2021
29. Center for Interactive Cinema Research. http://www.icinema.unsw.edu.au/about/icinema-overview/. Accessed 2 Dec 2021
30. Central Saint Martins. https://www.arts.ac.uk/colleges/central-saint-martins/student-life-at-csm/facilities/general/the-street. Accessed 2 Dec 2021
31. IUAV. http://www.iuav.it/DIPARTIMEN/LABORATORI/english/index.htm. Accessed 2 Dec 2021
32. DESIS Network. https://www.desisnetwork.org/labs/. Accessed 2 Dec 2021
33. NTNU. https://www.ntnu.edu/transark/about. Accessed 2 Dec 2021
34. Michigan Engineering. https://www.engin.umich.edu/research/research-centers/. Accessed 2 Dec 2021
35. Central Academy of Fine Arts. https://www.cafa.edu.cn/sp/nljg/?j=310. Accessed 2 Dec 2021
36. China Academy of Art. http://ycw.caa.edu.cn/yjzx/ygyjjg/cxsjxy/202001/36671.html. Accessed 2 Dec 2021
37. ICCI. https://icci.sjtu.edu.cn/icci/index/introduction. Accessed 2 Dec 2021
38. Friedman, K.: Design curriculum challenges for today's University. In: Davis, A. (eds.) Enhancing Curriucla: Exploring Effective Curriculum Practices in Art, Design and Communication, pp. 27–63. Centre for Learning and Teaching in Art and Design (CLTAD) (2002)

Cross-modal Representation Learning for Understanding Manufacturing Procedure

Atsushi Hashimoto[1]([envelope])[ID], Taichi Nishimura[2], Yoshitaka Ushiku[1][ID], Hirotaka Kameko[2][ID], and Shinsuke Mori[2]

[1] OMRON SINIC X Corp., Tokyo, Japan
atsushi.hashimoto@sinicx.com
[2] Kyoto University, Kyoto, Japan
https://www.omron.com/sinicx/en/

Abstract. Assembling, biochemical experiments, and cooking are representatives that create a new value from multiple materials through multiple processes. If a machine can computationally understand such manufacturing tasks, we will have various options of human-machine collaboration on those tasks, from video scene retrieval to robots that act for on behalf of humans. As one form of such understanding, this paper introduces a series of our studies that aim to associate visual observation of the processes and the procedural texts that instruct such processes. In those studies, captioning is the key task, where input is image sequence or video clips and our methods are still state-of-the-arts. Through the explanation of such techniques, we overview machine learning technologies that deal with the contextual information of manufacturing tasks.

Keywords: Procedural text generation · Image captioning · Video captioning · Understanding manufacturing activity

1 Introduction

The versatile fitting performance of deep neural networks has established a new paradigm, cross-modal processing, typified by image captioning. It is a natural ability for humans to explain what we witnessed by language or, inversely, imagine a scene from a text description. Such vision-language abilities are generalized as a projection of physical world observation into a symbolic world and vice versa.

The decisive difference between cross-modal processing and traditional classification problem is the non-existence of a format for symbolic expression. A traditional framework must have a pre-defined output format, limiting possible output patterns unnecessarily. In contrast, a linguistic expression has no such limitation. In this sense, captioning, for example, is an ultimate task for a machine learning (ML) model to extract information from a visual observation under no external limitations.

P.-L. P. Rau (Ed.): HCII 2022, LNCS 13312, pp. 44–57, 2022.
https://doi.org/10.1007/978-3-031-06047-2_4

We focus such captioning tasks on manufacturing, an activity to produce a valuable product from multiple materials through multiple processes. In manufacturing, the processes are described as procedural text. Humans can reproduce a product as long as the processes are described appropriately. Such an ability is vital for a system that displays instruction as work progresses by matching the situation and instruction. Similarly, it contributes to realizing a robot that obeys textual instruction and executes manufacturing; given instruction is compared with the current situation to identify the required robot's physical actions indicated by the textual instruction.

Considering procedural text generation from visual observation, the major difference from general captioning tasks is two-fold; it has a flow of material combination, and the materials change their state through processes. This paper introduces two techniques that model each of them: the state-of-the-arts to obtain cross-modal representation in manufacturing applications. Note that, due to the dataset availability, we evaluated those methods on the dataset of cooking activities.

2   Captioning on Time Series of Visual Observation

Since the success of image captioning by deep learning [29], its architecture of encoder (feature extractor) and decoder (text generator) has extended for other visual formats; visual story telling [8] and video paragraph captioning [31]. This section overviews manufacturing activity understanding from the viewpoints of these two problems.

2.1   Visual Storytelling

Visual storytelling is a task to generate a text for each image in a sequence, firstly proposed in [8]. This task is the most simple extension of image captioning to a time series observation; it should avoid duplicated mentions or track entities to refer to them appropriately. In manufacturing, the model should also consider an additional temporal context; how the materials have changed their state between two consecutive images. To model such changes, Chandu et al. [3] projected the latent space into discrete states and tried to imitate the state transition of real procedural text on a finite state machine. Two different approaches were made by us [19,21]. In [19], we have proposed a method that pre-trains the encoder by state-wise image-text retrieval. Training a model to discriminate state difference and use the retrieved sentences as references, we obtained more accurate description of each step than [3]. In [21], we have explicitly modeled the process of material mixing, which contributes to enhance the captioning performance independently with the other methods. We introduce the details of this method in this paper. Note that, in our method, we assume a given list of materials since it is often indistinguishable even for humans (e.g., white powders or clear liquid) without labels.

Since there are a number of how-to web contents with images, there are several datasets for this task in manufacturing, mainly in cooking [3,6,32].

2.2 Video Paragraph Description

Video paragraph description is a task to generate a text for each video segment [31], which makes a paragraph of a video. As visual storytelling, the primal challenge of this task is to reflect the context of the event sequence. Generally, a video clip does not focus on entities of interest as much as an image. In addition, it may include actions that an image can hardly represent. Hence, a spatio-temporal attention mechanism and action recognition should be considered with contextual information. When video paragraph description is firstly defined, segments are not given, and a model must identify segments of interest simultaneously with paragraph description [31,35]. However, due to its hardness, the problem was later re-defined as a simpler task with given segment boundaries [13,24]. In [20], we focused on state transition caused by actions observed in each video segment, with given segment boundaries and material lists. We introduce the details of this method in this paper, as well as [21]. In parallel with our studies, Shi et al. [25,26] proposed a method that utilizes transcript of narrated videos for generating fine-grained procedural text. Transcripts are a powerful resource to solve this task, but it is not always available because adding a transcript to a video requires an effort. Instead, our studies assume a given list of materials as a minimum external resource.

Since creating how-to content with videos is not a lightweight task, there are fewer datasets than images. YouCook2 [34] is almost only the dataset for this task, but the HowTo100M dataset [17] is often used for pre-training an encoder. We have also published a dataset with bio-chemical tasks [22], but the number of videos is quite limited. Note that there is a cross-modal dataset, YouMakeup [30], which is organized with videos of face makeup and instructions. This is slightly different from manufacturing because it is a task to paint cosmetics for different face parts rather than combining materials.

3 Procedural Text Generation by Modeling Material Merging Process

This section introduces our method that models merging processes of manufacturing, which is implemented on the problem of visual storytelling.

3.1 Tree Representation of the Merging Processes

Since manufacturing is a task to yield a valuable product from materials, it is essential to merge multiple materials. Among traditional graph representations of manufacturing process [9,10,18,33], we adopted Simplified Ingredient Merging Map in Recipes (SIMMR) [9], a graph representation of the manufacturing process whose node and edge models only material-merging actions. Based on SIMMR and the Cookpad Image Dataset [6], we have prepared a cross-modal dataset, visual SIMMR (vSIMMR) (Fig. 1).

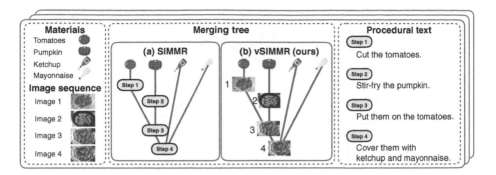

Fig. 1. The difference between SIMMR and vSIMMR (cited from [21]). Leaves of a tree graph refer to materials, and the other nodes refer to step-wise instructions in both SIMMR and vSIMMR. In addition, vSIMMR has an image corresponding to each step.

Each sample of this dataset consists of step-wise instructional texts, step-wise images, and a material list. Its annotation is given as a tree, whose leaves refer to materials in the list, and the other nodes refer to step-wise text and images.

3.2   Encoder-Decoder Model that Merging Processes

Based on the vSIMMR dataset, we aim to develop an encoder-decoder model that yields procedural text from given images and a material list. The overview of the model is shown in Fig. 2. There are encoder and decoder modules that consider the merging process. The additional tree-reprediction module aims to allow semi-supervision of the tree structure. We assume a situation where we can access a large number of image-instruction pairs collected on the web (the Cookpad Image dataset) and only a few percent of data with tree-structure annotation (the vSIMMR dataset). The following parts explain how the structure models merging process of manufacturing and how semi-supervised learning is realized. Please refer to the original paper [21] for a mathematically rigorous explanation.

Text Generator that Considers the Tree Structure. Utilizing this structure, we constructed a text generator (Process (iii) in Fig. 2) based on the child-sum tree LSTM [27]. The tree LSTM receives hidden states from multiple elements, children on a given tree structure. Thus, our decoder explicitly models the merging process of manufacturing.

Since the tree structure is not given at inference (other than leaf nodes of materials), we need to estimate the structure before calculating the decoder. We calculate attention-like weights for each material-image pair and image-image pair to estimate the edges, which we will explain in the next part. Regardless of the link weight calculation methods, we need to determine a tree structure by selecting edges based on the weights (Process (ii) in Fig. 2). Such deterministic

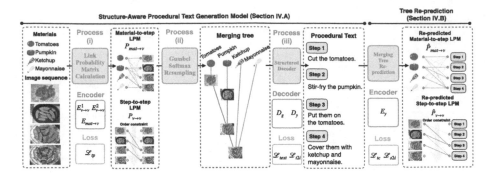

Fig. 2. The overview of proposed model (cited from [21]).

operation usually breaks the chain rule of differentiation and disable end-to-end optimization, which is crucial for neural networks to fulfill their potential. Hence, at estimating the tree structure, we use the Gumbel-max trick [5].

Material and Image Encoders with Tree Structure Prediction. Each material in the list is first embedded into a latent feature by a word2vec encoding. Then, it is further embedded through bi-LSTM, where all materials are input to consider the context in the list. We refer to the embedded feature of materials as z_m.

Similarly, each image is embedded by a ResNet50 model [7] pre-trained with an image-step retrieval task on the Cookpad Image dataset. Then, they are further embedded by two different LSTMs to obtain key and query features, z_v^k and z_v^q.

Let z_v^{max} be a feature obtained from z_v^k and z_v^q with an element-wise max-pooling. Calculating similarity $S(z_v^{max}, z_m)$ and $S(z_v^k, z_v^q)$, we obtain the material-step link weights and step-step link weights. z_m and z_q are re-used as the node feature of the tree at the decoder.

Tree-Reprediction Module for Semi-supervised Learning. We assume semi-supervision for tree structure prediction since tree annotation is costly. This means that we can calculate the loss for tree prediction only a few percentages of training data, which is generally hard to cover diverse recipes. To assist the prediction, we use a principle that the tree structure implied from an image sequence (input) and the procedural text (output) must be identical. Based on this principle, we add a tree-reprediction module that predicts the same tree structure from generated texts. We can regard the decoder and this module as tree auto-encoder. Since the decoder is based on Tree-LSTM, a better tree prediction facilitates a better text generation. Similarly, better text generation ensures a better tree-reprediction. Hence, we add loss for samples without tree structure annotation that evaluate inconsistency of re-predicted tree against the original estimation.

We add two βVAE-like modules that predict image features from the tree and step-wise sentences as additional modules for semi-supervision. For more details, please see the original paper [21].

3.3 Experiments

In this section, we introduce some of the key results of our method. Please refer to the original paper for the detailed conditions of experiments.

From the Cookpad Image dataset, we discarded recipes with steps without images, less than two steps, or less than two ingredients. After this selection, we got 200 k recipes with complete images, more than one step, and one ingredient. We divided them into train/val/test sets with a ratio of 80%/10%/10%. We have annotated the tree structure for c.a. 1% of samples in each set.

Since our method is compatible with many existing methods for visual storytelling, we implemented our method on the following four methods.

Image2seq [8] is the method firstly proposed for the visual storytelling task. It involves the temporal context with BiLSTM after encoding each image independently.

GLAC Net [11] considers the context by global and local image feature vectors.

SSiD and **SSiL** are methods both proposed in [3]. It projects continuous embedded features into discrete state space, where a finite state machine (FSM) models state transition. Feed-forwarding state information to the text generation enriches temporal contextual information (SSiD). SSiL is an extension of SSiD, which has an additional loss to better imitate the state transition of ground truth.

RetAttn [19] is the state-of-the-art method of visual storytelling on manufacturing activities. It cross-modally retrieves the ten most similar sentences for each step and concatenates the average feature of retrieved texts to visual feature for text generation.

As an ablation study, we prepared the **full model** and **half model**, which are with and without the tree re-definition module.

Table 1 shows the key results of the proposed method. Here, BLEU [23] and ROUGE-L [15] are major metrics for machine translation and captioning. Distinct [14] is a metric to evaluate diversity of description. Ingredient/action are scores calculated on sequences obtained by extracting only ingredient/action from generated texts, which show coherency of generated recipes. Overall, the table shows the proposed method's versatile ability of performance enhancement.

Figure 3 shows an example of generated procedural text and the tree structure predicted as a bi-product. In this example, our full model achieved an impressive description, "mix seasonings marked • in the ingredient list." "*bullet*" would be useful to re-predict tree structure from the text since it directly refers to the leaf nodes. This observation is supported by the predicted tree structure, where half model failed to predict the tree, but the full model succeeded.

Table 1. Word-overlap metrics for the five base models with half and full models. The scores in bold are the best for each base model. B = BLEU, RL = ROUGE-L, D = Distinct, I = Ingredient, and Ac = Action. * indicates statistically significant difference ($p < 0.001$) from the base models (original) through bootstrap sampling [12]. (cited from [21])

	B4	RL	D1	D2	I-B3	I-B4	I-RL	Ac-B3	Ac-B4	Ac-RL
Images2seq	5.1	18.4	38.3	54.7	0.5	0.1	9.7	3.8	2.0	18.4
+ Half	5.8*	20.6*	**51.1***	**75.0***	0.7*	0.2	12.7*	3.9	2.0	21.2*
+ Full	**6.3***	**21.7***	47.6*	71.0*	**0.9***	**0.3***	**13.8***	**4.3***	**2.1**	**22.9***
GLAC Net	5.9	21.4	46.6	69.0	0.9	0.3	13.2	4.3	2.1	22.8
+ Half	5.9	**21.8***	46.7	68.8	1.1*	**0.4**	15.6*	**4.4**	2.3	**23.1**
+ Full	**6.1**	21.3	**47.2***	**69.9***	**1.2***	**0.4**	**16.3***	**4.4**	2.3	22.5
SSiD	6.0	20.9	45.5	66.6	0.8	0.2	13.1	4.0	2.1	21.6
+ Half	6.2*	20.8	43.9	65.1	**1.3***	**0.4***	16.4*	**4.4***	2.2	22.1*
+ Full	**6.4***	**21.6***	**48.3***	**71.0***	1.2*	**0.4***	**16.7***	**4.5***	2.2	**23.5***
SSiL	6.3	21.4	45.5	66.8	0.7	0.2	12.5	4.0	2.0	22.1
+ Half	5.4	21.4	46.7*	68.2*	1.2*	**0.4***	16.9*	3.8	2.0	22.2
+ Full	**6.4**	**21.9***	**47.3***	**70.9***	**1.4***	**0.4***	**17.0***	**4.5***	**2.3***	**23.0***
RetAttn	6.5	21.6	40.2	60.3	1.0	**0.3**	14.5	3.2	1.5	21.2
+ Half	6.5	21.8	52.4*	77.8*	**1.2**	**0.3**	**14.8**	4.2*	2.0*	22.9*
+ Full	**7.1**	**22.1**	**52.7***	**78.6***	**1.2**	**0.3**	**14.8**	4.2*	2.0*	**23.1***

4   Procedural Text Generation by Modeling State Transition in Continuous Latent Space

This section introduces our method that models changing state of materials through processes of manufacturing. Such state change was modeled in SSiD/SSiL [3]. However, its projection from a continuous latent space to the discrete state machine model must have unavoidable information loss. It is also difficult to identify the optimal number of states. When modeling state transition directly in a continuous space, we do not face these problems. To learn such continuous state transition, we proposed a model that update latent feature in an action-driven manner. To observe actions, we implemented the model on the video paragraph description task.

4.1   Simulation of Materials State Transition

We model the material's state transition based on Neural Process Network (NPN) [2]. NPN is a model originally proposed for procedural text understanding, where input is procedural text and simulate the change of the states for each entity with the verbs in the sentence. We replace the entities with materials, which is given as the ingredient list. Similarly, we replace verbs in the text

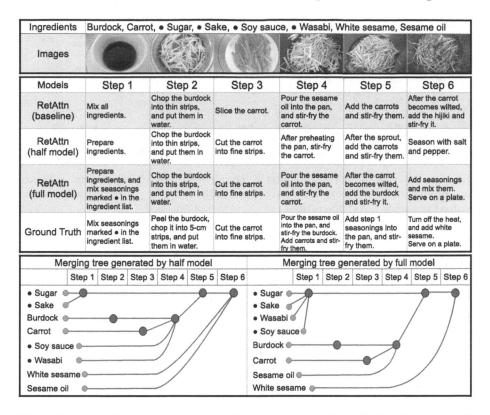

Fig. 3. Example of generated recipes and merging trees. Here, the baseline (original), half, and full models are compared with the ground truth. This sample has no ground truth of the merging tree. Note that the recipes are originally in Japanese and have been translated into English. (cited from [21])

with actions observed in video segments, where we train an action recognition model (and an involved material recognition model) with a distant supervision with procedural texts.

Figure 4 shows the action-driven operation on latent features of materials, which we call visual simulator. The input of this simulator is embedded features of materials and the n-th clip (=video segment). When $n = 1$ (at the first step), the material features are obtained as the method in the previous section. When $n > 1$, material features are those updated at n-th step. To train action and material selectors, we use distant supervision. Namely, we extract material names and verbs from the text for each step and use them as ground truth. Note that this supervision is unreliable, especially at later steps, due to zero anaphora or missing reference.

Based on the principle of identical state transition between visual observation and procedural text, we re-simulate the state transition on the generated text and minimize the inconsistency between visual and textural simulations. Please refer to the original paper for the architecture of the entire model [20].

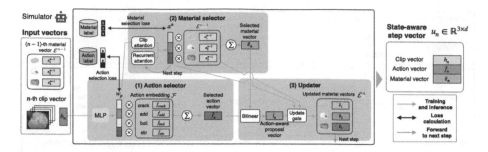

Fig. 4. An overview of the visual simulator. The simulator recurrently reasons the state transition of the materials at each step. Specifically, it predicts executed actions and involved materials in (1) the action and (2) material selectors. The selected material features are updated based on the selected action features. This update operation simulates the state transition in a continuous latent feature space (cited from [20]).

Table 2. Paragraph- and sentence-level word-overlap evaluation for the baseline and the proposed models with ablation studies. The scores in bold are the best among the comparative models. "I" indicates whether the model uses ingredient information or not. M=METEOR, C=CIDEr-D (cited from [20]).

Baseline	I	B1	B2	B3	B4	M	C	RL
Transformer-XL		39.0	22.0	12.1	6.7	15.2	22.7	30.9
+ Ingredients (Transformer-XL-I)	✓	37.7	22.5	13.4	8.2	15.4	35.4	34.2
MART		37.9	21.7	12.4	7.6	15.0	29.1	32.3
+ Ingredients (MART-I)	✓	42.3	26.2	16.1	9.9	17.6	48.2	36.2
Ours								
Video only (V)		43.2	24.5	14.0	8.1	16.6	32.4	31.9
V + Ingredients (VI)	✓	49.1	29.5	17.6	10.5	20.3	63.3	35.2
VI + Visual simulator (VIV)	✓	49.4	30.1	18.0	11.0	21.0	66.1	36.8
VIV + Textual re-simulator (VIVT)	✓	**49.4**	**30.9**	**18.3**	**11.3**	**21.1**	**67.1**	**37.1**

4.2   Experiments

We evaluated the above model on the YouCook2 dataset. Since the dataset does not have material lists, we prepared them by ourselves, which is accessible at https://github.com/misogil0116/svpc.

We compared our method with Transformer-XL [4] and MART [13], as the state-of-the-arts for general text generation tasks and the video paragraph description task, respectively. For a fair comparison, we prepared "+Ingredients" models for them (see the appendix of the original paper for more details). In addition to BLEU and ROUGE-L in Table 1, we show the scores of METEOR [1] and CIDEr-D [28]. Table 2 shows a clear superiority of our method against the baselines.

Ingredients	flour, eggs, baking soda, salt, pepper, water, shrimp, batter, breadcrumbs, oil		
	step 1	step 2	step 3
Clip sequence			
MART + Ingredients (MART-I)	add **flour salt** and **pepper** to a bowl and mix (✗ eggs, baking soda)	add milk egg and milk to the bowl and mix (✗ water)	coat the dough in the **batter** (✗ shrimp, breadcrumbs)
V + Ingredients (VI)	mix **flour salt pepper** and breadcrumbs (✗ baking soda, eggs)	mix flour salt pepper and breadcrumbs with the flour (✗ water)	coat the **shrimp** with the flour mixture (✗ batter, breadcrumbs)
VI + Visual simulator (VIV)	mix **flour eggs** and **salt** together (✗ baking soda, pepper)	add **salt pepper** to the eggs and mix (✗ water)	coat the **shrimp** in the **batter** (✗ breadcrumbs)
+ VIV + Textual re-simulator (VIVT)	mix **flour eggs baking soda salt** and **pepper** and **salt**	add **water** eggs breadcrumbs to a bowl of **water** and mix	coat the **shrimp** in the **batter** (✗ breadcrumbs)
Ground truth	add **flour eggs baking soda salt** and **pepper** to the bowl and stir	add cold **water** to the bowl and stir	cover the **shrimp** in the **batter** and **breadcrumbs**

	step 4	step 5
Clip sequence		
MART + Ingredients (MART-I)	fry the onion rings in **oil** (✗ shrimp)	remove the **shrimp** from the **oil**
V + Ingredients (VI)	heat **oil** in a pan and add the **shrimp** and fry	remove the **shrimp** from the **oil**
VI + Visual simulator (VIV)	heat **oil** in a pan and fry the **shrimp** in it	remove the **shrimp** from the **oil**
VIV + Textual re-simulator (VIVT)	fry the **shrimp** in **oil**	remove the **shrimp** from the **oil**
Ground truth	place the **shrimp** into a pan of hot **oil**	remove the **shrimp** from the pan

Fig. 5. An example of generated procedural text. Green bold and red bold words represent semantically correct and incorrect ingredients, respectively. Words in parentheses indicate missing ingredients that should be included in the sentence. Note that parallel words in a sentence are not comma-separated due to the format of the YouCook2 dataset (cited from [20]).

Figure 5 shows an example of generated recipes. Although the texts generated by our full model (VIVT) are not perfectly identical with the ground truth, the generated text still agrees with the content of each video segment.

Figure 6 visualizes two examples of state transitions caused by action "beat" on materials "flour" and "egg". Each raw ingredients (red) transit to other points (blue), where the two nearest samples are video segments from other recipes but with similar contents. To further confirm the realization of state transition in a continuous latent feature space, we demonstrated some arithmetic operations with latent features (Fig. 7). Here, the right-hand video segments are retrieved on the 2D t-SNE space in Fig. 6. Although it can fail in some cases, we observed that we could explicitly simulate the transition by simple operations.

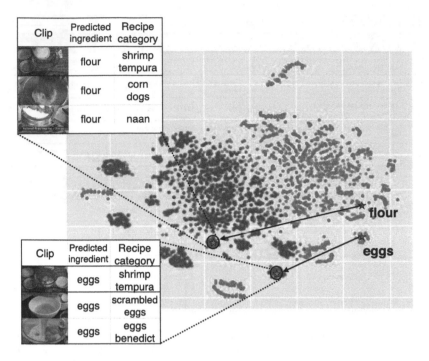

Fig. 6. A visualization of state transition in continuous latent space with tSNE [16]. Red and blue points represent raw and processed (updated) ingredient features, respectively (cited from [20]). (Color figure online)

	Ingredient	**+** Updated ingredient	**—** Raw ingredient	**=** Updated ingredient (nearest vector)
(a)	potatoes	**+** cut tomatoes	**—** tomatoes	**=** cut potatoes
(b)	flour	**+** add egg	**—** egg	**=** added flour
(c)	bacon	**+** fry onion	**—** onion	**=** fried bacon
(d)	meat	**+** fry onion	**—** onion	**=** chopped meat (fail)
(e)	chopped shallot	**+** add egg	**—** egg	**=** added chopped shallot
(f)	cut shrimp	**+** cover tortilla	**—** tortilla	**=** covered cut shrimp
(g)	cut potatoes	**+** add egg	**—** egg	**=** mashed potatoes (fail)

Fig. 7. Arithmetics using the learned latent features of ingredients. Examples (a) to (d) represent raw-to-processed transition, and (e) to (g) are processed-to-processed transition. Note that (d) and (g) shows failure cases (cited from [20]).

5   Conclusion

This paper introduced our recent attempts to model two major properties of manufacturing activities for cross-modal activity understanding. The first property is material merging processes, which we can model as a tree structure. Explicitly modeling the structure in the process of the visual storytelling task, we have enhanced captioning quality with any baseline methods. The second property is the state transition of materials, which we can model as an action-driven transition in continuous space, using NPN. After the training, we confirmed that we had obtained a cross-modal representation that explicitly simulates changes caused by actions.

At the same time, we still have several future works. First, we should develop a method to model both properties simultaneously. Second, we are currently assuming preliminary segmented videos as input; however, this assumption seriously harms the method's usability. Therefore, a model that works with unsegmented videos is crucial to developing a commercial system. Finally, we need to roll out these techniques to applications other than cooking. The current methods lie on the large-size datasets, which are not always available as cooking recipe websites. We are starting to collect data on biochemical experiments [22], but it is not realistic to assume the same scale of a dataset for such tasks. Thus, we need to transfer knowledge from cooking tasks to others.

Acknowledgement. This work was supported by JSPS KAKENHI Grant Number JP21J20250 and JP20H04210, and partially supported by JP21H04910, JP17H06100, JST-Mirai Program Grant Number JPMJMI21G2.

References

1. Banerjee, S., Lavie, A.: METEOR: an automatic metric for MT evaluation with improved correlation with human judgments. In: Proceedings ACL Workshop IEEMMTS, pp. 65–72 (2005)
2. Bosselut, A., Levy, O., Holtzman, A., Ennis, C., Fox, D., Choi, Y.: Simulating action dynamics with neural process networks. In: Proceedings ICLR (2018)
3. Chandu, K., Nyberg, E., Black, A.W.: Storyboarding of recipes: grounded contextual generation. In: Proceedings ACL, pp. 6040–6046 (2019)
4. Dai, Z., Yang, Z., Yang, Y., Carbonell, J., Le, Q., Salakhutdinov, R.: Transformer-XL: attentive language models beyond a fixed-length context. In: Proceedings ACL, pp. 2978–2988 (2019)
5. Gu, J., Im, D.J., Li., V.O.: Neural machine translation with Gumbel-greedy decoding. In: Proceedings AAAI, pp. 5125–5132 (2018)
6. Harashima, J., Someya, Y., Kikuta, Y.: Cookpad image dataset: an image collection as infrastructure for food research. In: SIGIR (2017)
7. He, K., Zhang, X., Ren, S., Sun, J.: Deep residual learning for image recognition. In: Proceedings CVPR, pp. 770–778 (2016)
8. Huang, T.K., et al.: Visual storytelling. In: Proceedings NAACL-HLT, pp. 1233–1239 (2016)
9. Jermsurawong, J., Habash, N.: Predicting the structure of cooking recipes. In: Proceedings EMNLP (2015)

10. Kiddon, C., Ponnuraj, G.T., Zettlemoyer, L., Choi, Y.: Mise EN place: unsupervised interpretation of instructional recipes. In: EMNLP (2015)
11. Kim, T., Heo, M., Son, S., Park, K., Zhang, B.: GLAC Net: glocal attention cascading networks for multi-image cued story generation. arXiv (2018)
12. Koehn, P.: Statistical significance tests for machine translation evaluation. In: Proceedings EMNLP, pp. 388–395 (2004)
13. Lei, J., Wang, L., Shen, Y., Yu, D., Berg, T., Bansal, M.: MART: memory-augmented recurrent transformer for coherent video paragraph captioning. In: Proceedings ACL, pp. 2603–2614 (2020)
14. Li, J., Galley, M., Brockett, C., Gao, J., Dolan, B.: A diversity-promoting objective function for neural conversation models. In: Proceedings NAACL-HLT, pp. 110–119 (2016)
15. Lin, C.Y., Och, F.J.: Automatic evaluation of machine translation quality using longest common subsequence and skip-bigram statistics. In: Proceedings ACL, pp. 605–612 (2004)
16. van der Maaten, L., Hinton, G.: Visualizing data using t-SNE. J. Mach. Learn. Res. **9**, 2579–2605 (2008)
17. Miech, A., Zhukov, D., Alayrac, J.B., Tapaswi, M., Laptev, I., Sivic, J.: HowTo100M: learning a text-video embedding by watching hundred million narrated video clips. In: Proceedings ICCV, pp. 2630–2640 (2019)
18. Mori, S., Maeta, H., Yamakata, Y., Sasada, T.: Flow graph corpus from recipe texts. In: Proceedings LREC (2014)
19. Nishimura, T., Hashimoto, A., Mori, S.: Procedural text generation from a photo sequence. In: Proceedings INLG, pp. 409–414 (2019)
20. Nishimura, T., Hashimoto, A., Ushiku, Y., Kameko, H., Mori, S.: State-aware video procedural captioning. In: ACMMM, pp. 1766–1774 (2021)
21. Nishimura, T., Hashimoto, A., Ushiku, Y., Kameko, H., Yamakata, Y., Mori, S.: Structure-aware procedural text generation from an image sequence. IEEE Access **9**, 2125–2141 (2020)
22. Nishimura, T., et al.: Egocentric biochemical video-and-language dataset. In: Proceedings ICCVW, pp. 3122–3126 (2021)
23. Papineni, K., Roukos, S., Ward, T., Zhu, W.J.: BLEU: A method for automatic evaluation of machine translation. In: Proceedings ACL, pp. 311–318 (2002)
24. Park, J.S., Rohrbach, M., Darrell, T., Rohrbach, A.: Adversarial inference for multi-sentence video description. In: Proceedings CVPR, pp. 6598–6608 (2019)
25. Shi, B., et al.: Dense procedure captioning in narrated instructional videos. In: Proceedings ACL, pp. 6382–6391 (2019)
26. Shi, B., Ji, L., Niu, Z., Duan, N., Zhou, M., Chen, X.: Learning semantic concepts and temporal alignment for narrated video procedural captioning. In: Proceedings ACMMM, pp. 4355–4363 (2020)
27. Tai, K.S., Socher, R., Manning, C.D.: Improved semantic representations from tree-structured long short-term memory networks. In: Proceedings ACL-IJCNLP, pp. 1556–1566 (2015)
28. Vedantam, R., Zitnick, C.L., Parikh, D.: CIDEr: consensus-based image description evaluation. In: Proceedings CVPR, pp. 4566–4575 (2015)
29. Vinyals, O., Toshev, A., Bengio, S., Erhan, D.: Show and tell: a neural image caption generator. In: Proceedings of the IEEE Conference on Computer Vision and Pattern Recognition, CVPR, June 2015
30. Wang, W., Wang, Y., Chen, S., Jin, Q.: YouMakeup: a large-scale domain-specific multimodal dataset for fine-grained semantic comprehension. In: Proceedings EMNLP-IJCNLP, pp. 5133–5143 (2019)

31. Xiong, Y., Dai, B., Lin, D.: Move forward and tell: a progressive generator of video descriptions. In: Ferrari, V., Hebert, M., Sminchisescu, C., Weiss, Y. (eds.) ECCV 2018. LNCS, vol. 11215, pp. 489–505. Springer, Cham (2018). https://doi.org/10.1007/978-3-030-01252-6_29
32. Yagcioglu, S., Erdem, A., Erdem, E., Ikizler-Cinbis, N.: RecipeQA: a challenge dataset for multimodal comprehension of cooking recipes. In: Proceedings of the 2018 Conference on Empirical Methods in Natural Language Processing, pp. 1358–1368 (2018)
33. Yamakata, Y., Mori, S., Carroll, J.: English recipe flow graph corpus. In: Proceedings LREC, pp. 5187–5194 (2020)
34. Zhou, L., Xu, C., Corso, J.J.: Towards automatic learning of procedures from web instructional videos. In: Proceedings AAAI, pp. 7590–7598 (2018)
35. Zhou, L., Zhou, Y., Corso, J.J., Socher, R., Xiong, C.: End-to-end dense video captioning with masked transformer. In: Proceedings of the IEEE Conference on Computer Vision and Pattern Recognition, CVPR, June 2018

Innovative Pedagogical Framework Based on Digital Collaborative Tools: A Design Education Practice of CADP Course for Freshmen in Design

Tiantian Li[1] (ID), Ningyi Dai[2], and Xuguang Zhu[1](✉)

[1] School of Art and Design, Zhejiang Sci-Tech University, Hangzhou, China
zxg761009@163.com
[2] School of Design, Hunan University, Changsha, People's Republic of China
dainingyi@hnu.edu.cn

Abstract. Under the background of "big design" and "post-formal education", the reform of design education is advancing to a deeper level, and online collaborative tools provide great potential for the development of design education. This paper puts forward an innovative pedagogical framework based on digital collaboration tools, discusses the new path of knowledge dissemination, and guides the reform of basic design courses. This paper proposes the communication dimension of digital collaborative environment. The research studies the students' participation and the types of knowledge creation in teaching cooperation, and carries out the integration of learning mode integration. We establish an innovative pedagogical framework of CAPD course empowered by online collaborative tool. The results show that the framework can achieve the goal of integrating design output. The combination of the innovation of pedagogical framework and digital collaboration tools may also contain greater potential in promoting the transformation of design education in the future.

Keywords: Innovative pedagogical framework · Digital collaborative tools · Teaching cooperation · Enquiry-based learning

1 Introduction

The current design knowledge system is transforming to the integration of interdisciplinary knowledge [1], and there is a "big design" trend in the design discipline that continues to integrate systematically. Gidley [2] believes that with social and cultural changes, the current education system is in a transitional stage from formal to post-formal education. In the field of design education, compared with the traditional engineering education model based on instruction-based learning (IBL), the learning method based on constructivist theory has ushered in extensive development in theory and practice [3]. In the era of artificial intelligence, designers design frameworks, and artificial intelligence provides users with personalized solutions based on data and algorithms [4]. In

P.-L. P. Rau (Ed.): HCII 2022, LNCS 13312, pp. 58–72, 2022.
https://doi.org/10.1007/978-3-031-06047-2_5

the field of teaching, students' creation of learning content has become a major trend in industrial design education. This is in line with the principles of constructivism in education, that is, learners apply knowledge in a similar environment as knowledge builders. There is no doubt that this environment includes both offline physical environment and online collaborative space. It can be considered that online collaborative tools provide great potential for the development of design education.

Since the post epidemic era, a large number of online collaboration tools have emerged ("Miro", or its Chinese counterpart "huiyizhuo"). They provide an accessible platform for collaborative design of diversified scenes, and are no exception in the field of education. It can be considered that the environment of online collaboration not only makes implicit thinking visible, but also promotes the transformation from distributed cognition to collective cognition.

In this context, the reform of design education is advancing to a deeper level. However, the reform of basic design curriculum is still very conservative, which is determined by the curriculum's own characteristics and objectives or status. Computer aided design practice (CADP) course is a basic course for freshmen of industrial design. Due to the steep curve of software learning, for the teaching mode of computer aided design practice (CADP), some universities adopt the "Instruction-based learning" (IBL) mode to passively teach software skills, while some directly ignore the stage of skill teaching to the use of software for design. The former model deviates from the needs and development of the times, while the latter model ignores the premise that the learning method based on constructivism theory requires to provide necessary guidance and support according to students' previous knowledge and skills. It can be considered that under the current background, the objectives of CADP course should meet the needs of changing from software skill learning to design integration work output, guide Freshmen majoring in design to broaden their horizons, make attempts guided by design purpose and curiosity, and provide preparation for docking with other directions in practical projects in the future. How to use the digital collaborative environment and tools to construct an innovative learning framework and system that integrates instruction-based knowledge learning and constructivist theory-based knowledge generation? How to re-discuss the relationship in design teaching cooperation and explore new ways of knowledge dissemination? How to guide the reform of basic design courses and enable design students, especially freshmen, to learn in complex fields under the background of "big design era" and post-formal education? The above questions have become the driving force of the research motivation and design education practice of this paper.

2 Literature Review and Theoretical Innovation

2.1 Digital Collaborative Tools and Environment as Carriers for Communication Between "Internal-External" and "Individual-Team" Dimensions

Creative design behavior is often regarded as a process in which internal thinking and external visualization interact simultaneously [5]. The generation stage in industrial design can be viewed as the iterative thinking and manual process of imagining future products (seeing as), concretizing concretized ideas, and evaluating what has been done (seeing that) [6]. Li [7] et al. proposed a process model of high-level semantic visual representation based on the "dual approach" in which internal thinking and external visualization in creative design occur simultaneously. From the perspective of cooperative design and participatory design, design problems are realized through teamwork. Christian et al. [8] studied participatory design in education from the perspective of computational empowerment. Karakaya et al. (2014) believe that a collaborative digital environment can enhance the creativity of designers, and an integrated design interface can bring an innovative design environment and enhance the ability to reflect on others' works.

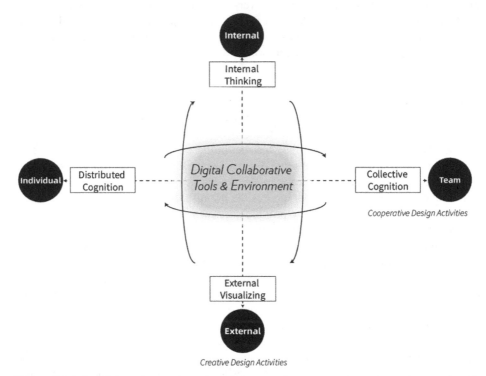

Fig. 1. Digital collaboration tools and environment that communicate internal-external and individual-team dimensions.

In the post-epidemic era, the digital collaborative environment empowers design behavior from both "internal-external" and "individual-team" dimension (Fig. 1). Among them, creative design behavior is formed by iterative interaction between internal thinking and external visualization, which is an internal-external dimension; while collaborative design behavior is formed by the transformation from the distributed cognitive process of the individual to the collective cognitive process of the team, which is an individual-team dimension. In the former, the digital collaborative environment provides an external carrier for the visualization of internal thinking; In the latter, the digital collaborative environment provides a communication environment for team collaboration, memory exchange, situational awareness and communication [10], which helps to realize collective cognition. Therefore, the digital collaborative environment can be used as an important platform for teaching mode practice in the field of design education.

2.2 Student Participation and Types of Knowledge Creation in Teaching Cooperation

Gidley [2] pointed out that although the so-called post-formal education lags behind other social and cultural changes caused by post-modern impulses to some extent, education is still in the transitional stage from formal education to post-formal education. She uses 14 post-formal characteristics (constructive consciousness, contextualization, creativity, dialogue, holism, etc.) [11, 12] as the identifiers of post-formal education and contrasts them with mainstream formal education. As the concept of co-creation has become increasingly popular in the context of disciplines and institutions, the idea of partnership between students and faculty members in teaching and learning has become popular too [13]. This not only involves the teaching cooperation relationship between educators and students, but also relates to the type and effect of knowledge dissemination, creation under different teaching cooperation relationships. Student participation in teaching cooperation can be divided into three levels from low to high, engagement, agency and empowerment [13]. In terms of the process and type of knowledge generation in teaching cooperation, the three types of knowledge creation, namely formal, informal and experiential knowledge, promote the learning process of design practice [14]. Auernhammer et al. [15] believe that in the learning cycle, the coach is the learning intermediary of the design team and can help the design team carry out design activities and experiential learning.

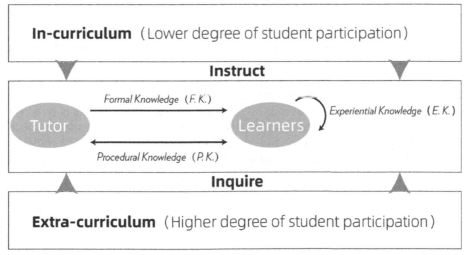

Fig. 2. Knowledge creation framework of CADP course: the source of knowledge creation and student participation in teaching cooperation, as well as the types of knowledge creation.

This article synthesizes previous research viewpoints and proposes a knowledge creation framework for computer-aided design practice courses (Fig. 2). According to Eris and Leifer's [14] point of view, product development knowledge is generated under the joint action of relevant personnel and resources. In this article, three types of knowledge (formal knowledge, informal knowledge and experiential knowledge) jointly promote the learning process of design practice. Relevant personnel refer to Tutor and learner (teams) in the teaching cooperation. In the context of design and system integration, the source of knowledge includes both the instruction of in-class knowledge and the enquiry of extra-curricular knowledge. In the Instruction level, students have a low degree of participation. In the enquiry level, students have a higher degree of participation. The different degree of students' participation can provide a basic reference for exploring the new teaching cooperation relationship and relate to different learning modes in design education.

2.3   Innovative Pedagogical Modes Integrating Instruction-Based Case Learning and Enquiry-Based Learning

The in-class teaching part of the CADP course is mainly oriented to the goal of skill learning, usually adopting an instruction-based learning (IBL) model, in which knowledge is passed to students through lectures, and students play a passive role. The possible reason why the constructivism teaching method has not become popular is that software learning has a relatively steep learning curve, and the concept of minimal guidance in the constructivist-oriented teaching method is not suitable for novice learners [16]. Given the traditional IBL model does not always produce the expected learning results [17], this article combines the characteristics of case teaching and instruction-based learning and teaching models, and proposes an Instruction-based Case Learning model (IBCL) that combines case teaching method and IBL. We try to adapt software teaching content into one case after another to improve the quality of software teaching.

The extracurricular enquiry part of the CADP course is mainly goal-oriented, through investigation from other sources, to expand the possibility of the final solution. Savery [18] pointed out that "enquiry-based learning" (EBL) is based on the philosophy of John Dewey, who believes that education begins with the curiosity of learners. In enquiry-based learning (EBL), on the one hand, the "lecturer" becomes the facilitator of problem-solving, rather than the statement of facts and information. On the other hand, educators construct and provide questions or problems, and then encourage students to follow a relatively linear process from the question or problem to the solution or answer [19]. It is essentially a model for teachers to build a framework and students to generate content [20]. Therefore, in "inquiry-based learning" (EBL), the question we need to face is what kind of a specific framework should be established to enable curiosity-driven learning to proceed in an orderly manner (Fig. 3).

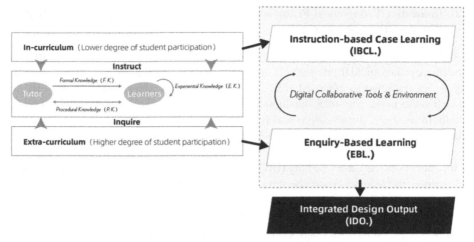

Fig. 3. The CADP course includes an in-class skill teaching part (corresponding to the IBCL. mode) and an extracurricular investigation part (corresponding to the EBL. mode) to achieve the goal of integrated design output in the CADP course.

3 Design Education Practice of Computer Aided Design Practice Course Based on Innovative Pedagogical Framework

3.1 Background of the CADP Course

Computer aided design practice (CADP) course is a basic course for freshmen of industrial design. The course originally adopted the "Instruction-based learning" (IBL) mode of traditional engineering education. The course teaches a 2D graphics software (Adobe Illustrator) and a 3D modeling software (rhinoceros), which focuses on the passive teaching of skills and does not emphasize the design output based on software skills. On the contrary, in some other colleges, the course directly ignores the stage of skill teaching and requires the use of software skills for design output. The former model is divorced from the needs and development of the times, while the latter model ignores the premise that the learning method based on constructivism theory requires to provide necessary guidance and support according to students' previous knowledge and skills.

It can be considered that under the background of the transformation from design to system integration and post formal education, the teaching goal of CADP course should realize the transformation from software skill learning to design integration design output. It should be noted that, as a course for freshmen, we hope CADP course can stimulate students' curiosity, let them independently try and explore different directions, and find the directions and fields of interest in the future from this attempt and practice. Therefore, an innovative pedagogical framework is established through the empowerment of digital collaborative tools and environment (Sect. 2.1), combined with student participation and knowledge creation types in Teaching Cooperation (Sect. 2.2), with the goal of integrated design output through Instruction-based case learning and Enquiry-based learning (Sect. 2.3).

3.2   Innovative Pedagogical Framework of CAPD Course Empowered by Digital Collaborative Environment

In order to achieve the goal of "integrated design output", this paper puts forward the innovative pedagogical framework of computer-aided design practice course, as shown in Fig. 4. The framework composed of IBCL, EBL and IDO. In the learning mode of IBCL and EBL, this paper combines the digital collaborative environment composed of online collaborative tools, presentations and feedbacks, and defines the teaching cooperation relationship between tutor and learners (individual and team).

- Instruction-based Case Learning (IBCL). The IBCL level is mainly for software skills learning. The teacher gradually starts the case teaching of two software (Rhinoceros, Illustrator), while students practice and review the basic cases of related software in class. Then, the teacher utilizes the digital collaborative desktop ("huiyizhuo") to comment and discuss the uploaded personal assignments to provide guidance and support for the teaching of software skills.
- Enquiry-based Learning (EBL). The EBL level is mainly based on data research and concept deduction of design objectives, which is essentially a model for teachers to build a framework and students to generate content. Here we have established an evolutionary procedural framework, in which the whole research process is composed of exploration framework (1.0), definition framework (2.0) and design framework (3.0). Among them, the teacher specified the research category of the exploration framework ("Industry News", "Case Applications", "Software Development", "Skills Know-how"), and the team filled the research content on the online collaborative desktop (huiyizhuo). We referenced part of the business of design consulting companies and proposed these four research categories the purpose of the four research categories is to open the horizons of freshmen, stimulate their curiosity, and enable them to quickly expand relevant information with the help of online collaboration tools. In the definition framework and design framework, teachers no longer specify the research category, and teams spontaneously organizes the content and category according to the previously found content and the goal orientation of the design. The teaching cooperation relationship is embodied in that teachers construct a "semi-open framework" and students generate content and categories; Teachers combine the feedback results to guide the direction and promote the research results to the ideal goal. Among them, the semi-open procedural framework is also one of the bold attempts of this research.
- Integrated design output (IDO). The integrated design output is achieved through the mutual drive and promotion of IBCL and EBL. In addition to the 2D and 3D software involved in the basic workload of the course, the comprehensive software skills acquired by the students also include other software for spontaneous learning based on research and practice for the purpose of meeting the design intent. The visualized process framework records and advances the design process. Together with software comprehensive skills, it can achieve multiple types of design submissions and integrated design outputs.

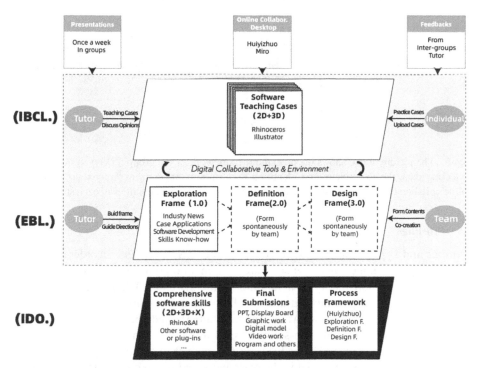

Fig. 4. Innovative pedagogical framework of CAPD course empowered by digital collaborative tools and environment to favor Integrated design output.

3.3 Research Purpose and Data Collection

This paper carries out the practice of design education based on the innovative teaching framework of the CADP course. The whole course lasts for 6 weeks from April to June 2021, with 30 participants, all freshmen majoring in industrial design, with an average age of 19.8 years.

All students are divided into 6 groups with 5 people in each group. The course aims to achieve the transformation from software skill learning to integrated design output. Therefore, the course attempts to indirectly reflect whether the goal of integrated design output is achieved by investigating from three aspects: comprehensive software skills, visualized process framework and design submission, and discuss the problems revealed.

In terms of software comprehensive skills, examine the number and types of software involved in the final submitted design works. The data source is the self-statistics of each group of students. In terms of the process framework, we examined the category of investigations established by 6 group at each stage in the evolutionary framework (exploration, definition, and design stage) and the number under each category. When collecting data, the researchers first identified the different stages from "huiyizhuo", the online collaborative desktops, and then counted the categories and quantities of each stage. In terms of design submission, the form of design submission and the type of output are investigated. The data source is the self-report of each group of students.

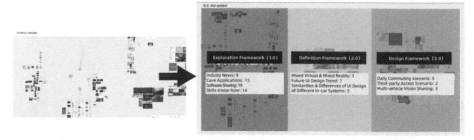

Fig. 5. The picture above shows the procedural framework of the group 5 (Vivi System). When collecting data, the researchers first identified the different stages from "huiyizhuo" (left), the online collaborative desktops, and then counted the categories and quantities of each stage (right).

3.4   Findings

Number and Type of Software Involved in the Final Submission. In order to achieve the design purpose, the number of software used in all 6 groups is 3–7 ($M = 5$). From the perspective of software type, in addition to the 2D and 3D software (Rhinoceros, Illustrator) taught in the course, it also involves illustration software such as Sai and procreate, game production software such as Unity3D and rpgmaker or lightweight plug-ins, lightroom or Animation software such as C4d. It can be seen that both the quantity and type of software involved are far more than the two types of software (Rhinoceros, Illustrator) involved in the basic workload of the course. These softwares are learned spontaneously by students (Table 1).

Table 1.   Number of software involved in the final submission of each group.

Name	Introduction	Software used	NO. of software used
The Nine Color Deer	The concept image design originated from "nine color deer" scriptures in Dunhuang	Photoshop, Illustrator, Aftereffects, Jianying	4
ROBOTOK	The dynamic poster design of futuristic concept robots	Cinema4D, Aftereffects, Photoshop	3
Against involution storm	The 2D role-playing game design	Unity3d, Aftereffects, Photoshop, Rpgmaker, Rhinoceros	5
MINECARFT	The scene and interface design based on Augmented Reality	Photoshop, Illustrator, Minecraft, Procreate, Lightroom, Rhinoceros, Cinema4D	7
Vivi system	The mixed reality in-car system design	Aftereffects, Rhinoceros, Illustrator, procreate	4

(continued)

Table 1. (*continued*)

Name	Introduction	Software used	NO. of software used
Tong Xin Tong Qu	The concept image design based on "innocence"	Cinema4D, Aftereffects, Sai2, Premiere, Procreate, Illustrator, Photoshop	7

Categories and Contents of Each Stage of the Process Framework. The category of exploration framework is specified by teachers ("Industry News", "Case Applications", "Software Development", "Skills Know-how"), and the content under the category is filled by students in Huiyizhuo. Among them, the total content under the four categories ranges from 30 to 63 (M = 47.5, SD = 11). It should be noted that both the categories and contents in the definition framework and design framework are generated spontaneously by students. Among them, the total number of categories of "definition framework" is 3 to 4, and the total number of contents ranges from 15 to 63 (M = 32, SD = 16). The total number of categories of "design framework" is 3 to 4, and the total number of contents ranges from 9 to 42 (M = 18.8, SD = 12). From the total number of categories and contents, it is not enough to determine whether there is "divergence" or "convergence" in the research process between exploration framework, definition framework and design framework, which may require further investigation on the basis of further data collection and improvement of research methods (Table 2).

Table 2. Categories and contents of each stage of the process framework

Group	Name	Exploration Framework (1.0)		Definition Framework (2.0)		Design Framework (3.0)	
		Total categories	Total contents	Total categories	Total contents	Total categories	Total contents
G1	The Nine Color Deer	4	51	3	18	3	26
G2	ROBOTOK	4	30	4	35	4	14
G3	Against involution storm	4	46	3	37	4	9
G4	MINECARFT	4	38	3	24	3	12
G5	Vivi system	4	57	3	15	3	10
G6	Tong Xin Tong Qu	4	63	4	63	4	42

Types of Final Submission. Figure 7 shows part of the final output of the CADP course. The topics of the final submission include in-car system, game program, augmented reality interface and concept image. The content of group 1 is the concept image design originated from "nine color deer" scriptures in Dunhuang, the content of group 2 is the dynamic poster design of futuristic concept robot, the content of group 3 is the 2D role-playing game design, the content of group 4 is the scene and interface design based on Augmented Reality, the content of group 5 is the mixed reality vehicle system design, and the content of group 6 is the concept image design based on "innocence".

The minimum requirements for design submissions are one PPT and two exhibition boards, and the types of other submissions are not limited. As a result, all 6 groups submitted more than the minimum requirements. Among them, 6 groups (100%) submitted more than one type of output, mainly graphic works including dynamic posters, scene renderings and other forms; Five groups (83%) submitted more than two types of outputs, involving graphic, video works or digital model; Three groups (50%) submitted more than three types of outputs, and two groups (33%) submitted more than four types of outputs, including game programs (Fig. 6).

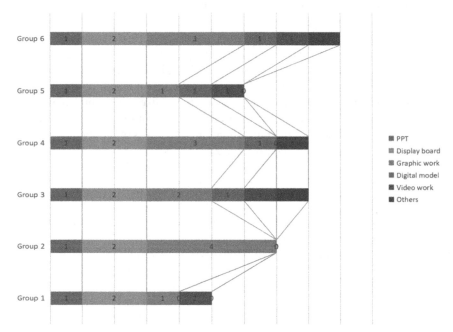

Fig. 6. The minimum requirements for design submissions are one PPT and two display boards, and the types of other submissions are not limited. In addition, the types of final submissions include graphic work, digital model, video work and other types, such as game programs.

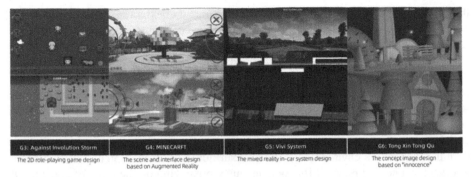

G3: Against Involution Storm	G4: MINECARFT	G5: Vivi System	G6: Tong Xin Tong Qu
The 2D role-playing game design	The scene and interface design based on Augmented Reality	The mixed reality in-car system design	The concept image design based on "innocence"

Fig. 7. Shows part of the final output from 4 groups, including 2D game design, augmented reality interface design, in-car system design and concept image design from left to right.

4 Discussion

4.1 Comprehensive Software Skills

The results show that both the amount of software involved (M = 5) and the types of software involved (drawing application, visual effect production, game development engine, etc.) are far more than the two taught in the course (rhinoceros, Illustrator). All other softwares are learned spontaneously by students. We believe that in order to make freshmen having this driving force for spontaneous inquiry, we should firstly open their horizons and stimulate their curiosity.

The four categories stipulated in the "Exploration Framework" are designed to open up their horizons. "Industry News" and "Case Application" enable freshmen to pay attention to the trends and related topics of top companies (Huawei, Alibaba Cloud, etc.), and "Software Development" enables students to quickly expand their knowledge and understanding of software (Lightweight software, cross-platform software, etc.), "Skills Know-how "provide operating methods for software applications, and some tutorials are collected from social media and short videos such as Weibo and tiktok, which has a certain eye-catching attribute.

In addition, through the use of online collaborative desktop (huiyizhuo) for multi-person collaborative exploration, not only the efficiency of information collection has been greatly improved, but also this activity is delightful and full of participation. Karakaya et al. [9] believe that a collaborative digital environment can enhance the creativity of designers. In an era when online learning resources and channels are abundant enough, it may be possible to integrate students together and provide such kind of collaborative inquiry environment and the connectivity of teaching cooperation is the value of the future classroom. As discussed in Sect. 2.1, this is also empowered by online collaboration tools.

4.2 Process Framework

The general idea of the ELM is that teachers build a "problem solving loop", a frame, and students generate content around the frame. An interesting phenomenon is that in the CADP course, students not only filled in the content of exploration framework (1.0), but also spontaneously constructed the categories and contents of definition framework (2.0) and design framework (3.0). For example, in group 5 (Vivi system), the category of definition framework is "mixed virtual and mixed reality", "future UI design trend", "similarities and differences of UI design of different in-car systems" (Fig. 5); The categories of design framework are "daily commuting scenario", "third-party access scenario" and "multi-vehicle vision sharing" (Fig. 5). These research categories and their contents are spontaneously constructed and improved by the team towards the goal. This enriches the specific meaning of "student-generated content" in the ELM, that is, in a digital collaborative environment, students can not only fill in content, but also begin to organize a new framework for spontaneously organizing on the basis of content. Of course, this spontaneity may have premises, one is derived from the directional opinions given by teachers during specific situation, the other is from the timely feedback from inter-group or teachers through questionnaires after each presentation. It also comes from the preservation of research content on the online collaborative desktop, which makes the previous content become a source of stimulation for students to further organize content and categories, so as to promote the process of research.

4.3 Integrated Design Output

In 2015, the International Council of societies of industrial design (ICSID), whose name has been used for 60 years, was renamed world design organization (WDO). The boundaries of different fields of design discipline have been broken and turned to collaborative development. As a course for freshmen, the original intention of the CADP course is to stimulate students' curiosity so that they can independently try and dabble in different directions, finding the direction and field of interest in the future from this trial and practice. There is no doubt that this needs innovative pedagogical framework design as methodological support.

Under the innovative pedagogical framework jointly promoted by IBCL and EBL mode, 83% of the groups submitted more than two types of outputs, involving graphic works, video works or digital models, and programs designed spontaneously. The design output includes in-car system, game program, augmented reality interface and concept image design. The design output between each group spans different fields, and the design output has a high degree of completeness. On the one hand, this is caused by the new teaching partnership, on the other hand, it also reflects that the interests of each group of freshmen are distributed in different fields. They are willing to spontaneously try and understand the fields of interest.

Although its standardization needs to be further strengthened, it provides preparation for docking with other directions in practical projects in the future. Through the course, students have the ability to independently explore and produce design schemes around unknown problems. To some extent, this reflects that the innovative teaching framework of CAPD curriculum empowered by digital collaborative environment can achieve the goal of integrating design output. In short, we believe that the innovation of pedagogical framework combined with the empowerment of digital collaborative tools can promote the transformation of design education in the postformal-education era. This combination has great potential to be explored.

5   Conclusion

The reform of design education is advancing to a deeper level under the background of "big design" and "post formal education". The combination of the innovation of pedagogical framework and digital collaboration tools may also contain greater potential in promoting the transformation of design education. This paper puts forward an innovative pedagogical framework based on digital collaboration tools, discusses the new path of knowledge dissemination, and guides the reform of basic design courses. This paper proposes the communication dimension of digital collaborative environment. This paper studies the students' participation and the types of knowledge creation in teaching cooperation, and carries out the integration of learning mode integration. We establishes an innovative pedagogical framework of CAPD course empowered by online collaborative tool. The results show that the innovative teaching framework of CAPD curriculum empowered by digital collaborative environment can achieve the goal of integrating design output.

Acknowledgements. We would love to thank all the students from the CAPD course participating in the research. This research is funded by the Collaborative education project of industry-university cooperation of the Chinese Ministry of Education, grant number 202102100014, and by the General Project of Zhejiang Provincial Department of Education, grant number 21086103-F, and by the research startup fund for Zhejiang Sci-Tech University, grant number 20082337-Y.

References

1. Jones, P.H.: Systemic design principles for complex social systems. In: Metcalf, G.S. (ed.) Social Systems and Design. TSS, vol. 1, pp. 91–128. Springer, Tokyo (2014). https://doi.org/10.1007/978-4-431-54478-4_4
2. Gidley, J.M.: Educating for evolving consciousness: voicing the emergency for love, life and wisdom. In: de Souza, M., Francis, L.J., O'Higgins-Norman, J., Scott, D. (eds.) International handbook of education for spirituality, care and wellbeing. IHRE, vol. 3, pp. 553–561. Springer, Dordrecht (2009). https://doi.org/10.1007/978-1-4020-9018-9_29
3. Barak, M.: Problem-, project-and design-based learning: their relationship to teaching science, technology and engineering in school. J. Probl. Based Learn. **7**(2), 94–97 (2020)
4. Verganti, R., Vendraminelli, L., Iansiti, M.: Innovation and design in the age of artificial intelligence. J. Prod. Innov. Manag. **37**(3), 212–227 (2020)
5. Sachse, P., Furtner, M.: Embodied knowledge in design. In: Leidlmair, K. (ed.) After Cognitivism, pp. 163–179. Springer, Dordrecht (2009). https://doi.org/10.1007/978-1-4020-9992-2_10
6. Rieuf, V., Bouchard, C., Meyrueis, V., Omhover, J.-F.: Emotional activity in early immersive design: sketches and moodboards in virtual reality. Design Stud. **48**, 43–75 (2017)
7. Li, T., Zhao, D.: Mood board tool on high-level semantics visual representation to favor creative design. In: Rebelo, F. (ed.) Advances in Ergonomics in Design: Proceedings of the AHFE 2021 Virtual Conference on Ergonomics in Design, July 25-29, 2021, USA, pp. 408–419. Springer, Cham (2021). https://doi.org/10.1007/978-3-030-79760-7_49
8. Dindler, C., Smith, R., Iversen, O.S.: Computational empowerment: participatory design in education. CoDesign **16**(1), 66–80 (2020)

9. Karakaya, A.F., Demirkan, H.: Collaborative digital environments to enhance the creativity of designers. Comput. Human Behav. **42**, 176–186 (2015)
10. Hung, W.: Team-based complex problem solving: a collective cognition perspective. Educ. Tech. Res. Dev. **61**(3), 365–384 (2013)
11. Arlin, P.K.: The wise teacher: a developmental model of teaching. Theory Into Pract. **38**(1), 12–17 (1999)
12. Cartwright, K.B.: Cognitive developmental theory and spiritual development. J. Adult Dev. **8**(4), 213–220 (2001)
13. Thompson, J.R.: From Engagement to Empowerment: Exploring the Potential for Pedagogical Partnerships in Design (2020)
14. Eris, O., Leifer, L.: Faciliating product development knowledge acquisition: interaction between the expert and the team. Int. J. Eng. Educ. **19**(1), 142–152 (2003)
15. Auernhammer, J., Lenzen, M., Leifer, L.: Dancing with Creativity: Changes in Conception in Design Thinking within Product Innovation Projects (2020)
16. Sweller, J., Kirschner, P.A., Clark, R.E.: Why minimally guided teaching techniques do not work: a reply to commentaries. Educ. Psychol. **42**(2), 115–121 (2007)
17. Balan, L., Yuen, T., Mehrtash, M.: Problem-based learning strategy for CAD software using free-choice and open-ended group projects. Procedia Manuf. **32**, 339–347 (2019)
18. Savery, J.R.: Overview of problem-based learning: definitions and distinctions. Essential readings in problem-based learning: exploring and extending the legacy of Howard S. Barrows. Interdiscip. J. Prob. Based Learn. **9**(2), 5–15 (2015)
19. Melles, G., et al.: Problem finding through design thinking in education. Inquiry-Based Learning for Multidisciplinary Programs: A Conceptual and Practical Resource for Educators. Emerald Group Publishing Limited (2015)
20. Brod, G.: Generative learning: which strategies for what age? Educ. Psychol. Rev. **33**(4), 1295–1318 (2020)

Status and Trend: The Application of Educational VR Games in Teaching Chinese as a Foreign Language

Zhen Luo[1] ⓘ, Zhifeng Jin[2] ⓘ, Linjian Li[1] ⓘ, and Zhejun Liu[1](✉) ⓘ

[1] Tongji University, 1239 Siping Road, Shanghai, China
{milkaholic08,2033670,wingeddreamer}@tongji.edu.cn
[2] No. 808, Institute of Shanghai Academy of Spaceflight Technology, Shanghai, China

Abstract. With more frequent international exchanges, the value of studying a foreign language is becoming increasingly apparent, and Chinese is becoming the language of choice for an increasing number of people. Virtual reality technology, with its ability to create fully immersive environments, has given foreign language learners a new lease of life, and academics believe that games have the potential to create virtual worlds rich of cultural and social value. As a result, the purpose of this work is to examine the current status and limitations of virtual reality games for Chinese language learning from three perspectives: academic literature, game applications, and online resources, as well as to recommend future research areas. According to the findings, the virtual reality games have shown a positive impact on Chinese learning, especially those adopting immersive VR system; most of the VR games are used to assist adult beginners in integrated language learning and cultural experience, with the impact on higher levels to be explored more; the suggestions on designing a better VR Chinese game are also given, including combining the characteristics of Chinese language, fully presenting the textbook content, and providing regular and timely corrective feedback. Limitations found in the previous studies are small sample size, single interaction mode, no placement test and so on. In the future, we expect to see more interdisciplinary experts work together and more VR games created to display characteristics of the Chinese language well, to completely exploit the capabilities of VR technology, and to produce lots of pleasure.

Keywords: Virtual reality · Game · Chinese language · Foreign language learning

1 Introduction

In recent years, with the development of full-scale globalization and ever more frequent international exchanges, the necessity of second language learning has become increasingly prominent. Overseas language learners often face the problem of lacking social and cultural context while learning a foreign language, so it is difficult for them to learn how to use the target language in real-life social interaction, which is important for foreign language learning.

P.-L. P. Rau (Ed.): HCII 2022, LNCS 13312, pp. 73–95, 2022.
https://doi.org/10.1007/978-3-031-06047-2_6

China is one of the fastest-growing economies in the world and Chinese has become an important option for many second language learners. The essential task of teaching Chinese as a foreign language is to cultivate the ability of cross-cultural communication. However, many Chinese language courses teach language skills and culture in a clumsy way, which can easily cause cultural misunderstandings and hamper learning enthusiasm. Moreover because of the Covid-19 pandemic, the number of offline Chinese courses has dropped sharply and many learners were forced to go online. Although technology breaks the limitations of time and space, it also introduces new problems such as the lack of interactivity, presence and interpersonal relationship, which are crucial to language teaching.

Therefore, it is urgent to change the pattern of foreign language and culture teaching in this new age by exploring new educational instruments and methods that may help learners to enhance their language ability and cultural cognition at the same time.

As a technology that is highly immersive, interactable and popular, virtual reality has already shown great potential in education and will promisingly benefit foreign language education as well. This new medium could break through the limitations of the traditional teaching environment by creating realistic virtuality, strong immersion, rich content and natural interaction [1, 2]. Benefitting from all these features, instead of being a passive viewer, a user becomes an active participant in a digital world where he/she may engage and receive feedback from interactions. While gamification techniques are believed to be beneficial in improving engagement further and then, the best possible results can be achieved if being introduced to VR technology [3].

The majority of researchers believed that games were capable of creating virtual worlds rich of cultural and social value. Gabe and Christopher [4] define gamification as the use of game elements and game thinking to engage users and solve problems. Simply put, the key to gamification is a reward dynamic, in which players who achieve the goals set forth by the game designers are rewarded in some measurable way, with some visible or audible mark of their accomplishment (such as points, higher game levels, winning badges, taking challenges, and visualizations of success in the form of a progress bar or leaderboards) [5]. In the educational games, learners might realistically feel and learn through perceiving, understanding, communicating and reflecting, which finally promoted retention and digestion of knowledge.

Games can be accessed through various platforms, such as mobile phones and desktop computers, but none of them can provide learners with a totally immersive experience as VR can. As immersion is a proven method of learning a foreign language [6], using virtual reality games to attain immersion brings new development opportunities.

VR and games, each in their own manner, have shown positive results in a variety of fields, and have been brought together over time for a variety of objectives from medicine and science research to education [7] and, more specifically, foreign language learning [8].

Mikropoulos and Natsis [9] published a ten-year assessment of empirical research on the educational applications of Virtual Reality in 2011. This study looked at 53 publications from 1999 to 2009 and found that the majority of them were done in schools and colleges, implying that VR may be used as a full-fledged instructional tool. It also pointed out the necessity of more research into the various multisensory interaction routes. There are other follow-up works that reviewed the application of VR in education field. For example, in 2019, Dorota et al. [7] presented the most recent VR applications used in education in several education areas, including general, engineering and health-related education. In the author's descriptions, it is clear that VR technology was applied in several forms and purposes, such as VR games was created to introduce civil engineering, and online laboratories was developed for learners to perform simple electronic laboratory activities. This review also pointed out the need for the creation of applications that can evaluate student's performance and consequently presented a collection of methods for creating scenarios and different approaches for testing and validation.

As for the specific education area this study concerns, that is, foreign language learning, scholars have long been interested in computer-assisted language learning (CALL). The literature review conducted by Liu et al. [10] in 2002 showed that, in 1990 to 2000, the advantages of the use of computer technology in foreign and second language learning were confirmed and well received. This is corroborated with the meta-analysis on CALL did by Chiu [11] in 2013, which examined papers from 2005 to 2011 and revealed that CALL has a positive effect in foreign language vocabulary acquisition. With the evolution of emerging technology, VR gradually attracts more attention from researchers in language learning, which is confirmed by the study of Lin and Lan [12]. According to their findings, the number of related studies has steadily increased from 2004 to 2013, with many showing that virtual environments promote learner autonomy, self-efficiency, and minimize learning anxiety. Their research also discovered that open-world social virtualities (Second Life, Moo, etc.) and massive multiplayer online games (MMOGs) (World of Warcraft and Civilization) were the most popular multi-user virtual environment (MUVE) technologies during that time period. Parmaxi [13] continued to review and analyze the use of VR to learn a foreign language during 2015 to 2018. The most popular VR applications, according to the author, are those that allow users to construct customized virtual environments, such as Second Life and Open Simulator.

It is noteworthy that VR systems can be categorized into three major types: non-immersive (desktop VR), semi-immersive VR, and immersive VR (iVR) [14, 15]. The desktop VR immersed users in a 3D Virtual Environment and one can only interact with it using a standard graphic workstation, which includes a monitor, keyboard, and mouse [15, 16]. Semi-immersive VR tries to maintain a high level of immersion while maintaining the ease and comfort of desktop VR or using a physical model [15]. Immersive VR (iVR) is usually the most expensive and provides the most immersion. This method allows users to interact with the virtual world as if it were genuine and true, giving them a greater sense of "presence", or the sensation of "being there" [17].

Because iVR technologies have been more widely available and less expensive in recent years, studies examining the benefits of iVR in foreign language education have remained small in comparison to the other two categories. Bruno et al. [18] did a comprehensive literature review to identify features, educational methods, technologies, and gaps of iVR for foreign language learning. In comparison to traditional pedagogical techniques, the author determined that the relationship between iVR and foreign language acquisition is rather beneficial, as is the connection between iVR and the user's motivation and satisfaction. Suggestions such as making more comparisons between VR and other forms of instruction and considering other aspects of multisensory immersion were also given to the future research in this review.

Despite the fact that there have been many studies on the use of virtual reality in foreign language education, all of which mention various forms of application, including games or learning system with gamification strategies, few scholars have conducted studies directly from the perspective of games. In order to understand whether the use of gaming strategies in VR is beneficial to the learning of a foreign language or not, Rafael et al. [3] conducted a systematic review of empirical research to characterize the state of the art, developed guidelines through the analysis of the outputs of the surveyed studies, and recommended future studies to use gamified VR technology as an assistant tool but not an entire replacement of traditional approaches in learning a foreign language.

Many studies have used English as the target foreign language to show that combining VR games and foreign language teaching is possible, but considering the differences between Chinese and other human languages, does this particularity affect the application of VR games to Chinese language teaching? Is it important to tailor the application strategy to the characteristics of various linguistic abilities? Given the need for a new pattern of foreign language and culture teaching, this systematic review aims to review the application of VR games in foreign language education, Chinese in particular. By describing the status and trends of the current application, it will hopefully help researchers, educators and teachers quickly understand the benefits and research perspectives regarding the use of VR games in teaching Chinese as a foreign language (TCFL), and open up new ways to develop and use VR games in the future. To summary, the main research question (RQ) of this systematic review (SR) is "Can virtual reality educational games or virtual reality technologies with gaming strategies, in general, be used to aid the learning of Chinese as a foreign language?" (RQ1). In order to answer it, this SR further examined the selected resources from the following perspectives:

RQ2. "The impact of VR educational games in TCFL". This question refers to the way of making impact, the nature of the impact (positive, ineffective or negative), and the way to assessed the impact.

RQ3. "The target educational stage and language level". This question is going to answer the following: Does the current research pay more attention to a certain educational stage, and what is the reason for choosing this educational stage? Does it mean that VR games are more suitable for a certain educational stage and Chinese level?

RQ4. "The target knowledge and language competencies". This is to figure out the trends that current research show in the selection of teaching content. For example, are there differences in learning outcomes when VR games teach different language skills? Does VR have an advantage or disadvantage in terms of a certain teaching content?

RQ5. "How to design a better VR game for TCFL?". To be specific, what should be considered when designing a VR Chinese game? How to better combine VR games with Chinese learning?

2   Methods

This systematic review was conducted based on PRISMA (Preferred Reporting Items for Systematic reviews and Meta-Analyses), which is a recognized approach from Liberati et al. [19] Following the procedures and guidelines established in The PRISMA methodology helps researchers to be clearer in identifying and analyzing relevant studies and, consequently, extracting knowledge and answering particular research questions.

2.1 Eligibility Criteria

Eligibility criteria are critical in determining a review's validity, applicability, and comprehensiveness [19]. It is worth noticing that the eligibility criteria listed below were applied to all sources reviewed in this paper, including academic literatures, commercial VR-based games or apps, and online resources.

Inclusion Criteria (IC)
IC-1. The manuscript has in the abstract, title or keywords the following phrases: "Virtual Reality" or "VR" or "Virtual Worlds" or "Virtual Environments", and "Second Language" or "Foreign Language" or "Chinese" or "Mandarin" or "TCFL", and "Gamification" or "Game" or "Gam*". Similarly, commercial VR-based games or apps and practical case studies have these aforementioned keywords in the official descriptions;

IC-2. The manuscript or the introduction of commercial apps was written in English or Chinese;

IC-3. The manuscript was published in a conference or journal;

Exclusion Criteria (EC)
EC-1. Not publicly available;
EC-2. Do not use Virtual Reality;
EC-3. The manuscript does not have an empirical study;
EC-4. Do not use games or gamification strategies;
EC-5. Language learning is not being evaluated;
EC-6. The target users are Chinese native speakers.

2.2 Search Strategy

The first stage of the search involved retrieving data from databases using a search string based on IC-1 in these databases: Scopus, Web of Science, ACM Digital Library, IEEE Xplore, and CNKI. These databases are recognized as important, dependable sources of high-quality publications in the fields of Computer Science and Engineering. We started with a simple string that represented this review's three major features, "Virtual Reality" AND "Chinese" AND "Game". However, to guarantee a more comprehensive search, synonyms and neighboring words were added. Thus, the following search string was defined: ("Virtual Reality" OR "VR" OR "Virtual Worlds" OR "Virtual Environments") AND ("Second Language" OR "Foreign Language" OR "Chinese" OR "Mandarin" OR "TCFL") AND ("Gamification" or "Game" or "Gam*"). The retrieved papers were imported to Endnote using the RIS format, which makes it convenient to delete the duplicated papers and export to a spreadsheet.

The second stage was the retrieval of VR-based games or apps. The selected applications were obtained from a search carried out on these popular commercial platforms: Steam (for games), Google Play Store (for Google Android OS) and App Store (for

Apple iOS), and the key terms used to identify the apps were "VR and Language Learning" and "VR and Chinese Learning". These keywords were also used to find related information on Google, YouTube, and Bilibili (China's equivalent of YouTube) so that more types of resources, such as web articles, practice examples, and gaming videos, can be found.

No time restriction was applied to the search.

2.3 Study Selection

The title, abstract, and keywords of each retrieved paper were compared with the eligibility criteria. This step evolved two researchers who independently read each abstract of the retrieved papers in an unblinded standardized manner. When there was no consensus, the articles were kept for a more thorough analysis during the full-text analysis phase.

2.4 Data Collection Process

For data collection, a form was created that incorporated all of the information extracted from each source for this systematic review. Because of the differences among these three sources, the form was separated into three sections.

For the academic literature, the following elements are extracted: title; type of publication (if it was a journal paper, book section or conference article or proceeding); VR type and displays (whether it was conducted with desk VR, semi-immersive VR or iVR system); platform and content type (an online platform, an application or a mobile app); target educational stages and language levels; evaluated factors (learning, motivation, immersions, among others); whether it was a comparison with different VR conditions or not; whether it was a comparison with other forms of instruction or not; how was learning measured; what educational theories are based on; any Chinese feature were considered; and how were the curriculum and game integrated.

The information of retrieved apps were manually imported to Excel, including: title; year of publication; operating devices and language supported; price; number of downloads; target educational stages and language levels; modes of instruction and learning approaches; learning scenarios and language competencies to practice; types of user interaction; kinds of feedback.

3   Results

3.1 Literature Selection and Results

Literature Selection

In the first phase, the databases listed earlier yielded 631 records. After removing the duplicate articles (n = 39), 592 unique papers were examined. A second step resulted in the rejection of 536 records based on titles, keywords, and abstract analysis, leaving 56 papers eligible for a complete review. After a study of full-text records, 31 records were eliminated, leaving 25 full-text articles for further examination.

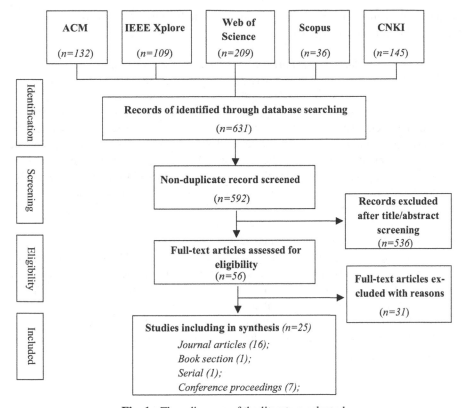

Fig. 1. Flow diagram of the literature selected.

Table 1. Selected papers.

Papers selected and analyzed
[20–44]

Table 1 lists all of the articles that were chosen and evaluated, and Fig. 1 shows a flow diagram with a report of the results acquired in each phase.

Results

Sample and Gender

The number of participants was mentioned in 13 papers out of all of them. These 13 full-text publications had a total of 535 participants, resulting in an average of 41.2 individuals per research, with a maximum of 159 and a minimum of 1. In terms of gender, 30.8% of the studies included information on the sample's gender. Males made up 41.2% of the sample, while females made up 58.8%. Only one study, however, considers the impact of gender differences on learning.

Which Educational Stages and Forms of Instruction Are Covered?

14 of the 25 studies mentioned the participants' educational stage, with college students being the most common (78.6%), followed by elementary school pupils (14.3%) and adolescent students (7%). The bulk of people (43%) who took part were Chinese language beginners or those who had never been exposed to the language before. The majority (60.9%) of the investigations were conducted outside of the curriculum, with the researcher picking and constructing the content and scripts for the experimental studies, or designing experiential content for the general public. In addition, eight experiments were conducted in a formal educational setting to monitor the study's findings and the influence of the VR game.

What Knowledge and Skills Are Targeted?

As shown in Fig. 2, many game-based VR learning systems (24%) focus on practicing several competencies at the same time, although more articles focus solely on one competency. The majority of articles (40%) examined the use in cultural learning. Three articles (12%) adopted VR tools to enhance speaking, and another three studies (12%) discussed VR enhanced vocabulary learning. In addition, VR game were used to promote development of language skills such as listening, pronunciation, Chinese character and writing.

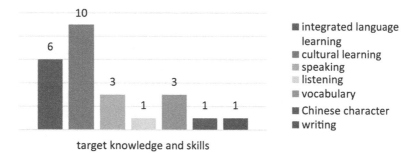

Fig. 2. Target knowledge and skills.

Which Kind of VR Systems and Displays Are Used?

Almost half of the studies (48%) used desktop VR to do research, with 8% used semi-immersive VR and 44% used immersive VR system. While one paper utilized and compared three types of VR systems and gave the conclusion about which kind of VR system is more efficient in learning motion. Regarding the Head-Mounted Display (HMD) setup of iVR system, only 2 studies mentioned that they used the Smartphone VR, while other studies did not provide the necessary setup type information. Desktop VR was employed in nearly half of the studies (48%), with 8% using semi-immersive VR and 44% using iVR. There is one article used and evaluated three different types of virtual reality systems to determine which one is the most effective at learning motion. Only two research indicated using the Smartphone VR for the Head-Mounted Display configuration of the iVR system, while the remaining studies did not give the requisite setup type information.

Platform and Content Type

In terms of platform, 56% of the research used a PC-VR application/software, while both mobile and online platforms tied with 12%, and the remaining studies did not specify which platform they used. In terms of content type, Virtual Environments were used in the majority of the research (84%), while Immersive 360 Video was used in 20% of the studies and Stereoscopic 3D Images were used in 12% of the studies. Three studies looked at different types of content. Interactive content was employed in 22 of the studies (88%), whereas passive content was presented in 12%.

What Form of the Environment Was Used?

The bulk of the environments (80%) were created so that the user may participate in the experience as if it were a real-world location, such as communicating with other players in real time and moving objects around as they want. 8 publications employed the settings as a virtual exercise scenario, while 2 papers used it as a virtual classroom. It is worth noting that all three types of setting were used in a total of 7 experiments, allowing users to do whatever they want based on their learning needs.

Is a Comparison Made with Other Forms of Instruction?

Almost half of the studies made no comparisons to other forms of instruction or different VR conditions (44%). Ten studies compared with traditional learning (face-to-face/picture-word/word-word association), 3 studies compared with different VR conditions, and one study compared not only with traditional 2D learning systems when testing usability, but also with non-education VR game software when testing likeability and knowledgeability.

What Instruments Are Used to Measure Learning

The measuring instrument was referenced in 64% of the full-text publications examined, and several papers utilized multiple instruments to assess learning. The most common method was "task performance", which was used in 50% of the studies, followed by "perception questionnaire", which was used in 43.8% of the studies, and "objective knowledge exam", which was used in 43.8% of the studies. The next three most popular instruments were "observation", "subjective knowledge exam", and "logs analysis", with 37.5%, 25%, and 12% respectively. The terms "course performance", "voice recognition and evaluation", "tutorial feedback", "time-spent", "user interface acquaintance", "cognitive", "interview", and "self-evaluated form" only occurred once.

Which Factors Are Being Evaluated?

With the exception of seven researches that did not identify the factors they analyzed, all of the remaining studies looked into more than one, and learning was the most common, appearing in seventeen (94.4%) of them, followed by motivation in eight (44.4%). Usability came in third position, with 27.8% of the articles considering it as a factor to be examined. Other aspects such as user perception, immersion, engagement, and playability are also taken into account.

What Educational Theories Are Referenced?

Eight out of 25 papers discussed the educational theories that were used to create the game-based VR learning system. Embodied learning was the most frequently stated theory (50%) [25, 26, 37, 43], followed by immersive Chinese teaching [38, 39], situated learning [37, 39], and cognitive load theory [25, 26], all of which were mentioned in two studies each. Multimodal education [43], effective learning environment theory [22], multiple intelligence theory [38], and task-based teaching [42] are some of the other theories highlighted.

What Adjustments Are Made in the Design of the Game According to the Characteristics of the Chinese Culture and Language?

Only four articles referenced Chinese language features and altered the design strategy accordingly. Two articles [24, 42] discussed the differences in pronunciation between Chinese and other western languages, two articles [40, 42] discussed the peculiarities of Chinese characters and teaching ideas, and one article [44] discussed cultural characteristics.

3.2 Game/APP Selection and Results

Game/APP Selection

A search of three of the most popular commercial app or game platforms, Steam, Google Play Store, and App Store, yielded the list of selected apps for the analysis. "VR Language Learning", "VR Chinese Learning", "language learning", and "Chinese" were the key phrases used to identify the software, with the tag "education" being used to narrow the search scope. A total of 924 games and applications were found after searching across all platforms (i.e., 171 games from Steam, 500 apps from Google Play Store and 222 from App Store). 902 software, on the other hand, had to be excluded because to the above-mentioned eligibility criteria. The majority of them were eliminated because they were primarily concerned with language learning and not with VR technology, while some were eliminated because they did not support Chinese language learning. In addition, the literature review revealed three more VR-based software programs that have been shown to be beneficial in Chinese learning. As a result, a total of 25 pieces of software were chosen to be thoroughly examined, from which, 15 from Steam, 6 from Google Play, 1 from the App Store, and 3 from academic literature (Table 2).

Results
Which Kind of VR Systems Are Used?

40% of the software can only be used with the iVR system, and 36% of the software can only be used with the desktop VR system, while 24% of the software can be used with both the iVR and the desktop VR systems for learning.

Table 2. Selected apps.

Name	Year of publication	Name	Year of publication
Second Life	2003	C-TAS: A Virtual Chinese Learning Game	2020
Influent	2014	EduVenture VR	2020
Fulldive VR - Virtual Reality	2015	Hanyu+ VR	2020
vTime XR: The AR & VR Social Network for Cardboard	2016	Terra Alia: The Language Learning RPG	2021
Mondly VR	2017	You, Calligrapher	2021
Witly - language tutoring in VR	2017	EON-XR	2021
VR chat	2017	ENGAGE Virtual Communications	2021
CoSpaces Edu	2017	ExpeditionsPro VR Tours	2021
The Dunhuang Grottoes	2018	Noun Town: VR Language Learning	2022
Earthlingo	2019	Chinese Architect	2022
Sheng Tian (升天)	2020	Chinese martial arts (kungfu) The 64 Hands of Bagua Zhang	2022
Chinese Brush Simulator	2020	VR Horoscope	2022
心境 VR/Mind VR Exploration	2020		

What Knowledge and Skills Are Targeted?

The majority of the software (40%) enables the acquisition of multilingual abilities such as vocabulary, grammar, listening, reading, and cultural awareness. Six (24%) of the remaining software helps vocabulary and pronunciation learning, with just one having non-contextual vocabulary learning; eight (32%) supports learning through cultural experiences, and one (4%) supports practicing communication skills. However, none of the software provides users a placement test of Chinese language proficiency, nor does it specify the appropriate educational stage and Chinese language level. Especially those cultural experience games whose interface language only supports Chinese, it is impossible for beginners to understand the mission statement and operate, let alone enjoy the game and learn something new.

What Kinds of Learning Scenarios Are Created?

As for the learning scenarios, seven (28%) games focus on everyday life scenarios to practice the most commonly used vocabulary and grammar; another 7(28%) are based on specific cultural scenarios, where learners are immersed in the culture to the greatest extent possible to perceive its charm and accelerate their learning; and 1(4%) game creates professional scenarios, such as campus, conference rooms, and so on, to better assist learners with this type of demand. It is worth mentioning that a lot of the software

(40%) we looked at allows users to build their own scenarios or upload photos and videos, so learning scenarios differ from person to person and can happen in a variety of situations.

What Learning Approaches Are Based?

The analysis showed that many of the games combined two learning approaches, either a task-oriented approach combined with a contextual approach (24%) or a task-oriented approach combined with experiential learning (8%), and one (4%) combined a constructive learning approach with a contextual approach. Of the remaining games that used only one learning method, it is clear that the contextual approach was the most popular method (36%), with practice oriented and experiential learning accounting for 12% of the total, respectively. We also found that more than half (64%) of the games we looked at solely enable individual learning, whereas the rest may be utilized alone or in collaboration and communication with other players to fulfill learning goals.

What Types of Interaction Are Provided?

With regard to the types of interaction, all games allow learners to use more than one type of interaction, except for one game that supports only visual contact. Of all these interaction methods, 11 games (44%) allow for both audio, visual and motion interaction, such as real-time conversations with other players or read after the example sentences; 8 games (32%) only support visual and motion interaction, i.e., users can only focus on the virtual objects by moving around or tapping the controller; and 5 games (20%) have built-in quizzes where learners need to choose the correct answers or solve the puzzles.

What Kinds of Feedback Do Are Given to Guide Learners Through Their Learning Process?

Unfortunately, 15 of the games (60%) do not provide any feedback on their own, including 5 games that allow online interaction with real players, which means learners may be able to get immediate feedback from the live tutor. The remaining 10 games (40%) provide visual (colors or icons) and sound information to indicate whether the learner is correct or incorrect. Based on this, one game added textual explanations aside the icons, and another one game gave hints or suggestions to the learner.

3.3   Web Searching

Selection of Online Resources (Web Articles and Videos)

We used Google and YouTube, as an implement resources to academic literature and commercial games currently available online, to conduct a more thorough investigation into the current state of VR games in Chinese language instruction. "VR language learning" and "VR Chinese learning", as well as other descriptive terms with the similar meaning, were again utilized as keywords. The first ten pages of each keyword search on Google were selected, and a total of nine websites pertaining to the topic of this article were screened, the particular classification and content of which will be discussed below. We explored YouTube until we found ten videos with unrelated content, at which point we found 233 videos and 13 related videos were determined to be analyzed in detail. At the same time, we used the same searching keywords in Bilibili and 17 out of 26 videos were sent to be further examined (Table 3).

Table 3. Selected online resources.

Videos	Web articles
[45–74]	[75–83]

Results
What Was Described and Showed in Web Articles?

Six of the nine web articles are about practical cases, one is about the use of VR in education in China [82], one is about the company's self-developed VR language learning game software and its own international competition [83], and one is about a virtual reality Chinese language education game developed by several authors with video clips explaining the game's theme and gameplay [75].

Although six articles describe practical cases, five articles [77–81] actually describe the same project, and two articles [34, 84] in the academic literature review section of this paper describe the same project as well. This project is conducted by the Rensselaer Polytechnic Institute (RPI) and IBM Research. The classroom used in this project is called the Cognitive Immersive Room (CIR), which is a circular classroom filled with screens and 360° video, so it can be considered a semi-immersive VR system. The project provides videos of various real-life scenarios in which students talk freely with the AI agent in the videos, thus learning the corresponding vocabulary and exercising their listening and speaking skills. It is worth noting that one [79] of the five articles mentions that the Chinese language is special due to the four tones, so the existing products that lack the functions related to tone learning may not be fully suitable for Chinese learning.

The other article [76] describes a study conducted by Professor Scott Grant of Monash University, focusing on the Chinese island on Second Life. It is worth noting that Monash University is also the organizer of the Chinese Island (a virtual campus for students to learn Chinese). This case uses a desktop VR system and is based on a textbook theme and a task-based approach. Students communicate and help with each other in the process of completing tasks, so that their communication skills can be developed. Unfortunately, there are no examples of Chinese language education using iVR in the Google search results.

An article [82], although not directly related to the research content of this paper, by describing the Chinese government's emphasis and initiatives on VR applications in education, we have some reasons to believe that applying VR games to Chinese language teaching is a promising direction.

When we filtering the searching results of "VR language learning", we found an article called "How to learn a Language with Virtual Reality" [85]. The article introduces many VR language learning methods and software, and mentions the ImmerseMe platform. Through the platform's website [86], we learned that ImmerseMe not only provides a VR language learning platform for teachers and students around the world, but also holds an international competition that attracts students from all over the world to participate. There were several sub-competitions divided by language, and students completed the game tasks and were ranked by their quiz scores, with the final winner in 2021 being a Year 12 high school boy from New Zealand [83].

Finally, in the web article [75] introducing the self-developed VR Chinese game, we can learn through text and video that the game introduces the background of the story mainly through narration, and players can learn the relevant cultural stories and the writing literacy of Chinese characters in the game.

What Was Described and Showed in Videos

Surprisingly, both Bilibili and YouTube have many players sharing videos of themselves playing VR games to learn Chinese, with the majority of videos (63.3%) showing VRchat, a social game, with one video receiving more than 10 million views [73]; one youtuber using Mondly VR [48]; and the other 5 videos [49, 51, 52, 54, 58] using and introducing different VR games, including LanguageLab, Altspace VR, Guessing Chinese Characters, You Calligrapher, and Crazy Kungfu. The remaining 4 videos did not mention the names of the games. .

There are four videos that show a multi-view screen used by players, in which VR headset devices can be found; the remaining videos do not provide a second view of the player, therefore we do not know what kind of equipment the players are using.

In terms of learning content, VR chat allows players to freely communicate with one another (learners with same targeted language or native speakers), allowing them to pick up some basic language and communication skills, which can be practiced in Mondly VR and Altspace VR as well; the other four videos depict traditional cultural experiences, and three show players learning and practicing writing Chinese characters in the game. Another video [53] is a presentation on the viability of utilizing virtual reality games to teach Chinese.

4   Discussion

The goal of this article is to examine the current state of VR games for learning Chinese as a second language and determine whether combining them is appropriate. As a result, this paper aims to broaden the scope of the search to include academic literature, commercial software, and online resources. We analyzed and organized the retrieved resources in terms of the target learners' language level, the type of VR used, the method of assessing effectiveness, and the method of combining the game with the learning content, and then discovered the limitations of existing solutions and proposed suggestions for future research directions.

The Impact of VR Educational Games in TCFL

Whether it is academic literature, commercial software or online resources, most of the papers indicate that VR games can have a positive impact on Chinese language learning. In contrast to traditional teaching methods, VR games can create real-life scenarios in which learners interact with virtual environments to gain a sense of immersion, presence, and realism, thereby increasing motivation and interest in learning [37], particularly among males [29] and learners who are struggling in second language learning [36]. In terms of the various VR systems, desktop VR continues to account for the majority of this paper, with only a small percentage using the iVR system, as technological advances have resulted in a reduction in the price of iVR, which has only happened in the last few years, but the number of studies and games published in the last two years indicates that there is a growing number of academics and game development companies focusing on the application of iVR in language learning. This is reasonable. Based on the comparison of the three VR systems, we can learn that iVR significantly improves learning efficiency and immersion time. However, when it comes to motion learning, taking into account the accuracy rate of learnt knowledge, semi-immersive system brings a higher learning efficiency [35]. However, we discovered that, while the learning effectiveness of VR games is encouraging, even in games supported by the iVR system, the interactions learners can have are only visual contact and clicking, implying learners' immersion is still very limited and the characteristics of VR have not been fully exploited. We expect future game developers to consider the immersion of other senses, i.e., incorporating all multisensory stimuli to increase learner's engagement [18].

In addition, the existing instruments that were used to assess learning outcomes only include objective knowledge test, subjective knowledge test, perception question-naire, task performance, logs analysis, observation, and course performance(grade). From a more rigorous academic research perspective, experimental findings from various physiological observations are more persuasive than the above-mentioned assessment methodologies.

The Target Educational Stage and Language Level
All the games and cases retrieved did not specify the applicable age and language level of learners, without setting any placement tests for learners, too. Only 14 academic literatures specify this, with the majority of them targeting adults (78.6%) [22, 25, 29, 30, 32, 36, 37, 39, 40, 43, 44] and Chinese beginners (42.9%) [25, 26, 30, 36, 41, 43]. At the beginning level, Chinese learning concentrates around daily life, such as everyday dialogues and physical nouns. In this regard, VR games have some natural advantages: firstly, from the learners' perspective, the most important element at the introductory stage of any language is to increase interest in learning so that learners can persist in learning [87]; from the other side, physical nouns can directly correspond to objects in virtual scenes, and if they are repeatedly in the learner's line of sight, the recurrence rate of vocabulary increases and thus the difficulty of memorization decreases. The intermediate and advanced levels are much harder to learn since there are more abstract nouns and grammars, and learners need more complete story logic to help with understanding. For the design of VR games for intermediate and advanced level, it is no longer sufficient to simply recreate everyday life, but rather to have a story script carefully written by professional Chinese teacher. The scripts need to cover all of the textbook contents and be careful of word choosing [39], while attempting to ensure the game is as enjoyable as possible [28]. Therefore, the development of VR games necessitates collaboration between game developers and experienced teachers. However, due to the lack of sufficient experimental studies, we do not know whether VR games are very effective in helping intermediate and advanced Chinese language learning or not. Overall, the VR games

can do a great help for beginner, and its applications in higher levels need to be explored more.

For those games and studies that do not explicitly state the applicable age and Chinese language level, a common missing is the level classification test. To help Chinese learners more effectively, the first step is to understand their level of Chinese, and then to create teaching plans that are tailored to their specific learning needs, resulting in learner-centered learning. One way to understand learners' Chinese level in the game is to set up learning content and game tasks for different levels, and allowing learners to choose their own levels to complete the game tasks; the other is to set up a pre-test in the game and automatically match learners with appropriate learning content based on the test results.

Furthermore, removing studies that did not indicate the participants, the average number of participants in the existing literature was 41.2, which is a small sample size in comparison to other academic studies. We expect that more experts will participate in future studies, that more participants will be invited, and that more segmented and in-depth investigations will be conducted dependent on the language level of participants.

The Target Knowledge and Language Competencies

When all of the searched resources (25 academic literature, 25 game software, and 39 online resources) were added together, the majority (46.9%) were concerned with improving overall language proficiency, followed by cultural awareness (27.2%) Unfortunately, "What type of language skills are VR games actually suitable for?" is not yet answered by research data. We look forward to a cross-sectional comparison of different language skills in the future, with credible data to answer this question.

A large part of the research and games that support integrated language learning are VR social games. In VR social games, by communicating with other players, learners can learn a variety of language competencies and practice communication skills; however, the disadvantages are also very noteworthy, such as learning content is not systematic, and very much dependent on the Chinese level of the one talk with: if he/she is a Chinese learner as well, then the two learners can help each other and progress together; if the he/she is a native speaker, something outside of the textbook can be learnt while the accuracy of grammar or pronunciation cannot be guaranteed; if he/she is a professional teacher, then the built-in rules of the game can be used to create scenarios or virtual classrooms so as to assist teaching. But due to the lack of research conducted on the comparison between virtual classroom and traditional one, we do not know how much learning effectiveness the virtual classroom can improve. From the teacher's point of view alone, the teacher needs to learn and master the game play in order to provide appropriate content for the students, which inevitably adds a lot of pressure to the teacher's lesson preparation [43].

Cultural experience accounts for the majority of studies that focus on single language skills. It is true that, whether it is a virtual environment that allows interaction or 360° panoramic videos and pictures, learners can feel the immersion from the first perspective that other learning methods cannot provide, and the virtual environment that allows exploration can also maximize the learning pleasure and the desire to understand the target language culture. However, the interaction mode in the current cultural experience games is very simple, and learners can only passively watch or click to switch scenes.

Besides that, nearly all of the research and examples connected to cultural cognitive ability development focus on traditional Chinese culture, showing learners scenes from ancient China but not scenes from modern Chinese life, which is consistent with Zhong's viewpoint [88]. Although the characteristics of VR help learners understand the complex traditional culture, many Chinese learners' learning purpose is to be able to communicate with modern Chinese people or to live in China. Learners' incapacity to integrate properly into contemporary Chinese society and grasp what Chinese people believe and feel is easily caused by the constant display of antique appearance without the introduction of contemporary culture.

How to Design a Better VR Game for TCFL?

Although many language learning apps support Chinese, many of them merely translate the language of user interface, task descriptions, and test questions, resulting in learners learning a different target language yet obtaining the same task subjects and scenarios. From the standpoint of a software developer, it is understandable that the more languages supported, the greater user numbers and benefits. However, while such a generic development model may be appropriate for fundamental Chinese language acquisition or simple daily conversations, it may not be adequate for higher-level learning and more precise comprehension. The distinctions between Chinese and other languages have been addressed in some research, and these variations have necessitated matching changes in game design. According to research analysis, the main difference between Chinese and other languages lies in Chinese characters and pronunciation. Chinese characters are difficult for western learners to understand, memorize, and write, but that understanding the evolution of Chinese characters, as well as learning the strokes and stroke order of Chinese characters, can do a great help [51]. And the difference on pronunciation refers to the prosodic and four tones. There are two ways to address this issue, one is to design the learning system by incorporating a prosodic model into the traditional speech recognition framework [24], while another [80] is to compare the pronunciation of the learner with that of the native speaker, and give feedback in a timely manner.

In the design of Chinese games, in addition to considering the characteristics of Chinese, it is also necessary to fully present the content of the textbook. Although only four literatures have answered this question "How can educational games be better integrated with textbook content?", they are still of great reference value. Firstly, it is believed that the learning system should first show the textbook content in its entirety before making adaptations, such as replacing obsolete terms [39]. For those abstract content that need to be rewritten into a story, it is crucial to not only ensure proper plot logic, but also include 2–4 extended vocabulary words in each scene [38]. Considering the role that VR games play in classroom teaching, [39, 43] it is claimed that they do not entirely replace traditional teaching techniques, but rather serve as supplementary teaching materials and a mechanism for students to evaluate and apply what they learned in class in this way, the feedback given by VR games is crucial. It is a pity that less than half of games provide learners visual or audible information to remind learners whether a choice is right or wrong. Among them, only one game provides correction information, and the learner needs to correct it before proceeding to the next task. For language learners, correcting mistakes in a timely manner is also a part of learning. It is hoped that future VR Chinese games can provide learners of regular and timely feedback on the students' learning process.

5 Conclusion

The purpose of this systematic review is to collect as much information as possible on the current application of VR games to the education of Chinese as a foreign in order to gain a more comprehensive understanding of the current situation of development in this field and to analyze future directions of exploration. Guided by the main question (RQ1) "Can virtual reality educational games or virtual reality technologies with gaming strategies, in general, be used to aid the learning of Chinese as a foreign language?", four sub-questions are proposed accordingly, which were: RQ2. "The impact of VR educational games in TCFL"; RQ3. "The target educational stage and language level"; RQ4. "The targete knowledge and language competencies", and RQ5. "How to design a better VR game for TCFL?".

Most of the articles had a positive answer to RQ1. As for RQ2, each study made its way of research to understand the impact of VR games, such as the impact of an application on a specific language skill, comparisons between different VR systems, gender differences, playability of games, etc. The target language level and educational stage (RQ3) in most studies were adult beginning learners, with children in the second place. The target language competency (RQ4) was an overall language proficiency improvement and cultural experience. With regards to "How to design a better VR game for TCFL?" (RQ5), based on the analysis, this SR gives answers from three aspects, even though there are many answers from other perspectives. Firstly, to consider the characteristics of Chinese, especially the pronunciation and Chinese characters that are the most different from other languages; secondly, to combine the game task with the textbook content, so as not to miss any knowledge; finally, the VR game that plays the role of an auxiliary teaching tool, it is important to give learners timely feedback.

Although many studies have explored VR games applied to Chinese learning from different perspectives, there are still many limitations. For example, most studies' positive results are less convincing due to a lack of physiological observations and a small sample size; many games are ineffective in helping learners due to the lack of user Chinese proficiency tests; the single interaction mode of the game causes learners to become bored and give up quickly; and the lack of research on the application of VR games in intermediate and advanced Chinese level.

In order to maximize the advantages of VR games to better help Chinese learning, there are still many challenges that need to be addressed. Amongst the primary challenges are especially the collaboration of interdisciplinary experts and scholars, both to fully utilize the immersive features unique to VR technology and to make the game fun, as well as to ensure that learners can learn Chinese while completing the game tasks. In detail, the challenges including to invite more participants of varied levels, to provide learners with more versatile opportunities to interact with the virtual environment, to be more learner-centered (e.g., implementing adaptive learning model based on their language level and regular feedback), to consider the characteristic of Chinese language and culture.

References

1. 张志祯. 虚拟现实教育应用:追求身心一体的教育——从北京师范大学 "智慧学习与VR教育应用学术周" 说起. 中国远程教育 (6), 11 (2016)
2. 叶新东, 仇星月, and 封文静. 基于虚拟现实技术的语言学习生态模型研究
3. Pinto, R.D., et al.: Foreign language learning gamification using virtual reality—a systematic review of empirical research. Educ. Sci. **11**(5), 222 (2021)
4. Zichermann, G., Cunningham, C.: Gamification by design: implementing game mechanics in web and mobile apps. O'Reilly Media, Inc. (2011)
5. Park, H.J., Bae, J.H.: Study and research of gamification design. Int. J. Softw. Eng. Appl. **8**(8), 19–28 (2014)
6. Savage, B.L.: Short-Term Foreign Language Immersion: How Does it Stimulate Language Learning? University of Colorado at Colorado Springs (2010)
7. Kamińska, D., et al.: Virtual reality and its applications in education: survey. Information (Switzerland) **10**(10), 318 (2019)
8. Shadiev, R., Yang, M.: Review of Studies on Technology-Enhanced Language Learning and Teaching. Sustainability **12**(2), 524 (2020)
9. Mikropoulos, T.A., Natsis, A.: Educational virtual environments: a ten-year review of empirical research (1999–2009). Comput. Educ. **56**(3), 769–780 (2011)
10. Liu, M., et al.: A look at the research on computer-based technology use in second language learning. J. Res. Technol. Educ. **34**(3), 250–273 (2002)
11. Chiu, Y.-H.: Computer-assisted second language vocabulary instruction: a meta-analysis. Br. J. Edu. Technol. **44**(2), E52–E56 (2013)
12. Lin, T.J., Lan, Y.J.: Language learning in virtual reality environments: past, present, and future. Educ. Technol. Soc. **18**(4), 486–497 (2015)
13. Parmaxi, A.: Virtual reality in language learning: a systematic review and implications for research and practice. Interact. Learn. Environ. 1–13 (2020)
14. Mujber, T.S., Szecsi, T., Hashmi, M.S.J.: Virtual reality applications in manufacturing process simulation. J. Mater. Process. Technol. **155–156**, 1834–1838 (2004)
15. Bamodu, O., Ye, X.: Virtual reality and virtual reality system components. Adv. Mater. Res. **765–767**, 1169–1172 (2013)
16. Bharathi, A., Tucker, C.S.: Investigating the impact of interactive immersive virtual reality environments in enhancing task performance in online engineering design activities. In: ASME International Design Engineering Technical Conferences & Computers & Information in Engineering Conference (2015)
17. Bowman, D.A., Mcmahan, R.P.: Virtual reality: how much immersion is enough? Computer **40**(7), 36–43 (2007)
18. Peixoto, B., et al.: Immersive virtual reality for foreign language education: a PRISMA systematic review. IEEE Access **9**, 48952–48962 (2021)
19. Liberati, A., et al.: The PRISMA statement for reporting systematic reviews and meta-analyses of studies that evaluate health care interventions: explanation and elaboration. J. Clin. Epidemiol. **62**, e1-34 (2009)
20. 潘自意. 新乘风(Zon)在对外汉语教学各环节中的作用——如何利用新乘风(Zon)进行对外汉语教学. 今日南国(理论创新版) (08), 78–79 (2009)
21. Chen, W., et al.: Animations, games, and virtual reality for the Jing-Hang grand canal. IEEE Comput. Graph. Appl. **30**(3), 84–88 (2010)
22. Cai, L., Liu, F., Liang, Z.: The research and application of education game design model in teaching Chinese as a foreign language. In: Proceedings of the 2010 IEEE International Conference on Progress in Informatics and Computing (PIC 2010) (2010)

23. Wang, X.F., et al.: Paper construction of a digital artistic system for paper-cut. In: 2010 International Conference on Multimedia Technology (2010)
24. Ming, Y., Ruan, Q., Gao, G.: A Mandarin edutainment system integrated virtual learning environments. Speech Commun. **55**(1), 71–83 (2013)
25. Lan, Y.-J., Fang, S.-Y., Legault, J., Li, P.: Second language acquisition of Mandarin Chinese vocabulary: context of learning effects. Educ. Tech. Res. Dev. **63**(5), 671–690 (2015)
26. Si, M.: A virtual space for children to meet and practice Chinese. Int. J. Artif. Intell. Educ. **25**(2), 271–290 (2015)
27. Ni, Z., Gao, Z.: Developing digital hall of prayer for good harvest software to promote historical culture by applying virtual reality technology. In: Proceedings - 2015 International Conference on Culture and Computing, Culture and Computing 2015 (2016)
28. Hu, X.Q., Su, R., He, L.: The research on Chinese idioms educational games in TCFL based on virtual reality. In: 3rd Annual International Conference on Information Technology and Applications (ITA), Hangzhou, People;s Republic of China (2016)
29. Coffey, A.J., Kamhawi, R., Fishwick, P., Henderson, J.: The efficacy of an immersive 3D virtual versus 2D web environment in intercultural sensitivity acquisition. Educ. Tech. Res. Dev. **65**(2), 455–479 (2017)
30. Lan, Y.J., Liao, C.Y.: The effects of 3D immersion on CSL students' listening comprehension. Innov. Lang. Learn. Teach. **12**(1), 35–46 (2017)
31. Xu, Y.J., et al.: The design and implementation of Chinese vocabulary learning case based on mobile VR for "The Belt and Road". In: 2017 2nd International Conference on Computational Modeling, Simulation and Applied Mathematics (CMSAM), Beijing, People's Republic of China (2017)
32. Sheridan, M., et al.: Investigating the effectiveness of virtual reality for cross-cultural competency training SIEDS 2018. In: 2018 Systems and Information Engineering Design Symposium (SIEDS 2018) (2018)
33. Zhang, L., et al.: VR games and the dissemination of cultural heritage. In: Lecture Notes in Computer Science (including subseries Lecture Notes in Artificial Intelligence and Lecture Notes in Bioinformatics), pp. 439–451 (2018)
34. Allen, D., et al.: The Rensselaer Mandarin project - a cognitive and immersive language learning environment. In: 33rd AAAI Conference on Artificial Intelligence (AAAI 2019), 31st Innovative Applications of Artificial Intelligence Conference (IAAI 2019) and the 9th AAAI Symposium on Educational Advances in Artificial Intelligence (EAAI 2019) (2019)
35. Chen, X.M., et al.: ImmerTai: immersive motion learning in VR environments. J. Vis. Commun. Image Represent. **58**, 416–427 (2019)
36. Legault, J., et al.: Immersive virtual reality as an effective tool for second language vocabulary learning. Languages **4**(1), 13 (2019)
37. Xie, Y., Ryder, L., Chen, Y.: Using interactive virtual reality tools in an advanced Chinese language class: a case study. TechTrends **63**(3), 251–259 (2019)
38. 张利红 and 谭学良. VR技术在沉浸式汉语口语教学中的应用初探. 汉字文化 (20), 34–35 (2019)
39. 张利红 and 谭学良. VR教学模式在对外汉语口语教学中的应用初探. 长春师范大学学报 38(05), 183–187 (2019)
40. Barrett, A., et al.: Technology acceptance model and multi-user virtual reality learning environments for Chinese language education. Interact. Learn. Environ. (2020)
41. Lan, Y.J.: Immersion into virtual reality for language learning. In: Federmeier, K.D., Huang, H.W. (eds.) Adult and Second Language Learning, pp. 1–26 (2020)
42. 冯东. 虚拟现实技术在对外汉语课堂中的设计与应用. 河北农机 (05), 79–80 (2020)
43. Hu, W.-C.: The theoretical foundation of virtual reality assisted language learning and its application in TCSL. J. Technol. Chinese Lang. Teach. **12** (2021)

44. 李晶津, et al.: 虚拟现实(VR)技术应用于对外汉语文化教学的设计初探. 汉字文化 (18), 165–167 (2021)
45. I Taught Chinese in VR - Does Teaching In VR Actually Work? I Totally Did Not Expect This! https://www.youtube.com/watch?v=Yv-geyXNZBA. Accessed 31 Jan 2022
46. Learn Chinese in VR - ChineseVR Gameplay. https://www.youtube.com/watch?v=I3iaMprV-AA. Accessed 31 Jan 2022
47. Learning Chinese in Virtual Reality. https://www.youtube.com/watch?v=duNzWUR2oyg. Accessed 31 Jan 2022
48. 我竟然在VR游戏里学中文? [信徒 | VR].   https://www.youtube.com/watch?v=eqHIvbAmcck. Accessed 31 Jan 2022
49. 用 Oculus Quest 在Altspace VR 虚拟现实语言交流聊天 VR Chinese Language Exchange. https://www.youtube.com/watch?v=crQmLu8MI_0. Accessed 31 Jan 2022
50. Learn Chinese in VR Chinese New Year Zodiac Signs. https://www.youtube.com/watch?v=zlAvU8QaVDg. Accessed 31 Jan 2022
51. Guessing Chinese Characters VR Game Introduction. https://www.youtube.com/watch?v=MjaQMGVhLy4. Accessed 31 Jan 2022
52. [元宇宙學外語:LanguageLab] VR多國語言學習遊戲應用介紹-Oculus-外語學習場景探索中文英文日文韓文泰文小語種生活化任務動作-室內戶外銀行餐廳活動學校車站辦公場景, https://www.youtube.com/watch?v=L6xWtv6apdM. Accessed 31 Jan 2022
53. TPET9 (7/6) 17:00~17:25 VR虛擬實境之華語文有效創意教與學 (賴飛鍾), https://www.youtube.com/watch?v=jaDyJgf9TIc. Accessed 31 Jan 2022
54. Learning to Write Simplified Chinese Letters in VR – You, Calligrapher Review. https://www.youtube.com/watch?v=OWdvJ9BRIB4. Accessed 31 Jan 2022
55. I Pretended to be Chinese in VRChat then Switched to Perfect English... https://www.youtube.com/watch?v=KIha4qQ5KOo. Accessed 31 Jan 2022
56. 外国小伙假装中国人，在国服遇上真老外?！ 还教育了他!, https://www.youtube.com/watch?v=TCDAe3qm6rg. Accessed 31 Jan 2022
57. American Sneaks Into VRChat CHINA with Perfect Mandarin, Hilarity Ensues. https://www.youtube.com/watch?v=y1GLR7Op2OQ. Accessed 31 Jan 2022
58. Crazy Kungfu. https://www.bilibili.com/video/BV1RX4y1c7Hf?from=search&seid=1984651877479939867&spm_id_from=333.337.0.0. Accessed 31 Jan 2022
59. 为什么英国日本土耳其人, 都爱在游戏里装中国人? https://www.bilibili.com/video/BV1TL4y147SF?from=search&seid=11889896400895171850&spm_id_from=333.337.0.0. Accessed 31 Jan 2022
60. 总有一天， 全服的德国人都要学优美的中国话. https://www.bilibili.com/video/BV1m34y1B7vx?from=search&scid=11889896400895171850&spm_id_from=333.337.0.0. Accessed 31 Jan 2022
61. 回忆暴击:泰国吉他手学中文, 超爱林俊杰和周杰伦. https://www.bilibili.com/video/BV1Tm4y1Q7HQ?from=search&seid=11889896400895171850&spm_id_from=333.337.0.0. Accessed 31 Jan 2022
62. 德国人早期驯服舌头珍贵影像. https://www.bilibili.com/video/BV1Zr4y1D7ZL?from=search&seid=11889896400895171850&spm_id_from=333.337.0.0. Accessed 31 Jan 2022
63. 汉语大战教学. https://www.bilibili.com/video/BV1PM4y1K7RT?from=search&seid=11889896400895171850&spm_id_from=333.337.0.0. Accessed 31 Jan 2022
64. 轮到英国人说英式汉语了!小哥分享英国教师面试经历.   https://www.bilibili.com/video/BV1BZ4y1d72e?from=search&seid=11889896400895171850&spm_id_from=333.337.0.0. Accessed 31 Jan 2022
65. 汉语鬼才1:教土耳其小哥说中文，而他教我德国历史?. https://www.bilibili.com/video/BV1w34y197jd?from=search&seid=11889896400895171850&spm_id_from=333.337.0.0. Accessed 31 Jan 2022

66. 不要总教外国人乱七八糟的中文了，还是教些美好的句子吧. https://www.bilibili.com/video/BV1CE411f7ht?from=search&seid=11889896400895171850&spm_id_from=333.337.0.0. Accessed 31 Jan 2022

67. 外国人试图通过动漫在线游戏学习汉语vlog05.   https://www.bilibili.com/video/BV1Xz4y1C77g?from=search&seid=11889896400895171850&spm_id_from=333.337.0.0. Accessed 31 Jan 2022

68. 我遇到了传说的热狗!他的法国小姐姐还给我化妆! [VRChat]. https://www.bilibili.com/video/BV1gJ411F76z?from=search&seid=11889896400895171850&spm_id_from=333.337.0.0. Accessed 31 Jan 2022

69. 那两个说中文的老外得知自己火了，高兴到说不出话! https://www.bilibili.com/video/BV1tJ411g7of?from=search&seid=11889896400895171850&spm_id_from=333.337.0.0. Accessed 31 Jan 2022

70. [vr游纪] 外国妹纸问我"老子"是什么意思. https://www.bilibili.com/video/BV12s411u76A?from=search&seid=11889896400895171850&spm_id_from=333.337.0.0.   Accessed 31 Jan 2022

71. [VRchat] 偶遇会日韩双语的韩国小姐姐，被要求教她汉语，怀疑我是韩国人. https://www.bilibili.com/video/BV1T4411T72G?from=search&seid=11889896400895171850&spm_id_from=333.337.0.0. Accessed 31 Jan 2022

72. [VRChat] 精通四门语言的老外!外国人说中文可以强到什么程度! https://www.bilibili.com/video/BV1xE411d7yC?from=search&seid=11889896400895171850&spm_id_from=333.337.0.0. Accessed 31 Jan 2022

73. 俩老外在中国服务器里疯狂飙中文!甚至还互相教学?   https://www.bilibili.com/video/BV1PJ411N7Ca?from=search&seid=11889896400895171850&spm_id_from=333.337.0.0. Accessed 31 Jan 2022

74. 汉语鬼才2:世界人民大团结万岁，而我被迫成为鬼子? https://www.bilibili.com/video/BV1sa411k7kf?from=search&seid=11889896400895171850&spm_id_from=333.337.0.0. Accessed 31 Jan 2022

75. Learning Chinese in VR. http://chinesevr.weebly.com/. Accessed 31 Jan 2022

76. Case Study 5: Virtual Worlds to Facilitate Chinese Language Learning (Paired Role-Play). https://blendsync.org/case-study-5-virtual-worlds-to-facilitate-chinese-language-learning-paired-role-play/. Accessed 31 Jan 2022

77. Mandarin Language Learners Get a Boost from AI. https://www.ibm.com/blogs/research/2018/08/mandarin-language-ai/. Accessed 31 Jan 2022

78. A Floating Panda, Tai Chi in China: Learning Mandarin in a VR Classroom. https://indianexpress.com/article/world/a-floating-panda-tai-chi-in-china-learning-mandarin-in-a-virtual-reality-classroom-5954848/. Accessed 31 Jan 2022

79. A new immersive classroom uses AI and VR to teach Mandarin Chinese. https://www.technologyreview.com/2019/07/16/65550/ai-vr-education-immersive-classroom-chinese-ibm/. Accessed 31 Jan 2022

80. This Classroom Uses AI and VR to Teach Mandarin. https://beebom.com/using-ai-vr-teach-languages-mandarin-chinese/. Accessed 31 Jan 2022

81. Virtual learning: using AI, immersion to teach Chinese. https://techxplore.com/news/2018-09-virtual-ai-immersion-chinese.html. Accessed 31 Jan 2022

82. The Good, the Bad and the Ugly: VR in China's Classroom. https://pandaily.com/the-good-the-bad-and-the-ugly-vr-in-chinas-classrooms/. Accessed 31 Jan 2022

83. Kerikeri Students Top The World in Virtual Language Contest. https://www.nzherald.co.nz/northern-advocate/news/kerikeri-students-top-the-world-in-virtual-language-contest/ZWQWDVHYYGKFWBBXMNFW2BKLYQ/?c_id=1503450&objectid=12344548.   Accessed 31 Jan 2022

84. Chabot, S., Drozdal, J., Zhou, Y., Su, H., Braasch, J.: Language learning in a cognitive and immersive environment using contextualized panoramic imagery. In: Stephanidis, C. (ed.) HCII 2019. CCIS, vol. 1034, pp. 202–209. Springer, Cham (2019). https://doi.org/10.1007/978-3-030-23525-3_26
85. How to Learn a Language with Virtual Reality. https://www.fluentin3months.com/virtual-reality/. Accessed 31 Jan 2022
86. ImmerseMe. https://immerseme.co/#media. Accessed 31 Jan 2022
87. Bowman, B., et al.: TEFL/TESL: Teaching English as a Foreign or Second Language. Manual M041. Class Activities **236** (1989)
88. 钟飞璐. VR技术辅助对外汉语文化教学浅析. In: *第十一届中文教学现代化国际研讨会. 中国澳门* (2018)

Social Impact in Design Education

Minqing Ni[1]([⊠]) [iD] and Tiziano Cattaneo[1,2] [iD]

[1] College of Design and Innovation, Tongji University, Shanghai, China
{niminqing,tiziano.cattaneo}@tongji.edu.cn
[2] Università degli Studi di Pavia, Dipartimento di Ingegneria Civile e Architettura, Pavia, Italy

Abstract. Social design has become a significant part of design education system. The paper takes transformation of design education as background and focuses on in-depth analysis of social design related degree programs, curriculums, methodologies, and intuitional influence of organizations towards social design education shift. The paper addresses that how social impact affects the development direction of related disciplines and its relationship, discusses its complexity and extension, and actively integrates social resources to develop new forms of design practice. The pedagogy for social design employs a collaborative, systems-oriented approach to design and social thought through emphasizing design-led research. It helps students understand their role, define their engagement, and develop creative practices to address emerging and complex challenges by considering social, economic, political, and environmental issues from multiple perspectives and scales to generate transformative multimedia strategies. The paper brings a new perspective for future social design learning and demonstrates the social impact in design education in a general framework, and which help emerging designers understand the role they play in design practice worldwide, as well as foster an understanding of civic engagement and contrasts it with the idea of design as service.

Keywords: Social design · Design education · Social impact · Social design curriculum

1 Introduction

The design has gradually expanded from the previous focus on the material world to the non-material realm. The objects of design are also constantly extending from symbols to objects, to activities, to relationships, services and processes, to systems, environments and mechanisms [1]. Design can not only drive innovation, but also promote social lifestyle changes and the transformation of the new economy. Design must change from passive to active, design emphasizes thinking while drawing, thinking while doing, and thinking while testing. Design requires a new and more active attitude to intervene in economic and social changes [2]. These statements make it possible for design to take on greater social missions more actively and proactively.

Now more and more design and art universities and institutions focus on organizational structure, interactive services and experience design on social impact. Many issues involve complex social and political factors, the problems faced by design are no

P.-L. P. Rau (Ed.): HCII 2022, LNCS 13312, pp. 96–108, 2022.
https://doi.org/10.1007/978-3-031-06047-2_7

longer just aesthetic issues, environment, urban system, education, medical care, elderly care, consumption, social interaction, entertainment, mobility, safety, etc., a series of complex social issues need to be responded by multifaceted solution, design could be one of the starting points to address on those issues. Design requires a new, more proactive approach to economic and social change. How the designers attempted to combine their professional skills toward social change? How the design school becomes effective agents of change in the contexts where they are situated? How the design education influenced by social impact?

2   What Is Social Design?

Victor Papanek is one of the first to address issues of social design in the 1960s. He was pointed out creating change within the design field and no longer account for the needs of all people and disregards its own environmental consequences [3]. Papanek also remarks on designing for people's needs rather than their wants and need to be socially and morally responsible. Victor Margolin is another important person who contributes to the development of social design. Margolin argues that designer's ability to envision and give form on material and immaterial products that can address human problems on broad scale and contribute to social well-being, the foremost intent of social design is the satisfaction of human needs [4]. Margolin also states his strong view that social design is an activity that should not be framed with connotations of charity, aid donations, help or even voluntary work, but it should be seen as professional contribution that plays a part in local economic development or livelihood.

Design has been approached as a profession that remains strictly answerable to market forces, social design envisages the possibility of a more distributive conception of surpluses, by ensuring that the benefits of services and systems reach a wider range of user groups who may often fall outside the market system, the foremost intent of social design is the satisfaction of human needs. Victor Margolin and Sylvia Margolin wrote about the social model involves a focus on human needs by taking inspiration from core social work literature and has an ecological perspective. Margolin suggests a multifaceted approach to solving problems, first accessing the situation by answering a few core questions, followed by survey research and interviews, content analysis of archival data, and/or participant observation [4].

Social design takes its reference mainly is using design thinking which is a human-centered approach to innovation that draws from the designer's toolkit to integrate the needs of people [5]. Social design is being mentioned more and more in the design education field, it focuses on the role and responsibility of designers in society by using the design process to achieve social change. Social design as a discipline has been practiced primarily in two different models, which implementing human centered design methodology in the social sector, or synonymously practiced by designers who undertaking into social entrepreneurship. "Social innovation" and "social design" should not be confused. Social innovation design refers to create new social forms, a way of constructing a society rather than be content with socially responsible design [6]. But now in current design filed, Manzini believes that the boundaries between social innovation and social design are blurring, and they are all going towards the direction of solving the wicked social problems.

3   Social Design Programs in Design Education

3.1   10 Social Design Related Programs

Here briefly introduced 10 social design related programs of design and art-oriented universities around Asia, Europe, Oceania and North America, which try to outline a general image on nascent discipline of social design in ten years (see Table 1). Among all the program statements, social design could be summarized as an innovative space that emphasizes "deign with" the community, by using collaborative methods to develop the comprehensive solutions.

The Hongkong Polytechnic University School of Design has four-year undergraduate admission of social design, within service design cluster. This program attempts to expand the scope of design beyond the current commercialised and compartmentalised professional practices by orienting towards the 'social dimension of design', with emphasis on civic participation, social engagement and collaborative design practices. Dedicated to the promotion of social and cultural sustainability, the program focuses on the realization of social innovations and civic goals through the framework of design

Table 1.   10 Social design related programs.

Universities	Program name and establishment time	Degrees	Design for social issues (in recent 3 years)
The Hongkong Polytechnic University School of Design	Social Design, 2017	BA(Hons)	Pandemic related issues, Family relationship, Elderly, Social cohesion …
Central Academy of Fine Arts, China	Social Design,2019	BA,MA	Rural-urban interaction, Design for poverty alleviation/migrates/visually impaired group…
The University of Technology Sydney	Creative Intelligence and Innovation, 2014	BA	Inclusive technology for aging populations, Artificial intelligence, Mental health…
College of Design and Innovation Tongji university	Environmental Design and other design studios, 2015	BA, MA	Social cohesion and community building, Neighborhood of Innovation, Creativity and Entrepreneurship
The Maryland Institute College of Art	Social Design, 2011	MA	Rain gardens maintain for the benefit of wildlifes, Safety for pedestrians and bicyclists, Family and child care…
The University of Applied Arts Vienna	Social Design- Arts as Urban Innovation, 2013	MA	Public space, City after dark, Speculative futures, Collective identity, Next generations, Rights

(continued)

Table 1. (*continued*)

Universities	Program name and establishment time	Degrees	Design for social issues (in recent 3 years)
Parsons school of Design, The New School	Integrated Design, 2017 Transdisciplinary Design, 2015	BFA MFA	Adapted kids, Digital society, Food Security, Woman in color... Air Pollution, Dying, Healthcare, Education reform...
New York's School of Visual Arts	Design for Social Innovation, 2011	MFA	Social emotional learning, Colorism, Food waste, Autism, poverty alleviation...
The School of Design, Ambedkar University Delhi	Social Design, 2013	MA	Health, Education, Transport, Waste, Governance Interfaces, Urban and Rural Commons, Intangible Heritage, Digital Technologies

thinking and solution prototyping. The program requests that the students learn independently and continuously develop cultural, social, technological and design literacy through local, regional and global contexts, and explore and address social and community issues through design research, experimentations and reflective implementation practices [7].

Central Academy of Fine Arts in China launched the first program named social design for undergraduate and graduate degree in 2019. According to program description, they stated that in contemporary Chinese context, social design is committed to using transdisciplinary system thinking and methods to provide strategic solutions for the sustainable development of urban-rural interaction, equity issues and observe in the "social process" of politics, economy and technology. Design can further integrate the methods of sociology and economics, study the combination model of social innovation, and form new productivity and driving force in the current Chinese society through the design strategies and its narratives [8]. They also clearly list how their education goal through curriculum, they wish the students have 5 abilities: People with keen perception, with questioning, systematic thinking and executive ability, as well as leadership and collaboration skills. The students can actively observe, acquire, analyze and judge "new problems", "new models" and "new technologies" in the social process.

The University of Technology Sydney launched the Bachelor of Creative Intelligence and Innovation (BCII)in 2014, it is not offered as a separate degree, but is completed only in combination with another professional core degree program, such as Business, Communications, Design, Science, Law, Health, Engineering. The program has been stated the complex problems we're facing in the world require solutions that transdisciplinary thinking can provide. The BCII goes well beyond the design-thinking and design-led innovation programs now common in the university environment, to examine how innovation is led from multiple disciplinary perspectives. It goes beyond the arts-based approach to creative thinking by including the sciences, IT, engineering, health, business and law in its field of enquiry [9]. It focuses on the development of novel solutions to social problems, enabling students to participate in a future-oriented, world-first interdisciplinary degree program that covers a variety of perspectives and integrates a series of industry experience, enable students to deal with the complex challenges. This degree program is not within the design school but as a university of technology, where graduates have an opportunity for thinking beyond their discipline to drive cross-disciplinary, industry and social change.

College of Design and Innovation Tongji university in Shanghai China, which opens a new frontier for social design education. In order to cultivate students' problem awareness and action ability, the college takes the initiative to break the gap between the school and the community and transform the community into a brand-new "learning by doing" environment. In 2015, the college has been initiated a research and design project called Open your space project, which helped the urban community acquire a better sense of sustainability, comfortability, and accessibility to public space. By synthesizing ideas of resilience, the project uses the placemaking approach to create the third place and social cohesion and how these relate to a new paradigm of spatial and social resilience [10]. BA/MA Environmental design mainly applied in their curriculum for deep learning and create speculative environment with creative methods from real practices. As the college is located within the community, thus, it is in a good position to apply design tools and strategies to create social impact and engage the social problem. It could also act as an effective agent for social change in the urban context. The most recent project of NICE 2035 (which is short for Neighborhood of Innovation, Creativity and Entrepreneurship towards 2035), is an experiment to help a residential neighborhood to develop into a design-driven citizens' community. The aim is to produce social innovation which can inspire and direct incubating processes towards sustainable and collaborative cities, which are perceived as an alternative asset to economic exploitation and building new forms of communities-of-place. The project established by the college that the students and professors could do research and practices under theme more collectively. Now 40% of the teaching and research space is in the community, including more than 10 laboratories such as the Design for Social Innovation and Sustainability Laboratory, the Future Mobility Design Laboratory, and the Sound Laboratory. The community as "living lab" integrated into teaching, research, co-creation process, it has been created to help students face the real society and solve social problems [11]. The social impact strategy of college which intends to connect people, generate public spaces, and improve the ecosystem that enables social actions with a hybrid collaborative platform.

The Maryland Institute College of Art (MICA) opened a social design graduate one year program in 2011. It is one of the earliest social design graduate degree programs offered by Center for Social Design in the United States, a decade of pioneering and experimental work to define and demonstrate new models of social design education and practice through human-centered design. They stated social design is a creative practice dedicated to understanding social problems and supporting positive social change. The curriculum introduces students to a broad theoretical framework for social design, exposes them to a variety of models for social impact, immerses them into the human-centered design process, and prepares them with a core set of skills necessary to pursue professional opportunities in the practice of social design. The program is committed to demonstrating the value of design in solving complex social problems and inspiring the young generation for innovative social change, elevating the social and design literacy of creatives, and building new pathways for professional practice. We can see the alumni have pursued a variety of socially based opportunities, such as design & innovation, health, government & public service, business & innovation, social entrepreneurship & start-ups, nonprofit organizations and academia & teaching [12].

The University of Applied Arts in Vienna offers a master's degree called Social Design- Arts as Urban Innovation, especially the art university is predestined to formulate these new, distinct perspectives on the inherent logic of cities and the corresponding dynamics of the processes. "Arts as Urban Innovation" listed in the program name clearly to show that focusing on art as a tool for urban innovation. Artistic practice in synergy with project-related methods and knowledge from the humanities, art, social, economic and health sciences, it could generate links between multifaceted disciplinary expertise and the problems posed by the urban realm. Their curriculum statement shows that artistic approach is reinforced as a positive power in the shaping of society, raising an awareness to take on social responsibility. They believed that art-based processes of communication and interaction in social systems can also provide social impact and relevance to certain forms of artistic praxis beyond the primarily market-oriented logics [13]. As the program required the core fields of expertise such as architecture, fine arts, design and theory, it adopts interdisciplinary research methods and knowledge for students in different research fields and important to predict the need for change but also to be able to react to acute crises great with fresh solutions.

Another two notable programs related to social design, it named BFA Integrated Design and MA Transdisciplinary Design by Parsons school of Design in New York. Integrated Design allows the students to engage in research-based studios while exploring a range of making techniques that can be applied to systems, services, and societies. The program promotes the self-directed & interdisciplinary could develop creative learning incorporating multiple design approaches. MA Transdisciplinary Design program could apply after BFA Integrated Design or other prior degree completion. This program employs a collaborative, systems-oriented approach to design and social thought, emphasizing design-led research. It takes big advantage and functions as an academic laboratory in New York City where the students can develop creative practices to address emerging and complex challenges by engage in projects that integrate ecological, economic, technological, and social systems to promote resilience, sustainability, community inclusion, and justice through design [14]. The program also opens the application for Design and Urban Ecologies, Strategic Design and Management, and Design and Technology programs, fostering interdisciplinary work from multiple perspectives and scales, in order to generate transformative multimedia strategies.

New York's School of Visual Arts has a two-year MFA degree program named Design for Social Innovation (DSI). The program offered the balance of academic and practical, which define design broadly by using system design, critical thinking, human-centered design, game mechanics and collective leadership to move people become more resilient and resourceful. The students examine issues related to food insecurity, healthcare, or poverty alleviation, and apply design principles to create a new solution or improve upon an existing product or methodology. In 2017, the program hosted an inspired

Measured Summit which social designers, researchers, foundation heads, monitoring and evaluation leaders, and data scientists gathered to take on these challenges, beginning with the impact of design on human health. The founding chair Cheryl Heller of DSI noted that it's important to define, measure, and scale the impact of social design and its potential [15].

The School of Design at Ambedkar University Delhi (AUD) in India also commenced a graduate practice-based program social design in 2013. They believe that social design can be more specifically rooted in the context of developing countries. The program is placed more inclusive and focused on the humanities and social sciences, with concerns of equity and ecology to create more accessible, inclusive and sustainable public services and systems through participatory and collaborative design methods [16].

3.2 Important Organizations Supported Social Design Programs

Beside the degree programs, the labs, institutions, and organizations all very important for social design development in design education. DESIS network (Design for Social Innovation towards Sustainability) was found in 2009 and established partnerships with other entities and evolving towards a network of Design Labs based in design schools and in other design-oriented universities and operating with local, regional and global partners to promote and support social change towards sustainability. Since September 2014, DESIS is a no-profit and cultural association, with the purpose to promote design for social innovation in higher education institutions with design discipline, which generate useful design knowledge and to create meaningful social changes in collaboration with other stakeholders [17]. The network introduced the notion of creative community and social innovation in various design schools worldwide, and they believe that design for social innovation could be a powerful driver towards sustainability and that design schools could help in supporting and accelerating the process. DESIS Labs are groups of academics, researchers and students who orient their design and research activities towards social innovation. Now 59 DESIS labs around world, they operate at the local scale with local partners and, in collaboration with other DESIS Labs [18], they actively participate in large-scale projects and programs, such as the recent design research initiative Design for Collaborative Cities(DxCC), which involves several design schools around the world that work at the crossroads of city making, social innovation and design, it has been adopted similar hypotheses of work, exchange experiences and produce an open and shareable design knowledge between the different stakeholders such as universities, local government and enterprises [19].

Another institute apply on the frontier of scientific research called The UAL Social Design Institute, their mission is to make a positive social and environmental difference through the art and design research and practice in social design and design for sustainability. They focus on three areas: i. Value and valuation through design. ii. Systems and design. iii. Policy contexts and implications. University of the Arts London (UAL) contains six colleges from different disciplines, the institute create the opportunities for improving the ways in which designers can develop a better understanding of the design value and the contexts they design for and in. Their work closely with colleagues across UAL including the Centre for Circular Design, Centre for Sustainable Fashion and Design Against Crime Research Centre [20]. These two examples show the social problem work with design solutions: Trash-2-Cash research project involved 17 part-ners from 10 different countries selected to represent the whole material life cycle in 3.5 year. The circular design concepts informed the materials development in an iterative co-design process to produce six sensational master case product prototypes through an experimental design-driven methodology was used to enable the collaboration along with new facilitation techniques and Life Cycle Thinking approaches [21]. The Design Against Crime Research Centre's award-winning Makeright project produced an anti-theft bag and accessory range co-designed with prisoners in the UK and India [22]. All these achievements demonstrate how the social impact could influence the design education.

The Hasso Plattner Institute of Design at Stanford, commonly known as the d.school. The Institute was founded by Stanford mechanical engineering professor as well as the IDEO founder David M. Kelley with six other professors in 2004. The school integrates business, law, medicine, social sciences and humanities into more traditional engineering and design education, this design thinking institute which inspired design education world a tremendous opportunity for students that learn design in this integrated way. Human-centered design is a powerful methodology and mindset to employ in their work. Thomas Both who is director of Designing for Social Systems Program at d.school states that both human-centered and systems-thinking methods fit within an effective design approach, and can work in conjunction to address social challenges(see Fig. 1) [23]. They have grappled with complex social challenges, such as how to redesign K-12 substitute teaching to ensure high-quality learning when regular teachers are absent; how to make access to nutritious food part of US health care and health insurance systems; how to make burial practices in the United States more environmentally in the face of the funeral industry and well-established societal expectations. The school use design thinking to create change at multiple levels, developing highly valuable skills such as empathy, the ability to collaborate, to deal with ambiguity and to create, and more important practice the ways of design for learning.

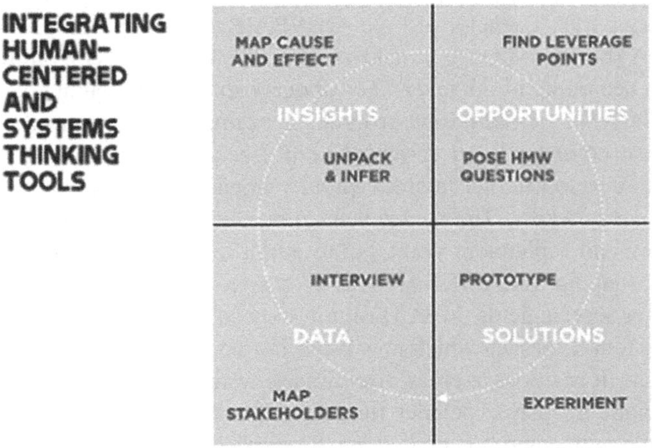

Fig. 1. The framework shown with a complementary human-centered and systems thinking tool in each quadrant (Source: Thomas Both [23])

4 Methodology and Curriculum of Social Design

Social design is regarded as a special method of social innovation. We may not explain the definition of "social design" explicitly, there are many program names related to it, whether call social design or not, we can dive inside to see the learning process to understand the context of social issues better, which emerging in the design education.

According to the description of each program statement, we can see in common four directions. 1. Apply professional skills of design to understanding of social needs and deliver outcome for the real-life social condition. 2. Introduce methods to students for social observation, ethnographic design research, participatory design and co-creation to part of design process, the social value produced through the collective creativity of people. 3. Engage students to communicate and collaborate with multi social institutions and communities address social issues and experiment with different approach and inaugurate design thinking with nondesign disciplines. 4. Prototype the design solutions for positive social change and develop strategy for relevant business, social and cultural circumstances [24].

Design activism is the main posture of social design. It is a spirit of "introspection" of design education. Students are expected to increase their critical knowledge and systematic ability through contextual research, design thinking and integrate conceptual and technical skills into the development and communication of creative ideas in the learning process, it explores new possibilities and paths for understanding the social literacy and design opportunities. Design activism as the development and evolution of the existing design logic, it focusses on generating alternatives, designers could play important role to transform the current system by using experimental and innovative approaches help to cope with new and complex situations. Co-design is other important methods used by social design, the co-design process encourages various participants to share skills and experience, this could lead to novel solutions and improvements in many areas, including processes of idea generation, decision-making, customer satisfaction and loyalty over the long-term [25].

There are two levels degree program on social design: undergraduate and graduate, which means BFA(Bachelor of Fine Arts)/BA(Bachelor of Arts), MFA(Master of Fine Arts), MA (Master of Arts). It makes sufficiently differences on requirements and its curriculum according to the levels. For undergraduate level, taking The Hongkong Polytechnic University social design program as example, students need to go through a freshmen year common to all current design specialisms, and join in the 3rd year and 4th year to develop further interdisciplinary mindset, professional knowledge and collaborative design skills. The senior year curriculum is set in coherence with that of the freshmen and sophomore years, but to admit students from a broader spectrum of disciplines, ranging from different areas of design to other social science, cultural, technological or service fields. MFA Design for social innovation of SVA in NYC, the curriculum for four semesters which now usual for the graduates' level program except the intensive one. It positions as cross-disciplinary, systems-level and hands-on. The first fall semester quite intensive, includes fundamentals of design for social innovation as start, combining with environmental ethics, disruptive design of research and insights, understanding natural and social systems, mapping and visualization design. The spring semester beside of the design studio and lecture series, in addition, it uniting games for impact, communication design, creative writing for social designers, and then introduction to thesis project, as the same of the other 2 years Master program, the second semester is mainly focus on thesis project's research, writing, presentation and implementation, as well as the leadership and entrepreneurship also professionally introduced to the curriculum, technologies for design change(design studio) and global guest lecture series come cross four semesters. This program also has opportunities to create an interdisciplinary path of study with other major in minor such as communication design, creative entrepreneurship and fashion communication.

For building social design curriculum that the partnership with other organizations also essential. The students have the opportunity to be exposed to and participate in a variety of initiatives within program partners and working across diverse contexts, disciplines, and themes. Students are expected to learn to identify issues critical to future professional and social conditions and take the initiative to tackle them in collaboration with corresponding partners or stakeholders. This is also a big consideration when the students apply the program. To design a social design curriculum is a complex social design project as well, this intervention will help contextualize the discipline and need to continue to attempt, observe, revise and constantly improve through teaching and learning feedbacks. The pedagogy for social design employs a collaborative, systems-oriented approach to design and social thought through emphasizing design-led research. It helps students understand their role, define their engagement, and develop creative practices to address emerging and complex challenges by considering social, economic, political, and environmental issues from multiple perspectives and scales to generate transformative multimedia strategies.

5   Conclusion

The rise of social impact in design education does optimistically reflect a wider shift in design. Design Thinking and Human-Centered Design (HCD) as one of its core principles of social design and applied mostly in design education. Through the research of programs above, we can see social design is contained of a set of principles, a process for organizing actions that propel progress from one stage to the next, and a specific set of skills required for the successful application of the principles and navigation of the process. According to the curriculum study, and the principles, process steps, and skills used in social design in relation to many other methods as stated this diagram (see Fig. 2) [26], such as collaborative research methods, problem reframing, idea generation, and prototyping. This is the big potential social design in broader collaboration with other disciplines, especially the multi disciplines universities take the advantages to collaborative with other programs and even offer dual degree to create innovative learning process. The design and art universities take part in collaborate with partners in the society, increasing the social literacy and examine the designer's role and responsibility.

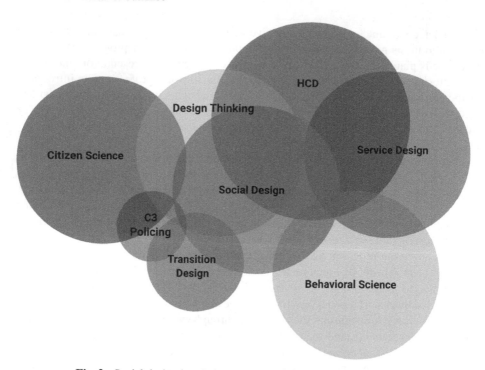

Fig. 2. Social design in relation to many other methods (Source: [26])

We have learnt that build effective social impact design curriculum and its critical role in preparing future designers to work more inclusively and sustainably. The selective courses promote meaningful social impact which combing with design thinking, social enterprise, engagement of citizenship, psychology and other multidisciplinary courses for developing products, services and systems. An engagement with diverse audiences through community field work and projects is built into social design curriculums, while skill development in iterative prototyping and participatory co-design allows students to improve their design thinking process. Collaborations with community stakeholders and local leaders represent the cornerstone of social impact design curriculum. If the role of design/designer is to move from serving a "want" to addressing a "problem", it is imperative that the education of these aspiring designers needs to be tailored to prepare them for that role [24]. Emerging design curricula needs to arm these designers with the right tools and train them with skills that will make them capable of handling complexities that social problems inherently pose.

Social design allowed designers to become responsible to and driven by the potential impact of their work, with the goal of fostering collaborative creation and thoughtful reflection, many programs focus on experiential learning which linking with economic, environmental and cultural contexts. They often do adjustment depend on the learning feedbacks and thesis projects show comments. We also need to consider that design education needs to rid itself of the master-apprentice instructional model and the reliance on subjectivist epistemologies, instead, design education needs to adopt user-centred and evidence-based approaches, and thus to move closer to design strategies that can facilitate a variety of successful social interventions [27]. Teacher-centered model will have big influence on how to define the "social problem", if we go back to the actual content of "social problem", there are also exist differences consideration in the context of social problems in China and the West society. The core principles of social design could explain more clearly the evolution: Solutions come from understanding and engaging communities in need of help, prototyping and observation are more effective than five-year plans, and all social issues are systemic and must be understood and acted upon that way [15].

Social Design is an emerging area where design is seen as having a wider impact by becoming a problem-solving tool for social innovation and change [28]. A design solution first be socially and environmentally responsible, then technically feasible, humanly desirable and economically viable, rather than only focused on aesthetics or functionality. Social design has the potential to address issues at a systems level, integrating human dynamics and relationships with new technologies and services. It integrates the wisdom and the experience of the people in need of help, giving them agency and a voice [28], most notably part which create empathetically alongside local communities and the most powerful outcomes come from diverse collaboration.

Our changemakers are all expected to learn how to incorporate the design skills, insights and knowledge into initiate the meaningful project that potentially generate positive impacts on societal systems. The paper brings a new perspective for future social design learning and demonstrates the social impact in design education in a general framework, and which help emerging designers understand the role they play in design practice worldwide, as well as foster an understanding of civic engagement and contrasts it with the idea of design as service. Through the social impact in design education, the emerging designers definitely get influenced by these paradigmatic shifts.

Acknowledgments. This research supported by the Foundational Research Funds for the Central Universities in China.

References

1. Buchanan, R.: Wicked problems in design thinking. Des. Issues **8**(2), 5–21 (1992)
2. Lou, Y.: Design activism in an era of transformation. In: Ni, M., Zhu, M. (eds.) Open Your Space: Design Intervention for Urban Resilience, pp. 68–75. Tongji University Press, Shanghai (2017)
3. Papanek, V.: Design for the Real World. Completely Revised Second Edition. Academy Chicago Publishers (1984)
4. Margolin, V., Margolin, S.: A "social model" of design: issues of practice and research. Des. Issues **18**(4), 24–30 (2002)
5. Brown, T.: Design thinking. Harvard Bus. Rev. **86**(6), 84–92 (2008)
6. Manzini, E.: Design, When Everybody Designs: An Introduction to Design for Social Innovation, p. 189. The MIT Press, Boston (2015)
7. Social Design Introduction Page. https://www.sd.polyu.edu.hk/en/assets/files/Programmes/2022-23/BAScheme/8_SpecialismDescription_SocialD.pdf. Accessed 10 Feb 2022

8. Social Design Introduction Page. http://design.cafa.edu.cn/detail.html?id=5d708687a310563 433dcac7e. Accessed 10 Feb 2022
9. The Bachelor of Creative Intelligence and Innovation Course Introduction Page. https://www.uts.edu.au/study/transdisciplinary-innovation/undergraduate-courses/creative-intelligence-and-innovation/degree-no-other. Accessed 10 Feb 2022
10. Ni, M., Cattaneo, T.: Design for urban resilience: a case of community-led placemaking approach in Shanghai China. In: Rau, P.-L. (ed.) HCII 2019. LNCS, vol. 11577, pp. 207–222. Springer, Cham (2019). https://doi.org/10.1007/978-3-030-22580-3_16
11. Ni, M.: Open your space: a design activism initiative in Chinese urban community. In: Rau, P.-L. (ed.) CCD 2017. LNCS, vol. 10281, pp. 412–431. Springer, Cham (2017). https://doi.org/10.1007/978-3-319-57931-3_33
12. MA in Social Design (MASD). https://www.mica.edu/graduate-programs/social-design-ma/. Accessed 10 Feb 2022
13. Social Design Art as Urban Innovation Curriculum. http://socialdesign.ac.at/images/PDF/Curriculum_SD_new2020.pdf. Accessed 10 Feb 2022
14. Transdisciplinary Design Program Introduction. https://www.newschool.edu/parsons/mfa-transdisciplinary-design/. Accessed 10 Feb 2022
15. Heller, C.: Designing a way to measure the impact of design. Stanford Soc. Innov. Rev. https://doi.org/10.48558/S26W-G090. Accessed 08 Feb 2022
16. Information for applicants applying for Master of social design. https://sls.aud.ac.in/uploads/1/admission/admissions2019/MDes%20in%20Social%20Design.pdf. Accessed 10 Feb 2022
17. About DESIS. https://www.desisnetwork.org/about/. Accessed 10 Feb 2022
18. DESIS Labs. https://www.desisnetwork.org/labs/. Accessed 10 Feb 2022
19. Design for Collaborative Cities (DxCC). https://desisnetwork.org/dxcc/. Accessed 10 Feb 2022
20. UAL Social Design Institute. https://www.arts.ac.uk/ual-social-design-institute. Accessed 10 Feb 2022
21. Trash 2 Cash. https://www.circulardesign.org.uk/research/trash-2-cash/. Accessed 10 Feb 2022
22. Makeright. https://designagainstcrime.com/Makeright. Accessed 10 Feb 2022
23. Both, T.: Human-Centered, Systems-Minded Design. Stanford Soc. Innov. Rev. https://doi.org/10.48558/DWBY-RF41. Accessed 08 Feb 2022
24. https://wdo.org/social-impact-design-education/. Accessed 08 Feb 2022
25. Steen, M.: Co-design as a process of joint inquiry and imagination. Des. Issues **29**(2), 16–28 (2018)
26. MeasureD. https://measured.design/what-is-social-design/. Accessed 28 Feb 2022
27. Souleles, N.: Design for social change and design education: social challenges versus teacher-centred pedagogies. Des. J. **20**(Sup 1), S927–S936 (2017)
28. Verma, N.: An eight-step pedagogy for teaching social design. SEGD Res. J. Commun. Place (2017)

An Analytical Study of Cross-Cultural Design Factors Affecting Virtual Reality Teaching Experience

Weilong Wu[1], Wu Wei[1], Yen Hsu[2(✉)], and Xin Cao[2]

[1] School of Film Television and Communication, Xiamen University of Technology, Xiamen, Fujian, China

[2] The Graduate Institute of Design Science, Tatung University, Taipei, Taiwan, China
wu_academic@163.com

Abstract. Objectives: With the COVID-19 epidemic, more and more schools are choosing online education and electronic devices for learning. Due to the uniqueness of the VR model, many teachers are introducing the use of VR in educational teaching activities. Generally speaking, virtual reality is widely used in the field of education and training because of its potential to promote interactivity and motivation. It also offers a new approach to teaching and learning due to the increasing number of online learners sharing and presenting educational content, and the technological possibilities of spreading knowledge over the global web and allowing students to participate in educational courses remotely.

Therefore, this study focuses on relevant design factors through the study of teaching scenarios such as VR experience teaching training in the field of product design. In the preliminary questionnaire survey, we concluded that the three key words that students care most about VR teaching tools are user interface, usability and interaction design, but from the questionnaire survey we cannot accurately understand the specific preferences of students for these three factors. Therefore, we want to understand specifically whether students care more about user interface, usability, or interaction design for VR teaching tools, that is, which of these three factors will be more preferred and valued by students, in order to consider how to weigh the three factors in the VR design and production process.

By studying the design factors of VR teaching and learning experiences, VR educational content developers can better understand the factors to be considered in this field. It can also guide VR content producers to produce more content that meets students' needs.

Methods: In this study, firstly, 80 questionnaires were mainly used to organize and collect the key words of relevant factors, and after the key words were obtained, the AHP tool was used to obtain the hierarchical model, and then according to the 1–9 scale method, 10 experts in the design field and 10 students were invited to score the three design factors of VR teaching tools in a two-by-two comparison, and finally the weight values were analyzed and organized according to the AHP calculation formula. Finally, the weight values were analyzed and sorted according to the AHP formula to determine the ranking of the weight values of the design factors of VR teaching tools.

© The Author(s), under exclusive license to Springer Nature Switzerland AG 2022
P.-L. P. Rau (Ed.): HCII 2022, LNCS 13312, pp. 109–119, 2022.
https://doi.org/10.1007/978-3-031-06047-2_8

Results: The AHP method is used to study the factors that influence students in the design and production of VR courses and software, and to form a hierarchy in which different factors are sequentially generated. Designers and content producers can determine the relative importance of each factor in the hierarchy through pairwise comparisons.

Based on the results, we can find that user interface is the most important VR design factor that students are concerned about, followed by interactivity. The findings can be used as a framework tool to design VR content according to students' needs and make the product a better experience.

Conclusions: According to the results, we can find that the user interface is the VR design factor that students are most concerned about, followed by interactivity, which also gives us a hint that when we are making VR teaching tools, we should pay more attention to the design and presentation of VR content, choosing appropriate VR materials, materials that are closer to the real world, and at the same time designing more beautiful, simpler, and more obvious buttons or The interface should be designed with more beautiful, simple and obvious buttons or prompts.

The user interface is also important, when students enter the virtual reality, they want to be as in the real world in general scenes, rather than poor quality 3D production of animation graphics, virtual reality to provide students with a realistic reproduction of the world, where they can operate, learn, practice and even experiment, and designers to do is to provide them with as much as possible to meet the needs of the VR tools.

Similarly, interactivity is also important in this process. If you can only watch, but not effectively interact with VR as if it were reality, then VR is obviously inappropriate. Therefore, the weighting of these three factors will hopefully provide some meaningful inspiration to the designers of VR teaching tools.

When students use VR educational products, it is very important for VR content providers and VR designers to improve the actual value of the product content, as it can help them design VR educational products that better meet the market demand.

Keywords: Virtual reality · Cross-cultural design factors · Teaching experience · Design education · Analytic hierarchy process

1 Introduction

Under the COVID-19 epidemic, VR education is receiving increasing attention. Due to the uniqueness of the VR model, many designers are introducing the use of VR in educational teaching or simulation teaching activities for medical students. Among them, the introduction of virtual reality in the teaching process is also becoming more and more common. VR is also often referred to as an immersive experience. A concept often mentioned in VR is "immersion" [1]. Jennett et al. [2] define the general concept of game immersion as participation in a game. This experience allows students to have a different experience in the teaching process of product design than in other teaching processes. A more intuitive experience in the classroom can stimulate the potential of students. Generally, virtual reality is widely used in the field of education and training because of its potential to facilitate interactivity [3] and motivation [4, 5]. Therefore, this study focuses on the design of virtual reality scene simulation in the field of education and medical education. It also offers a new pedagogical experiment due to the increasing number of online learners sharing and presenting educational content, and the technological possibilities of disseminating knowledge on the global web and allowing students to participate in educational courses remotely. By incorporating modern visualization technologies, these computer-based teaching concepts can be realized through virtual reality or mixed reality applications [6], as computer vision and digital technologies have developed to extensive levels, making it important to integrate new media into the curriculum [7].

To identify the factors of VR design experience in design and educational design process, this study focuses on the hierarchical analysis method (AHP) and virtual reality educational design. Professor Saaty proposed the hierarchical analysis method in 1971. Hierarchical analysis (AHP) has been widely used in design evaluation and decision making studies [8, 9]. In the preliminary questionnaire survey we concluded that the three key words that students care most about VR teaching tools are user interface, usability and interaction design, but from the questionnaire survey we cannot accurately understand the specific preferences of students for these three factors. Therefore, we want to understand the specific VR teaching tools, students will care more about the user interface, usability or interaction design, that is, which of these three factors will be more liked and valued by students, the purpose is to consider how to weigh the three factors in the process of VR design and production, which in essence, can be considered a decision analysis process, there are goals, factors, decisions, to These three factors are considered as our factor layer, the goal layer is "to determine the VR design experience factors", the decision layer is "factor weighting", so use the hierarchical analysis method.

The AHP method is used to study the factors that influence students in the design and production of VR courses and software, and to form a hierarchy in which different factors are sequentially generated. Designers and content producers can determine the relative importance of each factor in the hierarchy through pairwise comparisons. Conducting this study will facilitate VR content producers to follow these influencing factors more scientifically and rationally in the design process of VR educational materials to produce VR products that better meet the needs of students and teachers. Therefore, it is promising to study the relative importance of the influencing factors of VR teaching experience.

This paper focuses on the user experience factors for students using virtual reality for teaching and learning. The goal level is to select the best experience approach, the factor level is the three factors of user interface, usability and interaction design, and the decision level is to determine the best solution. This is a multi-objective, multi-criteria decision problem, so it is more appropriate to use hierarchical analysis in the process of virtual reality teaching experience to carry out the decision making process, and then determine the weighting of the influencing factors of VR teaching experience, understand the relative importance of the influencing factors, and clarify the ideas of students and teachers about VR devices, which is ultimately beneficial for VR producers to design VR products that better meet their needs.

2 Indicator System of Cross-Cultural Design Factors for Virtual Reality Teaching Experience

User interface, usability, and interaction design are relatively important for VR software production, and Nor'a & Ismail [27] argue that a user interface that is user-friendly and aesthetically pleasing can effectively increase students' interest and attention span in VR devices. Dalle & Abdul [26] and Rubio, Gertrudix & García [25] also suggest the importance of interaction design for VR design, which they argue provides a deeper sense of realistic VR experience. Therefore, in this study, we compare and analyze these three influencing factors in order to find out the interaction and feedback relationship between them.

2.1 User Interface

As a user interface for VR teaching scenes, the following considerations have been summarized based on previous studies, which should be taken into account when evaluating the user interface.

1. Information display: The keyword design should be obvious, the information should be displayed, and the keywords should be obvious. Irrelevant information should be excluded. Learners should be provided with enough information to be able to judge their own status and make appropriate decisions [14].
2. Menu options: In the process of teaching menu selection, multiple scenarios should be developed for application while meeting the needs of menu options between different disciplines [16].
3. Scene design: In the educational user interface, the design of its scene interaction interface is an important factor in the user's three-dimensional experience; therefore, different scene choices should be made in the scene design process [16].
4. Progressive access: saves the learning progress during the learning process, as learning is a long term phase, so this option is needed in the user interface [18].
5. Operation feedback: Novice actions are obvious, and positive feedback can be given quickly [15].
6. Input method: The input method should be easy to manage with appropriate sensitivity and responsiveness. The input method should allow for self-defined correlation mappings [14].
7. Visual setting: The learning process should give learners a clear and comprehensive understanding of their position and the visual information associated with that position [17].
8. Customization: Allows learners to customize various aspects of the user interface to a certain extent [19].

2.2 Usability

Usability reflects the efficiency and convenience of the VR teaching experience in achieving the pedagogical goals [6]. In order to understand the knowledge, the main function of

VR software for teaching and learning is the function of teaching and learning, therefore that function makes it a factor that should be considered by content producers [10]. At the same time, learners should be able to know exactly what is happening in the virtual environment, should be aware of failures, be allowed to make some mistakes, and easily recover after making them. activities in a VR repetition strategy teaching system should allow learners to participate multiple times and keep them entertained [21].

When performing the same task multiple times, it is important to be able to skip over content that is familiar and no longer appealing to the learner to ensure that the learner has a desire to stay engaged. The artificial intelligence in the system should be reasonable, visible to the learner, and consistent with the learner's expectations. In order to meet learner expectations and shorten the learning curve, learners can be given enough information to know how to get started right away. Learners can quickly access the system through tutorials and adjustment levels, and can view tutorials and adjust questions throughout the interactive teaching process. The various operating mechanisms in the tutorial system should feel very natural and produce the right level of physical and mental immersion [20].

In addition, the content presented in the system should be adapted to the situation the learner is facing. Learners should be able to identify elements such as roles, enemies, obstacles, threats, and opportunities in a virtual reality teaching system. These things should be so obvious that learners can spot them even if they have poor vision or are even color blind, and they should not be easily misunderstood. Moreover, when learners see these things, they can understand their purpose [22]. Virtual reality teaching systems respond to learner behavior in a predictable manner, including consistency across system elements, overall settings, and episodes [23].

2.3 Interaction Design

In the field of virtual reality simulation for educational interaction, human-computer interaction and interface interaction should be considered [22]. The concept of interaction model is derived from natural user interface. It refers to the use of multisensory channels such as vision, hearing, touch, taste, and smell to generate interactions with the system in a non-precise, parallel manner so that the interaction between the user and the computer is more efficient and natural [10].

Characteristics of Interaction: Natural interaction makes users feel natural and harmonious in the process of interacting with computers, thus lowering the threshold of human-computer interaction. Interaction is the application of the skills and experiences we learn when interacting with entities in our daily environment to the virtual environment created by the computer. Users can interact with objects in the virtual world as if they were communicating in the real world without any special learning [22].

Students focus on the experiential, interactive design learning process in the area of interactive feedback. Physiological and psychological influences on the teaching process are areas that need to be considered. The design and development of the software interaction interface is a key factor affecting the product experience [25]. VR is different from other smart devices because of its unique interactive immersion; it can bring users unprecedented experiences and feelings. A good interactive experience allows users to temporarily forget the real environment and integrate into the virtual world, while the ability to eliminate fragmentation when operating in the virtual world will largely determine the immersive experience of mobile VR [22–24].

All three are among the influential factors to be considered in the design of VR teaching tools, whether it is the user interface, usability or interaction design that should be considered and perfected before the VR tool is made. According to the requirements of the user interface, usability match, as well as ergonomic, human instinct interaction, in order to design a suitable, in line with the requirements of the public VR teaching equipment. However, the weight ranking of these three influencing factors and the inter-relationship among them are issues that are worth to be studied. Therefore, combining text analysis and survey, this study summarizes the design factors of VR teaching experience used for user interface, usability, and interaction design. Each index constructs a hierarchical model according to AHP analysis [12, 13], as shown in Fig. 1.

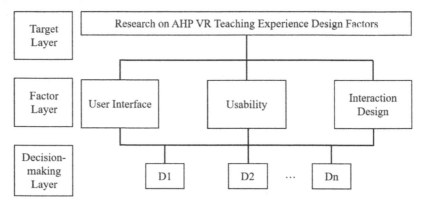

Fig. 1. Hierarchical model of VR teaching experience design factors [12, 13]

3 Experiment Design

3.1 Experimental Design

In this study, firstly, 80 questionnaires were mainly used to collate and collect the key words of relevant factors, and then the AHP tool was used to obtain the hierarchical model, and then according to the 1–9 scale method, 10 experts in the design field and 10 students were invited to score the three design factors of VR teaching tools in a two-by-two comparison, and finally, according to the Finally, the weight values were analyzed and sorted according to the AHP formula to determine the ranking of the weight values of the design factors of VR teaching tools. This study used a multi-criteria decision making approach to clarify the factors that students experience when using VR educational products.

3.2 Establish a Pairwise Comparison Matrix

In the case of a target, two factors at the same level should be compared. According to pairwise comparison, for example, 1, 2 and 3 to 9, set the ratio scale in numerical order.

Each scale represents judgment and pairwise comparison, A comparison matrix can be established to reflect the priority of different levels of factors [11]. When multiplied by standard numbers, this is a particular priority. Under reasonable assumptions, The geometric mean is used as the integration function to establish a pairwise comparison matrix. Each hierarchy element is evaluated under a component of the previous hierarchy, make a paired comparison n (n − 1)/2 pairwise are required for n elements, Place each comparison result in the upper triangle of the pairwise comparison matrix. The result of the lower triangle is the reciprocal value of the relative position of the upper triangle, that is Axn = 1/Axn. The comparison matrix is shown in Fig. 2. Experts use the level 9 scale to express the preference of each indicator, Grading the importance of VR teaching experience design factors. The table shows the 1–9 ratio, as shown in Table 1. According to the relevant criteria, The importance of each index layer is allocated by the 1–9 scale method, Constructed judgment matrices and computational weights, as shown in Table 2.

$$
A = \begin{bmatrix}
1 & A_{11} & \cdots & A_{1n} \\
1/A_{11} & 1 & \cdots & A_{2n} \\
\vdots & \vdots & \ddots & \vdots \\
1/A_{1n} & 1/A_{2n} & \cdots & 1
\end{bmatrix}
$$

Fig. 2. Establish a pairwise comparison matrix

Table 1. AHP assessment ratio scale and description

Scale aij	Define	Explain
1	As important as	Means i factors are as important as j factors
3	Slightly more important	Means i factors are slightly more important than j factors
5	Obviously more important	Means i factor is obviously more important than j factor
7	More important	Means i factor is more important than j factor
9	Extremely important	Means i factor is extremely important than j factor
2, 4, 6, 8	Median	The median value of the two adjacent judgments
Count backwards	Relative count backwards	When the j factor is compared with the i factor, the judgment value is aij = 1/aij

Table 2. Judgment matrix and calculation weight table

	User interface	Usability	Interaction design	Weight
User interface	1.00	2.00	1.50	0.44
Usability	0.50	1.00	0.33	0.17
Interaction design	0.67	3.00	1.00	0.39

3.3 Consistency Test

According to Saaty [12, 13], Because when policymakers make comparisons, Not easy to achieve consistency, Therefore, it is suggested to check consistency, Consistence Index (CI) and consistency ratio (CR) verification consistency. CI and CR values should be less than 0.1. Its consistency can meet acceptable requirements. That is to say, experts in the decision-making process of the factors are consistent. The more attributes, the easier it is to be inconsistent. The formula (1) and formula (2) to verify consistency are as follows:

$$CI = \frac{\lambda \max - n}{n - 1} \tag{1}$$

$$CR = \frac{CI}{RI} \tag{2}$$

The n is the number of factor layers, and the RI is the random index (Random Index, RI) of the comparison judgment matrix. The RI value varies according to the n, as shown in Table 3.

Table 3. Random indicator table

N	1	2	3	4	5	6	7	8
RI	0.00	0.00	0.58	0.90	1.12	1.24	1.32	1.41

By calculating the maximum eigenvalue $\lambda\max = 3.067$, CI = 0.034, when n = 3, RI = 0.58, CR = 0.058, and CI < 0.1, CR < 0.1, it can be concluded that all pairwise comparison matrices meet the requirements of consistency.

3.4 Ranking of Weight of Hierarchical Model

Sort according to the level calculation, as shown in Table 4:

Table 4. Ranking table of factor weights

	Weight	Sort
User interface	0.44	1
Usability	0.17	3
Interaction design	0.39	2

After calculating the weight value of factor level, the importance of factors in VR teaching experience design factors is sorted, and the results are as follows: user interface, usability and interactive design.

According to the above importance ranking results, in VR the teaching experience and developers to VR the content of education is to consider the user interface and then consider the interactive design.

4   Discussion and Conclusions

The purpose of this study is to examine the experiential factors in the virtual reality teaching and learning process. Considering the interactions and feedback relationships among the factors, a hierarchical analysis was used to calculate the weighting values. The relative influence of each attribute among all attributes was calculated through the analysis of the weight values. The purpose of the comparison is to select the best experience model.

Based on the three factors of user interface, usability and interaction design, this study found that user interface is the most concerned factor, followed by interaction design and finally usability. It can provide reference value for future VR content production and related work researchers, and provide suggestions for making more market-friendly VR educational content makers.

According to the results, we can find that user interface is the most important VR design factor that students are concerned about, followed by interactivity, which also coincides with the study of Nor'a & Ismail [26], which also gives us a hint that when we are making VR teaching tools, we should pay more attention to the design and presentation of VR content, choose appropriate VR material, the material should be closer to the real world, and also design more beautiful, simple, and obvious buttons or hints in the operation interface.

The user interface is also important, when students enter the virtual reality, they want to be as in the real world in general scenes, rather than poor quality 3D production of animation graphics, virtual reality to provide students with a realistic reproduction of the world, where they can operate, learn, practice and even experiment, and designers to do is to provide them with as much as possible to meet the needs of the VR tools.

Similarly, interactivity is also important in this process, and if one can only watch but not effectively interact with VR as in reality, then such VR is obviously inappropriate. Therefore, the weighting of these three factors will hopefully provide some meaningful inspiration to the designers of VR teaching tools.

Of course, the weighting of these three factors is only a reference value, none of them can be independent of the design process, they are all important, and the results of this paper only hope to provide some inspirational thoughts to future VR textbook producers. In VR teaching, there are more than three influencing factors, and this paper hopes that by studying these three relatively important influencing factors, researchers will be motivated to further expand their research to identify more influencing factors and provide a broader prospect for future VR teaching. In addition, the sample size of this paper is relatively small, and the choice of students' majors is not comprehensive enough for subsequent researchers to improve [28, 29].

References

1. Jones, P.H., Ott, M., Leeuwen, T.V., Smedt, B.D.: The potential relevance of cognitive neuroscience for the development and use of technology-enhanced learning. Learn. Media Technol. **40**, 131–151 (2015)
2. Jennett, C., et al.: Measuring and defining the experience of immersion in games. Int. J. Hum Comput. Stud. **66**(9), 641–661 (2008)
3. Roussou, M.: Learning by doing and learning through play: an exploration of interactivity in virtual environments for children. Comput. Entertain. **2**(1), 10 (2004)
4. Garris, R., Ahlers, R., Driskell, J.E.: Games, motivation, and learning: a research and practice model. Simul. Gaming **33**(4), 441–467 (2002)
5. Ott, M., Tavella, M.: A contribution to the understanding of what makes young students genuinely engaged in computer-based learning tasks. Procedia Soc. Behav. Sci. **1**(1), 184–188 (2009)
6. Pan, Z., Cheok, A.D., Yang, H., Zhu, J., Shi, J.: Virtual reality and mixed reality for virtual learning environments. Comput. Graph. **30**(1), 20–28 (2006)
7. Ebner, M., Holzinger, A.: Successful implementation of user-centered game based learning inhigher education: an example from civil engineering. Comput. Educ. **49**(3), 873–890 (2007)
8. Wang, Z.M.: Use grey relational analysis to construct a decision-making model for the deployment of quality functions. J. Desi. **11**, 43–57 (2006)
9. Huang, S.T., He, J.L., Peng, W.J., Zheng, Y.L., Liao, W.J.: Application of quality function deployment and grey relational analysis in green design: taking basketball shoes as an example. J. Eng. Technol. Educ. **6**, 127–147 (2009)
10. Sun, C.Y., Xu, M.Q.: Design and research of mobile VR natural interactive interface. Design **23**, 140–141 (2017)
11. Lin, M.C., Qui, G.P., Chen, J., Li, Y.G.: Image generation in product form for sustainable development. J. Environ. Protect. **20**, 74–83 (2019)
12. Saaty, T.L.: The Analytic Hierarchy Process: Planning, Priority Setting, Resource Allocation. McGraw-Hill, USA (1980)
13. Saaty, T.L.: Decision Making for Leaders: The Analytic Hierarchy Process for Decisions in a Complex World. RWS Publications, Pittsburgh, USA (1980)
14. Hsiao, S.W., Lee, C.H., Yang, M.H., Chen, R.Q.: User interface based on natural interaction design for seniors. Comput. Hum. Behav. **75**, 147–159 (2017)
15. Korableva, O., Durand, T., Kalimullina, O., Stepanova, I.: Usability testing of MOOC: identifying user interface problems. In: Proceedings of the 21st International Conference on Enterprise Information Systems, ICEIS 2019, January 2019, pp. 468–475. SciTePress (2019)
16. Johnson, J.: Designing with the Mind in Mind: Simple Guide to Understanding User Interface Design Guidelines. Morgan Kaufmann (2020)

17. De Rivera, J., Gordo, Á., Cassidy, P., Apesteguía, A.: A netnographic study of P2P collaborative consumption platforms' user interface and design. Environ. Innov. Soc. Trans. **23**, 11–27 (2017)
18. Lee, S., Lee, J.H., Kim, J.: User-friendly graphical user interface software for ideal adsorbed solution theory calculations. Korean J. Chem. Eng. **35**(1), 214–221 (2018)
19. Cremonesi, P., Elahi, M., Garzotto, F.: User interface patterns in recommendation-empowered content intensive multimedia applications. Multimedia Tools Appl. **76**(4), 5275–5309 (2016)
20. Quiñones, D., Rusu, C., Rusu, V.: A methodology to develop usability/user experience heuristics. Comput. Stan. Interfaces **59**, 109–129 (2018)
21. Wu, W.L., Hsu, Y., Yang, Q.F., Chen, J.J., Jong, M.S.Y.: Effects of the self-regulated strategy within the context of spherical video-based virtual reality on students' learning performances in an art history class. Interact. Learn. Environ., 1–24 (2021). https://doi.org/10.1080/10494820.2021.1878231
22. Chang, C.-Y., Sung, H.-Y., Guo, J.-L., Chang, B.-Y., Kuo, F.-R.: Effects of spherical video-based virtual reality on nursing students' learning performance in childbirth education training. Interact. Learn. Environ. **30**, 400–416 (2019)
23. Shin, D.H.: The role of affordance in the experience of virtual reality learning: technological and affective affordances in virtual reality. Telematics Inform. **34**(8), 1826–1836 (2017)
24. Wu, W.-L., Hsu, Y., Yang, Q.-F., Chen, J.-J.: A spherical video-based immersive virtual reality learning system to support landscape architecture students' learning performance during the COVID-19 Era. Land **10**, 561 (2021)
25. Rubio-Tamayo, J.L., Barrio, M.G., García, F.G.: Immersive environments and virtual reality: systematic review and advances in communication, interaction and simulation. Multimodal Technol. Interact. **1**(4), 21 (2017)
26. Dalle, J., Mutalib, A.A.: The impact of technologies in teaching interaction design (2020)
27. Nor'a, M.N.A., Ismail, A.W.: Integrating virtual reality and augmented reality in a collaborative user interface. Int. J. Innov. Comput. **9**(2), 11–15 (2019)
28. Wu, W., Yen, H., Chen, J.: The influence of virtual reality learning system on the learning attitudes of design history. In: Shoji, H., Koyama, S., Kato, T., Muramatsu, K., Yamanaka, T., Lévy, P., Chen, K., Lokman, A.M. (eds.) Proceedings of the 8th International Conference on Kansei Engineering and Emotion Research. AISC, vol. 1256, pp. 284–291. Springer, Singapore (2020). https://doi.org/10.1007/978-981-15-7801-4_30
29. Wu, W., Hsu, Y., Cao, X., Chen, J.: Cross-cultural education: the effects of AR technology and learning styles on learning achievements of sculpture course. In: Rau, P.-L. (ed.) Cross-Cultural Design. Applications in Arts, Learning, Well-being, and Social Development: 13th International Conference, CCD 2021, Held as Part of the 23rd HCI International Conference, HCII 2021, Virtual Event, July 24–29, 2021, Proceedings, Part II, pp. 241–250. Springer, Cham (2021). https://doi.org/10.1007/978-3-030-77077-8_19

Research on the Design of Children's Sensory Integration Training Product Based on Dalcroze Method

Xinyi Yuan, Zhitao Li, Yinglu Zhang, and Yun Liu[✉]

Industrial Design of Fuzhou University, Fuzhou, China
liuyun525@fzu.edu.cn

Abstract. According to scientific research, 3–6 years old is a critical period for children's sensory integration training, and proper training can be used to improve sensory integration ability. This study takes children aged 3–6 as the research object, with the purpose of improving children's sensory integration ability, based on the cognitive development structure of the child stage and the basic laws of physical and mental development, through market research and user research, combined with interviews, questionnaires, and observation method and other methods, using children's sensory integration training products as the carrier, combined with Diversified intelligent interaction methods that conform to children's psychological cognition, give full play to the role of Dalcroze method in children's sensory integration training, and help children to be active and happy. In the process of using this kind of products, the ability of sensory integration is unconsciously improved, so that children's physical and mental development can be healthy, and the comprehensive quality of children can be comprehensively improved. The principle of the research angle and the design method can provide references for other designs.

Keywords: Dalcroze method · Sensory integration · Children · User experience design · Intelligent interaction design

1 Introduction

The acceleration of urbanization, changes in urbanized lifestyles and family nurturing methods have led to the phenomenon of children's Sensory Integration dysfunction becoming more and more common, and they have also had a significant impact on children's physical, psychological and intellectual development. In recent years, in the research of sensory integration theory, the research on children's sensory integration training has gradually increased, and many scholars have put forward relevant insights and solutions. However, there are still gaps in the research on the combination of music education concepts and children's sensory integration training products. As an excellent music education method, Dalcroze method can not only improve children's aesthetics, but also have a strong extension. It has an irreplaceable role. It also emphasizes the use of children's body rhythms to improve overall motor skills, coordination and body

P.-L. P. Rau (Ed.): HCII 2022, LNCS 13312, pp. 120–136, 2022.
https://doi.org/10.1007/978-3-031-06047-2_9

awareness, which can play a certain role in promoting the development of children's sensory integration capabilities. Sensory training through music helps to form a musical sensory training model that integrates fun, pleasure, beauty, and coordination, which effectively stimulates children's physical balance and coordination capabilities and promotes multi-sensory perception. Effectively provides a practical and effective method to help parents develop their children's sensory integration capabilities.

2   Overview of Sensory Integration

2.1   Sensory Integration

In 1969, the American psychologist, Dr. A. Jean Ayres of the University of Southern California proposed the concept of Sensory Integration (SI), referring to the process in which the brain comprehensively processes and organizes sensory information from various organs of the body (ears, eyes, mouth, nose, skin, etc.) (Fig. 1) [1]. After sensory integration, humans can complete complex and advanced cognitive activities such as memory, attention, and speech organization.

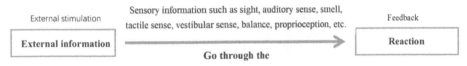

Fig. 1. Information input diagram

According to the questionnaire (Table 1), it is found that children aged 3–6 are in the best correction period of sensory integration, which is the most important stage of the development of children's sensory integration ability and the key period for the development of sensory integration ability. Children's physical and mental development and personality formation. Children aged 3–6 are lively, curious, susceptible to external interference, and have a strong ability to imitate. Therefore, choosing children aged 3–6 as the research objects of this article will help to further grasp the physical and mental characteristics of the target population, and conduct research and design of children's sensory integration training products on the basis of needs analysis. The research and application of child pedagogy, child psychology and other discipline theories laid the foundation for subsequent design research.

Table 1. Age cut-off table

Age	3-6 Years old	7-12 Years old	After the age of 12
Period	The best correction period for sensory integration (golden period)	Sensory integration best make-up period	Need psychological counseling and other means to intervene

2.2 Sensory Integration Dysfunction

Sensory integration dysfunction (SID) refers to the inability of external stimulus information to be effectively combined in the brain's nervous system. The brain loses control and combination of its various organs, unable to carry out effective analysis and comprehensive processing, and ultimately makes the whole body unable to function. People's attention, self-control ability, coordination ability and other abilities are all accomplished by the reasonable arrangement of the human brain's body movements. If the child suffers from sensory integration disorder, the development of cognitive ability and adaptability is slow, it will affect the child's learning ability and psychological quality, the child's socialization process is delayed, and it is prone to problems such as personality disorder and sensitive interpersonal relationship [1].

According to statistics from the National Health Commission of the People's Republic of China: In modern urban families, the proportion of children with sensory integration disorders is as high as 85%, and about 30% of them suffer from severe sensory integration disorders (see Fig. 2).

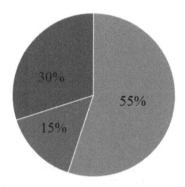

■ Children with severe sensory integration disorder

■ Children without sensory integration disorders

■ Children with mild and moderate sensory integration disorders

Fig. 2. Sensory integration disorder statistics chart

2.3 Overview of Children's Sensory Integration Training

The essence of sensory integration training is to combine sports and training products in a planned and targeted manner to enrich children's sensory stimulation, so that children can respond adaptively when receiving stimuli, improve the integration ability of the brain's nervous system, prevent or correct the sensory integration disorder. Children's sensory integration training has been valued and widely used in the process of children's growth and development, whether it is to correctly guide the growth and development of children with normal sensory integration capabilities, or to help rehabilitation training for children with sensory integration disorders.

Sensory Integration Training Content. According to relevant data, in the problem of sensory integration disorders in Chinese children, vestibular sense, tactile sense, and proprioception are the three important senses that affect children's sensory integration.

1. *Vestibular Sensation Disorder*
   Vestibular sensation is also called balance sense and static sense. It is the threshold of brain function. Vestibular sensation is one of the most important factors affecting children's growth and learning development. The vestibular sensation will receive the visual, auditory, taste, and touch information directly in front of the face, filter it, and then send it to the brain to select the appropriate information to respond. The vestibular imbalance is manifested as irritability, easy falling, carelessness, inattention in class, and naughty and willful.
   Vestibular sensation training is to stimulate the perception operation of vestibular sensation through sensory integration training products, so that children can continuously make coordinated sensory responses during the training process, so as to achieve the purpose of training.

2. *Tactile Disorders*
   The sense of touch is an important channel for people to understand the world. It affects people's judgment of the environment, and also affects people's emotional control of oneself and the emotional cognition of others. It has a great influence on personality and emotional intelligence (see Table 2).

Table 2. Classification table of tactile disorders

Classification	explain	Performance
Dull touch	For sensory information that is too little or takes a long time to respond, more intense information input will respond.	Slow response, inflexible movement, lack of self-awareness
Tactile seeking	The act of self-acquiring sensory input to perceive sensory input is more difficult to satisfy.	Bites, loves to hit people, loves to contain things
Sensitive to touch	Unable to tolerate normal sensory input	Sensitive to the touch, afraid of life,

Tactile training can activate tactile nerves by touching children's skin with products with different surface textures.

3. *Proprioception Disorders*
   Proprioception is the human body's perception of itself. Proprioception disorders can affect the body's control of various parts and cannot control muscle strength well. Common manifestations include: lack of self-confidence, negative withdrawal, frequent abrasions when playing; accurate actions; misjudgments of direction and information sources often occur, poor organization, poor language performance, etc.

Because the receptors of proprioception are distributed in the joints and muscles of the body, the training of proprioception needs to drive the whole body, often combined with different sensory exercises for training.

3 Children's Sensory Integration Training Products

Children's sensory integration training products are auxiliary training tools used in the process of sensory integration training. Such products are designed to help children carry out scientific and effective sensory training, promote the stimulation of children's various sense organs, so as to enhance children's sensory integration ability, and link children's brain, psychology and body coordination.

3.1 Analysis of the Status Quo of Children's Sensory Integration Training Products

In recent years, with the increase in the society's awareness of children's sensory integration ability, the demand for children's sensory integration training products has increased day by day, and a variety of sensory integration training products have emerged one after another.

According to different usage scenarios, the children's sensory integration training products on the market can be divided into two categories: home-based auxiliary sensory integration training products and large-scale sensory integration training facilities of professional training institutions:

1. *Home-Based Auxiliary Sensory Integration Training Products*
   The home-based auxiliary sensory training product is a small, low-cost home sensory training toy designed according to different sensory training methods such as balance, jumping, and rotation. Such products have a wide variety, small size, and easy storage. They are generally suitable for use in family situations. They can better help children perform sensory integration training with their parents, and help improve the effect of children's sensory integration training.
2. *Large-Scale Sensory Integration Training Facilities for Professional Training Institutions*
   The professional sensory integration training institution is composed of professional rehabilitation therapists, systematic sensory integration training courses and environmental space capable of accommodating large-scale training equipment. It has the characteristics of systematic and professionalism. Under the guidance of professional sensory integration training courses, children regularly conduct systematic sensory integration training, so as to get the effect of improving sensory integration ability.

   According to the six dimensions of venue, price, professionalism, systematic, continuous attractiveness, and effect feedback, different products were investigated and analyzed, and a comparison chart of children's sensory integration training products was obtained (Table 3).

Table 3. Analysis and comparison chart of children's sensory integration training products

Project	Site	Price	Professional degree	Systematic	Sustained attractiveness	Effect feedback
Sensory Integration training toys	Flexible	Cheap	Unprofessional	Scattered	Shorter	\
Sensory Integration Training Organization	Limited	Expensive	Profession	System	Curriculum arrangement is mandatory	Need to communicate with the agency in time

3.2 Problems and Development Space of Children's Sensory Integration Training Products

At present, domestic small-scale sensory training products have the advantages of being easy to store and suitable for parental companion training in family situations. However, there are also problems such as lack of innovation in function, single gameplay, boring training methods, and insignificant training effects. However, large scale professional sensory integration training institutions are generally expensive and parents cannot keep track of the training progress in time. Some sensory integration training products still have certain safety hazards and the training effect is not intuitive. They ignore the real needs of children's sensory integration training, resulting in the unpleasant sight of children's passive training, and hindering children's sensory integration ability to a certain extent. According to the analysis of the research results, sensory integration training products need to adopt a scientific and perfect teaching system, pay attention to the psychological path of children in the process of use, and combine functionality with fun to better enhance the effect of sensory integration training.

4 Analysis of Design Opportunities for Children's Sensory Integration Training Products Based on Dalcroze Method

4.1 Demand for Children's Sensory Integration Training Products

Through questionnaires, 25 effective people were interviewed by means of field observation and interviews, including staff of children's sensory integration training institutions, children and their parents, and sensory integration training product vendors. The survey results show that 80% of people believe that there is more room for development and improvement of sensory integration training products.

Summarize and analyze the needs of children's sensory integration training products as follows:

1. Conditional factors (pre-stage): clear and clear goals to achieve scientific and effective sensory integration training effects. Products should be safe and healthy, and product design and gameplay should match the children's construction ability. The training process and results can be displayed intuitively.

2. Experience factor (experience stage): Combining action and consciousness to stimulate children's curiosity, so that children can actively carry out sensory integration training. Gain a sense of potential control and let children have a better sense of participation.
3. Result factor (effect stage): Let children have a sense of pleasure in the process of using the product, and unknowingly carry out sensory integration training spontaneously.

4.2 Overview of Dalcroze Method

The Dalcroze method was proposed by the Swiss musician and educator Émile Jaques-Dalcroze in the early 20th century. The teaching method includes three basic teaching methods: Solfeggio, improvisation and Eurhythmics. Among them, Eurhythmics emphasizes the use of sports training to help students gain perceptual perception and musical experience, which is the most original and widely recognized teaching method by Dalcroze. Eurhythmics can stimulate the body's perception ability, especially with the help of the training of kinesthesia, so that students can obtain body awareness and sensory experience.

1. Correspondence Between Music Elements and Body Movement
Dalcroze believes that "the most powerful element in music is the rhythmic movement most closely related to life" [2]. Music is essentially the expression of human emotions. Translating inner emotions into music through body movement is the instinctive response of human beings [3]. Music education evokes the connection between the music and the body in the human body by guiding students to perform rhythmic movements, thereby cultivating students' musical sensibility, and gaining the ability to experience and express music.

There is a direct connection between music in the brain and the active body. The factors such as volume, intensity, speed, timbre contrast, and changes in the music performance almost all correspond to the strength, space, and time of the human body during exercise (see Table 4). The body is the best medium for perceiving music. Through body movement, we can feel, simulate and reproduce music [3].

Table 4. Correspondence between music and body movement

music	Pitch	Intensity	Timbre	Rhythm	Stop	Melody	Chord	Phrase	Harmony
Body movement	The direction and position of the gesture in space	Muscle strength	Representati-on of different parts of the body	Rhythm	Pause	Each action is continuous	Combinat-ion of various gestures	Action paragra-ph	Continuous combination of various gestures

2. The Serial Relationship Between Music Perception and Body Movement

Jean Piaget believes that "the more children see, perceive, and do, the more they want to see, perceive, and do" [4]. Gibson's research on perception and motor development concluded that perceptual learning and motor learning are inseparable. In many subsequent studies, researchers generally combined perception and action to explain the development of an individual, emphasizing that perception and action are interconnected in individual development. That is to say, the individual's perception and control of things need to rely on the sensitivity of the perception system and actions to explore the information feedback of things in order to be able to carry out coordinated activities. The Eurhythmics created by Dalcroze integrates body, music, and emotion. It requires students to make corresponding physical responses to music. As the number of exercises increases, students' perception of musical rhythm and emotional expression is gradually improved. Correspondingly, the students' physical coordination and control abilities have also been improved. In this positive cycle, students' perception and movement coordination with music rhythm will become more and more precise, and the coordination of hearing, kinesthesia, thinking, and emotion will be continuously promoted in teaching (see Fig. 3).

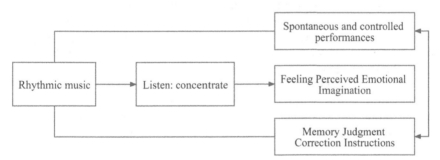

Fig. 3. Virtuous circle diagram

3. Teaching Methods Conforms to the Laws of Children's Psychological Development

According to Piaget's perception-action theory, when children's psychological development is in the stage of perception movement, the combined training of music and body movement are particularly in line with the child's nature and instinct. The Dalcroze method with "experience before cognition" as its core concept and its unique rhythm, improvisation, and play is in line with the characteristics and development requirements of children's physical and mental development. Dalcroze method breaks the traditional teaching method with its intuitive, individualized and gamified features. It can help children express their emotions through rhythmic movement, better stimulate children's enthusiasm and fun in learning music, and fully release the fun and active by nature, it can bring a relaxing and pleasant emotional experience to children.

5 Design Analysis of Children's Sensory Integration Training Products Based on Dalcroze Method

5.1 FBS Model Design Tool

Function-Behaviour-Structure ontology is referred to as FBS for short [5]. As a product design process, FBS mainly encourages designers to generate creative thinking in the process of deriving the relationship between function (F), behavior (B), and structure (S) [6]. FBS theory has been used as the basis of modeling design and design process in many design disciplines.

FBS is a product design process in which functional domains, behavior domains, and structural domains are mapped sequentially. In the process of introducing the FBS model design tool (Fig. 4 [7]), this paper deeply explores the relationship between the Dalcroze method and the sensory integration training, integrates the scattered pieces of knowledge into a knowledge collection with a logical structure, and constructs the corresponding Knowledge organization model. The modeling design and design process of this article is (Fig. 5): How to carry out effective sensory integration training is characterized as function F1, and the design problem is further subdivided into F2; looking for the design principle B1 that meets the realization of the function, and the specific principle performance the form is shown in B2, and analogy thinking is used to generate the original understanding of innovative design; the mapping relationship between behavior and structure is used to obtain the transformation of the principle to realize the structure S. The concrete realization of the whole process is mainly the result of the cross and integration of multidisciplinary knowledge under the support of various design resources. From the process of functional domain → behavior domain → structural domain, it presents a fuzzy to clear design state, and gradually evolves from abstract principle knowledge to specific domain knowledge.

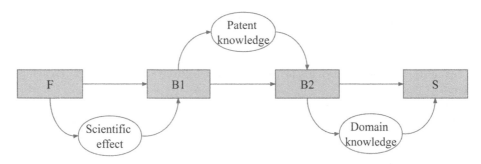

Fig. 4. FBS knowledge application process model [7]

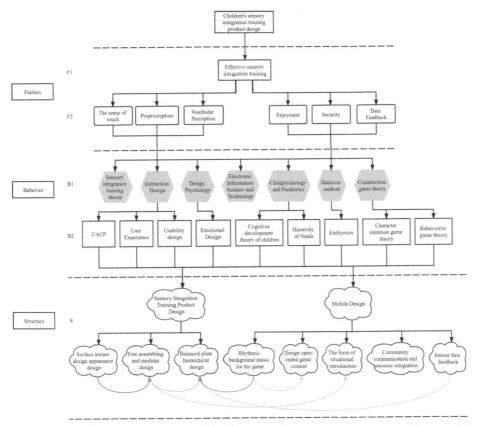

Fig. 5. Design process of children's sensory integration training products based on FBS model

5.2 Semantic Network Model Extension Based on FBS Model

The diffusion semantic network model of children's sensory integration training product is composed of previous research summaries and the semantic network innovation output based on the FBS model. The diffusion process of the semantic network model of the child sensory integration training product is shown in Fig. 6.

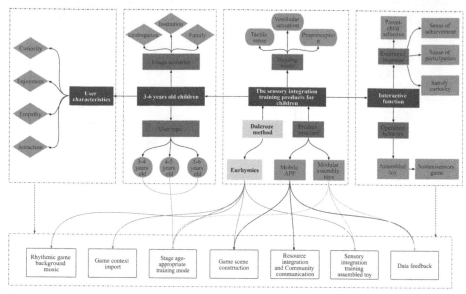

Fig. 6. Design of children's sensory integration training products based on FBS model extension

6 Design Practice

On the basis of the above research, with reference to the "3–6 Years Old Children's Learning and Development Guide" published by the Ministry of Education of the People's Republic of China, combined with relevant documents and teaching aid design specifications, the product design of sensory integration training was carried out.

6.1 Children's Sensory Integration Training Product Design

1. Modular Children's Assembling Toys
According to the constructive play theory, children can freely assemble different supporting components through interspersed pillars, which stimulates their strong curiosity and creativity. In terms of difficulties setting, the main toy blocks have different arcs to meet different training needs. At the same time, different bump textures are designed on the outsourcing contact surface of the assembled toys to train children's sense of touch and achieve the effect of more comprehensive training of children's sensory integration ability.

2. Children's Sensory Integration Game Design (see Fig. 7)
Based on interaction design theory and construction game design theory, a sensory integration training game is specially designed for children. In order to achieve effective sensory integration training, design a variety of game themes, open-ended game stories,

high-level two-way interaction, convey the meaning behind the story, in line with the children's characteristics of strong imitation and empathy.

3. Import Game Scenes
Refer to the teaching case of Dalcroze method, guide children to use their imagination in story situations, perform their own body rhythms, so that children have a better experience in the process of sensory integration training, stimulate children's curiosity, and let children take the initiative to feel Integrated training. At the same time, the potential sense of control allows children to use the product happily, and unknowingly conduct sensory integration training spontaneously, so that children have a better sense of participation.

4. Rhythmic Game Background Music
Rhythm is used in the Dalcroze method, allowing children to feel the music while using the body as an instrument. With the construction of the game scene and the changes in the speed, rhythm, intensity, and emotion of the music, children can improvise according to the changing rhythm and consciously control their movements to achieve effective sensory integration training.

Based on ergonomics, the three functions are studied in depth, and the ergonomic factors are considered as follows:

1. The height, angle, thickness, touch, hardness, weight, contact area and safety of the product.
3. Balance angle and balance strength.
4. Touch feeling: roughness size, surface texture design.

Fig. 7. Children's sensory integration training product hardware - Rhythm

6.2 Mobile Design of Children's Sensory Integration Training Products

Equipped with sensors on the hardware to collect children's movement status, real-time interaction with the game through Bluetooth connection, and a comprehensive score based on the number of game items collected by the child during the game and the balance ability. The sensor can collect and analyze data such as the child's movement accuracy, reaction sensitivity, and physical coordination ability and feed it back to the parents. It can help parents to have an intuitive understanding of the child's training process and training effects, and intervene when necessary. Parents on the mobile terminal can also exchange discussions and ask experts.

1. Mobile Terminal Software Design Planning (Fig. 8).

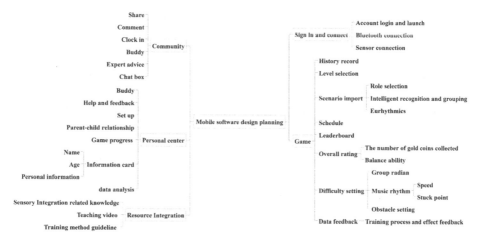

Fig. 8. Mobile software design planning

2. Mobile Terminal Software Interactive Prototype Design (Fig. 9 and 10).

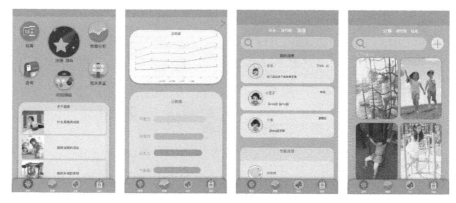

Fig. 9. Mobile interactive prototype design

Fig. 10. Game prototyping

7 Design Practice Evaluation

This design practice evaluation is for the usability test of "Rhythm", a child sensory integration training product based on the Dalcroze method. This test is for children 3–6 years old and their parents. The test content includes usability testing and usability testing of product functions. It aims to help the author team understand the target user's satisfaction with the product, discover the shortcomings of the product, and iterate.

1. Test preparation: build simple product prototypes, assemble sensors and Bluetooth modules, and design game prototypes.
2. Test subject: Invite three children and their parents, all children are 3–6 years old.
3. Test method: Task analysis, emotional behavior analysis, oral analysis and error analysis are performed on the testees through vocal thinking, user interviews and other methods.
4. Test procedure: First, before the start of the test, teach the children how to play games. After the participants have basically mastered the use of the product, let them start the free game. Each subject arranges 10 min of play time. During the test, the author's team recorded the observations of the whole process, and sorted out and analyzed the data.
5. Test result: Observe the test process of all subjects, and arrange the analysis as shown in Fig. 11.

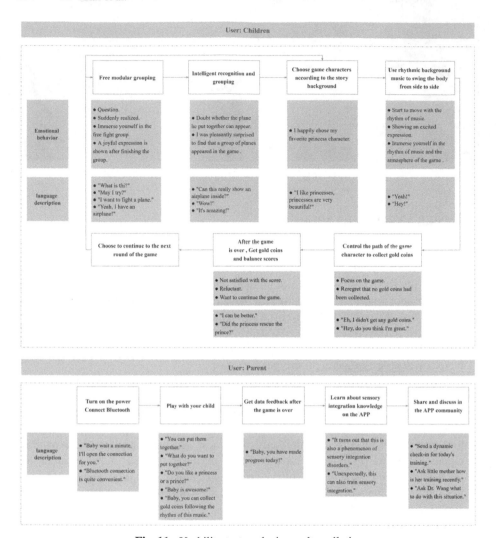

Fig. 11. Usability test analysis results collation

According to the results of this test, the author team found some issues that were not considered in the design stage, and made some adjustments, such as adding a stability score to the game scoring mechanism; adjusting the maximum swing angle of the product to improve safety etc. At the same time, the concept and interaction of the product have also been affirmed by the subjects and parents. The observation results will become the reference basis for the perfect iteration of the product in the future. At the same time, it is also hoped to expand the test sample size and increase the test methods to obtain a more comprehensive evaluation and feedback.

8   Concluding Remarks

This thesis is based on the design and research of children's sensory integration training products with children aged 3–6 as the target population. It focuses on the research on the core needs of children's sensory integration training products, and emphasizes the application of the Dalcroze method to children the positive effect of sensory integration training on the growth of children. Propose the experience design principles and strategies of children's sensory integration training products based on the Dalcroze method, find a new way to effectively link it with sensory integration training, give full play to the role of Dalcroze method in the training of children's sensory integration ability, and further expand the research ideas of the Dalcroze method in the experience design of children's sensory integration training products, and provide more possibilities for the design of such products.

The Remaining Problems

- Since the limited project time has limited the in-depth research progress, the author team selected a limited sample size in the analysis of children's psychological conditions and needs, which may have overlooked the subtle needs of some target users. The research in this article is further expanded to expand more test objects, so that the product fits the real needs of users, enhances the user experience, and achieves an effective sensory integration training effect.
- Sensory integration theory belongs to the field of neuroscience. Due to the limited professional ability, there are still limitations in its theoretical connotation and practical grasp, and further exploration is needed.

Prospects for the Future.   From the system point of view, users and purchase decision makers are included in the research scope, and the relationship between users and scenes is further coordinated to realize the improvement of the interaction design system. With the continuous maturity of interactive technology, its application will continue to extend to children's interactive products. In the future design of children's sensory integration training products, more attention will be paid to the interactivity and experience of the products. Will also explore more interactive methods, fun and in-depth experience in parent-child interaction.

Acknowledgment.   We would like to thank our esteemed supervisor – Dr. Yun Liu for her invaluable support which was really influential in studies during the course of writing a thesis. In addition, our gratitude extends to Fujian Student Research Training Program for the funding opportunity to undertake our studies. What's more, we would like to thank our research partners Ruizhe Liu and Zijing Zhang of Xiamen University for their technical support for the design and practice of this project. Finally, our appreciation also goes out to the participants for providing data feedback and improvement of this project during usability testing.

References

1. Fang, L.: Case study on sensory integration training to improve sensory integration disorder of young children. Inner Mongolia Normal University (2020)
2. (Switzerland) Dalcroze: Rhythm, Music, and Education. Springer Press, Germany (1935)
3. Limei, Y., Juemin, C.: Dalcroz Music Education Theory and Practice, vol. 24. Shanghai Music Press House (1995)
4. Qi, D., Sha, T.: Action and Psychological Development, vol. 136. Beijing Normal University Press (2004)
5. Gero, J.S.: Computational models of innovation and creative design process. Technol. Forecast. Soc. Chang. **64**, 186–196 (2000)
6. Galle, P.: The ontology of Gero's FBS model of designing. Des. Stud. **30**, 321–339 (2009)
7. Fan, F., Li, Y., Li, W.: Study on design knowledge organization and application strategy based on FBS. Mech. Des. **29**(10), 9–14 (2012)
8. Huang, Y., Wang, Y.: Test of sensory integration assessment scale in children aged 3–6. Chin. J. Mental Health **05**, 14–16 (1997)
9. Lin, W.: Research on the influence of sensory training on children's behavior. Chin. Off-campus Educ. **33**, 28–30 (2019)
10. Wang, A.: Practical research on musical sensory integration training in ordinary children aged 3–6 years old. Jiangsu Normal University (2018)
11. Ma, Z.: Research on product design of home sensory integration training for preschool children. Guangdong University of Technology (2020)
12. Yang, Q.: Analysis of psychological principles of darcross teaching method. Xi'an Conservatory of Music (2017)
13. Suh, N.P.: The Principles of Design. Oxford University Press, New York (1990)
14. Cheng, K.: Research on intelligent toy design based on audio-visual synesthesia education. Zhejiang University (2016)

The Effect of Virtual Reality Technology in Cross-Cultural Teaching and Training of Drones

Zhanpeng Zhao and Weilong Wu[✉]

School of Film Television and Communication, Xiamen University of Technology, Xiamen, China
wu_academic@163.com

Abstract. Objectives: With the rapid development of drone technology, drones have been used in various fields such as surveying and mapping, forestry, firefighting, emergency rescue, etc. In the face of a huge talent gap, drones market talents are in short supply. In order to cultivate reserve saving talents for drones, many universities already offer aerial drone survey courses. The traditional teaching mode requires a lot of time, manpower and material costs. In this paper, we take "virtual reality technology" as the core, and propose a "combination of virtual reality" and "combination of online and offline" teaching mode for the experimental course, in order to solve a series of traditional teaching. It also provides a valuable reference experience for the development and reform of other experimental courses. This study uses virtual reality and drone aerial survey technologies to allow students to visit and learn the basic theoretical knowledge of drone aerial survey and learn drone aerial survey technologies to achieve the purpose of the "online & offline" "virtual & reality" course teaching mode.

The drone aerial survey experiment course aims to cultivate excellent drone aerial survey talents. Drones aerial survey is a technology that has only been emerging for 4 to 5 years. The traditional teaching is mainly based on the offline mode, and the theoretical course is only based on the teacher teaching theoretical knowledge and demonstrating experimental operation, with fixed teaching content, single method and boring content. In course, if the teacher is inexperienced or inappropriate, it is easy for students to lose interest and initiative in learning. The students' professional knowledge is limited to superficial theories and basic operations, which cannot meet the course objectives, and due to the scarcity of teachers with operational and teaching experience, the effect of the drone aerial survey course is poor. As drone aerial survey course training is costly, restricted by the venue and many online courses today cannot meet the training needs, and as students come from different cultural backgrounds and living environments, culture becomes an important human-computer interaction issue if the interactive system is to be usable, useful and appeal to a wide range of users. Faced with students from different cultural backgrounds and living environments, the question of how to make drone teaching and training work better as an educational tool is one to ponder.

The use of virtual reality technology in the teaching process, through three-dimensional virtual simulation and virtual interactive technology to the course required equipment, scenes, experimental operation process, experimental results

© The Author(s), under exclusive license to Springer Nature Switzerland AG 2022
P.-L. P. Rau (Ed.): HCII 2022, LNCS 13312, pp. 137–147, 2022.
https://doi.org/10.1007/978-3-031-06047-2_10

for virtual display, real show the entire process of experimental operations. The use of virtual reality technology combined with traditional teaching can not only enrich the teaching content, but also overcome the extreme dependence on traditional experimental teaching equipment and environment. Under the reasonable control of teachers, students can carry out experiments independently, which effectively mobilises students' learning initiative and increases their learning interest, and also improves students' ability to relate theory to practice and improve learning efficiency. At the same time, the "virtual & reality" teaching mode can effectively extend the time for students to learn, operate and train, overcoming the traditional teaching mode's high limitation of time and space, enabling students to deepen their mastery of operations and key aspects, and more effectively cultivate a comprehensive quality of technical personnel.

Methods: In this study, 24 students were randomly selected as the control group and 26 students were selected as the experimental group. There were no major differences in the basic information of the two groups, and all of them had initially studied the drone course and had a preliminary understanding of drone knowledge. The control group used the traditional teaching mode, with the teacher teaching knowledge and operation demonstration, while the experimental group used virtual reality technology for teaching. A pre-test will be conducted before the teaching activities to ensure that there is no significant difference in the prior knowledge of the two groups, and a post-test will be administered at the end of the course and a questionnaire on learning interest and learning confidence will be administered.

Results: By comparing the test results of the control group with the experimental group and the results of the teaching questionnaire, it can be found that students in the experimental group had higher average test scores than those in the control group, and students in the experimental group had higher levels of classroom concentration, learning initiative and satisfaction with classroom teaching than students in the control group. Students in the control group indicated that the knowledge in the classroom was too boring and they did not pay attention in class, while students in the experimental group indicated that the classroom was more participatory and interesting, and they hoped that more experimental courses could be taught in this way.

Conclusions: This study found that traditional teaching courses do not fully meet students' learning needs, and that practical courses require more hands-on experience. The use of virtual reality technology combined with traditional teaching can be a good solution to this problem and improve students' learning efficiency.The 'virtual & reality' teaching allows students to have an immersive experience, which can effectively increase students' learning interest and learning confidence. In addition, there are a number of issues that need to be addressed. Due to the novelty of virtual reality technology, it remains to be seen whether or not it will have an impact on practical operations and how this can be addressed. More research is needed on how to make the best use of virtual reality in teaching and learning.

Keywords: Virtual reality technology · Drones · Cross-cultural training · Learning attitudes · Learning confidence

1 Introduction

Drones are now used in many fields such as mapping, forestry, firefighting and emergency rescue because of their high adaptability in different complex scenarios [1], and the drone market is in short supply of talents. In order to cultivate reserve saving talents for drones, several universities across the country have already offered courses on drone aerial survey [2]. Drone training courses are highly integrated with theory and practice. The traditional teaching model requires a lot of time, manpower and material costs, and is affected by high training costs, difficulty in realizing one drone per person, one-to-one training, viewing but not actual operation, and large venue restrictions. This paper proposes a "virtual reality combined" teaching model with "virtual reality technology" as the core, with the aim of solving a series of problems in traditional teaching and providing valuable reference experience for the development and reform of other experimental courses. This study uses virtual reality and aerial survey technologies to explore the impact of virtual reality technology on students' learning interest and learning confidence.

The purpose of the drone aerial survey course is to cultivate excellent drone talents, and drone aerial survey is a technology that has only emerged for 4–5 years [2]. The traditional teaching is mainly in offline mode, and the theoretical course is only based on teachers teaching theoretical knowledge and demonstrating experimental operations [3]. In the experimental course, if the teachers lack experience or operate improperly, they cannot achieve the course objectives, and it is easy for students to lose learning interest and learning confidence, and the effect of the drone aerial survey course is poor due to the scarcity of teachers with operational and teaching experience. Also as students come from different cultural backgrounds and living environments, culture becomes an important human-computer interaction issue if the interactive system is to be usable, useful and appeal to a wide range of users. The question of how best to train drones in the face of students from different cultural backgrounds and living environments is one to ponder.

The use of virtual reality technology in the teaching process, through three-dimensional virtual simulation and virtual interactive technology to the course required equipment, scenes, experimental operation process, experimental results for virtual display, real show the entire process of experimental operations [4]. The application of virtual reality technology to traditional teaching can overcome the over-reliance of traditional teaching on teaching equipment and teaching environment, effectively extend the time for students to study, operate and train, and enrich the teaching content, and students can learn independently, which can effectively improve students' learning interest and learning confidence. It will also enable students to deepen their grasp of operational and key aspects of the process, and more effectively develop a comprehensive and highly skilled workforce [5].

2 Literature Review

2.1 Drones and Drone Training

Drones, the collective name for unmanned aerial vehicles, are unmanned aircraft operated using radio remote control and airframe programmed controls. Originally used for military test training and reconnaissance surveillance, among other things, drones have seen rapid development in drone technology and their high applicability in many complex scenarios in everyday life. In agriculture, drones can provide real-time images and data of farmland, in medicine they can be used to provide disaster assessments when other avenues are limited, to deliver pharmaceutical resources to remote areas, and in certain areas involving national security, drones can be very good for border security monitoring and the timely return of information [6]. In addition to the advantages of drones in these fields, they can also be extremely useful in mapping, forestry and firefighting [1], and as a result, more and more people are engaging in research about drone education. Valente J, Kooistra L designed a MOOC agricultural drone online course to provide learners with aerial remote sensing with a focus on agricultural applications basics for learning about agricultural drones [7]. In today's epidemic situation, many industries have been hit hard and given the maneuverability and simplicity of drones, many researchers have started to think about what role drones could play in this epidemic, and the team of Jinkyung Jenny Kim, Insin Kim, Jinsoo Hwang used drones in their research on post-epidemic food delivery services. In their study of post-epidemic food delivery services, they used drones to deliver contactless products and concluded that they could do the job well [8].

According to reports and information from the Internet, drones have been used for some time in the educational field, which suggests that it is possible and necessary to introduce them systematically in the implementation of educational curricula, and there are already some examples of this in practice [9]. Drones can also be useful in interdisciplinary education, bringing together different fields, and researchers from the University of Puerto Rico, Mayaguez, have formed an interdisciplinary team to study the different characteristics of quadcopter drones for education in science, technology, engineering and mathematics [10]. Traditional drone training is mainly offline, which has a number of problems due to the complexity of the theoretical knowledge of drones and the more hands-on nature of the training. It is difficult to fully understand during the learning process and to have a drone to review the knowledge gained during the training afterwards. As drones have an extremely large learner population, many researchers have begun to try to propose solutions to these problems. Researchers at Sejong University in South Korea have proposed a remote training system for FPV drone flight in an MR environment that allows drone pilots to configure the environment in a virtual environment with the intention of what is needed in a real flight environment [11]. The development of an online training model is a necessary initiative in today's global offensive of the epidemic, where offline training is under attack.

2.2 Virtual Reality Technology

Virtual Reality (VR) technology, the principle of which uses electronic glasses to immerse the wearing individual into an environment simulated by a computer, is a tool that can provide users with greater participation and autonomy in academic research and some purposeful activities [12]. Due to the immersion that virtual reality technology can provide to users, many researchers' studies have shown that virtual reality technology is a viable tool in scientific fields such as engineering and medicine [13]. Due to the development of virtual reality technology, its role in the field of student education is also becoming apparent, with a greater impact on classroom teaching in higher education [14, 15]. Virtual reality, as a teaching tool in higher education, can facilitate a more immersive engagement with environments that are not normally easily accessible to students. it has a 360-degree immersion, with 3D models and interactive videos, to make people feel realistic about computer-generated virtual scenes [15, 16]. Jiang, Luchuan's team based on a virtual simulation experimental platform, studied based on an experimental virtual simulation platform, studied an online platform for training swimming in order to enable people to learn swimming strokes online and improve their swimming skills without the restriction of a swimming venue [17]. In today's pandemic environment, many schools and training institutions have to switch from offline to online teaching, which is undoubtedly a huge blow to some subjects with strong operational and abstract theoretical knowledge. Weilong Wu et al., developed a landscape architecture SV-IVR learning system using virtual reality technology, which effectively improved students' They used virtual reality technology to develop a landscape architecture SV-IVR learning system, which effectively improved students' academic performance, learning attitudes and self-regulation without negatively affecting them [18], demonstrating the effectiveness of virtual reality technology in education and its own great potential. Rui Wang et al. applied the virtual & reality teaching model to the optimisation of university classrooms and concluded that this teaching model can be effective in optimising the classroom [5]. In his study of civil engineering teaching, Ling Chen points out that traditional courses suffer from difficulties in theoretical teaching, shortage of practical teaching resources and insufficient innovation in teaching models, and that the emergence of virtual reality technology has solved these problems [19]. Cuicui Zhang pointed out that with the development of virtual reality technology, VR application in medical teaching has become a new trend and hot spot [20]. The drone aerial survey course studied in this paper, with its abstract theoretical curriculum and the need for strong operational skills, has more restrictions on offline training, and the development of online teaching is necessary in today's epidemic situation, we discuss whether virtual reality can work well in this course and provide some ideas for moving from offline to online teaching for other similar courses.

3 Experiment Design

In order to judge whether virtual reality technology can play an effective role in drone teaching and training, we aimed to combine virtual reality technology with a drone aerial survey course in a school in China, which is a compulsory course for drone learning and contains theoretical knowledge and practical operation knowledge. We arranged the course for the experimental group to learn theoretical knowledge and practical operation of drones using virtual reality technology, and for the control group to learn theoretical knowledge from the teacher, followed by a demonstration of practical operation by the teacher. The aim of our study was to investigate the effect of virtual reality technology on learning attitudes and confidence in drone training.

3.1 Participants in the Experiment

In this study, 24 students were randomly selected as the control group and 26 students as the experimental group. There were no major differences in the basic information of the two groups, and all of them had initially studied drone courses and had preliminary knowledge of drones. The control group used the traditional teaching mode, with the teacher teaching knowledge and operation demonstration, while the experimental group used virtual reality technology for teaching, with the teacher using virtual reality for classroom teaching and the students using VR for learning. All teaching activities are carried out by the same professor with many years of experience in education, who has a strong theoretical knowledge of drones and a high level of practical drones operation skills.

3.2 Measuring Tools

The research instruments for this study included a pre-test before the experiment and a post-test section after the experiment, as well as a questionnaire to measure students' learning attitudes and learning confidence. The questionnaire was divided into two sections, for learning interest and learning confidence, with the learning interest section containing five questions on a scale of 1–5 and the learning confidence section containing four questions on a scale of 1–5.

3.3 Experimental Procedure

The experimental process is shown in Fig. 1, where students in the experimental and control groups were given a pre-test before the course began, followed by an introduction to the drones aerial survey course and an initial presentation of relevant knowledge by the instructor. Afterwards, the students in the experimental group were taught using virtual reality technology, while the students in the control group were taught in a traditional way. Post-testing of all students at the end of the course, followed by the completion of a questionnaire to measure students' learning interest and learning confidence.

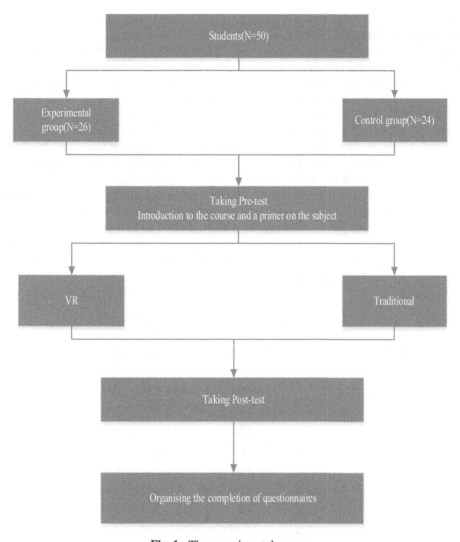

Fig. 1. The experimental process

4   Experimental Results

4.1   Analysis of Learning Interest

The independent sample t-test was used to analyse the students' interest in the drones aerial survey course under the traditional teaching mode and the virtual reality technology teaching mode, as shown in Table 1. The results of the study showed that the level of interest in the drones aerial survey course: showed a 0.01 level of significance (t = 3.349, p = 0.002), as well as the specific comparison differences can be seen that the mean of the experimental group (3.54), would be significantly higher than the mean of the control group (3.04). Conscientiousness during lessons in the drones aerial survey course: showing a 0.05 level of significance (t = 2.502, p = 0.016), as well as specific comparative differences can be seen that the mean of the experimental group (3.46), would be significantly higher than the mean of the control group (3.04). The initiative of learning in the drone aerial survey course: showed a 0.05 level of significance (t = 2.649, p = 0.011), as well as a specific comparison difference which shows that the mean of the experimental group (3.42), would be significantly higher than the mean of the control group (2.83). Satisfaction with the drones aerial survey course: showing a 0.05 level of significance (t = 2.643, p = 0.011), as well as a specific comparison difference that shows that the mean of the experimental group (3.77), would be significantly higher than the mean of the control group (3.25). The total score showed a 0.01 level of significance (t = 5.131, p = 0.000), as well as a specific comparison difference that shows that the mean of the experimental group (14.19), would be significantly higher than the mean of the control group (12.17). In conclusion, it can be seen that students who learn using virtual reality technology show significant differences in their attitudes to learning from those who learn using the traditional mode of teaching, and that the mean value of learning using virtual reality technology is higher than that of students who learn using the traditional mode of teaching.

Table 1. Research findings on learning interest

Learning interest	Group	N	Average	SD	t	p
Level of interest in aerial drone survey courses	Traditional	24	3.04	0.46	3.349	0.002**
	VR	26	3.54	0.588		
Conscientiousness during lessons in aerial drone survey courses	Traditional	24	3.04	0.46	2.502	0.016*
	VR	26	3.46	0.71		
Active learning in aerial drone survey courses	Traditional	24	2.83	0.76	2.649	0.011*
	VR	26	3.42	0.81		
Satisfaction with aerial drone survey courses	Traditional	24	3.25	0.61	2.643	0.011*
	VR	26	3.77	0.76		
Total	Traditional	24	12.17	1.37	5.131	0.000**
	VR	26	14.19	1.41		

$^{*}p < .05$ $^{**}p < .01$

4.2 Analysis of Learning Confidence

The independent samples t-test was used to analyse the students' confidence in learning the drones aerial survey course under the traditional teaching mode and the virtual reality technology teaching mode, as shown in Table 2, the results of the study showed that the perception of the difficulty of the traditional drones aerial survey course: showed a 0.01 level of significance (t = −3.336, p = 0.002), as well as the specific comparison difference can be seen that the mean of the experimental group (3.31), would be significantly lower than the mean of the control group (3.83). Acceptance of the instructor's knowledge about drones: This showed a 0.05 level of significance (t = 2.414, p = 0.020), as well as a specific comparison difference that showed that the mean of the experimental group (3.69) would be significantly higher than the mean of the control group (3.29). Mastery of the knowledge acquired in the traditional drones aerial survey course: showed a 0.05 level of significance (t = 2.559, p = 0.014), as well as a specific comparison difference which shows that the mean of the experimental group (3.73), would be significantly higher than the mean of the control group (3.33). Classroom efficiency: showing a 0.01 level of significance (t = 3.169, p = 0.003), as well as specific comparative differences it can be seen that the mean of the experimental group (3.58), would be significantly higher than the mean of the control group (3.04). The total score showed a 0.05 level of significance (t = 2.405, p = 0.020), as well as a specific comparison difference that shows that the mean of the experimental group (14.31), would be significantly higher than the mean of the control group (13.50). In conclusion, it can be seen that students learning with virtual reality technology showed significant differences in learning confidence from those learning with the traditional mode of teaching, with students learning with virtual reality technology perceiving the course to be less difficult than those learning with the traditional mode of teaching, and higher means in all other aspects of learning confidence than those learning with the traditional mode.

Table 2. Research findings on learning confidence

Learning confidence	Group	N	Average	SD	t	p
Perceived difficulty of the drones aerial survey course	Traditional	24	3.83	0.64	−3.336	0.002**
	VR	26	3.31	0.47		
Receptiveness to the teacher's knowledge about drones	Traditional	24	3.29	0.62	2.414	0.020*
	VR	26	3.69	0.55		
Knowledge of what you have learnt in the drones aerial survey course	Traditional	24	3.33	0.48	2.559	0.014*
	VR	26	3.73	0.60		
Classroom efficiency	Traditional	24	3.04	0.55	3.169	0.003**
	VR	26	3.58	0.64		
Total	Traditional	24	13.50	1.06	2.405	0.020*
	VR	26	14.31	1.29		

$^{*}p < .05 ** p < .01$

By comparing the test scores and teaching questionnaire results between the control group and the experimental group, students in the experimental group had higher average test scores than those in the control group, and students in the experimental group had higher classroom concentration, learning initiative and satisfaction with classroom teaching than students in the control group. Students in the control group said that the knowledge in the classroom was too boring and they did not pay attention in class, while students in the experimental group said that the classroom was highly participatory, the classroom was more interesting and the virtual reality technology effectively reduced the learning difficulty of the course, and they hoped that other experimental courses could be taught in this way.

5 Discussion and Conclusions

From this study we can find that the traditional drone aerial survey course is cumbersome and obscure due to the content, and the cost of the drone training course is large, and the site restrictions are also large, today's epidemic environment, the offline training course is even more impacted, and the universal online course can not meet the training needs, and the "virtual & reality" teaching model we proposed teaching model, which provides an opportunity to upgrade the development of the traditional teaching model, can solve the drawbacks of the traditional teaching model at the same time, can effectively improve students' learning interest and learning confidence, so that students have an immersive experience in the learning process, effectively improve the students' learning performance, to help cultivate talents [21–23]. At the same time, as students come from different cultural backgrounds and living environments, culture becomes an important human-computer interaction issue if the interactive system is to be usable, useful and appeal to a wide range of users. In the face of students from different cultural backgrounds and living environments, our proposed 'virtual & reality' teaching model, uses virtual reality technology to provide excellent cross-cultural training [24, 25].

Based on the results of this study, there are several suggestions for future research. Firstly, the size of the sample needs to be expanded, the selection of the sample needs to be more diverse, and the choice of experimental courses could be more varied. In addition, there are some issues that need to be noted, and it remains to be seen whether virtual reality technology, due to its novelty, will have an impact on practical operations and whether students will have technical problems while learning. More research is needed on how to better utilise virtual reality technology in teaching and learning.

References

1. Boccadoro, P., Striccoli, D., Grieco, L.A.: An extensive survey on the Internet of Drones. Ad Hoc Netw. **122**, 102600 (2021)
2. Ma, M.: Research on the experimental teaching mode of UAV aerial survey based on "online & offline" and "virtual & reality." Jingwei Tiandi **03**, 83–85 (2021)
3. Guan, Y., Yu, B.: Research on the reform of teaching mode of high-quality open courses in colleges and universities. Sci. Technol. Inf. **15**(34), 132–134 (2017)
4. Yi, Z.: Study on the design of teaching mode of VR technology. J. Sci. Educ. **26**, 10–12 (2021)
5. Rui, W.: The application of virtual/reality "double classroom" teaching mode in optimizing university classroom teaching. Wirel. Internet Technol. **18**(13), 118–119+131 (2021)
6. Ayamga, M., Akaba, S., Nyaaba, A.A.: Multifaceted applicability of drones: a review. Technol. Forecast. Soc. Chang. **167**, 120677 (2021)
7. Valente, J., Kooistra, L.: MOOC drones for agriculture: the making-of. In: 2020 IEEE Global Engineering Education Conference (EDUCON). IEEE, pp. 1692–1695 (2020)
8. Kim, J.J., Kim, I., Hwang, J.: A change of perceived innovativeness for contactless food delivery services using drones after the outbreak of COVID-19. Int. J. Hosp. Manag. **93**, 102758 (2021)

9. Ćosić Lesičar, J., Božić, D.: Current status of the use of drones in education in Croatia. Interdisc. Description Complex Syst. INDECS **19**(1), 160–167 (2021)
10. Yepes, I., Barone, D.A.C., Porciuncula, C.M.D.: Use of drones as pedagogical technology in STEM disciplines. Inf. Educ. **21**, 201–233 (2021)
11. Go, Y.-G., Kang, H.-S., Lee, J.-W., Yu, M.-S., Choi, S.-M.: Multi-user drone flight training in mixed reality. Electronics **10**(20), 2521 (2021)
12. Akdere, M., Acheson, K., Jiang, Y.: An examination of the effectiveness of virtual reality technology for intercultural competence development. Int. J. Intercult. Relat. **82**, 109–120 (2021)
13. Clark, D.B., Tanner-Smith, E.E., Killingsworth, S.S.: Digital games, design, and learning: a systematic review and meta-analysis. Rev. Educ. Res. **86**(1), 79–122 (2016)
14. Alhalabi, W.: Virtual reality systems enhance students' achievements in engineering education. Behav. Inf. Technol. **35**(11), 919–925 (2016)
15. Marks, B., Thomas, J.: Adoption of virtual reality technology in higher education: an evaluation of five teaching semesters in a purpose-designed laboratory. Educ. Inf. Technol. **27**(1), 1287–1305 (2021)
16. Elmezeny, A., Edenhofer, N., Wimmer, J.: Immersive storytelling in 360-degree videos: an analysis of interplay between narrative and technical immersion. J. Virtual Worlds Res. **11**(1), 1–13 (2018)
17. Jiang, L.: Research on 3D simulation of swimming technique training based on FPGA and virtual reality technology. Microprocess. Microsyst. **81**, 103657 (2021)
18. Wu, W.L., Hsu, Y., Yang, Q.F., et al.: A spherical video-based immersive virtual reality learning system to support landscape architecture students' learning performance during the COVID-19 era. Land **10**(6), 561 (2021)
19. Ling, C.: The application of virtual reality technology in civil engineering teaching. Ind. Technol. Forum **20**(13), 172–173 (2021)
20. Cui, Z.C.: Application of VR virtual simulation technology in medical teaching. Sci. Educ. Wenhui **06**, 116–117 (2021)
21. Topljak, A.: Equipping schools with information and communication technology for the needs of introducing the subject of informatics as a compulsory subject as part of the school for life project. In Croatian. Hrvatski sjever: književnost, kultura, znanost **15**(54), 95–114 (2020)
22. Xi, E.: Analyses of current status of domestic research on virtual reality technology in education. In: 2021 5th Annual International Conference on Data Science and Business Analytics (ICDSBA), pp. 588–591. IEEE (2021)
23. Moussa, R., Alghazaly, A., Althagafi, N., Eshky, R., Borzangy, S.: Effectiveness of virtual reality and interactive simulators on dental education outcomes: systematic review. Eur. J. Dent. **16**(01), 14–31 (2021)
24. Chan, C.S., Bogdanovic, J., Kalivarapu, V.: Applying immersive virtual reality for remote teaching architectural history. Educ. Inf. Technol. **27**, 4365–4397 (2022). https://doi.org/10.1007/s10639-021-10786-8
25. James, P.: The construction of learning and teaching in a sculpture studio class. Stud. Art Educ. **37**, 145–159 (1996)

Application of Digital Technology in Future Sculpture Teaching

Guang Zhu[✉]

Tsinghua University, Beijing, China
43445571@qq.com

Abstract. The model of traditional sculpture is affected by digital technology, and the form and process of sculpture teaching are changing, which puts forward new requirements for sculpture practitioners.

This paper analyzes the development history and status quo of modern sculpture teaching, combs the digital technology in sculpture field, and focuses on the analysis of sculpture's form, space, materials, technology and other issues in sculpture teaching. This paper analyzes and sorts out the application of digital technology in sculpture teaching, mainly including: the presentation of sculpture entity in virtual space, the simulation of sculpture material by using digital technology, and the interdisciplinary integration of digital sculpture teaching.

Digital technology has changed the traditional single mode of sculpture teaching. Digital software is not only used in the field of design, but also opens a new direction for sculpture teaching, changing the limitations of sculpture on space, site and site, enriching the materials of sculpture and breaking the limitations of sculpture discipline.

Keyword: Digital sculpture · Sculpture teaching · 3D software

1 Introduction

In the social background of the digital age, computer technology in the field of art has a lot of innovation and development. Digital technology first in games, animation, in foreign countries have more than ten years of development history, in the field of product processing is also widely used, the use of 3D modeling technology and printing technology rapid prototyping, and then mold production and processing.

In 1990, the concept of digital sculpture was first proposed and discussed at the American Society of Sculptors (ISC) Biennial Conference. In 1995, the first large-scale international exhibition with digital sculpture as the exhibition theme, "Digital Sculpture 95", was held in France. In this period, due to the relatively backward computer hardware and software, digital sculpture works showed the characteristics of geometry and abstraction, but it created the first digital technology for sculpture creation, so that the concept of digital sculpture was initially formed [1].

In recent years, the rise of 3D printing technology, the improvement of printing accuracy and printing volume, and the advantage of material price make the technology

P.-L. P. Rau (Ed.): HCII 2022, LNCS 13312, pp. 148–159, 2022.
https://doi.org/10.1007/978-3-031-06047-2_11

more widely put into production and manufacturing. The research and utilization of digital technology by sculptors and practitioners and designers is increasing year by year, and the use of 3D technology to make sculpture works has become a widely used means.

2 Application of Digital Technology in Sculpture Teaching

3d technology is the development of digital technology through a certain period of a new technology, its birth and development is based on the basis of the traditional digital 2d graphic design technology, through the two-dimensional plane will be digital, intelligent virtual 3d space fully, give people more intuitive experience. The processing capacity of computer software and hardware is not the computing capacity of computers in the last century, and the processing style and detail processing of some software have exceeded the effect of traditional ways to do sculpture. And through the actual operation of the virtual environment of light and shadow, the material and color of the object, movement track and way, geographical location and other details of the simulation display. In the field of digital basic education, it is generally believed that the basic courses of digital art in colleges and universities need to learn software such as 3DS Max and Maya. ZBrush digital sculpture has been rapidly accepted by sculptors in recent years. Advances in VR technology have made software such as Adobe Medium and Gravity Sketch, which are easier to use, popular.

The modeling process of Digital sculpture in ZBrush is highly modeled after the production process of traditional sculpture. The software is called "Sculptor's Assistant," and the process of making sculptures with the software is similar to traditional sculpture making. In the production process of ZBrush, we need to start from a simple shape and describe it step by step from the whole to the part. This engineering software, design software by accessories block the form and steps are completely different. For example, to complete a head, in traditional sculpture, it is necessary to "top the mud" first to complete an ellipse or sphere as a basic type, and then find a large surface and shoot a large surface of the figure's head. The production method in ZBrush is very close to that of traditional sculpture. It needs to build a ball as the basic shape of the head. After the model is transformed into polygonal mesh, the head block effect can be achieved. ZBrush software has rich functions. For students who have a basic knowledge of sculpture, as long as they master the skills of tools, they can be skilled in making sculptures after practice (Fig. 1).

There are a lot of functional brushes in ZBrush. These brush tools are derived from traditional sculpting, and you can get the same creative experience in virtual space as in actual sculpting. In the process of sculpting in ZBrush, you can define your own brush and become your own tool. Students can use the computer to sketch in front of plaster heads and human bodies, and use the mouse to make sculptures. The way of modeling is the same as the original sculpture. More conveniently, there is no need for mud, wire, and sculpture racks in preparation for the usual sculpture lessons. The sculpture that the work wants to become a physical object can be printed.

Fig. 1. Human sketching sculptures by Zhu Shangxi and Deng Wei

3 The Advantage of Digital Technology in Sculpture Teaching

3.1 Improving Efficiency of Sculptures Making

The production process of traditional sculpture is more complicated. From plane conception to sculpture forming, it involves the production of sculpture skeleton, clay sculpture, turning, mold dressing, casting and so on. In the process of production, sculpture collapse, damage caused by bad weather, and deformation in the process of turning over may also be encountered, which all trouble the creation process of sculpture artists. The addition of digital makes the production of large sculptures more convenient. Produced by tsinghua university academy of fine arts of the great cause and people's epic – "21 project" theme sculpture "great" have the courage to break through innovation, draft in the amplification stage by digital scanning, CNC machine carved 1:1 high density EPS foam, replacing the traditional zoom ring clay sculpture, its advantage lies in: 1, to avoid the risk of large-scale adjustment on the work. 2. It saves the time to make shelves, put on large mud and maintain sculptures, greatly reduces the basic labor consumption and avoids the large-scale gathering of people in dense space during epidemic prevention and control. 3, EPS foam light quality, high strength, fire safety; The working time at height is reduced and the working efficiency is improved. 4. Save costs and improve the efficiency of sculpture production [2] (Figs. 2, 3 and 4).

Fig. 2. Sculpture "weiye" three-dimensional scanning technology CNC engraving technology

Fig. 3. Neuron create Wang Yin

Fig. 4. Sui Jianguo sculpture

Fig. 4. continued

3.2   Achieve Results that Cannot Be Achieved by Conventional Means

Take advantage of the advantages of 3D printed materials for creation. 3D printing materials are becoming more and more extensive, from the original nylon material, photosensitive resin, to the cement material that can print buildings, the material that can print sand, the material that can print technology. Artist Jonty Hurwitz creates extremely small "nanosculptures" that can only be seen with the help of a microscope (Fig. 5).

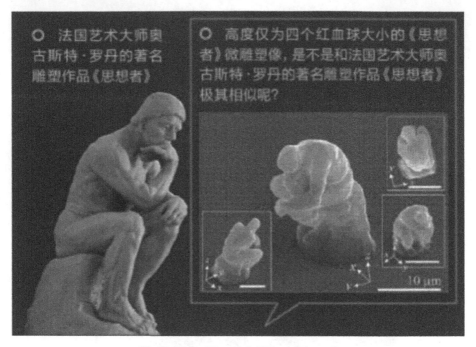

Fig. 5. Jonty Hurwitz's "Nanosculpture"

Shane Hope, an American artist, believes that 3D printers are no longer just mechanical data output tools, but can also create unique works of art. He tweaked the structure of a 3D printer to take advantage of the machine's errors in printing and create a series of random, accidental three-dimensional works. In creation, the advantages of digital materials can be used. Now 3D printing materials are also constantly enriched, providing a broader space for sculptors.

3.3 Stimulating Students' Interest in Sculpture

For based learning as a sculpture, sculpture digital technology can help learners to fully understand the knowledge of the anatomy of the human body structure, through the 3d model from the Angle of multiple observation and analysis, the students can accurately grasp the characteristics of the human form is more intuitive than traditional books and details, convenient for students to understand and master the structure of the human form. In addition, 3D software can simulate the multi-angle light source of the model. By adjusting the Angle and light and shade of the light source, the characteristics of the lines of each part of the human body can be further defined to help students further understand and master. At the same time, the 3D model further realizes the separation of muscle and skeleton, so that students can analyze and learn a specific muscle or skeleton, and realize the detailed characteristics of sculpture creation. At the same time, in the production of sculpture, it can also realize the editing and production of any part of sculpture in 3D software, adjust its structure, shape and dynamics, and further depict the details of sculpture, so as to achieve the purpose of improving the accuracy of sculpture.

3.4 Stimulate Students' Interest in Sculpture

There are a lot of rendering tools in the software, with the help of digital software to achieve sculpture in different scenes, lighting display effect. In the teaching display link, some sculptures can be scanned into a database, so that students can see European sculptures, African sculptures and some sculpture relics in class, which is very beneficial to students' learning.

3.5 Breaking Through the Restrictions on the Site

Traditional sculpture demonstration teaching must have strict site restrictions. Generally, teachers can demonstrate in the school studio. Once teachers leave this specific place, they cannot show their sculpture production process and method to students. And the student exercises also must have a fixed place, which greatly limits the teachers and students' production and learning space. In commercial sculpture, if the author wants to show the effect of the work to the business, there are only two ways, one is photos, the other is to bring to the production site. These problems are caused by the limitations of sculpture studios [3].

With the help of digital model making software, teachers can create art and teach sculpture techniques from their laptops anywhere and at any time. Students can also practice making sculptures in dormitories, libraries, dining rooms and even on the street. Need not put forward harsh requirement to skylight, light so, also do not spray water carefully with plastic wrap up, do not need to turn a stage more (Figs. 6 and 7).

Fig. 6. Classroom of sculpture Department, Academy of Fine Arts

Fig. 7. Photo taken by Zhu Shangxi of digital sculpture teaching in graduate class of School of Art, Beijing University of Technology

4   Digital Sculpture Case

Deng Wei is our country one of the earliest engaged in representational figures sculpture research colleges and universities teacher, he graduated from undergraduate course in LuMei, has a very deep sculpture basis, then access to the digital sculpture software, using ZBrush software digital representational sculpture achieve ideal level, use a brush to make simulation DiaoSuDao plastic mark, the simple sense of the clay sculpture. Both Professors Zhu Shangxi and Deng Wei emphasize the texture of clay sculpture in digital sculpture, and both of them have profound basic skills in sculpture. Zhu shangxi stressed that symmetry tools should be turned off in the process of making digital sculptures, not relying on the convenience of software. Deng Wei's digital sculptures have a strong sense of surface, decisive brushwork and bright shape, which can reflect the inner tension of the characters. In class, use the mouse instead of the sculpture knife, mouse click generated data instead of the sculpture clay. In Deng Wei's sculptures, you can see the precise structure modeling of the figures. The brushes are properly used and flipped in the virtual space. The rhythm of clay sculptures is relaxed.

Development is the Absolute Truth created by Deng Wei to commemorate the 20th anniversary of Xiaoping's speech during his southern Tour (Fig. 8).

For digital sculpture, realistic sculpture is a test of the author's basic skills, requires skilled grasp of the use of software skills, and make full use of the advantages of software performance. In the structure of the eagle group and modelling in the understanding of points, under the guidance of traditional sculpture modelling thought to compose, the academy of learning of anatomy, the center of gravity, dynamic structure, such as aesthetic elements play a crucial role, grasping the characters in the portrait sculpture, personality traits into a work type, the key to success, the use of this sculpture creation software skill is not important, It's just a tool [4] (Fig. 9).

Fig. 8. Sculpture by Deng Wei

Fig. 9. Sculpture by Wang Zhigang

5 Application of Digital Technology in Network Sculpture Teaching

Network teaching provides more extension and expansion for digital sculpture teaching, students and teachers can teach through the network platform. Screen sharing and remote operation have been very mature technology, teachers can use convenient technology to know remotely. For the difficulties encountered in teaching, teachers can record videos, and students can watch and learn repeatedly.

The era of digital technology has arrived, traditional sculpture is also facing challenges, while traditional sculpture also has more possibilities. Mankind has inevitably entered the era of digitalization and virtualization. Will traditional sculpture only appear in museums in the future, and digital sculpture can completely replace traditional sculpture? Such an example appears in the emergence of photography technology, painting also faces the same problem, today's digital photography and traditional film photography contrast. With the continuous development and change of The Times, we need to keep learning and clarify the development trend of The Times.

References

1. Sheng Zhang, F.: The core of digital sculpture is its new language rather than 3D printing. Sculpture **06**, 59–61 (2015)
2. Kun, Y.F.: Great cause and people's epic – discussion on the creation of "21 project" themed sculpture "great cause". Sculpture **04**, 12–13 (2021)
3. Shoumeng Ban, F.: Application of Digital Technology in Sculpture Teaching. Beijing University of Technology (2013)
4. Wei Deng, F.: 2012 Deng Wei's works. Sculpture **06**, 30–31 (2012)

Cross-Cultural Design in Arts and Music

Lyricism and Implicit Emotional Expression of Chinese Popular Music During 2001–2017

Pin-Hsuan Chen and Pei-Luen Patrick Rau[✉]

Tsinghua University, Beijing, China
rpl@mail.tsinghua.edu.cn

Abstract. Lots of music pieces are blooming with internet advancement, but only few studies focused on popular music and relevant social contexts. We can enhance the knowledge of popular music markets through the musical patterns. Therefore, this study aims to investigate prevalent styles of Chinese popular music from 2001 to 2017, and explore the trends. The convolutional neural network was exploited to analyze four music features (timbre, rhythm, pitch, and mode) extracting from melspectrogram and chromagram. Results indicated that (i) timbre and rhythm are critical among four music features. (ii) compared to expression styles far from realism, music related to audiences' behaviors and lifestyles are prevalent, such as lyricism and implicit expression. The proposed method accelerates the understanding of the evolution and prevalence of Chinese popular music. Meanwhile, this study might contribute to the future music markets, since musicians and marketers could comprehend trends efficiently and get inspired by this study.

Keywords: Popular music · Music feature · Popular music trend · Music market · Music creation

1 Introduction

With the dramatic advancement of technology in 2000s, the evolution of personal devices and internet influences people's music listening preferences and the musical business models. Nowadays, music streaming dominates listening behaviors and music creation. According to a report of the International Federation of the Phonographic Industry (IFPI), music streaming services have taken over half the total recorded music revenues worldwide since 2017. In China, the income proportion of streaming services is increasing yearly with the rapid growth of digital music platforms and musical programs. Lots of music pieces are created and getting popular with the fast-spreading of online short-form videos, which make the musical business model in China becomes unique compared to other countries [1]. In the light of this background, to preserve music and observe social and cultural cues from abundant music pieces efficiently are important. Therefore, this study aims to investigate the prevalent styles and trends of Chinese popular music from 2001 to 2017 by music feature learning.

This study applied the convolutional neural network (CNN) to train music features and derive music trends. Melspectrogram and chromagram were adopted to extract four features: timbre, rhythm, pitch, and mode. Then, this study concluded music categories and conducted trend analysis. This way, music could be preserved efficiently, and musicians could learn music preferences of the current market comprehensively.

2 Related Work

2.1 Representative Features of Chinese Popular Music

Many studies explored music genre classification and feature extraction with classical and folk music [2, 3]. But it is hard for popular music due to its complexity and diversity [4].

Popular music is a record of age, which is associated with culture and society. Mauch et al. (2015) studied music features of western popular music in Billboard from 1960 to 2010 and pointed out the connection between popular music and society [5]. Although Chinese popular music has developed since the 1920s, most studies focused on the algorithmic advancement for Chinese popular music recognition with content-based features [6–8]. Few studies further discussed the indications from the results of music feature analysis. Popular music in Chinese is different from the west because of different expression styles and cultural backgrounds. In light of the rapid growth of the Chinese music market in recent years, abundant music pieces could help facilitate understanding of Chinese society.

Popular music comprises several instruments and complicated arrangements, making timbre crucial for popular music feature extraction, particularly for the music influenced by multiple cultures [5, 7, 9]. For example, Chinese popular music learned from the western experiences after resuming from the historical incidents. Therefore, timbre is able to reveal Chinese popular music, which is of a variety of styles.

According to the research conducted by Moskowitz, stable rhythm and fewer syncopations were applied in Chinese popular music to arouse pleasure emotion [10]. And other studies about Chinese popular music also proved that rhythm was one of the obvious features [11, 12].

In addition, tonality, including mode and pitch, was reported to show the cultural elements in music [9, 13]. Chinese popular is influenced by different cultures, thus, tonality could be of benefit to reveal cultural indications of the evolution of Chinese popular music.

To sum up, this study gathered four features based on previous findings of Chinese popular music, including timbre, rhythm, mode, and pitch. Table 1 reports representative features of Chinese popular music. And both tables serve as instructions to define categories in this study.

2.2 Music Features Learning

Mel frequency cepstral coefficient (MFCC) is used to depict timbre and is useful quantitative statistical feature for music genre classification [7, 14]. Besides, Lidy et al. (2005) adopted temporal statistical spectrum descriptor (TSSD), the variation of frequency across time durations, to measure the rhythm [15]. Moreover, histograms graphed mode and pitch based on frequency [16–19].

Table 1. The representative features of Chinese popular music.

Music features	Types
Timbre	keyboard (e.g., piano); plucked string (e.g., guitar); string (e.g., violin); percussion; brass
Rhythm	simple meter; compound meter
Mode	Western musical mode; Chinese pentatonic musical mode
Pitch	C; C♯/D♭; D; D♯/E♭; E; F; F♯/G♭; G; G♯/A♭; A; A♯/B♭; B

Learning image features for classification, recognition, and generation is blooming in the light of CNN, and other deep learning algorithms. Most of the achievements are implemented with images in picture types, while few studies investigated those images demonstrating audio signals. For example, spectrogram is a transformation of sound, which is associated with music features extraction.

Melspectrogram, rhythmogram, and chromagram are three common music images, and previous MIR literature exploits them for further exploration. Chapaneri et al. (2015) and Nanni et al. (2016) indicated that using melspectrogram, a variation of spectrogram, to demonstrate timbre enhanced music classification performance [20, 21]. Besides, Barry et al. (2018) reported that melspectrogram is efficient to extract rhythm [22], while there was also a study illustrating rhythm with rhythmogram [23]. Moreover, chromagram was often used to demonstrate chords, pitches, and modes in music [24–26] since chroma was highlighted to be robust and meaningful enough to present music features [27].

Several studies have obtained superior results through extracting music features with music signals [28, 29]. For these reasons, this study would exploit melspectrogram for timbre and rhythm, and chromagram for mode and pitch.

2.3 Feature Learning of Chinese Popular Music

Taking advantage of CNN, Lukic et al. (2016) accomplished speech recognition with spectrograms [30], which method could facilitate feature learning and enhance the music classification performances [19]. As the results from Lee et al. (2017, 2018), the performances of music classification based on waveform and melspectrogram were of both accuracy over 80% [31, 32].

Dong et al. (2018) showed that music genre classification accuracy with melspectrogram matched the human-level accuracy [33], indicating that the cues from melspectrogram were close to human perception of music. Inspired by their achievements, learning music features with melspectrograms could be applied for broader applications.

Most of the studies performed supervised learning to conduct feature retrieval, whereas it is not suitable for unlabeled customized datasets. Transfer learning and fine-tuning based on pre-trained networks are introduced as alternatives to complete network training. In contrast, unsupervised learning is another algorithm to extract features from unlabeled data. Autoencoder was considered as a basic concept of unsupervised learning [34]. Le et al. (2012) carried out the image recognition with autoencoder and obtained favorable results [35]. Moreover, by combing autoencoder and k-means, Xie et al. (2016) further pointed out that image clustering could benefit from feature learning and reconstruction [36].

3   Methodology

3.1   Research Schema

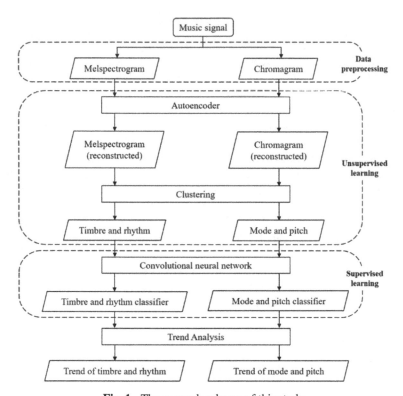

Fig. 1. The research schema of this study.

The procedure of music feature extraction and analysis could be divided into three stages: data preprocessing, unsupervised learning, and supervised learning. The first stage was to generate melspectrogram and chromagram. For the second stage, unsupervised learning was applied to strengthen and learn features, and then develop labelling rules of the studying dataset. As for the third stage, this study trained music features with supervised learning and carried out trend analysis for Chinese popular music. The overall research schema displays in Fig. 1.

The combination of unsupervised and supervised learning met two main properties of Chinese popular music dataset in this study. First, direct labelling with raw data was inefficient. Second, it could mitigate noises during feature extraction.

3.2 Dataset

There were 4805 songs released between 2001 and 2017 in the dataset. This study collected songs lists from the following awards: The Golden Melody Award, Top Ten Chinese Gold Songs Award Concert, and Global Chinese Songs List, while those in foreign languages were excluded. This study ensured all songs were with professional approval to present cogent arguments. Songs were obtained through being the membership in Kuwo.cn during the period October 9th, 2018 to January 31st, 2019.

No universal principles were proposed to suggest select suitable excerpts for music analysis because they remain arguing [7, 37]. Accordingly, this study selected the 120-s segment from the beginning of each recording. Every excerpt included intro, verse, and chorus, which were three main parts of a song.

3.3 Data Preprocessing

This study applied short-time Fourier transform to convert audio signals to melspectrogram and chromagram, with the size equal to 128 * 128 * 3.

The horizontal axis of melspectrogram and chromagram presented the time domain while different in the vertical axis. For the melspectrogram, it presented real-time frequency, and the measurement unit was Hz. The pattern of frequency illustrated timbre. Moreover, the density of frequency delineated the rhythm, particularly for rhythmic complexity. The chromagram displayed pitch class, which tuned frequency ranging in seven octaves into twelve chroma scales and exhibited music composition in terms of tone and tonic. Besides, chromagram explicitly indicated mode and pitch, which were associated with music arrangement.

3.4 Unsupervised Learning: Obtain Feature Categories

The dataset of melspectrogram and chromagram would serve for unsupervised learning, including autoencoder and k-means clustering.

At first, autoencoder was exploited to learn and strengthen significant features, and then, weaken others in the reconstruction process. After that, the k-means algorithm was performed for clustering. This study determined the k of melspectrogram and chromagram by exploring all k less than 10. The optimal value of k was selected based on the sum square of error and silhouette coefficient, which indicated cluster performance.

The structures of autoencoder for melspectrogram and chromagram started with stacking elementary layers. The encoding part stacked with convolutional and pooling layers, and the decoding part was with convolutional and upsampling layers. According to the learning processes, compared to melspectrogram, the processes kept more detailed features of chromagram. To deal with abundant image contents, there were two assumptions: 1) the batch size for chromagram was smaller than for melspectrogram. 2) the number of output features for chromagram was more than for melspectrogram. Therefore, the batch size was 64 for melspectrogram and 48 for chromagram. The number of output features for melspectrogram in the first encoding layer was 48, while it was 64 for chromagram. Both image types trained for 50 epochs each.

Moreover, the noise of data was likely to result in overfitting. Thus, this study randomly divided both datasets into 20% and 80% rather than using the whole datasets directly. The 20% of them were for feature learning and training classifiers, and the features of the remaining 80% would clarify with the generalization of classifiers.

According to the results of unsupervised learning, this study averaged the cluster of melspectrogram and chromagram, and output mean images, which demonstrated significant features of each cluster. Music categories were defined with mean images by researchers. Then, researchers randomly sampled 10% of the music used for unsupervised learning and listened to their original audio to check if their music features were consistent with the definition of the cluster. Compared the results of researchers to unsupervised learning, around 70% of the results were the same. This study then ensured that the results of unsupervised learning could be somewhat comparable to human perception.

3.5 Supervised Learning: Select Feature Extraction Models for Trend Analysis

The supervised learning was trained on the data used for unsupervised learning, which were annotated and served as ground truth data. This study picked the best model based on training performance with different parameters, which would be the classifier to identify features. And then, trend analysis would be conducted.

This study applied CNN to learn image features from melspectrogram and chromagram and select optimal models. This study found that the differences existed while processing both image types through autoencoder. The autoencoder might keep more chromagram details. Therefore, this study also assumed that more neural layers should be built for chromagram than for melspectrogram to enhance the training performances.

The neural network was initiated with the simple CNN. The convolutional layer would stack before the pooling layer, and the dropout layer was introduced to prevent the model from overfitting. Fine-tuning with the number of layers, batch size, and epochs were to obtain the final networks for melspectrogram and chromagram. With ratios of 70%, 20%, and 10%, labeled data were divided into three sets, in the order of training, validation, and testing. The training and testing accuracy of the chosen model were 73.18% and 72.91% for melspectrogram, and 68.64% and 75.79% for chromagram.

4   Results and Discussion

4.1   Feature Categories of Chinese Popular Music

The results suggested five clusters as the optimal number for melspectrogram and chromagram respectively. Because of the grayscale processing in autoencoder, the mean images were different from the original ones. Darkness meant signal with vigorous intensity, while brightness was with the low intensity (See Tables 2 and 3). The white lines in Table 3 denote the pitch class. Clusters were interpreted in terms of timbre, rhythm, mode and pitch.

Timbre and Rhythm. Timbre analysis focused on musical instruments, which was more distinguishable than human voices. rhythm analysis was based on the types of music meter.

This study derived results from the darkness and brightness in different parts of melspectrogram. For the brightness in high frequency, it might first indicate musical instruments that overtones decayed slowly in high frequency especially when the bright area was wide, for example, string and brass instruments: violin, and flute. Second, it depicted the diverse and unstable rhythm since complicated meters could present with the unclear distinction between darkness and brightness. As for the darkness in the low

Table 2. Timbre and rhythm explanations for Chinese popular music.

Feature annotation and characteristics	Mean image	Timbre	Rhythm	Example
TR-0 (Lyricism, and harmonics music)		Keyboard and plucked string instruments; Restrict to specific kinds of instruments	In simple meter	*Maybe one day* [38]
TR-1 (Influences, and orchestration music)		Intro: Keyboard or plucked string instruments; Verse and chorus: String, woodwind or brass instruments	Intro: Simple meter; Verse and chorus: compounded meter	*For myself in the future* [39]
TR-2 (Influences, and orchestration music)		Intro: Keyboard or plucked string instruments; Verse and chorus: String, woodwind or brass instruments; In contrast to TR-1, the differences in TR-2 is more obvious	Intro: Simple meter; Verse and chorus: compounded meter	*That girl said to me* [40]
TR-3 (Strong showing, rock, rhythmic,, and fast music)		Percussion or electronic instruments	In compounded meter	*Princess* [41]
TR-4 (Lyricism, harmonics, atmosphere, and slow music)		Keyboard and plucked string instruments; Structures are simpler than TR-0	In simple meter	*What do you want from me* [42]

frequency, it meant that instruments played in music were with fast-decay overtones, for example, plunk string and keyboard instruments: guitar, piano. Besides, meters tended to be simple in this case, which could result in the steady rhythm. Table 2 gathers musical descriptions for categories.

Different music production processes, such as machines, instruments, and environments, lead to the differences in timbre and rhythm, which indicates people's habits and behaviors. Thus, five categories of timbre and rhythm would be explained following the audience's living characteristics. TR-0 and TR-4 represented music with pure timbre

Table 3. Mode and rhythm explanations for Chinese popular music.

Feature annotation and characteristics	Mean image	Mode	Pitch	Example
MP-0 (Synthesizer, and electronic music)		Western musical mode and Chinese pentatonic mode	Indistinguishable	*Teenagers' clubs* [43]
MP-1 (Diverse music elements with the basis of western music)		Western musical mode	F, F#	*Say Goodbye* [44]
MP-2 (Poetic, easily-memorable, and folk music with the basis of Western music)		Western musical mode	E	*Heng xing* [45]
MP-3 (Poetic, easily-memorable, and folk music with the basis of Chinese music)		Chinese pentatonic mode	G	*Song hua jiang* [46]
MP-4 (Diverse music elements with the basis of Chinese music)		Chinese pentatonic mode	C, C#, D	*A painful stone* [47]

and steady rhythm. Both indicated the implicit and indirect expression ways, which were consistent with Chinese communication styles. In contrast, TR-3 was utterly different, its mean image showed a large area of darkness, which represented that TR-3 was of explicit and direct music expression style. Mean images of TR-1 and TR-2 were tranquility at the beginning, and then became intriguing and twisted gradually after prelude or verse. In other words, the music elaborated on details to attract listeners at the beginning, which was a coincidence with Chinese article structures and expression behaviors.

Mode and Pitch. The music arrangement was strict and regular when the darkness and brightness of mean images were distinguishable. As previous works proposed the significant connection between mode and pitch, and cultures, this study introduced Chinese pentatonic, and Western musical mode to interpret findings, which would be close to Chinese cultures and markets. The feature annotations with mode and pitch are in Table 3.

This study linked the musical mode and pitch to the development of Chinese popular music and found that Chinese popular music was not created only with Chinese musical system. However, it was noteworthy that Chinese musical elements were essential for popular music even though it has been influenced by western music these years.

The Chinese pentatonic mode demonstrated the compositions with the Chinese pentatonic scales (C, D, E, G, A). For MP-3 and MP-4, their mean images presented less power in F and B, which implied that Chinese musical systems had an impact on their music composition. In contrast, MP-1 and MP-2 depended on western composition styles because they covered a wide range of tones unusual in Chinese musical systems. Moreover, this study found that MP-2 and MP-3 followed strict music composition rules since they were more specific to some scales and were related to traditional folk music. Whereas, it was difficult to determine the mode and pitch of MP-0, which was defined as a combination of several music types according to results in this study, particularly in the initial period of music evolution.

Overall, the unsupervised learning established the labeling rules for Chinese popular music with four features, which benefited this study from three aspects. 1) from the music features aspect, the results overviewed Chinese popular music from 2001 to 2017. 2) from the automatic classification aspect, unsupervised learning was a way to understand music without human perception. 3) from the usage aspect, labeled data could be derived from the labeling rules and served as ground truth data.

4.2 Trend Analysis

This study evaluated trends of Chinese popular music with the percentage of the number of songs included in a category every year. Trends varied in terms of timbre and rhythm during the study period (See Fig. 2). It was evident that the pattern of TR-0 and TR-4 presented the opposite patterns, whereas there was no dramatic change in TR-1, TR-2, and TR-3. No tremendous growth or drop existed for the mode and pitch, except for MP-0. Figure 3 displays a decreasing trend in MP-0. To sum up, there were four findings for trends of Chinese popular music from 2001 to 2017.

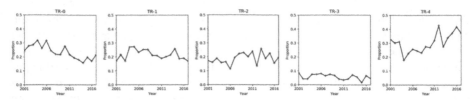

Fig. 2. Trends of timbre and rhythm in Chinese popular from 2001 to 2017.

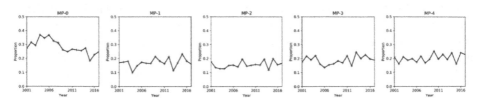

Fig. 3. Trends of mode and pitch in Chinese popular from 2001 to 2017.

No Significant Fluctuation Exists Once Music is Associated with People's Behaviors.
With regard to timbre and rhythm, TR-1 and TR-2 adopted soft and straightforward music styles in the beginning. Using instruments like a keyboard and plucked string helped present the bright sounds and simple rhythm, making listeners calm and then turning to the main plot. Diverse timbre and unstable rhythm twisted music to a captivating and inspirational ambiance. Hence, the instruments with long-lasting sounds were applied to deliver the core intentions of music and evoke emotions. The present finding was reasonable because of the following two explanations.

First, Chinese culture is a high-context culture, and people tend to elaborate on the embedded backgrounds in communication. Rather than directly showing thoughts, people used to narrate implicitly and then move to the topic. Music, a communication medium, is better to interpret it in a way that listeners were familiar with. Thus, music belonged to TR-1 and TR-2 was memorable and the spirits of music could be easily understood by Chinese listeners.

Second, the music arrangement of TR-1 and TR-2 was similar to the structures of Chinese poetry and article, which were usually in order: exposition, comparison, constructing the affective connections. In this way, Chinese listeners can understand ideas efficiently. Also, the music will be catchier while including rhyme.

Therefore, this study revealed that music aimed at resembling people's daily behaviors and listening habits usually matched listeners' preferences. In terms of the trends of TR-1 and TR-2, no dramatic decline and growth indicated that both music styles prevailed all the time.

Popular Music with Lyricism and Harmonics is Preferred in Recent Years. Taking TR-0 and TR-4 for example, this study found that songs involved in both categories presented naturally and transferred emotions moderately and conservatively. Despite that their trends were different, the total proportion remained at a certain level. It is worth notice that either TR-0 or TR-4 dominated the beginning and the final period from 2001 to 2017. Hence, both of them are the primary feature categories of Chinese popular music. The present finding is a coherent argument out of the research proposed by Moskowiz (2010), which implied that stable and simple rhythmic kept ahead in Chinese popular music [10]. Moreover, since timbre and rhythm could react sensitively in 17 years, they are selected as the critical music features of Chinese popular music.

Compared to the previous study investigated by Mauch et al. (2015), Western popular music trends are comparable to the result of this study [5]. They reported that music with harmonics and piano was growing after 2000. Likewise, the present study about Chinese popular music revealed that TR-4, with lyricism, harmonics, keyboard, and plucked string instruments, increased from 2001 to 2017. Both results indicated similar preferences across eastern and western for popular music.

However, music with different kinds of instruments and changeable rhythm types, such as TR-3, was in low proportion over 17 years. This music style mainly consisted of electronic and synthetic music and expressed emotion explicitly. Even though popular music covers a wide range of music types as globalization and internet advancements, this study discovered that rock and heavy metal music were hard to accept by Chinese listeners.

Popular Music with Plentiful Modes and Pitches Takes Over the 2000s. Mode and pitch could well demonstrate the cultural influences of Chinese popular music. The difficulties in determine the mode and pitch of MP-0 indicated the flexible and varied musical arrangement and composition. Besides, there were no significant features shown by MP-0. The reason was that Chinese popular music remained in a dynamic state since many producers and composers were dedicated to making music to meet the evolvement of the music industry in the 2000s. Although the trend of MP-0 decreased, it remained superior to others. This study summarized that various modes and pitches dominated in the 2000s, and Chinese popular music is evolving.

Chinese Musical Creation and Flexible Arrangements are Prevalent. To deal with music arrangements and composition, this study focused on two aspects: a) Which mode was often used to create Chinese popular music? b) Did it strictly obey a particular music principle?

This study introduced two creation properties of Chinese popular music: one was that the proportion of music with Chinese musical system (MP-3 and MP-4) was higher than with western musical system (MP-1 and MP-2). The trend analysis of the mode presented that Chinese musical creation was used more than Western.

The other was that Chinese popular music would relax some strict principles (MP-1 and MP-4) to compose and arrange music flexibly. Regarding trend analysis, the flexible arrangement was prevalent for listeners irrespective of the musical creation system.

5   Conclusion

This study has analyzed Chinese popular music from 2001 to 2017 through unsupervised and supervised learning. Timbre, rhythm, pitch, and mode are extracted from melspectrogram and chromagram to demonstrate for gathering trends of Chinese popular music. Results reveal that timbre and rhythm are vital for the evolution of Chinese popular music. Additionally, lyricism and implicit expression music styles are preferable, which matches with the consumers' behaviors and lifestyles. Moreover, exhibiting Chinese musical modes and rhyme schemes in popular music is becoming prevalent in this period, which reflects the enhancement of Chinese cultural identity.

The present study has proposed an efficient approach to overview the development of Chinese popular music and to understand social and cultural cues with abundant music pieces. In addition, the future human-machine collaboration of music creation might be a benefit from the idea of current study. It is because musicians and marketers could capture prevalent popular music features efficiently and put more effort on creativity and innovation.

This study suggests that future research could investigate music creation with style transfer and explore the potential of image-based music creation, such as melspectrogram and chromagram. Moreover, this study encourages neuroscience evidence to be included while analyzing audiences' preferences of popular music, since studies also reported the relationship between music features and emotions.

References

1. Shen, X., Williams, R., Zheng, S., Liu, Y., Li, Y., Gerst, M.: Digital online music in China - a "laboratory" for business experiment. Technol. Forecast. Soc. Chang. **139**, 235–249 (2019). https://doi.org/10.1016/j.techfore.2018.10.022
2. De Haas, W.B., Wiering, F., Veltkamp, R.C.: A geometrical distance measure for determining the similarity of musical harmony. Int. J. Multimedia Inf. Retr. **2**(3), 189–202 (2013). https://doi.org/10.1007/s13735-013-0036-6
3. Jondya, A.G., Iswanto, B.H.: Indonesian's traditional music clustering based on audio features. Procedia Comput. Sci. **116**, 174–181 (2017). https://doi.org/10.1016/j.procs.2017.10.019
4. Somerville, P., Uitdenbogerd, A.L.: Multitimbral musical instrument classification. In: IEEE International Symposium on Computer Science and its Applications, pp. 269–274. IEEE, New York (2008). https://doi.org/10.1109/CSA.2008.67
5. Mauch, M., MacCallum, R.M., Levy, M., Leroi, A.M.: The evolution of popular music: USA 1960–2010. R. Soc. Open Sci. **2**, 1–10 (2015). https://doi.org/10.1098/rsos.150081
6. Xia, Y., Wang, L., Wong, K.-F., Xu, M.: Sentiment vector space model for lyric-based song sentiment classification. In: Proceedings of the 46th Annual Meeting of the Association for Computational Linguistics, pp. 133–136. Association for Computational Linguistics, USA (2008)
7. Yang, Y.-H., Hu, X.: Cross-cultural music mood classification: a comparison on English and Chinese songs. In: Proceedings of the 13rd International Society for Music Information Retrieval Conference, pp. 19–24. International Society for Music Information Retrieval, Canada (2012)
8. Hu, Y., Chen, X., Yang, D.: Lyric-based song emotion detection with affective lexicon and fuzzy clustering method. In: Proceedings of the 10th International Society for Music Information Retrieval Conference, pp. 123–128. International Society for Music Information Retrieval, Canada (2009)
9. Moelants, D., et al.: The problems and opportunities of content-based analysis and description of ethnic music. Int. J. Intangible Heritage **2**, 59–67 (2007)
10. Moskowitz, M.L.: Cries of Joy, Songs of Sorrow: Chinese Pop Music and its Cultural Connotations. University of Hawaii Press, Honolulu (2010)

11. Jensen, K., Xu, J., Zachariasen, M.: Rhythm-based segmentation of popular Chinese music. In: Proceedings of the 6th International Society for Music Information Retrieval Conference, pp. 374–380. International Society for Music Information Retrieval, Canada (2005)

12. Jensen, K.: Multiple scale music segmentation using rhythm, timbre, and harmony. EURASIP J. Adv. Signal Process. **2007**(1), 1–11 (2007). https://doi.org/10.1155/2007/73205

13. Gedik, A.C., Bozkurt, B.: Pitch-frequency histogram-based music information retrieval for Turkish music. Signal Process. **90**, 1049–1063 (2010). https://doi.org/10.1016/j.sigpro.2009.06.017

14. Flexer, A.: Statistical evaluation of music information retrieval experiments. J. New Music Res. **35**(2), 113–120 (2006). https://doi.org/10.1080/09298210600834946

15. Lidy, T., Rauber, A.: Evaluation of feature extractors and psycho-acoustic transformations for music genre classification. In: Proceedings of the 6th International Society for Music Information Retrieval Conference, pp. 34–41. International Society for Music Information Retrieval, Canada (2005)

16. Gómez, E., Herrera, P.: Comparative analysis of music recordings from western and non-western traditions by automatic tonal feature extraction. Empirical Musicol. Rev. **3**(3), 140–156 (2008). https://doi.org/10.18061/1811/34105

17. Rauber, A., Pampalk, E., Merkl, D.: Using psycho-acoustic models and self-organizing maps to create a hierarchical structuring of music by musical styles. In: Proceedings of the 3rd International Society for Music Information Retrieval Conference, pp. 71–80. International Society for Music Information Retrieval, Canada (2002)

18. Rauber, A., Pampalk, E., Merkl, D.: The SOM-enhanced JukeBox: organization and visualization of music collections based on perceptual models. J. New Music Res. **32**(2), 193–210 (2003). https://doi.org/10.1076/jnmr.32.2.193.16745

19. Costa, Y.M.G., Oliveira, L.S., Silla, C.N., Jr.: An evaluation of convolutional neural networks for music classification using spectrograms. Appl. Soft Comput. **52**, 28–38 (2017). https://doi.org/10.1016/j.asoc.2016.12.024

20. Chapaneri, S., Lopes, R., Jayaswal, D.: Evaluation of music features for PUK kernel based genre classification. Procedia Comput. Sci. **45**, 186–196 (2015). https://doi.org/10.1016/j.procs.2015.03.119

21. Nanni, L., Costa, Y.M.G., Lumini, A., Kim, M.Y., Baek, S.R.: Combining visual and acoustic features for music genre classification. Expert Syst. Appl. **45**, 108–117 (2016). https://doi.org/10.1016/j.eswa.2015.09.018

22. Barry, S., Kim, Y.: "Style" Transfer for musical audio using multiple time-frequency representations. Unpublished article (2018). https://openreview.net/pdf?id=BybQ7zWCb

23. Jensen, K.: A causal rhythm grouping. In: Wiil, U.K. (ed.) CMMR 2004. LNCS, vol. 3310, pp. 83–95. Springer, Heidelberg (2005). https://doi.org/10.1007/978-3-540-31807-1_6

24. Tymoczko, D.: The geometry of musical chords. Science **313**(5783), 72–74 (2006). https://doi.org/10.1126/science.1126287

25. McVicar, M., Santos-Rodríguez, R., Ni, Y., De Bie, T.: Automatic chord estimation from audio: a review of the state of the art. IEEE/ACM Trans. Audio, Speech, Lang. Process. **22**(2), 556–575 (2014). https://doi.org/10.1109/TASLP.2013.2294580

26. Korzeniowski, F., Widmer, G.: Feature learning for chord recognition: the deep Chroma extractor. In: Proceedings of the 17th International Society for Music Information Retrieval Conference, pp. 37–43. International Society for Music Information Retrieval, Canada (2016)

27. Jiang, N., Grosche, P., Konz, V., Müller, M.: Analyzing Chroma feature types for automated chord recognition. In: AES 42nd International Conference, Germany (2011)

28. French, M., Handy, R.: Spectrogram: turning signals into pictures. J. Eng. Technol. **24**(1), 32–35 (2007)

29. Dieleman, S., Schrauwen, B.: End-to-end learning for music audio. In: 2014 IEEE International Conference on Acoustic, Speech and Signal Processing (ICASSP). IEEE, New York (2014). https://doi.org/10.1109/ICASSP.2014.6854950

30. Lukic, Y., Vogt, C., Dürr, O., Stadelman, T.: Speaker identification and clustering using convolutional neural networks. In: IEEE 26th International Workshop on Machine Learning for Signal Processing (MLSP). IEEE, New York (2016). https://doi.org/10.1109/MLSP.2016.7738816

31. Lee, J., Park, J., Kim, K.L., Nam, J.: Sample-level deep convolutional neural networks for music auto-tagging using raw waveforms. In: Proceedings of the 14th Sound and Music Computing Conference, pp. 220–226, Finland (2017)

32. Lee, J., Park, J., Kim, K.L., Nam, J.: SampleCNN: end-to-end deep convolutional neural network using very small filters for music classification. Appl. Sci. 8(2), 150 (2018). https://doi.org/10.3390/app8010150

33. Dong, M.: Convolutional neural network achieves human-level accuracy in music genre classification. Unpublished article (2018). https://arxiv.org/pdf/1802.09697.pdf

34. Baldi, P.: Autoencoders, unsupervised learning, and deep architectures. In: Proceedings of ICML Workshop on Unsupervised and Transfer Learning, vol. 27, pp. 37–49. PMLR (2012)

35. Le, Q.V., et al.: Building high-level features using large scale unsupervised learning. In: Proceedings of the 29th International Conference on Machine Learning, pp. 507–514. Omnipress, Madison (2012)

36. Xie, J., Girshick, R., Farhadi, A.: Unsupervised deep embedding for clustering analysis. In: Proceedings of the 33rd International Conference on Machine Learning, pp. 478–487. JMLR.org, USA (2016)

37. Yang, Y.-H., Chen, H.H.: Machine recognition of music emotion: a review. ACM Trans. Intell. Syst. Technol. 3(3), 40:1–40:30 (2012). https://doi.org/10.1145/2168752.2168754

38. Station, P.: Maybe One Day on *Man*. HIM International Music Inc., Taipei (2002)

39. Leong, F.: For Myself in the Future. On *Admire*. Rock Records Company, Taipei (2007)

40. Huang, Y.: That Girl Said to Me. On *Exclusive Code*. Sony Music, Taipei (2005)

41. Hsiao, J.: Princess. On *Princess*. Warner Music Taiwan Ltd., Taipei (2009)

42. Xue, Z.: What Do *You* Want From Me. On *Accidents* [CD]. Ocean Butterflies Music Company, Beijing (2013)

43. The Flowers. Teenagers' Clubs. On *Statement of Strawberry*. Newbees Music Production, Beijing (2001)

44. Li, Y.: Say Goodbye. On *Old If Not Wild*. EE-Music Ltd., Shanghai (2012)

45. Wang, F.: Star. On *Blooming Life*. Chuang Meng Music Company, Beijing (2005)

46. Li, J., Jiang, S.H.: On *Missing You*. Sirius Music, Liaoning (2007)

47. Hsiao, J.: A Painful Stone. On *Princess*. Warner Music Taiwan Ltd., Taipei (2009)

Non-linear Video Documentary Installation Frameworks, and Poetic Linkage in *Silk Road Stories: Life and Displacement on the Automated Highway*

Richard Cornelisse[✉]

Xi'an Jiaotong-Liverpool University, 111 Ren'ai Road, Suzhou Industrial Park, Suzhou 215000, Jiangsu, People's Republic of China
Richard.Cornelisse@xjtlu.edu.cn

Abstract. The entailed article details the creation of a non-linear, chance-driven, multi-screen video documentary installation that compiles interviews and daily moments from truckers along silk road routes in China within the context of emerging driverless commercial automated vehicles (AVs). The article will focus primarily on how Chinese non-linear poetry modalities such as xuanjitu and Japanese linked verse such as renga and poetic prose such as Zhitisu can serve as a unique format for non-linear documentary installation content delivery and exhibition. The entailed documentary installation utilizes this overall poetic framework to communicate an individualized participatory viewer experience that illustrates a highly subjective, ambiguous, meditative, and fluid documentation of people, places, machines, and traditions rather than broad informational summarization or reportage.

Keywords: Non-sequential · Interactive · Immersive · Modular · Linkage · Xuanjitu · Renga · Zuihitsu · Commercial automated vehicles · Chinese truckers · Geography · Documentary interview

1 Introduction

The entailed article details the underlying framework that comprises an automated, chance-based, non-linear multi-screen video documentary installation, which compiles video interviews, stories, daily moments, and personal perspectives of truck drivers along silk road routes in China within the context of emerging driverless commercial automated vehicles (AVs). In addition, the installation framework illustrated here will explore how non-linear traditional Chinese poetry systems and related Japanese poetic frameworks can function as a platform for modular, live-edited, automated video narrative and as a methodology for subjective documentary. Ultimately, the documentary and installation technical framework and methodology aim to privilege the viewer to form meaning and narrative from a more subjective lens than traditional Verite documentary and illustrate

P.-L. P. Rau (Ed.): HCII 2022, LNCS 13312, pp. 177–186, 2022.
https://doi.org/10.1007/978-3-031-06047-2_13

a multifaceted portrait of how automated vehicles may impact these truck drivers and cultural landscapes surrounding their livelihoods.

As developments in global shipping indicate, economies worldwide are undergoing unprecedented growth in shipping and delivery platforms in tandem with the deployment of semi-autonomous to fully autonomous vehicles. China, still the world's largest exporter, will undoubtedly play a vital role in how this convergence may reshape shipping and economic transactions both domestically and worldwide. According to the Berkeley Institute of Artificial Intelligence, China has already begun to incorporate commercial autonomous vehicles (AVs) in inter-province commercial truck delivery since 2020 in a logistics industry estimated to be worth USD 1.6 trillion [1]. Furthermore, at present, according to China's Ministry of Human Resources and Social Security, the current commercial truck freight industry comprises the largest group in China's logistics industry, with an estimated 16 million workers who carry more than 76% of the nation's goods [2].

Most current generation of commercial AVs vehicle operating systems run with automation conditional on driver supervision in what is known as Stage 2 Partial Automation within a five-stage criteria rating system for automation (Stage 5 indicating complete autonomy) [3]. However, these developments already illustrate a multitude of advantages in terms of centralization, cost efficiency, environmental impact, and safety. Computer simulations have already indicated that AVs may significantly reduce congestion, and traffic jams, such as the pile-up that paralyzed China's roadways in a two-week-long traffic jam in 2010, to further mitigate traffic accidents, cutting down on emissions, and reducing human to human contact [4]. The stark cost-benefit analysis may signal a move to replace human drivers faster than previously anticipated. However, what remains to be seen is how economic displacement patterns will reverberate through the personal lives of those directly impacted, namely truckers.

2   Installation Framework

Trucking serves as a thread to connect people across landscapes, cultures, and perspectives across complex economic, sociological, political, and cultural networks. This video documentary installation aims to create a poetic portrait of such truckers, their livelihood, and geography in the face of a nuanced cultural landscape and radical transformative technology that is difficult to ascertain fully. Therefore, the installation framework entailed here aims to underline an impressionistic collage of video vignettes that emphasizes a highly subjective viewpoint in a way that appeals more to an emotional register within a multifaceted issue.

The documentary incorporates a poetic video collage format made of a randomized three-screen audio/video installation framework that privileges the viewer to become the architect of meaning and narrative through engagement with the respective parts of work. Video, photos, text, and audio revolve in a fluid three-screen montage that links stories, landscapes, and people in a dynamic, ongoing re-contextualized shot to shot, screen to screen, and sound to image relationship that superimpose over one another in an accumulation of chance-based edits that is re-contextualized according to period and manner viewed (see Figs. 1 and 2).

In the end, this unique type of viewer/creator participation should elicit a sense of drama, tension, and aura that transports the viewer to a subtle yet emotionally heightened awareness of these relationships while highlighting a personal identification with them. Although the clips unfold in randomized edits arrays across three screens, components still operate within a type of global superstructure that illustrates trucking livelihoods, communities, family lives, and cultures interdependent with this industry along the silk road through themes, such as location, work, interview, cultural practice, and a social life that relies on a revolving pattern of inter-relational associations.

The documentary will explore how Chinese truckers identify with distinct cultures and economic systems along the silk road, how trucking serves as a means of financial independence in China, and how driverless automated vehicles could reshape China's cultural and economic landscape. A typical viewer may, in one case, for instance, hear an interview regarding one of these themes with a trucker and see a truck driver on the road. In contrast, in another instance, the viewer may hear the same interview and see a landscape unfolding through the perspective of a truck window, while yet another viewing may transmit the same voice juxtaposed over a video of a local musician playing folk music indigenous to the area. The installation will consist of fifty video clips ranging from ten seconds to three minutes split among three screens and fifty audio clips of a similar duration, creating nearly endless possible viewing possibilities.

3 Xuanjitu and Character to Character Relationship

At its foundation, non-linear classical Chinese poetry consists of a similar modular structure that incorporates interchangeability and metamorphosis of the poetic character unit or verse, which invite the reader to arrange respective compositional elements into a wide array of compositional outcomes and subsequent meanings. Xuanjitu, for example, written by Su Hui in the Sui dynasty in the 3rd century AD, was created as an embroidered love poem of 840 characters to be read in a variety of ways, forward, backward, horizontally, vertically, and diagonally with a possibility of 15,000 outcomes (see Fig. 3). The reader combines characters through imaginative play and inter-character pattern recognition to reformulate character relationships and re-contextualize them in a manner that forms a personalized yet flexible mental image that uncovers a sense of living dynamism both between individual character to character pattern formation and the more immense, transcendent superstructure within the work.

In Fig. 4 the detail from Wild Geese Returning: Chinese Reversible Poems, edited by Michèle Métail, provides some examples of compositional possibilities within the poem's center.

Right block according to the first way:
The cold year is recognizable in the dead pines
Of true things, one knows the end and the beginning.
The depressed look deforms a beautiful face
The virtuous sage is distinguished from the
wandering literati.

Second way:
In the pine that wastes away, one recognizes the
cold of the year
From the beginning to the end, one knows the truth
of things.
The beauty of a face is transformed by the
despondency of the look
The literati who leaves wanders far from the virtue
of the sage.

Fifth way:
The cold year is recognizable in the dead pines
From the beginning to the end, one knows the truth
of things.
The depressed look transforms a beautiful face
The literati who leaves, wanders far from the virtue
of the sage.

Ninth way:
The cold year is recognizable in the dead pines
The virtuous sage is distinguished from the
wandering literati.
The depressed look transforms a beautiful face
Of true things one knows the beginning and the
end.

Thirteenth way:
Of true things one knows the beginning and the end
The depressed look transforms a beautiful face.
The virtuous sage is distinguished from the
wandering literati.
The cold year is recognized in the dead pines [5].

As seen here, the character to character dynamics creates a subtle yet profound recursive variability lends the poem a sense of repetitive rhythm that further compounds the multidimensional network of associations, impressions, and experiences, which create a hypnotic feedback loop of interaction, composition, tone, and meaning. As Métail notes, "the important thing is not so much the exact number of poems, nor how exhaustively we read them, as it is the vertigo that grips the reader facing the open work, facing the infinitely unfurling meaning" [5].

The 20th-century Russian film pioneer and theorist Sergei Eisenstein underlines the inherent relational charge between character to character relationships not only to illustrate how characters can react with each other to transcend their meaning, but how they function as democratized individual building blocks that react to each other to "link different spheres of feeling - to create a single, unifying sound picture image" [6].

For Eisenstein, harmony between characters, as in his cinematic film shots, operates through an all-inclusive network of democratic layered interrelation, inter-being, and circularity. "Montage," as Eisenstein states, "is not built on particular dominants, but takes as its guide the total stimulation though all stimuli" [6]. The organization revolves around an inextricable synthesis of equal parts that serve to transcend literal asymmetrical compositional forms into a more expansive synesthetic polyphony, which in the case of xuanjitu is love and the sense of vertigo that can surround it.

Synthesis operates through an all-inclusive network of interrelation, inter-being, and circularity rather than the traditional cinematic form of linear, three-act structured, asymmetrical, conflicted oriented climatic documentary form. The subsequent non-hierarchy synthesis emphasizes a layered affinitive inner synchronization between the compositional pieces in terms of rhythm, emotion, meaning, and tone. It creates a transcendent meaning or "higher unity," as Eisenstein calls it, both in content and form within the framework itself [6].

4   Renga and Verse to Verse Association

In terms of cinema, xuanjitu resembles a puzzle of non-hierarchal shots, whereas renga in the Japanese linked verse literary canon is more akin to a collage of non-hierarchal shots and scenes. Although renga reflects many other early Japanese linked verse writing traditions dating to the 10th century, which share a commonality of form, style, and consequent breadth, it remains the most common in the Japanese literary canon with a level of sophistication that makes it particularly noteworthy for the sake of this particular study. At its foundation, renga consists of various interchangeable poetic verses that operate within a larger fluid body of 100 verses. Verses, in this case, can thus operate in any order, be omitted or added to others concerning the overarching theme. Much like xuanjitu, renga stresses the interchangeability and metamorphosis of the poetic unit within a larger framework, however, with the broader strokes of fixed, respective poetic lines dedicated to a specific mood and theme according to seasons of the year.

n renga, poems are composed in alternating turns in five lines composed of three 5-7-5 syllable verses, which one poet creates, and the remaining two 7-7 syllable verses made by the other poet collaborator. Each verse can act alone as a poem or can be removed and combined with other verses in the greater poetic structure to create a new composition with subsequent differing connotations. Although verses are changing aspects of the same picture again, they lend the poetry a broader imagistic compositional form in time and space that can transition from the specificity of a shot to the broader action. The poem quoted below by early 16th century poets Shohaku and Sogi provides an illustrative example of the fluid movement and context within such a framework and the shifting broad spatial, temporal, tonal, and aesthetic reinterpretations each verse brings to a whole.

A pine cricket   All in vain is chirping now,
    In my weed-grown house.
        On the mountain I staked out
    Now lodges only the moon
I awake from sleep   To the tolling of the bell
    My dreams unfinished
    I have piled upon my brow

The frosts of night after night
Autumn (pine-cricket). It   Chirps in vain because she does
        not hear it. The house is deserted
Autumn (moon).   Links to loneliness of preceding verse
With age his hair turns white,   as he remembers as he lies
        awake at night
        His plans for the future are
interrupted [7].

The broader multidimensional dynamics within such respective verses, when rear-ranged, illustrate a wide breadth of space, time, and perspective transitions from moment to moment, subject to subject, aspect to aspect, person to person, and person to a thing. The inherent sense of participation leaves the reader to combine pieces, reformulate meaning and re-contextualize it in a manner that forms a personalized, flexible mental image at a visceral level among inter-shot connections. Such poems further underline phenomenological reflections of experience within the "shifting changes between natural and human worlds and internal as well as external points of view" as Nobuyuki Yuasa states in her commentary on Matuso Basho's The Narrow Road to the North and Other Travel Sketches, which lends itself to a "kaleidoscopic beauty with infinite variety revealed to the reader in a slowly evolving movement" [8].

5   Zuihitsu and Juxtaposition

The Japanese prose genre of Zuihitsu also incorporates a similar resonance in its mal-leability, non-hierarchical interplay, and poetic resonance, however in this case with an emphasis on juxtaposition rather than the character to character and verse to verser asso-ciative relationships as discussed above. One illustrative example is in Sei Shonagan's 11th-century work The Pillow Book, which translator and commentator Ivan Morris describe as a record of "stray impressions" or "occasional writings, random notes," which includes "descriptions, diary entries, character sketches, and anecdotes" with no logical sequence or chronological order as can be illustrated by Shonagan's list of "Elegant Things" [9].

1. A white belt over a violet waistcoat
2. Duck Eggs
3. Shaved ice mixed with liana syrup and put in a silver bowl
4. A rosary of rock crystal
5. Wisteria blossoms. Plum blossoms covered with snow
6. A pretty child eating strawberries [10].

As a whole, these writings again transcend themselves in their relationship to each other in a way that Haruo Shirane refers to in his book Traces of Dreams: Landscape and Cultural Memory in the Poetry of Basho a "perspective by incongruity," that "moves from one world to another" in a double vision, which grants the reader "the ability to interact in playful dialogue [8].

This dynamic creates a duality between the parts and the whole, which as Katherine Higgens states in her book, Aesthetics in Perspective, "highlights the subjects in a new light in their discrete or respective existence as such, but also as a whole through various relational charge they hold with the other" [11]. The linkage between indirect and sometimes paradoxical parts serves as the fundamental operative agent that dramatizes and gives a heightened dynamism to the compositional elements through a singular participatory poetic experience that both invites the reader to create and combine meaning within fluid compositional forms.

In his book Sculpting in Time, Russian filmmaker Andrei Tarkovsky comments on the singular poetic charge inherent in such linkage in film stating, "[linkage] seem[s] to me perfectly appropriate to the potential of cinema as the most truthful and poetic of art forms. He goes on to say that "through poetic connections feeling is heightened and the spectator is made more active. He becomes a participant in the process of discovering life, unsupported by ready-made deductions from the plot or ineluctable pointers by the author. He has at his disposal only what helps to penetrate to the deeper meaning of the complex phenomena represented in front of him. Complexities of thought and poetic visions of the world do not have to be thrust into the framework of the patently obvious" [12].

6 Conclusion

Linkage between the examples provided of character to character, verse to verse, and juxtaposed poetic listing all highlight a uniquely potent form of empathetic connection through immersive creative engagement, which lends itself well to the shared dynamics inherent in this installation array, whether in the recursive shot to shot relationships, scene to scene movements or ostensibly non-sequitur linkage. This documentary installation aims to illustrate a fabric of life in a way that underlines the role of the viewer to weave the interconnected nuances of personal lives, experiences, struggles, and happenings of these truckers while celebrating the richness in language, diverse spiritual sensibilities, and conflicting histories as well as traditions within a broad, historically charged highly politicized, and culturally diverse geography.

The future of trucking in China deserves expansive discussion, creative depiction, and further questions. This highly subjective, participatory, and malleable portrait serves to bear witness to the complexities of diversity and identity in this landscape while highlighting an emotional tenor of how these socio-economic transformations may impact both truckers and related communities. In addition, these silk road routes have served as a means of religious, cultural, linguistic, artistic, technological, and genetic transmission that created regional, national, and global networks that continue to evolve in China's current Belt and Road Initiative.

When this vast, ancient, multifaceted, interdependent trade network becomes more digitized by transformative AI technology, what will it say about our relationship to each other and future generations? What will such displacement spell in China and the rest of the world? Can we learn to live with transformative AI technology in a way that benefits all humanity? As we tumble further into the digital unknown such questions and subjective viewpoints, if nothing else, can least illuminate a need for a broader range of perspectives into the subtle complexities of an ever-changing socio-cultural landscape.

Appendix

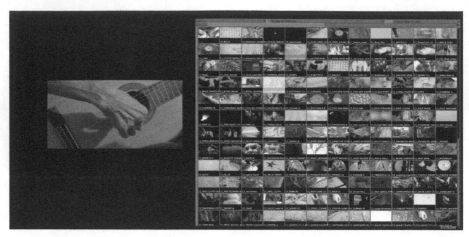

Fig. 1. Installation software layout (author's work in development). Note the audio/video clip array (right side) comprises a nonhierarchical media bank for a randomized edit output (left side).

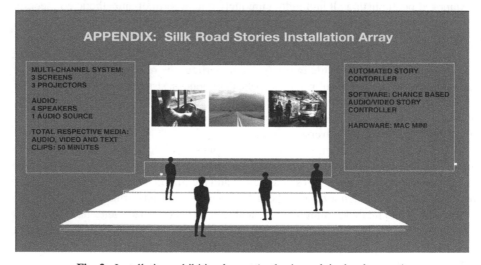

Fig. 2. Installation exhibition layout (author's work in development).

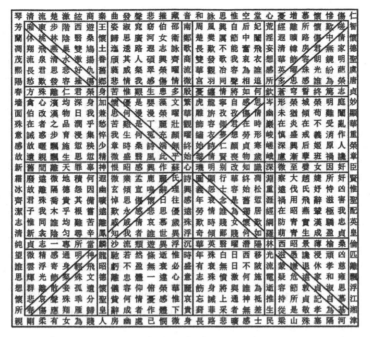

Fig. 3. Su Hui, *Xuanjitu.* Courtesy of the University of Hong Kong Press.

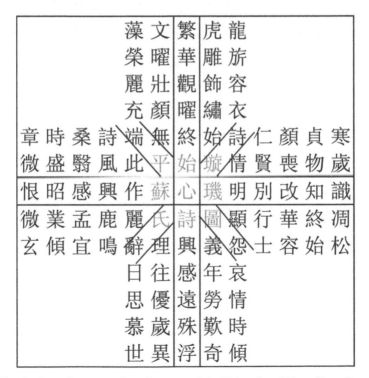

Fig. 4. Central cross-section. Courtesy of the University of Hong Kong Press.

References

1. Mejlak, P.: Independent Truckers in China Meet their (Freight) Match. International Finance Corporation World Bank Group, 1 May 2017. <https://www.ifc.org/wps/wcm/connect/news_ext_content/ifc_external_corporate_site/news+and+events/news/impact-stories/truckers-in-china-meet-their-freight-match>. Accessed 21 Dec 2021
2. Everly, R.: How Driverless Trucks in China Could Put 16 Million People Out of a Job. Forbes Magazine, 5 June 2017. https://www.forbes.com/sites/outofasia/2017/05/05/how-driverless-trucks-in-china-could-put-16m-people-out-of-a-job/. Accessed 16 Nov 2021
3. Larson, H.: Automated trucks: The good, the bad and the timeline. <https://www.transportdive.com/news/autonomous-trucks-levels-driverless-fleets-transport/586596/>. Accessed 8 Dec 2021
4. Vinitsky, E.: Autonomous Vehicles for Social Good: Learning to Solve Congestion. Berkeley Artificial Research, 3 June 2019. <https://bair.berkeley.edu/blog/2019/06/03/benchmarks/>. Accessed 14 Dec 2021
5. Menard, M.: 15 March 2017. <https://bombmagazine.org/articles/xuanjitu/>. Accessed 17 Dec 2021
6. Eisestein, S.: The Eisenstein Reader. Trans, Taylor, Richard. British Film Institute, London (1998)
7. Keen, D.: Anthology of Japanese Literature. Grove Press Inc., New York (1955)
8. Basho, M.: The Narrow Road to the North and Other Travel Sketches. Penguin, Baltimore (1966). Trans, Y.N. (ed.)
9. Shonagan, S.: The Pillow Book. Oxford University Press, London (1967). Trans, I.M. (ed.)
10. Shirane, H.: Traces of Dreams: *Landscape, Cultural Memory and the Poetry of Basho.* Standford University Press, Stanford (1998)
11. Higgins, K.: Aesthetics in Perspective. University of Texas Press, New York (1996). Brace, H. (ed.)
12. Tarkovsky, A.: Sculpting in Time. University of Texas Press, Austin (1986)

On the Possibilities of Light Environment Art in Digital Scenes: From the Perspective of Metaverse Research

Zihan Cui, Kaizhong Cao$^{(\boxtimes)}$, and Hantian Xu

Communication University of China, Beijing, China
77180256@qq.com

Abstract. This paper mainly explores the possibility of light environment art in digital scenes from the perspective of Metaverse research. Firstly, the concept of Metaverse is summarized and condensed on the basis of existing research results. The digital scene in the Metaverse is a digital society with a high degree of integration between virtual and reality. Continuous presence and a highly immersive experience. The light environment art, as the art of painting with light as the language, plays an irreplaceable role in both the real world and the digital scene. The light environment art stated in this article mainly refers to the virtual light environment art that plays a role in the digital scene. From the perspective of Metaverse research, this paper summarizes the three major characteristics of light environment art: hypermedia information transmission, surreal space construction of light images, and nonlinear light language and painting narrative mode; and further analyzes the light environment in the Metaverse space. The application of art includes: the symbol designation of the light environment in the virtual architecture, the visual presentation of the light environment in the virtual architecture, and the shaping of the light environment space in the virtual architecture.

Keywords: Light environment art · Metaverse · Digital scenes · Possibilities

1 Introduction

With the proposal of the concept of Metaverse, various possibilities of real space and virtual space are constantly being deduced. Based on the high immersion of the user subject, a multi-dimensional, multi-sensory and multi-quadrant super digital scene is constructed. In such a scene, the art of virtual light environment plays an irreplaceable role. No matter what kind of field, the light environment is the easiest and clearest way for us to perceive things. Light illuminates the real environment and the virtual environment, so as to make the two more. At the same time, light is also building the medium of content dissemination, including symbol designation, information transmission, and form perception. At the same time, there are also many scenes in the Metaverse where the real light environment and the virtual light environment are superimposed. The two transcend the limitations of time and space and build a surreal field of light language painting. The light environment of this field Design is also mastering its laws in continuous exploration, so as to realize the value of virtual light environment art.

Although there have been some studies on the Metaverse, including the technical basis of the Metaverse, its future development, and the changes to people's lifestyles, no research has paid attention to the art of light environments in the digital scene of the Metaverse, but the shaping of the light environment is the realization of the Metaverse. Therefore, it is of certain value to discuss the light environment art in digital scenes from the perspective of Metaverse research. This paper first expounds the concept of Metaverse and digital scene on the basis of domestic and foreign literature research; then analyzes the concept of light environment art and virtual light environment art, so as to further explore the characteristics of virtual light environment art in digital scene; Possibilities of light environment art in cosmic digital scenes.

2 The Metaverse and the Digital Scene

Zuckerberg, the founder of Facebook, once said: The Metaverse is the next generation computing platform after computers and mobile phones. As a highly immersive, Metaverse, which interacts the virtual world with the real world, it has become a new generation of computing platform that allows people to have an immersive feeling. It will also have brand-new operating systems, technologies and rules. The concept of Metaverse carries the most sophisticated technology industry chain today, including chips with high computing power and image processing capabilities, AI artificial intelligence, 5G communication technology, cloud computing, big data, allowing the real world and virtual environment to interact Operational 3D interactive physical Internet of Things, blockchain technology that makes everyone feel the center of the world, and so on. At the same time, the participant "human" subject participates in a series of activities such as social entertainment in such a virtual and real superimposed space field with a digital identity. As long as it can bring an immersive virtual world experience, it can become an application of the Metaverse. VR, AR and other head-mounted display devices can be regarded as the entrance to the Metaverse, and with the update and iteration of technology, the form of the entrance will be Gradually blurring, the boundaries between virtual and reality are no longer clear [1]. Roblox proposed eight key features of the Metaverse: Identity, Friends, Immersive, Low Friction, Variety, Anywhere, Economy, Civility [2], and the interaction of all things, integration of virtual and real, and decentralization are different from traditional environments obviously presented.

The term "scene" is often used in the field of drama, which refers to a certain task action or life picture that occurs in a specific time and space, which includes certain character relationships, event types, and activity backgrounds [3]. The digital scene in the Metaverse is a carrier constructed by the transformation of time and space under the action of media technology, theme, time and space, technology multi-element environment, in such a scene carrier, users participate in it as a digital human, and carry out a series of diversified social behaviors that can make friends and trade as in the real world [4]. In the digital scene of the Metaverse, the fusion of human and machine under the guidance of technology and the connection between the body and the virtual space are indispensable.

Through extensive literature reading and related research, the author believes that the digital scene in the Metaverse has two basic characteristics:

First, the super digital scene that transcends reality and virtuality. In real time and space, the physical world, the human world and the information world form a real ternary world; under the fusion of virtual time and space and real time and space, various digital technologies build an artificial ternary world that integrates real time and space [5]. Beyond reality refers to the final spatial scene effect that cannot be achieved in the real world, including some anti-gravity scenes, anti-scientific scenes and unconventional scenes. Such scenes are created by the creator or the user himself according to their own logic. With the creative play of cognition, the virtual construction of the scene blurs the boundary between true and false [6]. The transcendence of virtuality is reflected in the construction of digital scenes, from which the experiencer can obtain emotional experience and imagination space beyond the digital itself. They are not manipulated to form an independent writing subject, who can lead the overall narrative and integrate their emotions and brainpower. Use to break through the limitations of algorithms to form new digital scenarios.

Second, the user's body is continuously present and highly immersive interactive space, virtual and reality create perceptual presence, and digital twins create avatar presence. Users have their own identities in the Metaverse, and their implementation forms include links to various technologies, so as to realize the multi-sensory experience of users and the immersion of various perceptions such as experience and emotion. At the same time, in the Metaverse scene, people's digital avatars can socialize, shop, and entertain in diverse identities. In such a situation, the user's physical body also achieves continuous presence. At the same time, each user himself has become a pheromone to construct the scene information of the entire Metaverse. These pheromones provide a large amount of data and resource categories, forming a habitual orientation, so as to use digital technology to provide a more powerful body for the continuous presence of the body technical support. The high immersion in the Metaverse is no longer limited to enhancing the multi-sensory synesthesia experience of users, but an interactive way in which the digital avatars of different subjects coexist and interact with each other, including the construction of shared social, entertainment, and game scenes, different users can enter a common scene to chat and communicate, watch programs, listen to music, etc. This common participatory experience and hallucinatory scene constitute a highly immersive interactive space [7].

3 Light Environment Art and Virtual Light Environment Art

3.1 Concept Analysis of Light Environment Art and Virtual Light Environment Art

The concept of light environment art is defined according to the characteristics and attributes of its way of creation, expression and existence, whether it includes the elements of light language and painting in artistic creation, or the use of light environment design itself in artistic creation. The effect of the art type, all belong to the light environment art. In a broad sense, the physical light environment art refers to the comprehensive use of natural light and artificial light to design the environment lighting for the real space of human habitation, so as to provide the lighting needed for people's production and life [8]. At the same time, the lighting purpose is also dominated by functional lighting, with artistic lighting as the embellishment. The light environment art design uses the space scene as a stage, and conducts lighting settings and visual planning for the purpose of information communication and cultural construction. As a result, light environment art has become a public information carrier and public art action, an interactive landscape between people, space and culture [9]. The cultural attributes of light environment art enable it to culturally empower the places it serves, build its internal cultural value and content structure, so that the experiencer can feel the visual effects while feeling the visual effects. Different thinking and cognition create the spirit of place.

As the main body of light environment art design, light also plays a role in the creation process with various elements to realize the shaping of various light atmospheres in real and virtual scenes. These include light and shape, light and shadow, light and color, and dynamic effects of light [10].

Light and shape are shaped by light. Light can achieve special light environment effects while shaping the image of characters with exaggerated or implicit methods in various ways and ways of expression. According to the different functional directions of light shaping, it can be divided into main light, secondary light, contour light, ambient light, and decorative light. The key light, as the leader in the creation of spatial light environment effects, has a clear directionality and plays a decisive role in the tone and tone of the space picture. Auxiliary light, also known as auxiliary light, can supplement the light atmosphere of the light environment shaped by the main light in the space. The ratio of the main light and the auxiliary light can be used to form different spatial light environment effects. For example, when the space pursues the effect of the highlight ratio, the brightness difference between the main light and the secondary light can be increased to create a high-contrast light-dark effect. When the space pursues a soft light effect, the secondary light can supplement the shadow part formed by the main light, so that the brightness of the entire space is uniform. Contour light can outline the contour of the object and separate the subject from the background, so as to highlight the subject and increase the layering of the spatial image. Ambient light is the foundation of the spatial light environment. It can create ambient light effects such as dusk, dawn, and moonlit night. At the same time, it can also narrate the content, indicating the location, season, and time. Modified light refers to the detailed light effect achieved for the object of action. The purpose is to emphasize the spatial details and narrative clues. Its use method is flexible and can be presented from multiple angles and details.

Light and shadow, using light to create images and shadows to shape. The combination of light, object and shadow enhances the sense of form of space. As the saying goes, "form is content", and the form of light and shadow is also completing a certain metaphor. As the light expands and shrinks, the projection of the object will also change. Light is projected on multiple objects, and the shadows of multiple objects are combined, and the shadows will also mutate to form different spatial picture effects, combining the abstraction and imagination of shadows. Sexuality combined with the controllability of light will make space lighting more interesting when expressing objects and shaping the atmosphere of space lighting. This principle is used to embellish the local lighting of small areas inside the space, and objects that do not need to be displayed in the space can be hidden in the shadows by covering the shadows.

Light and color, which usually represent the emotional appearance of a space. The design of light and color plays an important role in rendering the mood and setting off the atmosphere. Vision is the primary way for humans to grasp the information of the external world, and color is the most contagious element in the perception process. When people define an object or field for the first time, in addition to the shape, the color impression is more important. This instinct for color judgment is the result of human development, and the use of light and color can effectively express emotions and emotions. The application of light color in space construction includes determining the main color of the space, forming the unique style of the space light environment, so as to realize the communication of different emotional elements. Starting from the concept of communication, the designer creates different light and color effects in the space. For example, James Turrell's light environment art works maximize the application of light color in the physical space. Under the establishment of the main color, adjacent light colors or contrasting light colors are mixed and rendered in the space, and the artist himself is also in the space. Experimented with the transition characteristics of light color and light color, either soft and hazy, or sharp separation. In such a stylized light and color space, people lose their judgment of time and perception of the original space, and then realize the reshaping of consciousness under the guidance of the designer.

The dynamic effect of light refers to the flow and interaction of light. In the presentation of light environment art, the dynamic effect of light is the most active and expressive element in visual art. The dynamic effect of light can realize its quasi-object characteristics and create a surreal picture. British artist Bruce Munro is committed to finding possible hazy luminous bodies in the natural landscape, so as to integrate his light sculpture into the natural environment in a more subtly way, using the dynamic process of light point conduction to simulate the flow of water ripples to create an unreal feeling of real space. The dynamic effect of light is also further trying to interact with the behavior of the main body of the space experience, thereby adding its interest. For example, the work "City Pinball" at the "Spotlight" Light Festival in Bucharest in 2019 uses 3Dmapping technology to achieve dynamic light effect presentation, people press the pressure-sensitive buttons in cooperation with each other to trigger different projection light effect content, so that the experiencer can be more immersed in the scene atmosphere created by the dynamic light effect.

The above design methods of light environment art are also applicable to virtual light environment art. Virtual is a system that uses computers and sensors to simulate real situations, so that people experience the same feeling as reality and make real responses [11]. Virtual also further implies the intangibility and multi-possibilities of existence, which is the scene reconstruction of people under the experience of embodied interaction. Under the concept of Metaverse, light environment art has gradually changed from reality presentation to digital environment creation, from real physical space to virtual scene. In the virtual parallel universe, sky light, natural light, digital light source and even UI interface have become the components of light environment art part. What the virtual light environment art provides is no longer the physical lighting presentation of a single functional attribute, but creates space and conveys emotions through the light environment. The virtual light environment art integrates the information characteristics of the times to move towards digital architecture, media environment and interactive space. It is an artistic interpretation and interpretation of light in a space that surpasses traditional lighting. After the combination of the five senses and the narrative of light, it presents a rich and interesting light and shadow atmosphere, thereby enriching and enhancing people's sense of space experience.

3.2   Characteristics of Light Environment Art in Metaverse Digital Scenes

Hypermedia Communication

The scenes of life, social interaction and learning in the metaverse are composed of a variety of new media technologies to form an environment where reality and digital media are integrated artistic presentation. Bringing together and re-creating various thoughts and various information contents makes the space in the metaverse a gradually expanding matrixed medium.

The visualization of light as a medium itself realizes the hypermedia presentation of light environment art. For example, in the oasis of "Ready Player One", the light environment of the block has long been separated from the reality of the block itself. The content of the lights in the block is mixed, and each light. The signs are conveying information such as store names, but under the superposition of countless light signs, the formed block space has already become a collection of light forms, and its content is no longer important. Instead, the focus will be on various light signs. The lighting modeling of the formed scene space allows participants to more intuitively perceive the transmission of their internal information elements. And the communication of this information also reflects enhanced urbanism, it becomes a demonstration of power, constructing the city's unique light language painting label, breaking the foundation of superimposing existing freedom perception preference, emphasizing the superiority of the communication form Semantic hegemony, under the guidance of thinking, further promotes virtual communication between people and between cities.

The Construction of Surreal Space of Light Image

Under traditional spatial cognition, time is considered to be linear, sequential and irreversible; space is considered to be enclosed, existing, and static; matter is considered to be real, concrete, and palpable; The enhanced virtual space is not simply the realization of material enclosure, but under the guidance of virtual objects, people's spirits are substituted into the virtual scene to strengthen the virtual experience [12], and the imaging of light will make these virtual objects Existence forms have been realized in various ways. Content empowerment of daily social activities in virtual space, and gamification design guidance of social interaction. On the one hand, light images are used to convey content and empower effects. For example, in the future education classrooms from the perspective of the Metaverse, they have broken through the flat images on the screen, and instead present the models of the knowledge conveyed in a three-dimensional and multi-dimensional manner. The superposition of light effects and light images realizes the effective communication and beautiful experience of content in the visual space (Fig. 1).

Fig. 1. Augmented reality in education © YouTube [13]

At the same time, the image of light also shows the characteristics of identity reference. Its presentation form does not appear as a completely realistic image, but is shaped by light effects on the basis of 3-dimensional contours. Participants who are not present are transformed from physical identity itself into a light body, participate in the interaction of social life and behavior, this kind of surreal space has expanded from the simple scene surreal to the surreal existence of the participating subjects. In this shaping process, the light environment art is no longer attached to the architectural space, but has become a digital extension of the subject's identity (Fig. 2).

Fig. 2. Augmented reality in education © YouTube [13]

Non-linear Light Language Painting Narrative Method

Through the disorder of time and the concealment of the plot, the interaction between the subject of creation and the subject of experience is further emphasized. In the real world, the night tour of theme parks is a night economic touchpoint that has attracted much attention, and the Metaverse provides infinite possibilities for the next generation of theme parks. Since the Metaverse provides a fusion of physical space and digital world, the narrative of content and the creation of light and shadow atmosphere make the theme park no longer a single material space, but a main body of storytelling. At the same time, in this process, the nonlinear narrative also presents a social integration experience. Disney, as a pioneer on the 'Metaverse' theme park track, presented it back at the 2020 IAAPA Conference – Disney's 'Metaverse Strategy': A Shared Sharing Combining Virtually Augmented Physical Reality and Reality Persistent Virtual Space Magical world (Fig. 3).

Fig. 3. The Metaverse according to Disney © Disney [14]

4   Possibilities of Light Environment Art in Metaverse Digital Scenes

4.1   Symbolic Referencing in Virtual Architectures

The origin of symbols is labor. As early as in primitive society, people began to have both practical and aesthetic needs, and began to enrich their daily life with unconscious symbolic behaviors. [15] Semiotics was first proposed by Swiss linguist Saussure and American philosopher Peirce. The former focuses on the meaning of symbols in social life and is related to psychology; the latter focuses on the logical meaning of symbols, which is closely related to logic and semiotics also affects the presentation of expressive thinking in the artistic design of light color and light intensity in light environment art. It is also because the use of semiotics enables the design element of "light" to more scientifically and accurately convey information, but also presents a variety of performance methods. Under the influence of light elements, symbol collage and scene construction are condensed into an organic whole, and vivid visual images are used to trigger the cognition and thinking of experiencers.

Simplified Cognitive Logic

The construction of different light and shadow spaces has certain cultural attributes and connotations, and the interpretation of the design purpose also requires further cognitive deduction. And cognition is like a key for people to enter the room. When the design brings strong cognition to the experiencer, people will be more willing to further explore and share their unique experience in the common sense. For example, the giant geisha hologram projected on the skyscraper in "Blade Runner 2049", the Chinese character signboards covered with the streets and alleys in "Ghost in the Shell" and the neon lights of the streets in each other's shadows [16], these works The unique and representative elements appearing in the book make people clear the cultural attributes at first glance, and at the same time indulge in the beauty of the conflict between the Eastern and Western cultures, and these different types of symbols are collaged in a simplified and clear way. The way is presented in front of the viewer, creating a sense of familiarity and belonging in the field of "alienation".

Familiar Identification Process

The purpose of design is to serve the economy and society. Designers need to find a design language that can be understood by both the host and the guest on the basis of their own inspiration and ideas, and skillfully combine ideas, language and emotion to achieve a sense of resonance in the design experience. This also includes aesthetic synaesthesia. This synaesthesia intuition is a positive emotional experience. The pleasant feeling of the experiencer comes from the central nervous system maintained at the optimal level of arousal. It is realized in the digital scene space in the Metaverse. The extension of human senses, the light environment constructs a new visual presentation in the virtual space, and on the basis of aggregating various symbolic elements, it is a high degree of "likeness" and "simulation" of real life, and the change of light effect symbols Triggering the experiencer's instinctive response and subconscious association, the experience subject is no longer one-way empathy, but seeks harmony and resonance in the round-trip response [17].

Specialized Presentation

Although "seeking common ground" is easy to understand, blindly "seeking common ground" in design will lead to serious problems of homogeneity of design, repeated designs of many similarities, and loss of initiative and uniqueness of design. For the same theme, designers need to find a variety of angles and various forms of expression to re-update and re-create the design. For example, in "The Matrix", digital light symbols are used to construct a space scene, which visually presents the artistic effect of light environment and the spectacle of resonance and mystery that do not exist in the real world. This kind of use of light color and light dynamic the realized "Digital Light Rain" scene deconstructs and reconstructs abstract data information, breaking people's inherent cognition and forming a unique visual style. [18] And this kind of spectacle also exists in the same form in the digital scene of the Metaverse and can also achieve a unique form of presentation (Fig. 4).

Fig. 4. The Matrix Digital Rain © Warner Bros. Pictures [19]

4.2   Synesthesia in Virtual Architecture

Starting from the visual dimension, light environment art in the Metaverse uses the scene light environment to construct an optical illusion experience of dynamic integration of light and color, and uses digital technology to extend the imaginary space in image production and light modeling to create an illusionary presentation, bringing visual On the other hand, with the development of virtual reality (VR), augmented reality (AR) and mixed reality (MR) technologies, the immersive experience brought by the traditional optical-based visual mode has gradually developed into a comprehensive light, shadow, sound Multisensory immersion and synesthesia brought about by interacting with perceptual patterns.

Superposition of Immediate Feeling and Diachronic Experience
On the one hand, a complete place is based on the foundation of material existence and rationality, and is manifested in the three basic elements of the place of existence. On the other hand, it is also necessary to introduce the perception of the subject, the experiencer, which includes local perception, contrast and change of perception, and overall experience. Human perception exists at two levels: immediate feeling and diachronic experience. Immediate feeling corresponds to a single place and its details. The diachronic experience corresponds to the integrity of the place, showing the overall process composed of fragmentary impressions according to certain clues, combined with the subject's personal memory, and finally obtains a sense of overall experience combining time and space.

The effect of light environment art on the feeling of the place is also reflected in these two levels. The first is the immediate feeling. By controlling the luminous intensity and color temperature of the light source, it can shape the atmosphere of light and shadow at a certain moment in the space. By emphasizing the shape, material, texture and depth, which can bring people an instant feeling of a specific place. The second is to enhance the diachronic experience, arranging and combining the instantaneous feelings of the experiencers in the space for the light environment according to a certain order. The people who are the experiencers are active in the place, experience the changes and extension of the light environment between places, and then after the informatization and emotional processing of the subject's feelings, a complete diachronic experience of the place is formed.

Superposition of Real Light Environment and Virtual Light Environment
The pursuit of humanized design in the Metaverse requires consideration of human feelings, visual effects, and environmental psychology. When people enter the Metaverse, the light environment carries the superposition of the real light environment and the virtual light environment. Taking color comfort as an example, light color can affect people's visual experience and psychological activities. Warm colors make people feel warm and comfortable, while cool colors make people calm and focused. Blue-purple is easy to cause fatigue. Older people generally prefer warm white light. In the Metaverse, the effects of light have been enriched in multiple dimensions. Light is no longer a fixed form or a fixed field, but an editable, changeable, and floating digital facade, which can be more intuitive. It is reflected in people's visual system and thus has an impact on it. In the Metaverse, the scene of changing light and color is constantly changing, and the multi-core linkage of the media interface, how to make these luminous virtual objects better adapt to the comfort of the human eye is the realization of the Metaverse. One of the keys to the humanized design of light environment art in the universe. The light environment design for non-real scenes can be infinitely close to the real world in terms of visual appearance, and exist as a simulacrum of the real world; on the other hand, it can make the virtual space surpass reality, no longer exist in a figurative form, and become an imaginative fiction Reality.

4.3 Spatial Shaping in Virtual Architecture

When mixed reality becomes the basis of our spatial cognition, after virtual reality is considered to have its own spatiality, the boundary between material space and "additional information" is gradually blurred [20], while the space carrying the light environment. It has also become a more generalized space itself. Light and space are complementary existences both in the real world and in the virtual world. As the virtual medium blurs the material itself, the true concept of spatial structure becomes difficult to define. Space is no longer defined and limited by a single material, but a mixture of material and virtual that form together and influence each other. The shaping of space is not a simulation of the real world, but the creation of a psychological space on this basis [21]. At the same time, with the openness of UGC user-generated content under the Metaverse, everyone can shape their own space. With the light environment, you can even change the appearance of the original virtual space scene according to your preferences and aesthetics on the basis of the original light environment design, forming a virtual field with a strong personal style.

Define Virtual Space Boundaries

Division of Fields and Boundaries

Through the interaction of light and shadow, light and dark, and the change of light color, the boundary of shadow or light is formed, and different areas in the space are divided. Domain refers to the place or space whose boundaries are defined, and is the interaction between the outward manifestation of human psychological state and the physical space. For example, in the XR scene of the Tencent Games Annual Conference in 2021, light-painting segmentation is adopted in the extension boundary of the virtual space, and the boundary division of the virtual space is realized from the cutting of light and shadow and the high contrast of the light ratio, so that people can clearly feel everything. The scope of the space is limited, so as to enhance the perception of scale in the virtual space (Fig. 5).

Fig. 5. XR scene of Tencent game annual conference in 2021 © Tencent [22]

Shaping Focus and Blur

Using the point, line and surface elements in the light painting language, people can focus on the spatial visual effect or be scattered and blurred. In the empty space, point elements are used to form the visual focus, and the point elements can also be processed to form a path to guide people's behavior. This also reflects the use of light in the enhanced virtual space to express people's subjective imagination and purpose instructions, integrate space poetics into it, and at the same time intersperse rational thinking to capture the formal meaning of space [23]. At the beginning of the XR scene at the 2021 Tencent Games Annual Conference, the focus of the experiencer can always be clearly attracted by the special-shaped luminous body in the space, that is, the triangular luminous body, so as to achieve visual guidance (Fig. 6).

Fig. 6. XR scene of Tencent game annual conference in 2021 © Tencent [22]

The focusing and blurring effects of light are more strongly reflected in the music festivals in the Metaverse. In November 2020, due to the popularity of the song "Old Town Road", Lil Nas X cooperated with Roblox to realize the realization of the music festival for musicians and bands in the Metaverse. Realize the construction of the concert in the middle of the year, the combination of the radiant light effect and the rhythmic music space surround feeling, the dynamic light and shadow effect in the virtual space can be re-created ignoring the physical constraints in the real scene, and it is difficult to achieve in the real space. The light effect, build fantasy together (Fig. 7).

Fig. 7. Lil Nas X held a concert at Roblox, the game platform that promotes the concept of "Metaverse" © Roblox [24]

Shape the Virtual Space

The virtual space has its inherent structural properties, and the light environment effect can further clarify the form of the virtual space and create a sculptural sense of the virtual space, so that the space is not only a function-oriented existence, but tends to shape the aesthetic value. The difference between space and real space is particularly important. The light environment effect that can be achieved in the real world is always limited by material conditions, while in virtual space, the construction of light environment space can transcend material conditions to meet demand, aesthetics or curiosity. Explore the many possibilities of virtual space light environment effects for directions.

Our perception will always follow a set of general principles when setting off the material form on the background, which, according to Gestalt theory, is both a purely optical activity and a semantic activity [25]. The light environment effect is gradually replaced by the line beam from the realistic lighting method, and the line light is used to outline the space form. For example, in the 2021 Tencent Games XR scene annual meeting for the light environment art of the virtual scene, while the light illuminates the enhanced virtual scene, it is also connected with the changes and changes of the space scene, using various forms of abstract light elements to carry out. The scene reconstruction of the different-dimensional space finally forms the super-real feeling of the light effect subject (Fig. 8).

Fig. 8. XR scene of Tencent game annual conference in 2021 © Tencent [22]

Create a Virtual Space Atmosphere

The diverse language and painting of light can induce different visual orientations, create a differentiated space atmosphere, and make people have different degrees of emotional changes. At present, the language and painting of light presents two trends, one is the trend of quasi-naturalization, and the other is the trend of surpassing reality. Pseudo-naturalization is obviously to restore and simulate the lighting phenomenon in nature as much as possible, such as restoring the abstract light environment art of the dynamic light and color process of sunrise and sunset in space. The bright and shining characteristics of sunlight can bring a positive atmosphere to the space, while the clear and bright moonlight can give the space a quiet atmosphere. This kind of space atmosphere can also create an illusion of the direct presence of objects involved, producing an embodied effect [26], digging out the deep emotions and psychology of the experiencers, and making the virtual space a direct and continuous continuation of their real and imagined lives (Fig. 9).

Fig. 9. Animal crossing friends club game scene © Nintendo Production Planning Department [27]

The quasi-naturalized light environment art can shorten the distance between designers and experiencers more conveniently, so that people can quickly establish a sense of familiarity with unfamiliar spaces. For example, in the light environment scene in Animal Crossing, its overall design is more suitable for reality under its animation style. Players turn into cartoon people to live in their own virtual homes, including growing vegetables, chopping wood, etc. The light in the scene exists in the form of time narration. The passage of time and the changes of light and shadow are completely in line with the real scene. On the basis of the two-dimensionalization of the overall design style, the quasi-natural presentation is used to achieve an immersive experience (Fig. 10).

The trend beyond reality is to explore the light and shadow effects that cannot be achieved in the natural world. All people can see are digital images with light effects. In an abstract way, people are immersed in the binary space to experience surreal images. In the virtual space, people's experience is a superposition of reality and virtuality, and light is used to create a serious, cheerful or tense atmosphere. The shaping of augmented reality scenes is attached to the real visual environment in the form of light barrages and light barrage windows. These contents are not meaningless presentations. The main purpose is to provide people with a better sense of life experience. The inconvenience of real life provides the most convenient feedback that can be achieved from the virtual dimension, and the light environment constructed by such elements is looking for its own functional properties beyond reality.

Fig. 10. Future life scenarios under the flood of AR © YouTube [28]

5 Discussion and Outlook

With the advancement of technology and the development of the Internet, the Metaverse will open a new social era, and light environment art is no longer limited to the old research paradigm, nor is the physical environment as a limiting factor, and can better understand the "human" "From the perspective of the main body, while ensuring comfort, the design expression of light environment art is built in the virtual world. The rapid update and iteration of digital and networked technologies will definitely bring more abundant creative resources to the creation of light environment art, and to a certain extent, it will also enable light environment art to innovate and continue to give full play to the design advantages in the new space scene form to realize the design. A vision to serve and lead life.

For the construction of digital scenes in the Metaverse, it blurs the boundaries between virtual and reality, realizes the perfect combination of sound, light and field under the intervention of light environment, meets the common needs of lighting and aesthetics in the virtual space, and allows the experiencer It can better extend cognition and feeling, and realize the two-way information interaction between the brain and the digital world, so that this virtual and real environment can better serve our production and life, and realize a variety of immersive perception and experience. It is our continuous exploration and pursuit of the future lifestyle. There are also many possibilities and expectations for future life scene styles.

References

1. Wang, R., Xiang, A.: 2020–2021 Metaverse Development Research Report. Tsinghua University New Media Research Center, Beijing (2021)
2. The Paper. The popular Roblox leads children into the "Metaverse" [EB/OL], 23 April 2021–10 December 2021. https://www.thepaper.cn/newsDetail_forward_12349573

3. Wang, Y., Weifeng, H., Tang, J., Li, S.: Scenario theory research in product interaction design. Packag. Eng. **06**, 76–80 (2017). https://doi.org/10.19554/j.cnki.1001-3563.2017.06.019
4. Zhang, H., Dou, W., Ren, W.: Metaverse: Scenario Imagining of Embodied Communication Press, vol. 1, pp. 76–84 (2022). https://doi.org/10.15897/j.cnki.cn51-1046/g2.20211228.001
5. Wu, J., Cao, Z., Chen, P., He, C., Ke, D.: User Information behavior from the Metaverse perspective: framework and prospect. J. Inf. Resour. Manage. **12**, 4–20 (2022)
6. Nevelsteen, K.J.L.: Virtual world, defined from a technological perspective and applied to video games, mixed reality, and the Metaverse. Comput. Anim. Virtual Worlds **29**(1), e1752 (2018)
7. Xiao, C., Zhang, M., Liu, H., Qin, B., Huang, B.: Analysis of spatial reconstruction of "Metaverse". Geogr. Geogr. Inf. Sci.
8. Zhang, L., Du, C.: Reality function, historical memory, cultural appeal: the overall conception of "Light Environment Design" of communication University of China Campus. Mod. Commun. (J. Commun. Univ. China) **10**, 130–134 (2014)
9. Zhang, L., Du, C.: Conception of light environment design discipline construction. Mod. Commun. (J. Commun. Univ. China) **12**, 118–121 (2013)
10. Li, X., Zhipeng, X., Zhang, L.: The Art of Lighting in TV Dramas. Communication University of China Press, Beijing (2012)
11. Ma, N.: Virtuality analysis of cyberspace. Reform Strateg. **12**, 14–17 (2003). https://doi.org/10.16331/j.cnki.issn1002-736x.2003.12.005
12. Ji, J., Lin, J., Song, B.: Construction of architectural space environment from the perspective of virtual reality. J. Archit. **S1**, 82–85 (2014)
13. Augmented reality in education. https://youtu.be/fI6VlHg25v8
14. The Metaverse According to Disney. https://www.google.com/amp/s/www.businessinsider.in/tech/enterprise/news/disney-ceo-bob-chapek-confirms-the-company-will-build-its-own-Metaverse/amp_articleshow/87641073.cms
15. Zhao, Y.: Semiotics. Semiotics Series, 201601.424. Nanjing University Press, Nanjing (2016)
16. Zhou, L.: Spatial construction, symbolic collage and field transformation: aesthetic analysis of binary opposition in cyberpunk films. Contemp. Films **8**, 36–40 (2020)
17. Bai, Y., Chen, J.: "Scene Symbols" and "Symbolic Scenes": the aesthetic experience pattern of online games in the age of convergence media. Journalism **7**, 48–55 (2019). https://doi.org/10.15897/j.cnki.cn51-1046/g2.2019.07.006
18. Ye, F.: Virtual spectacle: conceptual design concept of film in the era of digital media. Decoration **5**, 30–33 (2015). https://doi.org/10.16272/j.cnki.cn11-1392/j.2015.05.011
19. The Matrix Digital Rain. https://gss0.baidu.com/-Po3dSag_xI4khGko9WTAnF6hhy/zhidao/pic/item/f2deb48f8c5494eeeba842a42cf5e0fe98257e80.jpg
20. Yan, C., Yuan, F.: The duality of visualization: on the reconstruction of space materiality and virtuality. Urban Archit. **19**, 17–21 (2018). https://doi.org/10.19892/j.cnki.csjz.2018.19.003
21. Yin, J.: Research on space shaping based on digital video art. Mod. Decoration (Theory) **5**, 230 (2015)
22. 2021 Tencent Games Annual Conference XR Scene Display. https://www.bilibili.com/video/BV1Jv411V7tK?t=36.0
23. Soja, E.W.: Thirdspace, P. 57. Blackwell, Malden (1996)
24. Nas, L.: X held a concert at Roblox, the game platform that promotes the concept of "Metaverse". https://imagepphcloud.thepaper.cn/pph/image/166/279/71.jpg
25. Xu, D.: The perception of form: Roger Fry's research on the psychological motivation of art aesthetics. J. Fine Arts **2**, 100–105 (2021)
26. Wang, N.: The spatial poetics of digital immersion: a scene study in game narrative. Contemp. Anim. **1**, 36–42 (2020)

27. Animal Crossing. https://pic.zhuayoukong.com/d/file/news/gonglue/2020-03-27/868ca0647
    850a100f9c6b0c6bdd5d202.jpg
28. Future life scenarios under the flood of AR. https://www.youtube.com/watch?v=YJg02i
    vYzSs&list=PLw9037dd4hqHdGvoBLfzIKpmE2W6M_1fX&index=23

Research on Differences in the Emotional Cognition of Chinese Audience in War-Themed Films

Lijuan Guo[1] and Jun Wu[2(✉)]

[1] Anhui Normal University,
Wuhu 241000, Anhui, China
guolijuan1025@163.com
[2] Shenzhen University,
Shenzhen 518060, Guangdong, China
junwu2006@hotmail.com

Abstract. With the development of the global economy, consumption motivations have gradually shifted from practicality to pleasant experiences. Films watching in theaters has become one of the major ways for the public to get spiritual pleasure. As a type of genre films, war-themed films focus on real or fictional battles in history, occupying an important position in the film and television market, which can also help promote patriotism amongst audience. The emotional experience of audience watching war-themed films is an important and complex research topic. Exploring the differences in the emotional cognition of different audience watching war-themed films will not only help promote culture, but also provide reference for filmmakers. Taking Chinese audience as research objects, this research mainly studies the differences in the emotional cognition of war-themed films. The research results are as follows: 1. The emotional cognition of audience of different ages is relatively consistent, and the emotional recognition of female audience is significantly higher than that of men; 2. The emotional recognition of audience graduating from high school and below is significantly higher than that of postgraduates and doctors; 3. The emotional recognition of audience of arts-related and science-related majors is significantly higher than that of film and television-related majors; 4. The emotional recognition of audience working for public institutions, societies, or themselves is significantly higher than that of workers and farmers; 5. The emotional recognition of audience who do not understand historical events at all or understand only a little historical events is significantly higher than that of well-understood audience.

Keywords: War-themed film · Audience research · Emotional cognition · Chinese audience · *The Battle at Changjin Lake*

1 Introduction

As a kind of genre films, Chinese war-themed occupy an important position in the film market. This research has sorted out the box office of Chinese war-themed films from

P.-L. P. Rau (Ed.): HCII 2022, LNCS 13312, pp. 205–220, 2022.
https://doi.org/10.1007/978-3-031-06047-2_15

2020 to 2021 (shown in Table 1). There are 6 films with a box office of 1 billion yuan, of which 2 have a box office between 3–4 billion yuan, and 2 have a box office of more than 5 billion yuan. We can see from Table 1 that the war-themed films released in the past two years were successful as a whole, but three war-themed films performed poorly at the box office. Among them, *The Blood Battle of Occupying Xuchang* and *Breakout* performed poorly at the box office. How to make war-themed films gain double wins at the box office and word of mouth, to explore the experience by studying high-grossing films, especially the law of the emotional recognition of audience in war-themed films, can provide some references for the creation of war-themed films, can help promote the market of war-themed films, and can disseminate and promote patriotism. *The Battle at Changjin Lake* was released on National Day in 2021, which won the recognition and praise of the audience soon, with 124 million viewers and a box office of 5.775 billion yuan (as of January 25, 2022). Its box office even surpassed the film *Wolf Warrior 2*, becoming the highest-grossing film in China. With the rapid development of the cultural industry, film, as one of the cultural products, have attracted wide attention and love of the audience. Watching films in their spare time has become one of the most important leisure and cultural activities for people. War-themed films not only have great economic values, but also has great cultural and educational values. There are different consumption motivations for war-themed films, and emotion is one of the important ones. The audience's emotions when watching a film are complex and changeable. Understanding the rule of their emotional preferences when watching a film can better understand their psychological needs. Therefore, this research studies the highest-grossing film in China, *The Battle at Changjin Lake*, to explore the rules of emotional cognition of different Chinese audience in war-themed films, and the research results can provide a reference for the creation and research of future war-themed films. This research aims to explore:

1. The differences in the emotional cognition of audience from different backgrounds.
2. Difference in emotional cognition of audience with different levels of knowledge of historical events.

Table 1. 2020–2021 box office of Chinese war-themed films.

Film	Time	Director	Box office (billion)	Introduction
Wolf Warriors 2	2020	Jacky Wu	5.694	It tells the story of Leng Feng who was involved in a rebellion in an African country and launched a rescue operation on the battlefield
Operation Red Sea	2020	Lam Chiu Yin	3.651	It tells the story of the tragic victory of the Chinese Navy's "Jiaolong Commando" in the conspiracy to crush the rebel leader

(continued)

Table 1. (*continued*)

Film	Time	Director	Box office (billion)	Introduction
Operation Mekong	2020	Lam Chiu Yin	1.186	It tells the story of an action team trying to unravel the hidden conspiracy behind the deaths of Chinese merchant mariners in an attempt to uncover the culprit behind the drug trafficking case
The Taking of Tiger Mountain	2020	Tsui Man-Kong	0.883	It tells the story of a brave and skilled 203 squad of the People's Liberation Army fighting wits and bravery against the bandits who have been entrenched in the northeastern mountains for many years
The Eight Hundred	2020	Hu Guan	3.110	It tells the story of a reinforced battalion of the 524th Regiment of the 88th Division of the Third War Zone of the Chinese National Revolutionary Army, known as the "Eight Hundred Heroes", sticking to the Sixing Warehouse by the Suzhou River and blocking the Japanese army
The Sacrifice	2020	Hu Guan, Yang Lu, Fan Guo	1.126	It tells the heroic deeds of the volunteer soldiers who fought tenaciously with their flesh and blood in the case of the disparity of strength between the enemy and the enemy
The Blood Battle of Occupying Xuchang	2021	YuLin Fan	0.00011	It tells about the bloody battle scene in the spring of 1944 when the Anti-Japanese Self-Defense Regiment organized by the underground party and the new 29th Division of the National Army defended Xuchang and fought tenaciously against the Japanese invaders

(*continued*)

Table 1. (*continued*)

Film	Time	Director	Box office (billion)	Introduction
Sanwan Reorganization	2021	Hu Yang	0.05146	It tells the story of Mao Zedong's leadership of "Sanwan Adaptation" in Sanwan Village after the failure of the Autumn Harvest Uprising in 1927, and the creation of a whole new set of military strategies such as "the branch is built on the company" and "the equality of officers and soldiers"
Breakout	2021	Lian Wei	0.00018	It tells the story of He Kexi, the commander of the Eastern Zhejiang Column, calmly and calmly during the Chongqing negotiation between the Kuomintang and the Communist Party in 1945, and achieved a successful breakthrough at a relatively small price
The Battle at Lake Changjin	2021	Kai Ge Chen, Lam Chiu Yin Tsui Man Kong	5.775	It tells the story of the Chinese People's Volunteers' Eastern Front Combat Forces, with their steel will and brave and fearless fighting spirit, turning the battlefield situation and making important contributions to the victory of the Changjin Lake Battle

Source: [1].

2 Literature Basis

2.1 The Significance of War-Themed Films

Film is a barometer of social history, a gathering point of cultural change. The rewriting and shaping of history is an important part of ideological construction that a country and nation under rapid development cannot ignore [2]. In the more than 100 years since the birth of films, major historical events affecting human society, politics, economy and culture have become an important source of film [3]. Films participate in the writing of history with vivid visual language. While creating the continuity of historical memory, it is more conducive to let young people develop respect and love for their own nation, so as to build the common values of the nation [4]. War is the most dazzling stage for human beings, so war-themed films bring people more real and profound lessons than other types of films [5]. While watching and understanding heroes, we are influenced by patriotism and heroism deep inside, which makes us love our motherland even more and make our character stronger, so we will advocate heroism and patriotism even more [6]. As a result, in addition to the pleasure brought by other genre films, war-themed films also have certain cultural values and educational values, which are necessary for the research on the emotional cognition of audience in war-themed films.

2.2 Emotional Cognition

The research on emotions in art and design has attracted more and more attention. Don Norman [7] pointed out in the book *Emotional Design* that emotional design is divided into three levels, namely, visceral, behavioral and reflective. "Pleasure" is the intersection of visceral, behavioral and reflective design. Emotions enable users to make intuitive and quick decisions. In human society, the cognitive activities, behavioral activities and social activities at the individual level, group level and social level are all affected by emotions [8]. Emotions have become more and more important objects to be satisfied in life, and the methods of satisfaction are becoming more and more market-oriented and media-oriented [9]. As Gobe [10] said, emotional branding is the key to success in the 21st century. To maintain a long-term position in the market, a brand needs to communicate with consumers emotionally and pay attention to consumers' feelings. The product is a tool for brands to communicate with consumers. Emotional product design can not only drive users' preferences, but also create sustainable brands with competitive advantages [11]. Artwork is infectious, that is, a force that triggers the audience's emotions, feelings and even actions by the forms and elements of the work, including films [12]. Emotions in films can be divided into the emotions presented in the works and the emotional responses of audience when watching [13]. Emotional experience plays a non-ignorable role in the collective cultural memory, psychology, viewing methods, viewing pleasure, and audience's choice of films and their understanding of narrative [14]. Genre films and television works have different audio-visual representations, emphasizing the classification of different emotional stimuli to meet the viewing needs of different audience groups at different cultural levels, as well as the necessity between film and television works and the audience group to effectively establish a kind of positive interaction of emotions and feelings. Emotional responses determine the strength of the experience and restrict the participation of the emotion. Meanwhile, the experience will also react to the image itself, and even affect people's evaluation and attitude towards the image [15]. The major themed films with deep connotations can not only represent the personal emotions, ideological desires and social cognition of the main creators, but can also awaken the audience's in-depth accumulation of traditional culture, mood of the times, social emotions, folk psychology and other factors similar to the creative team. Only when the audience's inner emotions are awakened and their emotional resonance is aroused through the plots, can the connotation of the film and television works get a real and valuable response [16].

2.3 Film Audience

The artistic value and commodity value of film and television works is realized through the cultural market; in other words, it is the market that connects film and television production and film and television consumption. The support for the film and television cultural market come from consumers, who have the desire to consume film and television artworks with a certain purchasing power—the film and television audience [17]. In modern society, films have become the major form of cultural consumption in the daily life of many people. At the same time, the market popularity, box office, reputation, and even the success or failure of a film are closely related to the audience [18]. There are differences between audiences in age, academic background, cultural environment, personality and many other aspects [19]. Thomas Shatz stated: The filmmaker's motivation to innovate is adjusted according to his actual perception of certain conventions and audience responses: though audience demand innovation, change must occur in a familiar narrative [20]. The core of film and television creation is to touch audience with emotions and arouse their empathy. Emotion is the result produced by interacting with the content of film and television dramas during the viewing process [21]. The emotional heuristic theory reveals that the audience's choice, judgment, and evaluation of film and television works are consciously or unconsciously driven by subjective emotional responses. In the process of film and television creation and dissemination, emotional stimulation and experience are the core factors of audience research [22]. Therefore, accurately understanding the audience's emotional needs, preferences, experiences, and feedbacks, and integrating dynamic emotions into the viewing experience has become the key factor for the success of film and television works [23].

3   Research Methods

3.1   Questionnaire Design

This research adopts self-made questionnaires to analyze the audience's cognition of viewing according to the relevant theories of communication and emotional cognition. The questionnaire has six independent variables, including gender, age, major, education, occupation, the level of understanding of the history of the Battle at Changjin Lake; five dependent variables, including the degree of preference, the willingness to recommend it to others, the desire to watch war-themed films, the interest in understanding relevant historical events, and the willingness to join the caring for veterans of the Anti-Japanese War. A five-point scale is adopted for ratings (1 = strongly disagree, 5 = strongly agree) [24].

This research adopts online questionnaire, and the link is: https://www.wjx.cn/vm/QSTIaol.aspx. Random sampling is adopted and the respondents are all viewers of the film *The Battle at Changjin Lake*. Before answering the questionnaires, the purpose of this research and the operation method to correctly answer the questionnaires have been informed, their consent has been obtained, and the questionnaires have been filled out carefully.

3.2   Situation of the Questionnaire Samples

A total of 580 questionnaires were collected in this research, and 523 valid questionnaires were obtained after removing invalid ones, including 223 male respondents and 300 female ones. In terms of age, 63 aged 19 and below, 274 aged 20–29, 91 aged 30–39, 75 aged 40–49 years old, 20 aged 50 years and above. In terms of professional backgrounds, 66 related to the film and television industry, 158 related to the art industry, 65 related to the design industry, 38 related to the science industry, 29 related to the engineering industry, 101 related to liberal arts, and 66 related to other industries. In terms of educational background, 41 had a degree of high school and below, 52 graduated from junior colleges, 284 were undergraduates, 106 had a master degree, and 40 had a doctoral degree. In terms of career background, 205 were students, 14 were workers, 20 were farmers, 20 worked in state-owned enterprises, 121 worked at public institutions, 66 worked at private enterprises, 13 people are service provider, 13 worked at individual industrial and commercial households, 21 were freelancers, and 30 were others; In terms of their understanding of history, 154 did not know it, 278 knew a little bit, and 91 knew it. The number of valid samples in this research was 523, and the distribution of the number of questions in each variable is relatively balanced. The results can be used for exploratory research.

4   Research Results

4.1   Reliability and Validity Analysis

Statistical analysis found that the Cronbach's alpha was 0.908. Sapp pointed out that the Cronbach's alpha was acceptable when it was 0.8–0.9, and when it was above 0.9, it meant it had good reliability [25], which indicated that the questionnaire had good reliability. The total correlation for each dimension and item was from 0.721 to 0.827, and the "Cronbach's alpha after deletion" was 0.875 to 0.897, which can be seen that the internal consistency between the topics is relatively high and the topic selection is reasonable. Through the validity analysis, it can be seen that the KMO value was 0.847, which was of high value, the Sig value was 0.000, which was very significant, and the eigenvalue was 3.660, which can explain 73.204% of the variation of the preset use. The factor loadings of each question were from 0.821–0.886, and the commonality was from 0.674–0.802. Sapp pointed out that it is good when the factor loading is above 0.5, it was ideal when it is above 0.7. It is good when the commonality is above 0.3, and it is ideal when it is above 0.5. The factor loading and commonality of each question are both higher than the ideal value, indicating good validity.

4.2   Relevant Analyses Among Different Dimensions

According to the results of Pearson correlation analysis, it can be seen from Table 2 that there are significant correlations between the five general items, that is, the audience's preference for the film, their willingness to recommend the film to others, their desire to watch war-themed films, their interest in understanding relevant historical events, and their willingness to join the care for the veterans of the Anti-Japanese War. The five items affect each other. Among them, the correlation coefficient of preference and willingness to recommend reached 0.753; the willingness to recommend and the desire to watch war-themed films reached 0.764; the interest in understanding relevant historical events and the willingness to join the caring for the veterans of the Anti-Japanese War reached 0.752. It can be seen that the audience's preference for the film is highly correlated to their desire to watch war-themed films, their willingness to recommend the film is highly correlated to their desire to watch war-themed films, and their interest in understanding relevant historical events is highly correlated to their willingness to join the care for the veterans of the Anti-Japanese War.

Table 2. Related analysis.

Variable	f1	f2	f3	f4	f5
f1	1				
f2	.753**	1			
f3	.651**	.764**	1		
f4	.551**	.651**	.678**	1	
f5	.567**	.649**	.638**	.752**	1

(f1 = Preference; f2 = Willingness to recommend to friends; f3 = Desire to watch war-themed movies; f4 = Interest in knowing about relevant events in history; f5 = Join the will to care for war veterans)

4.3 The Differences in the Emotional Cognition of the Audience of Different Genders in the Film *the Battle at Changjin Lake*

Table 3. T-test analysis of differences in gender and trait evaluation.

Questions	Gender	N	M	SD	T	Sig	Scheffe comparison
Preference	Man	223	4.16	1.005	−3.102**	0.002	Man < Women
	Women	300	4.42	0.871			
Willingness to recommend to friends	Man	223	4.23	1.038	−3.537**	0.005	Man < Women
	Women	300	4.53	0.824			
Desire to watch war-themed movies	Man	223	4.20	1.061	−2.044*	0.017	Man < Women
	Women	300	4.38	0.923			
Interest in knowing about relevant events in history	Man	223	4.29	1.035	−2.813***	0.001	Man < Women
	Women	300	4.53	0.859			
Join the will to care for war veterans	Man	223	4.34	0.968	−2.677***	0.001	Man < Women
	Women	300	4.55	0.793			

$* p < .05.** p < .01. *** p < .001$

Taking gender as the independent variable and the five general questions as the dependent variables, the independent sample T test was used to explore the cognitive status of the audience of different genders. The results are shown in Table 3. There are significant differences in the five general items, and the scores of women are higher than those of men. There are significant differences in the interest in understanding relevant historical events and the willingness to join the care for the war veterans (sig = 0.001). It can be seen that the scores of female audience in the above five general items are significantly higher than that of male audience. Female audience get a better emotional experience when watching the film *The Battle at Changjin Lake*. *The Battle at Changjin Lake* mainly focuses on war scenes, with a large number of plots and audiovisuals used to show the important war to resist US aggression and aid Korea: *the Battle at Changjin Lake*, showing that the Chinese soldiers fought bravely without fear of difficulties in a harsh environment, even though the enemy far surpassed them in numbers, equipment and materials. However, after the bloody battle of the Chinese soldiers, they finally succeeded. In the film, the battle is fierce, the characters are passionate with distinctive personalities. The performance is vivid, as if they were on a real battleground. There are many scenes about the heroic stories and characters of the Chinese soldiers, and also scenes of casualties reflecting the cruelty of the war and the hardships of the Chinese soldiers in this battle. Although the whole film shows the image of male warriors, in addition to the fierce battle, the emotions of the characters in the film are sincere, directly showing the true feelings of the heroes, and bringing the characters to life. They bravely shoulder the heavy burden of safeguarding the country, even if scarifying their own lives. With the delicate emotions in the film, female audience recognized the film more than male audience, actively recommended the film to others, and were willing to watch more war-themed films. Their desire to understand the historical background of the film was stimulated, and they were willing to do whatever they can for the war veterans.

4.4   The Differences in the Emotional Cognition of the Audience of Different Ages in the Film *the Battle at Changjin Lake*

To conduct a test of difference of variance based on the age and the five general items, the scores of the above-mentioned five general items were relatively consistent, including the audience's preference for the film *The Battle at Changjin Lake*, their willingness to recommend it to others, their desire to watch war-themed films, their interest in understanding relevant historical events, and their willingness to care for the veterans of the Anti-Japanese War, with no significant difference. It can be seen that the scores of audience of different ages are relatively close, which showed no significant difference, meaning there was a relatively consistent opinion. *The Battle at Changjin Lake*, based on the war-themed history, uses realistic techniques to represent the historical battle, to further show Chinese soldiers defending their homeland in the historical battle. The film has a clear theme, which can arouse emotional resonance amongst audience of different ages, and can achieve good dissemination effects.

4.5 The Differences in the Emotional Cognition of the Audience of Different Majors in the Film *the Battle at Changjin Lake*

To conduct a test of difference of variance based on the major and the five general items, the results are shown in Table 4. Audience of different majors had relatively consistent scores in terms of their interest in understanding relevant historical events, with no significant difference. There are significant differences in the audience's preference, their willingness to recommend it to others, their desire to watch war-themed films, and their willingness to care for veterans of Anti-Japanese War. There is strongly significant difference in their willingness to recommend it to others and their desire to watch war-themed films (sig = 0.001). The scores of art-related audience were significantly higher than those of film and television majors. In terms of the desire to watch war-themed films, the scores of science-related audience and other majors were significantly higher than those of film and television majors. It can be seen from the above two questions that art-related audience had higher emotional recognition, and were more willing to recommend the film to others than those of film and television majors. Watching this film has stimulated the audience's desire to watch war-themed films. The scores of audience of art-related, science-related and other majors were significantly higher than those of film and television-related majors. In terms of the willingness to care for war veterans, the scores of art-related audience were significantly higher than those of film and television-related majors. By comparing the average scores, it can be seen that in terms of preference, the scores of audience with a science background were the highest, while the scores of audience with a film and television background were the lowest. Audience of art majors had relatively high scores in the above three items. Art-related audience have richer artistic expression techniques and higher artistic aesthetic abilities. *The Battle at Changjin Lake* is very professional whether in music, sound effects, color, scene design or the use of special effects, showing strong artistry and the presence of the war from details. The audience of art-related majors showed more recognition and resonance, they were willing to actively participate in the dissemination and promotion of the film, and they were willing to join the caring for the veterans of the Anti-Japanese War. The audience of film and television-related majors has rich experience in film and television creation, will pay special attention to the use of film and television skills while watching the film, and will pay attention to the exchange of technologies when watching films, so they generally have lower emotional experience while watching the film. The audience of science-related majors have strict logical thinking and they had the highest score in terms of preference, indicating that the film's logic is reasonable, and it has won the love of audience with a science background.

Table 4. ANOVA test analysis of differences between professional and characteristic reviews.

Questions	Source of variation	SS	DF	MS	F	Sig	Scheffe comparison
Preference	Intergroup	14.200	6	2.367	2.743*	0.012	
	Within group	445.238	516	0.863			
	Total	459.438	522				
Willingness to recommend to friends	Intergroup	19.436	6	3.239	3.851***	0.001	2 > 1
	Within group	434.044	516	0.841			
	Total	453.480	522				
Desire to watch war-themed movies	Intergroup	22.245	6	3.707	3.930***	0.001	2 > 1, 4 > 1, 7 > 1
	Within group	486.807	516	0.943			
	Total	509.052	522				
Join the will to care for war veterans	Intergroup	16.508	6	2.751	3.683*	0.041	2 > 1
	Within group	385.515	516	0.747			
	Total	402.023	522				

* $p < .05$. ** $p < .01$. *** $p < .001$ (1 = film and television industry; 2 = Art; 3 = design; 4 = science; 5 = engineering; 6 = liberal art; 7 = others)

Comparison of the average number of preference: 4(4.53) > 7(4.44) > 2(4.41) > 5(4.38) > 6(4.26) > 3(4.23) > 1(3.94).

4.6 The Differences in the Emotional Cognition of the Audience of Different Academic Backgrounds in the Film *the Battle at Changjin Lake*

Table 5. ANOVA test analysis of the difference between education and characteristics assessment.

Questions	Source of variation	SS	DF	MS	F	Sig	Scheffe comparison
Preference	Intergroup	12.622	4	3.156	3.658**	0.006	
	Within group	446.816	518	0.863			
	Total	459.438	522				
Desire to watch war-themed movies	Intergroup	12.551	4	3.138	3.274*	0.011	1 > 4
	Within group	496.500	518	0.958			
	Total	509.052	522				

* $p < .05$. ** $p < .01$. *** $p < .001$ (1 = High School and below; 2 = junior college; 3 = undergraduate; 4 = master degree; 5 = doctoral degree)

Comparison of the average number of preferences: 1(4.54) > 3(4.40) > 2(4.23) > 4(4.09) > 5(4.05).

To conduct a test of difference of variance based on the academic background and the five general items, the results are shown in Table 5. There is a significant difference between the audience's preference and their desire to watch war-themed films. In terms of preference, it can be seen from the average comparison that the scores of the audience with a high school degree and below were significantly higher than those with a doctoral degree. In terms of the desire to watch war-themed films, the scores of audience with a high school degree and below were significantly higher than those with a master degree.

It can be seen that in the above two items, the scores of audience with a high school degree and below were significantly higher than those with a master degree or above. The film *The Battle at Changjin Lake* is based on the historical event of *the Battle at Changjin Lake*. The film uses grand scenes and heroic stories of Chinese soldiers to represent *the battle at Changjin Lake* in visual language. Audience with a high school degree and below showed greater interest in war-themed films, who gave higher scores to *The Battle at Changjin Lake*. Audience with a master or doctoral degree had rich academic thinking skills. While watching the film, they paid attention to factors like the logic, history and culture of the film. The film is based on a historical event, which highly condenses and refines the event in a limited time. Compared with the real historical event, the plot is relatively simple, and a lot of details have been deleted. In order to achieve a great viewing effect, some parts have been adapted artistically, which may not meet the rigorous requirements of highly educated audience, so the scores were relatively low.

4.7 The Differences in the Emotional Cognition of the Audience of Different Occupations in the Film *the Battle at Changjin Lake*

To conduct a test of difference of variance based on the occupation and the five general items, the results are shown in Table 6. There was a significant difference between the audience's interest in understanding relevant historical events and their willingness to care for war veterans. From the average comparison, it can be seen that their interest in understanding relevant historical events was significantly higher than that of workers, farmers, and service providers. In terms of caring for war veterans, the scores of individual businessmen, students, and people working at public institutions were higher than workers and farmers. The audience working at public institutions had a high sense of social responsibility and stronger feelings for their homeland. Since they had been engaged in the work of serving the people for a long time, they can deeply understand the hard-won life of peace and happiness. They show respect and gratitude for the revolutionary martyrs. Students are still in the learning stage, who are familiar with history, and regularly participate in patriotic education activities at schools. For individual businessmen, many of them started from scratch, and their journey to start a business was no easy. Their struggle is arduous, so the film *The Battle at Changjin Lake* arouse their resonance, as the soldiers in the film fought bravely to defend the territory, their homeland, and honor of their country. The fighting spirit of the Chinese soldiers inspires the individual businessmen. Workers and farmers mostly work manual labor jobs, with low income. They still struggle for food and warmth, who have little knowledge of the historical event, so they resonated with the film poorly in emotion, and their scores were low.

Table 6. ANOVA test analysis of differences in occupational and characteristic evaluation.

Questions	Source of variation	SS	DF	MS	F	Sig	Scheffe Comparison
Interest in knowing about relevant events in history	Intergroup	18.200	9	2.022	2.318*	0.015	
	Within group	447.567	513	0.872			
	Total	465.767	522				
Join the will to care for war veterans	Intergroup	13.057	9	1.451	1.913*	0.048	
	Within group	388.966	513	0.785			
	Total	402.023	522				

* $p < .05.$** $p < .01.$ *** $p < .001$ (1 = Student; 2 = worker; 3 = farmer; 4 = state-owned enterprise; 5 = public institutions; 6 = private enterprises; 7 = service provider; 8 = individual businessmen; 9 = freelancer; 10 = others)

Comparison of the average number of Interest in knowing about relevant events in history:

5(4.58) > 8(4.54) > 1(4.49) > 9(4.48) > 10(4.43) > 4(4.30) > 6(4.29) > 2(4.00) > 3(3.95) > 7(3.77).

Comparison of the average number of Join the will to care for war veterans:

8(4.77) > 1(4.56) > 5(4.53) > 9(4.52) > 4(4.50) > 10(4.37) > 7(4.23) > 6(4.21) > 3(4.15) > 2(4.07).

4.8 The Differences in the Emotional Cognition of the Audience of Different Levels of Knowledge About the Film *the Battle at Changjin Lake*

To conduct a test of difference of variance based on the levels of knowledge of the film *The Battle at Changjin Lake* and the five general items, the results are shown in Table 7. There was a significant difference in the audience's preference, their willingness to recommend it to others, and their desire to watch war-themed films. In terms of preference, audience who knew a little about the history of the Changjin Lake campaign scored significantly higher than those who knew a lot about the history of *the Battle at Changjin Lake*. In terms of their willingness to recommend it to others and their desire to watch war-themed films, those who knew a little or nothing about *the Battle at Changjin Lake* scored significantly higher than those who knew a lot about *the Battle at Changjin Lake*. *The Battle at Changjin Lake* is a visual expression of the historical event, *the Battle at Changjin Lake*, which is based on real history. but film as one of the ways of artistic expression, in order to tell the story in visual language in an extremely limited time, all aspects such as narrative structure, character design and scene design are artistically processed, which has a certain difference with the real history. Audience who knew this historical event had a relatively complete understanding of the battle, will compare it to their previous understanding of the battle during the viewing process. When a big difference occurs between the real historical event and the artistically processed film, it is difficult to arouse their emotional resonance and recognition. For audience who knew a little about this history gained a lot of emotional recognition mostly based on the intuitive viewing experience of the film itself, such as the strong visual image, sound effects and rich and delicate performance.

Table 7. ANOVA test analysis of the difference between historical understanding and characteristic evaluation.

Questions	Source of variation	SS	DF	MS	F	Sig	Scheffe comparison
Preference	Intergroup	6.072	2	3.036	3.482*	0.031	2 > 3
	Within group	453.336	520	0.872			
	Total	459.438	522				
Willingness to recommend to friends	Intergroup	11.644	2	5.822	6.852***	0.001	1 > 3, 2 > 3
	Within group	441.836	520	0.850			
	Total	453.480	522				
Desire to watch war-themed movies	Intergroup	16.274	2	8.137	8.587***	0.000	1 > 3, 2 > 3
	Within group	492.777	520	0.948			
	Total	509.052	522				

$*p < .05. ** p < .01. *** p < .001$ (1 = Don't understand; 2 = Understand a little; 3 = Understand)

5   Conclusions and Suggestions

Based on the above research content, audience with different backgrounds showed both similar and different emotional experience of the film *The Battle at Changjin Lake*. The conclusions of this research are as follows:

1. Audience of different ages have relatively consistent emotional cognition to the film *The Battle at Changjin Lake*, with no significant difference; audience of different genders show significant differences in emotional cognition of *The Battle at Changjin Lake*, and female audience have more delicate emotional perception ability, and can gain more recognition and resonance for the rich and full emotions in the film. In the five research items, the scores of women are significantly higher than those of men.
2. Audience with different academic backgrounds have certain differences in the emotional cognition of *The Battle at Changjin Lake*. The scores of audience with a high school degree and below are significantly higher than those with a master and doctoral degree. Audience with a master degree or above have more rigorous academic training and have a better understanding of history, who have higher requirements and standards for the culturally related content, while audience with lower education background obtain more emotional recognition in the grand war scenes.
3. Audience with different occupations have a certain difference in the emotional cognition of *The Battle at Changjin Lake*. Generally speaking, the scores of audience of art-related majors are significantly higher than that of film and television-related majors. In terms of preference, the scores of audience with science and engineering-related majors are significantly higher than the audience related to film and television. Audience related to film and television pay more attention to the application of film and television technology, and their emotional recognition obtained while watching the film is lower.
4. Audience with different occupations have different perceptions of films. Audience working at public institutions, societies, and individual businessmen have significantly higher interest in understanding relevant historical events and more willing to

join the caring for veterans of Anti-Japanese War than workers and farmers. Audience of different occupations obtain quite different information in daily life, and the emotional experience obtained from watching war-themed films is also quite different.

5. Audience with different levels of understanding of historical events, show significant differences in emotional cognition. Audience who knew nothing or a little of the historical background score significantly higher than those who know a lot about the historical background. Although war-themed films are created based on real historical events, it is difficult for audience who know a lot about the historical events to gain more emotional recognition through artistically processed images.

This research is one of the major researches on the emotional cognition of audience, and the research on the emotional cognition of audience in war-themed films is a complex and important one. This research only selects Chinese audience as the research object, to study the highest-grossing film in China, *The Battle at Changjin Lake*. Subsequent researches can explore the important factors that affect the differences in the emotional cognition of audience based on different war-themed films and audience in different regions.

Acknowledgements. We would like to thank all the participants for their time and contributions. Specifically, we wish to thank Rungtai Lin.

Funding. This is a project supported by the Shenzhen University Young Teachers' Research Initiation Project: research on Audience's Emotional Perception of Melodramatic Films (860–000002112001).

References

1. Cat's Eye Movies. https://piaofang.maoyan.com/calendar, organized by this research. Accessed 4 Feb 2022
2. Chang, F.Y.: The eight hundred and the historical writing of ideology. Film Lit. **62**(21), 85–87 (2020)
3. Wang, L.L.: National memory and image lyricism: historical and cultural changes of Chinese antiwar films. Literary Theory Criticism **19**(04), 21–27 (2005)
4. Bai, W., Zhang, X.X.: Ideological communication strategies of melodramatic films: are search perspective based on youth audiences. Film Lit. **757**(16), 8–12 (2020)
5. Jiang, M.: Film and Television Art Education. People's Publishing House, Beijing (2013)
6. Feng, H.L., Zhu, H.L.: On the artistic function of military film and television. J. Shaanxi Normal Univ. (Philos. Soc. Sci. Ed.) **36**(S1), 378–379 (2009)
7. Norman, D.A.: Emotional Design: Why We Love (or Hate) Everyday Things. Basic Civitas Books, New York (2004)
8. Turner, J.C., Hogg, M.A., Oakes, P.J., Reicher, S.D., Wetherell, M.S.: Rediscovering the Social Group: A Self-categorization Theory. Blackwell, Basil (1987)
9. Guo, J.P.: Sociology of Emotion Theory-History-Reality. Shanghai Sanlian Bookstore, Shanghai (2008)
10. Gobe, M.: Emotional Branding. Allworth Press, New York (2009)

11. Kumar, M., Townsend, J.D., Vorhies, D.W.: Enhancing consumers' affection for a brand using product design. J. Prod. Innov. Manag. **32**(5), 716–730 (2015)
12. Zhang, D.: An analysis of the levels of artistic impact of The Eight Hundred. Film Lit. **767**(02), 85–87 (2021)
13. Bordwell, D., Thompson, K., Smith, J.: Film Art: An Introduction. McGraw-Hill, New York (1993)
14. Zheng, J.: Controlling audience emotions - a review of moving the audience: American Cinema and the audience experience. Film Art **54**(01), 150 (2010)
15. Sun, C.J.: Emotion: The Charm and Experience of Image Representation. China Film Press, Beijing (2010)
16. Bai, X.L.: The inspiration of War Wolf 2 and Operation Red Sea for the creation of China's melodramatic films. Film Rev. **618**(16), 50–53 (2019)
17. Huang, H.L.: Audience Theory of Film and Television. Beijing Normal University Press, Beijing (2007)
18. Xu, Y., Wu, Y.J.: An exploration of audience consumption psychology in Chinese film market. Film Lit. **61**(02), 3–6 (2019)
19. Ding, F., Huang, Y.F.: Research on Film Consumer Behavior. China Film Press, Beijing (2011)
20. Schatz, T.G., Schatz, T.: Hollywood Genres: Formulas, Filmmaking, and the Studio System. Temple University Press, Philadelphia (1981)
21. Lu, K.: How films stimulate the audience's emotions–a review of Karl Plantinga's cognitive-perceptual theory. J. Beijing Film Acad. **36**(06), 12–21 (2020)
22. Ji, L., Dong, W.: From the starting point of emotion research: a study of de-emotionalized emotions and media effects. Nanjing Soc. Sci. **28**(5), 110 (2018)
23. Lu, K.: A brief history of Chinese film audience studies. Film New Works **41**(2), 94 (2020)
24. Lewis, J.R.: Usability: lessons learned… and yet to be learned. Int. J. Hum. Comput. Interaction **30**(9), 663–684 (2014)
25. Sapp, M.: Psychological and Educational Test Scores: What are They? Charles C Thomas Publisher, Springfield (2002)

The Development of Virtual Production in Film Industry in the Past Decade

Haofeng Li, Cheng-Hung Lo[⊠], Arturo Smith, and Zhiyuan Yu

School of Film and TV Art, Xi'an Jiaotong Liverpool University, Suzhou, China
CH.Lo@xjtlu.edu.cn

Abstract. Virtual production (VP) is a computer-aided production and visualiza-tion filmmaking method, which was first officially applied in "Avatar" directed by James Cameron in 2009. After ten years of development, in the "Lion King" directed by Jon Favreau in 2019, VP's concept and technical level reached a new level, bringing a revolutionary impact to the film industry. This project's research objective is to explore the development trend of virtual filmmaking from 2009 to 2019 and make a reasonable prediction of the VP's future development in the film industry. This research selected four VP films as research cases: Avatar (2009), Jungle Book (2015), Ready Player One (2018), and Lion King (2019). The research method used is Historical Research (Longitudinal Studies), which collects secondary data in the form of text and videos related to the four cases in the database and other network sources for analysis and longitudinal compari-son to conclude. After data collection and data analysis, three reasonable global production trends are drawn in the past ten years: The digital models and tools for CG scene and character creation are transformed from traditional animation software to game engines. The participation and collaboration of various film-making roles in VP have gradually increased. The combination of VP technology and traditional filmmaking culture has steadily enhanced. This research also made reasonable predictions on the VP's future development prospects on "actor immer-sion and participation" and "popularization of VP." This research can be regarded as an introductory guide and historical review of virtual filmmaking. It may inspire and support readers who want to contact and understand the VP industry. It also provides some information about the latest developments in the industry for film-makers and virtual reality workers. This research can also provide an academic reference for filmmakers who want to make films through VP.

Keywords: Virtual production · Virtual filmmaking · Historical research

1 Introduction

A trend seems to be discovered that the film's function gradually transforms from record-ing reality world to creating a virtual world, and this transformation is positively related to the development of visual effect technology. Computer technology has made extraor-dinary developments and breakthroughs, which benefits the film industry as well. CG (Computer Graphic) techniques started to play significant roles in the film industry [1].

© The Author(s), under exclusive license to Springer Nature Switzerland AG 2022
P.-L. P. Rau (Ed.): HCII 2022, LNCS 13312, pp. 221–239, 2022.
https://doi.org/10.1007/978-3-031-06047-2_16

In the last ten years, filmmakers apply different CG techniques to film production and construct a fancy and realistic cinema world and unique audiences worldwide.

VP is a broad term referring to computer-aided production and visualization film-making methods. It combines Virtual and Augmented Reality with CGI and game-engine technologies to enable film crews to view their scenes unfold as they are composed and captured onset [2]. The authenticity of the simulated sets and the natural world are difficult to distinguish, giving users an immersive experience. Theoretically, the concept of Virtual Reality (VR) is a simulation system that users can create and experience a virtual world. James Cameron, the renowned film director, applied VR technology to the production of his science fiction film Avatar in 2009, which may be the milestone of virtual-production in the film industry [3]. James brought the concept into the industry and presented a wide range of prospects of this application to other filmmakers. In the following decade, some innovative film directors have continuously explored the possibilities of VR. The application kept developing, positively associated with the development of VR science. In 2019, Jon Favreau produced and directed Lion King, a film almost entirely constituted by CG shots. This film's advanced VR technology has amazed the whole film industry, showing excellent cooperation between VR and filmmaking [4]. It is undeniable that from 2009 to 2019, the development of VR in this decade has made revolutionary changes to the film industry, and it will make more significant changes in the future. The production model of CG movies has been changed, and new VR technology has been organically combined with traditional filmmaking technology. By analyzing the development trend of VR in film production during the decade, predicting this system's prospects provides wider opportunities and possibilities for filmmakers.

1.1 Research Questions and Cases

"The Development of the Application of Virtual Reality Concept and Technology in CG Film Production in the Past Decade" containing two specific research questions:

What is the development trend of the application of VP in the film industry in the past decade?

What is the prospect of the application of VP in the film industry?

Question one planned to be the central question in this project, occupying most of the research. The outcome of inquiry one will be a historical analysis of the past decade. Four films are selected to be the research cases of this project:

1. *Avatar (2009), directed by James Cameron*
2. *The Jungle Book (2015), directed by Jon Favreau*
3. *Ready Player One (2018), directed by Steven Spielberg*
4. *Lion King (2019), directed by Jon Favreau*

These four films are made during the past decade, and the production of them all applied VP to varying degrees. This article will analyze four films in chronological order of their output to draw VP's development trends in these films.

2   Literature Review

Unreal Engine is a game engine under Epic Games, published The VP Field Guide in 2019, a guide book of VP's concept and introduction [2]. VP is described as where the physical and digital worlds meet, and film artists can view the virtual scenes in real-time on the set, which benefits film production decision-making. The guidebook has laid out the difference between traditional CG film production and Virtual Filmmaking.

There are exceedingly complex production steps with highly compressed schedules in classic CG film production, including pre-production, post-production. The process is typically a highly linear mode, and the iteration is challenging and costly, while the development efforts are frequently isolated. For filmmakers, linear production causes an uncertain problem. It is difficult for directors and cinematographers to view the scenes similar to the final results on the set, so many creative decisions could not be made in real-time but wait until post-production. In VP, the final composition scene is presented in real-time low pixel through VR technology. What filmmakers see is no longer the green screen but the virtual CG scene. This production mode gives filmmakers more power on the set, allows them to control the filming details of CG scenes, encourages faster iterative, non-linear, and collaborative processes, and strengthens the cooperation of different departments in the crew [2]. The guidebook introduces four VP types: Visualization, Performance Capture, Hybrid Green Screen live, and full Live LED Wall, which have different functions and can achieve different production needs. The first three types have been applied to the four-film cases in this research, while Full Live LED Wall is still under investigation and testing and will be used in large feature film production in the future.

2.1   Avatar, 2009

In Liang Zhu's research published in the Journal of Beijing Film Academy [3], he gave a broad introduction of film technology behind Avatar's scene. An indication is that James Cameron had started to use primary VR concepts and techniques at that time, applying motion capture technology to the cinematic camera (capture the motion of real camera), creating a virtual-camera system called "Simul Cam." Some reflection marks were pasted onto the fusion 3D cinematic camera and recorded the camera's motion tracks. A virtual camera with the same track in the CG world was generated so that the live-action scene and CG scene were able to be composed in low quality, director and DOP could preview the CG shot in real-time. The "Simul Cam" technology was highly advanced at that time. Although it probably is considered low quality and primitive, it is undeniable that it laid a foundation for virtual-production in the film industry. Avatar's VR technology is described as the "shoulder of giant" and plays the role of inspiration in many reviews below.

2.2   The Jungle Book, 2015

Six years after Avatar, Jon Favreau brought his feature film Jungle Book to the public, taking VP of CG movies to a new level. Most of the shots in the film are done in a closed virtual-studio. This new production model is called the warehouse model [5]. In American Cinematographer, Michael Goldman [6] claimed that "Favreau opted for an essentially unproven VP methodology, and the result is an almost entirely digitally rendered and animated film that is intended to look completely photo-real." To achieve this goal, Favreau found Bill Pope, ASC, a traditional cinematographer, and Pope was considered a key man who pushed the boundaries of virtual cinematography mentioned by Goldman. Before the production, Pope thought he could make traditional photography decisions, but not sure in a digital place. However, Favreau admitted that he preferred a live-action photographer. According to Goldman, a new department named "Digital Domain" was highlighted in Jungle Book. "Digital Domain is the primary virtual-production vendor on the film, in charge of everything from supporting the virtual art department," said Girish Balakrishnan, the technical director of the digital domain. Balakrishnan introduced a unity video-game engine used in Jungle Book, called Photon. Photon was the first time a game engine was deeply applied to the feature film and previsualized the entire film from start to end. This innovation allowed Pope and Favreau made a precise cinematographic choice – camera movement, lens choice, depth of field, framing, and lighting, by virtual-camera, which referred to the previous experience in Avatar. "This is why Jungle Book looks and smells like a real film, shot on film." [6]. Through the review, virtual-production in The Jungle Book can be regarded as a revolutionary development, the game engine began to participate in the rendering work, and the physical camera was gradually replaced by virtual-camera. Some of these innovations were based on Avatar and improved on some of the time's rough technologies.

2.3 Ready Player One, 2018

Gary Roberts, the VP supervisor of Jungle Book, began working with Warner Bros. to prepare the VP for Ready Player One soon after finishing The Jungle Book. "The first thing we did was to set up a virtual art department at Digital Domain," said Roberts [7]. As Robertson wrote in Virtual Reality: Ready Set Go, the production of Ready Player One followed the virtual-production mode and technology started in Jungle Book, such as the DD system (digital domain). However, virtual artists in Ready Player One had to build up a bigger and more complicated virtual world named OASIS in the story [8], so the digital domain scale is more considerable than Jungle Book. Those virtual artists using Maya and other 3D modeling tools create virtual sets, props, vehicles, characters, and environments that could run in a modified version of Unity's real-time game engine. One of Jungle Book's changes was that filmmakers could scout the virtual sets in VR, which was considered an improvement after 2015. "Being able to walk around in a virtual set was super useful; it gave everyone a real-world sensibility for lighting and placing things," said Roberts [7]. In Ready Player One's production, Steven Spielberg could reach anywhere in OASIS with his virtual camera, like shooting films in the real world. He could even point, draw, write notes, create arrows, and make targets in the VR world with an annotation tool. The virtual-production in Ready Player One continued and developed the technology in Jungle Book. Compared with Jungle Book, Steven Spielberg owned more controls on the VR world created by the game engine, and it was more accessible and more flexible for filmmakers to scout and design the virtual scene by wearing VR glasses.

2.4 Lion King, 2019

Jon Favreau assembled 1.5 billion dollars to make his second Disney feature film four years after Jungle Book. With the previous experience, Favreau brought his team and other elements such as game engine and warehouse model into Lion King [9]. To create lifelike CG scenes, the team shot footage of wildlife in Kenya, Africa, and used them as references for rendering CG shots [4]. As Giardina Carolyn discussed in Hollywood's New King: 'VP' [10], the virtual-production team rendered an entire large CG landscape of Africa grassland, which helped relieve the physical limitations of filming, all the shots could be reshot at any time. Marc Snetiker [11] mentioned in Return of the King that, "We have built a multiplayer VR filmmaking game just to make this movie." explained by Favreau, which indicated that Lion King's virtual-production had moved to a level of gamification. The boundaries between filmmaking and game-making had been blurred gradually. However, Favreau still invited "traditional" cinematographer Caleb Deschanel to participate in the production, the same as Jungle Book's situation. "We needed a real cinematographer to impart artistry and wisdom," said the producer Robert Legato [4], which showed that live-action cinematographers are still playing significant roles in virtual-production and virtual-cinematography.

The reviews above are based on individual film cases. In the planned research, they should be connected and analyzed based on chronological order. Daniel Maddock [12] published research named Reframing Cinematography in 2019, which is similar to our research structure and methodology, belongs to the longitudinal study. It focuses on the development history of cinematography. Maddock's research mentions the development trend of virtual-cinematography, which is suitable as a source of our research. During the development of VR application in filmmaking, a significant change was the evolution of cinematography from traditional to virtual. Therefore, these two trends complement and influence each other.

Moreover, Maddock's research discusses that some film scholars and filmmakers present negative attitudes about VP. They argue that traditional cinematographers should be protected. These contents and arguments will provide valuable references for our research.

3 Methodology

This section will describe the critical method and technique used in this research. Firstly, the chosen method's methodological theory, referring to some academic resources of methodology and some research examples. Secondly, an instruction will describe how to use this method in this research. This question's answer is considered historical research since it asks about the development and changes in a period. According to Xiaotian Feng's thesis of the social research method, the time dimension is an essential aspect of social research design, divided into two types: cross-sectional studies and longitudinal studies [13]. Longitudinal studies refer to collecting data at several different points in time to describe the development and change of phenomena and explain the connection between various phenomena. According to this definition, longitudinal studies may be the appropriate method in this research. There are several straightforward methods under longitudinal studies, and "trend studies" are considered to be selected in this research.

The purpose of trend studies is to reveal and discover the changing trends and laws of social phenomena by comparing the attitudes, behaviors, or conditions of the general population at different times. In our research, "social phenomena" may be replaced by VR application phenomena in film production, while the mode of trend studies still matches the research. Xiaotian Feng [14] also claimed that the research method could be divided into four categories in terms of data collection: survey studies, experimental studies, literature studies, and field survey studies.

Since this research's target is film production, especially Hollywood CG film production, experiment and field survey are probably unavailable. Therefore, the research will follow the method of literature studies. Xiaotian Feng [14] emphasized that researchers can define "literature" as any form of information that contains the phenomenon that the researcher wishes to study, not just text materials. These types of materials are defined as "secondary data." Secondary data analysis requires researchers to reanalyze and reconstruct the existing data collected by previous researchers [15]. So in our research, the "secondary data" will be materials and information about the VP of those four-film cases collected by some Hollywood reporters and researchers, including videos, sounds, interviews, and texts. These secondary data will be assembled and connected, following the method of trend studies.

3.1 Data Collection

An extensive searching work toward the "behind the scene" information of the four-film cases is planned in this step. Reports, news, interviews, documentaries, journals, videos, blogs, TV shows, and other media about the virtual-production behind the four films' scenes will be considered data in this research. However, the data should be examined before collection and is expected to be valid and credible. Information from the filmmakers or crews who participated in the production will be valuable data, such as Steven Spielberg and Jon Favreau's interview or a documentary filmed during Lion King's output. The data may be messy and complicated after collection. It is necessary to extract the contents related to the topic, concentrating on keywords such as "virtual reality," "virtual-production," "virtual cinematography," "game engine," "ware-house model," and so on.

3.2 Data Analysis

After data collection, all the valid data will be analyzed based on longitudinal studies and trend studies mentioned above. Data will be divided into four-time points: Avatar 2009, Jungle Book 2015, Ready Player One 2018, Lion King 2019, and connected, compared in chronological order, aiming to reveal and discover the development trend changes. The method of analyzing the collected data, including article, video, sound recording, would be Close Content Analysis. A key factor of trend studies highlighted by Xiaotian Feng [14] is that the comparison at different time points must aim at the same research contents. More specifically, the questions asked at each time point should be the same; otherwise, they cannot be compared. This instruction indicates that the research should reach several specific aspects individually in the four films, avoiding general comparison, so that it could answer "what changed in this decade?" and "how did they change?" However, this research may not follow Feng's instruction strictly due to each film productions' uniqueness. In the film industry, every film is unique and individual. Therefore, it is possible and valuable to explore new and exciting characteristics in every new film. A journal by Yuting Gu and Wantong Cao [16] discussing the development trend of CG technology in Hollywood may be a negative example in this research. In that journal, the researchers merely presented a general trend study without discussing particular elements or aspects. The object focused on was the entire industry, so the conclusion it drew are statements like "CG animation image visual representation is under a certain characteristic of constant development" "CG animation in the decades is in the rapid development," only giving a conclusion that the industry is developing rapidly. However, it failed to answer what specifically changed and how they changed from a micro perspective. Therefore, our research should discuss the development trend and changes of specific aspects at different time points. This paper will discuss two elements in those four-film cases.

How are the virtual/CG scenes designed and rendered in the digital domain?

How do the director and cinematographer capture/film the shots?

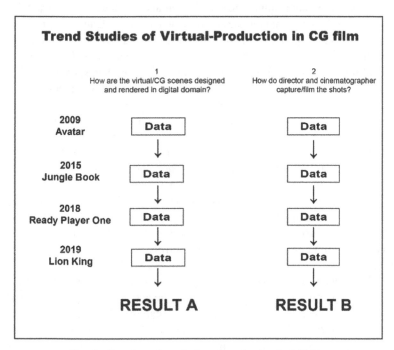

Fig. 1. Trend studies of virtual production in CG film

Each film case will answer these two questions, and the results will be compared and analyzed separately as showen in Fig. 1. The first aspect concentrates on the virtual scenes and sets design achieved by virtual artists and VFX artists, while the second aspect focuses on virtual-cinematography done by directors and cinematographers.

3.3 Result and Analysis

In this research, 16 literal data have been collected from the source of the XJTLU Library Database and other websites, including journal articles, research papers, web articles, and web news reports. 15 video data have been collected from the source of YouTube and Vimeo, including "Behind the Scene" documentaries, b-roll videos of the film production, interviews of filmmakers, live-talk about "virtual filmmaking," and recorded videos of a conference about "virtual filmmaking." These materials are chosen as the data of this study after a rigorous selection. They are closely related to the VP of the four-film cases in the research and can be used as credible research evidence. The data integration would be attached in the Appendix section.

After examining all the data, close text and content analysis of the four-film cases were completed, and the summary of significant findings and comparisons are as below in time orders.

Avatar, 2009

Avatar is the first feature film that widely applied VP and is also regarded as a milestone in the 10-year history of virtual filmmaking. From the present point of view, the technology of VP in Avatar is immature and elementary, but at the time, it was considered by filmmakers to be epoch-making and revolutionary. James Cameron first introduced the concept of virtual filmmaking into the film industry and brought essential inspiration to the other three film cases. Avatar tells the story of the alien planet Pandora, traditional live-action filmmaking is still used to film human scenes, and VP is mainly applied to the stages of the Navi aborigines of Pandora. The Navi characters were rendered by motion capture technology, and a computer also generated the environment and set. It said that the entire production process was utterly immersed in a virtual environment [17].

Before the production on set, the crew needed to create virtual CG elements. There was no department in Avatar responsible for constructing virtual scenes. These tasks were all undertaken by the visual effects team. The conceptual illustrator first designed an abstract image of the Pandora planet's environment, and then the VFX team performed 3D modeling based on the conceptual illustration to render the rough climate of the earth and the digital model of the set. The software used was still traditional VFX software such as Maya. These rough CG elements were completed in pre-production, waiting to be inserted into the computer system that controls the VP as a reference for virtual filmmaking [17].

Formal VP took place in a spacious studio with a white, empty stage for performance capture and computer clusters for VR rendering. The actors playing the Navi performed on the stage wearing costumes covered with motion capture markers. The motion parameters were recorded by multiple reference cameras installed on the studio's ceiling and transmitted to the VP system. The "Simul Cam" system loads the captured character actions onto the CG characters in real-time, then composed with the CG environment and set to render a low-quality grim movie picture, achieving the initial virtual preview. James held a virtual camera on the set, not a real camera, but a monitor connecting the real and virtual world. Through the virtual camera, James could view the environment of Pandora and the CG Navi's acted by actors. The system tracked the movement of the virtual camera. When James moved it, the camera angle also moved, just like manipulating a real camera. Such a VP system allowed the director to preview the movie's final screen in real-time on the set instead of looking at the green screen and relying on the scene's imagination. James could see the interaction between the character and the virtual camera's environment, directed the actors in real-time, adjust the position and movement of the essence, and preview the photographic composition of the final picture and the camera's movement track. James could also add, move and delete some virtual environment elements, such as stones and trees, which realize the first-level scene scouting and production design in VP, but it is carried out on a two-dimensional display [17]. Avatar's VP gave the director more control, allowing the director to play his role on set in real-time and make various decisions instead of waiting until post-production. However, the two crucial filmmaking roles: production designer and cinematographer, did not participate in Avatar's VP. The VFX team, VR technicians complete the design and modification of the virtual scene. The camera shots were made by James using a virtual camera after motion capture.

The Jungle Book 2015

As director Jon Favreau said in an interview, "The Jungle Book made using the Pandora box from Avatar six years ago" [18]. Jungle Book tells the story of a boy and a group of wild animals. In the movie, only the little boy Mowgli is acted by a live actor, and the rest of the animals are all virtual CG characters. These CG animal characters are anthropomorphic in the script, with rich body movements and facial expressions, and they have many dialogues and interactions with Mowgli. Unlike the static CG backgrounds and objects in Avatar, Jungle Book needs to render and manage the "live" CG characters. Traditional 3D modeling software is not enough to support the enormous rendering workload, so the production team applied the game engine. Photon, a game engine owned by Unity, participated in the rendering of virtual characters and environments in Jungle Book's scenes [6]. This movie is the first attempt at the game engine and movie production cooperation. The advantage of the game engine is the ability to render CG characters in real-time. It allows the animation department's CG animals to be "alive" in the virtual scene, transforming them into virtual actors and performing interaction with the boy actors. To better manage and distribute complex VP, a new department-Digital Domain has appeared in Jungle Book. Its role is to bring together talents in VR and assist traditional filmmakers in completing the production. This new department also extends to Ready Player One and Lion King.

Jungle Book and Avatar's VP's most noticeable difference are their combinations of live-action and virtual scene. In the movie, the little boy was played by a real actor, not motion capture, so he was filmed by a real camera. Jungle Book adopts Avatar's "Simul Cam" system, installs the sensor on the camera, tracks the camera's movement, and feeds it back to the virtual engine, realizing the connection between real and virtual. Following Jon's directing, the little boy actor performs dialogues and interaction with the air, while in the monitor, there are CG animal characters there, talking with the boy. There are also referenced objects in the studio that support the actors' performances, such as trees and stones, and the staffs in blue leotards act animals to provide reference points for the actors. Due to the live-action filming, it is also necessary to set up lights that match the set's virtual environment [19].

In general, Jungle Book has made improvements and breakthroughs in the rendering and control of virtual characters than Avatar, thanks to the game engine's participation.

The production model of Live-action and Virtual has higher requirements for coordinating live cinematography equipment and virtual systems, but Jon Favreau also admitted that the movement and use of many blue screens and reference props also make the filming process cumbersome. Avatar and Jungle Book's VR viewing angles are still in the two-dimensional stage, making the filmmakers lack the immersion in the virtual scene. In the following Ready Player One and Lion King, more and more VR devices were invented and applied to making movie production tend to be gamified, but there is no doubt that Jungle Book started the initial cooperation between movie production and games.

Ready Player One 2018

The VP in Ready Player One reached a new technological level, thanks to the progress and breakthroughs made by VR technology and equipment in 2018. In terms of the Digital Domain, Unity's game engine has become the primary support system for rendering the virtual world in movies, occupying a more significant proportion and role than it did in Jungle Book [20]. In Ready Player One, Unity has developed a set of VP tools specifically designed for filmmakers to convert complex VR technology into a more straightforward game-like operating system, which can be used by traditional film crews who have not been exposed to VR before. HTC Vive, a set of VR headsets and controllers developed by HTC, is used as an accessory to the Unity system [21]. This series of engines and hardware allows Steven Spielberg and his production designer to directly participate in the construction of virtual scenes in Ready Player One. Digital Domain first built a broad stage with a game engine and used 3D software to create various sets and props. Stephen and the production designer put on VR headsets on the location. They could enter the virtual world and reach any place for scene scouting by manipulating the VR game-pad. They could easily add, delete, and move CG objects with game-pads in a virtual scene, such as a vehicle, a house, and a computer [7]. While scouting, Stephen could also call up virtual cameras in VR and select lenses for each shots' composition to test each shot's composition in advance [21]. Compared with Jungle Book, gamified scene scouting and design allow the director and production designer to personally design scenes without passing commands to technicians, which improves the efficiency of production design. The application of HTC Vive allows the entire production preparation process and filming process to be carried out from a three-dimensional perspective, allowing filmmakers to truly "enter" into virtual scenes, visually observe all artistic details, and make decisions more efficiently. The progress from a two-dimensional perspective to a three-dimensional view is an essential breakthrough for Jungle Book to Ready Player One.

Like Avatar, the VP of Ready Player One's filming process is also performed in a spacious studio, and the motion capture system creates the virtual characters. With HTC Vive, actors can put on a headset before the performance and observe the virtual scene they are in advance so that they have a preliminary understanding of their environment, which is more conducive to their perspective from the virtual character, not just relying on imagination, this is a new advancement compared to Avatar. In Ready Player One, the form of virtual cinematography has also changed. Unity demonstrated their virtual cinematography tool for Ready Player One at Siggraph 2018 [21]. This set of tools has the same complete virtual cinematography equipment as the real crew, such as dolly track, rocker arm, drone, and lenses with different focal lengths. Distance, angle, focal length, aperture, color temperature, actual photography parameters are converted into digital format. Filmmakers only need to operate the VR handle to control a virtual camera and other auxiliary equipment in the virtual world to complete the shots. This set of Unity tools is widely used in Ready Player One. No real cameras, lights, or tracks are needed in the studio. Instead, VR controllers are used as virtual photographers standing in the field and filming in real-time. Virtual cinematography allows film artists to get the shots they want without being restricted by real conditions. However, the consequence is that the live-action photographers gradually lose control of the picture. Director of photography of Ready Playeobjectivee, Janusz Kaminski, said in an interview that he was only involved in 40% of cinematography in movies, and those were real-world shots. 60% of virtual photography is done by Stephen and Digital Domain staff. He showed his worries about VP, and as movies increasingly rely on digital technology and tools, the "image ownership" of cinematographers is disappearing [22]. In terms of this issue, in Lion King, directed by Jon Favreau a year later, a new solution appeared.

Lion King 2019

After Jungle Book and Ready Player One, many VP studios and technicians have appeared in the film industry, and they have accumulated much experience. It said that Lion King is a product of VP in an environment with sufficient technical conditions. Unlike the first three films, there are only animals but no humans in Lion King's story. The entire movie is made in a completely virtual state under this setting, without a real shot. This means that the amount of workload for virtual scenes and character construction will become huge. Jon has assembled many famous VR, games, and visual effects companies to help him complete Lion King. VR hardware technology companies Oculus and HTC Vive, game engine companies like Unity and Unreal Engine, and studio Magnopus, which integrates film and television production and game development, have all provided many supports for this film [23].

Before the production began, Lion King's team went to the African savannah and took many photos and videos of the environment and wild animals on the spot. These images will use as references for rendering the CG environment and animal characters [24]. Later, Digital Domain created a large 100-mile radius scene in the game engine, as if moving the African savannah into VR. Thousands of CG props, stones, grass, trees, and water flow are inserted into the virtual scene. To make them more realistic, the visual effects team used simulation plug-ins to increase the randomness of these elements, such as letting the grass grow at different heights, letting stones experience different degrees of corrosion, and letting water flow have different flow rates [23]. Jon Favreau explained that they are making movies in the same way as games. Before the first shot has been formally done, the entire virtual scene has been constructed according to CG games' standards.

Users could wear a headset to control the game-pad and travel in the "African Savannah" [25]. After the scene rendering was completed, the VFX team began to produce different animals in Lion King, giving each animal character bones and fur to make them move like real wild animals. The design and rendering technology of these animal characters inherited the Jungle Book. When all the virtual elements have been rendered, Jon and the director of photography Caleb Deschanel put on VR headsets to enter the virtual "Africa" and discuss each shot's positions [4]. This experience is familiar to Caleb, just like in the live-action movie, going to the filming location to observe, choosing favorite angle and composition. In Lion King's VP, the cinematographer's status and power have become as important as in the live-action film [24]. In scene scouting, Caleb is most concerned about the sun's position because in this movie, sunlight is the only light source, and the position of the sun affects the light and shadow of each shot.

Interestingly, in the game engine, the sun's position can be changed at any time, and Caleb can operate the game-pad to move the sun to the ideal position [24]. This is also an experience that traditional cinematographers cannot experience in live-action movies. In Lion King, VR technology and game engine truly become helpful tools in filmmakers' hands. Traditional filmmakers can still use these tools, combined with previous film production experience, to make creative decisions on the set.

The above technologies and processes for scene construction and scene scouting are not breakthroughs than Ready Player One. In Lion King, the most revolutionary development and progress are in cinematography. Jon Favreau and his team have reached a consensus before making Lion King a movie filmed by a human rather than a purely animated film. VFX supervisor Robert said that the difference between a live-action film and an animation is that those live photographers always accidentally capture some beautiful shots called "happy accidents," but the computer shots will eliminate these accidents and achieve 100% perfection. These perfections will make the movie feel digitally artificial and lose its charm [23]. Many sensors are installed on this actual equipment and connected to the virtual camera, so the camera operator could use these simple tools to objectively shots in the virtual scene, which is entirely different from the feeling of holding the VR game-pad. The Steadicam operator stood in the empty VR studio, having a sober and familiar Steadicam in his hand. He saw on the monitor a lion roaring in front of him [23].

4 Discussion

According to the result and analysis of all the data, the two research questions' reasonable answers could be drawn in this section.

Research Question 1:

What is the development trend of VP in the film industry in the past decade?

Digital mode and tools of CG scene & character creation, Production Design, and Scene Scouting transformed from traditional animation software to game engine.

Starting from the Jungle Book, the game engine's participation and contribution in VP have gradually increased. By Lion King 2019, the game engine has become an indispensable supporting system, maintaining the entire production's operation. Over the past decade, the game engine has gradually replaced traditional CG software and played an essential role in rendering CG scenes and characters, production design, and scene scouting. Such a change is caused by two main factors: the film industry's increasing requirement and the game industry's progress. From the film industry's perspective, the ratio of live-action scenes to VFX scenes in CG movies is changing in recent years. Traditional CG movies still focus on the production of live-action scenes. VFX is only inserted in the green screen as an additional effect. Even the live-action scenes in Avatar also occupy a high proportion. However, with the advancement of CG technology, film writers are more confident to create scripts containing more VFX scenes, and audiences are also happy to experience the visual excitement of VFX in cinema, which leads to an increase in the proportion of virtual scenes in movies, even exceeding live-action scenes.

The workflow of traditional VFX software is individual, and it cannot render large and complex scenes. When more than half of a movie is even composed of virtual scenes, this software cannot complete such a huge workload. In contrast, the game industry has devoted itself to improving the user interaction experience in the virtual space in the past decade. Many large game companies have designed the quality of virtual scenes and characters to a cinematic level, and the virtual engine they developed is also sufficient to support a continuously wide range of CG world rendering, which just meets the needs of virtual filmmaking. After the initial collaboration between the game engine and movie production in Jungle Book, game companies led by Unity and Epic Games have accelerated the development of virtual filmmaking systems and tools, intending to occupy a blank market of VP quickly. This cooperation model will be sustainable and continuously improving and change the structure of CG film production. The higher the virtual degree of production, the smaller the proportion of live-action scenes. Original budgets invested in location and equipment are now transferred to the game engine's construction and maintenance. The roles of the crew have also changed. Artists originally from the game company, such as "VR Supervisor" and "Digital Supervisor," have now joined the film crew.

The game engine's participation triggered another change in VP: Gamifying Film. It can be seen from the comparison of these four film cases that the production technology is improving, but the difficulty of the filmmaker's operation is gradually decreasing. In Avatar, James needed to give VR technicians instructions and asked them to execute if he wanted to move a stone in the virtual space. Nevertheless, when it came to Lion King, a director who has never been in contact with VR can personally adjust the sun's position through the game-pad. One of the characteristics of the game is the user's operability and interactivity. The game industry has been devoting itself to improving the user's operation experience. The game engine brings this feature of the game to film production. The tools developed by the game company can transform complex technology into a simple gamified operating system, making it easier for traditional filmmakers to work in VP. This is the trend of movie gamification, and the boundary between films and games has gradually become blurred. The participation and collaboration of various filmmaking roles in Virtual-Production increased gradually. This may be regarded as the most critical development trend finding in Research Question One. According to the VP Field Guide released by Unity, the film industry and the game industry generally believe that VP's core meaning is to change the linear production model of traditional CG movies to reduce the iterations of various departments in the production. In previous traditional visual effect movies, the filming team and the post-production team were two independent departments, which did not interfere with each other, and only existed the connection of footage delivery [2].

The directors, cinematographers, and production designers solely depended on the storyboards and concept illustrations for setting scenes and shots in the filming stage. On the set, they could hardly see any virtual CG elements, only large green screens. Directors and cinematographers could only film every green screenshot through their imagination of the CG picture. It can be said that their contribution only stayed in the performance of the actors and the necessary lighting and composition. Even in some cases, the lighting was inserted in post-production. These filmmakers did not have the opportunity to contribute professional skills and creativity to the set. As Jon Favreau said, a phenomenon caused by this production mode is that the entire movie seems to be reproduced once in the post-production stage. The film industry emphasizes collaboration between different roles, but the linear CG film production model significantly reduces cooperation, and the cumbersome iterative process also makes the entire project inefficient and costly.

The analysis of the four-film cases in this research shows that VP has transformed the original linear model into a non-linear real-time collaboration mode. CG production and filming process have become simultaneous events. Even different types of departments and roles can contact and participate in the whole process in person. The diversity of filmmaking roles involved in VP has shown a continuous increase in the past decade. In the VP of Avatar in 2009 and Jungle Book in 2015, the real-time preview of virtual scenes and CG characters resulted from revolutionary invention and development. This technology moved CG elements from post-production to the studio, and the director did not need to rely on his imagination to complete his work anymore. He could directly see the composed scenes and characters on the dedicated virtual monitor and guide the actors' performance and action paths. The director became the first traditional filmmaking role in this development history to participate in VP truly. Technology gave him the power to make real-time decisions, rather than just facing the green screen and fixed plans to complete the shooting.

However, in Avatar and Jungle Book, the VP technology is still in its infancy. At that time, the game engine's virtual filmmaking tools were still under development, making it difficult for other traditional filmmakers to contribute to this model except for the director. At the SIGGRAPH conference of Unreal Engine, Jon also said that the VFX team did the production designer and cinematographer's work in the Jungle Book [26]. When it came to Ready Player One in 2018, the production designer joined the party. The game engine's participation, the HTC Vive headset application, and the development of VR tools for constructing and scouting various scenarios, all these new technologies liberate production design from the technical team and leave it to more professional artists. The production designer of Ready Player One can make his artistic and creative contributions in a comfortable game environment and operating system. However, as a vital role in the film crew, the cinematographer, also a position with high professionalism and experience requirements, was not until officially participated in VP until Lion King 2019.

As a senior director, Jon has great respect and pursuit for live photography. He always believes that the shots taken by computer programs cannot be compared with those taken by real photographers. The model connected with the actual equipment and virtual camera developed by the Lion King team allows Jon to invite many professional live-action photographers to complete this epoch-making VP film. This may be the first CG movie production project in which photographers have such a significant role and power to produce movies in the virtual world with their standard equipment. Throughout the ten-year history, from Avatar in 2009 to Lion King in 2019, directors, production designers, cinematographers, and other filmmaking roles are gradually participating in VP, and the collaboration between them is also increasing. It is a process of exploration. The VP industry is working hard to eliminate traditional filmmakers' threshold to enter this new model. They hope that VP will become a universal production method accepted by the film industry in the future so that all filmmakers can benefit from it. "Virtual Filmmaking" is a combination of VR and Filmmaking, but Filmmaking is the most essential and fundamental in this cooperation. No matter how advanced the technology of VR is, the problem to be solved by this model is always how to make the film industry. Filmmakers adapt to the technology of VR and use the tools of VR to critical ideas and creativity in movies.

The combination of virtual filmmaking and traditional filmmaking culture was enhanced gradually. This development trend can be an extension and more indepth thinking and discussion of the last movement. As mentioned in the previous paragraph, the participation of different filmmaking roles in VP has gradually increased. They bring to the VP system their professional capabilities and the traditional moviemaking culture derived from their years of experience in the film industry. Some people may question that the emergence of VP has changed the film industry. The films made in VR are no longer films but digital products. It is undeniable that VP has indeed changed the way traditional movies are produced. This is driven by the development of the times and technology. However, advanced VR technology cannot replace the role and influence of traditional filmmaking culture. In this study, the directors of the film cases: James Cameron, Steven Spielberg, and Jon Favreau, who have been making films in Hollywood for more than two decades before participating in the VP, learn more about the significance of traditional filmmaking culture. In these four virtually produced film cases, they strive to achieve the organic integration of VR technology and traditional film culture. The former is used as a tool, and the latter is used as a carrier for using tools. In Ready Player One and Lion King, this combination is more significant.

Unreal engine demonstrated the virtual photography tool used in Ready Player One at 2018 Siggraph. Although the entire set of tools runs in the game engine, it covers almost all classic cinematography elements. Frame rate, resolution, light color temperature, shutter speed, aperture value, all professional parameters can be adjusted in the tool. The tool also contains a wealth of virtual cinematography equipment, tracks, Steadicam, drones, cinematic lenses. The parameters of all equipment are inserted into the game engine based on real values. There are many similar examples. Whether it is a game company or a VR company, they strive to retain the experience, skills, and culture of classic filmmaking in the VP products and tools they develop.

In Lion King, Jon Favreau even transplanted most classic movies' equipment and staff to the virtual studio. Every subtle job of the traditional crew, such as focus pullers and track operators, appears in the Lion King studio. Jon shared his views at Unreal Engine User Group at SIGGRAPH 2019, "We have 100 years filmmaking experience, we should not abandon them just because of the new technology, we should inherit the traditional skills of the great artists, inherit the culture of cinema" [26]. That is why he insisted on inviting Caleb and other excellent cinematographers to join Lion King's team. Jon is a pioneer and promoter of VP and an avid digital media technology enthusiast, but even so, he insists on retaining the traditional filmmaking culture in VP movies. This is his insight and understanding of the market and industry as a filmmaker: The audience is more willing to watch a realistic CG movie that looks like live-action rather than a 120-min game clip. The experience and skills of filmmaking can bring viewers a sense of authenticity. This is a movie-watching habit gestated in the history of 100 years. This will not change quickly, even in future development.

Research Question 2:

What is the prospect of the application of VP in the film industry?

According to the above analysis and discussion, VP's development during this decade has focused on the enhanced co-operation between VR technology and traditional film-making and enhancing the participation and experience of filmmaking roles in this model. It can be noted that there is a lack of essential parts in this development history, which are the actors and actresses. An actor is an indispensable part of filmmaking, and all the efforts made by all other filmmakers revolve around how to better film actors. However, in the four-film cases in this research, it can be found that the actors in the VP in Avatar and Ready Player One are performed on motion capture devices. There is only one live actor in Jungle Book, while there is even none in Lion King. During this decade, actors' participation and VP experience are not at a high level (Actors performing in a motion capture system cannot be regarded as fair participation). Current VR technology still needs external devices, such as VR headsets and virtual displays and virtual cameras, to provide users with immersion and realism. Actors as a unique role in the film crew; they are usually the people who receive the least information on the set. They cannot observe auxiliary monitors and other equipment and can only use their imagination to construct the visual picture in their minds. Obstacles to information reception and lack of immersion are why actors cannot benefit from VP. This is a limitation of the current virtual technology model. Improving the immersion and participation of actors in VP is likely to be the VP industry's prospect. VP studios and game engine companies in the sector are currently conducting product research and development in this area and have also made some progress. At Unreal Engine User Group at SIGGRAPH 2019, a new production model combining a large LED screen and a real-time preview engine was introduced. In this model, a substantial curved LED screen is installed in the set, and virtual scenes and virtual objects are displayed on the screen, creating a realistic environment. The actor is standing in front of the LED screen as if he is in a real scene. The immersion and interactivity of the actor in the virtual world are enhanced.

The picture in the LED is not static; it is connected to the camera, the movement of the camera will be tracked and fed back to the LED screen, and the virtual picture will change position and angle with the camera movement [18]. This new model is currently only tested in some demos and short films, but it brings new possibilities to VP's prospect. Actors can break away from the dependence on VR equipment in this model and directly observe the surrounding virtual scenes, which plays a significant role in their performance. Taking off the VR headset has always been the goal of research and development in the VR industry. There are currently research achievements on VR technology about getting rid of VR headsets, also named "Immersive Reality" [27]. Immersive Reality is now being tested in the military and other areas. In the future, not only LED screens but also other advanced technologies may be used in virtual filmmaking, breaking the barrier between the virtual world and people, allowing actors and filmmakers to enter virtual scene production with less equipment.

Popularization in the film industry may be another prospect of VP. The cases mentioned in this research are all massive commercial production with significant investment, and in the future, even small crews or filmmaking enthusiasts will be able to experience VP. In Unreal Engine User Group at SIGGRAPH 2019, a Cine Tracer tool developed based on the Unreal Engine was introduced. It is a cinematography & lighting simulator developed by cinematographer Mate workman. Filmmakers can use the late lighting and camera position of each shot in the virtual engine before shooting and make plans in advance. Cine Tracer is popular with many filmmakers. It is like a game and can be downloaded and used by ordinary people [18]. In the future, more VP software and tools may be developed for use by all filmmakers. VP will become more widespread; not only large production teams with huge investments are eligible to apply for VP, but it may also cover the entire film industry, which is an exciting prospect.

5 Conclusion

This research analyzes and discusses the development trend of Virtual Filmmaking from 2009 to 2019 based on the behind-the-scenes production information and data of film cases. The current virtual filmmaking technology's development direction makes a reasonable prediction of the production mode's future development prospect. The selected movie cases are Avatar 2009, Jungle Book 2015, Ready Player One 2018, Lion King 2019. These four films are all highly representative Virtual Filmmaking products in the global film industry in this decade, and the production time points are distributed in various stages of this history. It is meaningful to analyze the industry's development trends by putting them together and making a comparison. The primary research method used in this project is Historical Research (Longitudinal Studies). In the data collection, 16 literal data and 15 video data were collected, closely related to the VP of four movie cases and the VP's latest progress in the industry. Close Content Analysis is used as a research method in data analysis, and the information in the collected data is converted into academic analysis results.

In the Result & Analysis section, the four VP cases' production process and some crucial details are summarized and elaborated separately, including the inheritance of previous technologies and the breakthrough of new technologies. Four patients were compared on concepts, technology, and production mode. The purpose is to provide evidence support for summarizing the development trend in the Discussion section. In the province of discussion, the reasonable research findings are outlined based on two research questions. In question one, three development trends are elaborated as the conclusion of data analysis:

Digital mode and tools of CG scene & character creation, Production Design, and Scene Scouting transformed from traditional animation software to game engine. The participation and collaboration of various filmmaking roles in Virtual-Production increased gradually. The combination of virtual filmmaking and traditional filmmaking culture was enhanced gradually. These three development trends are based on the analysis and comparison of many data in this study, which can be regarded as scientific, reasonable, and credible answers to question 1. In research question two, some analyses and predictions on VP's prospects were elaborated, focusing on the discussion of "actor participation" and "popularization of VP."

VP is an advanced new production model and only has a short history. This research comprehensively reviews VP's birth and development in the film industry and summarizes the concept, technology, and impact of Virtual Filmmaking at various stages. The study macroscopically analyzes VP's development trend in this decade, expounds on the model's overall development direction in the film industry, and makes assumptions and discussions on some of its potential future development. This research cannot explore VP technology's details from the micro-level due to the research scale limitation. Simultaneously, some VP cases other than the four-film instances in the project are not involved. This research can be regarded as an introductory guide and historical review of Virtual Filmmaking. It may inspire and support readers who want to contact and understand the VP industry. It also provides some information about the industry's latest developments for filmmakers and virtual reality workers. This research can also provide an academic reference for filmmakers who want to make films through VP. The predictions prospects mentioned in Research Question 2 are the author's analysis conclusions, and the data referenced are the latest VP technology demonstrations in 2019. Unitized VP in filmmaking is a young model, and every day it will have new changes and progress. The concept and technology of Virtual Filmmaking are still continuously researched and developed. Its future is full of infinite possibilities. It will eventually become a significant milestone in the history of film production. All this is a natural result of the trend of the times.

Appendix

There are extra eight pages of the appendix containing 16 literal data and 15 video data from the source of YouTube and Vimeo.

These materials are chosen as the data of this study after a rigorous selection. They are closely related to the VP of the four-film cases in the research and can be used as credible research evidence. Here is the Appendix link of the network disk:

Link: https://pan.baidu.com/s/1oQN8YLSliEjlA8xpttosOQ.
Code: HCII.

References

1. Finance, C., Zwerman, S.: The Visual Effects Producer: Understanding the Art and Business of VFX. Focal Press, Waltham (2009)
2. Kadner, N.: The Virtual Production Field Guide (2019)
3. Zhu, L.: James Cameron and the digital 3D & virtual shot technology in Avatar. J. Beijing Film Acad. (2010)
4. Goldman, M., Fish, A.: To be king. Am. Cinematogr. 100(8), 58–73 (2019)
5. Nilles, B.: Motion capture and the future of VR computer graphics world, vol. 4, p. 6 (2017)
6. Goldman, M.: Welcome to the Jungle (cover story). Am. Cinematogr. 97(5), 32–45 (2016)
7. Roberston, B.: Virtual reality: ready set go. Comput. Graph. World 41(2), 7–15 (2018)
8. Breznican, A.: VIRTUaL INSaNITY (cover story). Entertainment Weekly, no. 1508, pp. 16–21 (2018)

9. Belloni, M.: Jon Favreau. Hollywood Reporter, vol. 425, no. 28, pp. 36–37 (2019)
10. Giardina, C.: Hollywood's new king: 'virtual production.' Hollywood Reporter, vol. 425, no. 24, p. 54 (2019)
11. Snetiker, M.: Return of the king (cover story). Entertainment Weekly, no. 1560/1561, pp. 18–27 (2019)
12. Maddock, D.: Reframing cinematography. Media Pract. Educ. **20**(1), 44–66 (2019). https://doi.org/10.1080/25741136.2018.1464735
13. Feng, X.: Social Research Methods, pp. 81–87. China Renmin University Press (2001)
14. Feng, X.: Social Research Methods, pp. 213–214. China Renmin University Press (2001)
15. Neuman, W.: Social Research Method Social Research Methods: Qualitative and Quantitative Approachess, p. 384. Pearson New International Edition (2014)
16. Cui, Y., Cao, W.: Research on the developmental trend of CG technology in hollywood and the influence on chinese film and television production, 35–38 (2016)
17. Daily Celebrity AVATAR, Making of and Behind the Scenes (2019). https://www.youtube.com/watch?v=_Y8Buy5b6DQ&t=22sDigitalMonarchMedia
18. Unreal Engine: Fox VFX Lab - Virtual Production and Collaborative Filmmaking | SIGGRAPH 2019|. Un-real Engine. https://www.youtube.com/watch?v=ai6PH61PMvM. Accessed 17 May 2020
19. Empty Popcorn Bucket the Jungle Book | Production B-Roll (2016). https://www.youtube.com/watch?v=69PWu5DIwI4. Accessed 19 May 2020
20. Parisi, P.: 'Ready Player One' Juxtaposes Real, Virtual Via VFX from Three Shops. https://variety.com/2019/artisans/production/spielberg-ready-player-one-vfx-1203144265/. Accessed 17 Apr 2020
21. Unity: Siggraph 2018 - Using a Real-Time Engine in Movie Production. https://www.youtube.com/watch?v=U_NG7WfoI7s. Accessed 7 Feb 2019
22. Giardina, C.: Cinematographer Janusz Kaminski Warns that Directors of Photography are Losing Control of Images they Shoot (2018). https://www.hollywoodreporter.com/behind-screen/cinematographer-janusz-kaminski-warns-directors-photography-are-losing-control-images-they-shoot-1101082
23. Movie Trailer the Lion King 2019 - Making of - How it was filmed in a realistic way. https://www.youtube.com/watch?v=KCnayCnM6Zk&pbjreload=10. Accessed 17 May 2020
24. Go Creative Show: The Lion King and Virtual Filmmaking (with Caleb Deschanel) GCS179 (2019). https://www.youtube.com/watch?v=9sjhdU9FB7Q. Accessed 27 Dec 2019
25. Variety: Jon Favreau on Directing 'The Lion King' in VR and Working with Beyonce (2019). https://www.youtube.com/watch?v=nBWg8PqBJPg. Accessed 15 Apr 2020
26. Unreal Engine: Unreal Engine User Group at SIGGRAPH 2019 (2019). https://www.youtube.com/watch?v=apLzZBqfqeU. Accessed 13 Mar 2020
27. Immersive Reality: Immersive Spaces (2020). https://www.immersivereality.ie/#work. Accessed 1 June 2020

The Spectacle Tendency of Contemporary Art–Reflections on Information Art

Tianming Liu(✉)

Academy of Arts and Design, Tsinghua University, Haidian District,
Beijing 100084, People's Republic of China
Liutianming0825@163.com

Abstract. In the information age, the network culture blessed by digital technology is deeply involved in our daily lives and is always shaping new public consciousness. The 2020 epidemic has indirectly accelerated the process of digitization and virtualization, and intensified the reflection on science and culture in the whole society. The rise of scientific culture seems to have provided quantifiable explanations and means of realization for all phenomena, including art, and the original cultural concepts need to be reinterpreted and reconsidered. Painting, as the main body of the traditional pure art discipline, intervenes in the conceptual context of the information age, and requires a deeper exploration of the language of painting. This kind of exploration is not only about painting itself. The new artistic environment and aesthetic appeals require painting. Participate in economic, social and other broader issues, especially scientific and technological factors and the huge changes that may be produced to analyze and integrate, so as to see the problems and difficulties it faces and give judgments on the future development trend of art.

Keywords: Information art · Concept art · Contemporary art · Image ·
Postmodern society

1 Issues of Concept and Information

1.1 Opposition Since Aesthetic Modernity

Since the Enlightenment, the development of European painting has been accompanied by self-criticism and self-subversive progress. In the later period of modernism, individualism and liberalism together, from artistic language, expression forms to artistic propositions, etc., have a great impact on European classical the art tradition of Doctrine has been thoroughly criticized and subverted in order to flaunt individuality and modernity. In less than a hundred years, all the possibilities of art seem to have been exhausted. More importantly, when all artists of the Western system have entered a frenzy of innovation, innovation itself has become a new public behavior, a certain obsolete mainstream, and therefore no longer possesses avant-garde. As Greenberg said: "When the media begin to explode... When everyone is revolutionary, the revolution is over." If modernism is a critique of art, then the later period of modernism is a critique of art. Criticism. It is

P.-L. P. Rau (Ed.): HCII 2022, LNCS 13312, pp. 240–254, 2022.
https://doi.org/10.1007/978-3-031-06047-2_17

against this background that contemporary art has turned to concepts, and conceptual art has developed to a new level in terms of rationality. It has changed the modernism's triumphant advancement in form and language, and has shifted to thinking about art itself and conveying concepts. The previous article discussed that the main difference between contemporary painting and modernist art lies in the emphasis on conceptuality. The conceptuality of works once became a contemporary alternative. While contemporary art pursues concepts and highlights contemporariness, the problems behind it are becoming more obvious. The typical problems are the various oppositions brought about by aesthetic modernity. The conceptualization of art leads art to philosophy. It seems that once again became a vassal of philosophy and finally triggered the conclusion of the end of art.

1.2 Contemporary Repression

The emergence of aesthetic modernity comes from the practical changes brought about by modern society to each individual's life. Changes in behavior are accompanied by changes in the way of thinking, followed by changes in all aspects of aesthetics, values, etc., in general, it can be called a comprehensive and deep-level conceptual change. In the field of contemporary art, conceptuality has become synonymous with contemporaneity, while the so-called contemporary art is actually the continuation of modernity. Contemporary art is constantly creating new problems while pursuing concepts and speculation to give artistic innovation. For the pursuit of contemporary sex, its negative effects have become more and more apparent, reflecting a multi-dimensional repression and deprivation of human nature.

First of all, the diversity of contemporary art reflects the confusion of value judgments and the disappearance of the mainstream. With the changes in the subject-object relationship between concepts and artistic phenomena in conceptual art, the value judgments about the artwork itself have gradually been replaced by conceptual judgments, and the artistic value judgments between different works have become diverse and incomparable. For artists, only the value choices of individuals or individual cases are left, and there is no mainstream or measurement standard. Only uncertainty has become the normal state that can be determined. If there is still a certain art mainstream in modernist art, such as the elements of modernity sorted out by Greenberg, etc., then this mainstream disappears completely in the contemporary art period, and the disappearance of the mainstream allows contemporary art to embrace more possibilities at the same time, is also full of uncertainty. This feature is not only embodied in conceptual art, but also deeply rooted in the overall context of contemporary art. The disappearance of certainty is an important feature that distinguishes contemporary art and contemporary society from classical art and classical society. Farming civilization works at sunrise and rests at sunset. It relies on the laws of nature and changes in four o'clock to accumulate tens of thousands of years of experience. Definite feedback allows people to have a stable expectation of the future. This certainty appears in the production and life of farming civilization. Every aspect, from the scope of life and life trajectory of the individual, to the coordination of production and governance of society and the country, is full of various types of certainty. In terms of culture and way of thinking, it is easier to form a collective and stable value, and then a certain mainstream value judgment will be formed over a long period of time and a wide geographical range, which of course also includes artistic concepts and aesthetics. Standards, critical criteria, etc. In contrast to modern society, with the industrial revolution and technological revolution, industrial production and commercial trade have replaced agriculture as the new economic foundation of modern society. The improvement of production efficiency, technological changes anytime and anywhere, and the iterative update of business models have greatly accelerated In modern society, the work efficiency and the range of movement of each person change the way of interaction between people, and what follows is the change of thinking mode and value judgment. Modern people must constantly adapt to new things and accept changes in order to continue to interact with others and achieve survival in modern society. The lives of modern people may suddenly get development opportunities because of a piece of news, or they may fail investment in an instant because of a policy. This unknowable sense of emptiness is the disappearance of the primitive certainty of farming civilization. At the same time, the division of labor and cooperation under the modern industrial and commercial system has made everyone a part of a huge social machine. Individuals can no longer complete production independently, but must rely on machines, systems, and collaboration with others. It is difficult for an individual to see the complete picture, and it becomes a part of a huge puzzle. This unknowable and uncertain affects the behavior and concept of every modern person, and people become the spinning feathers in the modern hurricane. In a nutshell, uncertainty is an important source of powerlessness and depression for modern people.

Second, the change in the concept of time in contemporary society has led to a general lack of self-consideration among contemporary people. In the era of farming civilization, each individual strictly follows the laws of nature, working at sunrise, resting at sunset, ploughing in spring and summer, harvesting in autumn and hiding in winter. The concept of time presents a continuous purposelessness and an associated economy. Activities are random and irregular, so people have more time for self-contemplation. In contemporary society, the popularity of electric lights makes night no longer a dividing point of time, and people no longer need to comply with the restrictions of day and night; heating facilities free people from dependence on weather and seasons; convenient and fast traffic makes people break through The constraints of region and space; developed network and rapid information transmission, even let people experience new space-time dimensions in virtual network, fragmented information fills all free time. When all needs can be met, people no longer have time for self-contemplation. As new needs continue to be stimulated and emerge, people are further constrained and trapped by industrial production and business models, and they no longer have time for self-contemplation, or even not with time again, the time cycle of human natural activities is replaced by the work cycle of going to work and leaving get off work, and the time awareness and concept of time that exist in the mind will also change accordingly. Time consciousness, including humans, is the basis of consciousness of all animals and changes in the concept of time seem to have given modern people more freedom. However, in fact, modern people have less time to have themselves, and they cannot observe themselves independently for a long time. It will make people feel the loss of free will, and they will not be aware of the existence of themselves, which will lead to depression and hesitation.

Third, the emphasis on conceptuality is the deep suppression of sensibility by reason. The efficiency and logic pursued by industrial production and business models have made the behavior and thinking mode of contemporary people more and more procedural. The negative effect is the suppression of human nature itself, and contemporary civilization must create more and fresher stimuli. Make up for people's repressed spirit. As a result, pan-entertainment floods, and more and more sensory-stimulating entertainment products are created to satisfy people's repressed instincts. More and more sensualized film and television entertainment works, dances full of symbols of desire, and music that can make ears pregnant have gradually become the mainstream of modern cultural consumption. If the division of labor since the Industrial Revolution has made people lose the ability to work independently, then today's information society has further lost the ability to imagine life. Everyone's vision of life is no longer affected by the media and the Internet all the time. And shaping. Behind every seemingly random short video push, every consumer choice, every human interaction encounter, are the results of the collection of countless personal information and the logical calculation of big data. The binding of human free will and real communication and consumption behavior makes every consumption behavior information that can be recorded and analyzed, and people eventually become data in the algorithm.

The American philosopher and sociologist Herbert Marcuse (1898–1979) criticized the combination of art and commerce in his 1964 book "One-Dimensional Man" (One-Dimensional Man). As a result of the commercialization of culture, the collusion between art and commerce has become a tool to suppress the spirit of modern people, and finally produced the phenomenon of "One-Dimensional" of culture and people. The so-called "one-dimensional" concept refers to a state of being kidnapped by reality, full of inertia, disheartened and critical, and lacking introspective spirit. Just as Marcuse described the situation: "If the mass media can blend art, politics, religion, philosophy and commerce harmoniously and seamlessly, they will give these cultural fields a common feature-commodity form. Music from the heart can be used as a marketing technique. Therefore, the important thing is exchange value, not real value. From the root point of view, the rationality of the status quo and the rationality of all aliens are subject to this." Marl Cousse saw that the commodity economy of modern society, under the blessing of art, combines commodity demand with people's aesthetic taste, and very implicitly and implicitly transforms commodity demand into people's deep-seated needs. "The so-called consumer society and politics of corporate capitalism has created the second nature of man, which links the aggressiveness and desire of human nature with the form of commodities. The demands of owning, consuming, and manipulating constantly give birth to new equipment, instruments, and engines in order to Satisfying the need to use these commodities even in the danger of self-destruction has become a biological' need."

The combination of commerce and art not only promotes elite culture to mass culture, but also enables culture to have the attributes of commodities and become a tool of the commodity economy. Marcuse keenly discovered the concealment of the cultural erosion of the capitalist commodity economy. The "one-dimensional" social phenomenon revealed that commodity clubs did not smooth the differences between elite culture and popular culture and various types of culture, but supported Encourage this difference, but the focus is on the dimensions of assimilation culture and commodity economy, so that both elite cultural behavior and mass cultural behavior are equivalent to the category of commercial behavior, and ultimately lose the critique and revolutionary nature of this assimilation behavior itself. "What is happening is not the degradation of high-level culture to mass culture, but the rejection of high-level culture by reality. Reality surpasses its culture… Today's novelty is through the elimination of opposition, alienation, and transcendence in high-level culture. Factors—they use high-level culture to form another dimension of reality—to eliminate the opposition between culture and social reality. The way to eliminate bidirectional culture is not to deny and reject various cultural values, but bring them all into the established order, and replicate and display them on a large scale." What is depicted here is exactly the scene where today's so-called multiculturalism is being produced and spread on a large scale under the coercion of commerce.

At the same time, Marcuse also pointed out the disappearance of the critical power of art to reality in the commodity society. The original truth attributes of art and the characteristics that are based on reality but distinguished from reality are also deprived in the commodity society. "They have been deprived of the antagonistic power and alienation from reality that were once the dimension of their truth. The meaning and function of these works have thus been fundamentally changed." Subsequently, in The Aesthetic Dimension: Toward a Critique of Marxist Aesthetics published in 1978, it was mentioned that the avant-garde negated and transcended the mainstream ideology and aesthetic experience, allowing people to regain criticality and avoid "One-dimensional" violations. In "Counterrevolution and Revolt" in 1972, he continued to emphasize the dual characteristics of the aesthetic form and historical structure of art—that is, the unity of the phenomenal world and the carrier of meaning. Among them, Marcuse also continued Marcuse's awareness of the non-single-dimensional nature of the truth attribute of art and the characteristics of "distance from reality", that is, the conservative nature of art affirming reality and the transcendence of negating reality, and finally pointed out that aesthetics is free from repressive society. The only discipline, only art, or the criticality in art, can further liberate humanity and transform society.

All in all, the pursuit of contemporaneity is an expedition without turning back. Reflecting on the various problems brought about by contemporaneity is not to oppose contemporaneity or conceptuality itself, because contemporaneity or conceptuality is part of contemporary culture and cannot be resisted. But it can still be introspected and reflected. Only with more knowledge more choices would show up, and one could gain new freedom from contemporary repression and deprivation. Otherwise, it will become a Marcuse-style "one-way". The status of a person of degree. The uncertainty caused by contemporaneity, the deprivation of self-consideration, and the suppression of human spirit by reason come from the binding of personal and social interests in contemporary society, that is, all the material and spirit that individuals want to obtain must rely on contemporary society. Obtain. Therefore, the problems caused by the conceptualization of contemporaneity are, fundamentally speaking, the complicity of every contemporary person.

2 Concept's Deprivation of Art

2.1 The Collusion of Image and Spectacle

The concept of "Spectacle" is the concept mentioned in the book "The Society of the Spectacle" (The Society of the Spectacle) published in 1967 by the French thinker Guy Debord (1931–1994). This book is considered to be a pioneering text introducing the concept of "Spectacle", which was subsequently refined in the sequel "A Review of the Society of Spectacle" published in 1988. The proposal of his concept coincides with the time when conceptual art appeared, and has profound critical significance for the development of contemporary conceptual painting and aesthetic theory.

The concept of "Spectacle" comes from the translation of "Spectacle" in French. The meaning of the word itself contains magnificent, fantastic, visual, and sensory pictures, but it also refers to and emphasizes that this kind of spectacle is deliberately created and superficial. The meaning of false, false and inverted. The combination of landscape and society more clearly points to a new look of modern society in the post-industrial era, not only on the material level, but also on the spiritual level. This concept was mainly put forward in the later stage of modernist society, under the background of the booming commodity economy, and aimed at the alienation of human life brought about by economic development, the shaping of values by the mass media, and other issues, and launched a symbiotic relationship with the social outlook. Criticism of the social and cultural outlook, as well as the impact of the spectacle society on all aspects of human production and life, values, and beliefs. The landscaping of modern society described by Debord is the result of a combination of various governments, policies, commodity economy, and mass media under the capitalist ideology. "Spectacle" is not only a phenomenon, but also a relationship and state, the most typical of which is the replacement of human social relationships by commodity relationships, and the subsequent changes in various forms of landscaping within the social scope. As Debord said, "All the once direct existence is transformed into a representation." In short, the process of social landscaping is a process of commercialization of all things within the whole society. It has become equipped with a commodity attribute, and has become focused on the appearance of display, the appearance of the surface, especially the image of a commodity transaction state, in other words, the "landscape". In this process, the real social production and life became representational, in Debord words: "Commodities successfully colonized the historical moment of social life." (Fig. 1).

On the other hand, the emphasis on commodity attributes and commodity relations within the social scope has directly led to human behavior, human-human interaction, and human social relations being gradually affected or even replaced by commercial behavior, commodity interaction, and commodity relations. In a landscaped commodity society, service is a labelled existence of a certain model. That is, what Debord said "passive identification with the Spectacle replaces real activity". At the same time, the Spectacle of human behavior and thinking patterns has made people simple and superficial, and blocked the progress of human perception and critical thinking. In reviewing the development of modern society, real social life has been replaced by extremely superficial "Spectacle". From the real "being" in life to the "having" in the commodity society, today, with the popularization of the Internet, the efficiency of information transmission

Fig. 1. Schematic diagram of social spectacle processing

has greatly improved, further shifting from possession and possession to a kind of the "appearing" that exists in the internet, social media, and communication channels, the "appearing" that Debord once described, has a more obvious and strong way to realize it. From the real-life experience, to the possession in the commodity society, and then to the instant appearance of the appearance in the information society, in this process, modern society has completed the landscaping.

The concept of "spectacle society" is mainly aimed at the criticism of contemporary consumer culture and commodity fetishism and the alienation of human nature brought about by it. It also involves many social issues such as class alienation, cultural homogeneity, and mass media. Just as Debord said "real social life is transformed into representation", what he refers to is the important composition of the concept of "representation" spectacle, and also summarized that the core problem of culture in contemporary society lies in representation, using Debord's concept to describe even landscaping. In the process of social spectacle, images have become the most effective carrier for landscaping. Spectacle are created and presented in images, and they are disseminated in the mass media in the form of images. But the relationship between landscape and image described by Debord is closer to the borrowing of the nature of the image, that is, the symbol of reality and the artificial and non-authentic characteristics of the image. The borrowing is used as a representational image to describe the relationship between representation and reality in the spectacle society. The inversion between people is a phenomenon in which commodity relations replace the inversion of interpersonal relations. As stated in his book, "Spectacle is not a collection of images; on the contrary, it is a social relationship between people through images." The interaction around images has replaced real human interaction. Today's information age is particularly profound and obvious. The developed Internet continues to attract users to stay on social software as much as possible, and allow users to stay on the Internet for as much time as possible. Various social media platforms continue to optimize user experience and continue to update with fresher and more exciting content. Not only provide users with opportunities to share their personal experiences, but also allow users to experience the experience of others through social software, and comment, like, and forward them. Under a series of instant feedback and long-term reward mechanisms, users are allowed to experience a closed loop formed by different temporal and spatial emotional experiences in a virtual network.

So far, when each individual's real-life experience is recorded, uploaded, and commented, it is the transformation of images into life. People in real life follow the "social logic" in social media, in fact, it fell into a state of interaction around images. Just as Debord said that people under the spectacle society lack a sense of reality and poor quality of life. In the information society where the Internet is developed, it can be said to be ubiquitous. One of the typical ones is the change in time experience. In the long-term Internet-immersed population survey, it is found that the sense of the passage of online time is very different from real life. The huge amount of information will weaken the passage of time in the Internet. Sense often consumes a lot of time without knowing it, but when returning to reality, both the mind and the body are empty and sickly. Popular global social software such as Facebook and Tic Tok can gain insights into users' aesthetic preferences, travel trajectories, consumption levels, behavior habits, etc. from the images uploaded by users. Through analysis of a large number of user data samples, it has further improved its information analysis capabilities, and even has the ability to predict user behavior. The push of each short video is based on the results of big data statistics and sample analysis. At the same time, the content pushed by social software stimulates users' needs and guides users' value orientation. The various comfortable, beautiful, and happy landscapes presented also shape users' imaginations of life. It can be seen that under the blessing of the Internet in the information age, images have become an important carrier of the landscape. With the blessing of social media, images continue to spread and ferment, accelerating the construction of a new contemporary landscape. The social landscape described by Debord is more extensive and thorough in the collusion with the image.

2.2 The Spectacle of Conceptual Art

The landscaping tendency of art began to emerge as early as the beginning of the 20th century when iconography intervened in art research. In 1939, Panofsky's "Study on Iconology: Humanistic Themes of Renaissance Art" mentioned at the beginning of the book: "The object of research is the theme of the work that is opposed to the 'form' of the fine arts. And meaning." It can be seen that the research method of iconology first refines the research objects into visible "form" and invisible themes and meanings behind "form". "Form" comes from observation and belongs to the category of vision. The significance mainly comes from the intervention of art criticism and the interpretation of the artist himself and critics. Panowski constructed the framework and model of early iconography, such as the three-stage image analysis method (description, Analysis, interpretation), and subsequent works such as "Image Research" and "The Meaning of Visual Art" in 1939, all laid the foundation for the development of modern iconology. The intervention of iconology separates paintings into "form" and "meaning" and conducts classification research. The analysis of "form" derives the study of visual elements such as color, composition, texture, light, and symbols. It is called internal research, or the internality of the work; the interpretation of meaning relies on a large amount of information behind the work, such as the author's age, region, country, and related national culture, national psychology, and social customs. The artistic trends of the same period, etc., are also called external studies, or the externalities of works.

It can be seen that the research on the form of works is biased towards phenomenological research methods, while the research on the meaning of works is similar to the research methods of anthropology, that is, it is widely connected with the background information related to the work to form a kind of work theme and research method. An open interpretation of meaning. It is this kind of research method that makes the phenomenon of interdisciplinary research in iconology extremely common, such as sociology, psychology, semiotics, phenomenology, and other disciplines and research methods. The study of painting works has gradually evolved into image research. When painting is included in a broader sociological category, it further highlights the characteristics of its visual research, that is, the "visuality" (visuality). American image scientist W. J. T. Mitchell calls it the pictorial turn. At the same time, the prerequisite for the multidisciplinary research method required for meaning interpretation is to eliminate the distinction between different disciplines and allow concepts to flow equally between different disciplines, otherwise they will not be able to communicate with each other. At this point, with the intervention of multiple disciplines and research methods, painting has transformed into a visual symbol that carries meaning, and the concept of painting and history has begun to slide: the transcendence of painting that symbolizes thought has slipped to the sensual and limited. Vision; the long, accumulated history has slipped into a short, labelled culture. This process is the sliding of knowledge and learning towards the senses, and it is also a process of landscape painting (Fig. 2).

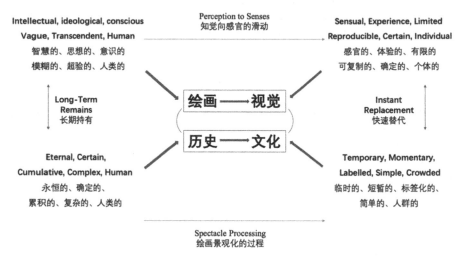

Fig. 2. Schematic diagram of art spectacle processing

For specific examples of landscape in paintings, you can refer to the hollow paintings of American artist Lisa Perez. In her works, there is no image, brushstroke, or color relationship similar to modernism. The painterly disappears; the irregular "frame" edges and hollow holes make the image of the work almost Disappearing; the way of hanging at a certain distance from the wall, the projection behind the work is intertwined with the hole of the work itself, the work itself is a flat painting, but at the same time it is displayed in a way similar to a three-dimensional installation, allowing the work to be displayed It is in a dual state of painting and "thing". At the same time, the hollows on the screen form a grid-like form, and the projections left on the wall behind are interlaced with the grid on the screen, forming new holes.

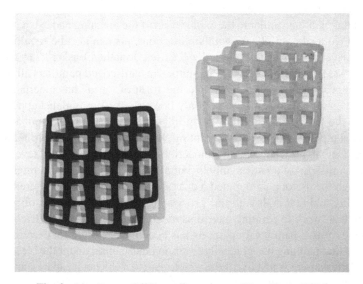

Fig. 3. Lisa Perez, Off Put, oil on canvas, 27 × 30 cm, 2016

The special feature of his work is that, firstly, the shape of the "picture frame" is no longer a standard square in the traditional sense, but an irregular shape; secondly, the hollowing out on the surface of the work makes the picture no longer It is a closed plane, the vision no longer stays on the surface of the painting, light can also penetrate the surface of the work, and the space behind the work is related; third, the change in the way of hanging allows the work to float on the wall instead of tightly. Paste it on the wall, let the projection of the wall interlace with the grid in the foreground, and appear together. Furthermore, the projection behind it has become a necessary part of the work, participating in the composition of the form in the picture, becoming a supplement to the artistic language and a closed loop of the artistic form. At the same time, the concept and meaning of the work is also achieved in the interlacing of the projection and the grid. Finished speculatively. That is, the shadow of the wall is projected to the picture, that is, the symbol of the projection of the painting to the reality. The projection is not only an interesting way to help form the picture, but also a metaphor for the meaning, function and way of existence of the painting.

In another of her works, the concept presented by the interlacing of the projection and the foreground grid is better demonstrated. In this work, the picture itself is distorted, and the grid presents a kind of uneven "fluctuation". Due to the simulation ability of the painting and the viewing habit of a single perspective, the viewer cannot confirm that this "fluctuation" is the brushstroke. The change in the orientation and shape of the painting still comes from the twisting of the canvas itself. At this time, the projection on the background wall produces a different degree of "fluctuation" from the picture, which further proves the state or nature of the work itself. By showing the difference between the two, that is, the difference between plane and three-dimensional, it symbolizes the plane nature of painting and the simulation of space by painting. Its concept is not only a symbol of the existence and meaning of painting, but also the difference between the subject's cognition and the objective world metaphor.

Conceptual painting similar to the exploration of the meaning and existence of painting is not an isolated case. Works with similar concepts can also be seen in the works of other artists, such as Richter's "Window" series, Jonathan Lasker's large number of "grids" "Works, Al Held's (1928–2005) geometric hard-edged paintings all have a similar "grid" appearance. It can be seen that the form of "grid" has a certain degree of universal recognition among artists, not only because of its minimalist appearance, but also because the sense of composition of "grid" symbolizes the movement and transformation between plane and space. For painting, it is naturally critical. From the comparison of Fig. 3 it can be seen that the connection between the works of several artists is not only the similarity of artistic symbols, but also the deep-level conceptual relevance, that is, through the use of painting media characteristics to show the difference between painting reality and real reality. In this process, the historical tradition of painting and the sense of handwork in painting have disappeared one after another, leaving only the symbol of the form of painting, or painting has become a medium for carrying concepts. It can be said that painting has gradually become landscaping under the blessing of concepts. This landscaping is just like the characteristics of the landscape society described by Debord, that is, the sliding from "existence" to "appearance". Although the blessing of concepts has given painting a new dimension of freedom, as far as painting itself is concerned, from the perspective of conceptual painting since the 20th century, painting has become closer to concept, and painting has its own "existence" characteristics. The weaker, the more obvious the "showing" feature.

3   Conceptual Inspiration from the End of Art

Conceptual art's emphasis on conceptuality brings the discussion of the value and meaning behind artistic phenomena to the forefront, which once again connects artistic behavior with philosophical speculation. If conceptual art is concept-oriented, then it can also be said that conceptual art is philosophy-oriented. The emergence of the idea of the end of art has pushed the issue of the relationship between art and philosophy to the culmination, and has continuously triggered intense and in-depth debates on a global scale. The debate about the end of art actually points to fundamental issues such as how art exists, its function, and its value and significance. In the field of contemporary art, when concepts are involved in art, the issues of art disciplines are generally connected with social disciplines and philosophical issues. Thinking about the end of art has profoundly inspired the emergence and development of conceptual art.

In fact, the end point of art and painting has long existed in Europe. In Baudelaire's anthology "The Painter of Modern Life", it is mentioned that as early as BC in Ancient Rome, the architect Marcus Vitruvius (Marcus Vitruvius) Pollio referred to painting as "dying art." The emergence of photography in 1839 completely deprived the narrative function of painting to record reality. After that, a large number of artists, critics, and supporters of new technology have been ruthless on painting. Suddenly, countless views of "painting is over" and "painting is dead" rose rapidly. However, most of the above criticisms or comments are based on artistic phenomena, and do not go deep into the fundamental problems of art, and most of them are out of the system. The true criticism of the fundamental function and significance of art from a historical perspective depends on American art critics. Arthur Coleman Danto's criticism is the most systematic and profound. Danto's theory inherited the ideas of art and philosophy from Plato's aesthetics to Kant's aesthetics, and basically inherited Hegel's views on art and philosophy. The emphasis is different from the art stage described, but they are all in the end. Put forward the conclusion of "the end of art". However, due to translation problems, the term "end" appears extremely harsh and even biased. It is often directly understood as the end of artistic phenomena and artistic behaviors, as if art came to an abrupt end because of its theory. However, art is still happening all the time. Changes are taking place all the time, and a lot of debates and thinking up to this day have come from misunderstandings and misunderstandings of the "end" view.

Arthur Danto's book "The Transfiguration of the Commonplace" (The Transfiguration of the Commonplace) published in 1981 mentioned the end of modernist art towards the Hegelian end, which caused widespread controversy; then, in 1986 The publication of "The Philosophical Disenfranchisement of Art" (The Philosophical Disenfranchisement of Art) caused an uproar in the academic world, but the translation of the name of this book is actually not accurate. Named directly after the end of art; in 1987, the German historian Hans Belting published "The End of Art History?" "Responds to Danto's thesis on art history; in 1997, Danto continued to publish "After the End of Art" (After the End of Art) to unfold what kind of art will look like after the end, and where is the mission of art going. The 1999 article "Hegel's End of Art" (Hegel's End of Art) further elaborated Hegel's point of view, and further sorted out and proved the inheritance relationship of Danto's end of art. Danto combed through the discourses on the relationship between art and philosophy from Plato to Kant, Schopenhauer, and Hegel, and detailed the history of art, especially the history of the relationship between art and philosophy, and finally pointed to the end of art. As soon as the thesis on the "end of art" came out, it triggered discussions and thoughts that lasted for decades and continued to this day.

In Danto's 1999 thesis "The End of Hegel's Art", the opening quoted Hegel's explanation of the concept of art: "Art, in terms of its highest mission, is a thing of the past for us. So it loses the true truth and life for us, but is transferred to our thoughts, instead of maintaining its early necessity and occupying its higher position in reality." Summarized Haig Er's core view of art: that is, the mission of art has become the past, the essence of art has shifted, and the existence of art is no longer necessary to maintain the same way. The "highest vocation" of art proposed by Hegel refers to: "The universal demand for art…is the rational need for human beings to elevate the inner and outer world to his spiritual consciousness as an object, He re-understands himself in it." It can be seen that Hegel's understanding of art is more inclined to art as a symbol of truth, a model of knowing truth, approaching truth, or a way of knowing truth and self. It has a certain acceptance. The religious color of worship and the mission of art also point to the function of adult education and helping people. Therefore, from this perspective, art is a derivative of religious or philosophical truth and is in a subordinate position. By the time Hegel was living, art had drifted away from religious or philosophical truths, and art was no longer the necessary carrier of the "highest mission." Hegel thus saw the sacred and limited behavior of art. The trend towards personal, universal behavior. But then Danto said, "Of course, art will continue to be produced. There will be art after the end of art." He also quoted another passage from Hegel: "Art can be used as a fleeting drama, providing entertainment. And entertainment, decorate our environment, bring joy to the outside of our lives, and make other objects stand out through art decoration." It can be seen that the art after the end mentioned by Danto can represent any role, have any function, and pass any the medium is symbolized, manufactured, and expressed, in Hegel's words, it has become a carrier of the "objective spirit" of society. Therefore, artistic performance and artistic phenomena will continue, but they are different from the previous art, and they no longer have the highest vocation of art. Regarding the conclusion of the end of art, the definition of art is not different. Art before the end is not art after the end, and "end" is not the cessation of artistic creation, but a change of artistic mission.

Therefore, in the follow-up discussion, Danto tried to discuss the basic definition of art in the face of "art after the end", especially the various emerging artistic phenomena in the twentieth century art and the problems behind them. "Art" is a concept that is constantly being debated and changes with history. Today's artistic concept, scope, and meaning are very different from the past. Various books and articles have defined the question of "What is art?". In a general sense, or from a historical perspective, art is basically classified as a macro sociological category. Danto's "institutional definition of art" defines art as an art school, Museums and artists consider art without further formal and detailed definitions. In his "The Transmutation of Ordinary Objects", Danto believes that: "art works are entities that give meaning". In the original text, the word "embodiment" is used, and its original meaning includes materialization, making it an entity meaning. Danto further explained in the Veery magazine: "Art criticism, in addition to content, is actually a way of giving meaning." It further pointed out the connotation of artwork as a meaning-carrying entity, as well as the way in which the artwork gains meaning and the meaning of art criticism. In articles in the 1960s, a series of new titles of art were proposed. For example, in 1964, Danto used the term "artworld" to implicitly indicate the cultural context or "atmosphere of art theory" (atmosphere of art theory), which had a considerable influence on later art criticism and the integration of aesthetic theory and philosophy.

After about 2005, Danto tried to simplify his definition of art into two basic principles: "First, art must have content or meaning; second, art (artwork) must embody this meaning in some appropriate way." From Danto's "principles" we can see that the definition of the conceptual change after the "end" of art has expanded from a certain type and category in history to the combination of substance, content and meaning, that is, the concept and meaning of art. A combination of artistic phenomena; the source of the definition of art or artwork has also expanded from limited groups and organizations in history, such as courts, churches, and literati and intellectual groups serving mainstream values, to broader groups and classes, such as Danto said that the artist group and art academies, art collection institutions and even the general public, the definition of art today is more derived from the general recognition and conventions of the above groups rather than a certain limited mainstream. In short, from the perspective of Danto's "principles", the first principle summarizes artworks as a combination of phenomena and concepts, while the second refers to the level of artistic quality of artworks, that is, the relationship between phenomena and concepts. The level of expression and bearing issues include issues such as work techniques, presentation effects, and the depth of artistic language. It also points out the intervention methods of art criticism, that is, the value and meaning of artworks come from the intervention of art criticism. And give. All in all, from Danto's discourse on the end of art since Hegel, it can be seen that the discourse on the "end" mainly comes from the difference in the definition and mission of art, and the "end" refers to the Hegelian "top the end of the art of "mission", and the art after the "end" no longer has the "highest mission", or at least the purpose and function of art no longer only serve the "highest mission", but become broader and more comprehensive. Ordinary and close to daily life. If art still exists after the "end", and new artistic phenomena, artistic concepts, and broader artistic behaviors are constantly emerging, it can be said that this "end" is a limited "end", the end of a certain stage of art and the direction of art, rather than the end of the overall art. However, it is precisely because of the end of art that contemporary artists are reminded to return to the fundamental and basic problems of art, to intervene in the work with concepts, and to find the value and meaning of the work. From a certain point of view, the "end" thesis testifies to the conceptual turn of contemporary art, proves the rationality of conceptual art, and becomes the theoretical basis of conceptual art. On the other hand, it also stimulated the return of painting, which is an ancient and basic pure art subject. The combination of painting and concept has allowed painting to find new outlets and attachment points in the contemporary era.

References

1. Greenberg, C.: The Collected Essays and Criticism, volume 4: Modernism with a Vengeance, 1957–1969, p. 292. The University of Chicago Press, Chicago (1993)
2. Marcuse, H.: An Essay on Liberation. Beacon Press, Boston (1969)
3. Hegel's Aesthetics: Lectures on Fine Arts, vol. 7. The Clarendon Press, Oxford (1975). Translated by T. M. Knox
4. Danto, A.: The Transfiguration of the Commonplace: A Philosophy of Art. Harvard University Press, Cambridge (1981)
5. Philosopher art critic Arthur C. Danto. Veery J. (2020)
6. Danto, A.: Remarks on Art and Philosophy, pp.113–114. Acadia Summer Arts Program ASAP available through D.A.P./Distributed Art Publishers, New York
7. Dessoir, M.: Aesthetics and the philosophy of art in contemporary Germany. Monist 36(2), 299–310 (1926)
8. Greenberg, C.: The Collected Essays and Criticism, vol. 4, p. 86–87. University of Chicago Press, Chicago (1997)
9. Dufrenne, M.: In the Presence of the Sensuous: Essays in Aesthetics, edited and translated by Mark S. Roberts and Dennis Gallagher, p. 145. Humanities Press, Atlantic Highlands (1987)

10. Polanyi, M.: What is a painting? Am. Sch. **39**(4), 655–669 (1970)
11. Gombrich, E.H.: Art and Illusion: A Study in the Psychology of Pictorial Representation, 6th edn., pp. 4–5. Phaidon Press, London and New York (2002)
12. Polanyi, M.: Science, Economics and Philosophy: Selected Papers of Michael Polanyied. R.T. Allen, pp. 313–328. Transaction Publishers, London (1997)
13. Currie, G.: The Ontology of Art, p. 72, 65, 75. St. Martin's Press, New York (1989)
14. Liscomb, K.: The lyric journey: poetic painting in China and Japan China (review). China Rev. Int. (2011)
15. Liu, J.T.C.: China Turning Inward: Intellectual Political Changes in the Early Twelveth Century. Harvard University Press, Cambridge (1988)
16. Cahill, J.: The Distant Mountains Chinese Painting of the Late Ming Dynasty, pp. 1570–1644. Weatherhill, New York (1982)
17. Jullien, F.: The Great Image Has No Form, on the Nonobject through Painting. The University of Chicago Press (2009)

A Study on the Innovation of Traditional Lacquer Art: The Creation of Paper-Based Lacquer Paintings as an Example

Jin-Shan Shen, Yu-Meng Xiao, and Rungtai Lin[✉]

Graduate School of Creative Industry Design, National Taiwan University of Arts,
New Taipei City 220307, Taiwan
rtlin@mail.ntua.edu.tw

Abstract. With exchanges in politics, economy and culture growing worldwide in recent years, homogeneity has become increasingly serious, which also throws down challenges to the traditional lacquer painting art in the market. This paper attempts to analyze the merits and demerit of traditional lacquer painting art creation so as to apply its merits to the creation of paper-based lacquer paintings, and to explore the possibility of reducing the stereotype of thickness and heavy colors featured by traditional lacquer painting art by changing the materials used in creation. By viewing 3 pieces of paper-based lacquer paintings respectively created at technical, semantic, and effect levels (3 groups of paintings, totaling 9 pieces), viewers were asked to answer three questions in questionnaires related to subjective evaluation. After relevant statistics and analysis, the results show that the innovative paper-based lacquer paintings successfully resonated with the subjects. The innovation in this study helps artists to provide a possible sample for the innovation of traditional lacquer art. There are still many possibilities for the innovation of lacquer art, which will be worth discussing in further research.

Keywords: Artistic creation · Traditional lacquer art · Paper-based lacquer

1 Introduction

The history of Chinese lacquerware shows from the culture of Hemudu that the history of human beings using lacquer is far longer than that of human beings using Chinese characters. From the Neolithic period to the present, Chinese lacquerware has undergone a transformation from simplicity and practicality to artistic quality. With the elapse of time and the change of society, the craftsmanship of lacquerware has become more complicated, delicate and practical. Whether it is traditional lacquerware or contemporary lacquer paintings, "lacquer" is used as the material to realize the corresponding functions and construct its value. The history of traditional Chinese lacquer paintings can be traced back to the slave society. The red lacquer painted wooden bowl unearthed in Zhejiang has a history of more than 7,000 years. Traditional lacquer paintings have reached a high artistic level as early as the Warring States Period. Most of the lacquer paintings

P.-L. P. Rau (Ed.): HCII 2022, LNCS 13312, pp. 255–267, 2022.
https://doi.org/10.1007/978-3-031-06047-2_18

in this period were created on daily utensils, rather than stand-alone easel-based lacquer paintings. Red and black colors were dominant, together with yellow, blue, green, brown, etc. With exquisite shapes and vivid expressions, the paintings on lacquerware created in the Han Dynasty were an important part of the paintings of the Han Dynasty and were influenced by the Chu culture in the adoption of themes. In the early Western Han Dynasty, lacquer paintings were characteristic of cloud, dragon and phoenix, and geometric patterns in diverse forms, as well as many figures and animal patterns. In the middle and late Western Han Dynasty, lacquer paintings were created with more abundant expression techniques, such as lacquer line drawing, oil color line drawing, cone painting, etc. In the Three Kingdoms Period, the lacquerware tended to be of diversification and practicality, and the inlaying technique and color painting technique used in lacquer paintings became more mature. In the Period of Wei, Jin, Southern and Northern Dynasties, the use of a large number of ceramic utensils impacted the leading role of lacquerware in daily utensils, and prompted a change in lacquerware. Lacquer paintings gradually transformed from the practical function to the decorative function. The first monograph on lacquer crafts in the history of China was born in this period, which laid the foundation for traditional lacquer paintings.

Traditional lacquer paintings are mainly created on lacquerware. As a kind of painting material, lacquer needs to be attached to some carriers, commonly known as base or blank, such as woods, bamboos and rattans, leathers, metals, ceramics, horn bones, etc. After painting, the base or blank becomes lacquerware. In addition to lacquer, traditional lacquerware also includes gold, silver, lead, tin, eggshells, shells, stone chips, wood chips and other media materials.

Modern lacquer paintings refer to paintings that exist independently rather than being used as decoration or auxiliary for other handicrafts and utensils, and are created based on a variety of craftsmanship techniques, combining the craftsmanship and pictorial nature. The difference from traditional lacquer paintings is that modern lacquer paintings are completely independent, with more pictorial manifestations, and more emotional and spiritual expressions [1].

Since the launch of the "Chinese National Folk Culture Protection Project" in 2003, traditional lacquer painting techniques have been included in the first batch of national intangible cultural heritage lists [2, 3]. Then, as far as China's current situation is concerned, there are certain difficulties in the dissemination of the lacquerware industry. The disadvantage of the development of modern Chinese lacquer art lies in the limitation of its practicality. In order to enhance the practicality of lacquer art, it is necessary to enhance its sense of design and originality at the beginning of creation. Through multiple thinking and exploration, attempts have been made to increase the experimentation and creativity of the works by inheriting and innovating on the traditional lacquer art, integrating contemporary elements, and organically combining theory and practice. It should be deeply realized that the single road to develop traditional lacquer art is quite narrow, and we must start to pay attention to the diversity of lacquer materials, attach importance to cultural expressions, try to combine lacquer with a variety of new media materials in order to make breakthroughs and get more room for development in the field of lacquer art. In the creation of traditional lacquer painting creation, it presents a relatively heavy and ancient effect visually due to the limitation of the plane space of the lacquer painted wooden frame. If we can break through and change the materials, a light and cheerful visual effect can be realized.

Based on the above background and motivation, the detailed purpose of this study is to: discuss the viewer's degree of resonance with paper-based lacquer paintings at the "semantic level", "effect level" and "technical level" after the application of traditional lacquer painting to paper-based creation.

2 Literature Review

2.1 Craftsmanship of Traditional Lacquer Paintings

The raw materials used in the lacquer painting process is "natural lacquer" obtained by cutting the original sap from the lacquer tree, which turns brown after contact with the air and the surface of which solidifies and hardens to form lacquer after a few hours. Lacquer paintings are characteristic of unique craftsmanship, exquisite materials, and excellent production and so on, and are purely hand-made in the entire craft process, so it is difficult in the craftsmanship. The processes include: plate making, copying, material inlaying, paint filling, colored drawing, lacquer covering, grinding, brightening and so on [4]. Lacquer paintings feature anti-corrosion and moisture-proof, stable form, strong color stability, long-lasting, etc. It has strong technological characteristics and unique artistic value [5].

As far as a lacquer painting concerned, the most important craft techniques mainly include the following: First, inlaying. Second, over-dyeing. Third, maki-e making, namely color painting by use of maki-e powder. Fourth, colored drawing. Fifth, variable coating. Sixth, embossed lacquer. Modern lacquer paintings are created in relatively common processes. The first is the bottom layer drawing, which requires a certain treatment of the bottom plate. After the bottom layer meets the requirements of smoothness and flatness, it is further processed through various techniques such as grinding or inlaying to lay a solid foundation for subsequent creations. The second is the middle-layer painting, which generally forms the prototype of the work through techniques such as inlaying, pre-embedding, and maki-e making. The third is to complete the painting, which is the last stage of the lacquer painting technique, and determines the basic tone of the picture. In this stage, main painting methods include the lacquer decoration, the over-dyeing method and the multi-layer method. After grinding and painting decoration, and other techniques, the works shows the final effect. The above just shows a general procedure and creative process. Different lacquer works have more detailed technical requirements. Through the integration of more techniques, lacquer works can finally be created completely and expectations are met according to the ideas of lacquer painters, and even bring unexpected surprises. According to the different types of lacquer paintings created, some of the lacquer paintings are covered with a layer of transparent varnish after the final completion so as to protect the effect of the picture and prolong the shelf life of the works.

Based on the essential characteristics of lacquer paintings, craftsmanship is an indispensable part of lacquer paintings. In the absence of the craftsmanship, the works cannot be called lacquer paintings. In this regard, this is even admitted by the lacquer painters who are in a pure pursuit of the pictoriality. In the process of realizing the pictoriality, they still need to rely on certain craftsmanship, which is the premise and foundation. From this point of view, the display of pictoriality will not affect the development of craftsmanship, and the two are complementary to each other.

2.2 Predicament and Development of Traditional Lacquer Paintings

Traditional handicrafts must be based on the development and inheritance of contemporary life, but when it comes to a lacquer painting, the first impression is a work of art. Lacquer paintings are expensive and mysterious, passively in a state of "too high to be popular". With a long creation period and expensive price, lacquer paintings are in the high-end market, far away from daily life.

Creation of lacquer art is a complex process. Traditional lacquer paintings are produced in a long cycle and the output is low [6]. The bases are made after basic materials are fully prepared. It usually takes three to four months to make the base body. The fabric, scraping ash, and painting of each process need to be polished and should meet the specific process requirements and standards; it takes a long time to carve the body and dry the paint layer. These are mechanically irreplaceable [7]. A good piece of work often takes one to two years, resulting in lower production volumes and correspondingly higher product prices [2]. Therefore, the lacquer painting industry cannot meet the market demand, hindering its development.

Traditional lacquer art has a history of thousands of years, and in the process of creating modern lacquer paintings, traditional media materials are still attracting attention, and the use of various new media materials has brought great help to the creation of lacquer paintings. In order to achieve innovation based on inheritance of tradition, it is necessary to explore new media materials and new artistic language of media materials so that modern lacquer painting creation has more choices so as to create a richer form of media language. Combining traditional craft techniques to promote the diversified development of lacquer painting creation is the inevitable choice for the sustainable development and growth of modern lacquer paintings in the future, and it is also the inherent development needs.

A single path to develop traditional lacquer art is quite narrow, and we must start to pay attention to the diversity of lacquer materials, attach importance to cultural expressions, try to combine lacquer with a variety of new media materials in order to make breakthroughs and get more room for development in the field of lacquer art.

2.3 Mentality of Artistic Creation

The American empiricist philosopher John Dewey said: "Most of us want to be artists, all that we lack is not the emotion to activate, nor the skill to operate, but the ability of thought and emotion to express a vagueness according to a certain medium" [8].

The Chinese believe in the philosophy of the unity of man and nature, and follow the principle of freehand brushwork in creation, and regard both form and spirit as a specific requirement for carrying out activities. As early as the 4th century AD, Xie He, a native of the Southern Qi Dynasty during the Period of Wei, Jin, Southern and Northern Dynasties, proposed "six methods" in his art theoretical work "Paintings", namely vigorous artistic conception, vigour of strokes, similarity in form, colors assignment according to the types, composition of a picture, and imitation and heritance. Zhang Yanyuan, an art theorist in the Tang Dynasty, also mentioned in his "Records of Famous Paintings in the Past Dynasties" that in the artistic creation, if a painting is "stiff, similar in shape without vigour of strokes, weak in brushwork, and only good in coloring, it is not wonderful" [9]. Among them, "vigorous artistic conception" is the highest realm that artists expect to see in creative practices.

Therefore, artists are the subject of artistic creation, and their subjectivity and self-cultivation are essential. At the same time, the source of spirit is also the basis of artistic creation. Only by integrating various basic creative techniques can they "work out the plot before putting pen to paper". For the realm of "beautiful or talented painting" in artistic creation, it is necessary to deal with the relationship between conception and brush use (see Fig. 1).

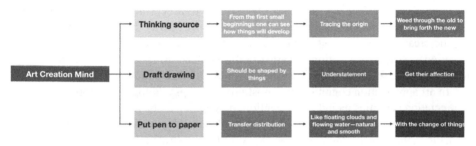

Fig. 1. Flow chart of the new artistic creation method.

2.4 Viewers' Resonance with Lacquer Works

Artists are getting an increasingly stronger connection with viewers. For effective communication in artworks, they need to be meaningful, understandable, memorable, etc. [10]. To evaluate a works of art, we need to better understand the communication between the artist and the viewer, not only to participate in the social context, but also to develop the interactive experience between the artist and the viewer [11]. On communication researching, questions have been identified in communication researches at three levels: technical, semantic, and effect levels. At the technical level, it requires to learn the attractive force against the viewer through his/her sense organs. At the semantic level, it requires the viewer to understand exactly what the message means through his/her implementation. At the effect level, it involves the way the viewer properly reflects through his/her influence [12, 13].

3   The Methods of Study

3.1   Research Structure

This study has been conducted in four stages: clarifying research questions, reviewing and sorting out the literature, analyzing and practicing the creation, and research findings and discussion (see Fig. 2).

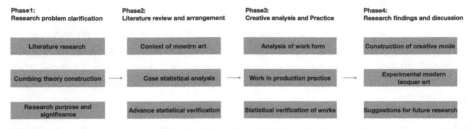

Fig. 2. Flow chart of this study.

Artists have different understandings of artistic creation, and their creative methods are also inconsistent. Some artists emphasize improvisation and intuition, and are very optimistic about creative passion and imagination. However, some artists tend to be rational and ideological, and they will choose to accept the guidance of aesthetic theories, the selection of themes and the application of methods. In terms of the entire artistic creation process, both are inseparable from three specific links, namely artistic experience, artistic conception and artistic communication. These also correspond to the technical level, semantic level and effect level of artistic creation.

In art appreciation cognition, the most prominent psychological factors in aesthetic appreciation activities include the attention, perception, association, imagination, emotion and understanding. They are independent of each other while they also interact with each other, forming a complete aesthetic psychological structure. Under the active action of this structure, the aesthetic re-creation of art appreciation activities can be realized. The conduct of art appreciation activities is inseparable from the interaction of various aesthetic psychological factors, mainly composed of three levels: aesthetic intuition, aesthetic experience and aesthetic sublimation. It has the established characteristics of the present, and it seems that an aesthetic appreciation activity is completed in an instant without thinking [14].

According to the cognitive model as the research framework, after a traditional lacquer painting is created on paper, the paper-based lacquer painting has a resonance for the viewers at the "semantic level", "effect level" and "technical level" (see Fig. 3). Nine descriptive expressions are used as the metrics to evaluate the creation of paper-based lacquer paintings. At the semantic level, the metrics include incomparable grace, vivid charm, and vigorous artistic conception; At the effect level, the metrics include fine resemblance, lifelikeness, and acme of perfection; At the technical level, the metrics include prominent personality, talented painting and high degree of professional proficiency.

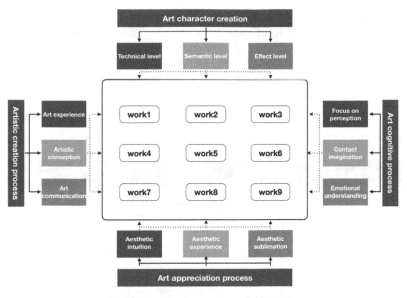

Fig. 3. Research structure of this study.

3.2 Tested Samples

The research samples were created by the creators who transfer the merits of traditional lacquer paintings into the creation of paper-based lacquer paintings. A total of 9 pieces of works were selected as the tested samples (see Fig. 4). The lacquer painting works are mainly selected from the series of abstract figures, which are analyzed and discussed through 9 metrics.

Fig. 4. Samples tested in this study.

3.3 Data Collection Method

The questionnaires are distributed in the form of an online questionnaire. The questionnaires include two parts. The first part is the basic data, and the second part is the subjective evaluation. The 9 tested samples were evaluated according to the metrics at "technical level", "semantic level" and "effect level". This study uses the Likert scale to explore the degree of resonance of the viewers with paper-based lacquer paintings at the "technical level", "semantic level" and "effect level" (see Table 1). Scores were measured by use of Likert scale, 1 = Strongly Disagree, 2 = Disagree, 3 = Neutral, 4 = Agree, 5 = Strongly Agree.

Table 1. Questionnaire on the degree of resonance of viewers with paper-based lacquer paintings.

Pictures	Metrics	Levels
P1 P2 P3	prominent personality	technical level
	talented painting	
	high degree of professional proficiency	
P4 P5 P6	incomparable grace	semantic level
	vivid charm	
	vigorous artistic conception	
P7 P8 P9	fine resemblance	effect level
	acme of perfection	
	lifelikeness	

4   Result and Discussion

4.1   Questionnaire Results

In this study, 130 questionnaires were distributed through the Internet, and 109 valid questionnaires were recovered. 59 boys and 50 girls; 38 persons aged 18–25, 31 persons aged 26–30, 27 persons aged 31–40, 13 persons aged 41–50; 0 person with high school education or below, 24 persons with high school education, and 72 persons with bachelor's degree, 10 persons with graduate degree and 3 persons with doctoral degree; 35 persons from the design department, 42 persons from the art department, and 32 persons from other departments (see Table 2).

Table 2. Demographics.

		Frequency	Percentage (%)
Sex	Male	59	54.13
	Female	50	45.87
Age	0–18	43.9	43.9
	18–25	38	34.86
	26–30	31	28.44
	31–40	27	24.77
	41–50	13	11.93
Level of education	Below high school	0	43.9
	High school	24	22.02
	Bachelor degree	72	66.06
	Graduate degree	10	9.17
	Doctoral degree	3	2.75
Educational background	Design department	35	32.11
	Art department	43	38.53
	Others	32	29.36

This study uses spss26.0 for statistical analysis and verification. The reliability and validity of the questionnaire were analyzed. The results show that the overall Cronbach α value of each dimension and scale is >0.7, which means that the scale has high homogeneity and good reliability. The results of the reliability analysis show that the standardized reliability coefficient is 0.942. Because the reliability coefficient after item deletion is less than the 0.942, the scale is of high internal consistency and high reliability (see Table 3). In the validity analysis, the method of exploratory factor analysis was adopted to realize the test process. The KMO sampling suitability test and Bartlett's spherical test were performed on the questionnaire sample data. The test results show that the KMO value is 0.942, and the X2 value of Bartlett's spherical test is 731.114, reaching a significant level ($P = 0.000 < 0.05$), indicating that the questionnaire data are suitable for factor analysis. The mean and standard deviations (see Table 4 and Table 5) were obtained after evaluating the 9 samples of all subjects at the "technical level", "semantic level", and "effect level".

Table 3. The reliability results of this study.

Dimension	Cronbach Alpha	Number of items
Technical level	0.841	3
Semantic level	0.836	3
Effect level	0.806	3
Overall scale	0.942	9

Table 4. Overall evaluation scores (P1–P5).

Metrics	P1	P2	P3	P4	P5
Prominent personality	4.06 (1.145)	3.91 (1.159)	3.98 (1.247)	3.83 (1.190)	3.83 (1.221)
Talented painting	3.91 (1.183)	3.95 (1.057)	3.83 (1.258)	3.88 (1.275)	3.84 (1.256)
High degree of professional proficiency	4.03 (1.118)	4.02 (1.202)	3.89 (1257)	4.05 (1.109)	3.99 (1.159)
Incomparable grace	4.08 (1.029)	3.91 (1.183)	3.92 (1.131)	3.85 (1.145)	4.02 (1.138)
Vivid charm	4.02 (1.130)	3.91 (1.159)	3.85 (1.238)	3.83 (1.213)	3.88 (1.223)
Vigorous artistic conception	3.93 (1.025)	3.99 (1.058)	3.85 (1.193)	3.86 (1.058)	3.99 (1.050)
Fine resemblance	4.06 (1.141)	4.01 (1.243)	3.81 (1.280)	3.81 (1.280)	3.87 (1.285)
Lifelikeness	4.03 (1.190)	3.99 (1.167)	3.75 (1.263)	3.85 (1.193)	3.91 (1.221)
Acme of perfection	4.04 (1.071)	3.96 (1.146)	3.83 (1.261)	3.90 (1.239)	4.03 (1.158)

Table 5. Overall evaluation scores (P6–P9).

Metrics	P6	P7	P8	P9
Prominent personality	3.83 (1.253)	3.72 (1.292)	3.89 (.972)	3.98 (1.186)
Talented painting	3.90 (1.146)	3.78 (1.166)	4.17 (.887)	4.06 (1.161)
High degree of professional proficiency	4.03 (1.158)	3.86 (1.205)	4.17 (.967)	3.93 (1.144)
Incomparable grace	3.94 (1.212)	3.87 (1.226)	4.24 (.912)	3.90 (1.097)
Vivid charm	3.84 (1.263)	3.84 (1.218)	4.13 (.914)	4.03 (1.023)
Vigorous artistic conception	3.94 (1.116)	3.97 (.995)	4.33 (.850)	3.98 (1.194)
Fine resemblance	3.96 (1.105)	3.79 (1.255)	4.17 (.995)	4.01 (1.190)
Lifelikeness	3.92 (1.218)	3.79 (1.123)	4.21 (.924)	3.81 (1.174)
Acme of perfection	4.01 (1.101)	3.89 (1.220)	4.23 (.968)	4.22 (1.100)

The Friedman test was used to evaluate the metric scores of each picture. The P values of the first eight pictures are all greater than 0.05, that is, there was no difference between the metric scores. Only the picture 9 has an X2 value of 24.70 and a P value of 0.002, indicating that the picture 9 has differences in the metric scores. After pairwise comparison, in the comparison of only the score of acme of perfection with the score of lifelikeness, the adjusted significant P value is 0.003, and in the other pairwise comparisons, all P values are >0.05. This shows that although the picture 9 has the highest score of acme of perfection, it is only significantly higher than the score of lifelikeness, but not significantly higher than the scores of other metrics (see Table 6 and Table 7).

By taking the technical-level metrics as dependent variables, analysis has been conducted on the influence of sex, age, educational background, and educational level on the technical-level values. The results of ANOVAs analysis show that the significant P values of sex, age, educational background, and educational level are all >0.05. Therefore, differences in sex, age, educational background, and educational level would not affect the technical-level values. At the same time, the interaction between sex, age, educational background, and educational level would not affect the technical-level values.

By taking semantic-level metrics as dependent variables, analysis has been conducted on the influence of sex, age, educational background, and educational level on the semantic-level values. The results of ANOVAs analysis show that the significant P values of sex, age, educational background, and educational level are all >0.05. Therefore, differences in sex, age, educational background, and educational level would not affect the semantic-level values. At the same time, the interaction between sex, age, educational background, and educational level would not affect the semantic-level values.

By taking effect-level metrics as dependent variables, analysis has been conducted on the influence of sex, age, educational background, and educational level on the semantic-level values. The results of ANOVAs analysis show that the significant P values of sex, age, educational background, and educational level are all >0.05, and only the P value of educational background is <0.05. Therefore, differences in sex, age, and education level would not affect the effect-level values, but educational background would. However, the interaction between sex, age, educational background, and educational level did not affect the effect-level values.

In general, the subjects will not have different perception at the "technical level", "semantic level" and "effect level" of paper-based lacquer paintings out of sex, age, educational background and educational level, indicating that the innovation of paper-based lacquer paintings can be accepted by the public.

Table 6. Friedman test results of pictures 1–4 metrics.

	P1		P2		P3		P4	
	Mean	Std.	Mean	Std.	Mean	Std.	Mean	Std.
Prominent personality	4.06	1.145	3.91	1.159	3.98	1.247	3.83	1.190
Talented painting	3.91	1.183	3.95	1.057	3.83	1.258	3.88	1.275
High degree of professional proficiency	4.03	1.118	4.02	1.202	3.89	1.257	4.05	1.109
Incomparabe grace	4.08	1.029	3.91	1.183	3.92	1.131	3.85	1.145
Vivid charm	4.02	1.130	3.91	1.159	3.85	1.238	3.83	1.213
Vigorous artistic conception	3.93	1.025	3.99	1.058	3.85	1.193	3.86	1.058
Fine resemblance	4.06	1.141	4.01	1.243	3.81	1.280	3.81	1.280
Lifelikeness	4.03	1.190	3.99	1.167	3.75	1.263	3.85	1.193
Acme of perfection	4.04	1.071	3.96	1.146	3.83	1.261	3.90	4.01
Chi-square value	7.407		4.177		9.025		7.303	8.903
P value	0.493		0.841		0.340		0.504	0.351

Table 7. Friedman test results of pictures 5–9 metrics.

P5		P6		P7		P8		P9	
Mean	Std.	Mean	Std.	Mean	Std.	Mean	Std.	Mean	Std.
4.06	1.145	3.91	1.159	3.98	1.247	3.83	1.190	3.98	1.186
3.91	1.183	3.95	1.057	3.83	1.258	3.88	1.275	4.06	1.161
4.03	1.118	4.02	1.202	3.89	1.257	4.05	1.109	3.93	1.144
4.08	1.029	3.91	1.183	3.92	1.131	3.85	1.145	3.90	1.097
4.02	1.130	3.91	1.159	3.85	1.238	3.83	1.213	4.03	1.023
3.93	1.025	3.99	1.058	3.85	1.193	3.86	1.058	3.98	1.194
4.06	1.141	4.01	1.243	3.81	1.280	3.81	1.280	4.01	1.190
4.03	1.190	3.99	1.167	3.75	1.263	3.85	1.193	3.81	1.174
4.04	1.071	3.96	1.146	3.83	1.261	3.90	4.01	4.22	1.100
7.407		4.177		9.025		7.303	8.903	24.698	
0.493		0.841		0.340		0.504	0.351	0.002	

5 Conclusion and Suggestion

In line with the changes of the times, the main consumers are young and middle-aged people. Therefore, this survey was conducted in the form of online questionnaires distributed to respondents aged 18–50. Analysis on metrics at the "technical level", "semantic level" and "effect level" shows that young and middle-aged people can resonate with innovative ways of lacquer paintings. The innovation in this study helps artists to provide a sample for the researching into the innovation of traditional lacquer art. The creation of lacquer paintings should also constantly update the concepts so as to give lacquer paintings more connotations and make lacquer paintings reflect richer artistic charm. There are still many possibilities for lacquer art innovation, which will be worthy of further research and discussion.

References

1. Wu, P.L.: On the future of lacquer painting. In: Popular Literature and Art, vol. 15, p. 36 (2012)
2. Xu, S.S.: Analysis of the protection, inheritance and development of Chinese lacquer art. Mass Lit. **22**, 37 (2014)
3. Liu, X.: From ware to art: evolvement of Chengdu lacquer art. J. Hundred Sch. Arts **1**, 172–176 (2012)
4. Chen, E.S.: Contemporary Lacquer Painting. Chongqing Publishing House, Chongqing (2003)
5. Wang, H.: The spread of lacquer art (2003)
6. Teke, S.G.: Living heritages and fixed traditions in the lists of the convention for the safeguarding of intangible cultural heritage. Milli Folk **120**, 19–31 (2018)
7. Song, B.: Traditional Handicraft Techniques in the View of Intangible Cultural Heritage Protection—Beijing Lacquer as an Example. China Academy of Art, Beijing (2010)
8. John, D.: Art as Experience, p. 74. Minton Balch, New York (1934)
9. Zhang, Y.Y.: Records of Famous Paintings in Past Dynasties. On the Six Laws of Painting, vol. 1. People's Fine Arts Publishing House (1963)
10. Porter, A., McMaken, J., Hwang, J., Yang, R.: Common core standards the new US intended curriculum. Educ. Res. **40**(3), 103–116 (2011)
11. Goldman, A.: Evaluating art. In: The Blackwell Guide to Aesthetics, pp. 93–108 (2004)
12. Craig, R.T.: Communication theory as a field. Commun. Theor. **9**(2), 119–161 (1999)
13. Fiske, J.: Introduction to Communication Studies. Routledge, London (2010)
14. Tong, Y.: Ten Lectures on Art. Xiamen University Press, Xiamen (2014)

Research on the Relationships Between Humans and Printed Photos in the Digital Era

Lintao Tang[1,2] and Qiuhua Li[1(✉)]

[1] Academy of Arts and Design, Tsinghua University, Beijing, China
82978032@qq.com
[2] Alexander Von Humboldt Foundation, Berlin, Germany

Abstract. In the digital era, there are still a large number of photos being printed instantly. These instant photographs can be seen as an indispensable approach for human beings to perceive their interactions with the society. In this study, ethnographic interviews, visual diaries and a creative workshop are conducted to investigate photo-printer users' motivation and to explore their photo-using scenarios. From sociological and designing perspectives, four relationships between humans and printed photos are explored—documentary, narrative, self-representation and anchor. This study contributes to increasing the understanding of the relationship and will inspire designers in developing relative innovative products, services and systems.

Keywords: Cross-cultural product and service design · Design research · Interdisciplinarity · Design methods · Product design · Printed photo

1 Introduction

The popularity of smartphones makes photo-taking a common behaviour in ordinary people's daily lives. These photos are normally stored digitally and spread widely via social media. The mass production, aggregation, dissemination and consumption of such private images mentioned above are an important part of "visual culture". However, in the time of digital images and social media networking, there are still a large number of photos being printed "instantly". The hot sales of Mi® photo printers is a strong proof of this phenomenon. The product was launched for crowdfunding at Mi.com in December 2018, and it exceeded 20,000 units within just 8 h. At present, the annual sales volume of this product is approximately 500, 000 units, accounting for about half of the market share in China. Its avid users print more than 300 photos per year, which means almost once a day on average.

Questions raised by this phenomenon are as follows. Devices such as cellphones, computers, portable hard disks, cloud servers and digital photo frames have already enlarged the space to store photos. Besides, with the help of information and communication technology (ICT), social networking platforms such as Facebook®, Twitter® and WeChat® have become the main media for photo spreading and sharing. Nonetheless, why on earth are photo printers still in high demand? What types of differences exist on

P.-L. P. Rau (Ed.): HCII 2022, LNCS 13312, pp. 268–282, 2022.
https://doi.org/10.1007/978-3-031-06047-2_19

using experiences between "digital photos" and "printed photos"? The issue discussed here seems to concern about the relationship between humans and photo printers, but actually about the relationship between humans and printed photos. The printers are no more than a bridging tool to acquire photos. An ultimate question is what kind of relationship exists between humans and printed photos in this digital time?

This essay will apply ethnographic interview, visual diary and lead a creative workshop to analyse the process of people's photo printing behaviour and the scenarios of using photos and to explore the reasons of photo printing for people living in the time of digital images, so that the relationship between humans and printed photos can be constructed and the evidence can be provided for future design innovation of relevant products, services or systems.

2 Methodology

2.1 Methods in this Study

This study mainly uses the method of qualitative research to explore the relationship between humans and printed photos. Three specific methods for the investigation, namely, ethnographic interviews (Spradley 2016), visual diaries (Wimmer and Dominck 2003) and creative workshops (Steen et al. 2011) were adopted. Firstly, the ethnographic interview (Spradley 2016) analysed the relationship between humans and printed photos by investigating motivations and behaviours of photo printer users and observing photo-using scenarios. Secondly, the visual diary (Wimmer and Dominck 2003) acts as a supplementing method and reveals relevant contents that are not discovered by the first ethnographic interview method. Lastly, in the creative workshops (Steen et al. 2011), representative users and experts with different academic backgrounds, including professions in designing, sociology and communication, are invited to co-design (Kohtala et al. 2020), discuss and reflect findings from the previous two methods. The purpose is to verify the hypothesis in the theory and explore possibilities of innovation for future products, services and systems (See Fig. 1). Using more than one research method can provide multiple perspectives and greater effectiveness, thereby increasing the credibility of the results (Robson and McCartan 2016).

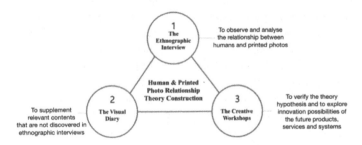

Fig. 1. The investigation methodology

2.2 Sampling

Considering how factors such as users' gender, status, household structure influence the motivation of photo printing and scenarios of using photos, a non-probability sampling, as Babbie (2013) refers as quota sampling, was used in this study with reasonable distributions for each characteristic. Participants of both males and females are sampled; the dimension of status covered students, white-collar workers, caretakers and the retired; the household-structure dimension covered families of single persons, couples and families with children. Based on the fact that more photos are printed by the females, the quota for female samples was increased. Frequent users who printed more than 300 photos per year and regular users were sampled. The above-mentioned investigations select 32 participants in total. Based on Nielsen's experiences, in some qualitative studies, more than 80% of the problems can be found with 8 samples, while in quantitative studies, statistically significant results can be reached with 30 samples. The total number and detailed description of participants in each investigation are shown in Table 1.

Table 1. Descriptions about the investigation participants

Investigation	Total number of participants	Gender (M/F)
The ethnographic interview	15	5/10
The visual diary	6	1/5
The creative workshop	11	6/5

2.3 Ethnographic Interview

Fifteen typical users who purchased the household printer were interviewed and observed (Wimmer and Dominck 2003) in the first ethnographic interview. Aspects such as printing causes, theme preference, printing process as well as the scenarios of using photos are investigated. The purpose is to find out users' deeper demand of printing photos under the surface and the possible relationship between humans and printed photos, which is conducive to lay a foundation for the upcoming methods of visual diary and creative workshop. The interview used Krippendorff's (2006) semi-structured design theory. Three sections were included in the interview, ice-breaking section (questions about personal background and lifestyles were included), motive and behaviour section (questions concerning the frequency and process of photo printing were included), and scenario section (questions investigating the space, place and way of positioning photos were included). A voice recorder was used during interviews, with approximately 30 min duration of each time. The audio files were transcribed into the text file afterwards.

2.4 Visual Diary

The subsequent investigation invited six representative users to accomplish their visual diaries (Blighe et al. 2008) that contain images and texts. Researchers provided the participants with the framework for the content of diaries so that the submitted diaries were relevantly and effectively aligned with the theme of this study. The framework was composed of three parts, namely a participants' persona (age, gender, household type), home environment and the story behind a typically printed photo. The frame of the photo story, in specific, should contain the theme, time, place, event of this photo. Besides, contents such as the reason for printing the photo, the location of the photo and the significance of the photo were also necessarily consisted. Visual diaries in details represent how the photos were used. They reflect the relationship between the human and the printed photo. Therefore, the second investigation verifies and supplements the findings found from the first ethnographic interview.

2.5 Creative Workshop

In the following creative workshops (See Fig. 2), 11 participants were invited and divided into two groups. These participants were composed of students in the fields of designing, sociology and communicating and retired professors, who also have a habit of printing photos daily. Participatory design (Cooper 2019) and design as research (Lawson 2002) were applied. Through note-taking and voice-recording, the whole investigation process of the creative workshop was recorded. In the initial ten minutes, the host introduced the theme of the workshop and the instructions of ice-breaking activities. Then, formal activities were divided into three sections. In the first section, all the participants expressed how they print and use photos daily as printer users. In the second section, the host first shared with the participants the findings discovered from the previous two types of investigations. Then, participants were asked to express their opinions and insights from different academic perspectives concerning the relationship between humans and printed photos. In the third section, participants with various academic backgrounds were invited to co-design the future products, services and systems in the greatest prospect.

In order to collect all the opinions of the participants and to minimise the distraction from each other, participants were asked to write down their opinions and insights on stickers and then discuss them in groups, especially on key questions such as the motivation of printing photos, scenarios of using photos and the possibilities of innovating. By organising the workshop in this structure, each participant's opinion was fully expressed and exchanged with others. After the discussion, these opinions were classified, summarised, analysed and completely comprehended by researchers.

Fig. 2. The creative workshop

3 Data Analysis

In the recent decade, smartphones have replaced conventional digital cameras and become the main gadget for people to acquire photos. The convenience of the equipment enables individuals to produce, store, share and use photos. The photo stands for a captured personal experience, which is a grammar that can be visualised. It is the photo that puts humans into a position that connects with the outer world (Sontag 2010). Nowadays, as long as smartphones are at hand, everything around us will be potential objects to be acquired. However, acquiring the photos is merely the onset of connecting with the world, the subsequent storing, selecting, editing, online sharing, printing and using further present the existing relationship within the human, with others and with the outer world (See Fig. 3). Notwithstanding the internet age makes digital photos a mainstream of sharing photos, this study still focuses on analysing and contemplating how people use printed photos to establish various relationship: documentary, narrative, self-representation and anchor.

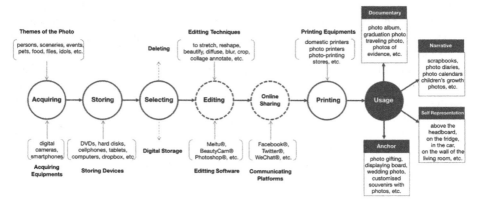

Fig. 3. The production and use of photos

3.1 Acquiring

The acquisition of the photos is intentional, therefore it is a process of subjective perceiving. The time, space, person and objects that intentionally captured by photographing might be a classmate reunion, a family ceremony or an emergent event. The theme and content of the people's photo-taking reveal what they see, or to be precise, what they see intentionally. In the context of a consumer society and a spectacle society, the themes of the photos are no longer constrained in those traditional persons, sceneries or events. The themes can also include pets, food, files, idols, etc., which lead to a statement of the French sociologist Barthes (1980), a photo is a 'Tuche', meaning an opportunity, a contemporary encounter between subject and the world.

3.2 Storing

Digital photo storing methods include digital video discs (DVDs), hard disks, the cell-phone, the tablet, and the dropbox. The advantages of digital storing of photos are the large storing space, and the convenience for duplicating and online editing; the obvious disadvantage is that it is difficult to find out one particular photo from a large number of unclassified photos. Some photos are even hardly seen for another time. To avoid the damage or change of the storing equipment, people may store these photos in multiple devices, which further undermines the photo management.

3.3 Selecting

When confronting with a large number of digital photos, people usually select the photos with conscious and caution and then delete, remain or edit the photos afterwards. Selecting is a prerequisite of the following three actions, which can be seen as a judgment of the value on the good or the bad, the beautiful or the ugly, the useful or the useless, the worthwhile or the unworthy. Selecting implied and signifies a series of standards on values. The standards may evolve from the psychology of individuals, the shape of the society or the cultural concepts. Selecting acts as a filter of the photos, which is similar to the behaviour of house cleaning. In this sense, the space-purifying process is also a self-purifying journey. Those deleted or stored digital photos are not the studying samples of this essay. The emphasis is on printed photos.

3.4 Editing

Editing is a form of reality distortion. Due to the popularity of image-editing software such as Meitu®, BeautyCam® and Photoshop®, people prefer to use the techniques to edit their real self into an ideal-self prior to sharing these photos online or printing them. By editing, the connection between humans and the world is stretched, reshaped, beautified, diffused, blurred, cropped, collaged and annotated. In a nutshell, a new relationship between self and the world, an illusion, is created. After taking, storing and selecting the photos, editing becomes a filtering lens that embedded between the self and the world. Unedited photos can be regarded as the raw materials, which can be stored yet are not entitled to be spread, presented and viewed.

3.5 Online Sharing

Sharing photos via network communication is the current mainstream lifestyle and will be in the future. In such a lifestyle, people show their life stories in public and reconfirm their existence on social media, WeChat® for instance. Everything happens behind the screen. The use of the photos in an above-mentioned way is out of the range of this essay. However, photo sharing in the virtualised world may become the innovation source of real things. The garbage bins existing in the real world have become a metaphor of deleting files, therefore it is the turn for the current design to attempt to transfer symbols, approach and relationships in the virtual world into the reality.

3.6 Printing

Whether it is food pictures taken by food lovers, children pictures taken by the elderly or scenery pictures taken by tourists, as long as they are printed, the moments of those pictures are selective, highlighted beautiful memories, a chosen eternity of that-has-been (Barthes 1980). Printing is a key step to materialising and objectifying images, where there are normally two ways of accomplishing it.

In the age of the film and sheet, photos can only be obtained with the help of photo printing stores. In 1998, Epson®, a Japanese technology company, had its product launch of Stylus Photo 700 printer, which is the onset of serving households to achieve the output of the photos. Household printers are more convenient and effective, while photo printing stores not only print photos but also provide extension services of manufacturing annual calendars, albums, brochures, customised photo artworks and souvenirs. In recent years, photo printers are smaller-sized professional domestic output applicants. By the technique of the heat sublimation, photo printers reached the standard of printing stores on colour quality and realise the real-time image processing by information and communication technology (ICT), which is a permanent demand developed in the time of Polaroid®. The latest photo printer usually has the effect of camera filter, the processing techniques of cropping and picture composing and the technique of automatic lamination that increase the durability of the photo.

3.7 Usage

After printing, the most common way of using photos are displaying, gifting, collecting and making scrapbooks (See Fig. 4), which are the focus of this study. In the ethnographic interview, it is found that the printed photos are frequently displayed on the wall of the living room, on the refrigerator, above the bedroom headboard, on the table or the bookshelf and on the television cabinet. The position of the photos turns these spaces into places. A place means security, indicating the core of people's values, a place that they can rest their vision, emotion and thoughts. For instance, a family photo on the refrigerator is a company and a symbol of living together, which implies "we are being together all the time".

Photos are printed to send to others as a gift. One of the participants in the creative workshop claim that once on a birthday party of his classmate, he printed out photos of two of them, their favourite idol and some special sceneries of their shared memories and made them an exhibition board with words. He then raised the board highly to celebrate his classmate's birthday. Such behaviour imitates how the fans interact with the superstar. One of the senior participants told the researcher, as a frequent patient of the hospital, she occasionally prints out photos with annotation as a gift card to show her gratitude to the doctors, which assembles the gift flags that materialise their compliments. Besides, in the occasion of a family reunion, to send out photos that are instantly printed out to others as the gifts have more sense of ritual than sending digital photos on social media thereby is more emotional on the scene.

Additionally, people have a careful arrangement for those printed photos. They organise these photos into chronological order or logic of their interrelations and make a photo collection in the family albums, which is a rigorous sorting and filing process. Collecting photos is virtually recollecting memories. For example, one student selected some of the best photos to edit and collect them physically into an album; a mother sorted and collect printed photos of her child according to different stages of children's development; an elderly printed out his photos and force his children to make a collection.

Further, photos are the necessary raw materials to make scrapbooks. A young participant printed her selfies, photos of the pet, food and superstars and made them into a scrapbook. Scrapbook making behaviour is a process of compiling her personal life stories. Printed photos are indispensable materials of images, which are a kind of visual evidence.

Fig. 4. The usage of the printed photos

4 Finding

From the findings mentioned above, this essay classifies the relationship between humans and printed photos into four categories, namely documentary, narrative, self-representation and anchor (See Fig. 5). Such comprehension is based on an assumption and explanation of the objective facts, a probable judgement under the logic of retrospect.

4.1 Documentary

All the photos being printed are carefully selected and significantly memorable moments being documented, which are worthy of travelling back in time. Human beings live in the river of time. The printed photos are not random clips of the dotted memory in the flow

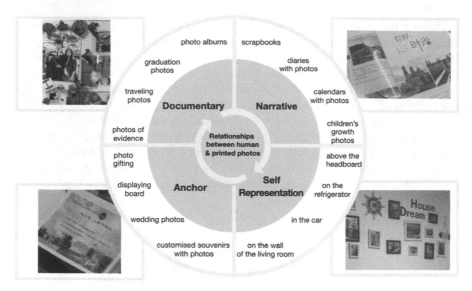

Fig. 5. Four relationships between human and printed photos

of time (Bergson 1912), rather they are a collection of the dotted memory (Bachelard 1969). Life is like a necklace made by those dots. Therefore, printing is a process of selective storage. It is an extract of memory, a materialised and objectified highlighted moment. Photos that are printed have been put in the documentation. To put the printed photos into the places of people's daily life is to replay them without the constraint of space and time to review that particular moment. Photos are proof of the eternal, retractable that-has-been (Barthes 1980), conveying people's memories.

With the development of digital storing technology, individuals have owned an increasing number of digital spaces, resulting in larger and larger quantities of digital photos stored in those spaces. Few people will have the chance to flip over these data again, for it requires a mass of time to locate some particular photos. Printed photos are the substance of the materials and are tangible memories. Photos to be printed can be larger in size, can be positioned in any places, triggering the functions of viewing and commenting automatically and increasing the duration and frequency of being viewed. Digital photos, on the other hand, exist in virtual space and can be defined as things that both exist and do not exist. Having physical photos at hand makes people feel authentic, assured, reliable, which make up the limitation of human memories. They allow us to truly grasp the moment and recall the memories that have been forgotten. Examples of participant comments:

- *"I have printed many travelling photos taken in my retirement. I hope that when I am too old to walk, I can flip over these photos at home. These are photos that help me record those places I have been to and those interesting people and things that I have encountered."*

- *"Things that are stored digitally are quite easy to be lost. Usually, I have two backups and have those important photos printed and reserved, so that I can have a look at these photos over and over again."*
- *"When I was in the army, I took the photo album to my dormitory. When I was alone at night, I would flip them over, because they are the memories with my family."*
- *"I put my graduation photos on top of my piano since they are the important moments in my life."*
- *"These printed photos record honestly those memorable persons, things and emotions. Whenever I think of those situations, memories at those moments are refreshed."*

4.2 Narrative

By organising, deleting, arranging the "dotted" photos in different themes, people are telling stories using a series of pictures (See Fig. 6). Occasions like graduation, wedding, reproduction, relocating, promotion, travelling, feast, reunion, represented by each frame of printed photos, consist every chapter of the whole life story of each individual. People narrate their stories through photos, expressing their emotions and significance. The uniqueness of the life stories is represented and extended, which is a form of interaction with themselves and others. Parents use the photos of their child to make a displaying wall or an album according to their preference, witnessing the growth of the children. Such memory organised by others becomes the only memory for children during their pre-memory phase. Parents also give photos of their own to their children after editing, beautifying and filing, hoping their children may remember the parents in a way they are supposed to be. Some elderly deliberately selects some well-taken or even carefully edited photos as their portrait for the funeral. By managing the photo for a lifetime, people in these photos become heroes with unique characteristics of the story. It is acknowledged that they takes the initiative of making life histories of themselves and others. By using images to narrate, they are entitled to roles of playwrights, directors, actors and actresses. Examples of participant comments:

- *"This photo album contains the most memorable days of the year. Each year, I will pick and print some meaningful photos about travels, birthdays and festivals to make an album with text. It is a representation of life in that year."*
- *"I will use photos to make calendars. Photos taken last year in that month are used to be the picture to decorate the same month in calendars. Also, I send the calendar to relatives as a gift, which is a pragmatic way of sharing our life stories."*
- *"Photos on this wall are selected during my child's growth. I order them chronologically, so that it is easy to distinguish different stages of children's physical and intelligent development, and is easy for children to remember themselves in different period."*
- *"I'm 83 years old now. I can use printers to print photos. Six years ago, I printed a photo of myself, not to show them to myself, but to leave them to my child. After I pass away, my child is able to see these photos."*

Fig. 6. Photo albums & calendars

4.3 Self Representation

In interacting with the printed photo, people can perceive, understand and express them-selves. They print out traveling photos to show their expanded horizon, photos of deli-cious food to reveal their good taste, photos with celebrities to express their cultural identity and social status. People choose "this photo" rather "that photo" to be printed behind which is their decision to publicise "that" part of the life. Printed photos present an ideal and flawless self. These contents are both true and false, which are what Goffman (1959) defines as the presentation of self in social life.

Front region and backstage are concepts put forward by Goffman (1959). Living rooms are the font region of the family, which are open, public and displaying, while bedrooms are at the backstage, which is exclusive and private. When placing photos of graduation, birthday party and traveling in the living room, people express their exclamation of "How happy our life is!". Photos in the living room are openly publicised, which creates topics of communication for the visitors and friends and presents a self in others' eyes. However, when photos of the loved ones are placed in the bedrooms, it expresses the determination of "willing to be with their partners and children either when being awaken or asleep". These photos construct a private space for people and mirror a presence of a self in their own eyes and a self in other's eyes. By behaviours of photo printing, people are managing their social images, maintaining their character masks, recognising themselves by photos and understanding the ultimate big question of "who I am". The physical photo allows the identity, role, character and dream to be realised and are more direct, systematic and visualised. Examples of participant comments:

- *"The purpose of printing these photos is to show to others who have seen the photos that my life is colourful."*
- *"Photos being printed represent an ideal me. In other words, it describes a person that I hope to be."*
- *"Guests in the house usually will take a look at these photos in the living room, such as my daughter's graduation photo and my son's wedding ceremony photos."*
- *"These photos are taken when happy moments. I hope that they can reflect my positive energy to others."*

4.4 Anchor

The printed photo anchors the relationship within the self and between self and others. When the photographer, the subject of being photographed and the viewer of the photograph are identical, in the succession of the changing roles, the relationship between different self has been strengthened and anchored (Mead 2015). The self in the past and the self at the present confide and listen to each other calmly and quietly, comforting each other's hearts. The subjective self continuously objectifies itself, because only by doing this, love will be given to the self again in a way of narcissism and the self will be reshaped into a more ideal and perfect one. The objectified ideal self will be accompanied by the subjective self permanently in such absolute loneliness.

When printed photos are given to others as a gift, such social interaction sends friendly regard to others. By sharing life experiences, exclusive comprehension and memory are established where the sympathy and relationship between each other are strengthened and deepened. Gift sending generates social connections (Mauss 1924). Gift of a materialised photo makes this relationship more visible and existential. If comparing sending digital images to others with handing printed photos to others in person, it is manifest that the anchoring of the latter has a more solid and lasting relationship.

The implication of the term "Anchor" is to offer people a sense of security and mental support. People who make scrapbooks use this media as an anchor to strengthen the relationship with themselves, between self and the child, self and the pet, and between self and the celebrity. Anchoring is a stabiliser for us in the lifetime ups and downs. Only by having an anchor, we can be assured and relaxed. The scrapbook is a good example of an anchor. Examples of participant comments:

- *"Sending printed photos taken with friends during the journey arouses shared memories and intimates the friendship."*
- *"Photos for the wedding are usually being printed. By placing them at key areas, the statement of the couples are married is made clear. The wedding photos are also a great conversation-opener for friends and relatives."*
- *"These photos are fantastic feedback for me emotionally. By looking at these photos, I can see the happiness experienced by the old me."*
- *"When holding the birthday party of one classmate, I print out photos of him as a photo displaying board and write down my best wishes as a special gift for him."*

5 Discussion

The popularity of the Mi® photo printer is the motivation for this study. It is based on two questions. First, why do people still need printed photos in the digital image era? Second, what kind of relationships are there between human and printed photos? By three qualitative research methods, this study summarises the human-printed photo relationships into four categories, documentation, narrative, self-representation and anchor. Having said that, the relationships between human and printed photos are not confined to the four types mentioned above. For instance, hanging a photo of the child inside the car signifies conventional meanings of amulets and prayers, which can be seen as another relationship between human and the printed photo. Besides, in specific usage scenarios, the above-mentioned four relationships may exist alone, yet more often than not, they appear in a combinational form. For example, the printed photos as a gift to others are in one relationship of anchor, while photos in the living rooms reflect the whole four relationships of documentation, narrative, self-representation and anchor.

The study takes place in the time of digital photos and online social networking. Whether it is in the era of films and sheets thirty years ago, or it will be in the future time of artificial intelligence and internet of things, the four relationships of documentation, narrative, self-representation and anchor all exist. Such a relationship between human and things in the materialised and the real world last long and will not fade. These relationships are how people live conventionally, existentially and materialised. This essay aims to reveal these relationships and to inspire the designers. By a better product, service and system designing practice, the above-mentioned relationships are further expanded, strengthened and enriched.

As for the methodology, the study combines ethnographic interview, visual diary and creative workshop. The results of the three investigations supplement and cross-verify each other. The total number (N) of the participants (N = 32) is a relatively small sample amount. Three inter-supplementary methods are adopted to increase the validity of the small sample amount. A participatory approach is used in the creative workshop. Participants, printer users and designers of different academic backgrounds are gathered together to have a profound discussion about the fundamental questions of the study, which is to generate further thoughts and innovation.

The future researchers, on one hand, are suggested to implement investigations of larger samples to deepen the comprehensions and insights about the research questions. On the other hand, they are recommended to implement innovative practice based on these comprehensions and insights. In the approach of design as research, practice and research are aligned seamlessly (Manzini 2015). What the people need is printed photos, rather than photo printers. Furthermore, they need these photos as media to document, narrate, self-represent and anchor relationships. Therefore, the original design intention can be printing for the sake of documenting. For example, the design of adding photo-taken information (e.g. time, place & person) at the margin of the photo or a photo paper of index with customised logo (e.g. index card in the library) fall into this category. Also, the original intention can be printing for the sake of narrating. For instance, the design of printing multiple photos on one piece of paper in a collage manner (See Fig. 7). In the creative workshop investigation, many innovative concepts are put forward in the findings. For example, designing ideas of the time machine, electronic photo frame with commenting function, cellphone Polaroid®, etc. Such innovative novel products, software, services and systems may not be realised easily, however, they further the depth and range of the study.

Finally, this study is to understand the human-photo relationship from the sociology scientific perspective. Only based on this understanding, designers are able to have inspirations. Design is not about simple artificial creating, rather, it is about creating all types of new social relationships through things. To be more precise, the design is not on printers, but on the new way of using photos to establish a good social relationships between self and self as well as between self and others.

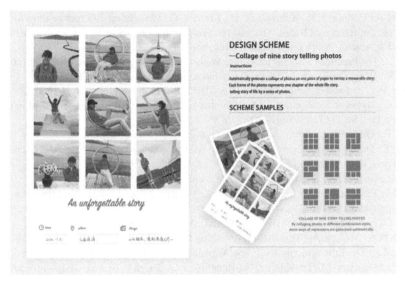

Fig. 7. A conceptual design scheme

6 Conclusion

In the digital image era, the demand of printing photos still exists. These photos are printed for different uses in people's daily life. Acquiring physical photos instantly is a dispensable approach to perceiving the self and interacting with society.

Three methodologies of the ethnographic interview, visual diary and creative workshop are adopted in this study. Four human-printed photo relationships of documentation, narrative, self-representation and anchor are summarised. It is concluded that printed photos have recorded people's life journeys, which is an extract, assistance and replay of the memories and a proof of that-has-been; photos are printed to narrate experience subjectively and compile life histories of themselves and other; they are a self representation of the real-life experience; photo printing anchors the relationship with selves and between the self and the other. This study not only enriches the knowledge of the relationship between human and images but also inspire and influence designers to further develop innovative products, services and systems.

Declaration of Competing Interest. This research is supported by Tsinghua University Initiative Scientific Research Program.
    Program Number: 2021THZW.

References

Bachelard, G.: The Poetics of Space. Beacon Press, Boston (1969)
Barthes, R.: La Chambre Claire: Note Sur La Photographie. Gallimard, Paris (1980)
Bergson, H.: Time and Free Will: An Essay on the Immediate Data of Consciousness. George Allen, London (1912). (Pogson, F. L., Trans.)

Blighe, M., O'Connor, N.E., Rehatschek, H., Kienast, G.: Identifying different settings in a visual diary. In: Conference of Image Analysis for Multimedia Interactive Services [WIAMIS 2008], Ireland & Austria. Ninth International Workshop on May 2008, pp. 24–27 (2008)

Babbie, E.: The Practice of Social Research. Wadsworth Cengage Learning, Belmont (2013)

Cooper, R.: Design research: its 50-year transformation. Des. Stud. **65**, 6–17 (2019)

Goffman, E.: The Presentation of Self in Everyday Life. Doubleday, New York (1959)

Kohtala, C., Hyysalo, S., Whalen, J.: A taxonomy of users' active design engagement in the 21st century. Des. Stud. **67**, 27–54 (2020)

Lawson, B.: Design as research. Archit. Res. Q. **6**(2), 109–114 (2002)

Manzini, E.: Design, When Everybody Designs: An Introduction to Design for Social Innovation. MIT Press, Cambridge and London (2015)

Mead, G.: Mind, Self & Society. University of Chicago Press, Chicago (2015)

Mauss, M.: Essai sur le don: Forme et raison de l'échange dans les sociétés primitives. Année Sociologique **1**, 30–186 (1924)

Robson, C., McCartan, K.: Real World Research. Wiley, London (2016)

Sontag, S.: On Photography. Translation Publishing House, Shanghai (2010). (Huang, C.R. Trans.)

Spradley, J.P.: The Ethnographic Interview. Waveland Press, Long Grove (2016)

Steen, M., Manschot, M., De Koning, N.: Benefits of co-design in service design projects. Int. J. Des. **5**, 53–60 (2011)

Wimmer, R.D., Dominck, J.R.: Mass Media Research: An Introduction. Wadsworth Publishers, California (2003)

A Study of 3D Stereoscopic Image Production of "Triadic Ballet" of the Theater of the Bauhaus

Yi-Wen Ting[1(✉)], Po-Hsien Lin[1], Rungtai Lin[1], and Ming-Hong Shi[2(✉)]

[1] Graduate School of Creative Industry Design, National Taiwan University of Arts,
New Taipei City 22058, Taiwan
ading1113@gmail.com, {t0131,rtlin}@mail.ntua.edu.tw
[2] Shenzhen Technology University, Shenzhen, Guangdong, People's Republic of China
jun101786@126.com

Abstract. The Bauhaus covered all aspects of the visual arts: architecture, graphic design, sculpture, industrial design and stage performance, during its short 20th century life. Central figure Oskar Schlemmer (1883–1943) ushered in the golden age of the Bauhaus theatre and is known for his dedication to spatial design. His experience of the space comes not only from visual observations but also from the movements and physical interactions of the dancers with the performance space. He observes the trajectories of the human body in the space and transforms them into abstract geometric figures to explain the inner meaning of the dancers in the "stage cube". Our team has been working on the Theater of the Bauhaus, and in 2020 received funding from the Ministry of Science and Technology of Taiwan for our research on 'Triadic ballet'. We successfully reproduced fragments of three ballets that Schlemmer exhibited in Stuttgart in 1922. Through this reproduction, we learn more about Schlemmer's research; and his thoughts on "people and space" and "artistic images," including his belief that new theatrical forms will eventually unfold over time. This research uses the principle of Pepper's Ghost to create 3D virtual images. The results not only fulfill the prediction of Schlemmer's space experiment but also force us to rethink how he transformed the concepts of "rational numbers" and "emotional people" into abstract art forms.

Keywords: Triadic ballet · 3D images · Pepper's ghost

1 Introduction

The Bauhaus, an art school founded in the early 20th century, encompassed the entirety of the visual arts over its short period of operation, including architecture, graphic design, sculpture, and industrial design [1]. Many studies have explored the Bauhaus's influence on art. However, few have focused on the Theater of the Bauhaus, although the artistic experimentation of the Bauhaus considerably influenced modern dance and theater [2]. Oskar Schlemmer (1888–1943), a central figure in the history of the Bauhaus although he only taught at the school for 9 years, ushered in the Golden Age of the Theater of the Bauhaus. Schlemmer was most famous for his interpretation of space, producing

P.-L. P. Rau (Ed.): HCII 2022, LNCS 13312, pp. 283–293, 2022.
https://doi.org/10.1007/978-3-031-06047-2_20

paintings that represented space in a manner that was visually similar to that of his ballets and theatrical stage pieces. Schlemmer experienced space not merely through vision but through perceived space that could be achieved through the overall positioning of dancers' and actors' bodies. He observed the trajectories of the human body in space and used these observations to transform the dancers of his productions into geometric, abstract representations of the human form, through which he questioned the meaning and value of "man as dancer" on a cubic stage. The goal of the Bauhaus was to develop a unity of artistic ideals through a comprehensive inquiry into the creative elements of craftsmanship and, through all its components, to understand the nature of "construction" and the development of creativity [3]. The ideology of the Bauhaus was also the ideology of the Theater of the Bauhaus, whose first consideration was visual space. In Schlemmer's most famous work—the Triadic Ballet—he deconstructed the human body through costumes, subtly abstracting the body into a moving organism. He succeeded in conveying his own interpretation of space and articulated human emotions through color. In modernist art, form is extremely abstract and pure. This study is a research project on the Theater of the Bauhaus on the occasion of the Bauhaus' centenary. In this project, a segment of Schlemmer's Triadic Ballet, which premiered in Stuttgart, Germany, in 1922, was reproduced, and a public rehearsal was held at the OPOP seminar at National Taiwan University of Arts. The audience awarded the reproduction an average rating of 4.5 (out of 5), indicating that Schlemmer's Triadic Ballet remains relevant to contemporary audiences.

This research on and reproduction of the "Triadic Ballet" facilitated understanding of Schlemmer's lifelong exploration of "man and space" and his beliefs regarding artistic imagery. Schlemmer's book, The Theater of the Bauhaus, discussed his experimentation with space on the stage, which created visual curiosities through the visual abstraction of the dancers. The popularization of new theatrical forms requires only time, materials, and techniques [1]. Therefore, this study proposed that the core concept of the "human body as a moving building" of the theatrical form Schlemmer developed could be articulated through the perspective of modern technology with virtual three-dimensional (3D) images. Accordingly, in this study, 3D stereoscopic images were created to reproduce segments of the Triadic Ballet (2020) to execute Schlemmer's vision of experimental space and to understand the effects of 3D stereoscopic imaging of artistic works.

In this study, the ideology of the Bauhaus and the theory of the Theater of the Bauhaus were used as the horizontal and vertical axes, respectively, to enable study of spatial interpretation in the Triadic Ballet. Virtual 3D stereoscopic imaging of the dances was presented using modern technology along with the Pepper's Ghost illusion technique to realize Schlemmer's vision of a new theater proposed in his The Theater of the Bauhaus. In addition, although the coronavirus-2019 (COVID-19) pandemic has resulted in new problems, it has also led to breakthroughs in art. When audiences are unable to view live performances in theaters, 3D imaging may enable them to continue viewing live performances. In this study, a 3D image of Triadic Ballet was created based on the principle of "Pepper's ghost", trying to present the relationship between dancers and space with virtual images, and to develop different forms of dance performances.

Accordingly, the objectives of this study are as follows: (1) to review the literature on space in the Bauhaus design ideology and (2) to discuss the application of the Pepper's Ghost illusion in the Theater of the Bauhaus.

2 Literature Review

2.1 The Theater of the Bauhaus "Triadic Ballet"

The Theater of the Bauhaus program was established at the school's founding in 1920. When the school moved to Dessau in 1926, an exclusive theater was established, presided over by the Schlemmer. The purpose of the program was to teach students about the relationship between the human body and space through theater and to develop student's creating thinking through creative demonstrations of the performing arts. As noted on Bauhausdance.org, "Oskar Schlemmer's concept of theater has influenced the performance theories of modern and postmodern dancers, such as Merce Cunningham, Alwin Nikolais, and Robert Wilson." Most studies on the Bauhaus have primarily focused on its influence within the fields of design and architecture; few have investigated the Theater of the Bauhaus. *The Theater of the Bauhaus* (Die Bühne im Bauhaus) [3], a book series published in 1925 and translated into English in 1961, contains an introduction by Walter Gropius and four short essays, including Schlemmer's *Man and Art Figure* and *Theater (BÜHNE)*; Moholy-Nagy's *Theater, Circus, Variety*; and Farkas Molnár's *U-Theater*. *The Theater of the Bauhaus* shocked readers in that it deconstructed traditional understandings of theater from two perspectives: theater space and the human body in space. Theater space focuses on the building itself and the potential of the performances that can be produced there. The human body in space refers to the maximization of the performing arts. Schlemmer proposed four laws of the human body in space, which were a breakthrough in the narrative form of traditional dance. Through these laws, the focus of dance was no longer the characters of the performance but rather the creation of art through bold experimentation that reflected the purity and abstraction of modern art. In *The Theater of the Bauhaus* [3], Schlemmer remarked, "Man, the human organism, stands in the cubical, abstract space of the stage. Man and Space. Each has different laws of order. Whose shall prevail? Either abstract space is adapted in deference to natural man and transformed back into nature or the imitation of space... Or natural man, in deference to abstract space, is recast to fit its mold... Invisibly involved with all these laws is Man as Dancer (Tänzermensch). He obeys the law of the body as well as the law of space... whether in free abstract movement or in symbolic pantomime, whether he is on the bare stage... the *Tänzermensch* is the medium of transition into the great world of theater." Dancers began performing the Triadic Ballet in workshops as early as 1912, and it was partially released in 1915. The ballet premiered in Stuttgart in 1922, and its first public performance was held at the Weimar National Theater in 1923. In a decade-long experiment, Schlemmer used the metaphor of dance and machines to explore the potential of theater. The extremely unballet-like ballet became a crucial means of understanding the transformation of modern art and the stage ideals of the Bauhaus [4]. The Triadic Ballet has different iterations, all of which contain three acts and three dancers. The performance includes solos, duets, and trios, with the 12 dance segments expressed using geometric shapes, and contains 18 sets of costumes that are divided into three series: yellow, rose, and black. In the performance, two male and one female dancer complete the 12 segments wearing the 18 costumes.

2.2 Virtual Reality Dance

The application of digital imaging technology in performance theater has altered perceptions of dance, means of creation, and the dissemination of dance. Rosenberg noted in *The Oxford handbook of screen dance studies* that [5], compared with live performances, contemporary dance viewed through media can be transformed through control of space and kinetic energy. The incorporation of multimedia has given rise to a trend of digitalization, leading to the emergence of different forms of dance. The digitalization of dance and development of virtual reality technology have also challenged the physicality and liveliness of dance, further changing the audience's aesthetic experience of viewing dance. Applications of digital technology in dance have expanded to include videos, motion capture technology, virtual reality, and network interactions. The development of digital technology and its application in dance can be traced back to the postmodern dancer Loïe Fuller's experimentation with new technology and dance performance. Fuller combined projected films with shadow effects to visually alter her body shape during performances, even creating dances in which clothes glowed. Her complex manipulation of light extended the perceived space and transformed her physique and visual form. Schlemmer's Light Plays (1923) combined the human form, shadow effects, and projection to pioneer explorations of technological performances. Furthermore, in the 1920s, Schlemmer optimized the abstract expression of narrative, space, and dance [6]. In the 1960s, experimental and avant-garde postmodern dance moved beyond the traditionally framed stage, with dancers moving performances to different spaces, such as natural spaces or outdoor buildings. In the 20th century, German dancer Bina Bausch's dance theater (Tanztheater) altered the form dance performances would take in the future; she promoted spatial aesthetics within a space and forming a polyphonic viewing relationship with the audience [7]. Following the advent of the fourth industrial revolution of the 21st century, technology was gradually integrated into dance. The combination of new media and dance has since become an artistic cross-domain experiment. The development of virtual reality has facilitated dancers breaking through the boundaries of space in dance performances, enabling the performance to progress from a physical (real) field of view to a real, interweaving virtual field of view. Thus, the audience's perception of dance has become increasingly complex, and the relationship between the dance and the viewing of the performance has complexified. The spatial designs of stages convey figurative symbols in visualizing dance performances. The introduction of modern scientific and technological means has disrupted traditional space composition on stages and created a new spatial concept with the assistance of various elements [8].

Dixon explored the transformation of the performing arts and digital theater through the three perspectives of body, space, and time and expanded the perceived theatrical space, creating an immersive and dynamic theater stage design [6]. In this unique space, the audience's perceptions of time are altered through their physical perceptions of the performer and their perceptions of their own movements through space. Traditional performing arts require a collective response (for example, for the audience to look in the same direction), which leads to conception of a "group audience." However, the viewing mode is constantly challenged with the addition of digital technology [9].

Moreover, the audience's viewing behaviors are subjected to reexamination; from the perspective of an individual viewing experience, the audience is encouraged to become a part of the performance, which then becomes experiential. Technology theater empha-sizes "how the audience imagines and processes the meaning of the work" and how the intertextuality of multiple inputs occurs during the interaction [10].

Whereas traditional theater regards fiction as a projection of an alternative world, the environmental simulation involved in virtual reality is not confined by the mimetic concepts of traditional art; rather, it enables formation of a self-sufficient ontological world. That is, the simulated world is no longer a replica of or reference to the real world but rather contains meaning in itself [11]. When the theater acts as a mediating entity between the audience and the performance, the audience's views and perceptions change with the form and medium of the work. Compared with the immersion of traditional theater, the audience experiences a transference into the fictional plot, integrating their mind with the plot as an inseparable whole. The implementation of digital technology in theater enables the audience to experience the perceived and imagined world through their senses.

2.3 Pepper's Ghost

Dating back to the 16th century, Pepper's Ghost was one of the earliest means through which ghosts and illusions were created in theatrical performances. The theory of the illusion was first proposed for use in theaters by scientist Henry Dircks in 1858 and was subsequently modified in 1862 by Professor John Pepper, the director of the Royal Polytechnic Institution. The illusion, often referred to as Pepper's Ghost, became a practical device that can be used in any theater [12]; it simply involves using glass to reflect objects onto dark spaces. That is, the device uses the relationship between glass and light to simulate ghosts. A space hidden from the audience with a black cloth is created under the stage to reduce interference from external light. The image of the actor is reflected on a mirror and then reflected on sloping glass at the stage entrance. When the light in the space underneath the stage is turned off, the image of the actor, or "ghost," disappears. The illusion was patented by Pepper and Dircks in 1863; although it was extremely popular at the time, it eventually faded in popularity because it could not be used in many mainstream theatrical performances.

However, Pepper's Ghost is still used in Disneyland's Haunted Mansion and Phantom Manor attractions. German electrical engineer Uwe Maass modified the bulky glass used for the original Pepper's Ghost and developed special metal sheets to replace them. After Maass patented the sheets, he founded Musion, a holographic projection service, with British businessmen James Rock and Ian O'Connell. Use of holographic projection technology has increased over the years; such technology was used in performances by the singer Madonna and the musical group the Gorillaz in 2006. In 2007, holographic projection enabled a performance by the deceased Elvis Presley [13].

Pepper's Ghost has been applied with considerable success for use in museums, theaters, television, and movies. Pepper's Ghost is notably still being replicated and adapted four centuries after its conception [14]. The Triadic Ballet spatial interpretation project in this study applied the principles of Pepper's Ghost and modified these principles to complete a 3D spatial interpretation of dance performances.

3   Research Design and Method

3.1   Research Process

This research first analyzes and understands the relevant literature of the Bauhaus Theater and Triadic Ballet, and then analyzes the concept of Triadic Ballet's works. After the re-production of the works, the production of 3D images and the production of virtual images of Pepper's ghost are carried out (Fig. 1).

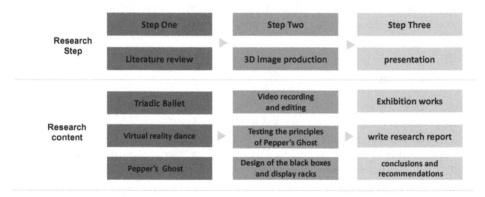

Fig. 1. Research process

3.2   Research Samples

In this study, the Triadic Ballet from the Theater of the Bauhaus was used as the research sample. 3D images were produced using the National Taiwan University of Arts reproduction (2020). Because the Triadic Ballet consists of 18 dance segments, a segment was selected from each scene of the ballet, including the solo dances in the yellow, rose, and black segments, for the 3D images, as presented in Fig. 2.

Fig. 2. Reproduction of triadic ballet, 2020. (Choreography by Oskar Schlemmer, 1921)

4   Producing Stereoscopic Images of the Triadic Ballet

Schlemmer stated that the arrival of a new form of theater is only a matter of time and technology. This study examined Schlemmer's most famous work of art, the Triadic Ballet, for an experiment in a new form of performing art. This study was the first to apply the principle of Pepper's Ghost in real–virtual integration in theater performance to create 3D imaging of the Triadic Ballet.

The production process was divided into four stages. The first involved video recording and editing; the second concerned testing the mirror reflection principles of Pepper's Ghost; the third involved designing the display box and rack; and the fourth involved production of the display rack and exhibition. The stages of the production process are detailed in the following:

Step 1. Video Recording and Editing. After analyzing the creation model of the 2020 production of the Triadic Ballet, the research team applied its core conceptual shapes, colors, space, expression, choreography, costume design, and stage design as the basis

Fig. 3. Recorded in virtual studio (Color figure online)

for reproduction. A subsequent public performance was held for verification of the reproduction of the work, after which the recording of the Triadic Ballet commenced. To achieve the full effects of Pepper's Ghost, the background of the images had to be removed and changed to black. To achieve a more accurate and efficient postproduction of the images, they were recorded in Virtual studio and shot in front of a green screen (Fig. 3). This facilitated constant-color matting of the background. After video recording, the video editing software Adobe After Effects was used for image matting (Fig. 4).

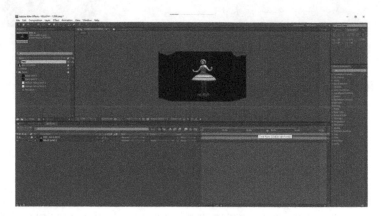

Fig. 4. Video editing

Step 2. Testing the Mirror Reflection Principles of Pepper's Ghost. According to the principles of Pepper's Ghost, the reflective glass used for the illusion must be presented at an angle of 45° in relation to the image plane (Fig. 5). However, because the relationship among the reflection of the glass, the intensity of the light source of the image, and the black box display were unclear, a mirror reflection test was conducted. The recorded video image was displayed on a 12-in. iPad using the playback software KMPlayer. First, the afterimage effects of the glass reflection needed to be removed. The effects of three types of paper, namely aluminum foil, black transparent cellophane, and automotive sun control film, were tested. The results indicated that the effects of the automotive sun control film were superior to those of both the aluminum foil and black cellophane. Therefore, the automotive sun control film was selected as backing for the mirrored glass. A light source test of the black box was then performed. Generally, stage lights are used for application of Pepper's Ghost in theater or concerts. However, the original black box design was considered to be nonideal in the absence of the light source of a projector; the goal of this study was for the effect produced with the viewing equipment to closely resemble that of theater black boxes. Therefore, the lighting design of theater stages was applied in a light source test. A light emitting diode light with an adjustable brightness was used as the projected light source and was placed at the center of the top of the black box to produce the effect of a stage spotlight. Subsequently, light fixtures with adjustable light sources were used to adjust the brightness of the light source in the black box in relation to the lighting of the exhibition site.

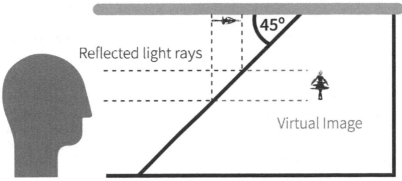

Fig. 5. The mirror reflection principles of Pepper's Ghost.

Step 3. Design of the Black Boxes and Display Racks. The black boxes and display racks designed in this study are presented in Fig. 6. These designs enabled optimal mirror reflection at the angle from which the audience would be viewing the Triadic Ballet. In addition, to present the Triadic Ballet in a manner that imitated a frame-like stage, the vehicle of the presentation was presented as a black box. The images of the dancers in the black box were displayed at the point of the viewer's focus. The size of the black box was determined according to the size of the iPad screen. The display rack, which adopted a simple concept design, was 160 cm high and conformed to Bauhaus design; that is, it had

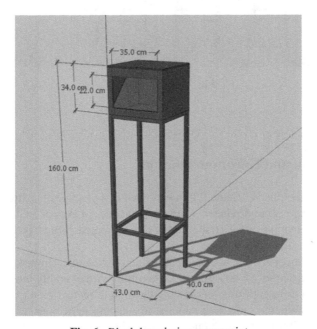

Fig. 6. Black box design manuscript

an ergonomic viewing height and highlighted the Bauhaus focus on geometric shapes. Because the Triadic Ballet segments displayed in this study comprised three segments (yellow, rose, and black), to create a sense of color in the space, the backgrounds in the black boxes were painted yellow, rose, and black. This was meant to convey a sense of wit, seriousness, and mystery.

Step 4. Display Rack Production and Presentation. Through the recreation of the Triadic Ballet, the Pepper's Ghost illusion, and the design of the display racks, this study established a method of 3D spatial interpretation of the Triadic Ballet and produced display racks. After the display racks were completed, their positioning at the exhibition site was adjusted according to the onsite space, and the lighting of the displays was adjusted based on the onsite light source. The Triadic Ballet was performed at the Exhibition Hall of National Taiwan University of Arts on December 6–10, 2021(Fig. 7).

Fig. 7. Exhibition site

5   Conclusion and Recommendation

In this study, Schlemmer's Triadic Ballet was used in a practice of spatial interpretation of dance. 3D images were produced using the principles of Pepper's Ghost. In addition, 3D stereoscopic imaging of the Triadic Ballet was presented through production of black boxes and light source adjustment.

Traditional dance performances generally offer onsite value. However, advancements in technology, particularly with respect to integrating virtual reality into the performing arts, has enabled different forms of viewing through the integration of virtual and real performing arts. Whether audience patterns in viewing performances in theaters will change after the COVID-19 pandemic remains unknown. However, this study presents a new medium of dance performance as well as a new application of technology that can be used in the future in the performing arts industry. The results of the 3D Pepper's Ghost imaging of this study can enable simulation of 3D space in live performances. Nevertheless, whether the audience's experience of viewing the live performance of the Triadic Ballet differs from that of the 3D stereoscopic images and their subsequent perceptions of the dance performances warrants future exploration.

Acknowledgment. This study was partly sponsored with a grant, MOST-110-WFAA-410018, from the Ministry of Science and Technology, Taiwan.

References

1. Schlemmer, O.: The Letters and Diaries of Oskar Schlemmer. Northwestern University Press (1990)
2. Smock, W.: The Bauhaus Ideal Then and Now: An Illustrated Guide to Modernist Design. Academy Chicago Publishers, Chicago (2004)
3. Schlemmer, O.: Man and art figure. In: Gropius W., Wensinger, Ar.S. (eds.) The Theater of the Bauhaus, Wesleyan University Press, Middletown, CT (1961)
4. Liu, C.: Humanity Dance and Mechanical Laws-Speaking from "Triadic Ballet" (2018). https://kknews.cc/zhtw/culture/pgkz88j.html. Accessed 21 Dec 2020
5. Rosenberg, D.: The Oxford Handbook of Screen Dance Studies. Oxford University Press, Oxford (2016)
6. Dixon, S.: Digital Performance: A History of New Media in Theater, Dance, Performance Art, and Installation. MIT Press, London (2015)
7. Huang, R.: The allocation and construction of two performance forms in dance theatre creation. J. Beijing Dance Acad. 26(4), 58–66 (2019)
8. Wang, R.: Research on dance stage space from the perspective of technical aesthetics. J. Beijing Dance Acad. 25(1), 46–50 (2018)
9. Chiu, C.Y.: Stand-in performance: the "variant" and "machine/human" in digital performing arts. J. Taipei Fine Arts Mus. 38, 4–32 (2019)
10. Oddey, A.: Re-Framing the Theatrical: Interdisciplinary Landscapes for Performance. Palgrave Macmillan, New York (2007)
11. Chiu, C.Y., Cheng, H.Y.: The immersive somatic experiential aesthetics of techno-theater. Tsing Hua J. Art Res. (1), 1–16 (2019)
12. Burdekin, R.: Pepper's Ghost at the Opera. Soc. Theatre Res. 69(3), 152–164 (2015)
13. Li, D.C.: "Ghosts" in Drama - Pepper's Ghost. Art Educ. (10), 84–85 (2017
14. Duckworth, J.: Pepper's Ghost. Stage Direction, pp. 30–31 (2021)

Preference Diversity and Information Activities: A Study on Korean-Drama Fans' Information Behavior

Tien-I Tsai[1][✉] [iD], Juo-Hsuan Hung[1], Kai-Lin Hsiao[2], and Chu-Han Hsu[1]

[1] National Taiwan University, Taipei 10617, Taiwan
titsai@ntu.edu.tw
[2] University of Washington, Seattle, WA 98195, USA

Abstract. Korean Wave (or "Hallyu") started since the 1990s, and K-dramas have been even more popular among young people. As over-the-top (OTT) media services and smartphone devices grow rapidly, people have a wide variety of choices to watch video contents. In order to examine the information behavior of K-drama fans, a web survey was conducted with 325 college students. Follow-up interviews were conducted to help explain the results. The findings indicate that K-drama fans are typically clear about their preferences and have a moderate preference diversity. They do not consult information sources or perform information activities very frequently, but they search and browse K-drama-related information more often than deeply engage in reading or constantly monitoring relevant information. They usually receive information passively from social media and other interpersonal sources. Nevertheless, those rated higher on preference diversity tend to perform various information activities more frequently. Future research and suggestions are proposed based on the findings.

Keywords: Information behavior · Information activities · Preference diversity · Korean Drama Fans · College students

1 Introduction

Korean Wave (or "Hallyu") has been starting since the 1990s, and among various types of Korean popular culture spreading worldwide, Korean television dramas were remarkably attracting young people's attention after the 2000s [1, 2]. It was even more popular after 2008 when South Korea's cultural exports increased by 10% each year, and among Korean-Drama Fans in Taiwan, one of the major groups is the college student [3, 4]. These young adults grew up during this Korean Wave. And watching Korean dramas (K-dramas) is one of the popular leisure activities among young adults [5].

As over-the-top (OTT) media services and connected television (CTV) platforms grow rapidly, people have a wide variety of choices to watch K-dramas. In 2018, 40.5% of those who are over 16 years old watched video contents through smart phones; in 2020, the population who watched videos through smart phone reached 54.5% [6, 7]. On the contrary, those who watched video contents through traditional television dropped

P.-L. P. Rau (Ed.): HCII 2022, LNCS 13312, pp. 294–303, 2022.
https://doi.org/10.1007/978-3-031-06047-2_21

from one-third to one-fourth during 2017–2020. [7] This phenomenon implies that users' information behavior regarding accessing video contents have changed, and it is worthy of further investigation.

Additionally, K-drama fans may not only watch the dramas but also pay attention to different genres of information to stay up-to-date with the latest news regarding K-dramas. According to Yeh's research on the information behavior of undergraduate students' online video viewing, information needs may be triggered before, during, and after viewing the video, and the information behavior involves different active and passive activities such as seeking, monitoring, exchanging (includes receiving and sharing), and using information [8].

Hektor's model of information behavior provides a framework for examining infor-mation behavior with emphasis on everyday-life information activities; he identified four modes of information behavior—seeking, gathering, communicating, and giving, and eight types of information activities—search and retrieve, browse, monitor, unfold, exchange, dress, instruct, and publish [9]. Hartel, Cox, and Griffin acknowledged that Hektor's model of information behavior allows comparative and more precise research, and they applied this model to analyze three different forms of serious leisure [10]. Based on the above works, the current study applied this framework to investigate the infor-mation activities in college students' K-drama watching information behavior. Mapping the information activities identified in Yeh's research [8] with Hektor's model [9], five out of eight activities (i.e., search, browse, monitor, exchange, unfold) were identified in examining undergraduate students' video viewing information behavior. The current study further examines the frequencies of these five information activities in college students' K-drama watching contexts.

When discussing leisure engagement with information, Tang, Ke, and Sie proposed the concept of user preference diversity to examine users' reading interest; specifically, they developed a 10-item scale to examine how narrow or wide an individual's reading interest is and discussed how individuals' preference diversity may influence reactions or recommendations on an online social bookshelf platform [11]. Later on, Tang, Chang, and Lin have tested and validated the 10-item scale in the context of movie goers [12]. The current study adopted this preference diversity scale to examine how college students are interested in different topics and genres of K-dramas, and whether or not students' preference diversity is related to their information activities.

Drawing upon the aforementioned literature, the current study investigates K-drama fans' information behavior through the following research questions: 1. What K-drama watching preferences and patterns do K-drama fans exhibit? Do K-drama fans' have a wide preference diversity? 2. How frequently do K-drama fans consult different sources and perform different information activities (i.e., search, browse, monitor, exchange, unfold)? Are there correlations between preference diversity and information activities?

2 Methods

2.1 Data Collections

A web survey and follow-up interviews were conducted to collect data. The survey includes three parts: demographics, K-drama-related background and preferences, K-drama-related information behavior. The first part includes demographic questions such as gender and level of study. The second part includes K-drama watching preferences such as when they started watching K-dramas, what types of K-dramas they watched, number of K-dramas they watched during the past year, K-drama watching pattern, genres, occasions, and a 10-item preferences diversity scale on 5-point Likert derived from Tang, Ke, and Sie [11] and Tang, Chang, and Lin [12]. The third part includes frequencies consulting various information sources (e.g., search engines, online forums, magazines, derivative works, family and friends), and frequencies of information activities (i.e., search, browse, monitor, exchange, unfold) based on Hektor's framework [9].

The web survey was built on the DoSurvey platform and distributed through multiple Facebook groups affiliated with a large public research university in northern Taiwan. College students who had watched at least three different K-drama series during the past six months were invited to participate in the survey. In order to better explain the quantitative results, participants who expressed their interest in participating in the follow-up interviews were invited to the in-depth interviews.

The interview guide includes three parts. First, participants were asked to describe the role of K-drama in their life and their motivations for watching K-dramas. Second, participants were asked to describe and explain their watching patterns and preferences. Third, participants were asked to describe their information behavior, including their information needs and information-seeking behavior, as well as the information activities involved.

2.2 Participants

As shown in Table 1, 325 participated in the current study. While students came from different year in college, most were female (84.9%). Nearly half of the students (40.9%) have been watching K-dramas since they were in high school, and most students have been watching K-dramas prior to college (80.3%). And since participants were self-reported as K-drama fans, all participants watched at least 6 K-dramas during the past year. While almost 70% of the participants watched 6–10 K-dramas during the past year, 14.5% watched more than 15 K-dramas during the past year.

Table 1. Demographics of the participants ($N = 325$).

Demographics	Frequency	Percentage
Gender		
Female	276	84.9%
Male	49	15.1%
Year in college		
Freshman	73	22.5%
Sophomore	68	20.9%
Junior	70	21.5%
Senior or above	114	35.0%
Started watching Korean dramas		
Since elementary school	38	11.7%
Since junior high school	90	27.7%
Since high school	133	40.9%
Since college	64	19.7%
Number of Korean dramas watched during the past year		
6–10	225	69.2%
11–15	53	16.3%
16–20	34	10.5%
More than 20	13	4.0%

Three follow-up interviews were conducted to clarify the results derived from the web survey. The interview participants were all female in their senior year.

2.3 Data Analysis

Descriptive statistics were used to examine students' K-drama watching preferences, preference diversity, and information activities. The Cronbach's α of the 10-item preference diversity reached .849, which means the reliability is good. Correlation tests were performed to examine whether or not preference diversity has a significant correlation with specific information activities (i.e., search, browse, monitor, exchange, unfold). Interview data were first open coded and then coded based on themes that could possibly help explain the survey results.

3 Findings

3.1 K-drama Watching Preferences and Patterns

General Preferences and Patterns. Most participants in the current study typically watched K-dramas on K-drama websites (84.9%) and/or other general social media sites such as YouTube or other online forums (76.3%). Only about one-third (34.2%) watched K-dramas on TV. And very few (0.9%) watched K-dramas through renting or buying DVD. This phenomenon is somewhat similar to the results in the survey conducted by the National Communications Commission [6, 7] that fewer people used TV as their primary device when accessing video contents during recent years.

As to K-drama fans' preferences and patterns in Table 2, most of the participants (93.2%) typically watched K-dramas alone. Participants tended to watch K-dramas with a concentrated pattern—only about one-third (32.3%) of the participants watched K-dramas almost every day regularly, others (67.7%) tended to watch many episodes of K-dramas all at once. Among those who watched K-dramas regularly, most of them (59%) watched K-dramas for one to two hours a day, and more than one-fourth (27.6%) watched

Table 2. K-drama watching preferences and patterns ($N = 325$).

Preference and pattern	Frequency	Percentage
Watch alone or with others		
Watch alone	303	93.2%
Watch with others	22	6.8%
K-drama watching pattern		
Distributed	105	32.3%
Concentrated	220	67.7%
Number of hours watched per day ($n = 105$)		
Within 1 h	11	10.5%
1–2 h (less than 2 h)	62	59.0%
2–3 h (less than 3 h)	29	27.6%
3 h and above	3	2.9%
Length of the K-drama (frequency)	*Mean*	*SD*
Less than 16 episodes	3.64	1.209
16–24 episodes	3.59	.979
25–50 episodes	1.97	.814
Over 50 episodes	1.51	.679
Genre of K-drama (frequency)	*Mean*	*SD*
Romance	4.12	.794
School	3.33	.946
Mystery	3.26	.938
Comedy	3.24	1.088
Historical	3.05	1.044
Medical	3.04	1.056

for two to three hours a day. The preferences and patterns can be largely explained by the role of students.

In the follow-up interviews, participants also explained their preferences by describing their daily life as a college student. Since participants in the current study are college students, their typical day is somewhat occupied by coursework and other student activities. Therefore, even if students identified themselves as K-drama fans, they typically cannot afford to spend a great amount of time watching K-dramas on a regular basis. Those who watched K-dramas with a distributed pattern typically spent within 3 h per day during mealtime to relax; those who watched K-dramas with a concentrated pattern tended to watch it on weekends and during holidays.

Table 2 also shows that students tended to watch K-dramas less than 25 episodes. Students often watched K-dramas with fewer episodes. The three top genres students watched more frequently include: romance, school, and mystery. Other genres with a higher variation include: comedy, historical, and medical dramas. Students also explained that they do not have time to watch lengthy K-dramas with too many episodes. They also consider a shorter drama series may be of better quality.

Preference Diversity. Table 3 shows students' self-perceived K-drama preference diversity. Students had a moderate overall score on preference diversity. While they tended to be willing to try K-dramas recommended by others ($M = 4.10$, $SD = 0.72$), and enjoyed discovering K-dramas ($M = 4.08$, $SD = 0.72$), they tended to disagree that their K-drama preference is difficult to categorize ($M = 2.89$, $SD = 1.01$). It's interesting to examine the variations on these items, especially the last five items in Table 3. The standard deviations of these lower-rated items vary a lot. This means K-drama fans may be quite different in terms of their preference diversity. While most K-drama fans enjoy

Table 3. K-drama preference diversity ($N = 325$).

Preference diversity	Mean	SD
I am willing to try K-dramas recommended by others	4.10	0.72
It gives tremendous pleasure to discover K-dramas that I like	4.08	0.79
I am willing to try K-dramas recommended by media or online sources	3.92	0.83
I always feel there are many good K-dramas out there waiting to be discovered	3.87	0.86
I often learn about new K-dramas through different sources	3.77	0.90
My K-drama preference is not limited to certain styles or genres	3.53	1.01
I often view K-dramas of different subjects, genres, and styles	3.52	0.97
I am able to discuss K-dramas with people of various kinds of K-dramas preferences	3.44	0.88
I have watched many non-mainstream K-dramas	3.39	0.98
It's hard to categorize the K-dramas that I like	2.89	1.01
Overall	3.65	0.59

Note. Scale adapted from Tang, Ke, and Sie [11], Tang, Chang, and Lin [12].

discovering K-dramas, some may have specific K-drama preferences and would like to simply delve into it; others may be more open to trying different genres and styles.

This phenomenon can be further explained by the interviewees. While students tend to believe they have a diverse preference to some extent, they are typically very clear about what they do not like. Therefore, sometimes they can be quite selective when it comes to the information they receive.

3.2 Information Behavior

Based on the above findings regarding preference diversity, we found that no matter K-drama fans have a wider or narrower preference, they tend to be willing to obtain information from different sources, including interpersonal communication. This helps us further discuss K-drama fans' information behavior. The following findings first discuss information sources consulted when participants obtain K-drama-related information, and then discuss the information activities performed.

Information Sources. Table 4 shows the information sources consulted by K-drama fans. In general, when students were asked how frequently they consult different sources to obtain K-drama-related information, they tended to rate between sometimes to often. Among which, social media ($M = 3.75$, $SD = 0.91$) and interpersonal sources ($M = 3.55$, $SD = 1.08$) seem to be consulted more often in general. Search engine ($M = 3.50$, $SD = 1.04$) ranked the next. And K-drama fans seldom or never consult derivative works ($M = 2.11$, $SD = 0.93$) or magazines ($M = 2.04$, $SD = 0.97$). The large variations again show the discrepancies among K-drama fans' information source use behavior.

Table 4. K-drama-related information sources ($N = 325$).

Information source	Mean	SD
Social media	3.75	0.91
Interpersonal sources	3.55	1.08
Search engine	3.50	1.04
Derivative works	2.11	0.93
Magazines	2.04	0.97

Note. 1 = never; 5 = always.

In the follow-up interviews, students explained that social media are their top choice because it's the most convenient way to obtain information, and using social media is part of their everyday-life activities. They also highly value friends' recommendations, especially when they believe they share similar tastes. They also value the information derived from the latest Korean news on social media because they can get an overview of how popular these dramas are, and they can easily follow the latest news about the actors/actresses they love.

However, they typically would not make extra efforts to read derivative works or magazines because the main reason they watch K-dramas is to relax and to release stress. This may also explain why the overall frequencies are not very high. Students emphasized they are busy with coursework and other errands. Watching K-dramas could help them escape from reality. They typically follow specific social media groups or pages, but do not actively consult many sources.

Information Activities. Figure 1 shows the frequencies of information activities performed by K-drama fans. The pattern of information activities performed by students is similar to their information source use patterns. Students tend not to actively perform information activities. Therefore, when students were asked how frequently they performed information activities, they tended to rate between sometimes or seldom. Only "search" ($M = 3.63$, $SD = 0.61$) and "browse" ($M = 3.45$, $SD = 0.89$) are relatively higher than other activities.

When further examining Table 5, we found that there is are greater variances in "exchange" ($M = 3.35$, $SD = 1.03$) and "monitor ($M = 2.52$, $SD = 0.97$)." Based on the findings from the interviews, students explained that they only exchange information when they are with K-drama friends, so it depends on how frequently they meet one another. As to monitor, students seem not to consider following social media passively an active monitor activity, and therefore, they rated it with low frequency because they only follow new pages or groups once in a while and do not check the pages or groups regularly. This explanation reflects the complexity of information behavior, and it could be further discussed how we should define "monitor" in the social media world.

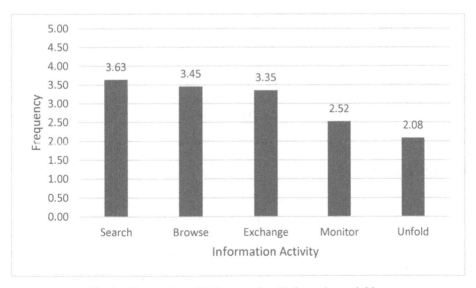

Fig. 1. Frequencies of K-drama-related information activities.

In addition to watching K-dramas, students tend not to engage in other K-drama-related information too deeply unless it is related to the drama they watched or the

Table 5. K-drama-related information activities ($N = 325$).

Information activity	Mean	SD
Search	3.63	0.61
Browse	3.45	0.89
Exchange	3.35	1.03
Monitor	2.52	0.97
Unfold	2.08	0.84

Note. 1 = never; 5 = always.

actors/actresses they love. As mentioned earlier, students highlighted they do not make extra efforts in performing information activities, and therefore, they browse much more frequently than they really unfold information.

Preference Diversity and Information Activities. As shown in Table 6, preference diversity is positively correlated to all five information activities. The higher the preference diversity is, the more frequent information activities are performed.

Table 6. Correlations between preference diversity and information activities ($N = 325$).

Information activity	Search	Browse	Exchange	Monitor	Unfold
Preference diversity	.313**	.423**	.300**	.318**	.345**

Note. *** $p < .001$.

Based on the interview findings, we learned that students typically have a clear sense of their K-drama preferences. If they have a wider preference diversity, they tend to be open to more information sources, and thus are likely to perform various information activities more frequently.

4 Conclusion

College students as K-drama fans typically consider watching K-dramas a relaxation. The findings of the current study can be largely explained by their role as undergraduate students. Students tend to emphasize their busy college life and how they would like to "escape" through watching K-dramas. As a result, they tend not to consult information sources or perform information activities that require extra effort.

Overall, students tend to search and browse more often than deeply engage in reading or constantly monitoring information. They usually receive information passively from social media and other interpersonal sources. Specifically, they use social media in their daily lives, and occasionally exchange information with friends with similar K-drama tastes. K-drama fans are clear about their K-drama preferences and have a moderate preference diversity. Although they do not consult information sources or perform information activities very frequently in general, those who rated higher on preference diversity tend to perform various information activities more frequently.

The current study found that the information behavior of college students as K-drama fans may not necessarily reflect characteristics of information behavior in serious leisure contexts. Future research may further investigate the similarities and differences of individuals' information behavior in non-serious leisure versus serious leisure contexts. Additionally, students in the current study emphasized that they watch K-dramas for relaxation. Future bibliotherapy research can further identify K-dramas that meet different needs. This type of research can implement in academic and public library programs in order to help maintain college students' well-being.

References

1. Wikipedia: K-pop. https://en.wikipedia.org/wiki/K-pop. Accessed 11 Feb 2022
2. Rawnsley, M.-Y.T.: Korean wave in Taiwan: cultural representation of identities and food in Korean TV drama Daejanggeum. In: Kim, J. (ed.) Reading Asian Television Drama: Crossing Borders and Breaking Boundaries, pp. 215–237. I.B. Tauris, London (2014)
3. Kuwahara, Y.: The Korean Wave: Korean Popular Culture in Global Context. Palgrave Macmillan, New York (2014)
4. Shim, D.: Hybridity and the rise of Korean popular culture in Asia. Media Cult. Soc. **28**(1), 25–44 (2006)
5. Lee, A.-G.: The Rise of K-Dramas: Essays on Korean Television and its Global Consumption, McFarland (2019)
6. National Communications Commission: A survey on ICT market development and trends (NCCT109008). https://www.ncc.gov.tw/chinese/files/21021/5190_45724_210217_3.pdf. Accessed 11 Feb 2022
7. National Communications Commission: 2020 Taiwan digital convergence survey. https://www.ncc.gov.tw/chinese/files/21022/5364_45750_210223_1.pdf. Accessed 11 Feb 2022
8. Yeh, N.-C.: Exploring undergraduate students' casual-leisure information behaviors of online video viewing. J. Libr. Inf. Sci. **41**(2), 106–126 (2015)
9. Hektor, A.: What's the use: Internet and information behavior in everyday life. Linkoping, Sweden: Linkoping University. http://liu.diva-portal.org/smash/record.jsf?pid=diva2%3A254863&dswid=6661. Accessed 11 Feb 2022 (2001)
10. Hartel, J., Cox, A.M., Griffin, B.L.: Information activity in serious leisure. Inf. Res. **21**(4), paper 728. http://InformationR.net/ir/21-4/paper728.html. Accessed 11 Feb 2022 (2016)
11. Tang, M.-C., Ke, Y.-L., Sie, Y.-J.: The estimation of aNobii users' reading diversity using book co-ownership data: a social analytical approach. In: Jatowt, A., et al. (eds.) SocInfo 2013. LNCS, vol. 8238, pp. 274–283. Springer, Cham (2013). https://doi.org/10.1007/978-3-319-03260-3_24
12. Tang, M.-C., Chang, M.-M., Lin, S.C..: The development and validation of "preference diversity" and "openness to novelty" scales for movie goers. In: Proceedings of the Association for Information Science and Technology, pp. 486–493 (2018)

Welcome to Heshan: An Installation to Create Immersive and Entertaining Experiences with Local Art Through Interactive Media Technologies

Le Zhou$^{(\boxtimes)}$ and Fuqi Xie

Xi'an Jiaotong - Liverpool University, Suzhou, People's Republic of China
le.zhou@xjtlu.edu.cn

Abstract. In this paper, we proposed an interactive art installation titled "Welcome to Heshan" with an application of emerging technology, which aims at having a more profound impression on participants, including locals and tourists, and engaging audiences with interactive and immersive experiences. In this project, we welcome participants to entertain and impress them with FONG TSE KA's art through designed interactive visual elements. The visual presentation consists of different designs of the Chinese calligraphy and other patterns found from FONG TSE KA's painting, including "calligraphy waterfalls", "calligraphy snowflakes", re-designed abstract background referenced to the paintings and human profiles filled with vivid colours. The installation will, by default, show a running calligraphy waterfall over a repeating background series as the presentation mode. When the participant walks in the interactive area, the installation will detect their presence and switch to interactive mode in which the waterfall will partially switch to snowflake with falling and bouncing effect. Moreover, the installation will project the participant into the screen as color blocks in profile shape, and the participant can virtually catch and hold the calligraphy snowflakes as in the physical world. Through this installation, we have successfully conveyed a warm welcome to visitors in an entertaining and engaging format within the constraints of the specific location and cultural context.

Keywords: Interactive installation art · Motion capture · Physical simulation · FONG TSE KA

1 Introduction

Rapidly evolving digital media technologies have provided a solid foundation for new media art, facilitating interactive installations. Interactive installation art, developing from installation art, emphasizes real-time interactive experiences supported by emerging technologies [1, 2]. In contrast to traditional installation art, which is created by artists and appreciated by the audience, interactive installations emphasize interaction and on-site experiences [3]. With a dynamic art form, the interactive installation presents

P.-L. P. Rau (Ed.): HCII 2022, LNCS 13312, pp. 304–317, 2022.
https://doi.org/10.1007/978-3-031-06047-2_22

Fig. 1. Participant interacts with the installation

uncertainty and encourages a collaborative relationship between the audiences and the artwork through various interactions [4]. It varies in size and medium, but generally, this form requires different computer technologies for information acquisition, processing, editing, and communication and appropriate software and hardware equipment to complement them [5]. These characteristics distinguish interactive installation art from the traditional art experience and make it unique and widely accepted by audiences in this information era [6]. While many interactive installations nowadays work mainly on abstract visual effects as attraction to participants, this project investigates in the cultural connotations and focuses on innovative expressions of traditional culture heritage. This paper presents a wall-size interactive screen to provide interactive cultural immersion through entertaining experiences. Participants will, in real-time, see their full-body profiles projected into the screen as vivid-colour-filled outlines. Moreover, there are curated Chinese calligraphy characters, falling and bouncing from the designed backgrounds, which participants and their projected profiles can interact with these virtual elements in the screen through our customized physical behaviour simulation (Fig. 1).

2   Background

This project extract and redesign materials from traditional culture and art and combine them with emerging technologies. Aiming at a new creation of existing local artistic content and presenting them in a new format, we look in the artwork of a local artist FONG TSE KA.

2.1   Project Location and Background

The interactive installation is in Heshan Town - Tongxiang City, a small water town located in eastern China, where FONG TSE KA, was born and raised. The local government designed and built a resort village that referred to the story and art of the artist and named it "The Painter's Ideal Village" to attract visitors worldwide. There is an

Innovation Center and exhibition hall, next to the village entrance and the tourist centre, to host public gathering events and exhibitions [7]. In the exhibition hall, the architect planned a permanent interactive wall that serves as a welcoming installation to welcome visitors and aims at promoting the local culture and the local artist - FONG TSE KA's art to the audience in a modern and entertaining way.

2.2 FONG TSE KA's Arts

FONG TSE KA (T.K.), the 'Progenitor of Modern Chinese Cartoons, was a native of Tongxiang, Jiaxing City, Zhejiang Province. He is also a famous modern Chinese calligrapher, published over 160 books, encompassing such diverse fields as calligraphy and painting collections, essays, art theory and music theory. FONG TSE KA usually wrote some verses on the paintings. Xun Ouyang influenced the brushwork of his calligraphy at the beginning, and then he switched to the Northern Wei following master Shutong Li and eventually formed his style [8]. In both running and cursive calligraphy arts, his strokes flow naturally in the brushwork. The style demonstrates a unique flavour of the strokes, which initially had a clear tendency towards the regular script, with an additional reflection as distinctive as his cartoon paintings.

Main Contribution. Regards of the local cultural context and the demand for innovative expression of traditional art, we proposed this interactive art installation titled "Welcome to the Heshan" with the application of emerging technology, which aims at having a more profound impression on participants, including locals and tourists, and engaging audiences with interactive and immersive experiences.

In this project, we welcome participants to entertain and impress them with FONG TSE KA's art through designed interactive visual elements. The visual presentation consists of different designs of the Chinese calligraphy and other patterns found from FONG TSE KA's painting, including "calligraphy waterfalls", "calligraphy snowflakes", re-designed abstract background referenced to the paintings and human profiles filled with vivid colours. The installation will, by default, show a running calligraphy waterfall over a repeating background series as the presentation mode. When the participant walks in the interactive area, the installation will detect their presence and switch to interactive mode in which the waterfall will partially switch to snowflake with falling and bouncing effect. Moreover, the installation will project the participant into the screen as colour blocks in profile shape, and the participant can virtually catch and hold the calligraphy snowflakes as in the physical world.

We have explored the design and development of this interactive installation with motion capture techniques and projection display, using a depth capture camera and image processing technology to capture participants' human contours. And we applied physical simulation to the captured contour and other visual elements such as gravity, bounce and etc. in the physical-engine-powered world scene simulation. Through this installation, we have successfully conveyed a message of warm welcome to visitors in an entertaining and engaging format within the constraints of the specific location and cultural context.

3 Installation and Interaction Design

The system has two main modes - presentation and interaction modes - along with a shared debugging interface. The two display modes will automatically switch based on the state controller, the real-time detection of whether participants are playing in the interactive area.

3.1 The State Controller

The system switches between the two modes by detecting human and other moving objects in the interactive area while no static object exists in the interactive area in the physical setup. Thus, we use human detection to describe the system's initial state (0) and the presentation mode later in this manuscript. When the number of the active objects, human, detected exceeds the set range, which is zero, in the interactive area, we consider there is human entering the area and note state (1), exit the presentation mode and switch to the interaction model. When the number of detected human-less is greater than the set range, we consider no human in the interactive area and note the system state (0), exit the interactive mode and execute the presentation mode. When the system does not detect any human and notes state (0), we execute and display the presentation mode.

3.2 The Presentation Mode

Fig. 2. Presentation mode

When in the state (0), the system will execute presentation mode. This presentation mode consists of a Chinese calligraphy waterfall in different shades and a group of repeated coloured backgrounds that change regularly. There are 11 different poems arranged in 28 columns horizontally distributed on the screen from left to right. The font size and transparency parameters follow a sin wave, whose peaks are on the left and right sides, and the valley is at the centre. The scrolling speeds, strokes and size of adjacent verses are randomly different (Fig. 2).

3.3 The Interaction Mode

When the state (1), participants, enter the interactive area, the system will execute inter-action mode. The participants will see their real-time profiles projected on the screen, and they can open arms or use other parts of the body to catch or bounce away from the text blocks. The Chinese text blocks, which means "Welcome to Heshan", appear from the top and fall in the middle interactive zone. Otherwise, they will bounce away, fall to the ground, fade over time and eventually disappear (Fig. 3).

Fig. 3. Interaction mode

Real-time human profile projection is presented by superimposing several overlaying colour blocks. The colour block appears filled with external outlines of the human body with a certain transparency. The top layer is the currently detected human, while the layers of the human body in the past four frames are stacked downwards in sequence with different colours. When the human moves fast enough and with significant position changes, the different layers of the frames will be staggered to show a coloured track like a long exposure image of movements.

We name this effect: the calligraphy character, previously described as text blocks, will fall like snowflakes, "calligraphy snowflakes". The snowflake will slightly collide and bounce with the contour of the human and the ground - the bottom edge of the screen. The participants can raise arms to grab, hold, or bounce away from the snowflake and keep them on or in the shape or area formed by gestures. When lowered the arms or any other gesture not to block the snowflake, they will continue to fall, bounce from the ground and pile up. All the snowflakes will gradually disappear after a certain period.

3.4 The Debugging Interface

The debugging interface can real-time modify three essential parts of the installation, including detection, interaction and the objects' behaviours, control the interactive enter-tainment and behaviours, and tweak the installation to align with the physical environ-ment for better performance. This interface is mainly used on-site and during the setup and could activate with the space bar. All adjustable parameters are arranged in the panel located on the left side of the screen. Sliders and drag can adjust the parameters to left or right between the bar's minimal and maximum value, and all the adjustments show in real-time in the interactive zone (Fig. 4).

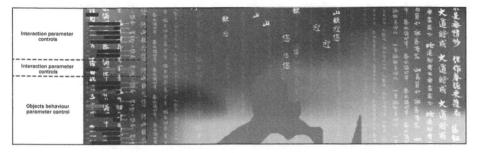

Fig. 4. Debugging interface

Detection Parameter Controls. The parameters in the detection part control the dimension of interactive areas, including the depth range and the width and height. There is a ShowMoitor button that controls whether to display the depth image that catches by the camera. Int-width and int-height limit the size of interaction areas. Depth Min and Max control the depth of the capture area, so is the size of the interactive area. The OpenCV blur value and the OpenCV threshold affect the recognition and the filters.

Interaction Parameter Controls. The parameter in the interaction part corresponds to the human contour, and the calligraphy snowflake controls during the interaction mode. DrawEdges affects whether to stroke the contour. Start_collusion activates the collision in the physics engine. The start object controls the initialization of the falling snowflakes.

Objects Behaviour Parameter Control. The parameters in the part of the objects affect the snowflakes' number, size, frequency and lifespan. Both the text size, randomTextSize, miniSize and maxSize decide the size of the snowflake. ParticleRate and lifespan are about the frequency and lifespan, while the polygonRate and polygonStop Threshold is about the sampling rate of the human contour polygon.

3.5 Visual Design Iterations

The elements of this interactive system are derived from the paintings of FONG TSE KA to bring traditional culture, local flavor and interactive technology together. There are many calligraphic inscriptions in FONG TSE KA's paintings, and we have extracted all the characters as the essential part and though which, we enabled interaction with participants. We arranges the verses in the painting vertically, flowing from left to right in varying shades, sizes and speeds, creating a waterfall of poetry (Fig. 5).

Fig. 5. Three color schemes: from left to right are schemes one, two, and three

We tried three different color scheme options for the text and backgrounds. The first is to visually simulate a traditional scroll with a beige paper pattern as the background and black colored texts in the foreground. The second uses contrasting solid colors with a black background and white colored texts moving above, which refers to inscription on an ancient tablet. The third uses a richer palette and displays a stronger sense of modernity and design. The background is a mix of different colours of rose-coloured clouds, taking on the mood of a natural landscape. They flow into each other and blend to make the image more prosperous and vivid. In the foreground is a white waterfall of poetry, contrasting with the rich colors of the background. Aiming at more substantial visual impact with a modern aesthetic, we chose the third color scheme and designed eight different backgrounds in a series (Fig. 6).

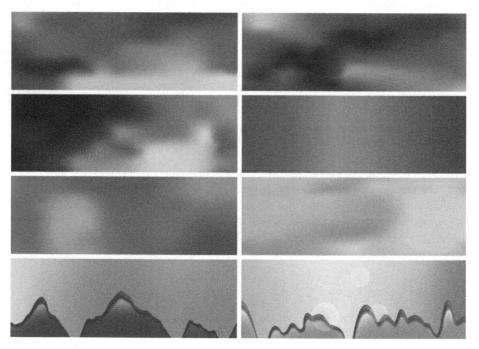

Fig. 6. Eight backgrounds

4 Software Implementation

The interactive system includes the presentation and interaction modes and several functional modules, including human detection, "calligraphy waterfall", human contour detection and "calligraphy snowflakc" physical simulation. The system's initial state is the presentation mode, and it switches to interactive mode on positive human detection. The former mode forms a calligraphy waterfall with moving calligraphy images. The latter will sequentially several function modules obtain human contour and add them, along with calligraphy images, to the physical engine to simulate collision and other physical effects. Furthermore, when setting up the interactive installation on-site, we also use the space bar to activate the debugging panel and adjust the parameter and settings.

4.1 Software Architecture

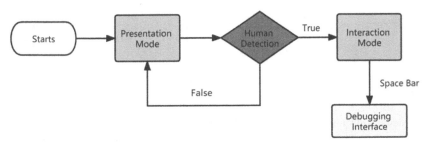

Fig. 7. System structure

The Presentation Mode and Interaction Mode are affected by the human detection module, the state controller, deciding which mode the system plays. After the system starts, the presentation mode is run by default and display the "calligraphy waterfall" over the dynamic background images. When Kinect detects the participant entering the interactive area, register the state as 'true', and switch to interactive mode [9, 10]. In this mode, the flow speed of the "waterfall" and the transparency of the intermediate interactive zone will be reduced. Furthermore, in the interactive zone of the screen, the physics simulation engine applies gravity and bounce to the Chinese calligraphy blocks, which enable them to collide and bounce with the ground and the outlines of the human body—the captured result from the human contour detection module (Fig. 7).

4.2 The 'Calligraphy Waterfall'

In the presentation mode, we set different positions and speeds for different calligraphy images and regularly repeated them with eight background images, forming the calligraphy waterfall. In order to make it scroll and repeat seamlessly within the display area, the height of the calligraphy image is twice the height of the display area. Initially, we place the images and align their bottom edge with the display, and the images gradually

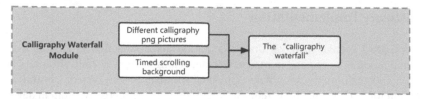

Fig. 8. Calligraphy waterfall

move downwards. When the top of the image hits the top edge of the display, it returns to its initial position. Therefore, the calligraphy images show a smooth animation and repeat on the display (Fig. 8).

4.3   The Human Detection and the Human Contour Detection

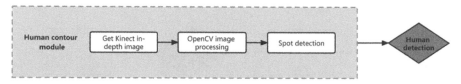

Fig. 9. Human detection module

Human detection runs in the background as the state controller and switches the system between modes. The program uses the getRawBodyTrack function in the KinectPV2 library to find humans in the current picture. The first step will sequentially obtain the depth image, apply OpenCV image processing, and apply contour detection to acquire the human contour information [11]. The second step is to obtain depth information from the depth camera with detecting humans. It uses the getRawDepthData function in the KinectPV2 library to obtain the depth image update and return the corresponding gradient colour depth map according to the depth value. The third step is to perform OpenCV image processing on the updated depth map [12]. Use the OpenCV methods including blur, threshold, dilate and erode functions in the OpenCV processing library to pre-process the image, filter out small objects, fill in small gaps, and return the processed image [13]. The fourth step is contour detection, which uses the setThreshold, compute-Blobs, and getEdgeNb functions in the blobDetection library to filter dark areas, calculate counter and blobs, and return a list of contour arrays that meet the conditions [14–16]. The outline of the human body obtained in this process will be passed to the physical engine for simulation and presented on the screen with our visual designs (Fig. 9).

4.4   The Physical Engine and Simulation

There are three main tasks to build the physical engine: environment setup and the simulation of both the human contour and the "Chinese calligraphy snowflakes". With the box2d library, we set these elements with corresponding classes and functions, and the physical engine will perform the simulation (Fig. 10).

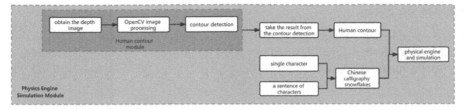

Fig. 10. Physics engine simulation module

Environment Setup. The initializing environment contains the physical engine environment and the simulated ground. The physical environment is initialized by creating a "world" with gravity in the engine. This installation needs a physical ground at the bottom of the screen, so the programme used a boundary collider to simulate the virtual ground and place it correspondingly. Thus, the calligraphy snowflakes will bounce when they contact the ground.

Human Contours. We take the previous contour detection result and apply multiple processing methods. The first step is to convert the detection results into correspondence key points of the boundary, optimize them in the case of false edge detection and returns an array list containing all the points of the human profile boundary. The second step is to create a chain collider with the key points array list in the physics engine, which involves calling the Surface class to do the conversion and then setting its collision properties and displaying them on the screen. The third step is to recalculate the contour key points and the chain with the real-time detected result in each frame.

Chinese Calligraphy Snowflakes. We have designed two forms of calligraphy snowflakes, including a single character as a square collider and a sentence of characters as a rectangular collider. The square collider uses the Particle class and produces a circle in the physical engine. The collision properties of those particles can also be controlled with the control panel in debugging interface. The rectangle collider uses the Polygon class to produce a polygon in the physics engine, and its collision properties can also be real-time modified. Both elements move from the top of the screen along different tracks while the opacity decreases as the number of frames increases, and the snowflakes will eventually disappear when reaching the given threshold.

5 Hardware Solutions and Installation Setup

5.1 Basic Configuration

This interactive system runs on Windows 7 and above, developed in Java language, using a creative coding framework - Processing 3.5.4 with libraries including controlP5, Kinect for Windows, OpenCV for processing, blob detection and box2d. The system requires a computer with at least a 1-core processor, 1G RAM and a 20 GB hard disk working with the Microsoft KinectV2 depth camera.

5.2 On Site Setup

Based on the location for this interactive installation, the double innovation centre's site conditions in Heshan Town, we used two 8000 lm projectors and anti-light curtains as the display medium (Figs. 11 and 12).

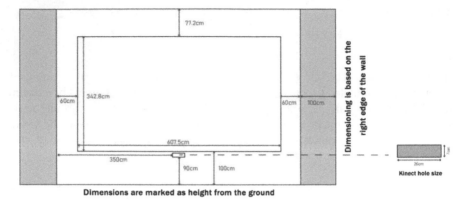

Fig. 11. Installation dimension design

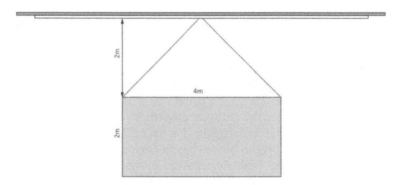

Fig. 12. Interactive area in front of the screen

The recommended interactive area for this interactive system is 1 m to 4.5 m far in front of the device with a width of 4 m. The running computer needs configuring Processing and all dependent libraries and installing the Kinect v2 driver. The maximum frame rate of the interactive system can reach 60 fps, and the average of the interactive mode is 30 fps.

6 Testing and Feedback

After the installation was set up, we, along with visitors, played and tested the interactive installation. Participants showed significant interests in this new form of cultural

Fig. 13. Participants interact with the installation

experience. Some will open their arms to take the Chinese calligraphy snowflakes and let them pile on their arms until the snowflakes disappear. Some treat the snowflakes as balloons and repeatedly touch certain ones with their arms. Others like to grab and then embrace the snowflakes and walk around, waiting for it to disappear and then move on to the next one. The system's interaction design is simple and straight forward, with an instinct mapping to real life experiences. Participants can quickly master the gameplay and explore the more interesting interactions. Some participants mentioned that the way the human contours appears on the screen is somewhat different from other visual effects, creating a psychological gap between virtual and real. Some believe that integrating traditional cultural elements into interactive installations demonstrates a sense of novelty and makes them look forward to more interactive installations. Others said that this interactive format interested them in exploring the art further because they wanted to double-check whether the elements were from FONG TSE KA's paintings (Fig. 13).

7   Conclusion and Future Developments

This paper introduces an interactive system designed and developed with FONG TSE KA's paintings as inspiration and material and installed at the Heshan Town, which aims to create new experiences and represent traditional culture in an innovative format. Through interactive design, we apply new technologies to achieve the purpose of making tradition and local art more attractive and easy to access. Combining with the message of warm welcome, we extracted the form of Chinese calligraphy characters from the poems of FONG TSE KA's paintings as the main visual design element. And we then built an interactive system consisting of two modes and three main functional modules to showcase the design and experiences.

As an exploration of both art and technology, this installation could apply several improvements in future in terms of visual design and system stability. Firstly, the different visual design elements of this interactive installation is not harmonious enough. In the current visual appearance, the human profile differs in style from the overall interface, creating a sense of disparity for the participants. This design has highlighted the participant with different colours and transparency as well as overlaps over the frames, and the overlaid area gets darker as the number of layers increases. In contrast, the background is in a macaroon-colour scheme with a gradiently blurred brightness. In future work, we will apply modification to the visual style of the human profile and fit the overall visual style. Secondly, the system stability could be improved. When there are too many participants in the interactive area, the frame rate decreases, resulting in a noticeable lagging effect. We believe that the platform and programming language - Processing limited the performances. In future work, we will try to build an interactive system with Unity which is more capable of heavy loads of physical simulation. Thirdly, the installation could introduce more cultural content and present different interactions. Different elements can be found and processed to fit the contexts. This project could be a continuing exploration of various combinations of art and technologies and various interactive experiences.

References

1. Schraffenberger, H., van der Heide, E.: Interaction models for audience-artwork interaction: current state and future directions. In: Brooks, A.L. (ed.) ArtsIT 2011. LNICSSITE, vol. 101, pp. 127–135. Springer, Heidelberg (2012). https://doi.org/10.1007/978-3-642-33329-3_15
2. Hu, J., Funk, M., Zhang, Y., Wang, F.: Designing interactive public art installations: new material therefore new challenges. In: Pisan, Y., Sgouros, N.M., Marsh, T. (eds.) ICEC 2014. LNCS, vol. 8770, pp. 199–206. Springer, Heidelberg (2014). https://doi.org/10.1007/978-3-662-45212-7_25
3. Ahmed, S.U.: Interaction and interactivity: in the context of digital interactive art installation. In: Kurosu, M. (ed.) HCI 2018. LNCS, vol. 10902, pp. 241–257. Springer, Cham (2018). https://doi.org/10.1007/978-3-319-91244-8_20
4. Zhang, Y., Gu, J., Hu, J., et al.: Learning from traditional dynamic arts: elements for interaction design. In: 2013 International Conference on Culture and Computing (2013)
5. Nardelli, E.: A classification framework for interactive digital artworks. In: Alvarez, F., Costa, C. (eds.) UCMEDIA 2010. LNICSSITE, vol. 60, pp. 91–100. Springer, Heidelberg (2012). https://doi.org/10.1007/978-3-642-35145-7_12
6. Price, S., Sakr, M., Jewitt, C.: Exploring whole-body interaction and design for museums. Interact. Comput. **28**, 569–583 (2015)
7. Ceconello, M.: Smart artefacts and spaces to interact, promote and transfer cultural knowledge. In: Advances in Intelligent Systems and Computing, pp. 644–652 (2018)
8. Luo, H.: The interaction of China calligraphy and Chinese characters. J. Chin. Characters **19**, 31–40 (2017)
9. Processing. https://processing.org/
10. Kinect for Processing Library – Magic & Love Interactive. http://www.magicandlove.com/blog/research/kinect-for-processing-library/
11. Alouache, A., Wu, Q.: Evaluation of an OpenCV implementation of structure from motion on open source data. In: Fox, C., Gao, J., Ghalamzan Esfahani, A., Saaj, M., Hanheide, M., Parsons, S. (eds.) TAROS 2021. LNCS (LNAI), vol. 13054, pp. 158–167. Springer, Cham (2021). https://doi.org/10.1007/978-3-030-89177-0_16
12. Han, L.: Object detection module based on implementation of Java and OpenCV. J. Comput. Appl. **28**, 773–775 (2008)

13. Tong, W., Li, H., Chen, G.: Blob detection based on soft morphological filter. IEICE Trans. Inf. Syst. **E103.D**, 152–162 (2020)
14. Wang, G., Lopez-Molina, C., De Baets, B.: Automated blob detection using iterative Laplacian of Gaussian filtering and unilateral second-order Gaussian kernels. Digit. Signal Process. **96**, 102592 (2020)
15. Li, D., Bei, L., Bao, J., Yuan, S., Huang, K.: Image contour detection based on improved level set in complex environment. Wirel. Netw. **27**(7), 4389–4402 (2021). https://doi.org/10.1007/s11276-021-02664-5
16. Cheng, X., Sun, J., Zhou, F.: A fully convolutional network-based tube contour detection method using multi-exposure images. Sensors. **21**, 4095 (2021)

Creative Industries and Cultural Heritage under a Cross-Cultural Perspective

A Framework for Corporate Museums to Build Customer-Based Brand Equity

Shu-Hua Chang[✉]

Department of Arts and Creative Industries, National Dong Hwa University, Hualien, Taiwan
iamcsh0222@gms.ndhu.edu.tw

Abstract. Traditionally, corporate museums have focused on company history, whereas today they not only play a service role, but are also used as a vehicle for creating brand marketing advantages. The role of corporate museums has expanded to be a new marketing device for building corporate brand identity strategies. To date, corporate museums have been little-explored in the general brand management or marketing literatures. It is difficult to build brand equity for corporate museums. Unlike products, corporate museums' branding is quite multifaceted, as there are many aspects involved in their branding, given the cultural, social, economic, and technological issues associated with museums as products. The objective of this study is to address this important issue and present a modified framework for building the customer-based brand equity of corporate museums. The cases study was carried out in two historic corporate museums in Taiwan: Kuo Yuan Ye Museum of Cake and Pastry, and Chihsing Tan Katsuo Museum. In-depth semi-structured interviews were conducted to explore the brand elements, according to the different phases of the brand equity related to each corporate museum's brand, products, and experiences. This study proposed five experience design elements, namely knowledge acquisition, relevance of activities to life, exhibition experience, product experience, and interactions with staff, that affect the formation of brand equity. This study contributes a framework upon which corporate museums can build sustainable brand equity to enhance their competitiveness.

Keywords: Corporate museum · Brand equity · Customer-based brand equity · Brand experience · Experience design

1 Introduction

1.1 Research Background

Corporate museums have existed for over a century [1] and have become a popular destination in cultural tourism. Nowadays, corporate museums are considered to be exhibition-based facilities that are owned and operated by publicly traded or privately held companies, often fulfilling roles such as public relations and marketing [2: 536]. The role of corporate museums has expanded to be a new marketing device for building corporate brand identity strategies [2]. Traditionally, corporate museums have focused on company history, whereas today they not only play a service role, but are also used as a

P.-L. P. Rau (Ed.): HCII 2022, LNCS 13312, pp. 321–333, 2022.
https://doi.org/10.1007/978-3-031-06047-2_23

vehicle for creating brand marketing advantages. To date, corporate museums have been little-explored in the general brand management or marketing literatures, with studies by Carù, Ostillio, and Leone [3], Nissley and Casey [2], and Piatkowska [4] being the few works in this area. Carù et al. [3] pointed out that corporate museums help customers identify the brand and enhance brand authenticity. Furthermore, corporate museums can enrich the brand image through storytelling and the visitors' experience [3].

Brand is regarded as the most valuable asset for enterprises, and it is found to be important to build strong brands that have brand equity, to influence loyalty [5–7]. According to Gilmore and Pine [8], consumers are increasingly searching for experiences and authentic brands. Keller [6, 7] stated that enterprises need to choose brand elements to build brand equity, such as brand names, logos, symbols, slogans, packages, etc. However, it is difficult to build brand equity for corporate museums. Unlike products, corporate museums' branding is quite multifaceted, as there are many aspects involved in their branding, given the cultural, social, economic, and technological issues associated with museums as products.

Based on the development of the tourism industry and social culture, corporate museums can not only strengthen their brand identity and corporate image, but also contribute to the cultural sustainability of the industry. However, corporate museums have been underexplored in the brand management or marketing literatures.

1.2 Purpose

The objective of this study is to address this important issue and present a modified framework for building the customer-based brand equity of corporate museums. The cases study was carried out in two historic corporate museums in Taiwan: Kuo Yuan Ye Museum of Cake and Pastry, and Chihsing Tan Katsuo Museum. The two museums were invited to participate in this study because of their specific industrial history that provides similar traditional industry restructuring and upgrading backgrounds. This factor was used as a common denominator, allowing the extraction of the most important elements from the particular cases. In-depth semi-structured interviews were conducted to explore the brand elements, according to the different phases of the brand equity related to each corporate museum's brand, products, and experiences. This study builds an experiential design framework by illustrating how the corporate museums create a brand relationship with visitors by manipulating the social and physical context. Hence, this study contributes a framework upon which corporate museums can build sustainable brand equity to enhance their competitiveness.

2 Literature Review

2.1 Corporate Museum

Corporate museums have been developing for over a century [1], but academic research on marketing is still limited [4]. Previous studies focused on the role and function of corporate museums. For example, Daniel [9] defined a corporate museum as a corporate facility with physical objects or displays designed to communicate the history of the enterprise to internal employees, customers, and the general public. Nissley and Casey [2: p. 536] proposed that corporate museums were "exhibition-based facilities that are owned and operated by publicly traded or privately held companies, often serving roles such as public relations and marketing". In recent years, research has gradually extended to examine corporate museums' relevance to customer experience and brands, such as Piatkowska's [4] study from the perspective of marketing, which explored how the corporate museums of Porsche, Mercedes-Benz, and BMW (BMW Welt) contributed to brand marketing. The study proposed that corporate museums, in addition to their social value, contribute to the establishment of brand identity, and leverage the advantages of marketing strategies and selling branded products.

Recently, studies on corporate museums have been expanded to the issue of visitors' experience and branding. Regarding marketing, Piatkowska [4] explored the value of Porsche, Mercedes-Benz, and BMW Welt's corporate museums for brand marketing. The study proposed that corporate museums not only have social value, but also contribute to the brand identity and leverage the advantages of marketing strategies and product sales.

Piatkowska [4] found that the Porsche Museum was designed to give visitors a proposed mystical journey, through the creation of sensual experiences, which can verify the authenticity of the branded products and quality of service. Hence, corporate museums contribute to the stability of brand imagery, and this also highlights their importance as a corporate brand strategy. In a case study of the Salvatore Ferragamo Museum, Carù, Ostillio, and Leone [3] proposed that corporate museums can help customers identify with and perceive the authenticity of the brand, and that museums can enrich the brand image through storytelling and the design of the visiting experience. In terms of communicating the museum's message, temporary exhibitions can be a strategy to broaden its offering through innovative content that expresses its modernity; this attract potential visitors with valuable experiences, who will become loyal to the brand [3].

Traditionally, the role of corporate museums has concentrated on the firm's history, such as the story of the founder or other important individuals, by displaying documents, photographs, and products. Nowadays, the meaning of the corporate museum has been extended as a strategy for corporate brand marketing [2]. Although this is one of the strategies that encourage consumers to experience the company brands, the relevant literature has not yet explored the topic of corporate museums' experience design and branding. Therefore, the study will fill this gap, to examine the museums' experience design and its association with brand equity.

2.2 Experience Design

Reviewing the literature, Pullman and Gross [10] claimed that experience design refers to how organizations can create an emotional connection with customers through delivering intangible and tangible components. In terms of tourism, experience design is described as creating and managing touchpoints with tourists, to achieve the practice of a successful customer experience [11]. Tussyadiah [11] proposed that experience design refers to interactivity, including the interactions with tourism objects (such as scenes, cultural relics), interaction with social elements of the destination (such as other tourists, locals, employees of tour providers, other relevant social networks), and interactions with media elements (such as mass media, marketing media, etc.).

In the cultural sector, experiences are often created by the physical and social contexts [10, 12, 13]. The physical context of experience design refers to the tangible aspects in the settings, such as the architecture and interior design, supporting facilities [10], and the layout and type of exhibits [13], which is similar to "mechanics clues," according to Carbone and Haeckel [14]. Minkiewicz et al. [13] found that the spatial features of the museum influence customers' attitudes and behaviors. The social context refers to the interaction with other visitors, locals, service providers, and so on, at the destination [10, 11]; this is similar to "humanics clues," defined by Carbone and Haeckel [14]. According to the study of VIP tents by Pullman and Gross [10], both physical and social elements have impacts on the perceived quality of the customer experience. However, experience design is still a relatively new topic, which can pose considerable challenges to cultural businesses [15]. Although marketing research in the cultural context has increased lately, there is limited literature on experience design, to understand and explain how to build a valuable customer experience in corporate museums. The study will fill the research gap by employing qualitative in-depth interviews on the experience of corporate museums.

2.3 Brand Equity

In the 1990s, the term of customer-based brand equity (CBBE) was proposed in marketing. Brand equity is "a set of brand assets and liabilities linked to a brand, its name and symbol that adds to or subtracts from the value provided by a product or service to a firm and/or to that firm's customers" [5]. In terms of customers, Keller [6] defined brand equity as "the differential effect of brand knowledge on consumer response to the marketing of the brand." Brand equity can be divided into two levels: brand response and brand knowledge [6]. In the marketing aspect, brand equity refers to a customer's perception and learning related to a brand, through strategic marketing activities of a firm [5, 6]. According to Keller's [6] study on CBBE, brand equity is divided into brand awareness, brand association, brand feeling, brand performance, brand judgment, and brand resonance. Aaker [5] argued that brand equity includes brand awareness, brand association, perceived quality, brand loyalty, and other proprietary brand assets (e.g., patents, trademarks, channel relationships, etc.); the first four elements are from the customer's viewpoint, and the last one is from the corporation's perspective. According to what customers learned, saw, felt, and heard about the brand, this would lead to customer-based brand equity [6]. The challenge of brand marketing is how to connect customers' thoughts, feelings, images, and experiences with the brand.

The construct and variables of brand equity have been adjusted in different fields of research, such as space cleaning [16, 17]; spatial attractiveness [18], which is included in the quality of perception; and activity as a measure of brand imagery [19, 20]. This implies that customer-based brand equity is not yet universally applicable [21, 22].

Brand awareness refers to how well a customer can identify or recall a brand [5–7]. Brand awareness comprises two components: brand recall and brand recognition [6, 7]. Brand recall is defined as the consumer's ability to remember a brand when thinking of that product class, while brand recognition is regarded as more important, in terms of making product decisions regarding the brand [6, 7]. Brand awareness is the first step in building customer-based brand equity [6, 7].

Brand association refers to the characteristics that consumers can associate with the brand, which will help them create and organize their memory of a brand [5]. Brand association can include product and non-product features [23]. Similarly, Keller [6, 7] proposed that brand association is derived from brand attitudes, emotional features, and experiential benefits.

Perceived quality is defined by Zeithaml [24] as a consumer's judgement regarding the product's superiority or excellence. Similarly to Aaker [5] and Keller [6], Zeithaml [24] refers to perceptual quality as a consumer's perception of the overall product or service quality in comparison to its competition.

Brand loyalty consists of two components, namely behavioral loyalty and attitudinal loyalty [25, 26]. In tourism, behavioral loyalty refers to the tourist's frequency of repeat visits. Attitudinal loyalty is concentrated on the tourist's intention to revisit and positive recommendation to others. Reviewing the literatures, previous studies proposed that visitors could be loyal to a destination even if they could not revisit the destination [16, 27, 28]. Therefore, attitude loyalty can be used as a tourist's loyalty to a destination brand [16]. In corporate museums, attitudinal brand loyalty is more suitable than repeat visit.

3   Research Methods

This study explores how experiential design elements relate to brand equity, which is still in an exploratory research phase; Yin's [29] case study methodology is applied to collect questions about why or how this occurs. Few studies have examined the experience design in corporate museums by means of a qualitative research method. Benbasat, Goldstein, and Mead [30] proposed that a multiple-case study provides powerful materials for descriptive analysis or the establishment of theory. Therefore, a qualitative multiple-case research is suitable for this study. Two corporate museums were invited to participate in the study via email: the Kuo Yuan Ye Museum of Cake and Pastry (Shilin Branch), established in 2002, which is located in Taipei; and the Chihsing Tan Katsuo Museum, established in 2003, which is located in Hualien. Both of the corporate museums have delivered a remarkable performance to their parent company. The sites were chosen because their operations have similar general characteristics; this was used as common standard, allowing the extraction of the most important features from specific cases.

3.1   Data Collection

This study examines how the elements of experience design that are associated with brand equity in corporate museums, which are important for corporate museum operators and visitors, can be assessed; this will help to determine how the experiential design affects visitors. The study employed purposive sampling to recruit visitors who had experienced either one of the research sites, who might offer individual perspectives on the visiting experiences. The purpose was to invite active respondents who could contribute to the research, rather than to maximize the size of the representative sample [31]. The interview respondents included fourteen participants who had visited either the Kuo Yuan Ye Museum of Cake and Pastry (Shilin Branch) and Chihsing Tan Katsuo Museum. To safeguard the reliability of data analysis and interpretation, the author illustrated the exemplars and the operational definitions of the study to the participants.

On this basis, the semi-structured questions were formulated as follows:

1. What experiences of the museum inform you about the characteristics of the brand? Why?
2. What experiences of the museum affect how you view the meaning of the product or service offered by the brand (e.g. product, service, design style)? Why?
3. How did the visiting experiences enable you to generate a positive assessment of the brand?
4. How did the visiting experiences influence your intention to visit again?

3.2 Data Analysis

Following the qualitative content analysis techniques of Dey [32], Elo and Kyngas [33], and Zhang and Wildemuth [34], the data analysis approach was employed in this study. All interviews were transcribed verbatim, and content analysis was used to analyze and interpret the interviewed visitors' data. First, the author generated the initial codes through segmenting the terms according to the experiential design characteristic implemented at the research sites. Second, the texts that frequently appeared in the recording were labelled and grouped together into categories [33]. Third, the codes were categorized by identifying common themes, with relevant meanings. Finally, each theme was assigned to one of the social and physical contexts corresponding to brand equity. Because individual themes were used as the coding unit, the author repeatedly read the contexts of the interviews according to the theory of experience design and brand equity.

4 Results

The study collected the elements of experience design corresponding to brand equity in the two corporate museums through conducting interviews. The elements of experience design were organized using the aforementioned data analysis method, as shown in Table 1.

Table 1. Summary table of elements of experience design corresponding to brand equity

Experience design elements	Brand awareness	Brand association	Perceived quality	Brand loyalty
Relevance of activities to life	Immersing in DIY activities	Experiencing traditional ritual	The details of activities	Innovations on activities
Knowledge acquisition	Thematic guided tours	Learned by making products through practical experience		
Interactions with staff		Hospitality and the joy of service interaction	Customized tour commentary	
Product experience			Experiencing authenticity and reliability through product	
Exhibition experience	Experiencing the exhibition of traditional cultural ritual	The collection of exhibition objects	Characteristics of the exhibition design	New themed exhibitions

4.1 Elements of Experience Design and Brand Awareness

Brand awareness refers to the ability of customers to recognize or recall a brand under various conditions. The results showed that knowledge acquisition, relevance of activities to life, and exhibition experience were likely to increase brand awareness.

Regarding knowledge acquisition, the corporate museums enabled visitors to acquire knowledge and recognized the characteristics of the brand through thematic guided tours. The relevance of activities to life refers to respondents immersing themselves in DIY activities at the corporate museum, to acquire knowledge that contributed to their awareness of the company brand. For example, bonito flake making offered by Chihsing Tan Katsuo Museum, or traditional cake making provided by Guo Yuanyi Cake Museum (Shilin Pavilion), enhanced visitors' recognition of the company brand. One of the respondents mentioned: "…experiencing the DIY allows us to better understand the brand" (C2-e). The exhibition experience also plays an important role in attracting visitors' involvement, which can encourage visitors to perceive brand authenticity. Visitors experienced the exhibition of traditional wedding and funeral culture at the Guo Yuanyi Cake Museum (Shilin Pavilion), which made them deeply understand the relevance of cakes in their lives.

4.2 Elements of Experience Design and Brand Association

Brand association refers to images, thoughts, and beliefs [6, 7] that are formed in the consumer's mind by a brand. Knowledge acquisition, relevance of activities to life, the exhibition experience, and interactions with staff lead to brand association, as a result of experience design.

With regard to the exhibition experience, the collection of exhibition objects being related to the theme of the corporate museum enhanced visitors' positive associations with the brand. For example, the guide at the Chihsing Tan Katsuo Museum explained in detail the geographical location of Qixingtan, and the development of fisheries, which made visitors feel the authenticity and reliability of the brand. Guo Yuanyi Cake Museum (Shilin Pavilion) exhibited more than 100 years of cake history, which made customers trust the brand. Regarding the experience design elements of knowledge acquisition, the results of the study showed that visitors learned by making products through practical experience, which enabled them to form reliable associations with the brand.

In terms of the relevance of activities to life, visitors felt a sense of fun by participating in activities such as a traditional Chinese wedding ritual at the Guo Yuanyi Cake Museum (Shilin Pavilion). Respondents personally participated in programs such as bonito flake making, takoyaki making, and cake cooking provided by the corporate museums, which made customers associate the brand with friendliness and fun. One respondent explained: "The most surprising thing was that they design a funny activity like embroidered ball throwing to experience the traditional wedding culture, which made us feel very interested" (C1-c).

The service quality of the staff's interaction with visitors led customers to associate the brand with professionalism and pleasure. One of respondents stated: "… I felt it was interesting that in the exhibition area of wedding customs, the guide interpreted slang in Taiwanese, which could be heard in the past…. Through the guide's explanation, I found it interesting and impressive." The results of the study showed that the quality of service interaction, such as hospitality and the joy of service interaction, improved customers' association with the brand.

4.3   Elements of Experience Design and Perceived Quality

Perceived quality refers to the customer perception of a brand's superiority and performance in comparison to other products/services. The interactions with staff, exhibition experience, relevance of activities to life, and product experience affect customers' perceived quality of a brand. The interactions with staff refer to service reception, style and appearance, and tour expertise, as a result of experience design. When museums provide customized tours for particular customers, this can enhance visitors' perceived good service quality of the brand. One respondent mentioned: "The whole service process is quite complete: they provide a customized tour commentary, such as designing different tours for disadvantaged groups, children, adults or foreign visitors, and foreign language tours are provided, such as Japanese, English, etc., which made me perceive that this museum is professional" (C4-b). A thorough interpretation of the museum's exhibition can also lead to good perceived quality. For example, one interviewee mentioned: "Very professional: when we asked questions whether it is about the ocean or about the culture of Qixingtan beach, the guide responded in great detail" (C3-d).

The elements of the exhibition experience are reflected in the characteristics of the exhibition design, including the history of cultural relics, industrial cultural knowledge, and the beauty of the display design. The selected exhibition subjects of the two corporate museums, such as the cultural relics of Taiwan's wedding culture, the mold for cake making, and the cultural context of the bonito industry, made customers feel the uniqueness of the brand. The industrial cultural knowledge displayed by the museum, such as the production process and the industrial life culture, led visitors to perceive the museum's trustworthy professionalism.

The product experience is reflected in how the museum enables visitors to experience the authenticity and reliability of products from the company brand. At the Chihsing Tan Katsuo Museum, the demonstration of the bonito process, bonito making, and other related product experiences enabled customers to trust the brand's professionalism. The relevance of the activity to life relates to the detail design of activities such as DIY, so that customers feel a pleasant visiting experience.

4.4   Elements of Experience Design and Brand Loyalty

Attitudinal brand loyalty refers to the positive feelings towards a brand. Furthermore, the influence of experience design on brand loyalty is achieved through the innovation of visitors' experience.

New tours, exhibitions, new product development, and innovative experiential activities can enhance visitors' revisit intention. Regarding the Chihsing Tan Katsuo Museum, most respondents suggested that a new tour design, such as real fishing experiences, fishing village cultural experiences, innovations in product and exhibition themes, and workshops, could attract the participation of younger consumers. Regarding the Guo Yuanyi Cake Museum (Shilin Pavilion), most respondents were looking forward to more diverse experiential activities (such as experiencing different cake-making programs) and new themed exhibitions, to enhance visitors' revisit intention.

5   Discussion

This study aims to explore the relationship between experience design elements and the dimensions of brand equity. Brand equity consists of four dimensions, namely brand association, perceived quality, brand awareness and brand loyalty in the study. A framework of experience design and brand equity is proposed in corporate museums (see Fig. 1). This study provides novel insights into how to construct the customer experience in corporate museums which extends to the existing experience design literature [3, 4, 15]. This section discusses the results refer to related existing literature, considers the implications of these results for theory and practice.

Elements of experience design   **Dimensions of brand equity**

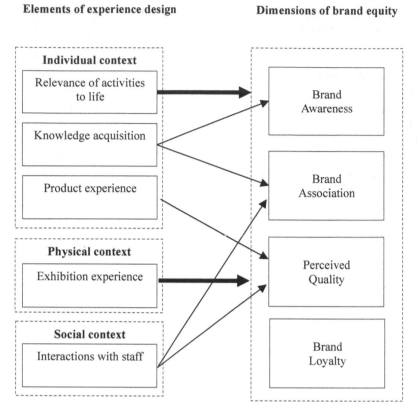

Fig. 1. Conceptual framework between experience design and brand equity.

First, the results of the study show the elements of experience design have influence on brand awareness, brand association, perceived quality, and brand loyalty. The study demonstrates that elements of experience design are associated with brand equity to a different degree in corporate museums. Research conducted by Carù et al. [3] in the case of Salvatore Ferragamo Museum showed storytelling and the visiting experience influencing the brand image and loyalty. Piatkowska [4] in his research also emphasized the crucial role of the visiting experience in building corporate identity and brand image. The current study extends visitors' experience in corporate museums to have influence on brand equity.

Second, the findings show the relevance of activities to life and exhibition experience have influence on brand awareness, brand association, perceived quality, and brand loyalty. The results of the study also showed the relevance of activities to life and exhibition experiences in a corporate museum have more influence on the dimensions of brand equity. The elements of the relevance of activities to life (e.g., experiencing traditional Chinese wedding ritual, DIY activities) are designed for connecting with visitors on a personal level which have influence on dimensions of brand equity. The results of the study extend the role of exhibition-based facilities [2] to activity-based events in corporate museums context. Consistent with Nissley and Casey [2] who had claimed that corporate museums to be exhibition-based facilities.

Third, the findings show the element of interaction with staff has influence on brand association and perceived quality. Most visitors reported interacting with the staff. Visitors emphasize the availability, professionalism, and caring attitude of staff member. This is consistent with Ponsignon et al. [15] who claimed that staff members played a key role in creating visitor experience.

Fourth, the results of the present study show knowledge acquirement has influence on brand awareness and brand association, and product experience has influence on perceived quality. Knowledge acquirement refers to learning by playing in corporate museums. This finding is consistent with previous research that emphasize the crucial role of learning and entertainment in creating a successful visitor experience in cultural sectors [10, 15]. According to Danilov [9], the aim of a corporate museum is to create a buying atmosphere for selling products through exhibiting the development of product lines and brand products. The findings show the product experience enable visitors to perceive the authenticity and reliability of brand products. Visitors understand the ins and outs of production, and experience the design process of a brand product through visiting experiences that enable visitors to trust the brand. This resonates with Danilov [9] who find that the features of corporate museums influence the product knowledge of visitors.

Finally, the findings extend physical and social contexts of two important experience design decision areas to individual context. Previous research suggested that experience design elements consist of physical and social contexts [10, 12, 13]. The results of the study show that interaction with staff is corresponding to social context, and exhibition experience is corresponding to physical context. Further, the relevance of activities to life, knowledge acquirement, and product experience that contribute to individual context. In corporate museums, the findings show individual context as an important experience design decision area as well as social and physical contexts.

6 Conclusion and Suggestions

The objective of this paper was to explore the relationship between the elements of experience design and brand equity. This study proposes a framework that advances academic understanding of experience design and brand equity in corporate museums. The framework includes design elements of social, physical, and individual context, which support the dimensions of brand equity in a different degree.

This study provides several implications for corporate museums operators and researchers. One theoretical contribution is that this study extended the scope of experience design and brand equity to corporate museums setting. Previous studies have focused on tourists' experiences and brand equity in tourism, little research has been conducted in the field of corporate museums. The findings show that each element of experience design had a different degree influence on the dimensions of brand equity.

In practice, this study identifies different elements of experience design that can facilitate brand equity. The elements of experience design should be considered as a guide for designing the corporate museums settings, events, programs. This study can provide valuable insights for corporate museums operators to tap the benefits by creating better visiting experiences to enhance brand equity. Corporate museums operators should not focus only on physical and social contexts of experience design, but also providing valuable experiences based on individual context.

This study has some limitations. Selecting two corporate museums as the research subject, this study serves as an empirical reference for the relevant museums. However, the generalizability might be limited because of the diversity of corporate museums. The current study does not aim to produce generalized results, but rather proposes a new perspective on corporate museums. In the future, a quantitative study could be conducted to explore the relationship between elements of experience design and brand equity for improved model applicability.

Acknowledgments. The authors gratefully acknowledge the support for this research provided by the Ministry of Science and Technology, Taiwan, under Grants MOST 108-2221-E-259-004. The authors also wish to thank those who contributed to the research.

References

1. Lane, J.B.: Oral history and industrial heritage museums. J. Am. Hist. **80**(2), 607–618 (1993)
2. Nissley, N., Casey, A.: The politics of the exhibition: viewing corporate museums through the paradigmatic lens of organizational memory. British J. Manag. **13**, S36–S45 (2002)
3. Carù, A., Ostillio, M.C., Leone, G.: Corporate museums to enhance brand authenticity in luxury goods companies: the case of Salvatore Ferragamo. Int. J. Arts Manag. **19**(2), 32–45 (2017)
4. Piatkowska, K.K.: The corporate museum: a new type of museum created as a component of company marketing. Int. J. Incl. Mus. **6**(2), 29–37 (2014)
5. Aaker, D.A.: Managing Brand Equity. The Free Press, New York (1991)
6. Keller, K.L.: Conceptualizing, measuring, and managing customer-based brand equity. J. Mark. **57**, 1–22 (1993)
7. Keller, K.L.: Strategic Brand Management: Building, Measuring, and Managing Brand Equity, 4th edn. Pearson Education, Boston (2013)
8. Gilmore, J.H., Pine II, B.J.: Authenticity: What Consumers Really Want. Harvard Business Review Press, Boston (2007)
9. Danilov, V.J.: A Planning Guide for Corporate Museums, Galleries, and Visitor Centers. Greenwood, Westport, CT (1992)
10. Pullman, M.E., Gross, M.A.: Ability of experience design elements to elicit emotions and loyalty behaviours. Decis. Sci. **35**(3), 551–578 (2004)
11. Tussyadiah, I.P.: Toward a theoretical foundation for experience design in tourism. J. Travel Res. **53**(5), 543–564 (2014)
12. Lanir, J., Bak, P., Kuflik, T.: Visualizing proximity-based spatiotemporal behavior of museum visitors using tangram diagrams. Comput. Graph. Forum **33**(3), 261–270 (2014)
13. Minkiewicz, J., Bridson, K., Evans, J., Russell-Bennett, R., Kowalkowski, C.: Coproduction of service experiences: insights from the cultural sector. J. Serv. Mark. **30**(7), 749–761 (2016)
14. Carbone, L., Haeckel, S.: Engineering customer experience. Mark. Manag. **3**(3), 8–19 (1994)
15. Ponsignon, F., Durrieu, F., Bouzdine-Chameeva, T.: Customer experience design: a case study in the cultural sector. J. Serv. Manag. **28**(4), 763–787 (2017)

16. Bianchi, C., Pike, S., Lings, I.: Investigating attitudes towards three South American destinations in an emerging long haul market using a model of consumer-based brand equity (CBBE). Tour. Manag. **42**, 215–223 (2014)
17. Kim, W.G., Kim, H.-B.: Measuring customer-based restaurant brand equity. Cornell Hotel Restaur. Adm. Q. **45**(2), 115–131 (2004)
18. Šerić, M., Gil-Saura, I., Mikulić, J.: Customer-based brand equity building: empirical evidence from Croatian upscale hotels. J. Vacat. Mark. **23**(2), 133–144 (2017)
19. Kim, S., Schuckert, M., Im, H.H., Elliot, S.: An interregional extension of destination brand equity: from Hong Kong to Europe. J. Vacat. Mark. **23**(4), 277–294 (2017)
20. Konecnik, M., Gartner, W.C.: Customer-based brand equity for a destination. Ann. Tour. Res. **34**(2), 400–421 (2007)
21. Christodoulides, G., De Chernatony, L.: Consumer-based brand equity conceptualisation and measurement: a literature review. Int. J. Mark. Res. **52**(1), 43–66 (2010)
22. Tasci, A.D., Guillet, B.D.: It affects, it affects not: a quasi-experiment on the transfer effect of co-branding on consumer-based brand equity of hospitality products. Int. J. Hosp. Manag. **30**(4), 774–782 (2011)
23. Park, C.S., Srinivasan, V.: A survey-based method for measuring and understanding brand equity and its extendibility. J. Mark. Res. **31**(2), 271–288 (1994)
24. Zeithaml, V.A.: Consumer perceptions of price, quality, and value: a means-end model and synthesis of evidence. J. Mark. **52**(3), 2–22 (1988)
25. Boo, S., Busser, J., Baloglu, S.: A model of customer-based brand equity and its application to multiple destinations. Tour. Manag. **30**(2), 219–231 (2009)
26. Odin, Y., Odin, N., Valette-Florence, P.: Conceptual and operational aspects of brand loyalty: an empirical investigation. J. Bus. Res. **53**(2), 75–84 (2001)
27. Chen, J., Gursoy, D.: An investigation of tourist' destination loyalty and preferences. Int. J. Contemp. Hosp. Manag. **13**(2), 79–85 (2001)
28. Nam, J., Ekinci, Y., Whyatt, G.: Brand equity, brand loyalty and consumer satisfaction. Ann. Tour. Res. **38**(3), 1009–1030 (2011)
29. Yin, R.K.: Case Study Research: Design and Methods, 3rd edn. Sage, London (2003)
30. Benbasat, I., Goldstein, D.K., Mead, M.: The case research strategy in studies of information systems. MIS Q. **11**(3), 369–386 (1987)
31. Kensbock, S., Jennings, G.: Pursuing: a grounded theory of tourism entrepreneurs' understanding and praxis of sustainable tourism. Asia Pac. Jo. Tour. Res. **16**(5), 489–504 (2011)
32. Dey, I.: Qualitative Data Analysis: A User-Friendly Guide for Social Scientists. Routledge, London (1993)
33. Elo, S., Kyngäs, H.: The qualitative content analysis process. J. Adv. Nurs. **62**(1), 107–115 (2008)
34. Zhang, Y., Wildemuth, B.M.: Qualitative analysis of content. In: Wildemuth, B. (ed.) Applications of Social Research Methods to Questions in Information and Library Science, pp. 308–319. Libraries Unlimited, Westport (2009)

Research on User's Value Cognition Evaluation of Huizhou Handmade Ceramics Skills

Yanlong Guo[✉] [iD]

Anhui University, Hefei 230601, China
20106@ahu.edu.cn

Abstract. Huizhou handmade ceramic products are part of the intangible cultural heritage, with extremely high artistic value and use value. This paper divides the cognitive value of Huizhou handmade ceramic products into six evaluation indicators, namely historical and cultural value, spiritual and cultural value, scientific and technological value, artistic aesthetic value, economic development value and social harmony value. Through the method of questionnaire survey and literature analysis, the survey users evaluate and analyze the value cognition of 6 value indicators. The questionnaire was designed in combination with the improved method of the Lister scale, and the numerical cognition level from 0 to 9 was gradually increased. This time, 80 questionnaires were distributed, and 72 questionnaires were recovered, with 72 valid questionnaires. The preliminary investigation was collected, and SPSS25.0 software was used for data analysis. Some phenomena of the value cognition of Huizhou handmade ceramics production techniques are obtained: First, in the evaluation of users' value cognition of Huizhou handmade ceramics product design, the respondents attach great importance to the historical and cultural value and artistic aesthetic value of this intangible cultural heritage. and economic development value. Second, ordinary workers have insufficient awareness of the importance of the historical culture, spiritual culture and artistic aesthetic value of Huizhou handmade ceramics production skills. Third, the young group will become the main inheritor of Huizhou handmade ceramic product design, but the level of cultural awareness and value awareness is low, etc.

Keywords: Ceramic design · Value cognition · Huizhou

1 Introduction

1.1 Introduction of Huizhou Production Techniques

From the perspective of Huizhou's cultural and geographical boundaries, the classic Huizhou includes one prefecture and six counties, namely: Huizhou prefecture administers She County, Xiuning County, Yi County, Qimen County, Wayman County, and Jixi County, which are actually six counties [1]. But in 2008, it was approved as a national-level Huizhou cultural and ecological protection experimental zone. In accordance with

© The Author(s), under exclusive license to Springer Nature Switzerland AG 2022
P.-L. P. Rau (Ed.): HCII 2022, LNCS 13312, pp. 334–347, 2022.
https://doi.org/10.1007/978-3-031-06047-2_24

the construction principles put forward in the "Huizhou Cultural and Ecological Protection Experimental Zone Master Plan" officially implemented in 2009 [2], centering on the implementation of Tunxi Liyang Old Street, Huangshan District Gantang-Xianyuan, Huizhou District Qiankou, Xiuning County Wan'an, She Seven cultural heritage-intensive areas, including Huizhou Prefecture in Huizhou County, Xidihong Village in Yi County, and Lixi Comprehensive Learning Center in Qimen County, have vigorously promoted engineering construction [3].

As a national cultural and ecological protection experimental area, Huizhou's characteristics of intangible cultural heritage are undoubtedly closely related to the cultural characteristics of the region and evolved and developed in a unique regional space and historical framework [4]. Specifically, the classic cultural design of ancient Huizhou, such as the patriarchal system from the immigrant culture of the nobility in the Central Plains, the integration of Confucian and merchants and the Huizhou merchant's cultural system of the Ming and Qing dynasties, the Huizhou mountains and rivers and the life culture system supported by the concept of feng shui, etc., are very distinctive in the Chinese cultural system [5]. There is no doubt that these characteristics have the functions of forging muscles and bones and tempering the endoplasm of the regional intangible cultural heritage, and finally endow Huizhou's intangible cultural heritage with a distinct regional cultural form.

Another feature of the intangible cultural heritage created by the millennium Huizhou culture is the unforgettable quality of the project. Unlike the usual intangible cultural heritage projects with small circulation and application scope and limited influence, ancient Huizhou can be regarded as a model sample due to the essence of culture, so a considerable number of intangible cultural heritage projects that have been passed down to today represent the country's top skill level and national inheritance. Affect surface.

1.2 Introduction to the Craftsmanship of Handmade Ceramics in Huizhou

The craftsmanship of Huizhou handmade ceramics is one of the representatives of typical Huizhou cultural skills. China is the birthplace of ceramic production skills, with high historical and cultural value and economic and practical value. Song Yingxing in the Ming Dynasty edited the production method of ceramics in "Heavenly Creation" (Fig. 1) [6]. Unlike many Chinese intangible cultural heritages that originate from local people, although many intangible cultural heritage techniques in Huizhou culture also originate from the people, they have a very significant aesthetic interest of scholars and literati. The "earth" atmosphere of the folk culture is very weak, which is a very special regional cultural tendency. Huizhou handmade ceramics are mainly concentrated in Qimen County, Huangshan City, which is an important channel for the central and western provinces to enter Jiangsu, Zhejiang, Shanghai and Fujian. Located in the mountainous area, the climate is warm and humid, which is suitable for the production of ceramics throughout the year. The Qimen crust is mostly quartz banyan veins, and the reserves of porcelain ore are abundant. In the Ming Dynasty, people from Qimen built many kilns for production, and they were mass-produced during the Kangxi period of the Qing Dynasty [7]. In the Qing Dynasty, Jingdezhen used the porcelain clay of Qimen Zhuangling for the porcelain fired for the Empress Dowager Cixi, so the Zhuangling Mine became known as the "Queen Mother's Pit". Taihe Pit and Linjiawu Porcelain Stone and Porcelain Clay participated in the Panama World Exposition and won the Class A Award and Silver Medal. "Porcelain Making Map" records the porcelain making process in Jingdezhen in the Qing Dynasty (Fig. 2) [8], Huizhou handmade ceramics also attracted attention [9], gradually became a popular commodity overseas.

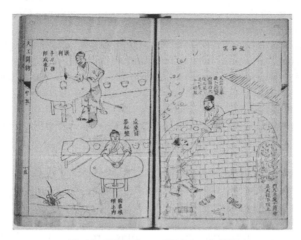

Fig. 1. T'ien-kung K'ai-wu (1637)

Fig. 2. Porcelain production map (collected by the Hong Kong Maritime Museum)

After the founding of New China, Huizhou Handmade Ceramics insisted on pioneering and innovating, and successively established Qimen Porcelain Clay Factory, Qimen Porcelain Factory, Changjiang Porcelain Factory, Empress Dowager Porcelain Factory, Jinzipai Porcelain Factory, Chishan Porcelain Factory and Ruokeng Porcelain Factory.

From processing china clay to producing porcelain. In 1980, the Qimen Porcelain Factory produced a batch of blue and white art porcelain and gold-painted welcome pine vases and tea sets for the Anhui Hall of the Great Hall of the People in Beijing. It is necessary to use a better and more effective form to inherit and develop the craftsmanship and culture of Huizhou handmade ceramics.

1.3 Problems Faced by Huizhou Handmade Ceramics Production Skills

With the development of science and technology, the traditional craftsmanship of Huizhou handmade ceramics has been gradually replaced by modern craftsmanship, and the value cognition of Huizhou handmade ceramics has gradually decreased. After preliminary investigation at the macro level, the following questions were initially drawn:

A: **single funding channel, accelerated resource loss**
In recent years, the central government's financial investment in the protection of intangible cultural heritage has continued to increase in Huizhou's handmade ceramics making skills transfer subsidy funds, but the Anhui provincial government has very little matching subsidy funds, and Huangshan City has never been used for intangible genetic inheritance activities.. At this stage, the investment is asymmetric with the rich intangible cultural heritage resources in Huangshan City and the requirements for protection and utilization, which to a certain extent affects the depth and breadth of the protection of Huizhou's handmade ceramics production skills.

Huangshan City has many intangible cultural heritage projects covering a wide range of areas. The lack and lack of government financial support has affected the enthusiasm of Huizhou handmade ceramics production skills intangible heritage projects to pass on, help, and lead, resulting in the phenomenon of "masters are willing to teach, no one is willing to learn" in related projects, and the ability to utilize subsequent resources rapid decline.

B: **the tendency to focus more on individuals and less on groups**
Since 2006, in the process of protecting intangible cultural heritage, in addition to strengthening the investment in the protection of intangible cultural heritage projects, the state has also gradually increased the protection funds for inheritors, which has played a very large guiding role in the protection of intangible cultural heritage and guaranteed the protection of intangible cultural heritage. Fundamental inheritance funds for a large number of inheritors.

However, many inheritors believe that the inheritance funds directly allocated to the inheritor's name are personal subsidies and living expenses, and it is entirely up to the individual to decide whether to use part or most of it for the inheritance of intangible cultural heritage.

When such confrontation occurs, the group of inheritors should not be blamed. It is suggested that the state should implement overall protection for the inheritors of intangible cultural heritage in addition to the protection of the intangible cultural heritage projects with strong group and strong coordination and strive to make every role able to Get the benefits of inheritance and development.

C: **the tendency to focus on tradition and less on innovation**

There have always been two different mainstream concepts about the craftsmanship of Huizhou handmade ceramics, namely sticking to tradition and the key to innovation. First of all, due to the classics of Huizhou handmade ceramics production techniques and the continuation of Huizhou research traditions, many people believe that Huizhou intangible cultural heritage products are rare and rare treasures left to us by our ancestors, especially those artifacts and techniques that have survived to this day. The purest and most traditional craftsmanship and product methods are strictly protected, and hand-made in strict accordance with the traditional craftsmanship to ensure the authenticity of their products, and the craftsmanship and style cannot be changed to pursue innovation.

Secondly, a large bottle of high-end intangible cultural heritage in ancient Huizhou actually appeared with the consumption interest of Huizhou merchants and Huizhou officials and gentry. Strictly speaking, it should belong to the category of luxury goods, and its price is also surprisingly high. It can only be a sigh of relief. Therefore, some experts and practitioners in the survey believe that walking on two legs can be completely adopted. On the one hand, they are strictly following traditions, and on the other hand, they can develop more through innovations in design, materials, production techniques, tools and equipment. The high-quality and low-cost intangible cultural heritage derivatives for the contemporary consumer allow those intangible cultural heritage items that are closely related to life to continue to exert their value. Let Huizhou's intangible cultural heritage products truly become tourism consumer goods with local characteristics in the Southern Anhui International Tourism Zone, so that people can "buy it, take it away and keep it".

2   Questionnaire Design and Survey

2.1   Questionnaire Design

In order to explore the value cognition of Huizhou handmade ceramics production skills and products more truly in the public, the researchers conducted research in the form of questionnaires. Select the fourth-level inheritors of intangible cultural heritage related to the protection and utilization of intangible cultural heritage in the Huizhou Cultural and Ecological Protection Experimental Zone, officials of intangible cultural heritage/cultural tourism/competent departments of provincial/city/district and county governments, experts in intangible cultural heritage protection and research, and intangible cultural heritage products Promoted enterprise employees, etc. Through questionnaire survey and literature analysis, survey users evaluated and analyzed the value cognition of 6 value indicators (Table 1), using an improved version of the Likert scale, and the numerical cognition degree increased from 0 to 9.

Table 1. The evaluation index system of value cognition of Huizhou handmade ceramics production skills.

Index	Extremely unimportant ← Importance → Very important
Q1	0---1---2---3---4---5---6---7---8---9
Q2	0---1---2---3---4---5---6---7---8---9
Q3	0---1---2---3---4---5---6---7---8---9
Q4	0---1---2---3---4---5---6---7---8---9
Q5	0---1---2---3---4---5---6---7---8---9
Q6	0---1---2---3---4---5---6---7---8---9

Q1: Historical and cultural value refers to the role of users in historical cognition such as social and historical development information of Huizhou handmade ceramics, reflecting the process of cultural and ecological changes.

Q2: Spiritual and cultural value refers to the role of users in the construction of consciousness of Huizhou handmade ceramics accumulated and passed down from generation to generation in long-term production and life practice, as well as enriching the regional value system and optimizing regional personality.

Q3: The value of science and technology refers to the user's exploration of the development law of the natural world for Huizhou handmade ceramics, reflecting the level of science and technology and social productivity, prospering traditional skills, inspiring people's technological innovation capabilities, and providing natural and social scientific research information and other scientific and technological research and development aspects of the role.

Q4: The aesthetic value of art refers to the user's role in the development of literature and art such as the characteristics of literature, music, art and craftsmanship of Huizhou handmade ceramics in folk traditions, stimulating the enthusiasm for literary and artistic creation and life expression, and creating aesthetic experience.

Q5: The value of economic development refers to the role of users in the economic utilization of Huizhou handmade ceramics in developing cultural tourism projects, developing cultural industries, and building regional, enterprise and product brand images.

Q6: The value of social harmony refers to the role of users in Huizhou handmade ceramics in improving the quality of life, enhancing happiness, promoting social stability and harmony, promoting the construction of new countryside, and expanding foreign exchanges and cooperation.

In the process of questionnaire survey data statistics, two analysis modules were selected: the cognitive evaluation table of the value of Huizhou handmade ceramic products and the data interpretation of the cognition survey data of all the respondents in each area on the cultural and ecological protection value of intangible cultural heritage in Huizhou. Five analysis modules including gender, age, education, occupation, and professional title make cross-statistics.

3 Analysis

In this study, SPSS 25.0 software was used for statistical analysis of questionnaires, combined with the previous macro survey. Judging from the demographic information of the respondents, in terms of age, they are mainly 30–49 years old (41 people, accounting for 56.9%); in terms of the nature of the units, they are mainly other enterprises and institutions (26 people, accounting for 36.1%), Followed by schools and research institutions (19 people, accounting for 26.4%); in terms of educational level, the main ones with bachelor degree or above (50 people, accounting for 69.4%); accounting for 30.6%), followed by intermediate titles (18 people, accounting for 25%).

The reliability of the collected questionnaires was tested by SPSS 25.0 reliability analysis. The data shows that the scale's Cronbach's Alpha coefficient is 0.882. It is generally believed that the Cronbach's Alpha coefficient above 0.6 indicates that the data results of the questionnaire have good consistency, [10] so the data of this questionnaire has high reliability.

The descriptive statistics of the questionnaire was obtained through statistical analysis of the mean value of the value cognition evaluation of Huizhou handmade ceramics production skills (Table 2). The data shows: First, the variance of Q1 is 0.415, and the variance of Q5 is 0.562. The variance values of these two indicators are relatively small, indicating that different groups are aware of the historical and cultural value of Q1 and the value of Q5 economic development in Huizhou handmade ceramic products. relatively consistent. Second, the variance of Q3 is 0.700, and the variance of Q4 is 0.716. Among the six indicators, the variance value is medium, indicating that different groups are aware of the Q3 scientific and technological value and the Q4 artistic aesthetic value in Huizhou handmade ceramic products. The divergence is relatively concentrated on multiple factors, but the degree of cognition is relatively non-centralized. Third, the variance of Q2 is 0.998 and the variance of Q6 is 1.110. The variance values of these two indicators are relatively large, indicating that there are serious differences in the cognition of Q2 spiritual and cultural value and Q6 social harmony value in Huizhou handmade ceramic products among different groups., the cognition of these two indicators in different groups is quite different.

Table 2. Descriptive statistics of the questionnaire

	N	Minimum	Maximum	M-means	Standard deviation	Variance
Q1	21	7.00	10.00	8.3005	.64412	.415
Q2	21	6.67	10.00	8.0324	.99918	.998
Q3	21	6.50	10.00	7.9990	.83661	.700
Q4	21	6.50	10.00	8.0657	.84593	.716
Q5	21	6.00	10.00	7.7781	.74934	.562
Q6	21	5.17	10.00	7.0424	1.05340	1.110
Valid N (list state)	21					

The data of the questionnaire were processed by SPSS 25.0, and the mean variance analysis table was obtained (Table 3). The data shows that the significant value is 0, which is less than the significance level of 0.05. Therefore, it is considered that Q1 historical and cultural value, Q2 spiritual and cultural value, Q3 scientific and technological value, Q4: artistic aesthetic value, Q5 economic development value, Q6 social harmony in the survey There are significant differences between the indicators of value, and the average value between the indicators can be analyzed.

Table 3. Mean Analysis of Variance (ANOVA) Table of Questionnaires

		Sum of squares	df	Mean square	F	Sig.
Between groups		56.639	20	2.832		
Within the group	Between items	20.161	5	4.032	12.087	.000
	Residual	33.360	100	.334		
	Total	53.521	105	.510		
Total		110.160	125	.881		

3.1   The Perceptions of Respondents of Different Genders on the Value of Huizhou Handmade Ceramics Production Skills

Longitudinal analysis of respondents of different genders, the survey results show that among all respondents' value evaluation of Huizhou handmade ceramics production skills, historical and cultural value is the highest (8.26), followed by artistic aesthetic value (7.8) and economic development value (7.77)), the protection and utilization status (7.71) score is high(Fig. 3).

From the perspective of different genders, women's scores on the six value indicators of Huizhou handmade ceramics production skills are higher than men's, and the scores on the cognitive evaluation indicators of Q5 and Q6 are higher than men. It can be seen that women have a strong perceptual understanding of the economic development value and social harmony value of Huizhou handmade ceramics production skills, but in the Q6 indicator, men and women among the respondents generally believe that the value is not high. The influence of Huizhou handmade ceramic production skills on the value of social harmony is weak. In the evaluation indicators of Q3 and Q4, the value cognition of men and women is relatively stable.

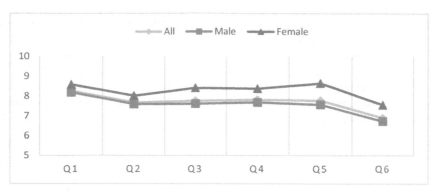

Fig. 3. The mean value of the cognitive evaluation of the craftsmanship value of Huizhou handmade ceramics by respondents of different genders

3.2 The Perceptions of Respondents of Different Ages on the Value of Huizhou Handmade Ceramics Production Skills

In terms of age, the 30–69-year-old samples of the respondents scored higher than 30 on the historical and cultural value, spiritual and cultural value, scientific and technological value, artistic aesthetic value, economic development value and social harmony value of Huizhou handmade ceramic production skills. under-age groups. In addition to artistic aesthetic value, the respondents' evaluation of various values showed a general rule: the older the person, the higher the value score of various Huizhou handmade ceramics production skills, and the two showed a clear positive correlation. To a certain extent, this reflects the age structure characteristics of the value cognition of Huizhou handmade ceramics production skills, and the younger group pays less attention to the value of Huizhou handmade ceramics production skills. However, the older the respondents were, the lower the evaluation of the indicators of Q5 and Q6. They believed that the economic development value and social harmony value of Huizhou handmade ceramics production skills had relatively little impact. The index evaluation of and Q6 is relatively high, and it is believed that the economic development value and social harmony value of Huizhou handmade ceramics production skills have a high impact. It can be seen that the young and old groups have a social and economic impact on Huizhou handmade ceramics production skills. There are differences, and the cognitive elements are very different(Fig. 4).

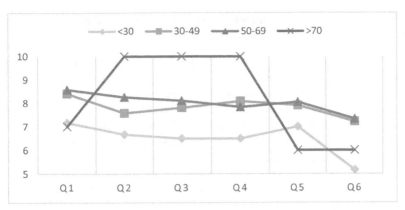

Fig. 4. The average value of the cognitive evaluation of the craftsmanship value of Huizhou handmade ceramics by respondents of different ages

3.3 The Perceptions of Respondents with Different Educational Backgrounds on the Value of Huizhou Handmade Ceramics Production Skills

From the perspective of education, in the evaluation of various values of Huizhou hand-made ceramics production skills, in the indicators of Q1, Q2, Q3, Q4, Q5 and Q6, it shows that the higher the education level, the value evaluation of Huizhou handmade ceramics production skills The lower the score, the lower the score for those with a mas-ter's degree and above than for those with a bachelor's degree or below. In the score of artistic value utilization prospect, respondents with different educational backgrounds have large fluctuations in evaluation cognition, which means that there is no unified standard for the artistic value of Huizhou handmade ceramics production skills(Fig. 5).

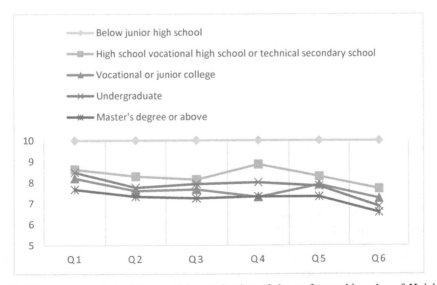

Fig. 5. The average value of the cognitive evaluation of the craftsmanship value of Huizhou handmade ceramics by respondents with different educational backgrounds

3.4 The Perceptions of Respondents from Different Units on the Value of Huizhou Handmade Ceramics Production Skills

Judging from the nature of the respondents, schools and research institutions have lower scores on the various values of Huizhou handmade ceramics production skills than state organs, party-mass organizations and other enterprises and institutions. From the point of view of sub-item value evaluation, the scores of other enterprises and institutions for historical and cultural value, spiritual and cultural value and social harmony value are higher than those of state organs party and mass organizations, while the scientific and technological value of state organs party and mass organizations to Huizhou handmade ceramics production skills, artistic aesthetic value and economic development value scores are higher than other enterprises and institutions. In terms of protection and utilization status and prospects for protection and utilization, the scores of other enterprises and institutions are also higher than those of state organs, party and mass organizations(Fig. 6).

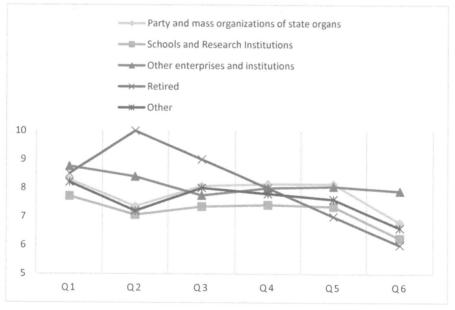

Fig. 6. The average value of the cognitive evaluation of the craftsmanship value of Huizhou handmade ceramics by respondents from different units

3.5 The Perceptions of Respondents with Different Professional Titles on the Value of Huizhou Handmade Ceramics Production Skills

From the perspective of professional titles, among the six value evaluations of Huizhou handmade ceramics production skills, respondents without technical titles scored the lowest, and workers without technical titles had little awareness of the importance of their value. Among them, there is a deviation in the cognition of different investigators with different professional titles in the Q2 indicator. The primary professional title believes that the spiritual and cultural value of Huizhou handmade ceramics production skills is higher (9.00), and the respondents without professional titles think that the spiritual and cultural value of Huizhou handmade ceramics production skills are relatively high. Low (6.77), there are two clear perceptions among investigators with low professional titles, but the gap is relatively large. However, the evaluation of the spiritual and cultural value of Huizhou handmade ceramics production skills with intermediate professional titles (7.47) and senior professional titles (7.95, 8.40) is relatively stable. It can be seen that the spiritual and cultural value of Huizhou handmade ceramics production skills needs to be further shaped(Fig. 7).

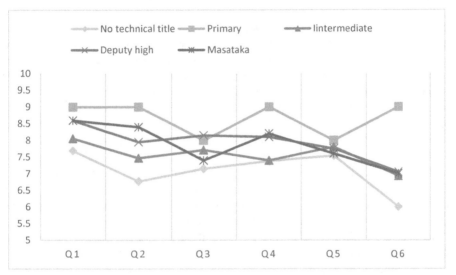

Fig. 7. The average value of the cognitive evaluation of the craftsmanship value of Huizhou handmade ceramics by respondents with different professional titles

4   Conclusions and Recommendations

4.1   Conclusion

The following conclusions were drawn from the analysis:

First, in the evaluation of users' value perception of Huizhou handmade ceramic product design, the respondents valued the historical and cultural value, artistic aesthetic value and economic development value of this intangible cultural heritage. Young people under the age of 30 attach less importance to the value of Huizhou handmade ceramics making skills, which is not conducive to its subsequent inheritance and development.

Second, ordinary workers have insufficient awareness of the importance of the historical culture, spiritual culture and artistic aesthetic value of Huizhou handmade ceramics production skills, so they should increase their popularization and education, so that they can truly perceive its uniqueness in actual work. Value and cultural connotation, and then enhance the general public's cognition level and protection awareness of intangible cultural heritage.

Third, young people will become the main inheritors of Huizhou handmade ceramics production skills, but their cultural awareness and value awareness are relatively low. The general public's aesthetic and cultural awareness of Huizhou handmade ceramics production skills needs to be improved. The government's recognition of Huizhou handmade ceramics production skills is lower than that of enterprises, and the value attributes of Huizhou handmade ceramics production skills need to be developed and disseminated.

4.2 Recommendations

It can be seen from the survey that the variance of historical and cultural value of Huizhou handmade ceramics production skills is relatively small, and the public of different ages and occupations have relatively consistent cognitions on this dimension. It is believed that the historical value of Huizhou handmade ceramics production skills is relatively high, and the development of classic Huizhou culture has the characteristics of strong systematisms and strong autonomy, and this characteristic is produced when the system as a whole reaches a high level. However, there are cognitive biases of different groups in other indicators, so it is recommended to improve from the following aspects:

First, take institutional innovation and mechanism innovation as the guide, further enrich and enhance the experience of talent team building, improve the subsidy system for representative inheritors at all levels to pass on learning activities, [11, 12] implement the academic aid system, and encourage innovation with richer resource allocation. Bring apprentices to pass on art, learn art from teachers, and promote living inheritance.

Second, the ability of inheritors to move towards modern society is cultivated. According to the training idea of "strengthening the foundation, increasing the education, and broadening the horizons", relying on the colleges and universities to regularly hold popular training for non-genetic inheritors, to help them make up for the lack of cultural accomplishment, the lack of art foundation, the lack of design awareness, [13] and the market awareness The lack of enhances the responsibility and ability of a craftsman to actively face the challenges of contemporary society [14].

Third, resolve the crisis of intergenerational inheritance, and combine the old and the young to grasp the inheritance. In order to "strengthen the material support and spiritual respect for the inheritors, especially the inheritors of aging, endangered projects, and difficult-to-industrial development projects, [15, 16] Strengthen the radiation effect of the young group of the inheritors, and alleviate the aging and generational difficulties of the inheritors" In order to make a breakthrough, promote the construction of Huangshan City's non-genetic inheritance team to solve the crisis of intergenerational inheritance.

Fourth, optimize the practical path for intangible cultural heritage to enter the campus. Improve the practice of intangible cultural heritage entering the campus and realize the creation of a more three-dimensional atmosphere from knowledge popularization to skills training to knowledge and brand communication [17, 18]. Effectively promote deeper and more effective cooperation between schools and representative inheritors of intangible cultural heritage or their enterprises, achieve mutual benefit and win-win results, and establish a model of virtuous circle and coordinated development of intangible cultural heritage undertakings.

Acknowledgments. The author is very grateful to the support of Anhui University's 2020 Talent Introduction Research Start-up Fund Project Fund, project number: S020318019/001. The authors also wish to thank those who contributed to the research.

References

1. Wang, S.: Anhui Province Huizhou Prefecture Chronicle. Chengwen Publishing House Co. Ltd, Taipei (1985)
2. Xu, M.: Research on the current situation and countermeasures of intangible cultural heritage protection——taking Huizhou Cultural Ecological Reserve as an example. J. Anhui Admin. Inst. **7**(2), 88–95 (2016)
3. Zhang S.: Discussion on regional protection strategies of cultural ecology——taking Huizhou cultural ecology protection experimental area as an example. J. Tongji Univ. Soc. Sci. Edit. **20**(3),27–35+48(2009)
4. Wu, L.: A brief analysis on the protection and development of Huizhou's intangible cultural heritage. J. Huangshan Univ. **11**(4), 20–23 (2009)
5. Bian L.: Problems existing in the construction of cultural and ecological protection areas and their solutions: taking Huizhou cultural and ecological protection experimental area as an example. Cultural Herit. **13**(4),24–30+66 (2010)
6. Song, Y.: Heavenly Creation. Guangdong People's Publishing House, Guangzhou (1976)
7. Wang, Y.: Qimen County Chronicle (1–4). Chengwen Publishing House Co. Ltd, Taipei (1975)
8. Zhao H.: Porcelain production map: a real record of the export of porcelain in Jingdezhen in Qing dynasty and the activities of barbarians in Guangzhou. Decoration **337**(5), 56–65 (2021)
9. Xiong Y., Chen Y., Li W., et al.: Huizhou's contribution to the economic development of Jingdezhen porcelain industry. China Ceramics **44**(9),82–85+57 (2008)
10. Leontitsis, A., Pagge, J.: A simulation approach on Cronbach's alpha statistical significance. Math. Comput. Simul. **73**(5), 336–340 (2007)
11. Yang, Z.: Discussion on the protection of intangible cultural heritage from the perspective of cultural ecology. Acad. Exchange **241**(4), 204–207 (2014)
12. Shen, H., Wang, M.: research into protecting and developing intangible cultural heritage in database of government, colleges and enterprises in cloud computing. Int. J. Database Theory Applicat. **9**(6), 145–150 (2016)
13. Han, L., Yan, Q., Wang, X., et al.: Design of daily ceramic tableware based on Huizhou culture. Art Sci. Technol. **29**(10), 10–11 (2016)
14. Zhang, Y.: The artistic interpretation and design innovation of Huizhou ceramic elements in Hefei subway space. J. Beijing Inst. Graph. Design **25**(6), 46–48 (2017)
15. Gao B., Song H.: Intangible cultural heritage protection in the construction of cultural and eco-logical protection areas and urbanization process: mechanism and policy thinking. Northwest Ethnic Res. **89**(2),198–204+23 (2016)
16. Wei, T., Cai, H., Gao, Y., et al.: The transmission and practice of intangible cultural heritage in the perspective of geographies of the body. Acta Geograph. Sinica **75**(10), 2256–2268 (2020)
17. Zhang, M.: A new model of cultural and creative design talents training in the context of non-genetic inheritance and innovation. Heilongjiang High. Educat. Res. **272**(12), 139–141 (2016)
18. Lu, Z.: Live streaming in China for sharing knowledge and promoting intangible cultural heritage. Interactions **27**(1), 58–63 (2019)

Relationship Between Taiwanese Audience Preference and Cultural Values in Korean Dramas

Shih Hui Hsueh[1(✉)], Rungtai Lin[1], and Sandy Lee[2]

[1] Graduate School of Creative Industry Design, National Taiwan University of Arts,
New Taipei City 220307, Taiwan
hsueh17@gmail.com, rtlin@mail.ntua.edu.tw
[2] Sandy Art Studio, New Taipei City 24352, Taiwan
slee195600@gmail.com

Abstract. Although Taiwan has recently produced a few dramas that have enjoyed high ratings and topicality, its development in the film and television market has stagnated. However, as indicated by the preceding information, the film and television market of Taiwan is still sizable, and there is a demand for more productions including Korean dramas. A questionnaire survey was used to investigate the implicit cultural values perceived by Taiwanese audiences when they watched Korean dramas and then compare them with the audiences' preference for the drama. Due to the viewing habits of Taiwanese audiences have changed in recent years and online streaming services and platforms have gradually become a major channel for viewing film and television productions, the top three Korean dramas chosen as the research samples were selected by calculating the scores of individual Korean dramas on the 2021 Weekly Top 10 Lists released by Netflix for the Taiwan region. And cultural values in this study comprised family and marriage values, personal values, and social values. The results of this study would like to investigate whether relevant production personnel can develop content by adapting and selecting content that matches the cultural values and viewing preferences of the Taiwanese audience based on the ratings performance and experience of Korean dramas in Taiwan.

Keywords: Cultural values · Korean drama · Audience preference · Cultural proximity

1 Introduction

1.1 Taiwanese Dramas in the Domestic Market

The 2020 Taiwan Cultural Content Industries Survey Report II: Television, Motion Picture, Animation, and Radio Industries [1] published by the Taiwan Creative Content Agency indicated the total revenue of the Taiwan television industry in 2019, including television program production, distribution, channels, platforms, online program production, and digital distribution and broadcasting, was estimated to be approximately

NT$148.298 billion, which was a 4.33% increase from that of 2018. In 2019, a total of 95,531 h of television programs were broadcast in Taiwan, during which Taiwanese dramas (including dramas in the Mandarin, Minnan, and Hakka languages as well as Mandarin anthologies) were broadcast the most (36.21% of total broadcast hours), followed by Mainland Chinese dramas (32.53%) and Korean dramas (25.61%).

Taiwan premiered 56 new dramas in 2019 (including dramas that crossed over different years of production), among which love and romance (39.71%) and family (19.12%) dramas were the genres most featured. Although some of the Mandarin dramas such as *The World Between Us* produced by Taiwan Public Television Service Foundation garnered the public's favor and were widely discussed, Minnan dramas continued to have the highest average rating in 2019 at 0.69, followed by Mandarin dramas at 0.14 [1].

Taiwanese dramas, such as *Meteor Garden* (2001) and *Fated to Love You* (2008) had been hugely popular. However, the quality of Taiwanese dramas has been inconsistent due to production conditions and cost factors [2]. In addition, audience preference and tastes have also evolved; romance dramas and those with cliché story plots no longer draw viewership [3].

The present audience have diverse choices as global markets have become increasingly open and with the Internet boom. Hence, in addition to domestic competition, Taiwanese dramas are now also faced with challenges presented by the diverse range of audio and visual products from around the world [3, 4]. In particular, in failing to highlight its local cultural characteristics and meet the trend of the export market, Taiwan's radio and television industry has failed to take off in the international stage and showcase its economic value [5].

Despite such challenges, some production teams have attempted to use different themes and methods to try to reverse the status quo [2]. Consequently, some of the later drama productions such as *Close Your Eyes Before It's Dark* (2016) of *Qseries*, *The Teenage Psychic* (2017), *A Boy Named Flora A* (2017), and *The World Between Us* (2019) have been able to garner high ratings and become popular topics of conversations among the public. These dramas demonstrate the potential of Taiwanese television dramas and web series and that they still have room for development.

1.2 Taiwan as the Third-Largest Market for Korean Dramas

The 2020 Broadcasting Industry White Paper [6] released by the Korea Creative Content Agency stated that the total export value of the broadcasting industry of South Korea amounted to US$539.21 million. Among the various exporting countries, Japan ranked first in export value (US$91.76 million; 30.3% of the total global export value), followed by the United States (US$77.21 million; 25.6%), and Taiwan (US$27.39 million; 9.1%).

The popularity of Korean dramas in Taiwan can be traced back to *Fireworks*, a Korean drama broadcast by Gala Television in 2000, which received record ratings and ushered in the "Korean Wave" in Taiwan [7]. This was followed by the successive broadcast of other hugely popular Korean dramas such as *Autumn in My Heart* (2001), *Winter Sonata* (2003), and *Dae Janggeum* (2004), which cemented the trend of Korean dramas in Taiwan and secured them a place in the Taiwanese market [8]. The popularity of the Korean dramas not only realized the interests of the dramas; merchandize related to the dramas, products endorsed by the Korean cast, makeup and skin care products, Korean cuisine, and tourism in Korea all benefited from the dramas. Additionally, they even piqued the interest of the Taiwanese audience on Korean culture, which propelled the development of industries related to Korean language learning as well as related books and publications [8].

Related research in Taiwan on the Korean Wave and Korean dramas have mainly focused on the impact of Korean dramas on tourism, fashion consumer products, and the wedding industry. Some studies have analyzed the culture as well as the interpersonal and social values presented by the characters in the dramas [9–14]. While several research have extended their analysis from the dramas to other industries or examined the implicit character roles and values presented in the dramas, few have examined audience preference and identification regarding the drama content.

Although Taiwan has recently produced a few dramas that have enjoyed high ratings and topicality, its development in the film and television market has stagnated, and its film and television industry is experiencing a brain drain as relevant professionals increasingly seek jobs and development opportunities abroad. However, as indicated by the preceding information presented in this paper, the film and television market of Taiwan is still sizable, and there is a demand for more productions. Therefore, this paper examined how Korean dramas have continued to maintain their popularity among the Taiwanese audience during a time when ratings for local dramas have stagnated in Taiwan. In addition, what does this phenomenon represent in terms of audience preference and the implications of cultural values? Accordingly, the author investigated whether relevant production personnel can develop content by adapting and selecting content that matches the cultural values and viewing preferences of the Taiwanese audience based on the ratings performance and experience of Korean dramas in Taiwan.

2 Literature Review

2.1 Cultural Proximity

Straubhaar [15, 16] adopted the concept of cultural proximity to demonstrate the importance of cultural distance on the success of exporting and importing program productions and asserted that audiences prefer content that is similar to their own culture when all other conditions are held constant. Straubhaar emphasized that language is the most crucial factor affecting cultural proximity, and other related factors including cultural similarities such as clothing, skin color, body language, gestures, story pace, music traditions, and religious beliefs, all affect reception of the media content by local consumers. Straubhaar [15] mentioned that due to cultural proximity, when domestic programs fail to satisfy the needs of the audiences, they will prefer programs from neighboring countries that share cultures similar to their own, rather than programs with culture that differ considerably from their own. Hence, transnational media aiming at the global market need to address the differing needs of the various markets, including lingual and cultural differences, and formulate content accordingly [17].

2.2 Cultural Values

Discussions on the concept of culture generally cite the definition proposed by anthropologist Edward B. Tylor in 1871. Numerous discussions have since been made on the concept and definition of culture, and Huang [18] collated the definitions of several scholars and concluded that they share a central concept of culture as being something that is "common or shared within a society," which may be a characteristic or presentation shared by members of a nation, group, or region.

The definition of "values" largely encompasses the two components of the individual and culture. In the past, Western scholars have explained values as the orientation chosen by oneself or an organization, that values are inseparable from character, and that they lead the individual or organization in choosing the methods and means of action [18]. Wen [19] summarized values as: (a) an indicator that influences individual behavior; (b) an organic connection to culture or society; and (c) general principles for interpersonal relationships and relationships between people and the environment.

2.3 Culture Values of Ethnic Chinese Society

In 1992, Yang [20] proposed the Multidimensional Scale of Chinese Individual Traditionality (MS-CIT), which suggested individual traditionality to comprise the five psychological components of submission to authority, filial piety and ancestor worship, conservation and endurance, fatalism and defensiveness, and male dominance. Regarding the Multidimensional Scale of Chinese Individual Modernity (MS-CIM), he proposed individual modernity to comprise the five psychological components of egalitarianism and open-mindedness, social isolation and self-reliance, optimism and assertiveness, affective hedonism, and sex equality. Later, on the concept of traditionality in ethnic Chinese society, Huang [18] grouped cultural values into five levels: individual behavior and attitude, family relationship, social interaction, social structure, and the relationship between the individual and the universe.

Lee [21] compared the cultural values of American, Japanese, and Taiwanese television and found that while the values depicted in Japanese and Taiwanese television were very similar, they were markedly different from those in American television. Lee suggested that such values can be called "Asian values." Wen [19] also noted that values in Asia have been deeply influenced by Confucianism and a small extent of which have also been influenced by Buddhism.

However, related research have shown differences in values between various cultures and societies in Asia. Tsai, Li, and Li [7] examined Korean dramas broadcast in Taiwan between 2001 and 2005 to determine whether differences existed in the values depicted in Korean dramas popular in Korea and Taiwan. The results showed that Taiwanese audiences acknowledged the family values of filial piety and patriarchal consciousness and the social values of karmic retribution and leniency toward others (but strictness in self-discipline); regarding love, themes that showcased dedication and sacrifice as love resonated more highly with Taiwanese audiences. In comparison, the Korean audiences were more accepting of the personal values of looking out for oneself. This suggested that although Taiwan and Korea are both Asian countries, the values preferred by the Taiwanese and Korean audiences in Korean dramas differed. Ho [22] studied the films of renowned Korean director Park Chan-wook and noted that his works connected with the antagonism of the entire nation and the narrative context of his films were clearly based on the notion of revenge. Such a narrative is markedly different from the cultural basis of Taiwan, which has been influenced by Confucianism.

Despite sometimes similar cultural origins, various regions in Asia have developed their own cultural similarities and differences. Aside from the technical aspects of screenwriting, filming, post-production, or promotion that may have contributed to the widespread popularity of Korean dramas, this paper investigated whether the cultural values depicted in the dramas perceived by the audience influence audience preference and ratings.

3   Methodology

The research subjects of this study were individuals who had watched Korean dramas. A questionnaire survey was used to investigate the implicit cultural values perceived by Taiwanese audiences when they watched Korean dramas and then compare them with the audiences' own values. In doing so, this study analyzed the relationship between the preference of Taiwanese audiences for Korean dramas and their cultural values. Owing to labor, temporal, and financial constraints, the author adopted an online questionnaire to collect data.

3.1   Research Framework

This study used a questionnaire survey to explore the implicit cultural values perceived by Taiwanese audiences when watching Korean dramas, and compared them with their own values. Subsequently, the author analyzed the relationship between the Taiwanese audience preference for Korean dramas and their cultural values. The analysis involved four parts, with the first part being an analysis of the participant demographics, which included variables such as sex, age, educational attainment, profession, and place of residence. The second part involved variables on watching Korean dramas such as average weekly hours spent watching Korean dramas, methods of watching, average duration of watching, and Korean dramas watched during the past three years. The third part dealt with cultural values perceived when watching Korean dramas such as family and marriage values, personal values, and social values, and included an analysis on the relationship of the values that the audiences identified with when watching Korean dramas and their preference.

3.2   Research Participants

This study aimed to analyze the relationship between Taiwanese audience preferences and the cultural values of Korean dramas. Therefore, the research subjects were limited to Taiwanese audiences who had previously watched Korean dramas.

3.3 Research Samples and Sampling

The viewing habits of Taiwanese audiences have changed in recent years, and online streaming services and platforms have gradually become a major channel for viewing film and television productions. Therefore, when selecting research participants and samples, only those who used legal online video streaming services were considered. According to the *2020 Digital Convergence Development Report* issued by the Taiwan National Communications Commission, Netflix accounted for 61.9% of all paid streaming services subscribed by Taiwanese audiences.

The top three Korean dramas chosen as the research samples in this study were *Hospital Playlist* Season 2, *Hometown Cha-Cha-Cha*, and *Squid Game*. They were selected by calculating the scores of individual Korean dramas on the 2021 Weekly Top 10 Lists released by Netflix for the Taiwan region. Specifically, the Country Lists—Weekly Top 10 published by Netflix was used to score the various Korean dramas by allocating scores (1–10 points) according to their weekly rank (10th to 1st). The Country Lists—Weekly Top 10 were accessed on January 19, 2022, and the period referenced for the ranking data was July 4–December 31, 2021.

3.4 Research Instruments

This study adopted the questionnaire survey method to collect data on the relationship between the preferences of Taiwanese audiences and the implicit cultural values in Korean dramas. The online questionnaire is divided into four parts. The first part collected data on participant demographics; the second part inquired participants of their extent of watching Korean dramas; the third part concerned the cultural values perceived by the participants when watching Korean dramas and their identification with the values; and the fourth part measured the relationship between audience preference and cultural values.

Demographic Variables. This first part collected data on the sex, age, educational attainment, profession, and place of residence of the participants. The age groups were divided into 12 years and below, 13–18 years, 18–25 years, 26–35 years, 36–45 years, 46–55 years, 55–65 years, and 66 years and older. Educational attainment were divided into junior high school or below, general and vocational high school, college, and postgraduate. Professions included students, government employees, medical personnel, finance and insurance, agriculture, forestry, fishery and animal husbandry, service, electronic information, construction, manufacturing, commerce, mass media, freelance, homemaker, unemployed, retired, and others. The places of residence include northern Taiwan, central Taiwan, southern Taiwan, eastern Taiwan, and the offshore islands.

Variables on Watching Korean Dramas. The participants were asked about the weekly number of hours they spent watching Korean dramas and their method of watching. The time spent watching Korean dramas were divided into the four groups of 5 h or less, 6–10 h, 11–20 h, and 21 h or more. Methods of watching included cable television, paid streaming services, free online platforms, paid mobile apps and platforms, free mobile apps and platforms, and others. To determine whether the participants were familiar with Korean dramas, the questionnaire also asked whether they had watched at least one Korean drama (including television and web series) in full between 2019 and the time of data collection and whether they had watched the aforementioned top three dramas. Participants who have watched the dramas were then presented with related questionnaire items to fill out.

Variables on Cultural Values. Few studies have analyzed the cultural values in dramas. Hence, this study adapted the MS-CIT and MS-CIM scales of Yang [20] to collect and analyze the data on cultural values.

In this study, cultural values comprised family and marriage values, personal values, and social values. The item choices for family and marriage values included filial piety, reverence for ancestors, family unity, authoritative parenting, democratic parenting, patriarchy, and spousal respect. Regarding the item choices for personal values, they include looking out for oneself, knowing one's place, mutual help and friendship, standing up for oneself, optimistic views, self-pity, fatalism, seize the day, and long-term planning. As for social values, the item choices comprised egalitarianism and open-mindedness, submission to authority, followership, emphasis on individual will, class distinction, and respect for the rule of law. After the participants selected the aforementioned values, they were then asked to choose the values that they identified or did not identify with.

Variables on Korean Drama Preference. The preference for Korean dramas was determined by asking the participants about the top three Korean dramas of 2021 as calculated by scoring the Weekly Top 10 Lists released by Netflix. They were asked about their understanding of the content, and their preference for the dramas.

4 Research Results

4.1 Participant Demographics

A total of 102 online questionnaires were collected in this study. Considering the participants' familiarity with Korean dramas, after deducting the samples of Korean dramas that have not watched at least 1 complete series (including TV series and web series) so far in 2019, there are a total of 91 valid questionnaires.

First, in terms of biological sex, 79 women (86.8%) were the most, followed by 11 men (12.1%) and 1 (1.1%) others. In terms of age, the participants of this questionnaire are mostly 26–35 years old ($n = 32$, 35.2%), 36–45 years old ($n = 26$, 28.6%), followed by 46–55 years old ($n = 13$, 14.3%), 19–25 years old ($n = 8$, 8.8%), 56–65 years old ($n = 8$, 8.8%), over 66 years old ($n = 3$, 3.3%).

In terms of educational attainment, college ($n = 59$, 64.8%) is the most, followed by postgraduate ($n = 26$, 28.6%), and general and vocational high school ($n = 6$, 6.6%). In terms of professions, government employees accounted for 28.6% ($n = 26$) the most, followed by finance and insurance 13.2% ($n = 12$), service 8.79% ($n = 8$), and students 8.79% ($n = 8$).

In terms of place of residence, the northern Taiwan accounted for the most at 84.6% ($n = 77$), followed by central Taiwan accounted for 12.1% ($n = 11$), and southern Taiwan accounted for 3.1% ($n = 3$).

4.2 Participants' Extent of Watching Korean Dramas

In terms of the weekly number of hours that participants spent watching Korean dramas, 5 h or less ($n = 58$, 63.7%) is the most, followed by 6–10 h ($n = 23$, 25.3%), 11–20 h ($n = 7$, 7.7%), and 21 h or more ($n = 3$, 3.3%).

In terms of methods of watching, paid streaming services (68.1%) is the most, followed by free online platforms (48.4%) and cable television (25.3%).

Participants' Preference for Korean Dramas. In this study, the results were filled in by the participant ($n = 32$), and preference for Korean dramas was used to score by preference scores (1–5 points) according to their level of preference (5th to 1st), and calculate the average preference score according to the proportion of the number of respondents. *Hospital Playlist* Season 2 and *Hometown Cha-Cha-Cha* scored 4.41 points and 4.18 points, respectively, for "highly-favored" dramas, and *Squid Game* scored 3.62 points for "moderately-favored" dramas. In addition, the ranking of the average preference score is the same as the ranking of Weekly Top 10. The following Table 1 gives a summary of the ranking of the average preference.

Table 1. The ranking of the average preference of Korean dramas.

Drama name	*Hospital Playlist* Season 2	*Hometown Cha-Cha-Cha*	*Squid Game*
The ranking of Weekly Top 10	1	2	3
The average preference score	4.41	4.18	3.62

4.3 Cultural Values Perceived by the Participants When Watching Korean Dramas

According to the result of the questionnaire, this study analyzes three aspects of "family and marriage values", "personal values" and "social values".

Frequency Distribution of Family and Marriage Values. Frequency distribution of family and marriage values that were perceived by the participant ($n = 411$), family unity (27.0%) is the most, followed by filial piety (24.8%), and patriarchy (16.1%). The following Table 2 gives a summary of the frequency distribution of family and marriage values.

Table 2. Frequency distribution of Family and marriage values

Cultural value	Feature type	Percentage (%)
Family and marriage values	Filial piety	24.8%
	Reverence for ancestors	5.7%
	Family unity	27.0%
	Authoritative parenting	10.6%
	Democratic parenting	7.7%
	Patriarchy	16.1%
	Spousal respect	8.2%
	Total	**100.0%**

In addition, the analysis was conducted according to the participants' preference and perceived family and marriage values. The following Table 3 shows there is a significant difference in the frequency distribution between the participants' preference and their perceived family and marriage values, $\chi^2(12, N = 404) = 93.75$, $p < .001$, Cramer's $V = .34$. When watching highly-favored dramas, participants perceived "family unity" (31.7%, 34.5%) the most, and followed by "filial piety" (24.8%, 19.4%). When watching moderately-favored dramas, participants perceived "patriarchy" (34.6%) the most, and followed by "filial piety" (31.7%). From this, it can be seen that the "family and marital values" perceived by participants watching highly preferred dramas have similarities, while the highly and moderately preferred dramas have part of similarities.

Table 3. Cross-analysis of participant preference and perceived family and marriage values

	Feature type	Filial piety	Reverence for ancestors	Family unity	Authoritative parenting	Democratic parenting	Patriarchy	Spousal respect	Total
Participant preference	Highly-favored 1	40 (24.8%)	6 (3.7%)	51 (31.7%)	12 (7.5%)	23 (14.3%)	14 (8.7%)	15 (9.3%)	164 (100.0%)
	Highly-favored 2	27 (19.4%)	17 (12.2%)	48 (34.5%)	12 (8.6%)	6 (4.3%)	15 (10.8%)	14 (10.1%)	139 (100.0%)
	Moderately-favored	33 (31.7%)	0 (0.0%)	10 (9.6%)	19 (18.3%)	2 (1.9%)	36 (34.6%)	4 (3.8%)	104 (100.0%)
	Total	100	23	109	43	31	65	33	404

Chi-Square $= 93.75$, *df* $= 12$, $p < .001$; "Highly-favored 1" refers to Hospital Playlist Season 2, "Highly-favored 2" refers to Hometown Cha-Cha-Cha, and "Moderately-favored" refers to Squid Game.

Frequency Distribution of Personal Values. Frequency distribution of personal values that perceived by the participant ($n = 632$), mutual help and friendship (17.2%) is the most, followed by standing up for oneself (15.7%). The following Table 4 gives a summary of the frequency distribution of personal values.

Table 4. Frequency distribution of personal values

Cultural value	Feature type	Percentage (%)
Personal values	Looking out for oneself	11.4%
	Knowing one's place	6.3%
	Mutual help and friendship	17.2%
	Standing up for oneself	15.7%
	Optimistic views	13.3%
	Self-pity	6.2%
	Fatalism	10.6%
	Seize the day	13.8%
	Long-term planning	5.5%
	Total	**100.0%**

In addition, the analysis was conducted according to the participants' preference and perceived personal values. The following Table 5 shows there is a significant difference in the frequency distribution between the participants' preference and their perceived personal values, $\chi 2(16, N = 632) = 45.61, p < .001$, Cramer's $V = .19$. When watching highly-favored dramas, participants perceived "mutual help and friendship" (20.3%, 17.2%) the most, and followed by "optimistic views" (18.8%, 16.0%). When watching moderately-favored dramas, participants perceived "standing up for oneself" (16.9%) the most, and followed by "looking out for oneself" (15.3%). From this, it can be seen that the personal values perceived by participants watching highly preferred dramas have similarities, while the highly and moderately preferred dramas have no similarities.

Table 5. Cross-analysis of participant preference and perceived personal values

	Feature type	Looking out for oneself	Knowing one's place	Mutual help and friendship	Standing up for oneself	Optimistic views	Self-pity	Fatalism	Seize the day	Long-term planning	Total
Participant preference	**Highly-favored 1**	10 (5.0%)	13 (6.4%)	41 (20.3%)	29 (14.4%)	38 (18.8%)	8 (4.0%)	15 (7.4%)	31 (15.3%)	17 (8.4%)	202 (100.0%)
	Highly-favored 2	22 (13.0%)	13 (7.7%)	29 (17.2%)	26 (15.4%)	27 (16.0%)	7 (4.1%)	14 (8.3%)	23 (13.6%)	8 (4.7%)	169 (100.0%)
	Moderately-favored	40 (15.3%)	14 (5.4%)	39 (14.9%)	44 (16.9%)	19 (7.3%)	24 (9.2%)	38 (14.6%)	33 (12.6%)	10 (3.8%)	261 (100.0%)
	Total	72	40	109	99	84	39	67	87	35	632

$Chi\text{-}Square = 45.61$, $df = 16$, $p < .001$; "Highly-favored 1" refers to Hospital Playlist Season 2, "Highly-favored 2" refers to Hometown Cha-Cha-Cha, and "Moderately-favored" refers to Squid Game.

Frequency Distribution of Social Values. Frequency distribution of social values that perceived by the participant ($n = 373$), followership (22.8%) is the most, followed by class distinction (19.0%). The following Table 6 gives a summary of the frequency distribution of social values.

Table 6. Frequency distribution of social values

Cultural value	Feature type	Percentage (%)
Social values	Comprised egalitarianism and open-mindedness	17.7%
	Submission to authority	13.9%
	Followership	22.8%
	Emphasis on individual will	15.8%
	Class distinction	19.0%
	Respect for the rule of law	10.7%
	Total	**100.0%**

In addition, the analysis was conducted according to the participants' preference and perceived social values. The following Table 7 shows there is a significant difference in the frequency distribution between the participants' preference and their perceived social values, χ^2 (10, $n = 373$) = 40.19, $p < .001$, Cramer's $V = .23$. When watching highly-favored dramas, participants perceived both "comprised egalitarianism and open-mindedness" (25.8%, 25.0%), and "followership" (20.2%, 29.5%). When watching moderately-favored dramas, participants perceived "class distinction" (26.7%) the most, and followed by "followership" (21.1%). From this, it can be seen that the social values perceived by participants watching highly preferred dramas have similarities, while the highly and moderately preferred dramas have part of similarities.

Table 7. Cross-analysis of participant preference and perceived social values

	Feature type	Comprised egalitarianism and open-mindedness	Submission to authority	Followership	Emphasis on individual will	Class distinction	Respect for the rule of law	Total
Participant preference	**Highly-favored 1**	32 (25.8%)	13 (10.5%)	25 (20.2%)	21 (16.9%)	18 (14.5%)	15 (12.1%)	124 (100.0%)
	Highly-favored 2	22 (25.0%)	7 (8.0%)	26 (29.5%)	10 (11.4%)	10 (11.4%)	13 (14.8%)	88 (100.0%)
	Moderately-favored	12 (7.5%)	32 (19.9%)	34 (21.1%)	28 (17.4%)	43 (26.7%)	12 (7.5%)	161 (100.0%)
	Total	66	52	85	59	71	40	373

Chi-Square = 40.19, *df* = 10, *p* < .001; "Highly-favored 1" refers to Hospital Playlist Season 2, "Highly-favored 2" refers to Hometown Cha-Cha-Cha, and "Moderately-favored" refers to Squid Game.

5 Conclusion and Follow-Up Research

5.1 Conclusion and Discussion

After comprehensive analysis and comparison, this study finds that Korean dramas that audiences highly-favored have common values when they watch Korean dramas. However, the values perceived by watching moderately-favored Korean dramas have some similarities and differences with highly-favored Korean dramas. The main findings of this study are as follows:

1. Consistent with existing research findings, influenced by Confucian culture, the Korean dramas that Taiwanese audiences highly-favored have the same characteristics in terms of family and marriage values, personal values, and social values, and are consistent with the values emphasized by Confucianism [7, 19]. The Korean dramas that Taiwanese audiences highly-favored, that family and marriage values perceived by audiences are mainly "family unity" and "filial piety", and their personal values are mainly "mutual help and friendship" and "optimistic view". Although social values are different in order, they are mainly based on "comprised egalitarianism and open-mindedness" and "followership". It shows that Taiwanese audiences can perceive content that conforms to their own cultural values when watching Korean TV dramas, which resonates.

2. The Korean dramas that Taiwanese audiences moderately-favored are consistent in the presentation of family and marriage values, social values with highly-favored dramas. The Korean dramas that Taiwanese audiences moderately-favored, that family and marriage values perceived by audiences are mainly "family unity" and "filial piety ". And "filial piety" can be perceived in Korean dramas with highly or moderately-favored, which is consistent with existing research findings, indicating that Taiwanese audiences are more accepting of the value of filial piety [7]. In terms of social values, there is "followership", which shows that Taiwanese audiences prefer to have a group consciousness socioculturally.

3. In terms of personal values, Taiwanese audiences perceive different types of characteristics when they watch Korean dramas with high and moderate preferences. Existing research has found that Korean audiences are more accepting of personal values of "self-consciousness" [7] and it's consistent with the personal values perceived by Taiwanese viewers (daring to standing up for oneself, looking out for oneself). It shows that although all parts of Asia have common cultural origins, they are influenced by different national conditions and social customs. Although they have similarities with Taiwan in terms of family, marriage and social values, they have differences in personal values. However, due to changes in the social environment, Taiwanese audiences have also increased their acceptance of values that value personal interests and demands.

Based on the above discussion, starting from the audience's perception, this study found that Taiwanese audience prefer content consistent with their own culture in terms of family, marriage, and social values when watching Korean dramas, but less consistent in terms of personal values. In addition, in terms of family and marriage values, the

Korean dramas that Taiwanese audiences like to have the characteristic value of "filial piety", while social values all have the characteristic value of "followership". Therefore, although South Korea and Taiwan have their cultural differences, they are both influenced by Confucian culture. If Taiwanese audiences can perceive cultural values that match their own when watching Korean dramas, they will have a higher degree of acceptance and preference.

And in recent years, the development of Taiwan's film and television market is still stagnant. In addition to discussions on industry and technology, whether the values contained in film and television content can resonate with Taiwanese audiences can also be explored in depth.

5.2 Suggestion for Follow-Up Research

This research uses a questionnaire survey method to explore the relationship between Taiwanese audiences' preferences for Korean dramas and cultural values that they perceived but no other variables such as genre of drama. It is recommended that follow-up research incorporate drama genres into the analysis in order to obtain a more holistic view of cultural value preferences.

In addition to the values perceived by the audience, the values that the film and television content itself intends to convey, and how to use plots, dialogues, and scenes to shape these values are also the key points of inquiry.

References

1. Taiwan Creative Content Agency: The 2020 Taiwan Cultural Content Industries Survey Report II: Television, Motion Picture, Animation, and Radio Industries. https://www.taicca.tw/article/26bcd207. Accessed 3 Oct 2021
2. Hsu, C.H., Lien, S.C.: Research on online word-of-mouth marketing of Taiwanese dramas. J. CAGST, 140–155 (2019)
3. Wu, Y.K., Jiang, Y.H.: A Diachronic analysis of the industry transition of Taiwanese trendy drama. In: Chinese Communication Society Proceedings. http://ccstaiwan.org/word/HISTORY_PAPER_FILES/1275_1.pdf. Accessed 14 Nov 2021
4. Lee, T.D.: Strategies and policy planning commissioned research projects for the development of Taiwan's film and television media in the era of global competition. Research project commissioned by Government Information Office, Executive Yuan, project number: EL-95091. Government Information Office, Executive Yuan, Taipei (2006)
5. Lee, J.L.: The role and effect of TV dramas in the culture creative industries: using "guardian: the lonely and the great god" as an example. Res. Educ. Commun. Technol. **118**, 47–64 (2018)
6. The Korea Creative Content Agency (KOCCA): 2020 Broadcasting Industry White Paper. https://www.kocca.kr/cop/bbs/view/B0000146/1844047.do?searchCnd=&searchWrd=&cateTp1=&cateTp2=&useAt=&menuNo=201826&categorys=0&subcate=0&cateCode=&type=&instNo=0&questionTp=&uf_Setting=&recovery=&option1=&option2=&year=&categoryCOM062=&categoryCOM063=&categoryCOM208=&categoryInst=&morePage=&delCode=0&qtp=&pageIndex=1. Accessed 3 Oct 2021
7. Tsai, J.L., Li, S.C., Li, Y.C.: An examination on the relationship between popular Korean dramas and their cultural values: a cultural proximity perspective. Commun. Soc. **16**, 55–98 (2011)

8. Kuo, C.W.: Korean wave in Taiwan: implications for coping strategies. Taiwanese J. WTO Stud. **18**, 127–190 (2011)

9. Lin, C.M., Chan, C.E.: The new trend of the fashion consumption market in Taiwan-an analysis of the marketing strategies of Korean cosmetic shops. J. Int. Esthet. Sci. **6**(2), 103–128 (2009)

10. Lin, R.Y., Chen, C.M.: Factors influencing Taiwanese females' bridal photographs taking in Korea: an exploratory study. J. Int. Esthet. Sci. **13**(2), 35–58 (2016)

11. Wu, S.H., Wang, T.Y.: The relationships of likability of Korean drama toward the premium of Korean product and travel intention. J. Int. Bus. **11**(1), 59–84 (2017)

12. Chen, M.C.: A Study on motherhood and mothering in Korean female script writer Su-Hyeon Kim's family dramas: taking mom's dead upset, life is beautiful, childless comfort as examples. J. Audio V. Media Technol. **41**, 41–87 (2021)

13. Choung, H.: Korean culture in Korean TV drama and movies–focused on affection, " Han" and Shinmyoung. East Asian Stud. **1**(1), 1–13 (2016)

14. Wang, E.H., Chueh, Y.T.: Korean TV drama fans' interpretation patterns-a study on my name is Kim Sam Soon's Chinese audience. Commun. Soc. **16**, 99–122 (2011)

15. Straubhaar, J.D.: Asymmetrical Interdependence and Cultural Proximity: A Critical Review on the International Flow of Television Programs, London (1992)

16. Straubhaar, J.D.: Beyond media imperialism: assymetrical interdependence and cultural proximity. Crit. Stud. Mass Commun. **8**(1), 39–59 (1991)

17. Cheng, K.Y.: Research on the localization strategy of international marketing of overseas satellite TV channels. Department of Journalism, National Chengchi University (2001)

18. Hwang, J.H.: Online discussions concerning current events - elucidation of cultural values. Mass Commun. Res. **95**, 1–54 (2008)

19. Wen, C.: Chinese Values. San Min Book Co. Ltd., Taipei (1993)

20. Yang, K.S., Yu, A.B., Ye, M.H.: Chinese Personal Tradition and Modernity: Concepts and Measurements. Laureate Book Co., LTD, Taipei (1991)

21. Lee, P.S.: A Comparison of the cultural values of American, Japanese, and Taiwanese TV. Mass Commun. Res. **78**, 45–69 (2004)

22. Ho, P.L.: Naming "Vengeance" Tyrannous, desire, and devilishness/humanity in park Chan-Wook's films. J. Aesthet. Vis. Arts **7**, 95–108 (2015)

A Study of the Impact of the Incubation Mechanism in the Cultural and Creative Industry

Yu-hui Huang[✉]

Graduate School of Creative Industry Design, National Taiwan University of Arts,
New Taipei City 22058, Taiwan
Yuhui4241@gmail.com

Abstract. With the recent changes in the industrial environment, incubators have come to play an important role in the promotion of the cultural and creative industry. Incubators started from technical incubation for traditional industries and have now turned to providing services for specific industries. A professional training and guidance mechanism for the cultural and creative industry is the need of the hour. This study interviewed enterprises in the cultural and creative industry that have taken assistance and guidance from the National Taiwan University of Arts to understand the impact of incubations. Our study shows that the incubation mechanism is highly beneficial for a comprehensive growth of the enterprises. Through the incubators, they receive training on how to solve business problems and seek out business resources. We suggest that incubators should provide diversified choices as the industrial environment changes further and promote innovation and development of enterprises. And we look award for that more incubation center join in and focus on the cultural and creative industry through our research.

Keywords: Culture and creative industry · Incubators · Incubation mechanism

1 Introduction

With creative industries being promoted globally, creative products or innovative services have increasingly started entering the market. As a medium of transmission between industry and consumers, brands transmit cultural value to consumers. As cultural and creative industries evolve, more creators have launched new brands, invested in the industry, and are trying to highlight the value of art and culture. They have found a sustainable balance between artistic creation and commercialization.

In recent years, both micro-entrepreneurship and brand awareness among consumers have grown. Many creators with innovative products have launched new brands by setting up personal studios to sell their goods or services. However, a new brand inevitably encounters several difficulties when it enters the market; this is where an incubation center's role comes in. When we think about how to increase the output of the cultural and creative sector, incubation is highly effective in brand development.

© The Author(s), under exclusive license to Springer Nature Switzerland AG 2022
P.-L. P. Rau (Ed.): HCII 2022, LNCS 13312, pp. 363–373, 2022.
https://doi.org/10.1007/978-3-031-06047-2_26

Earlier, most incubation centers were engaged in incubating technology manufacturers and used a general incubation mechanism to provide services to enterprises in the cultural and creative industries. However, the cultural and creative sector differs from general industries [7], and traditional technology entrepreneurship and cultural entrepreneurship have marked differences in terms of entrepreneurial conditions and requirements [26]. For the cultural and creative industry, a general mechanism is not applicable. In recent years, with changes in the industrial environment, incubation centers have begun to shift from being technical incubators for traditional industries to providing specific industry guidance for cultural and creative industries [26]. Therefore, a professional training and guidance mechanism dedicated to the cultural and creative sector is important. However, much of the literature focuses on the role and function of the incubation center for technology or manufacturing industries. There are very few studies on the incubation mechanism for the cultural and creative industry.

The cultural and creative industry in Taiwan is more than ten years old. With the rapid changes in the industrial environment, incubation strategies also need to adapt accordingly, and there is a need to re-examine the current incubation mechanism for the cultural and creative industry. Therefore, this study focuses on the brands assisted by the National Taiwan University of Arts (NTUA) through its incubation center. We will discuss the impact of the current strategies and resources invested on the enterprises and the requirements of the enterprises in their process of growth. We also explore the impact of the current mechanism and strategy for the cultural and creative industry and propose suggestions for further improvement.

2   Literature Review

2.1   The Challenge of Marketing in the Cultural and Creative Industry

The products in the cultural and creative industry focus on the development of spiritual value and artistic creation with the effect of the consumption process of modern culture [8]. The cultural and creative industry is not just about selling creative products, it is also about embodying life. At the core of the cultural and creative industry is a "business (industry)" based on "creativity (design)" that is derived from "craftsmanship (culture)" [14]. The ultimate goal is the development of brands, which is critical for sustaining the enterprises in the cultural and creativity industry.

As a communication medium between the industry and consumers, brands play an important role in transmitting cultural value to consumers. The value of the cultural and creative industry depends on the needs of consumers and the intangible value of cultural and creative products; the utility and experience of consumers determines the value of these products and services [12]. The cultural and creative industry has a deep emotional connection with its consumers and needs to interact with them frequently. Therefore, it has an industrial structure that is dominated by small enterprises. Further, small enterprises have the advantage of not needing large capital investments and can quickly respond to market changes [23]. Hence, most new ventures in this industry tend to be small.

Creative businesses tend to be quite small, individualistic and highly risky which are the characteristics [5]. From the perspective of manufacturing, there are four factors:

changes in manufacturing, manufacturing methods and places, products and services, and the market [4]. It contributed to the production with small scale in the cultural and creative industry. From the perspective of economic development, the emergence of new and small enterprises is the result of many structural changes. It reflects a shift from an emphasis on economies of scale and mass production to an emphasis on knowledge, initiative, and flexibility [23]. In an economic system that emphasizes knowledge and creativity, the focus of economic activity is information, including its acquisition, processing, and transmission. The application of information and communication technology helps teams work together through the internet, so that many people can organize themselves and engage in innovative activities on their own [17]. Small enterprises have the advantage of flexibility and agility, which helps them quickly respond and adjust to changes in the industrial environment.

In developed countries, entrepreneurship is an important policy route for economic and social development [23]. Entrepreneurs have to first develop a new product and market it with limited resources; since most new entrepreneurs do not have adequate resources in equipment, funds, contacts with potential customers and other aspects, incubators become a supportive service partner in the entrepreneurial process by providing complementary resources [13, 19]. Network resources are crucial for entrepreneurs. Therefore, if the incubation center can provide access to a rich external network, it provides more opportunities for success.

2.2 Intervention from the Incubation as a Mechanism in Culture and Creative Industry

Innovation incubators promote new and small enterprises, and they also promote industrial development. Just as incubation helps premature babies survive safely to term, incubation centers help fledgling business ventures overcome environmental challenges in the early stages of growth [1]. Incubation centers first originated in the United States in the 1950s. They assist in economic development in four ways: develop regional growth; assist regional enterprises in preventing outward migration; help disadvantaged groups develop useful human resources within the community; and guide skilled entrepreneurs in the technology industry [22]. The current creative institutions include co-working spaces, entrepreneurial bases, incubation centers, accelerators, and so on, and have different names according to the services they provide.

The Centre for Strategy and Evaluation Services (CSES) developed an incubator model for the European Commission (Fig. 1) [11]. The inputs are operator management resources and collaborative projects proposed by entrepreneurs, and the outputs are the potential growth of successful enterprises and the employment and wealth generated. As a mediator, an incubator connects the resources of all parties, intervenes in the process, and enhances the efficiency and stability of an enterprise.

The functions of an incubation center are: selection, mediation, and business support [3]. There are three main periods in the evolution of incubation centers. First-generation incubation centers were facility renting services, providing low-cost land or space for long-term residency; second-generation incubation centers provided professional consulting and training services and connections to ensure that entrepreneurs can stably maintain operations; third-generation incubation centers provide networking, with the

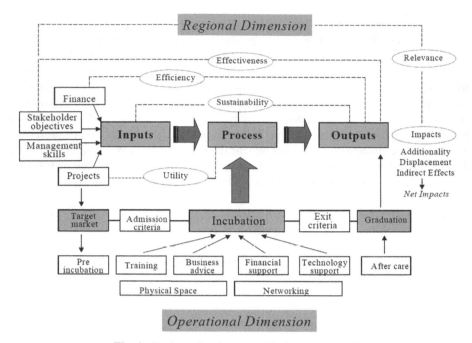

Fig. 1. Business incubator model (CSES, 2002: 25)

focus on start-up network matchmaking in the early stages of the business, to integrate the cultivators into the regional innovation ecosystem [3]. Incubation centers have begun to shift from traditional technical training focused on general industries to specific guidance for cultural and creative industries. The incubation function has gradually transformed from commercialization of technology to that of a role of a regional platform [21].

3   Research Methods

3.1   Procedure

To understand the impact of the incubation mechanism, this study adopts multiple case studies from the perspective of the mentored enterprises. We used semi-structured interviews with company leaders to gain an in-depth understanding of the impact and changes in new ventures after coaching.

   Based on the literature [21], we divide the incubator's functions into: selection, business support, and mediation, and use the business incubator model [11] to synthesize the current strategy of incubation and propose the following study framework (Fig. 2). The interview structure is based on the service content of business support. We used the interview records and secondary data for analysis. The secondary data is collected from the particular projects, industry report and public materials.

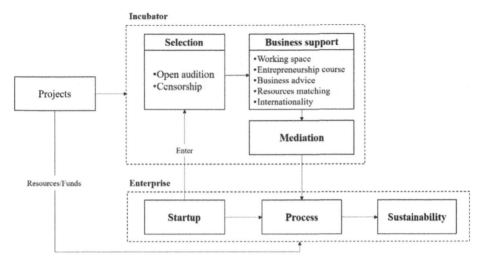

Fig. 2. Research framework

3.2 Case Selection and Company Profiles

Incubation centers specific to cultural and creative industry are relatively new in Taiwan, with most of them being university or government agencies. NTUA has been running an incubation center for the cultural and creative industry for more than ten years, and its coaching structure is complete and successful. Hence, we interviewed some of the cultural and creative enterprises mentored by NTUA. Our focus is on the craft and visual arts industry to avoid the influence of differences between industries.

NTUA assists new ventures in the cultural and creative industry with pre-incubation through the government project. They provide business support and resource matching to help new ventures achieve stable development. We selected five startups that have been assisted by NTUA between 2017 and 2019 and received relatively similar incubation and environment. Two of these enterprises are in the visual arts industry and three are in the craft industry. We interviewed seven leaders with the interview time ranging from 60 to 90 min. Each interview was recorded and transcribed with 74 pages in all. The collected case data is shown in Table 1.

Firms A and D are in the visual art industry, while Firms B, C, and E are in craft design. Firms A, C, and D have participated in more than 2 incubation centers. Startup entrepreneurship can be divided into five stages: seed, startup, expansion, mezzanine, and turnaround. Firms A, B and C entered the incubation center at the seed stage, mainly seeking working space and entrepreneurial resources, while Firms D and E entered the incubation center during the startup stage to seek entrepreneurial resources. At present, all firms have moved into the expansion stage, an indication that their products or services have been accepted by the market. Furthermore, the enterprises have gradually strengthened their marketing and productive abilities to expand their scale of enterprise.

Table 1. Company profiles

	Firm A	Firm B	Firm C	Firm D	Firm E
Established	2016	2016	2016	2012	2014
Industry	Visual Arts	Crafts	Crafts	Visual Arts	Crafts
Entered incubation	2017	2017	2017	2018	2017
The number of incubators	2	1	2	2	1
Under counseling	3 years/1 year	3 years	2 years/3 years	2 years/1 year	3 years
Necessity for seeking incubation	Working space/Entrepreneurship resources	Working space/Entrepreneurship resources	Working space/Entrepreneurship resources	Entrepreneurship resources/Technology	Working space/Entrepreneurship resources
Startup stage before incubation	Seed	Seed	Seed	Startup	Startup
Startup stage after incubation	Expansion	Expansion	Expansion	Expansion	Expansion

4   Main Findings

4.1   The Requirements of Enterprises in Creative Environments

Most enterprises enter incubation centers due to their need for working space. However, Firms D and E entered the incubation center 6 and 3 years after their establishment, respectively, and were focused on enterprise transformation. Although firm E initially needed a workspace, their ultimate goal was transformation, to change their production and research and development (R&D) models. Firms A, B, and C had an acute need for workspace, so they entered the incubation center soon after their establishment.

Cheap rent is an important factor, but there are other perks too. There is dust or noise during production, and it is impossible to rent a factory. If you rent a place in a residential area, other residents would protest, so it is important to have an unconstrained environment for creators. (Firm A)

As stated earlier, most of the firms in the cultural and creative industry are micro and small enterprises making customized orders on a small scale and so, require working space for micro-mass-production. If the products need to be mass-produced in the future, then production outsourcing model can be adopted. Consequently, the requirements for starting a factory is relatively low. At present, many incubators provide only office working spaces. Creative enterprises, especially, also need space for R&D and small-scale production. Therefore, it is important for enterprises in the cultural and creative industry to have a working space.

The environment of NTUA, where there is a high degree of interaction with similar brands, is what attracted us. If the brands in other places are not artistic or cultural and creative, then there is low commonality and that leads to a communication gap. In NTUA, we have interactions with others based on common interests. (Firm D)

Working space is required not just for production; Firms D and E believe that it is better to separate the production and living areas. The space should also provide additional functions, such as product display, conference rooms or visitors' area. Additionally, most enterprises tend to congregate in the same area to form industrial settlements, which have both tangible and intangible advantages. The tangible advantages of industrial agglomeration are reduction in production and operation costs, easy access to professional labor and services, and efficiency in production [17]. At the same time, it can also render intangible effects, such as knowledge sharing and invisibly increasing technology and innovation capabilities. All the interviewed enterprise leaders agreed with this point of view and stated that information sharing is key to decision making in the cultural and creative industry. In summary, industrial clusters can not only create high demand, but can also stimulate innovation through interactions between enterprises in the cultural and creative industry.

4.2   Develop the Ability to Solve Business Problems

Apart from the demands of workspace, enterprises also require professional coaching. NTUA's incubation center assists them with entrepreneurship courses, such as product development, brand marketing, finance, commodity photography, proposal writing, and international fairs. Most entrepreneurs come from an artistic background, and, therefore, lack practical business knowledge in the cultural and creative industry. Hence, business courses are important for them. However, different enterprises need different set of courses depending on their needs (Fig. 1). For example, Firm A's CEO is graduated from department of business and management, so they have a grasp of basic concepts, such as finance and marketing. In such cases, when enterprises are faced with a difficulty, they often obtain solutions through professional coaching. To sum up, coaching with others who have had similar experiences leads to greater learning.

What we want is practical experience or a discussion of industry case studies with objective suggestions. (Firm C)

We would like to create the same path for artists and enterprises. That is why we need experience sharing when we encounter real-life difficulties. (Firm D)

When we enrolled in these courses, we expected the lecturer to be a collaborator. I had an opportunity to work with several lecturers because I thought that we need more proactive exchanges and get more from the lecturers. (Firm A)

The interviewed enterprise leaders pointed out that the sharing of practical experience in the industry is very important for new ventures. They can receive more information from the seniors in the industrial settlement and from guest lecturers at the incubation center. Lecturers have rich industry experience, so new ventures can get a better understanding of the current industry situation and existing business models.

When we were involved in another incubation center, they would track the progress every month and give more professional and substantive suggestions. It's helpful for us. Sometimes it was through group discussions with people from different industries. If this was applied to the cultural and creative industry, everyone could share their problems more easily. (Firm D)

However, not everyone proactively asked for assistance. Firms B, C, D, and E rarely used this service. This was because they did not much knowledge about the kind of difficulties encountered or how to ask for assistance. They also thought the lecturers were not able to give substantive solutions. Firm D had participated in other incubation centers, where they learnt to share problems and resolve them through discussions. This reflects the importance of peer groups in industry; they can help find feasible solutions quickly through sharing of experiences.

4.3   Resource Mediation from Incubators

During the incubation period, the center provides a lot of opportunities for marketing, like pop-up shops, sale on consignment, Creative Market, domestic and foreign fairs, and so on, which help enterprises get exposure. Most of these are business-to-customer (B2C) channels. Enterprises additionally hope to mine professional ideas on marketing strategies. For example, what kind of media exposure to choose and how to distribute marketing channels and increase opportunities for cooperation. Firms B, C, and E expressed the hope that the business-to-business (B2B) channels could be available from incubation center. Before the Covid-19 pandemic, the incubation center provided opportunities for international fairs, allowing enterprises to operate internationally and proactively match with buyers who purchase in large quantities. However, most buyers want lower purchasing costs, large shipments, and instant deliveries. Unfortunately, most enterprises in the cultural and creative industry cannot undertake large orders because of their small scale. Therefore, selection and matching of suitable fairs is important for the enterprises from the incubation center.

At present, we only have a social media presence, but we want to know more about how print and TV media operate, find more exposure opportunities and channels, so that our brand marketing can be more comprehensive. (Firm E)

During the incubation in NTUA, they wanted to guide the growth of brands in an all-round way. Whether it is physical channels or exhibition sales, there are very few digital resources. But not every enterprise can go for mass production or expand internationally. For those enterprises, it is necessary to deepen brand management through digital transformation. (Firm A)

Lastly, the role of digital platforms is also worth a mention in the process of brand internationalization. Due to the digitalization of the global economy, there are more diversified marketing channels available, such as digital platforms, online marketing, and purchasing agents. Enterprises no longer need a high threshold for expanding internationally. New ventures look for exposure opportunities at international fairs as well as assistance with overseas marketing resources and acquiring new business [18]. In conclusion, the incubation center, as a mediator, not only strengthens the business knowledge of the enterprises but also provides suitable business strategies based on industry trends.

5   Discussion

5.1   The Incubation Centers Dedicated to the Cultural and Creative Industry

The enterprises in the cultural and creative industry try to convey brand concept with aesthetic value rather than technological innovation. Therefore, it is impossible to apply the incubation concept of the technology industry; there is need for an incubation strategy exclusively for the cultural and creative industry. In the future, it can be expected to develop towards an incubation model for specific industries [24].

The participating enterprises thought that digital platforms were not being used strategically during the incubation period. The incubation strategy should change in response to the growth stage of the enterprise and differences in the industrial environments. Accordingly, the fourth generation of incubation service can be expected to focus on virtual services, supply of digital business model, and creation of intellectual capital [9]. Thus, digital transformation can be expected to become an important part of the incubation mechanism in the future.

5.2 The Incubator as a Mediator

As the entrepreneurial ecosystem grows internationally, it would become necessary to find ways to measure the connection between internal and external business environment in the future [25]. In addition to providing a dedicated space, the incubation center also plays the role of a mediator in the industrial environment, such as holding exchange meetings, competitions and other activities to promote healthy competition and cooperation between enterprises. When there is competition and cooperation between enterprises, it helps them understand their market positioning and product characteristics, which is conducive to their growth [16].

Regardless of the change in the incubation center's services according to industry trends, its role of a mediator would continue to be relevant, where it provides diversified resources to the enterprises, thereby promoting enterprise innovation and development. Incubators should move away from "providing counseling resources" or "accelerating management ability" to helping enterprises develop own their competence with the ability to internationalize and manage themselves in a specific industry. Overall, it would be more effective to guide new ventures and achieve sustainable development by highlighting their core competencies and resource cooperation in the business ecosystem [18].

5.3 Limitations and Future Research

This study focuses on pre-incubation strategies in the cultural and creative industry. The participating enterprises indicated that they continue to encounter problems in operating even after leaving the incubator. These include issues with organizational management, marketing strategies, establishment of digital platforms, and transformation of the overall business model. Incubation centers are gradually becoming centers of knowledge dissemination and business internationalization [2, 10, 15]. A significant issue confronting incubation centers would be how to continuously provide resources flexibly to enterprises. Future studies can focus on the growth strategies of accelerators, highlighting the differences between incubators and accelerators in the cultural and creative industry.

References

1. Aernoudt, R.: Incubators: tool for entrepreneurship. Small Bus. Econ. **23**, 127–135 (2004). https://doi.org/10.1023/B:SBEJ.0000027665.54173.23
2. Aerts, K., Matthyssens, P., Vandenbempt, K.: Critical role and screening practices of European business incubators. Technovation **27**(5), 254–267 (2007). https://doi.org/10.1016/j.technovation.2006.12.002
3. Bergek, A., Norrman, C.: Incubator best practice: a framework. Technovation **28**(1/2), 20–28 (2008). https://doi.org/10.1016/j.technovation.2007.07.008
4. Bianchini, M., Maffei, S.: Could design leadership. Be personal? Forecasting new forms of "Indie Capitalism". Design Manage. J. **7**(1), 6–17 (2012). https://doi.org/10.1111/j.1948-7177.2012.00029.x
5. Bilton, C., Leary, R.: What can managers do for creativity? Brokering creativity in the creative industries. Int. J. Cultural Poli. **8**(1), 49–64 (2002). https://doi.org/10.1080/10286630290032431

6. Bruneel, J., Ratinho, T., Clarysse, B., Groen, A.: The evolution of business incubators: comparing demand and supply of business incubation services across different incubator generations. Technovation **32**(2), 110–121 (2012). https://doi.org/10.1016/j.technovation.2011.11.003

7. Caves, R.: Creative Industries: Contracts Between Art and Commerce Cambridge. Harvard University Press, MA (2000)

8. Chen, H.Y.: A study on the information design of cultural product. Doctoral thesis, Ming Chuan University, Taipei, Taiwan (2009). https://hdl.handle.net/11296/wab5md

9. Costa Junior, J.F.: A study on the internationalization barriers to incubated companies: defining the constructs to develop an effective research instrument. Eur. J. Sci. Res. **153**(3), 334–359 (2019). ISSN:1450-216X/1450-202X

10. Engelman, R., Zen, A.C., Fracasso, E.M.: The impact of the incubator on the internationalization of firms. J. Technol. Manag. Innov. **10**, 29–39 (2015). https://doi.org/10.4067/S0718-27242015000100003

11. European commission: benchmarking of business incubators centre for strategy and evaluation services Kent, UK (2002). https://ec.europa.eu/docsroom/documents/2767/attachments/1/translations/en/renditions/pdf

12. Feng, K.H., Tai, S.C., Lai, W.S.: Value co-creation in local cultural and creative industry: the perspective of tri-sector partnerships. Soochow J. Econ. Bus. **82**, 1–33 (2013)

13. Hackett, S.M., Dilts, D.: A real options-driven theory of business incubation. J. Technol. Transfer **29**(1), 41–54 (2004). https://doi.org/10.1023/B:JOTT.0000011180.19370.36

14. Lin, R.T.: Preface – the essence and research of cultural and creative industries. J. Des. **16**(4) (2011). https://doi.org/10.6381/JD.201112.0002

15. Mian, S., Lamine, W., Fayolle, A.: Technology business incubation: an overview of the state of knowledge. Technovation **50–51**, 1–12 (2016). https://doi.org/10.1016/j.technovation.2016.02.005

16. Narver, J.C., Slater, S.F., MacLachlan, D.L.: Responsive and proactive market orientation and new product success. J. Product Innovat. Manage. **21**(5), 334–344 (2004). https://doi.org/10.1111/j.0737-6782.2004.00086.x

17. Ouden, D.E.: Innovation Design: Creating Value for People, Organizations and Society. Springer, London (2012). https://doi.org/10.1007/978-1-4471-2268-5

18. PwC Taiwan, Taiwan Institute of Economic Res: 2019 Startup ecosystem survey in Taiwan. Taipei, Taiwan (2019). https://www.pwc.tw/zh/publications/topic-report/2019-taiwan-startup-ecosystem-survey.html

19. Rice, M.P.: Co-production of business assistance in business incubators: an exploratory study. J. Bus. Ventur. **17**(2), 163–187 (2002). https://doi.org/10.1016/S0883-9026(00)00055-0

20. Rosenfeld, S.A.: Networks and clusters: The Yin and Yang of rural development. In: Proceedings of Rural and Agricultural Conferences, pp. 103–120 (2001)

21. Soetanto, D., Jack, S.: The impact of university-based incubation support on the innovation strategy of academic spin-offs. Technovation **50–51**, 25–40 (2016). https://doi.org/10.1016/j.technovation.2015.11.001

22. Tasi, S.L.: A close examination of the effectiveness and the appropriateness of innovative incubation centers in Taiwan. Commerce Manage. Quart. **1**(43), 417–445 (2000)

23. Tung, F.W., Huang, P.Y.: A study on value chain analysis of design entrepreneurship in Taiwan. J. Des. **20**(2), 49–64 (2016)

24. Vanderstraeten, J., Matthyssens, P.: Service-based differentiation strategies for business incubators: exploring external and internal alignment. Technvation **32**(12), 656–670 (2012). https://doi.org/10.1016/j.technovation.2012.09.002

25. Wang, L.J.: The continuous improvement is for entrepreneurial ecosystem in Taiwan. Taiwan Econ. Res. Monthly **41**(9), 113–120 (2018). https://doi.org/10.29656/TERM.201809.0015

26. Yang, C.H.: Value network creation of university incubator for cultural and creative-based start-ups: a multilevel stakeholder analysis. J. Technol. Manage. **24**(3), 1–36 (2019)

The Multiple Effects of Digital Archaeology in the Future Space

Jiawei Li[1(✉)], Mingdong Song[1], Yanwei Li[2], and Yinghui Shang[2]

[1] Royal College of Art, London W12 7FN, UK
799974@network.rca.ac.uk
[2] Tianjin College of Commerce, No. 23 Yaguan Road, Haihe Education Park, Tianjin, China

Abstract. Today, as the global ecological crisis continues to assault mankind, we are all faced with a worrying ecological fate, yet we all share the desire to escape from it and to live happily ever after. In the context of the growing global ecological crisis, the construction of a future ecological community has also become a real need. Well-understood archaeological research has intrinsic value in terms of innovative knowledge and the development of innovative research methods. Examining historical narratives can make us aware of different cultures and ways of life throughout history, while techniques from the archaeological past and understanding and using them can also contribute to the renewal and development of design research. This paper plans to investigate the role and significance of digital archaeological technologies in the transfer of information about the sensory features of material and immaterial culture from the analogue to the digital realm in a future context, in conjunction with innovative design thinking tools of the retrospective method, in order to contribute to the construction of a future organic ecological network system composed of the natural world, the sensory world and the meta-universe.

Keywords: Digital archaeology · Ecological Community of the Future · Retrospective method · Innovative design thinking tools

1 Introduction

Historical and cultural heritage has a unique and significant role in spreading culture, conveying friendship, preserving the world's cultural diversity and creativity, promoting the exchange and mutual appreciation of civilisations, and facilitating the building of a community of human destiny. Today, cultural relics have become the most important signposts, connecting historical accumulation with contemporary development and prosperity, linking a country's vast and profound culture with the magnificent and diverse civilisations of the world, and building bridges of dialogue between different civilisation forms and social systems. Archaeology is a very important discipline. The history of human origins over millions of years and the history of prehistoric civilisations over tens of thousands of years have been constructed mainly on the basis of archaeological results. Even the history of civilisation after written records has to be referred to, corroborated, enriched and improved by archaeological work. Historical and cultural heritage not only tells a vivid story of the past, but also profoundly influences the present and the future.

Janus, the Roman god of beginnings and threshold space, is often depicted in iconography as having two faces pointing in opposite directions [1]. Despite the close proximity of the faces of the two-faced gods, they cannot see each other. In many ways, Janus' predicament is a good metaphor to describe the current relationship between science-oriented archaeology and social disciplines. While archaeologists were among the first users of digital technologies such as GIS, disciplinary boundaries between fields such as anthropology and history have led to a loss of intellectual and material opportunities.

Although there is no academic consensus on the definition, the discipline of digital society entails the use of computational methods to study social issues. Scholarship that explores what digital social disciplines are or speculates about their future form has turned out to be an important issue. Speculating on their future forms has become a genre piece. Like archaeology, the digital social discipline is an interdisciplinary field characterised by a collaborative project-based approach to research. In addition to these features, it promotes open-ended, exploratory research designs rather than the use of empirical models of hypothesis or model testing. As a result, there is a tendency to favour the avant-garde or visionary when looking for alternatives to traditional models of knowledge production. In archaeology, by contrast, geospatial technologies are often considered powerful tools for analysis or data capture [2], although there are important exceptions to the general trend, such as applications in cultural heritage management, museum studies or joint methods surveys [3].

The future of technologies such as GIS in science-oriented based archaeology depends on how practitioners envision the nature of their intellectual endeavours. Are archaeologists scientists engaged in model testing to develop universal theories, or are they humanists using scientific methods such as GIS to answer historically specific and contingent questions? The study of the epistemological shifts that have emerged in landscape studies is particularly revealing. Recent decades have seen a shift in the theoretical focus of regional landscape studies in Anglo-American archaeology [4]. The cultural ecology approach that prevailed in the mid-twentieth century has been challenged by various postmodern, post-positivist philosophies [5]. While some archaeologists previously equated the concept of landscape with the physical environment, a growing number of scholars now embrace a socio-historical perspective on the study of past landscapes. As a result, the scope and focus of GIS research has also shifted to the exploration of humanities and social science questions. In response, landscape archaeologists [6]. have called for approaches that combine social and spatial theory [7] leading to a shift in the field from an emphasis on patterns of interacting behaviour to the social dimension of landscape production [8].

A review of the current literature shows that archaeologists have internalized criticisms of postmodern, post-positivism in recent decades [8] and are examining traditional humanist lines of research, such as spatial experience or tracing historically specific developments. Given that the concept of landscape has shifted from the environment to social history, it is useful to define the areas in which geospatial approaches can be broadened through engagement with digital disciplines and spatial history, as landscape archaeology has many intersections with traditional humanities and social science inquiry.

This thesis will therefore analyse the role and significance of digital archaeological technology in the transfer of sensory information from the analogue to the digital realm of material and immaterial culture in a future context, combined with the innovative design thinking tools of retrospection, in order to contribute to the construction of a future organic ecological network consisting of the natural world, the sensory world and the metaverse.

2   Concept

Over the last few decades, the understanding of what cultural heritage is and how it is defined has changed and expanded its scope. Important international bodies, such as ICOMOS and UNESCO, representing reference points for documentation and conservation, have revised the definition of cultural heritage to include not only elements associated with historical art and testimonies of civilisations, but also their surroundings. In other words, the meaning of cultural heritage has been extended to include the concept of cultural landscapes.

Well-understood archaeological research has intrinsic value in terms of innovative knowledge and the development of innovative research methods. Examining historical narratives can make us aware of different cultures and ways of life throughout history, while techniques from the archaeological past and understanding and using them can also contribute to the renewal and development of design research.

David Sless, Director of the Australian Institute of Communication said in Design or 'Design' - Looking to the future of design education:- "Previously the agenda for change in design has been seen as ambitious, but in my view we should have a more modest vision of design:doing thoughtful, useful, evidence-based work to help progressive, informed and sustainable improvement, considering areas where we can consider and do no harm" [9]. In this vision, creativity is no longer at the centre of the design enterprise, but is seen as a useful part of the treasure trove of design information. More importantly, he mentions that we need to pay attention to two groups of people: those who have already created design tools and methodologies, and those who are happy to evaluate the design systems that have been created. the vision proposed by David Sless cuts through the traditionally perceived radical claims that design is revolutionary and transformative, and replaces them with design as a reconstructive activity embedded in existing social and natural systems.

How can we use digital technology to transcend (disrupt) the boundaries of perception and develop new understandings of self and others, society, life or embodiment? Can we work with digital media and technology to develop new perspectives on a past that transcends the human? Is it possible to grasp and cultivate other non-human moving entities through digital media and technology to create multisensory experiences? How is digitisation changing the relationship between archaeologists, the archaeological record and the public?

The closely related disciplines of archaeological research, anthropology, history and heritage studies offer a new way of thinking about future design: by connecting the past with the future, a retrospective perspective can be found. Whereas in the past future design has mostly been practised through foresight and anticipation, the intrinsic value of archaeology can help us to be able to look back, critique the present and look forward, and develop research methods oriented towards specific problem analysis, thus helping to address a range of challenges facing contemporary society and even the world.

3   Research Cases

Academic research into digital archaeology itself started late, with the Oxford Institute for Digital Archaeology (IDA), the Media Lab at the Helsinki University of Art and Design (DAMD), and Stanford University all currently beginning professional and research studies in the field.

The Oxford Institute for Digital Archaeology (IDA) has developed projects such as 'Olfactory Heritage - The Smell of History', 'Portable Heritage: The Evolutionary History of Books', 'Digital Syria' and 'Heartbeat of the City: 500 Years of Personal Time', all of which involve the use of digital technology and artistic creation to digitally simulate scenes from the past and to future-proof existing things. In "Smelling Heritage - The Smell of History", the IDA director explains that heritage assets take many forms. Some, such as old buildings and huge sculptures, display a strong physical presence. At the other extreme are purely ephemeral forms of cultural expression - dance, gastronomy, music - which have as much connection to our collective past as any building or statue, and are shaped by them. From the very beginning, the IDA has been preserving heritage in a variety of ways. In addition to pictorial and physical reconstructions, considerable effort and resources have been expended on observing, documenting and studying ephemeral heritage. IDA's current focus is on the concept of smell as ephemeral heritage. IDA has developed a suite of olfactory experiences for upcoming exhibitions at the Bodleian Library, Oxford University and the New York Public Library. Rare books and manuscripts for these installations include Edmond Malone's First Folio, a copy of the Magna Carta of 1217, James Madison's Federalist Papers, books from the private collections of CS Lewis and JRR Tolkien, and a range of rare Egyptian papyri, including fragments One of the earliest known copies of the Iliad. Each one has its own distinctive scent that tells its history, in Fig. 1. In 2020, the IDA will be collaborating with Vacheron Constantin, the world's oldest watchmaking company, on a travelling exhibition of clocks and other horological materials. This autumn, at the University of Oxford's Museum of the History of Science, visitors will be able to walk through the heart of a giant watch escapement and learn more about the workings of these precision machines. The installation - part of a joint venture with Vacheron Constantin - will incorporate an olfactory element, in Fig. 2.

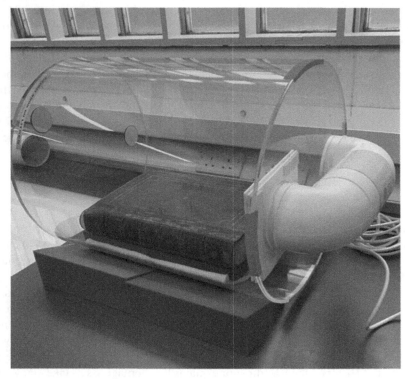

Fig. 1. Edmond Malone's first folio in IDA's proprietary odor extraction device at the Bodleian

The sense of smell is a complex sense with the unique ability to construct or access memories. The study of ancient spices has led to an awareness of the immense history and science contained in scent. working with palaeobotanists and olfactors in the USA, Europe and Central Asia, IDA has explored a range of heirloom varieties of traditional spice plants, recovering scents that in some cases have been forgotten by the world for centuries. They are establishing a herbarium as a living library of these ancient plants, preserving not only their genomes but also their fragrances, as an emerging form of historical conservation that will contribute greatly to the knowledge base of future and future generations.

Digital Archaeology is a design/research discipline being developed at the Media Lab (DAMD) at the University of Art and Design Helsinki, Finland. Emphasising the important contribution of artists to the development of the information environment, it aims to reconstruct and make previously inaccessible cultural artefacts as widely available as possible. Issues of access and preservation, research and intellectual enquiry, and the metaphorical nature of technology are invoked as building blocks for the future. Looking at historical narratives allows us to be aware of the differences between cultures

Fig. 2. Preparing the scents for the 2020 Bodleian library "Sensational Books" Exhibition

and ways of life throughout history, says project organiser Lily Diaz in the discipline description. New technologies facilitate artists' contributions to the knowledge base by collecting suggestions, researching data and other materials used in innovative ways to create art. The advent of digital archaeology is an important step towards building the future of the humanities [10].

The Stanford JANUS Initiative is an interdisciplinary study focused on past, present, and future human experiences of innovation and design, which is co-sponsored by the Center for Design Studies and the Center for Archaeological Studies in the School of Engineering at Stanford University. The initiative combines features from the fields of design thinking, strategic foresight, scenario planning, design-based research, planning and implementation, organisational studies, archaeology, history, ethnography and anthropology. Its research focus on digital business archaeology, such as the work of historians and museums can be used to document the history of a business for good a good outcome, which links past business and corporate experiences to today's business challenges and concerns, using retrospective methods to build innovation capacity for desired future outcomes. The creation of the JANUS initiative's business archaeology knowledge base has become a way to collect examples of archaeological data positively influencing the future innovation capabilities of businesses and organisations.

It is thus clear that digital archaeology is able to make effective use of retrospective methods, focusing on collecting data from the past and summarising the experiences of known cases positively contributing to the future. Digital archaeology has been addressed by academics but has not yet been studied as a broad discipline.

4 Thematic Significance

4.1 Pilot Program

Firstly, a phenomenological analysis and systematic inquiry based on the theoretical foundations of archaeology, communication, sociology and humanities, collecting existing cases of digital archaeology and exploring them in depth in different fields and in different ways of expression.

Secondly, an attempt to connect with the meta-universe: the interpretation, reconstruction and communication of retrospective datasets taught to users using the information provided by the virtual participatory platform allows to work together in the same cyberspace, interacting with models of artefacts, monuments and sites in real time. The study and analysis of archaeological virtual reconstruction processes will contribute to the contextualised reconfiguration of spatial archaeological datasets. The creation of the platform can also be envisaged as an open laboratory, with mechanisms built through an interactive ecosystem. The result will be the creation of new learning, research and educational processes in the virtual archaeological world, communicating and interacting in a 3D cyberspace [11].

Then attempting to make connections with the sensory world: archaeology is often thought of as a visual discipline. With many sites and objects trapped behind walls, isolation strips and glass, the visual dimension of these materials has historically been the only point of contact for all people, trying to use senses such as smell, sound visualisation and touch to change the way people interact with objects [12].

Finally, attempting to make connections with the natural world: attempting to design the documentation of cultural heritage in areas affected by natural disasters and creating online image databases, including through the use of new digital technologies, to preserve the memory of the past and reduce the risk that valuable cultural assets may be damaged or lost.

4.2 Pilot Projects

'E-Trace' is our research project for our second year at the Royal College of Art. The background is based on the value of archaeology in the search for memories that have been lost in the history of human civilisation. The relics of the past can inspire our future and re-examine our present. So, as people living in the 'now', have we ever wondered how humans will explore our lives a hundred years from now? What will be part of the valuable 'artefacts' of our everyday lives and how they will be stored?

The main goal of the project is to create a meta-universe space, set in a future world, where users facilitate the interpretation, reconstruction and communication of archaeological datasets through remote virtual participation. In the first phase, we plan to use our custom-developed application to build the spatial database and create different interpretations of the archaeological model. At this point, the framework is not intended to facilitate interaction between large numbers of users, for example in a massively multiplayer game, but rather to allow interactive communication between small groups of up to five users. In the second phase, the data and results of the interpretation process will be disseminated to a wider audience of educators, students and others via the Internet. In this respect, we plan to make use of emerging multi-user virtual communities, such as the OpenSimulator environment.

OpenSimulator is an open source 3D application server that can be used to create virtual worlds that can be accessed by others over the Internet using various protocols. The engine is also compatible with SecondLife® protocols and client applications, making it potentially possible for SecondLife® users to enter OpenSimulator virtual worlds [13]. In our web archaeology framework, spatial databases created by our collaborative applications can be synchronised with SQL Grid databases supported by these environments. Users of openSimulator can access virtual archaeological sites and explore artefacts linked to other data sources. Due to the exceptional limitations of this environment, models need to be greatly simplified (e.g. reduction of texture resolution, optimisation of geometry) to allow remote access to interactive imagery, in Fig. 3.

Fig. 3. Grady Booch presentation at Opensimulator community conference 2013

Archaeological datasets can also be shared with virtual communities through the Open Cobalt environment, an open source project that aims to create, share and hyperlink virtual workspaces for research and educational purposes (Open Cobalt 2010). The platform allows the creation of simplified virtual worlds that can be connected to each other through portals. The interactivity and reliability of the platform is currently quite limited (note that the project is in alpha phase); however, 3D datasets can be imported and presented in a simplified form in these virtual environments, and our research on remote immersion plans to create realistic and dynamic personas that can be integrated into these and existing virtual communities (e.g. OpenSimulator) [14]. This will allow users with stereoscopic cameras to achieve a higher level of immersion, while allowing users with limited technical capabilities to interact in the same environment. Dynamic avatars will allow users to express their emotions and body language, which will make the use of applications more intuitive than using predefined scripts, such as pointing out different features or making eye contact with other users [15]. The metaspace is seen as a social space where groups of active users create avatars and can share the space and communicate and interact with each other in three dimensions.

5   About E-Trace

The goal of this space is to teach the interpretation, reconstruction and communication of archaeological datasets using all the information provided by the virtual participatory platform. Users from different geographical locations, represented by 3D avatars, can work together in the same web space, interacting with models of artefacts, monuments and sites in real time. This prototype collaborative application for data archaeology - built on an open source virtual reality framework - aims to demonstrate real-time collaborative interaction with 3D archaeological models associated with video streaming technologies, including lightweight 3D tele-immersion using stereoscopic cameras. The study and analysis of the archaeological virtual reconstruction process will contribute to the recontextualisation and restructuring of spatial archaeological datasets by the virtual community, from the first draft (where data is not yet interpreted) to the final level of communication. The learning activity will involve a bottom-up approach, whereas the analysis of archaeological remains and finds requires a top-down approach, such as the reconstruction of ancient architectural styles, materials, shapes, etc. The field of virtual reality collaboration is a simulated environment where advanced behaviours, actions and new research and training methods will be tested. It can be conceived as an open laboratory: a place where the construction and validation of interpretive processes can be compared, where new relationships between spatial and temporal data can be studied, and where opportunities can be established through interactive ecosystems. The result will be the creation of new learning, research and educational processes in a virtual archaeological world, playing and interacting in a 3D cyberspace.

5.1   Background

The value of archeology is to search for the memories that have been lost in the history of human civilization. The remains from the past could inspired our future and re-examine our present. So as people living in the "present", have we ever imagined how humans in a hundred years time will explore OUR lives? What in our daily lives will form part of valuable 'artifacts' and how they will be stored? Our project presents a hypothetical answer to these questions. By reflecting on today's mechanized society and the phenomenon of information digitalization, we pictured a future which humans existence is endangered and the human senses- our direct connection with the physical world is preserved in the form of data and becomes the most precious artifacts for post-human to excavate.

5.2 Trailer

We used C4D to create a trailer to give the audience an idea of the background of the story, in Fig. 4. The animation is in Chinese style, interspersed with traditional Chinese elements such as stone lions, lanterns and hexagonal pavilions. Abandoning the original sci-fi futuristic style of green, blue and black, we boldly experimented with the use of reversed colours for the expression of the RGB world. The soundtrack uses oriental instruments such as bamboo flute, Chinese Zither and drums to reflect the majestic and harmonious mood. A geographical message is prompted at the end of the trailer and the viewer is only allowed to proceed to Part 2 once this message has been obtained.

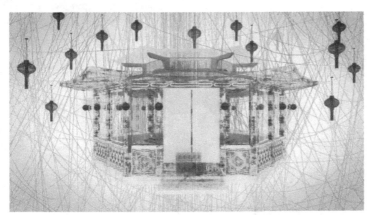

Fig. 4. Pilot film scenes in the E-Trace virtual space

5.3   Virtual Space Archaeology

Our space destination - the Biobank, in Fig. 5. It is a space made up of data, taking out our mobile phones to scan the X-language floating in space and get the sensory information we have been dreaming of. This is one of the most innovative new ways of future storytelling in the whole project - the first attempt to use AR in VR, in Fig. 6.

Once the five sensory data have been collected, the five-digit code formed by combining the first digit of each gene sequence number is the key to gaining sensory abilities, in Fig. 7. (All biosensory prototypes and data are from Protein Data Bank https://www.rcsb.org/).

Fig. 5. E-Trace Biobank

Fig. 6. E-Trace AR

6 Conclusion

In terms of direction, in order to conform to the current trend of the times - the common destiny faced by all humanity is ecological destiny - one of the connotations of constructing a community of destiny is to construct an ecological community, i.e. to integrate the construction of an ecological community into the vision and process of building a community of human destiny. In terms of its role, digital archaeology captures the virtual nature of information environments such as digital communication infrastructures and the internet, with the fundamental goal of developing the use of these environments to reconstruct previously inaccessible artefacts and to store modern things. We believe that its greatest strength is its ability to subtly infuse data information from both the natural and artificial worlds on the basis of the creation of virtual spaces such as metaverse, as digital archaeology has already had cases of sensory data preservation as far as developments are concerned, so it can to some extent help build organic ecological network systems for the future.

References

1. Hamer, J.: The physiognomy and artistic representation of Janus with special reference to the coinage in Southern Italy. In: Alfaro, C., Marcos, C., Otero, P. (eds.) XIII Congreso Internacional de Numism?atica, Madride2003. ActasePro-ceedingseActes, pp. 619–624 (2005)
2. Comer, D.C., Harrower, M.J.: The history and future of geospatial and space technologies in archaeology. In: Comer, D., Harrower, M. (eds.) Mapping Archaeological Landscapes from Space, pp. 1–8. Springer, New York (2003)
3. Price, D., Koontz, R., Lovings, L.: Curating digital spaces, making visual arguments: a case study in new media presentations of ancient objects. Digit. Humanit (2013)
4. Patterson, T.C.: The history of landscape archaeology in the americas. In: David, B., Thomas, J. (eds.) Handbook of Landscape Archaeology, pp. 77–84. Left Coast Press, Walnut Creek, CA (2008)
5. Ashmore, W.: Social archaeologies of landscape. In: Meskell, L., Preucel, R.W. (eds.) A Companion to Social Archaeology, pp. 255–271. Blackwell Malden, Malden (2004)
6. Knapp, A.B., Ashmore, W.: Archaeological landscapes: constructed, conceptualized. Ideational. Archaeol. Landsc. Contemp. Perspect. 1–30(1999)
7. Harvey, D.: Social Justice and the City. University of Georgia Press, Athens (1973)
8. David, B., Thomas, J.: Handbook of Landscape Archaeology. Left Coast Press, Walnut Creek (2008)
9. Sless, D.: Design or design-envisioning a future design education. Vis. Lang. **46**, 54–65 (2012). Cincinnati
10. Díaz, L.: Digital archeology: design research and education- connecting historical narratives and digital environments. Leonardo **31**(4), 283–287 (1998)
11. Díaz-Guardamino, M., Morgan, C.: Human, transhuman, posthuman digital archaeologies: an introduction. Eur. J. Archaeol. **22**(3), 320–323 (2019)
12. Ruffino P.A., Permadi D., Gandino E., Haron A.: Digital technologies for inclusive cultural heritage: the case study of Serralunga d'alba castle. ISPRS Ann. Photogrammet. Remote Sens. Spat. Inf. Sci. **IV-2-W6**, 141–147 (2019). DOAJ
13. Sequeira, L.M., Morgado, L., Pires, E.J.S.: Simplifying crowd automation in the virtual laboratory of archaeology. Proc. Technol. **13**, 56–65 (2014). Elsevier

14. Christopoulos, A., Conrad, M., Shukla, M.: Co-presence in the real and the virtual space: interactions through orientation. In: Costagliola, G., Uhomoibhi, J., Zvacek, S., McLaren, B.M. (eds.) CSEDU 2016. CCIS, vol. 739, pp. 71–99. Springer, Cham (2017). https://doi.org/10.1007/978-3-319-63184-4_5

15. Earley-Spadoni, T.: Spatial history, deep mapping and digital storytelling: archaeology's future imagined through an engagement with the digital humanities. J. Archaeol. Sci. **84**, 95–102. ScienceDirect (2017)

The Application of Geometric Abstraction of Chinese Traditional Cultural Symbols in the Design of Daily Utensils–Taking Fengyang Phoenix Painting as an Example

Huifang Li[1,2](✉)

[1] Industrial Design, Department of Mechanical Engineering, School of Mechanical Engineering, Anhui University of Science and Technology, No. 9, Donghua Road, FengYang, Huainan 233100, Anhui, China
306648166@qq.com

[2] Educational Management, School of Management, Stamford International University, No. 2 Khwaeng Prawet, Khet Prawet, Bangkok 10250, Thailand

Abstract. With the upgrading of consumption, personalization and customization have become the consumption characters of the new generation [1]. Modern daily-use utensils need not only practical value, but also personalized and cultural design. Fengyang is the largest silicon industry base in China. Glass daily-use utensils are sold all over the world. Phoenix painting is a form of folk painting circulating in Fengyang County, Anhui Province. It has a history of more than 600 years [2]. This article starts from the function and use situation of daily utensils, connects the phoenix painting, splits its semantic and modeling elements, and thinks about the materials and craftsmanship of daily utensils. Designing daily utensils with Fengyang cultural characteristics by using the innovative creation methods of abstract symbols and the design methods of mind maps. In the course of practice, we fully consider the application of plane patterns to the three-dimensional form and decoration of products, unify the relationship between cultural modeling, product three-dimensional modeling and production technology, and summarize its design methods. This paper combs the related theories on the geometric abstraction of cultural symbols, and redesigns the local intangible heritage-phoenix painting, which not only inherits the local culture of Fengyang, but also applies abstraction theory to product design practice, and obtains practical operating methods Model. The Phoenix culture, which represents Fengyang and even China, is spread to all parts of the world through products, and it brings not only economic value, but also cultural value.

Keyword: Chinese traditional cultural symbols · Geometric abstraction · Daily utensils · Fengyang phoenix painting

P.-L. P. Rau (Ed.): HCII 2022, LNCS 13312, pp. 387–399, 2022.
https://doi.org/10.1007/978-3-031-06047-2_28

1 Background

1.1 Daily Utensils Design Requirements

Fengyang County is "China's daily-use glass industry base". With its resource advantages, it focuses on the development of the glass industry. Glassware products basically cover 80% of the cities and counties in the country, and are currently exported to all over the world [3]. The current characteristics of Fengyang glass industry are resource-based and high-consumption type. It is very urgent for enterprises to transform and upgrade. Innovation is an important development driving force for transformation and upgrading [4]. Design innovation is vital to the daily utensils industry.

With the rapid social and economic development, people's living standards have made great strides. Aesthetic requirements have also come up [5]. With the improvement of people's consumption level, modern daily utensils not only need practical value, but also need personalized, cultural and aesthetic design. More and more famous designers use Chinese elements to improve the value and attention of products [6]. Therefore, mining Fengyang local cultural symbols, applying them to daily utensils, and redesigning and applying cultural symbols is achievable, and has social value and significance.

1.2 Fengyang Phoenix Painting

Phoenix painting is a form of folk painting circulating in Fengyang County, Anhui Province. It has a history of more than 600 years. The phoenix is often the theme, symbolizing auspiciousness and happiness. Fengyang Phoenix Painting is now one of the intangible cultural heritage projects in Anhui Province [7].

Both the dragon and the phoenix are totems of the Chinese nation, and were regarded as symbols of power and dignity by the emperors of the past dynasties. Phoenix, also known as "Phoenix Emperor", is the king of birds in ancient legends. Divided into two birds, male and female. They are collectively called phoenix, also known as pill bird, fire bird and so on. Often used to symbolize auspiciousness, The phoenix flying together is a symbol of auspicious harmony and has been an important element of Chinese culture since ancient times. From the beginning of Qin, the image of Feng began to turn from yang to yin, and was gradually "feminized" [8]. In addition to symbolizing happiness, harmony and auspiciousness, Fengyang people's paintings of phoenixes also combine the concept of phoenix with the concept of imperial power [7].

Although the phoenix painting has been preserved as an intangible heritage, its popularity is much lower than before. Although it has a high artistic value, it cannot keep pace with the times. "Phoenix painting has rich cultural connotations, and its cultural value will be greater if its cultural symbols are attached to daily necessities through design methods.

2 Geometric Abstraction of Chinese Traditional Cultural Symbols

2.1 Geometric Abstraction

What is Abstraction in any of the arts? "Abstract" works of art are sometimes contrasted to "representational" (or "figurative" or "objective") ones [9]. Mondrian, the master of the Dutch style school, believes that "all complex and tedious forms can be replaced with the most concise abstract graphics. "[10] Abstract" is the term most often used to describe the more extreme effects of this urge to break away from "natural". Pure abstraction refers to works composed of abstract elements such as geometry or amorphous [11]. Nearly abstract works, the artist starts from natural forms and transforms them into abstract or almost abstract forms. "The meaning of abstraction lies in the refinement of the essence, transforming it from a blunt description to a vital reconstruction [10].

Geometric abstraction is a geometric figure formed by people's high-level overview and abstraction of the forms of all things in nature in social practice, as well as visual choices. It has both the beauty of orderly reason and the beauty of artistic sensibility [12].

2.2 Chinese Traditional Cultural Symbols

Traditional culture is the wealth of the nationalities. The traditional culture of China has a long history and ethnic characteristics. As an important part of traditional culture, the traditional cultural symbols affect the thinking and behavior of each generation [5]. Chinese traditional art is the crystallization of people's long-term social practice. Combined with people's aesthetic experience and self-worth identification [13].

Chinese traditional cultural symbols have been applied in various design fields, and their forms, colors, and semantics have collided with different modern fields to produce rich results, such as visual communication, clothing, product design, architecture, etc. [5, 13–15].

Both the dragon and the phoenix are totems of the Chinese nation, and were regarded as symbols of power and dignity by the emperors of the past dynasties. The phoenix painting is one of the many traditional Chinese arts. It also belongs to the traditional Chinese cultural symbol.

2.3 Geometric Abstraction and Chinese Traditional Cultural Symbols

The abstract symbols of traditional culture are the essence and spirit of national culture, and traditional culture is also the basis for the survival of design culture. Some people say that Chinese modern design is undergoing earth-shaking Westernization and innovation. In fact, from a historical perspective, our design has never been too far away from the abstraction of traditional culture. Modern design inevitably stems from traditional design, design is the product of the combination of culture, art and science and technology [16]. At the same time, traditional cultural abstraction and modern design have an interactive influence.

At present, industrialized mass production of products requires a certain degree of unity. What culture presents is diversification and complexity. How to combine products and culture has both diversity and unity. Symbolic abstraction is the best design method. Can convey information and beauty in a concise and rational way, and is widely used in the field of design. Since the industrial revolution, under the mass production mode, geometric products that are easy to produce and reduce costs have been favored by producers. At the same time, the simplicity and modern artistic characteristics have also made geometric products more popular.

According to Mondrian, Dragon and Phoenix, as a more complex cultural symbol, can also be refined by geometric abstraction to make it concise and closer to the essence. The phoenix painting has a complex shape, and it can only be applied to the three-dimensional shape of daily utensils through geometric productization to achieve mass production.

3 Research Content and Implications

3.1 Research Content

By sorting out the relevant theories on the geometric abstraction of cultural symbols, this paper redesigns the local intangible cultural heritage-phoenix painting, applies the abstraction theory to the practice of product design, and obtains a practical operation method model.

3.2 Research Implications

With the continuous expansion of consumption scale, consumers' personalized demands are becoming increasingly obvious [16]. With the improvement of people's consumption level, modern daily utensils need not only practical value, but also cultural, artistic and aesthetic designs. Through research, this paper designs products that meet the needs of consumers by integrating the production process requirements of glass products and local culture, and summarizes the design methods to provide experience support for designers.

Fengyang is the production base of daily glassware, and its products are exported to all over the world. The phoenix culture of Yang and even China is spread all over the world through products, which bring not only economic value, but also cultural value.

4 Glass Forming Process

Glass can be formed in a variety of ways to meet the shape and size required for design and use. Various molding methods such as blowing, drawing, pressing, pouring, press-blowing, die-casting, calendering, winding, sand core, and moldless free forming are used [18]. Glass can be processed into fibers, microbeads, rice beads, inlaid beads, hollow beads, tubes, rods, plates, bottles, utensils, lamps, sculptures, etc. The size ranges from nanometer and micrometer products to urban sculptures of more than ten meters [18].

Glass can also be used to make complex handicrafts by a variety of hot and cold processing methods, such as lamp molding, hot melting, hot bending and lost wax (lost wax) casting; grinding, polishing, engraving, frosting, sand carving, etching, etc. cold working method.

There are various methods of surface treatment such as matching and cold working coating, gold decoration, color glaze, pile flower, diffusion coloring and so on. Local glass companies can use these processes.

The local glass daily-use utensils in Fengyang mainly use molding methods such as die and pressure-blowing mold casting, and produce low-cost and cost-effective glass daily-use products through cold processing such as coating, polishing, and sand carving.

5   Daily Utensils Redesign

5.1   Theoretical Model of Practice

There are many kinds of daily utensils. This article takes daily tableware as an example. According to eating habits, glass tableware modeling technology, semiotic meaning and geometric abstraction of phoenix painting, relevant theories and design methods are used to establish relevant practical models. The main theoretical basis and methods include aesthetics, semiotics, semantics, morphology, manufacturing technology, creative thinking and other aspects (see Fig. 1).

Daily tableware with the characteristics of phoenix painting is represented by PDt. PDt as a result of design, taking into account function, craftsmanship, form and semantics. The new design not only has the function of tableware, but also has the meaning of phoenix painting. The prototype of phoenix painting is represented by P, as a symbol, the medium is represented by P(M), the Object is represented by P(O), the Interpretant is represented by P(I). Daily products are represented by Dt. The three-dimensional model production process is represented by PPm, and the graphic design production process is represented by PPg. Geometry types use Gtg for planes and Gtm for 3D model. Food types are denoted by Ff. There is a cross connection between the craftsmanship or function of a product and cultural symbols or semantics. Functional symbols and product semantics can be seen from the shape of the product, and cultural symbols also have functions and require related craftsmanship. In the process of creation, divergent thinking is required, and more shapes are created through association, imagination, and application of mind maps (see Fig. 1).

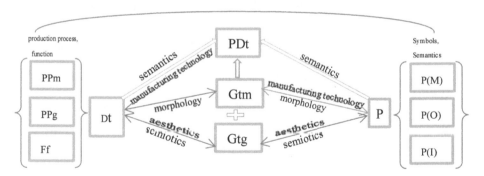

Fig. 1. Daily tableware design practice model, taking tableware as an example.

5.2   Analysis of Symbols in Phoenix Painting

According to the American pragmatist philosopher Peirce's symbolic triangle model, Any symbol consists of three elements: Medium (M), Object (O), Interpretant (I). According to Peirce's symbolic theory, the decomposition of the phoenix painting is shown in Table 1.

Table 1. Phoenix painting (P) dismantling

Medium (M)	Object (O)	Interpretant (I)
	Snake head; eagle beak; eagle beak; goat's beard; slender eyes	The snake is recognized by the people as the little dragon; wishful
	Five peaks of neck	The ups and downs of life
	turtle back, fish scales	Longevity, auspicious, wishful
	crane legs	It is a symbol of longevity,auspiciousness and elegance
	nine tails, peacock tail	Fengyang Prefecture governs nine prefectures , auspicious, wishful, prosperous
	eighteen wings	Fengyang Prefecture governs eighteen counties,prosperous, soaring
	Ink,Multicolored, plain color	Different colors represent different meanings, and different colors are used in phoenix paintings, which are very rich in meaning.Including auspicious, prosperous, warm, artistic conception
	The phoenix sings towards the sun, and the birds face the phoenix	Symbol of prosperity and peace

The picture comes from Hua Rongsheng's "Hundred Birds Chaofeng" and 360 Encyclopedia8.

Fengyang phoenix painting has been continuously created by generations of artists, and gradually formed a unique traditional art style. The phoenix shape must be "snake head, turtle back, eagle mouth, crane legs, wishful crown, nine tails and eighteen wings", etc. There are three color expression techniques of "five colors, plain colors and ink" [8].

Influenced by culture and politics, each feature of phoenix painting represents a certain meaning. With the changes of the times, some of the meanings are no longer up to the times, but their symbolic shapes can be used for modern design.

5.3 Daily Utensils Form and Geometric Abstract Form

Daily utensils are artificial forms, including three-dimensional and two-dimensional, and their forms carry practical functions, symbolic cognitive functions and aesthetic functions. Most of the practical functions are presented in three dimensions, and the plane mainly plays an aesthetic function. Whether it is a solid or a plane, it belongs to the symbol.

The first thing to consider when designing glass tableware is the functional form. The practical function corresponds to the form, including the operation mode of the form, the space occupied by the form, the weight of the form, and the storage and transportation of the form and other functions.

The geometric abstract form is beneficial to the cost control of products, saves materials, and is convenient for production and transportation. It is a relatively ideal form. In the development of modern art, a unique beauty of rationality and order has gradually formed. At present, geometric forms in artificial forms have become very common.

Utensils include daily utensils. In a broad sense, utensil glass refers to the general term for daily utensils, decorations and art glass. In a narrow sense, utensil glass refers to glass utensils that hold food and beverages, such as water cups, small plates, cold dishes, wine utensils, etc., so it is also called glass tableware [18]. Therefore, this article takes the design practice of tableware as an example.

Three-Dimensional Modeling Geometric Design. The design of utensils with geometric abstract forms and the beauty of phoenix paintings needs to be combined with the local production technology level. The shape of daily utensils in Fengyang enterprises is restricted by technology and equipment, mainly mold press-blowing, and also has hot and cold processing technology to make the surface texture of the utensils, such as Grinding, engraving, frosting, sand carving, etching. The surface texture has certain ups and downs, which is not only decorative, but also has certain practical functions, such as anti-scalding, anti-skid and so on.

Aiming at the eating habits of central and eastern China, tableware includes bowls, Plates, chopsticks, spoons, etc., according to the shape of the daily ingredients, the required tableware diameter, depth, thickness, shape, etc. are different.

The functional form of the product is affected by the production process and the type of food. For example, the soup bowl requires a large space, the shape with a deep bottom. The cost is high, or the more complex shape that the local craftsmanship does not meet the requirements cannot be mass-produced.

The main categories of food include soup, no soup, cold dishes, hot dishes, meat dishes and vegetarian dishes, etc. The shape is mainly affected by the amount of soup. Therefore, the analysis of food form in this paper is divided into solid, liquid, and a combination of solid and liquid. Hot dishes and cold dishes also have a certain impact on the functional form, and hot dishes need at least anti-scalding shapes. At the same time, the form of the complete set of utensils requires consideration of packaging that is easy to transport and saves space.

In short, the basic function of the floor-standing glass tableware design needs to consider the shape characteristics of the tableware itself, as well as the ingredients, eating habits, production technology level, and the combination of geometric abstract forms (see Table 2).

Table 2. Three-dimensional modeling design elements

Daily tableware (Dt)	Food form (Ff)	Geometry type (Gtm)	Production process (PPm)
Rice bowl	Solid, liquid (hot)	Cube	Press-blowing
Small plate	Solid (cold)	Sphere	Grinding
Plate	Solid and liquid (hot)	Cylinder	Engraving
Soup bowl	Liquid (hot)	Cone	Frosting
Spoon	Liquid	Square cone	Sand carving
Chopsticks	Solid	Prism	Etching

The four are closely related, But not all are one-to-one.

Graphic Design Geometric Abstraction. The geometric abstract types in the plane include points, lines, and surfaces (geometric shapes), and the geometric shapes are small to a certain extent, that is, points. Summarizing and summarizing complex graphics has become a major feature of the development of modern graphic design [19]. Modern graphic design abandons the cumbersome and detailed description of patterns, and focuses on the performance of points, lines, surfaces, color blocks, and volume. The figurative form gradually transitions to the abstract form, and the sense of order and rational thinking are reflected in the graphics [19].

In local businesses, there are many surface treatment processes for glass tableware, which mainly play the role of decoration and beautification, such as electroplating, ion plating, color spraying, stickers, printing, polishing. These create a variety of possibilities for the appearance of glass.

When designing the flat decoration of tableware, in addition to considering the craftsmanship, it pays more attention to the beauty of form. It needs to conform to the laws of formal beauty, such as contrast, unity, order, repetition, etc. (see Table 3).

Table 3. Graphic design elements.

Daily tableware (Dt)	Flat Form beauty	Geometry type (Gtg)	Production Process (PPg)
Rice bowl	Symmetry and balance	Straight line	Electroplating
Small plate	Change and unity	Curve	Ion plating
Plate	Contrast and harmonize	Square	Color spraying
Soup bowl	Rhythm	Round	Stickers
Spoon	Structure and repetition	Triangle	Printing
Chopsticks	Image beauty	Polygon	Polishing

The four are closely related, But not all are one-to-one.

5.4 Design Practice

In design practice, not only the support of aesthetics and semantics is needed, but also divergent thinking is needed. Through the mind map, the product shape, function, geometric abstract form and the phoenix painting shape symbol can be closely linked. Considering the actual craftsmanship level and modern eating habits, different styles of tableware with the phoenix painting shape characteristics can be designed.

Vessel shape, phoenix painting shape and geometric abstract shape need to be combined with the semantics to be expressed through creative thinking methods to form a series of glass tableware designs. Table 4 summarizes the main modeling elements. The design has functional requirements, is full of aesthetics and semantics conveyed by phoenix paintings, and requires rich professional experience and imagination.

This paper selects the classic tail decorative shapes in phoenix paintings to carry out the practice of transforming three-dimensional and plane shapes. Shown in Fig. 2 and 3, by simplifying and summarizing its modeling characteristics, a basic shape is formed, which is mainly transformed from a circle. This shape can be changed in depth, thickness, colour and size, and combined with the basic shape of the utensils, to form tableware with functionality and shape, including small plates, large plates, bowls, soup bowls, and spoons. Through the selection, extraction, simplification, change and transformation of the phoenix painting shape, a new three-dimensional shape of the vessel is formed. The designed three-dimensional shape meets the process requirements, and the shape suitable for pressure blow molding and one-time molding is better, ensuring low cost and high cost performance.

Table 4. Graphic design elements.

Daily table-ware (Dt)	Phoenix painting dismantling(P)	geometry type(Gtg)	geometry type(Gtg)	geometry type(Gtm)	geometry type(Gtm)
Rice bowl		straight line	——	cube	
small plate		curve	⌇	sphere	
plate		square	▭	cylinder	
soup bowl		round	○	cone	△
spoon		triangle	△	square cone	△
Chopsticks		polygon	⬡	Prism	

The six are closely related, But not all are one-to-one.

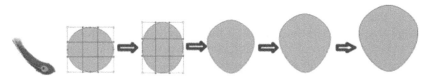

Fig. 2. Deformation process of phoenix tail geometric three-dimensional vessel.

Fig. 3. The change of width, height and thickness of glass tableware, it can meet the needs of basic functions.

The basic shape of decoration is established, and it is arranged and reorganized according to the basic method of formal beauty, and laid on the tableware of different three-dimensional shapes to play a decorative role. Only by paying attention to the laws of formal beauty can we design beautiful patterns. The basic shapes are arranged and combined according to the basic bones. The bones can be points, lines, planes, squares, circles, triangles, and polygons, which can form rich and diverse geometric abstract patterns. There are various forms of color expression in phoenix paintings. There is no need to be too restrained in the expression of colors. According to the expressive semantics of colors, it can be combined with the design goals and the colors that consumers like today (see Fig. 4). Refer to Table 3 for the specific rules of formal beauty.

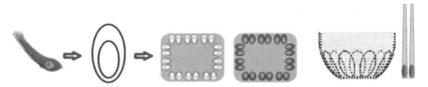

Fig. 4. The evolution process of phoenix tail geometric plane decoration.

Wang Changeling divides the "realm" of poetry into "object realm", "situation" and "artistic realm". Poetry and painting have the same origin, and artistic design can also be adopted. Pursuing the beauty of artistic conception is the highest state of aesthetic art [20]. The beauty of artistic conception goes deep into the heart. If you want to design a design work with beautiful artistic conception, you need to have a deeper understanding of people's thoughts, emotions and human culture. The following design works are combined with Chinese calligraphy brush and ink to form a curve, form a basic shape, and have a certain artistic conception. According to the flowing curve of the phoenix tail and the shape of the raindrops, the plate is designed with an aesthetic and anti-slip handle, and the graceful curvature of the spoon, it forms a functional structure, making the work more vivid (see Fig. 5).

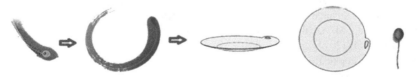

Fig. 5. The evolution process of the combination of the plane shape of the phoenix tail and the functional shape of the vessel.

6 In Conclusion

This article mainly combines local enterprises and local cultural characteristics, with distinct regional and craft restrictions, through daily tableware and a simple demonstration of the tail part in the phoenix painting, according to the design practice model demonstrated in this article, it is expected that there will be more abundant Design results. All designs are inseparable from creative thinking. In this article, we mainly focus on the discussion of product technology and function, as well as the process of geometric abstract transformation of phoenix painting with symbolic and semantic meaning. The method of creative thinking is relatively simple.

The practical model (see Fig. 1) of daily utensil design in this paper can be used in any design of abstract modernization of traditional cultural symbols. Pure geometric abstract forms can no longer meet people's spiritual needs. Unchangeable traditional cultural symbols cannot be loved by consumers either. Cultural symbols that have been tested by history are the source of inspiration for designers. Designing works recognized and loved by modern people, is conducive to the inheritance of traditional culture.

References

1. Wei, W.: Research on consumption upgrading and retail innovation development based on mobile internet technology. IOP Conf. Ser. J. Phys. Conf. Ser. **1176**, 042070 (2019)
2. Baidu Encyclopedia. https://baike.baidu.com/item/%E5%87%A4%E7%94%BB/4401186. 2022/1/25
3. China Glass Network. https://www.glass.com.cn/2021/2/4
4. China Glass Network. https://www.glass.cn/glassnews/newsinfo_48263.html2021/2/4
5. Li, Y.: Study on the application of traditional cultural symbols in visual communication design. In: 2018 International Conference on Arts, Linguistics, Literature and Humanities (ICALLH 2018) (2018)
6. Zhu, S., Li, S.: Redesign of Liangzhu pottery based on form style recognition. Appl. Mech. Mater. **268–270**, 1970–1973 (2013)
7. Encyclopedia. https://baike.so.com/doc/6446675-6660356.html2021/2/4
8. Encyclopedia. https://baike.so.com/doc/5350121-5585577.html2021/2/4
9. Walton, K.L.: What is abstract about the art of music. Aesthet. Art Crit. **46**(3), 351–364 (1988)
10. Wang, Z., Li, Y.: Research on the application of abstract graphics in graphic design teaching. J. Dalian Univ. Natl. **22**(4), 380–384 (2020)
11. Barr Jr., A.H.: Cubism and Abstract Art. The Belknap Press of Harvard University Press Cambridge, Massachusetts, London (1986)
12. Xie, Z.: Characteristic analysis of traditional dragon patterns and research on geometric abstraction. J. Sichuan Univ. Natl. **28**(2), 79–84 (2019)
13. Wu, X., Wang, M.: On the application of Chinese traditional symbols in modern packaging. Packag. J. **4**(1) (2012)
14. Shi, N.: The application of Chinese traditional cultural symbols in architectural design. In: 2018 4th International Seminar on Education, Arts and Humanities (ISEAH 2018)
15. Wu, C., Zhang, H.: Application of traditional Chinese cultural symbols in modern clothing design: deductive method and its design model. J. Zhejiang Univ. Sci. Technol. **23**(4) (2011)
16. Li, Z.: Speculation on abstract symbols of traditional culture in modern design. Grand View Fine Arts Art Des., 90–91 (2013)
17. Guo, L., Zhang, D.: EC-structure: establishing consumption structure through mining e-commerce data to discover consumption upgrade. Hindawi Complex. **2019**, Article ID 6543590, 8 p. (2019). https://doi.org/10.1155/2019/6543590
18. Wang, C., et al.: Daily Glass Manufacturing Technology, pp. 2–8. Chemical Industry Press, Beijing (2014)

19. Li, H.: Graphic Creativity and Design Basis. China Construction Industry Press, Beijing (2010)
20. Dong, W., Liu, X.: The connotation and innovative design of traditional cultural symbols in tea sets. Study Res. Explor. Prod., 1003–0069 (2018). 06-0100-03

The Interactive Design and User Experience of Virtual Museums: Case Study of the Virtual Palace Museum

Wenhua Li[1]([✉]) and Xiaoli Huang[2]

[1] Guangzhou Academy of Fine Arts, No. 257, Changgang East Road, Haizhu District, Guangzhou 510000, China
vivian.lee8686@gmail.com
[2] Guangzhou Nanfang College, No. 257, Changgang East Road, Haizhu District, Guangzhou 510000, China

Abstract. One of the fundamental functions of a museum is to collect and preserve ancient cultural relics. Nowadays, some museums also undertake the roles as learning center, communication and social place, leisure center, and cultural communication center, by offering comprehensive experience of multisensory feelings, intelligence, aesthetics, social communication. As active participators and operators in virtual environment, the visitors show stronger engagement and better use experience when using virtual reality applications. A good interactive design in the virtual museum system will enhance the quality of remediation, which will encourage users to be active and immersed in the virtual tour. This study aims to analyze the interaction design of the virtual Palace Museum and examine virtual experience designed for visitors. After analyzed the virtual applications of the Palace Museum, we found that virtual museums can deliver knowledge in an attractive and accessible way for better cultural experience. Virtual reality is not to replace the unique experience of appreciating real objects, but it can greatly improve our understanding of artifacts and allow us to better understand their stories. The virtual museum enables immersive sense, good storytelling, interactive learning, and sharing between peers, which turns passive visitors to active explorers. In the digital age and the epidemic, we must re-examine the positioning and mission of museums from a longer-term perspective, dig and interpret the diverse values of cultural heritage, and give new vitality to cultural heritage.

Keywords: Virtual museum · Virtual reality · User experience · Human-computer interaction · Culture heritage

1 Introduction

One of the fundamental functions of a museum is to collect and preserve ancient cultural relics. Nowadays, some museums also undertake the roles of learning center, communication and social place, leisure center, and cultural communication center, by offering a comprehensive experience of multisensory feelings, intelligence, aesthetics, and social

P.-L. P. Rau (Ed.): HCII 2022, LNCS 13312, pp. 400–409, 2022.
https://doi.org/10.1007/978-3-031-06047-2_29

communication. With elaborate curation by museum experts, general visitors can easily understand the exhibitions and the stories behind ancient cultural relics. With the development of interactive technologies, the exhibitions become more interactive, immersive, and interesting. After visiting museums, the audiences may acquire knowledge, contemplation, relaxation, sensory pleasure, new social relationships, and long-lasting memories. With the development of digital technology, the digital museums meet challenges to create new experiences for their online and offline visitors. Visitors can read a lot about museums online before going to them. We take mobile phones and tablets into museums and use mobile devices for space navigation and content query. Robotic facilities, sensors, and real-time data allow museums to bring different personalized, multi-sensory experiences, and learning opportunities.

Nowadays, many museums offer virtual tours and online exhibitions for global visitors without time and space restrictions. The Google Art Project provides virtual tours of thousands of museums, like Google Maps Street View. Visitors can virtually browse these galleries and click to enjoy high-resolution images of artworks. The virtual museums in The Google Art Project are 360-degree panoramic scenes, which can be viewed directly without the need for head-mounted devices. Some virtual museums interact with visitors with virtual reality technologies. The visitors need to use head-mounted devices to enjoy virtual tours. As active participators and operators in a virtual environment, the visitors show stronger engagement and better use experience when using virtual reality applications [1]. This study aims to analyze the interaction design of the virtual Palace Museum and examine the virtual experience which has been designed for visitors.

2 Theoretical Background

Experience is formed when a person's mental, physical, intellectual, and spiritual levels are in a highly stimulated state [2]. Every experience is unique. Experience originates from the interaction between unique time, environment, and the spiritual and existential state of the person. Museums transfer their roles from knowledge providers to experience makers, offering a comprehensive service that is rich in feelings and resonates with every visitor. The value of experience is that the experiencing memories can be kept for a long time. Carter and Gilovich [3] found that, purchasing experience is more pleasing than purchasing products, which produces a greater sense of satisfaction. Pine and Gilmore [2] depicted the process of business model transformation as an agrarian, industrial, service, and experience economy. Experience is the result of the participation and interaction among people, objects, and environments. The experience economy offers users special interaction and creates memories for people. In the experience economy, consumption is not only performed to purchase a product but to consume physical, emotional, and even spiritual experiences. The paradigm shift of the economy inspires us to rethink the challenges of using experience design in changing social and economic environments. Pine and Gilmore [2] proposed the model of the Four Realms of an Experience, analyzing experience design in two dimensions: participation and environmental relationship. The first dimension of user participation contains two user groups: active groups and passive groups. Passive groups will not affect the performance at all. Museum visitors are used to being passive participators, who are immersed in the museum by a professionally curated environment. Museum visiting is an "aesthetic" experience according to the Four Realms of an Experience model. Digital museums have been changing the situation by turning passive visitors to be active operators, who can navigate in the virtual environment with their own routes and even build their own collections and exhibitions. A good interactive design in the virtual museum system will enhance the quality of remediation, which will encourage users to be active and immersed in the virtual tour [4] (Fig. 1).

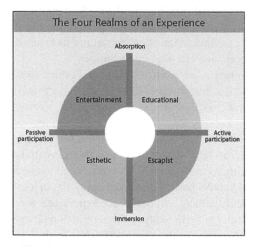

Fig. 1. The four realms of an experience [2]

Virtual reality is a computer simulation system that can create and experience the virtual world. It uses computers to generate a simulated environment and immerse users in the environment. Users can experience the most real feelings in the virtual reality world. The authenticity of the simulated environment is indistinguishable from the real world, making people feel like they are in the real world. The simulation system of virtual reality can realize human-computer interaction, so that people can operate at will and get the most realistic feedback from the environment during the operation.

Virtual reality applications are designed to meet the requirement of the 3i characteristics: immersion, interaction, imagination [5]. One important selling point of virtual reality applications is "real", to take the audience into an authentic and exciting digital world. Virtual reality applications used in a museum can enrich the experience in museum spaces and change the way people interact with each other [6]. Virtual reality technology can be used in a physical visit and online virtual tours. User experience can be enriched with innovative storytelling and entertainment. Virtual reality technology is valuable in preserving cultural relics in a digital database. The destroyed artifacts can be virtually reconstructed and observed in detail with the help of virtual reality. Many factors influence the virtual user experience, for example, motivation, visual attractiveness, ease-of-use, usability, engagement, satisfaction perceived by the visitors, etc. It is possible to design a better user experience for virtual museums after identifying the key factors that affect user satisfaction.

3 Methodology

This study is a case study of a leading digital museum in China, The Palace Museum. We acquired data and materials from secondary sources, including official websites, official virtual reality applications, journal articles, and research books.

The Palace Museum, one of China's foremost-protected cultural heritage sites, was established in 1925 and launched its digital museum in 2001. The Palace Museum has 1.86 million collections, and only about 30,000 collections can be displayed through exhibitions every year. To allow more people to appreciate the collections of the Forbidden City and allow the audience to appreciate more collections, the Forbidden City has launched a digital exhibition hall and a digital cultural relic library to display cultural relics in various digital forms.

The Palace Museum started to adopt virtual reality technologies in 2001 and offered virtual reality tours on its website in 2015. The Palace Museum has three approaches to create virtual reality experiences: first, it uses 3D digital modeling techniques to generate an accurate virtual representation of its physical space, which allows users to navigate through the virtual palace via head-mounted displays; the second approach is to use a 360-degree panoramic technique to show thousands of the architectures and exhibitions in the Palace Museum. The users can use regular displays, such as a mobile phone, computer or television to take a virtual tour of the Palace Museum online; the third approach is that the Palace Museum has produced VR films and games to deliver the knowledge of culture heritage. Different approaches may lead to different interactive experiences.

4 Discussion and Analysis

The user experience design of the virtual Palace Museum is now examined and analyzed based on The Four Realms of an Experience model.

4.1 Digital Treasure Pavilion–3D Digital Modeling Application

The form of digital architecture and digital cultural relics can exhibit the fragile and difficult to-display cultural relics among the precious cultural relics. The content that is difficult to show in a physical exhibition to the audience can be transferred to digital form. 3D digital models can meet the communication needs of important and especially fragile cultural relics. It ensures the safety of cultural relics and can also stimulate the interest of the public in the preservation and restoration of cultural relics. 3D digital models can be created with CAD software, while 3D scanning can produce the most accurate record of an item. The advantage of this technique is that it does not touch the objects, so it can be used to record the most fragile or large collections. 3D digital scanning is the beginning of different forms of display for the collections in the Palace Museum. As a digital database, the digital treasure pavilion of the Palace Museum can be inexpensively and efficiently shared around the world and can also be shared by multiple researchers at the same time. Digital models of cultural relics can be used to monitor the deterioration of cultural relics and help in their restoration in the future.

Researchers can zoom in on the digital versions of rare cultural relics without being limited by the physical environment. Moreover, scanned artifacts can be explored in all directions, and changing the parameters such as lighting conditions can reveal details that are imperceptible to the naked eye. Fragments of objects can be recombined, large objects can be compared side by side, and logos and patterns from different objects can be overlapped and compared. Besides all of these advantages, digital cultural relics enable innovative and imaginative interactions between museums and the audience.

How to lead users to quickly understand the massive collections and the stories behind them in an interesting way is a problem that designers have always wanted to solve. The Digital Treasure Pavilion abandons the traditional catalog classification, uses patterns as guide clues, and selects totems with beautiful meanings from cultural relics, such as dragon patterns, cloud patterns, bat patterns, flowers and birds, geometric figures, and replaces "text" with "patterns", connecting the cultural relics with patterns to create a brand-new cultural relic browsing experience. When the user selects a pattern to start exploring, the pattern will lead the user to browse the cultural relics with the same pattern all the way. Each cultural relic has two patterns, making the encounter between the user and the cultural relic full of surprises. When you feel fatigue in browsing, you can stop at any time, and the system will generate an exclusive footprint map of the cultural relics according to the user's browsing trajectory. Finally, a fun and playful philosophical poster is generated for the user to post in social networking sites or to share with friends. The users transfer their roles from passive viewers to positive viewers. The social factors are designed in an interesting way that the users are willing to share with friends (Figs. 2, 3 and 4).

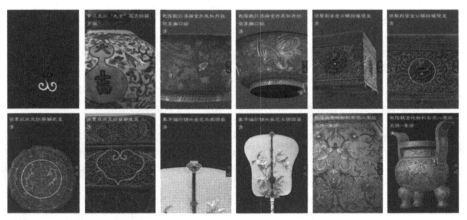

Fig. 2. Patterns as entrance in browsing procedure in digital treasure Pavilion (Source: https://www.dpm.org.cn/shuziduobaoge/html.html)

Fig. 3. The whole experience procedure of digital treasure Pavilion (Source: screen captured from WeChat Mini Apps of Digital Palace; the website of digital Palace www.dpm.org.cn)

Fig. 4. Philosophical poster generated according to the user's browsing trajectory (Source: screen captured from WeChat Mini Apps of Digital Palace; the website of digital Palace www.dpm.org.cn)

4.2 Panoramic Palace: 360-Degree Panoramic Applications

360 panoramic technology is the core technology of panoramic applications. Its essence is to record the real scene in 360 degrees through a professional camera, capture the image information of the entire scene, and then group the photos according to the points and order, and use software to synthesize the pictures. The two-dimensional floor plan is simulated into a real three-dimensional space and presented to the viewers. Different from "virtual reality", 360 panoramic technology records and digitizes reality through panoramic views and street views. The scene presented by the 360 panoramic technology has the advantages of strong realism, more expressive information, good interactive performance, and strong immersion. At the same time, the generated files are small, easy to transmit, and can be launched in various formats, which are suitable for various forms of network applications.

The Panoramic Palace project was first released in 2001, using 360-degree panoramic techniques to represent the Forbidden City online, which is the largest and most complete timber-framed building complex around the world. The application has been updated to the fifth version, with many improvements in its user experience design. The visitors can use common display devices, such as mobile phones, laptops, computers, or smart televisions to start the virtual tour.

On the homepage of this application, the designers have designed the introduction pages of the main buildings of the Forbidden City. The audience can learn about the main palaces and the historical stories behind them in an all-round and multi-dimensional way through pictures, text, audio, and video materials. It is convenient for the visitors to find information on the homepage. The designers added historical photos to the panorama of the Hall of Supreme Harmony, making the visitors feel like they have traveled back to the historical moments. Through the introduction parts on the homepage, visitors can easily find the architecture they want to see and link to the page they need. The Panorama Palace has added the function of time axis, which enables users to enjoy the scenery of the Forbidden City in different seasons and different weather. The charming views can satisfy the user's imagination of the Forbidden City in different seasons. The latest version of the Panorama Palace has optimized the tour recommendation mechanism. According to the updated classification of the Palace Museum areas, the data logic of thousands of panoramic materials is reconstructed. The system can recommend the surrounding scenic spots according to the location of the visitor, which improves their virtual experience (Figs. 5 and 6).

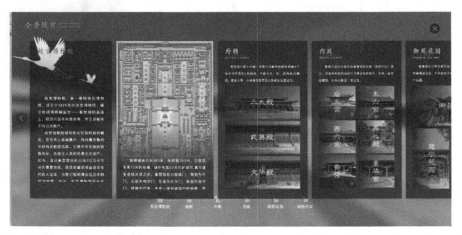

Fig. 5. The introduction parts in the homepage of the Panoramic Palace Museum (Source: https://pano.dpm.org.cn/gugong_pano/index.html)

Fig. 6. Four season scenery of the Forbidden City in Panoramic Palace (Source: screen captured from WeChat Mini Apps of Digital Palace; the website of digital Palace www.dpm.org.cn)

4.3 V Palace: Virtual Reality Applications

The Palace Museum has launched several virtual reality applications, including 7 virtual reality works based on the theater environment, namely, "The Emperor's Palace in the Forbidden City", "Three Halls", "The Hall of Mental Cultivation", "Juan Qin Zhai", "Ling Zhao Pavilion", "The Corner Tower", and "The Imperial Garden"; 2 virtual reality interactive experience projects with head-mounted devices: "The Hall of Mental Cultivation" and "Royal Garden"; 3 web-based online interactive experience projects: "The Hall of Mental Cultivation", "Ling Zhao Pavilion", and "Juan Qin Zhai".

Some palaces in the Forbidden City are too dilapidated to meet the criteria for public visiting. Some palaces have been restored, but they are not suitable for many audiences to visit. Many cultural relics can only be displayed in a concentrated space and cannot be placed in their original positions. In order to solve these problems and create a better experience, a virtual reality theater was built to play virtual reality movies produced by the Palace Museum. When viewing a virtual reality movie, the audience will first watch along the preset path, accompanied by the on-site commentary by the commentator. The audience can ask questions and communicate with the commentator. After the preset event ends, the audience can freely select the objects in the three-dimensional scene through the controller, becoming an active explorer. With a highly immersive and interactive mode, the virtual reality theater helps the audience experience the charm of the Forbidden City and traditional culture in the shock of audio-visual effects (Fig. 7).

The "Royal Garden" VR film is the latest released film, which not only reproduces the architectural style of the Royal Garden, but also represents the ecosystem in the Royal Garden, including vegetation, animals, pools, rockeries, plants, etc. Royal Garden was used to raise deer and fishes, which are reappeared in the VR film. The film used a 3D engine to render light and shadow in real time changing during a day. While displaying the historical features of the Royal Garden, it creates a lively and dynamic garden space. In the virtual film, a vibrant royal garden is created. This film adopted the interactive technique of large-screen and small-screen synergy, to enrich the interactive experiences for the audience. The interaction in the "Royal Garden" VR film reveals richer hidden knowledge about the Royal Garden and provides a more personalized in-depth experience.

Wearable virtual reality system refers to people entering a virtual and innovative space environment through a head-mounted display device, and interact in the virtual environment with trackers, sensors, data gloves, and other sensing equipment. The Palace

Fig. 7. The virtual reality theater in the Palace Museum (Source: https://www.sohu.com/a/500 67792_119586)

Museum has launched 2 virtual reality works displayed with head-mounted devices. Wearing VR glasses, users can enter the Hall of Mental Cultivation, and observe from the emperor's perspective. With artificial intelligence, automatic speech recognition and image recognition technologies, users can interact with the system in different ways. In the virtual building of The Hall of Mental Cultivation, users can explore the architectural details from different perspectives. Users can sit on the emperor's seat, review memorials, and interact with ministers. The system will tell the user the quality of the memorials he has reviewed. Each virtual minister can speak more than 500 sentences and be able to chat with users. It is easy to prepare the physical environment for wearable virtual reality works. Therefore, two virtual reality works by the Palace Museum have been exhibited in many cities in China, allowing more audiences to participate in.

The Palace Museum has launched 3 web-based online interactive experience projects, which have used a first-person perspective to create the sense of immersion. The visitors can either wear VR glasses to start an immersive tour, or use simulated Web VR mode, or choose naked eye mode to view it on the screen of personal mobile devices. In the project, designers have created two non-player roles: an old craftsman and a young cultural relics restoration expert. There are two levels of interaction with non-player roles: first, users can communicate with virtual cultural relic restoration experts to appreciate architecture and cultural relics; second, users can learn from virtual craftsmen about traditional decoration skills. Non-player roles can tell the visitors about the history and stories about the palaces and play puzzle games with the visitors. Visitors feel engaged when they travel with non-player characters. Visitors can choose to set the route or use free mode to enjoy their tours. The mechanism of gaming brings a lot of fun to the visitors and enriches the user experience.

5 Conclusion

The application of virtual museums is the exploration of new forms of artwork appreciation. Virtual museums can deliver knowledge in an attractive and accessible way for better cultural experience [7]. Virtual reality is not to replace the unique experience of appreciating real objects, but it can greatly improve our understanding of artifacts and allow us to better understand their stories. Virtual museums enable more people to view the artifacts and create more forms of interaction. Using virtual museums, users can observe artifacts from perspectives that are impossible in real life. The fragile artifacts can be studied by users with virtual reality applications.

This study has examined the virtual reality applications being used in the Palace Museum. The Palace Museum adopts different virtual reality interaction solutions to meet different needs. The virtual applications being utilized in the Palace Museum have been examined and analyzed. The purposes of the virtual Palace Museum include museum visiting, culture display, information communication, public education, leisure, and entertainment. Virtual tours online and a virtual reality room in the physical museum meets the basic needs of museum visiting and culture display. Virtual reality films, documentaries and games have been designed to meet the need for entertainment and education. With the ultimate target to build a digital museum community, the Palace Museum has explored all the paths of digitalization to integrate into our lives. The virtual museum enables immersive sense, good storytelling, interactive learning, and sharing between peers, which turns passive visitors to active explorers. In the digital age and the epidemic, we should re-examine the positioning and mission of museums from a longer-term perspective, dig and interpret the diverse values of cultural heritage, and give new vitality to cultural heritage.

References

1. Chang, H.-L., et al.: Using virtual reality for museum exhibitions: the effects of attention and engagement for National Palace Museum. In: PACIS 2018 Proceedings, vol. 145 (2018). https://aisel.aisnet.org/pacis2018/145
2. Joseph, P.B., Gilmore, J.H.: The Experience Economy. Harvard Business Press, Boston (2011)
3. Carter, T.J., Gilovich, T.: I am what I do, not what I have: the differential centrality of experiential and material purchases to the self. J. Pers. Soc. Psychol. 102(6), 1304 (2012)
4. Lee, J.W., Kim, Y., Lee, S.H.: Digital museum and user experience: the case of Google art & culture. In: International Symposium on Electronic Art (2019)
5. Burdea, G.C., Coiffet, P.: Virtual Reality Technology. Wiley, New York (2003)
6. Sylaiou, S., et al.: Leveraging mixed reality technologies to enhance museum visitor experiences. In: 2018 International Conference on Intelligent Systems (IS). IEEE (2018)
7. Zhang, H.: Head-mounted display-based intuitive virtual reality training system for the mining industry. Int. J. Min. Sci. Technol. 27(4), 717–722 (2017)

Research on Innovative Ways of Contemporary Display Porcelain Under the Background of Longyao Culture in Jing County

NaNa Li[✉] [iD]

Art and Design, Hefei University of Economics, No. 1, Xuefu Road, Hefei 230000, Anhui, China
78340668@qq.com

Abstract. After a long history of development, Longyao culture has strong local characteristics at each stage. The art of Longyao culture in Yixian County, Anhui has precipitated the craftsman spirit and historical sentiment of Xuanzhou Kiln. Furnishing porcelain is a reflection of modern people's color requirements and aesthetic orientation of home decoration. It has the demand of exquisite traditional craftsmanship and contemporary decoration. It is also a carrier of traditional ceramic firing process and social culture. This topic mainly studies the characteristics and artistic creation style of furnishings in the background of Longyao culture in Yi County, Anhui, analyzes the decorative features and aesthetic significance of contemporary furnishings, focuses on the innovative ways of contemporary furnishings, and concludes in the context of Longyao culture. Significance and Market Potential of Contemporary Contemporary Furnishing Porcelain Decoration Art.

Keywords: Jingxian · Longyao culture · Display porcelain · Modeling and Decoration

1 Introduction

With the development of social economy, people's standard of living, the concept of life and consumption concept has changed dramatically. Display porcelain has been widely used in modern home environment decoration, as part of the family culture and personal taste, home porcelain is gradually playing their own decorative charm. Contemporary decorative porcelain not only gives people a special sense of visual beauty and artistic enjoyment, but also in terms of color and decorative techniques to build the home environment and atmosphere provides a new approach. Display porcelain has been called "the perfect combination of heart and hand". In the current home environment decoration, modern furniture porcelain decoration is increasingly used to become an important part of the home environment.

2 Jing County Dragon Kiln Development Background

Tao Yao Village in Jing County has a long history of pottery making. From the late Qing Dynasty to the early Republic of China, more than 60 dragon kilns in Jing County were

P.-L. P. Rau (Ed.): HCII 2022, LNCS 13312, pp. 410–421, 2022.
https://doi.org/10.1007/978-3-031-06047-2_30

concentrated in Tao Yao Village. During the war against Japan, Jing County's ceramic industry declined. Product sales were affected by the war, sales fell sharply, kiln factories have closed. There were only three large kilns and small kilns in the county. Only 40 workers remained, Jing County's entire pottery industry was greatly affected. At the beginning of the founding of the People's Republic of China, with the establishment of the Jing County Pottery Kiln Cooperative, the ceramic industry was restored and the development of ceramic products reached its peak. However, in the early days of reform and opening up, with the decline of the national ceramic industry, Jing County dragon kiln industry once again into the trough. For ten years, Jing County has been looking for ways to revitalize the traditional pottery (Fig. 1).

Fig. 1. Jingxian kiln factory.

3   Features of Jing County Long Kiln and the Artistic Creation Style of Porcelain for Display

3.1   Characteristics of Jing County Long Kiln

The characteristics of Jingxian Long Kiln can be explained in three aspects: (1) Firing temperature: As the original material taken from Jingxian is pottery, the soil is red fusible clay, and there are more impurities and larger particles in the soil. Therefore, most of the vessels produced were pottery. With the improvement of mud refining technology, the proportion of impurities in the soil was reduced, forming the porcelain clay needed to make porcelain. The firing temperature also increased from the original 900 °C to 1100 °C. (2) Glaze: In the early days, the kiln was poorly sealed due to the internal structure of the long kiln. During the firing process, the mineral elements contained in the clay (such as iron oxide) were difficult to burn fully, which led to the color of the glazing material on the product being red or reddish brown during this period; with the development of modern kiln technology, the color of Jingxian's ceramic glaze also tends to diversify, and can be divided into high-temperature flower glaze and low-temperature lead glaze. (3) Pattern decoration on the vessels: traditional ceramic vessels are still made of clay in large pieces, while small pieces of porcelain are hand-kneaded, so most of the patterns are decorated with natural and traditional patterns.

3.2 Contemporary Display Porcelain Art Creation Style

Jing County ceramics mainly to the production of daily-use pottery, so decorative porcelain modeling also tends to be practical, its artistic style lies in: 1, the shape, Jing County still retains the most traditional modeling production methods: a, the clay bar plate into type from the original pottery period, the traditional ceramic modeling prevailed in small pieces of hand-kneaded into shape, large pieces of clay bar plate into type; b, pounding molding will be processed clay group made of rectangular or Round mud pier, the size of the mud pier according to the needs of the product. The mud dun is easy to store and carry, and there are still a few areas in Yunnan where traditional black pottery is produced by the pounding method. c. The special technique of making large pieces by pounding, which only exists in Jingxian and Ningguo, has a thick and sturdy structure, and is more free in size than the billet shaped ware, which cannot be replaced by modern shaping techniques. 2, decorative style, Jing County ceramic glaze color tends to diversify, can be divided into high-temperature glaze and low-temperature lead glaze, and kiln glaze is a high-temperature glaze in the boutique, high-temperature kiln is due to the direct impact of the temperature in the dragon kiln glaze color changes, the temperature of the dragon kiln are higher than the traditional firing kiln temperature, the glaze on the surface of the porcelain in the high-temperature environment has a strong chemical reflection, thus forming a non-artificial The kiln change glaze (Fig. 2). (Fig. 3)

Fig. 2. Hand made mud blank.   **Fig. 3.** Ceramic products.

4 Jing County Dragon Kiln Products Production Status and Market Difficulties

4.1 Jing County Dragon Kiln Products Production Status

Jing County Dragon kiln ceramic products production and business model can be divided into the following two kinds.

1. Individual Production and Operation Mode

There is a long kiln about 20 m long near the ancient kiln site in Jing County, and this kiln belongs to the private assets of a local family of potters. In this long kiln, the kiln owner made his own pottery, while employing a number of potters, kiln burners and other personnel. When the products produced in the kiln were piled up in the kiln, the owner could fire up the kiln. There was no limit to the variety of pottery that could be produced. The kiln is smaller than the former state-owned factories of the long kiln, but the kiln process is still the same. After the kiln is filled with kiln loaders, after 6 days of firing and 3 days of cooling, the products in the kiln can be sold out of the kiln. There are local middlemen who specialize in the wholesale of such products. Wholesalers by telephone on the same day the porcelain out of the kiln will drive the truck to the kiln factory to buy, or rent their own cars to transport products to the town or other places to sell, which is the traditional mode of individual production and operation.

2. Joint Household Contract Management Mode

After the closure of the former state-owned pottery factory, the original factory, including the long kiln, was retained. Despite the poor condition of the houses and the urgent need to repair the long kiln, four or five families in the village still insist on making a living from ceramics. Most of them are employees of the former state-owned factory. They spend the rest of their time making porcelain, except for those families who do not make porcelain from New Year's Day to the Qingming Festival. They do not have their own private kilns, so they have to use the former state-owned factory. After the bankruptcy of the former state-owned factory, the remaining large dragon kiln firing kilns jointly contracted for the construction and repair of the factory. Among them, another person was elected factory director, responsible for some external business contacts and overall planning arrangements, and several other people were their subordinates and shareholders. However, they did not build a formal factory. Instead, they worked on a per-family basis, with each family making a different type of pottery. It became a workshop separately, and several workshops together formed a factory. This form got rid of self-employment and self-marketing. Traditionally, it is inevitable that there will be some conflicts and opinions on the distribution and interests of some people, which is not conducive to the long-term development of ceramics. The owner of each workshop not only makes porcelain, but also participates in other tasks, such as firing the kiln and configuring the mud. To increase sales and avoid unhealthy competition, each family made as many different products as possible. The difference between Jing County's billet makers is in making large and small pieces. Sometimes they also hire people to make varieties that they cannot make. Usually the dragon kiln can be fired every 15 days when there are no rainy days. Usually, on the day the product comes out of the kiln, the factory manager will contact the wholesaler who bought it. After the products are removed from the kiln, they will be loaded directly onto the wholesaler's car, and this sales model ensures that there is a small inventory of products. There are also foreign customers who need pottery and they need to rent a car in order to transport it to their local area, the cost is paid by their relatives and when the customer receives the payment, the public costs, such as the kiln manager, labor costs for clay and fuel, are removed. Depending on the profit of the pottery produced by each family, the owner of each workshop pays the labor costs of the owners employed. Typically, pottery sales can reach 20,000 to 23,000 per kiln at a cost of about 12,000 to 15,000. These daily pottery pieces are typically sold to Wuhu, Maanshan, Chaohu, and nearby Anhui, Jiangsu and Zhejiang.

4.2 Jing County Long Kiln Ceramic Market Dilemma

The Impact of Modern Pottery Making and Industrial Products. Large-scale industrial production has led to rapid socio-economic development, and people's requirements for quality of life and aesthetics are constantly updated. For example, the existing market of stainless steel kettles, cups, bowls, pots and some plastic products, as stainless steel than ceramic is stronger, harder and more modern, so it has gradually been accepted by most people. The appearance of glass has also had an impact on porcelain, which looks more sophisticated and popular than ceramic due to its crystal clear texture and vibrant colors. However, it is plastic products that have dealt a fatal blow to traditional everyday ceramics. Industrial production lines producing cheap and easy-to-use plastic products have penetrated every corner of people's lives. Replacing the traditional everyday pottery as the main protagonist in people's daily lives. In short, modern industrial civilization brought by a variety of new materials made of daily tableware gradually replaced the traditional daily ceramics, traditional porcelain is gradually disappearing from people's daily life.

The Dilemma of Inheritance and Development of Traditional Pottery Making in Taoyao Village. Only four to five households in Tao Yao village of Jing County have been engaged in pottery for a long time. The age of potters is between 45 and 58 years old. Young people are reluctant to engage in pottery because not only is it difficult to make pottery, but the labor and rewards are disproportionate. They prefer to work in the city. Not only do they have access to the colorful life outside, but it is easier to make money than making pottery. Making pottery is a manual labor, especially for large pieces of porcelain making is even more difficult, so we can only rely on some skilled but older pottery artisans to continue to pass on this dying art. Because of the importance attached to this traditional handicraft culture and the lack of protection measures in the policy, most people in Jing County do not understand the importance of this fine traditional folk culture, which also leads to the lack of ceramic crafts of the Long Yao culture.

Weak Perception of Product Culture. The ceramic production of the Long Kiln in Jing County is only used for subsistence. After their everyday porcelain gradually lost its market, most people had to accept this situation. In Yixing and Jingdezhen, ceramics are constantly adjusting their product mix and style to suit the market and using various platforms to promote their products and find business opportunities. Although Jing County's pottery products have developed compared to the past, they still do not meet the demand for material and cultural development. In the survey, Jing County potters are very proud of their engagement in this craft, and from their words can feel the rural people for the traditional pottery making craft of the unrequited love. As the craftsmen suffer from their own cultural level and the reality of the environment, they have begun to realize that this ancient craft should be carried forward, but helpless in reality, can only be limited to the paper.

The Problem of Environmental Protection. The clay used to make ceramics in Jing County is taken from the local mountains, and the long-term collection of large amounts of soil has destroyed the local vegetation environment. At the same time, burning the long kiln requires a large amount of firewood, which is also taken from the local mountain forests, which has caused damage to the local forest environment. For example, the existing long kiln in the area consumes about 100,000 kg of firewood per year. For the sake of environmental protection, the government will not plan local industrial projects in such a way that this dying and environmentally destructive industry will be included in the village planning and development plans and will be passed on.

5   Contemporary Porcelain Display Forms and Shapes

5.1   The Way of Furnishing in the Interior Environment

Modern home decoration generally uses the type of furnishing porcelain are porcelain sculptures and flower arrangements, vases, porcelain prints, etc. Porcelain modeling and home space structure combined to create a decorative space environment. Porcelain decorative area is relatively independent, with a strong individual aesthetic orientation, regional decoration has not fixed, so the porcelain can be placed in the study, living room, bedroom and other areas.

Contemporary furnishing porcelain with the continuous prosperity of the cultural and creative market, but also continue to enhance the cultural value of the brand. The design of display porcelain needs to add connotation design in the background of traditional culture, but also to meet the quality requirements of young designers for interior decoration, the visual enjoyment brought by the display porcelain can release the designer's communication of traditional culture, the designer's design emotions will be affected by the unique artistic charm of the display porcelain.

Ceramics and Interior Environment. The art of beautifying the home can be called environmental art, and its main beautifying technique is the use of highly infectious furnishings to shape a think environmental art. But today's furnishing environment and the relationship between people occurred some irreconcilable contradictions, such as the use of modern materials to decorate the home environment and bring the hard home furnishing atmosphere, such as the rapidly changing industrial technology to create mechanical products, are ignoring the environment and human emotional communication, human emotional needs are not only material satisfaction, people in the spirit of dialogue with the furnishings needs to force the design of modern furnishing ceramics Consider more human factors. Young designers are more and more interested in using materials like clay with the original atmosphere of life as their design vehicle, designing some elegant furnishing ceramics to add interest to the interior decoration.

5.2   Different Types of Furnishings in Home Decoration

Display ceramics in the home environment is also very important, placement and the overall style of the family does not match not only can not show the characteristics of display ceramics, but also make the room becomes crowded and messy. In the ancient layout of the home more attention to the "East bottle West mirror", such as the design of the hall furnishings, in order to highlight the role of the owner of the welcome to visitors, most people will choose some stable and atmospheric furnishing ceramics, as a way to highlight the cultural atmosphere of the whole room. For the literati, in order to show its elegant taste, more will be placed in the study some furnishing ceramics, most people choose some rustic, ancient, elegant ceramics, so as to appear the master taste elegant not vulgar.

Modern pottery in the home decoration is mainly used to place type and three-dimensional type. Placement type pottery is a single piece of individual can also be a combination, according to the indoor entrance, corridor, study, balcony, living room and other different space environment needs, placed in different sizes, different shapes of ceramic works as furnishings. Designers for the ground, wall, countertop three types of furnishings, in-depth exploration of its different furnishing characteristics, understanding the placement of furnished ceramics and space to come up with the following regional decorative features.

Fig. 4. Home furnishing porcelain.   **Fig. 5.** Interior view of the Forbidden City (Sanxi Hall).

1. above-ground area decoration: above-ground area usually refers to the home environment in addition to furniture placement position outside the free area, people for these space area decoration will mostly choose a strong sense of decoration, and has a certain symbolic meaning of furnishing ceramics placed therein, the most common ceramic decorations are porcelain vase, clay sculpture, ceramic screen, etc. As furnishings and placed in the classroom ceramic vase, generally more to take the meaning of peace, the vase inserted in different objects also represents a different moral, such as inserting three painted halberds next to the placement of a sheng, meaning a flat rise three; bottle inserted peony means rich and safe, the bottle inserted in the moon flower means four seasons of peace and so on. From the point of view of decorative techniques, porcelain vase soft shape curve and home space decorative straight line echoes each other, breaking the dull home environment, porcelain vase because of its harmonic sound and "Ping" the same word, is widely used in the home space, these furnishings ceramic placement not only to send people's good wishes, but also enhance the overall tone of the home environment These ceramics are widely used in the home space (Fig. 4).

wall area decoration: wall area usually refers to the use of ceramic decorative wall in the home environment, wall decoration is widely used in architectural decoration, in large outdoor buildings and indoor home decoration often see ceramic decorative wall figure. Ceramic decorative wall in the process of using the same need to pay attention to some issues, such as in order to reconcile the conflict between wall decoration and the environment, it is necessary to pay attention to the symbiosis of art furnishing ceramics and decorative environment, both to harmonize and to have a certain difference, in order to achieve the purpose of creating a space environment art atmosphere. Wall ceramic furnishings can make the indoor space is no longer full of steel and concrete indifference, enriching the interior space levels, adding a touch of interest to the interior space. Ceramic wall decorations mainly include outdoor large ceramic murals, mosaic tile ceramic murals, colorful painting landscape ceramic plate, thin ceramic wall lamps, etc. These beautiful and durable wall furnishing ceramics show a unique cultural atmosphere, not only shows the artistic beauty of traditional ceramics, but also for the indoor living room to create a relaxed and pleasant atmosphere. Figure 5 shows the interior of the "Sanxi Hall" in the Qianlong Emperor's Hall of Health. The area of the Sanxi Hall is small, only 4.8 square feet, but it is in this small study that the Qianlong Emperor furnished a total of 110 pieces of cultural relics, including 11 ceramic wall vases hung on the east wall of the house as decoration. The whole house is a clever integration of interior decoration, stationery, cultural relics, playthings and architecture.

2. Table top area decoration: modern home furnishings in the table decorative furnishings is the development of ancient rituals evolved, the placement of furnishing objects also have a lot of attention, table top placement and "should be short and small, kiln ware such as paper mallet, goose neck, eggplant bag, flower zun, flower sac, short small party clear for", table top display can According to the needs of life to place pots, vases, ceramic penholders, ceramic antiques, ceramic artifacts, etc., "painting table can be placed stones, or the genus of seasonal flowers and bonsai, placed bottles, with the size of the bottle system placed on top of the Japanese few, spring and summer with copper, autumn with porcelain...", "Dream of the Red Chamber" also The bottle furnishings are mentioned, these descriptions highlight the role of the bottle on the table furnishings.

5.3 The Beauty of the Modeling Art of Contemporary Ceramics

Home space in the design of furnishing ceramics to meet the material needs at the same time, more should pursue a breakthrough in modeling, the law of beauty integrated into the design of ceramic furnishings such as flower vases, incense stoves and a variety of exquisite ornaments. With the level of production techniques and aesthetic concepts, the shape of ceramics has undergone an evolution from simple to complex. Looking back at the history of the development of China's ceramic modeling, many forms of diverse, well-conceived traditional furnishing ceramic modeling moved us, designers should continue to innovate on the basis of inheritance, to abstract the free approach to form their own unique modeling language, so that the design of furnishing ceramics and the aesthetic of today's times.

6 Jingxian Long Kiln Cultural Atmosphere on the Impact of Contemporary Furniture Design

Long Kiln porcelain development to today, the product is still mainly ornamental collectibles and daily-use porcelain with high prices, this phenomenon has a great limitation on the development of contemporary furnishing porcelain industry, in order to better inherit the spirit of this ancient Long Kiln culture, but also to break the bottleneck of the development of modern furnishing porcelain industry, to space environment decoration as the entry point, from the perspective of interior furnishing art to explore the idea of product innovation and development.

6.1 Influence of Kiln Firing Process on Contemporary Porcelain Decorati

Traditional dragon kiln firing process is largely reflected in the kiln temperature and kiln position. The temperature of the dragon kiln directly affects the change of glaze color, thus producing kiln glaze. The temperature of the dragon kiln is higher than the traditional kiln firing temperature, the glaze on the surface of the porcelain in the high temperature environment produced a strong chemical reaction, thus forming a non-artificial kiln glaze. Glaze kiln change and porcelain placement is also closely related, dragon kiln firing kiln temperature is from low to high, gradually heating up, kiln masters in the kiln head firing material heating all the way to the end of the kiln, due to the poor closure of the dragon kiln, the kiln body is long, easy to lead to the kiln environment into an oxidizing atmosphere, in the dragon kiln on both sides of the porcelain is easy to produce kiln change in the environment of oxidizing atmosphere.

6.2 The Influence of Extended Traditional Kiln Glaze Color on the Color of Contemporary Porcelain

Traditional dragon kiln firing technology is not subject to human control, glaze color will be affected by the kiln temperature factor, the dragon kiln porcelain products are often called "into the kiln a color, out of the kiln a thousand colors", in short, the main reasons affecting the dragon kiln porcelain glaze color kiln change are glaze ratio, kiln temperature, kiln placement, glaze thickness, firing atmosphere and other five factors by.

Dragon kiln glaze color after the previous people's continuous summary, its kiln type is mainly divided into the following kinds: 1, beeswax yellow: beeswax yellow glaze color is more like the beeswax in the ore, color glaze surface has a hazy feeling, seemingly transparent, glaze texture is very strong, has a high artistic ornamental value, is the dragon kiln glaze color kiln change in the representative glaze color. 2, fried rice yellow: with fried rice yellow glaze color of porcelain overall hair color is light yellow, color glaze 3, crab shell green: porcelain glaze color is more like the color of the crab shell in late autumn, the overall presentation of dark gray-green, giving a sense of simple digging thick. 4, ugandan black: porcelain exterior color is more like the obsidian in the gemstone, black bright color, the surface glaze color is extremely fine, giving a sense of calm in the elegant.

6.3 Contemporary Porcelain Modeling Innovation in the Furnishing

Traditional dragon kiln modeling has three most traditional production methods: First, the clay bar plate building: clay bar plate building into a shape is the most primitive technique of ceramic vessels, from the original pottery period onwards traditional ceramic modeling prevailed in small pieces to hand pinch molding, large pieces are built into the shape of the clay bar plate. Second, pounding molding: will be processed into a rectangular or round mud dun, the size of the mud dun according to the needs of the product. It is easy to store and carry, and there are still a few areas in Yunnan where traditional black pottery is produced by beating. Third, beaten piece forming: beaten piece forming method to produce large products of special skills, and now this technique only exists in Jingxian and Ningguo area, the finished structure is thick and strong, the size of the production is more free than the billet forming ware, is the modern forming technology can not replace, worthy of contemporary young porcelain artisans to pass on.

7 The Innovation Way of Contemporary Porcelain

With the improvement of the quality of life, people's requirements for the home environment and consumer attitudes have changed. From the initial royal artifacts to appear in the most common furnishings of ordinary people's homes, furnishing ceramic decoration is undergoing a bit of a traditional transformation. Today's furnishings are widely used in the decoration of the new China as a representative of family culture and personal taste. Potters have used their wisdom to lay a deep cultural and technical foundation for traditional ceramic art, but due to objective conditions and market constraints, traditional furnishing ceramics have failed to meet the needs of modern consumers. This suggests that contemporary decorative ceramics must find innovative ways to inject new vitality into the decorative ceramics market and incorporate the popular elements of modern society into ceramics to make them more in line with the aesthetic interests of today's society. Next, from three aspects through the contemporary decorative ceramics, to find out the innovation path of decorative ceramics.

7.1 The Innovation of Existing Ceramic Product Categories

Jing County Dragon Kiln produces products aimed at the local residents of the basic daily necessities market, the practicality of everyday pottery is much higher than the artistic qualities of the ceramics themselves. Jingxian existing market in the ceramic shape is too traditional, a common shape without innovation can be used for decades. Patterns are crudely designed, and the number of pieces produced has increased at the expense of innovation in product variety. In order to cater to the sales market, the local people only do a few of the more popular mainstream product modeling, making Jing County ceramics sales market gradually become narrow. According to the survey, most of the daily porcelain shapes produced in Jing County are sold to the townships, these areas are economically backward, living conditions are low, the purchasing power is relatively low. In the first- and second-tier cities near Jingxian, such as Nanjing, Hangzhou and Shanghai, modern people have increasingly high requirements for quality of life, and modern furnishing porcelain designs with a strong country flavor are becoming increasingly popular, including high-end hotels, nostalgic restaurants and the pursuit of fashionable life commercial environment decoration. Modern pottery designers can take advantage of the natural and simple characteristics of wood-burning dragon kiln, combined with the mainstream of modern society's food culture, tea culture, etc., to produce cultural restaurant tableware and antique ceramic decorations suitable for special decoration requirements, adjusting Jing County's existing industrial structure, combining artistry and functionality, and gradually create its own brand of pottery under the Jing County dragon kiln culture, can be combined with cross-industry, cross-field other traditional crafts Combined with other traditional crafts across industries and fields, creating a pottery production path belonging to the cultural characteristics of Jingxian Longkao.

7.2 Broaden the Traditional Ceramics Business Model

Jing County, Anhui Province has a long history of ceramic production, high-quality clay resources and a long history of firewood and pottery technology. At present, Ningguo City is building a national character town of Qianxi Long Yao town, located in Liangting Village, Port Town, with a planning area of 2–3 km^2 and a core area of 1 km^2. Highlighting the characteristics of "ancient handicrafts and ancient villages", the town is positioned as a "famous international dragon kiln culture town in Yangtze River Delta", implementing "industrial transformation and upgrading + 4A-level scenic spot + national heritage declaration". The town will focus on building a "thousand-year dragon kiln town" and become a town with national influence and cultural charm. Tao Yao Village can combine tourism with local traditional handicrafts in the area, and then the government will provide preferential policies to support the formation of a new business sales model. The local traditional pottery making experience tour, together with some famous tourist attractions in Jing County, has established a cultural dissemination platform with integrated tourism experience. Can also be closely linked with the local tea culture and culture, joint development from tea picking → fried tea → boiled tea → burned tea → tea tasting in one of the sensory experience tourism route, the government side to strengthen the local tourism industry in Jing County publicity and promotion activities, with the unique local tea culture to drive the sales model of tea sets, home decorations and other modern pottery products.

7.3 The Establishment of College Creation Practice Base

At present, it is difficult for pottery students in Anhui Province colleges and universities to come into contact with the traditional dragon kiln ceramic production process in the classroom. Jing County dragon kiln culture in the use of materials, molding techniques and firing aspects of the wood kiln, there are many places worthy of research and promotion of modern college students, especially during the normal study period is difficult to contact the wood kiln firing techniques, wood burning in the firing process of atmosphere control and other traces can also enable students to recognize and experience the traditional pottery and modern pottery modeling from the design concept and artistic expression of the difference. Jing County government can encourage the surrounding influential universities to establish teaching experimental bases in the local area, individual operators can teach students the skills of pottery making while engaged in pottery production. In the process of learning in the teaching experimental base, students can also participate in the manufacture of ceramics and kilns, through this method of teaching, on the one hand, students can have a deeper understanding of traditional pottery, on the other hand, can improve their enthusiasm for learning this profession, attracting more people to learn the traditional pottery of pottery kilns. And experts and scholars in the university can organize and launch various academic seminars regularly for the development and excavation and protection of dragon kilns in Jing County. The seminar will be held for Jing County to create a solid foundation for the international influence of the Dragon Kiln Expo Group. Not only enrich and enhance the connotation of Jingxian thousand-year-old dragon kiln town, but also provide a higher platform and broader space for cultural exchange and technical creation of dragon kilns.

For the local ceramic craftsmen, they must constantly improve and refine their cultural and professional skills, and combine theoretical knowledge with practical experience in order to better inherit the traditional regional culture. This will enable the design of ceramics with regional culture to be in line with the world and expand the sales space of ceramic products. Ceramic production is an industry with a long cultural history and must conduct artistic exchange activities in specific regions to form a category and a wide applicable market. Only by attracting artistic colleagues from other regions or abroad to join our artistic culture can we promote the sustainable development of the contemporary furnishing porcelain design market. At the same time, strengthening the construction of innovative and entrepreneurial practice bases in colleges and universities can improve the single undergraduate teaching environment, lead contemporary college students to learn innovative ideas beyond the classroom, broaden their horizons, learn new techniques and information about traditional ceramic art, keep up with the times, innovate, and bring into play the artistic charm of contemporary porcelain for display in the world economic market system.

References

1. Zhi, J.: Jing County Local History Compilation Committee. Fangzhi Press (1996)
2. Dr. Li, H.: Lin: compilation. History of Jingxian County, Anhui Province (eight volumes). Office of local chronicles Compilation Committee of Jing County, Anhui Province (1987)
3. Xuancheng City Archives Bureau (Fangzhi Office): Xuancheng geographic names. Huayi Publishing House (2009)
4. Yu, X.: Inheritance and Variation of Chenrezig Ceramic Art. Hunan Normal University (2016)
5. Yan, H., Tan, T.: The development prospect of display art porcelain. Popular Literature and Arts (2011)
6. Sha, L.: Investigation and research on traditional pottery making process in Tao Yao Village, Jing County, Anhui. Nanjing Art Institute (2011)
7. Lv, J.: Research on the art of handmade living ceramics. Shandong Fine Arts Press (2008)

Fluency and Aesthetic Models Revisited in the Context of Museum Management Design

Hanlin Mi[1] and Rui Xu[2(✉)]

[1] School of Art and Design, Fuzhou University of International Studies and Trade, Fuzhou 350200, Fujian, China
[2] Institute of Design Science, Tatung University, Taipei 11604, Taiwan
520031111@qq.com

Abstract. In addition, innovativeness and originality are more strongly influenced by experts, who expect more surprises from artworks. Changes in aesthetic mood are associated with many possible variables, and what is particularly important to consider in the context of a comprehensive psychological theory of artwork appreciation is the relationship between interest, confusion, and surprise as a function of the observer's perception of artworks and other stimuli that are often presented as potentially mediating appreciation, namely, mood and level of expertise. The experimental data concluded that there is indeed a moderating relationship between users' fluency status and aesthetic emotions represented by interest, confusion, and surprise. Users with higher fluency are generally believed to be more interested in design works, less confused and surprised. On the contrary, most users with low fluency present an incredible sense of surprise for their creation, which provides a new thinking direction for the later integration of artificial intelligence and emotional design.

Keywords: Museum management · Design · Fluency · Aesthetic models · Digitization

Since the 21st century, information technology, digital technology and graphics technology, including Virtual Reality Technology, Digital Image Processing, Computer Graphics, Multimedia Technology, Sensor Technology, Interactive Digital Board, Cloud Computing Services and Internet of Things Technology have been constantly updated, iterated, innovated and developed. In the process of wide application and rapid development of these technologies, they have been closely integrated with various industrial institutions and have made many remarkable achievements [1]. In the development process of these high and new technologies, thousands of data are generated every minute. In the face of such diversified data types and huge data scale, the traditional data processing tools and models are obviously difficult to deal with. Therefore, in the era of big data, how to manage and use big data scientifically and efficiently has become a highly concerned issue in all walks of life. Under the current development, the support of these high and new technologies is also needed by the museum industry. It is an urgent need for this new data management mode based on the big data technology, and big data technology and related management modes are born with the trend. In this context, the heritage and museums industry shall grasp the opportunity and establish the big data in a timely and accurate manner; Popularize the knowledge of big data, deepen the concept of big data, and continuously pay attention to the development of big data; Take the museum as an important site for collection, collection, display and research on the representative natural and human cultural heritage; Adhere to the purpose of learning, education and entertainment; Remain open to the public; Actively think and try to solve the problems found in the current museum operation and management through digital technology and big data, so as to further enhance the service effect and overall value of the museum.

In short, in the era of big data, core formats, associated formats and derivative formats are constantly upgrading. Especially since the 13th Five-Year Plan, China's ability of big data analysis and application has been constantly strengthened, which has prompted great changes in traditional museums and related fields of the heritage and museums [2]. In addition, with the continuous development of social economy and the improvement of people's living standards, more and more people tend to visit museums in their spare time as an important means to further improve the construction of spiritual civilization. The annual increase in the number of visitors has put unprecedented pressure on the current traditional museum operation and management model. Therefore, the management model combined with big data technology has become an unstoppable trend, which can not only better adapt to the current environment of the times, but also meet the aesthetic needs of young people as the main group.

1   Big Data Technology

Theoretically, big data technology is not a pure technical term, but a collection of data processing tools and technical achievements. Big data, as a product in the digital era, is in the process of continuous refinement, and its value and impact on people's life and work are in the stage of continuous rise. In March 2012, the United State government represented by Obama announced the world's first big data promotion policy – "Big Data Research and Development Plan" [3]. In 2014, the White House released the report "Big Data: Seizing Opportunities and Protecting Values" again, which even more closely linked big data with the industrial transformation [4]. Then, the China Academy of Information and Communications released the "China Big Data White Paper" five times in 2014, 2016, 2018, 2019, and 2020, detailing the warm-up, start-up, landing and deepening stages of China's big data applications [1]. The most recent retrospective analysis is the Big Data White Paper 2020, released in December 2020, which highlighted that data has become a key strategic resource influencing global competition. Only when more authentic and reliable data resources are acquired and mastered can it occupy a dominant position in a new round of global discourse competition [5]. Big data technology can not only help consumers, micro, small and medium-sized enterprises and traditional industries achieve transformation breakthroughs, but also show its irreplaceable value-added value. Especially in the face of the sudden outbreak of COVID-19, big data technology has shown its irreplaceable core role in both epidemic prevention and control and resumption of work and production. In daily life, big data technology is widely used in industry detection, marketing detection, public opinion reports and personnel flow analysis and other practical fields. However, there is relatively little research on the use of the big data technology to help the heritage and museums industry to carry out the big data management and display mode. According to the existing studies, it has been found that big data has five main characteristics: Volume, Velocity, Variety, Vraisemblance, and Value [5]. Volume refers to the huge data generated in the era of information explosion, and uses this to define and name innovative technologies related to it. In general, the amount of information that is considered big data starts at least in terabytes. The current big data technology has achieved a qualitative leap from TB to PB or even ZB [6]. Velocity refers to when the data reaches this level of measurement, existing information technology and data processing tools are utilized to efficiently and systematically perceive, collect, manage, analyze and store the data within a specified period of time. Diversity refers to the wide variety of big data types, including not only traditional formatted data, but also text, pictures, videos, geographic locations and other content from multiple channels. Vraisemblance is a new dimension added to the feature of big data 3V in the big data press conference of IBM (International Business Machines Corporation) in 2013, which has the ability to transform data into quantitative information generated by audience interaction. Some scholars have concluded that only real and accurate data can give real meaning to data management and application [7]. Finally, in the face of massive data, how to use data fusion and advanced mathematical methods to further improve the quality of data to create higher value is an important topic that needs to be discussed in big data technology. With the full combination of big data and special scenes deepening, it is predictable that the work of the museum is showing a trend of transition to the big data mode, and gradually forming a mature ecosystem of digitization, media and diversification. It can be predicted that the big data management model will become a new hot spot in the construction of digital museums in the future [8].

2 Management Mode of Big Data Museum

The audience is not only the basis of the operation of the museum, but also the main object served by the museum [9]. Most of the museum's big data digital information comes from the audience. These digital information mainly covers two dimensions of big data collection (acquisition) and big data fusion. Figure 1 clearly shows the main components of big data in the digital museum. In fact, this big data information is already generated before the audiences even enter the museum. For example, the big data generated by the audience inquiring and locking the location of the museum and the surrounding main environmental components by using the Internet search platform; the big data generated by the audience purchasing or booking tickets for the museum and its special exhibitions; the big data generated in the process of the audience obtaining the detailed information of the museum's exhibition collections; the big data generated by the audience participating in various online and offline related activities hosted by the museum; or the big data generated by the audience planning the tour itinerary in the museum and publishing fresh and interesting content on the new media social platform.

In addition to the variety of data information itself, the variety of audience is also a point that big data technology needs to pay close attention to. Audiences may come from different countries and regions in the world, with different age levels and greatly different

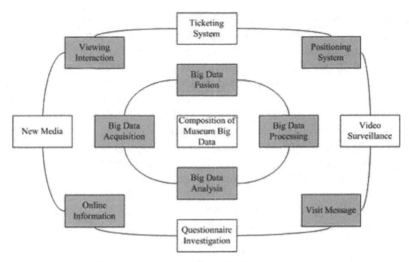

Fig. 1. The model of the big data of museum

interest preferences [10]. Therefore, they come to the museum for different purposes, and the digital information related to the audience can be generated and stored in the digital museum's big data system. Through the application of various data processing means, the value of these data can be effectively used and played, and then economic benefits and social benefits are generated. It is worth mentioning that since the outbreak of COVID-19, based on the support of big data from the government, the public, and enterprises for epidemic prevention and control, the major museums have carried out all-round and multi angle real-time display of personnel, vehicle flow, resource distribution, logistics and transportation and other information in and out of the museum, so as to realize the prevention and control of the epidemic and disease diagnosis, and establish an effective prevention and control network. Big data management mode not only provides digital services for the audience, but also helps the museum greatly improve its management level and service quality through crowd statistics and customer source analysis, as well as formulating more targeted exhibition strategies. More reasonable personnel layout and allocation can be carried out for different time periods, busy periods and quiet periods, which is especially important for flow control during the epidemic period.

At present, the National Museum of the Netherlands, the Van Gogh Art Museum, the New York Metropolitan Museum, the National Museum of Washington and the National Museum of China have also successively established big data museums, and on the data content page, the museum's collection catalogue and the metadata of each exhibit have been provided [11]. Taking the British Museum, the most popular tourist attraction in the UK as an example, the big data management system initially established by it and Microsoft Corporation enables managers to effectively analyze the interaction methods of nearly 6.9 million people each year with the 800000 feet of museum space, and to understand personally how the audiences experience the exhibition space, what route the audiences take, and how long the audiences stop in front of a piece of work. Siorna, senior manager at the British Museum, said: "I thought most audiences would start their tour at the Rosetta Stone on the ground floor. But, based on the big data, to let me and my team know exactly, there are also many people who start on the second and third floors." Similarly, the Louvre museum in France has embarked on big data practices. Since the beginning of 2020, the scientific research team jointly formed by the United States, Switzerland and Spain has conducted quantitative and visual research on the movement of Louvre audiences through three big data research framework and Bluetooth detector so as to not only better analyze the viewing preferences of different groups, but also roughly understand which audience has the potential to consume art works, which is the core value of big data. The traditional museums often go to great lengths to inform their audiences, but neglect to use big data to understand and better serve their audiences.

The full use of the technology of big data analysis and processing can collect, analyze, store and present the relatively valuable contents in the massive audience's digital information, and realize the in-depth mining of the internal connection between these data links. The mining of a large amount of valuable data has achieved the transformation of the "Data-Information-Knowledge-Wisdom (DIKW)" hierarchical structure [12], which can not only help museum managers discover problems in museum operations in a timely manner, but also help to promote the intelligent work of digital museums, thus escorting the future decision-making of curators and managers.

Based on the above problems and the museum big data module mode, in this paper, some suggestions have been proposed on the big data collection (acquisition) and big data fusion of the big data museum management system.

2.1 Big Data Collection

The data collected by the traditional museums mainly cover two types of unstructured data and structured data, and the data volume is small. In the era of big data in which unstructured data accounts for more than 90% of the total data, these data are far from enough to study the psychology and behavior of the audience. The establishment of the big data collection system provides a more in-depth understanding of the audience for the management and operation of the museum. Big data collection systems rely on multiple approaches and sources. What data is collected usually depends on the current scientific and technological means, knowledge level and the specific needs of museum personnel. The way of data collection mainly consists of traditional (questionnaire form), online (website visitor analysis, website sales, digital museum, social media, intelligent voice guide, etc.), ticketing (point of sale, gift shop), Internet of things, indoor location tracking (visitor heat map, consume flow analysis, audience dynamic map) and other possible data.

Among them, social media is an economic and efficient data collection tool, which can be used to create museum related "fan" files, measure social participation, and attract target audiences based on interest through later data analysis. Taking Weibo as a social platform, for example, as of August 2021, the official Weibo of the Palace Museum has attracted 10.15 million followers, the National Museum of China has attracted 5.08 million followers, and the Sanxingdui Museum in Guanghan, Sichuan has attracted 4.1 million followers. Social media, such as Weibo, Wechat, Douyin, Kuaishou, Instagram and even Taobao Live, not only provide a platform for the promotion and marketing of museums, but also fully record the statistical data of the interaction between audiences and social media pages. Social media with a large number of consumers leads to a large and rich collection of consumers information, so targeted interest marketing can be easily carried out, while the size of the potential audience can also be measured. These social platforms, which combine knowledge, interaction and entertainment, provide direct contact opportunities between the audience and the museum, and greatly enhance the interaction and communication between the museum and the audience. In addition, the installation of Internet of things connection equipment is also of great significance for big data collection. For example, with the use of Bluetooth ibeacons, WiFi router or UWB anchor in the museum, the accurate motion analysis of the audience can be provided, the quantitative data information of the interaction between the audience and the museum space can be obtained more systematically, and the real trend of the guests can be captured. After the data is further visualized, it can help the staff easily identify how the audience moves in the museum, which exhibits are popular (or unpopular), and identify some dead corners, so that the staff of the museum can make better use of space, exhibit layout and moving line design [10].

2.2 Big Data Fusion

1) *Integration of big data and cultural and creative products*
   In 2016, The State Council forwarded "Several Opinions on Promoting the Development of Cultural and Creative Products in Cultural relics Units" (hereinafter referred to as the Opinions) released by the Ministry of Culture, and discussed how to make museums and other excellent resources inject new vitality through the development of cultural and creative products [13]. In the Opinions, there are two unified requirements for cultural and cultural relics units including museums to develop cultural and creative products. The first is to "make full use of creative and scientific means to promote the integration of cultural resources and modern production and life so as to realize the organic unity of cultural value and practical value". Therefore, the integration of big data technology and the cultural and creative products may have to be made.

On the one hand, through the collection of various resources, big data can deeply investigate the real needs of the public and deeply grasp the interests and preferences of consumers, so as to develop products that meet the needs of the audience and contain traditional culture. For example, according to the "New Cultural and Creative Consumption Trend Report" jointly released by the Institute of Cultural Economics of Tsinghua University and Tmall, it has been found that the cultural and creative market of museums has been growing rapidly in recent years - more and more consumption Consumers tend to buy cultural and creative products online. Nearly 80% of consumers are born in the 1990s, and most of them are students. Obviously, cultural and creative products have become a new way to connect museums with young people [14].

On the other hand, big data can also help designers of cultural and creative products choose the most appropriate collection among the large volume of cultural relics as cooperation objects. Based on the big data, after mastering the consumption preferences and differentiated consumption of the audience, Shanghai Museum has developed a special bronze ware - spring and autumn sacrificial Zun series magnetic bookmarks, which sell for around 20 yuan and are highly praised once launched [15].

2) *Integration of big data and e-commerce*

The depth of big data mining has become an important factor affecting the development of e-commerce. In 2014, the concept of "culture + e-commerce" was first introduced in the "International Forum on Cultural Trade" held at the cultural industry expo held in Shenzhen. With the help of the new transaction mode of e-commerce, the greatest limit is to push the once "secret" sales mode of cultural and creative products to the popular sales platform. The new business form of "big data + cultural relics + e-commerce" is combined with strong powers to integrate into modern urban life in a more diversified form. The integration of big data, cultural relics and e-commerce can be realized in the following ways:

First of all, official channels: B2C self-operated commercial sales mainly refer to the establishment of official museum online stores on various B2C shopping platforms, such as Taobao, Jingdong, Dangdang, Weidian, Amazon and so on. The integration with big data technology can help reduce the existing risks of proprietary B2C. For example, the backlog of goods and overdue goods [16]. It speeds up the updating of consumer's demand, consumption data and other information, and provides strong technical support for consumer's personalized needs. At present, the Palace Museum, the National Museum of China, Shaanxi History Museum, Suzhou Museum and other well-known cultural and museum institutions have landed on Tmall and established official flagship stores. In the era of big data, traditional museums have paid attention to the e-commerce. The Palace Museum, for example, has 1.43 million followers since its arrival two years ago. According to the data, it has been found that, in the past six months, the sales of the museum flagship store on Tmall have maintained a rapid growth, with an average growth rate of nearly 200%. In terms of the international market, the British Museum is the first to enter and reached a business partnership with Tmall London in 2016. Among them, the most important cooperation content is to promote the museum's new "IP" derivatives, other internationally renowned museums are also actively following. Similarly, the cooperation between cultural institutions and e-commerce can also be promoted through the B2C third-party operation mode. B2C third-party mode mainly refers to that e-commerce platforms transfer orders to other small and medium-sized enterprises and earn profit margins [16]. The advantage of this model is that it can make use of the supply chain of cross-border retail products, or operate both B2B and B2C e-commerce platforms. This mode not only provides the cultural products developed based on the collection of cultural relics resources for consumers to buy, but also provides businesses with materials and cultural resources for secondary creation and development. At the same time, it also realizes the production, supply and marketing trading services of cultural products such as books, paintings, audio-visual products, so as to realize the maximum of benefit.

Big data integration can further promote the integration of big data, cultural relics and e-commerce by broadening data acquisition channels, optimizing overall operation mode, integrating supply chain, improving marketing strategy and network promotion. This good data collection and fusion method can help the museum to establish automatic feedback systems for surplus cultural and creative products and defective cultural and creative products, so as to timely reflect the product status and improve the overall efficiency. In the context of big data, the diversified integration tried by the museum is not only an important channel to enhance the national cultural soft power, but also an important means to enrich the people's spiritual and cultural life and meet the diversified consumption needs. Expanding the functions of museums is of great significance to promote the integration of cultural resources and modern production and life.

3 Conclusion

To sum up, in the era of big data, digital technology will continue to be organically combined with more fields. As mentioned above, with regard to the deeper cooperation between big data and the heritage and museums industry, the management, integration, analysis and processing visualization of big data can better use information technology as an intuitive presentation of data to a certain extent, and play a broader role. For museums, the digital museum management mode based on big data technology has the opportunity to become the core part and important cornerstone of various businesses in the cultural and museum industry in the future. It can realize the functions of multi screen interaction, data communication, data cooperation, data sharing, data storage and so on by visualizing the display equipment in the digital system, so as to not only break through the traditional operation mode of the museum, but also eliminate the information island between people, people and things, and things and things. This not only makes the digital museum meet the personalized needs of the audience under the background of the times, but also plays a great role in helping the decision-making level and management level of the digital museum.

References

1. General Office of the CPC Central Committee, General Office of the State Council, Outline of Action for Promoting Big Data Development, National Issue, no. 50. People's Daily (2015)
2. Zhang, X., Dong, Z.: Discussion on information construction and management of museums. Natl. Mus. China (2), 6
3. Ye, Y., Ye, Y.: Talking about the role of big data in promoting the exhibition and teaching work of science and technology museums——taking Zhejiang Science and Technology Museum as an example. Sci. Technol. Bull. (2021)
4. Cao, L., Ma, C.: Research on the application practice of big data of public culture at home and abroad. Libr. J., 9–15 (2015)
5. Chinese Academy of Communications: Big Data White Paper 2020 (2020)
6. Liu, J.: A Preliminary study on the application of museum big data – taking the Shanghai Museum Data Center project as an example. Sci. Conserv. Archaeol., 20–22 (2017)
7. Qiu, Y.: Brief analysis of the dynamic audience service system of museums in the era of big data. Natl. Mus. China, 68–71 (2014)
8. Zhang, X.: Using museums from the perspective of digital museums. In: Research and Practice of Digital Museums, p. 6. Beijing Association for Science and Technology, Beijing Municipal Cultural Heritage Bureau, Beijing Municipal Bureau of Economy and Information Technology, Beijing Digital Science Association (2010)

9. He, Q.: Research on tourists' demand preference for interpretation system of China Geological Museum. J. Huaihai Inst. Technol. (Human. Soc. Sci.), 116–118 (2017)
10. Zhang, X.: Discussion on the construction conditions and methods of wisdom museum. Natl. Mus. China, 110–115 (2018)
11. Dai, T.: Research on standardization of museum cultural relics digital image metadata based on CIDOCCRM – taking the design of cultural relics image metadata system of National Museum of China as an example. Natl. Mus. China, 131 (2020)
12. Fang, J.: Research on data visualization design based on DIKW hierarchical structure. Master thesis of Nanjing University of Aeronautics and Astronautics
13. The Central People's Government of the People's Republic of China: "Several Opinions on Promoting the Development of Cultural and Creative Products in Cultural relics Units" forwarded by The State Council Office (2016)
14. Institute of Culture Economy, Tsinghua University, Cultural and Creative Consumption Trend Report (2019)
15. Chen, Q.: Application of big data analysis in museum scene – taking Shanghai Museum Data Center as an example. Sci. Educ. Mus., 188 199 (2018)
16. Xiong, L.: Prospects and reflections on the e-commerce development of museum cultural and creative product sales. Mus. Dev. Collect., 70–76 (2017)

Cultural Gene: The New Enlightenment from the Display Design of University History Museum

Mengyao Wang[✉]

Tsinghua University, 30 Shuangqing Road, Haidian District, Beijing 100084, China
625427399@qq.com

Abstract. In the context of globalization, "mobile modernity" has become the norm in modern society. In today's cultural integration, how to make designs with "personal characteristics", "local characteristics" and "national characteristics" has become an increasingly urgent task. But design innovation never happens by accident. Every designer innovates and merges on the basis of a certain cultural context. Looking for Chinese design in global design and exploring individual design in Chinese design is a design exploration of collective identity and individual identity. At the same time, in the process of cultural evolution, "cultural gene" with interdisciplinary research was discovered and gradually recognized, "gene" this element, through the biological to social level of discussion. The origin of the birth of cultural genes is biological genetics. Like biological genetic genes, it has the functions of replication, selection and mutation. Biological genes determine biological diversity, and cultural genes determine cultural diversity. Today, when China is vigorously developing the construction of cultural museums and promoting the construction of campus culture and spirit, facing the university history museum, which is still a "young" education exhibition space—for this space, whether it is in terms of definition or specific design mode, and its impact on the university itself The significance of is still in an "ambiguous" stage. The discovery and concept of "cultural genes" have given the author new enlightenment on the design of the exhibition space of the school history museum.

Keywords: Cultural genes · University history museum · Display design

1 Cultural Genes and University History Museum

1.1 A Brief Analysis of Cultural Genes

"Meme" appeared in British scientist Richard Dawkins' best-selling book "The Selfish Gene" in 1976. The word "Meme" originated in Greek and can be understood as memory. In French culture, "Meme" means clone. The Chinese translation is "cultural gene", which is used to describe the basic unit of social and cultural transmission and evolution. Culture has similar characteristics to biological evolution through non-hereditary methods. At the same time, the dissemination of concepts has brought a positive effect to the development and research of cultural gene theory.

P.-L. P. Rau (Ed.): HCII 2022, LNCS 13312, pp. 431–441, 2022.
https://doi.org/10.1007/978-3-031-06047-2_32

The book "The Meme Machine" by Susan Blackmore, a student of Meme founder Richard Dawkins, further explains that in various cultural phenomena, Meme, as a replicator, is closely related to genes in the biological world. There is similarity and equivalence in function and effect. Compared with the different definitions of many scholars, the most authoritative is the interpretation of Meme in the Oxford English Dictionary in 1988. As follows, meme: An element of culture that may be considered to be passed on by non-genetic means, esp. imitation.

In this article, the perspective of cultural genes is based on the recognition that "cultural genes" and genes are both a "replicator", that is, the process of recognizing the analogy between cultural transmission and gene transmission, "the development of culture", patterns of dissemination and diversification have characteristics similar to biological evolution." When we talk about biological evolution, we will refer to the "Origin of Species" published in 1859. Darwin believed that the evolution of living things needs to have three characteristics: mutation, selection and inheritance. Organisms need to mutate, resulting in differences between individuals; secondly, the conditions provided by the environment are suitable to different degrees for the survival of organisms with different characteristics; thirdly, the characteristics of the previous generation of organisms must be able to pass some pathway to the next generation of organisms. Through these three aspects, the characteristics of organisms that are conducive to their survival in this environment will inevitably show an expanding trend. The evolution of biology seems to have a certain distance from the culture and design discussed in this article, so the author borrows the research of comparative linguists on language to make a connection [1].

Language provides an excellent example of the evolution of culture, and the organizational structure of language is inseparable from cultural transmission. Steven Pinker (1994) explicitly applies evolutionary thinking to the analysis of language development. He examines the effects of inheritance, variation, and dissociation of language, thereby theoretically accepting the cumulative effects of combinations of variation. In his book "Language Instinct", he mentioned that language differences, like species differences, are the result of long-term effects of three evolutionary processes. The first is "variation", which is called "mutation" in biology and "innovation" in linguistics. The second is "hereditary", biologically speaking, all species retain the variation results of their ancestors, that is, genetic inheritance; linguistically speaking, this is expressed as the ability to learn. The third is "isolation," which is biologically represented by geographic factors, breeding seasons, or genital anatomy, and linguistically represented by population migration or social segregation. For languages and species, isolated groups will gradually accumulate different mutational results, and over time, differentiation will occur [2].

Combining the conditions of "biological evolution" and "language evolution", the author believes that the evolution process of cultural genes mainly includes "inheritance (replication), selection and innovation". Culture needs to reproduce its parts that are conducive to survival in some way; the diversity of culture also depends on the selection of the external environment of culture, and different external environments breed different cultural groups; finally, culture needs innovation, it depends on Because culture occurs in the process of heredity and selection, culture is an important source of individual differences.

1.2 Cultural Genes with University Cultural

The performance of culture in universities varies greatly according to the carrier. The author believes that the evolution of university cultural genes is dominated by dominant carriers, recessive carriers and active carriers. The dominant carrier is mainly expressed by the dominant carrier such as the geographical location of the university, the architectural landscape of the university, the research results of the university, and the major events of the university. The spiritual temperament is mainly expressed; the carrier of activity is all the people, things and projects in the university that translate materialization into connotation. And from connotation to materialization, people, things and projects that show the spirit of university culture.

The author believes that the activity carrier is the key to the "carrying vitality" in the process of cultural gene transfer. They are all carrying processes of human creation, human production and human life that take place as the origin of human beings. At the same time, the inheritance and creation of university cultural genes is also based on the vitality and creativity of generations of teachers, students and employees who live and study in the university. However, it is different from the general biological evolution, biological genetics and other families, races, etc., which have a certain biological bond to maintain. The "gene" relationship between them is based on the cultural genes of a university to form a cultural group for inheritance and connection. At the same time, the stability, development and vitality of this university group also depend on the inheritance and creation of the cultural genes of the university people from generation to generation.

Therefore, the dissemination of cultural genes of a university to itself is an important part of university development, and the content of its dissemination is also multi-level and diversified content around the university. The richer the connotation of a university's cultural genes, the deeper its development.

The author has investigated the contents displayed in the History Museum of China University and conducted in-depth interviews with relevant practitioners, and based on the three processes of cultural gene inheritance, namely "**inheritance (replication), selection and innovation**". The composition of the university cultural gene content is divided into six major sections: campus landscape planning, scientific research achievements, famous humanities, and commemorative events with the core of the history and the spirit of the university.

"University History" is the origin and development of a university. It generally describes the main development process of a university. The origin and development of a university profoundly determines the future development direction of a university, that is, the fundamental source of innovation vitality and development direction; "University spirit" is a cultural connotation with human temperament closely connected with the origin of the university. It endows a university with a unique temperament that exists in society and is the basis for cultivating the values and ideas of university people. "Campus landscape planning, scientific research results, famous humanities, commemorative events" and other university-related content are the essence of a university's dissemination and absorption from each generation of university students.

We can see that the content of university cultural genes has great differences in nature. They are a mixture of concrete material form and ambiguity, but how can these be better inherited and displayed? Since the 1980s and 1990s, under the influence of the rapid development of China's economy and cultural education, Chinese universities have begun to build "University History Museums" in order to better preserve their high-quality cultural content and spiritual characteristics. In 1999, Shanghai Jiaotong University established China's first mature university history museum.

1.3   University History Museum with Cultural Genes

The University History Museum of China belongs to a special category of history museums in terms of the content of its collection. The school history museum belongs to the university in terms of administration. Relevant research shows that the content displayed by the school history museum is a complete picture of the culture and history of colleges and universities in a specific period, including campus construction, scientific research results, and comprehensive information about teachers and students. The school history museum takes the collection of a specific area as the collection standard, and is not fixed on certain topics or disciplines [3]. The university history museum is different from the general history museum. The main function is not only research, teaching and preservation of collections. It also has an important role in education, publicity and connection with alumni. The display is not only to satisfy people's curiosity or entertainment, but also to educate college students and the general public. In terms of personnel functions, the staff of the school history museum is usually linked to the party history office, archives and other institutions. Due to this characteristic, the functional requirements of different school history museums sometimes have big differences. Foreign universities pay more attention to the preservation of department history and scientific research results, so the research and preservation work is relatively independent between departments and schools.

The University History Museum is not only a place for historical research, but also a powerful educational means in the process of higher education. Therefore, in addition to displaying university historical materials, contacting university alumni, and displaying university scientific research and academic achievements, the Chinese University History Museum is also an important place for moral education in each university. It is a centralized training base for university cultural education. And the creation of the university history museum has a strong university culture place spirit [4].

So far, Chinese university history museums have gradually become one of the main carriers of university cultural genes. As a relatively "young" cultural display space, the University History Museum is the "one body and two sides" of university culture and university history. At the same time, it also has strong social and temporal attributes.) is the production content of the carrier of university activities, and is centrally constructed, transmitted and stored in the space of the university history museum. At the same time, due to the different composition of "cultural genes" in the social environment, it has brought about the display of the inherent collective identity and uniqueness of different groups.

In the early stage of school history exhibitions, most of them simply display the development history of universities, key event nodes, and universities in national development as the main display objects and purposes. Now, although it may not be fully reflected in the display design, through literature and research, the author finds that more and more university history museums use the shaping of university historical and cultural space as a means and purpose, and gradually become a constant update and iteration. It is the main carrier of the university's cultural genes, and it is a concentrated display space for the material and non-material achievements and spirits of the university's stage genes.

2 Display Design of University History Museum Based on the Cultural Genes

Based on the "Tsinghua University School History Museum Exhibition Design Project", the author will explain how the university cultural gene has a new perspective on the display design of the school history museum in terms of content and form. The author believes that the content formation of the university history museum is the inheritance (replication), selection and innovation of university cultural genes. The design method of constructing the exhibition space of the university history museum can also be inherited (replicated), selected and innovated on the basis of the exhibition content.

The author hopes that, different from the traditional way of planning the content and design of the university history museum based on the narrative structure, but starting from a university cultural gene, it can provide some new curatorial ideas for the continuous construction of the university history museum.

2.1 The Inheritance (Replication)

This kind of replication not only replicates and conveys the content of single or continuous events, characters, etc. in the history of the university, but also greatly affects the design strategy of display design in the university history museum. This kind of copying is usually displayed as a secondary communication of "design symbols" in the curatorial content, such as the design and utilization of the main visual elements that have been formed in the campus, etc., forming a strong echo of cultural visual elements in the school history museum., so that the viewer can receive the visual cultural symbols in the space where they are located.

On the first floor of the History Museum of Tsinghua University, visitors can feel this strong "Tsinghua Wind" coming from the moment they enter the front hall. Among the four major buildings of Tsinghua University, the "gate of the Science Building" was designed to be placed at the entrance of the front hall. The audience was immersed in the atmosphere of Tsinghua the moment they entered the exhibition hall. At the same time, the material transformation that has a more collective memory is that the entire first floor uses red bricks as a wall treatment method, and the interior of the exhibition hall also uses a continuous arch wall shape. Although Tsinghua University is an institution of higher learning in China, its unique development history emphasizes the school-running characteristics of "Western Learning" and "Eastern Integration". At the same time, Tsinghua University still has a very typical old western building complex on campus. In shaping the environment of the exhibition hall on the first floor of the History Museum, elements full of western architectural features such as "red bricks" and "arch walls" have been preserved and even used on a large scale (see Fig. 1 and 2).

Fig. 1. Front hall of the University History Museum 1 (Photo source : taken by the author)

Fig. 2. Front hall of the University History Museum 2 (Photo source: taken by the author)

2.2 The Selection

The "Selection" means that some cultural genes have been favored by cultural heritage, which may be based on the fact that this part of genes has an important influence on the further development of university culture, or the core content that needs to be continuously copied and inherited, and it may also be another An important part of a university's ability to maintain its uniqueness. And this "choice" depends on the ability of the content of this part of the meme to gain and maintain attention in the current environment.

In the history of Tsinghua University, "sports spirit" and "sports activities" are very important cultural genes. Whether it is Tsinghua University's emphasis on students' physical health in the past, or the comprehensive development of young people's "morality, intelligence, physical beauty and labor" in the context of the times, the design team chose the history of Tsinghua Sports School to focus on depicting. The historical exhibition has been injected with vitality because of the moral subject of "sports", and the

Tsinghua sports spirit is displayed in a fluid and rich layer through design. The historical environment at that time is restored through scene shaping, in order to allow visitors to have a deeper memory and a more immersive viewing experience. And through the design of the plot, the exhibits, the "remaining fragments of the past order", are placed in a new contextual order (see Fig. 3 and 4).

Fig. 3. The display space about the campus sport spirit in the University History Museum 1 (photo source: author photo)

Fig. 4. The display space about the campus sport spirit in the University History Museum 2 (photo source: author photo)

In the second exhibition hall, there is a separate memorial space related to the event in the original exhibition design plan. The main purpose of the design is to be in this area, build a about the event, from past to now, break the existing one-way event line, and through different from other space material for display difference, is given priority to with a mirror reflective material, through multi-level graphic display, image, interactive display, form the event cultural echo memory. By constructing the memory field of pure the event culture, activating the emotion and memory of persistent events covered by great history, thus a new exhibition order and connection can be established (see Fig. 5 and 6).

Fig. 5. Memorial space design (drawn by design team)

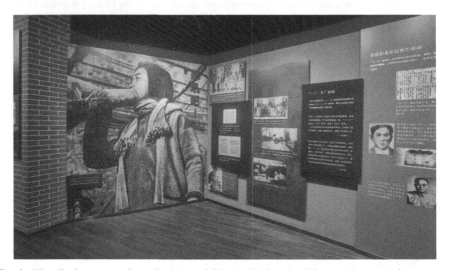

Fig. 6. The display space about the Memorial in the University History Museum (photo source: author photo)

2.3 The Innovation

The evolution of genes is also often subject to mutations, bringing new changes.

In the transmission of university cultural genes, new content and design methods are reflected in every update of the university history museum. The university history museum is different from the general resident exhibitions. It has a certain frequency of updating the design.

The better the development of a school, the greater the probability that it will be updated on the anniversary of the school anniversary such as 5 years, 20 years and 100 years. Because of the rapid accumulation of development content such as training methods and research results in each generation of universities, and the development of Chinese universities is often closely integrated with national development, the occurrence and accumulation of "innovation" is very fast.

In the display design, innovative display methods for "things" are constantly increasing, but at the same time, it also breeds a display form that is "innovative" for the past. That is to use the creation of artistic design to display and explain, what is achieved is the communication between souls and the transmission of information.

In the university history museum, the most difficult thing to display is the "invisible carrier" mentioned above - the university spirit, etc. There is no specific material form. In the display design of the university history museum, because of the way the space itself narrates history. It is artistic, so in each update, the designer tries to present some university history, full of contemporary spirit and aesthetics, to the audience again through art through the creation of artworks.

In the Tsinghua university history museum, the head sculpture of the early president of Tsinghua University, the large-scale sculpture of Tsinghua heroes and the miniature sculptures of the "Four Great Mentors of Chinese Studies", the large-scale handmade tapestry work "Lotus Pond Moonlight" and The graphic design pattern of the Tsinghua school flower "Bauhinia" used to decorate the ceiling of the second floor of the School History Museum and other art works from non-university history are on display. Among these art and design works, the research on the correlation between commemorative sculpture works and commemorative space and memory is the most mature.

In a general interpretation, a "monument" is defined as a large man-made object built to preserve the memory of something/someone. According to Wu Hong's article "The 'Monument' in Global Art", can commemorative sculptures only be huge, permanent and in public spaces? This is a clear example in the newly-added sculpture of the "Four Great Teachers of Chinese Studies" in the History Museum of Tsinghua University. In the exhibition space of the school history museum this time, the work will be displayed for a long time in the size of the entire group of sculptures that do not exceed 1200 mm in length, height and width. The sculpture placed in the exhibition space of the first chapter of the University History Museum, although the scale is reduced, but in the atmosphere of the exhibition hall and related historical background introduction, whether it is the four depicted and commemorated by the sculpture itself A great master of Chinese studies, and even about the Tsinghua Institute of Chinese Studies, at the time, it was fortunate that a group of such outstanding tutors represented by Liang Qichao, Chen Yinke, Wang Guowei, and Zhao Yuan were able to promote Tsinghua School and even China's academic independence to go further and further. The history of is more clearly presented.

The author believes that in the exhibition space of the school history museum, the miniature version of the sculptures of the "Four Great Mentors of Chinese Studies" is displayed on the spirit of the four great men Academic pursuits have become a gene of the era, being displayed and retrospected, and because of this emphasis, the viewer is allowed to interpret and reflect when "watching" (see Fig. 7).

Fig. 7. The picture of the sculpture in the University History Museum (Photo source: Author photo)

3   Conclusion

"The people we are today are by no means the people of today, they must be people of the past. The evolution of the physique gave the me of yesterday to the me of today, and the transmission of culture also gave the me of yesterday to the me of today. Through 'evolution' and 'transmission', we live in yesterday and today, it is yesterday that determines today, and today also continues yesterday" [5].

Through the exploration of the inheritance method of cultural genes, the author believes that the university history museum is one of the symbols of the inheritance of university cultural genes. University cultural genes have a better and more stable carrier form in university history museums, and cultural genes have become an important source of design expression and content for university history museums.

At the same time, based on the inheritance method of cultural genes, the author believes that for the display and dissemination of cultural genes of a university, from curatorial script to display design, "inheritance (copy), selection and innovation" are the three main design thinking directions of designers. University is an important field of world cultural education. We cultivate young talents in the university who are beneficial to the future of the world. It is equally important to use display design to convey the precious spiritual civilization of the university while inheriting the tangible material civilization. And establishing the brand heritage of each university's culture contributes to the diversity of the world's universities, thereby maintaining academic vitality and academic uniqueness.

The curation and design of the university history museum is a search and expression of university brand culture. In the display design practice of the university history museum, the author believes that searching for a brand's cultural genes and in-depth study is an important source of brand display. It is the content of the brand display and the design basis of the brand display.

The current research is more about the influence and association of cultural genes on the cultural content of a brand, but the design method of cultural genes cutting into the display of cultural genes itself still requires us to further research, experiment and try. The author hopes that through the display design of the university history museum, we can get new enlightenment on the display design method, so as to better promote the display design quality and content of the brand culture.

References

1. Blackmor, S.: The Meme Machine, 1st edn., p. 19. Jilin People's Publishing House, Changchun (2001)
2. Pinker, S.: The Language Instinct: How the Mind Creates Language, 1st edn., p. 252. Zhejiang People's Publishing House, Zhengjiang (2015)
3. Yang, L.: Research on the Development Trend of Contemporary Western Museums. Xueyuan Publishing House, Beijing (2005)
4. Qin, Y.: University History Museum Design Study - Tsinghua University History Museum as an Example. Tsinghua University (2009)
5. Wu, Q.: The Theory of Cultural Genes, 1st edn., p. 55. The Commercial Press, Beijing China (2017)

Digital Museum Visualization Digital System Based on Big Data Technology

ZiQiong Yang[1], Rui Xu[1,2(✉)], and JinMeng Zhang[1]

[1] School of Art and Design, Fuzhou University of International Studies and Trade, Fuzhou 350200, China
635524937@qq.com
[2] The Graduate Institute of Design Science, Tatung University, Taipei, Taiwan

Abstract. With the development of various electronic and computer technologies, augmented reality With the establishment of (AR) technology, virtual reality technology (VR), artificial intelligence (AI), big data technology, and the concept of meta universe, it is imperative to deepen the cooperation between electronic information technology and various industries. Therefore, in the era of big data, how to manage and use big data scientifically and efficiently has become an issue of great concern to all walks of life. This article attempts to overcome some of the shortcomings of the current traditional museum display design in the modern and contemporary digital era, and proposes a digital museum visualization digital system that includes the concept of a museum display design model based on digital technology and big data technology. The system will fully integrate computer technology, such as big data platform, virtual reality technology, and multimedia technology, and will perceive, collect, process, analyze and store data in various links of the museum according to the characteristics of museum big data. Based on this, the system will also use advanced visualization technology to present the processing results and analysis results of museum big data to users in various forms, involving three parts: the client, the content management server, and the database. Through preliminary investigation and related experiments, the results show that the system can accelerate the transformation and upgrading of traditional museums, and to a certain extent can improve the economic and social benefits of museums.

Keywords: Digital museum · Visualization technology · Digitization · Digital art · Exhibition design

1 Introduction

Museums, like a train passing through time tunnel, have always been a bridge as a cultural center: the traditional future is an existence that can't be ignored, which represents the local historical and cultural flavor, and also bears a stage of historical and cultural inheritance, and can invisibly reflect the spiritual and cultural thickness of a city, a region and a country. The function of museum is the main way to meet social needs, realize social values and interact with society. Including collection, protection, research, dissemination, exhibition, etc., one of its important missions is to spread and inherit the traditional excellent culture, so as to make the cultural relics collection glow with greater value. Museums collect the past, shape the present and inspire the future. It has the power of connecting the past, present and future three time dimensions. Social practice in every historical stage of human society is inseparable from the basis of historical conditions and the reference of historical experience [10].

In the ever-changing technological update and iteration, it has penetrated into all social cells without exception, and intelligent products represented by digital museums have emerged. And it has greatly changed the appearance of traditional museums. Compared with traditional museums, digital museums are the products of the protection, research, development and utilization of cultural heritage in the information age under the new situation, and become a brand-new way of cultural communication, which is characterized by interactivity, playfulness, virtuality and openness. Think about the problem from the perspective of visitors, Introduce scientific and intelligent solutions to the needs of visitors.

In this digital age, the museum is no longer a storehouse or display space for cultural relics, but it is gradually developing towards perception, inheritance, permanence, sharing and portability. To a large extent, the museum is also gradually turning the previous traditional, rigid and old-fashioned pronouns into vulgarity, showing people as a complex. Use the interaction with culture to arouse visitors' emotions, and pay attention to "people-oriented, emotional people".

From the visitor's point of view, although the entities exhibited in traditional museums are more friendly and appealing, compared with the limitations of space, time and region of traditional museums, digital museums have broken through these barriers. Using visualization technology, augmented reality (AR) technology, virtual reality technology (VR), artificial intelligence (AI) and holographic projection technology to display some more comprehensive cultural relics can bring visitors a sense of being there. With the progress of the times, Apple introduced a new function, iBeacon technology, which was installed on the OS for mobile devices (IOS 7) released in September 2013 to meet the requirement that people can accurately locate in closed places. IBEACON technology can replace the positioning scheme of GPS indoors [4] accurately and plan the viewing route for users. From the point of view of cultural relics protection, the two are mainly differences in exhibit carriers. There are many kinds of cultural relics left over from ancient China. If exposed to the air for a long time and some of them are exposed to the flashing lights of visitors, it will inevitably lead to unfavorable conditions such as color degradation. The digital museum formed by blending digital technology with museums can copy or virtually restore cultural relics and scenes through holographic projection, digital sand table, VR, AR and other technologies. Fully display its history, culture and connotation, without the help of actual objects, visitors can fully appreciate the beauty of cultural relics through the projected pictures, detailed drawings and 3D drawings. From the perspective of cross-regional appreciation, compared with traditional museums, digital museums enable people to stay at home and share resources across regions. See the diverse history and culture of various places; For the current epidemic prevention and control, the mass gathering is reduced, and all kinds of rich resources are shared with the public through space. In terms of education, digital museums can promote cultural exchange and dissemination to the greatest extent. Traditional local museums need to open and close the museum due to time constraints, while in contrast, Digital museums circumvent this problem.

With the popularization of digital technology, such as Metropolitan Museum of Art in New York, Detroit Art Museum, Palace Museum in Beijing, National Museum of China, etc., museums of all sizes are repositioning, integrating digital technology into them, becoming more interactive, flexible, adaptable and mobile, and using digital technology to make cultural relics "speak". Civilization is colorful because of communication, Civilizations are enriched by mutual learning. The formation and development of museums have convinced modern people that mainstream museums are real material records from art treasures, historical relics, natural specimens and other human beings, while digital technology museums are all curious people behind the walls, a digital world composed of those pictures and data. It seems that it is not the same as the museum, but also youthful and energetic. This strongly shows that the deep logic of the integration of museums and digital technology is two basic behaviors of human beings, and with the progress of digital technology, it is becoming an important driving force for the development of museums today [3]. Using digital technology, museums can flexibly change the displayed content. This not only enriches people's visual experience, but also improves the exhibition effect of the museum and adds a more effective management mode. Literature Review.

2   Theoretical Basis

2.1   Digital Museum

1) *Analysis of the Current Status of Digital Museum.*

With the development of modern science and technology, the relationship between science and production is getting closer and closer. Science and technology, as a productive force, are playing an increasingly important role in all walks of life, and museums in cultural industries are no exception. Big data, multimedia technology, smart wearable technology, information technology, digitalization and visualization technology are increasingly being used in museum exhibitions. The dynamic, interactive, immersive, convenient, online, experiential and other activation expressions brought by simulation, virtual and exhibition-free technologies can bring the audience a fresher feeling. For the museum exhibition of Chen Zhong, intangible history is combined with cultural relics and historic sites, which provides new technical support for showing history and activating and displaying cultural relics. The director of the Art Museum of the Central Academy of Fine Arts pointed out: "In the 14th Five-Year Plan," culture "was mentioned 47 times and" innovation "was mentioned 51 times, which means that museums, as cultural production units, must build a new knowledge system. Become the power source of knowledge production and cultivate people's creative thinking."

Since the beginning of the 21st century, the international community has also made new orientation and requirements for museums. In 2015, the 38th General Conference of UNESCO adopted the Recommendation on Protecting and Strengthening Museums and

Collections, Their Diversity and Social Functions, calling on museums around the world to unite together to face new challenges and opportunities. This requirement for museum sociality is more prominent and urgent in the post-epidemic era [10]. The museum has also become an important out let for spreading culture.

Digital museum is a special form of information art in the current historical stage, and it is a new museum form in the transition from industrialization to informationization of human society [1]. On the premise of not tampering with the nature of traditional museums, it carries out technological innovation on them. At the moment of the epidemic, according to the report of China Research Network, "the epidemic may cause 13% of museums in the world to close permanently", Wang Kunxin, deputy secretary-general of the World Tourism Alliance, said: "Digital museums have turned crisis into opportunity, and digital museums have done it in a real sense. The exhibition will not end, the service will not be closed, and the wonderful events will not be discounted." At the moment of epidemic prevention and control, it has fundamentally prevented visitors from close contact. More and more museums have begun to study and explore digital museums, Some theoretical and practical achievements have been made, and the digital wave of museums has also been listed as the focus of work. The implementation of digital museums is conducive to the spread of history and culture and the development of the museum industry.

Under the background of digitalization, the big data platform is used to integrate the historical data of regional museums, to promote the development of small and medium-sized museums in this region and the rapid construction of digitalization, and to realize the regional balance of museum construction. At the same time, the construction of digital platform should not only be limited to data fusion, but also update new cultural relics in real time when they are introduced. Meet the needs of intelligent museum construction, so as to achieve long-term development.

At present, the digital exhibition of museums has formed the exhibition mode of "enlarged space exhibition" and "virtual exhibition space" [9].

2) *Augmented Space Display in Digital Museum.*

Due to the inflexible display of exhibits in traditional museums, there will be a lack of emotion in displaying exhibits in digital museums. These phenomena prompt the real space in museums to integrate virtual space, which is a brand-new space with interactive and navigation features.

Through the digital intelligent positioning system, visitors can choose their favorite exhibits and enter their virtual information space, and the system will give visitors exhibits information tips. For example, when visiting Jingdezhen Ceramic Culture Digital Museum, when visitors stay in front of a piece of pottery, visitors enter the space of reality and virtual docking through the digital intelligent navigation system. The digital intelligent navigation system will provide relevant information about this pottery. If the same dynasty or related exhibits as this pottery are nearby, the digital intelligent navigation system will advise visitors to visit and plan the route to guide the related exhibits area. If visitors are not interested, then the system will respect visitors' choices and will not recommend them accordingly. From the above case analysis, How to establish the interface of the digital positioning system, the modules for visiting exhibits and their interactive relationship reflects the regenerative value of the display and provides opportunities for the personalization and flexibility of the display.

The guiding way of "expanding space display" embodies "people-oriented, serving the people". Visitors can compare physical information in reality with material information in virtual space, so as to increase visitors' interest in exhibits and provide a software and hardware platform for museum education and research [11]. Under such circumstances, visitors, You can explore the mystery of the exhibits more deeply, and observe the subject and the details of the subject at 360 in the simplest and clearest way.

The digital intelligent navigation system of the museum's "augmented space display" not only provides visitors with personalized and diversified display and interaction modules, but also helps visitors explore interesting visiting spots in real space, making visitors' viewing routes more reasonable [11] (Fig. 1).

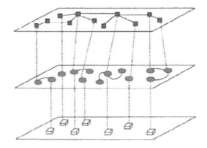

Fig. 1. Dynamic formation of virtual space in augmented space

3) *Virtual exhibition space in digital museum*

The development of smart wearable device technology and high-tech in contemporary society has put forward new requirements and goals for museums, which will eventually lead to the renewal of the exhibition discipline. Therefore, the exhibition design will certainly produce a design civilization corresponding to it in the digital age.

With the rapid development of digital economy, virtual display design has also ushered in a vigorous spring. Virtual exhibition space is one of the components of digital museum, which is mainly divided into: fully immersive virtual exhibition system, semi-immersive virtual exhibition system and non-immersive virtual exhibition system. It consists of modern digital display equipment, Virtual Reality technology, digital media technology, multimedia technology and other digital technologies create an entity display space, among which virtual reality technology (English name: virtual reality, abbreviated as VR) is a brand-new practical technology developed in the 20th century. Virtual reality technology includes computer, electronic information, simulation technology, The basic realization way is to simulate the virtual. Environment by computer, thus giving people a sense of environmental immersion [6]. Make the system in the digital museum more humanized, better meet the individual needs of visitors, and truly achieve "people-oriented, serving the people." The use of VR technology has increased the use of smart wearable devices in museums. At the same time, it also improves the grade and style of the pavilion. Undoubtedly, the combination of popular science and technology has gradually become the popular trend of museum display. Virtual exhibition system can form an independent, barrier-free and immersive "museum" that can communicate with the audience with the support of interconnection.

To achieve this effect presentation, it is necessary to import data into VR glasses for users. Data in virtual reality technology refers to raw materials that have not been processed, and effective knowledge classification will contribute to the value of data. Museums have rich and complicated data of display contents, The content display from offline to online needs reasonable Categorical Data, and the original data can be effectively sorted by classifying or grouping the specific display content according to some attributes [7]. The way of Knowledge Classification after classifying these data is based on the classification, naming and grading of museum collections on the one hand, For example, according to the texture, use, age, source and country of the collection, ensure the scientificity and practicability of data collection and classification; On the other hand, the classification of digital characteristics of data can be divided into text, sound, video, pictures, three-dimensional models and other forms. Different museum collections and contents need to consider different data presentation methods at the same time. For example, ceramic collections are more suitable for data knowledge presentation of three-dimensional models, so as to ensure that the contents of museum collections are optimally adapted to online learning of the public [8].

For example, when people browse all kinds of cultural relics in museums, they can't observe ancient cultural relics at close range and for a long time due to the limitation of conditions and time. In order to solve the space and time limitations of the history museum [5], the traditional museum needs additional design to increase the exhibition space, rearrange the display order, and stipulate the height of the showcase according to the size of the exhibits. Width and size, the exhibits should be arranged neatly in the showcase, and the showcase should also be arranged neatly in the museum. In this process, apart from other factors, the consumption is enormous in terms of materials, manpower, material resources and time, while the digital museum uses virtual reality technology to solve the problems of small space and complicated display design of the former. And provide visitors with a brand-new experience. If they are not satisfied with static, there are dynamic vr full-motion video and AR experiences to choose from.

Visitors can enjoy the interactive explanations provided by the museum when browsing the exhibits in the digital museum, so that visitors can feel the immersive visiting experience in it, truly make the audience interact face-to-face with cultural relics on the spot, and further enhance the interest, interactivity and flexibility of the exhibition. At present, many museums are gradually entering the digital age and introducing advanced science and technology.

For example, VR technology, the modern digital museum introduced its technology and created VR venues. Using high-definition VR technology in VR venues, with the help of 3D scanning, VR, 360 panorama and other technologies, visitors can break through the limitations of time and space, cross the Millennium history, become ancient people in the scene, walk, touch and experience the customs and historical relics of the selected dynasties. It brings visual, tactile and auditory feelings and forms an interactive experience with all props and cultural relics. At the same time, it also provides some smart wearable devices for the audience to choose independently. After browsing the exhibits, the audience can search the exhibits information through inquiry and create with some digital application software. Rearrange the exhibition according to your own understanding of the exhibition after visiting it. These all depend on the development of computer graphics and computer visualization technology in today's science and technology.

2.2 Visualization Technology

Visualization has gradually developed into a comprehensive discipline involving data mining, human-computer interaction, computer graphics and so on. There are many kinds of visualizations: Data visualization, information visualization, content visualization, etc. In daily life, information visualization and data visualization are the most common contacts. How to apply data visualization in digital museum? It needs to retrieve data and materials related to exhibits from multiple websites and systems for cleaning by using interfaces or other searching and grabbing technologies. Convert the cleaned data into a format acceptable by association rule algorithm, and at the same time, conduct topic mining, find out the main viewpoints and discourses that are relatively concentrated in the data, analyze the captured and cleaned data, and try to find out the valuable information and rules hidden behind the data, and finally save them in the database in the museum.

The value of data visualization lies in that it not only belongs to experts, but also breaks the phenomenon of "information island" and slow data transmission in the past. Instead, it pays more attention to serving people. No matter how the data is mined and analyzed, the ultimate goal is to present the information contained in the data to the viewer in the most concise and understandable way. Let the viewer experience the situation, development and story behind the information through data visualization design. To achieve this goal, data visualization needs a common requirement, that is, accurate, efficient, concise and comprehensive transmission of information and knowledge, so that the data can speak for itself as much as possible.

It can be used in the digital museum to compare the number of online and offline visits, the statistics of the number of visitors to the museum during the offline period, the comparison between the number of visitors and previous data, and the comparison between the economic development of the museum and other museums in the past year, or even in the current epidemic situation. Visitors' body temperature scanning and feedback in the museum have greatly improved people's work efficiency.

2.3 Digitization

With the people's growing need for a better life gradually improving, based on Maslow's hierarchy of needs theory, which mentioned that the demand for knowledge, study and aesthetics between respect demand and self-realization demand wants to be realized, the museum in the modern sense appears. It will exist as a public space of service and perception to seek knowledge as a whole and meet its aesthetic needs, and it will also integrate communication, aesthetics, collection, research, appreciation, education, culture, etc., and become an important part of urban cultural construction, which is conducive to improving the aesthetic needs of the audience. The development of museums is also in urgent need of digital assistance [2]. To appreciate the exquisiteness of artifacts, witness the development of history and absorb the essence of the times, the emergence of digital museums has largely met people's growing spiritual and cultural needs.

What is the digital transformation of museums? That is to say, using computer information technology to transform the information of cultural relics into measurable, editable digital and data forms, and then using these data to build a suitable digital model, combining with data information such as words, sounds, images and colors, so as to achieve the purposes of archiving, browsing and management. The digital museum management system based on 3D data improves the management level of the museum and realizes the synchronous promotion of social, economic and cultural benefits of the museum. Under the restriction of space, time and place, a large number of wonderful exhibits can only be put behind the scenes in the online physical museum. "According to statistics, there are about 350,000 registered cultural relics sites in China, with 12 million pieces of cultural relics collected in various museums, and a large number of cultural relics unearthed every year. However, due to the limitations of time, space, place, protection conditions, storage conditions and protection technology, only a small number of cultural relics can be exhibited and provided for research. How to better display the museum's functions of exhibition, appreciation, education, culture and research, and how to better serve the society and the public, and promote the museum's own development and younger development are the major challenges facing modern society.

1) *Digitization of cultural relics*

Part of the concept of digital protection of cultural relics is to use digital technology to collect all-round data of cultural relics, and each cultural relic has an online model, so that the public can visit the cultural relics on the Internet, watch them through video playback, and the public can inquire about the information of the cultural relics they want to know, so as to fully understand their existence time and parameters, etc. Let the public visit the exhibits at home and get spiritual and cultural satisfaction. For example, digital technology can restore the true historical features of Yuanmingyuan, and digital means such as panoramic shooting, 3D data collection and modeling, and artificial intelligence can be used to let the audience truly understand the history of Yuanmingyuan and see the Yuanmingyuan in history. The restoration of Yuanmingyuan by digital technology not only presents the rich cultural connotations of royal garden culture and gardening art to the audience, but also shows the value and charm of China's cultural heritage represented by Yuanmingyuan.

When the digitization of cultural relics is realized, the reuse of space level makes it easier to watch exhibitions-National Museum of China, Detroit Museum, etc. can appear in exhibition halls all over the world after digitization; Some exhibits that can't be fully displayed due to limited space, such as long scroll exhibits in calligraphy and painting exhibitions, murals, etc., with the help of digital technology, Not only can we get a glimpse of the whole picture for people, but we can even let the audience enjoy it in a slowly unfolding mode and restore the original appreciation mode of the long scroll. Data reuse to gain higher freedom, thus bringing more fluent knowledge structure and narrative logic to visitors.

For example; when organizing exhibitions; we are often troubled by some exhibits; some exhibits have already appeared of other exhibitions; and an exhibit is the main part for this historical story for this dynasty; which runs through a period for historical development; but the exhibition for another period also needs this exhibit. This will make the staff face such a dilemma in the state of exhibition, and the arrival of digital technology will solve this dilemma, because cultural relics can be used as "doppelgangers" of cultural relics themselves under the "replication" of digital technology.

2) *Digital collection management*

The cultural relics in the museum have a history of one hundred years or even one thousand years, which is unique and rare.

In the past, cultural relics were managed and protected by formulating systematic protection measures, but as time goes by, cultural relics will be damaged for various reasons. Using digital technology to scan the cultural relics in three dimensions and retrieve the historical information contained in the cultural relics can keep the information forever. It is not enough for a digital museum to have a large number of digital collections. It not only needs an easy-to-present way and easy-to-display technology, but also needs to consider its practicality and aesthetics while satisfying the functionality from the perspective of product concept, so as to enhance the browsing experience of users. And as the next new cultural product of the Internet. At the same time, with the development of knowledge sharing resources in China, the economy and society are promoted to turn to paper-based information, offline to online, manual to system, individual control to big data control, improving information exchange and efficiency while taking into account digital data and analysis.

Digital collection and management of collections is the basis of digital museum's survival. By using digital means, the visualization display and management in the tube are more standardized and normalized, and the collection database is established, including collection shooting, scanning, sound recording, animation production and image color output. With the support of digital technology, On-line service and collection display have been greatly improved in efficiency, and the contradiction between collection protection and collection utilization in the museum has been well solved, so that every treasure can be displayed to visitors, and every treasure can be best protected.

At present, through digital technology, precious artifacts are moved to the digital museum on the line, thus breaking through the tradition, breaking the time, space and regional restrictions, shortening the distance between cultural relics and the public, accelerating the integration of tradition and modernity and promoting the stable development of museums. As far as the present situation is concerned, The digital construction of museum cultural relics protection and management can be divided into two links. First of all, it is necessary to collect the specific data of cultural relics, and master the external shape, patterns, colors, internal inscriptions and time characteristics of cultural relics, so as to facilitate the classification of cultural relics and contribute to data entry, arrangement and collection in the future. Collection can be divided into two categories, The first is the collection of text data; The second is the collection of cultural relics entity images.

Secondly, simply process and use the collected information, sort out the collected information, and then enter it into the system. While completing information management, resources can also be shared, which is conducive to communication and reference among museums and better protection of cultural relics.

3) *Dissemination "digitalization"*

Digitalization not only helps the development of Wenchuang, but also plays an important guiding role in Wenchuang product marketing and museum brand communication.

In the current epidemic situation, the surrounding areas of traditional museums will face the phenomenon of "pressing boxes" and slow sales, which has caused troubles for the economic development of museums. The emergence of digital museums has driven the sales of these surrounding areas, and the public can place orders for their favorite products through the smart phone line, which just meets the current online shopping craze and designs an exclusive APP and logo for the museum. Integration in the surroundings can promote the promotion of museum brands.

As early as 2012, Baidu Encyclopedia cooperated with eight famous museums such as Comrade Liu Shaoqi Memorial Hall and Shanghai Museum in depth, and used VR virtual reality technology to make realistic simulation effects on rare exhibits such as the animal head of Yuanmingyuan, and realized the synchronous display of computer and mobile phone. Among them, 3D scanning laser technology is another technological revolution after GPS technology, which is also called real-life replication technology. The obtained real-life data has the characteristics of high sampling rate, high resolution, high precision, full view, full coverage and true three-dimensional, which significantly improves the public's experience.

Focusing on the current education era, how to make students better improve efficiency and save time won't worry about the high cost and considering where to go to a certain museum after careful consideration. The Digital Museum has launched to enjoy the spectacular terracotta warriors and horses and the beauty of the Louvre anytime and anywhere through the Internet. Appreciating the magnificent relics left by history for people also improves people's learning efficiency with the development of the information age. Using the network platform can let the younger generation know about China's history and culture, effectively improve their cultural literacy and aesthetic standards, and the elegant taste and profound connotation of traditional culture can also meet the cultural pursuit of young people.

3 Overview of Digital Museum Visualization Digital System Based on Big Data Technology

The museum itself is the most intuitive and concise way as the main link with society, which can reflect the social phenomenon of a period of time. From this, it can be seen that the visualization book is brought by the museum itself, and it is gradually formed with the digitalization of the museum. When the data visualization is cited in the museum, When visitor data, exhibit data, museum data, collection management data and so on are included in the scope of retrieval and collection data, how to better reflect the function of these data, present these data more intuitively and give full play to the value of these data becomes a problem worthy of consideration at present. Museum visual data system can also better guide visitors to find problems through data.

The digital museum visualization digital system based on big data technology designed in this paper is classified management-centralized comparison design mode. Each department mainly collects and conducts the first screening based on the data of people, collections and museum economy, and then manages the collected visitors, collections and museum data separately. Then the data will be collated and fed back to the general management for comparison.

The collection scope of the visualization system covers the collection data, visitors' traffic, behavior capture of visitors in the exhibition area, click-through rate of exhibits information, sales around Wenchuang and other data, as well as the three fundamentals of museum collection, analysis and cultural communication. Digital museum staff can collect data through various resource channels such as the Internet entrance, the on-site service entrance of the exhibition hall and the entrance of the local area network in the museum, so that the staff can "overlook" the data and observe and study it through the general data office, and accurately, timely, comprehensively and comprehensively reflect the real-time operation of the museum. It can be expected that, Through the long-term accumulation, research and analysis of the above-mentioned data, the data portrait of the public service effect of the museum is obtained, and the trend forecast and business forecast of the development of museum culture communication are obtained, which will provide the evaluation and decision-making basis for the museum to implement the precise service based on the museum collections and audience needs.

Realize the management and display of various visual modules such as museum records, collection management, exhibition information, activity management, ticket management, digital assets, and cultural and creative shops [12].

This design system covers subsystems such as exhibition scheduling, staff management system in the exhibition hall, exhibits and appliances management system, etc., and realizes the correlation of data in the exhibition hall. Users can bind their identity information through their mobile phones and log in with one click to obtain individual knowledge and information sharing.

When visitors enter the exhibition hall, they will first monitor their body temperature by automatic portrait temperature measuring machine, and the monitoring data will be uploaded to the department personnel for analysis and integration at different times. Then, visitors will log in to the local area network of the museum through their mobile phones for binding, authentication and identification, select the exhibition hall area according to their own preferences, and the system will make route planning according to the visitors' options. And attach an explanation function. The system will collect visitors' behaviors in front of each exhibit, analyze and count the data such as the number of times of using relevant smart wearable devices in the exhibition hall and the number of visitors' clicks on the exhibits, and upload them to the total data office for centralized comparison.

4   Concept of Museum Display Design Mode Based on Digital Technology

Today's museums are facing problems:

Improvement of visitors' experience demand With the rapid development of contemporary economy, science and technology, people's demand for spiritual level is increasing day by day, showing a diversified trend. The purpose of people's exhibition is not just to get the information conveyed by exhibits as in the past. Under the influence of "user experience design" in the information age and "experience economy" in the economic field, the word "experience" has attracted more and more public attention. At present, there is no universally accepted definition of "experience". Experience is explained in Modern Chinese Dictionary as "knowing things through practice and personal experience". In Phenomenology of Perception, maurice merleau-ponty interprets experience as "the movement of human body in the environment establishes contact with the world, making the perception of the body become a series of persistent experiences, And perception is to perceive the world through five senses" [14]. Therefore, the research of museum exhibition space design should pay attention to human behavior, psychological activity, emotional level and space creation in the museum as consideration factors, and join the museum space design, so that visitors can participate in the exhibition activities in a brand-new interactive way.

4.1   Emotional Experience Level Design Based on Visitors

Museum exhibition design mode should pay attention to emotional design of exhibition design according to the emotional level of participants. The emotional experience of visitors is a high-level experience triggered by human perception. Museum emotional experience can be divided into three levels: instinct level, behavior level and reflection level [15]. The instinctive layer is the instinctive behavior reaction triggered by the visitors' sensory experience at first, and the first real reaction obtained by receiving the physical information through the senses. Behavior layer is a process for visitors to feel and experience the museum, which urges designers not only to consider the features of space modeling, color expression, illustration and typesetting, but also to pay attention to the space design. Emotional experience for visitors. The reflection layer is a kind of psychological activity of visitors after the exhibition, and the feedback and evaluation after visiting the museum, so that the museum can revise and improve according to the feedback of visitors.

4.2   Design Based on Space Atmosphere Digital Museums Need to Convey Corresponding

Information through virtual objects, interpret scenes with space, and situational narrative space can not only provide functional space for visitors, but also bring them into corresponding situations, so that visitors can personally experience the designer's scene conception or historical and cultural plot. The scene organically combines the cross-media narration such as static images, dynamic images, sounds, words and information through digital technology, and makes use of new technologies such as sound, light and images [16], based on the integration of physical information and virtual technology, to make visitors feel more involved and experienced. From the deep cultural transmission, we should pay attention to the metaphorical design of the museum.

4.3 Building Online Display Design Based on Digital Museum

Digital museum experience activities permeate offline and online, and building an online virtual experience hall is also an important measure to spread museum culture and education. In online space, the audience intuitively understands and analyzes with the concept of spatial interaction rather than just plane interaction. Visitors are encouraged to participate in online viewing and experience, Try to maximize the connection between entity and virtual space context. The combination of online and offline gradually constitutes a new social and cultural experience and becomes an important form of museum cultural communication.

Take the Palace Museum as an example. During the current epidemic, the Palace Museum launched the "Palace Museum Exhibition" APP, opened the Palace Museum official website, the official Weibo and the official WeChat, and obtained the latest exhibition news, experienced online exhibitions, visited the 360 panoramic exhibition hall, looked at pictures and introductions of cultural relics, and watched new exhibitions on the cloud without leaving home. After downloading the APP, users will see the "Forbidden City" and its background, and the word Hui will change with the sun's rays, and enter the interface to log in. What comes into view are the exhibitions such as "Dunxing for a long time-Dunhuang Special Exhibition of the Forbidden City" and "Danchen Yonggu-600 Years after the Forbidden City was built". Users can enter the corresponding exhibitions according to their own needs, leave a message on the exhibition, and view the introduction, exhibits and 360 panorama. You can screen all exhibitions, exhibitions in progress or past, temporarily closed and upcoming exhibitions. When you enter the 360 panorama, you can show online through the instructions in the interface, and you can also learn about the key booths through the map function in the interface for transmission.

5   Conclusion

To sum up, the digital museum is leading the development direction of museums in the future. The new technologies it uses and the combination of online and offline have changed the unchangeable way of viewing exhibitions in the past, and prompted visitors to acquire knowledge and understand history more comprehensively and deeply. Guide visitors to be more active in viewing and collecting information. Digital display enables the museum's traditional cultural knowledge, with the help of modern science and technology, to go further and broaden on the road of knowledge dissemination and cultural education [13]. It meets the people's growing spiritual and cultural needs and promotes the development of China's cultural and cultural undertaking.

References

1. Yang, Y., Wang, Y.: Exploration of interactive design of digital museum based on cultural communication. Integration, innovation and development—digital museum promotes the construction of cultural power. In: Proceedings of Beijing Digital Museum Symposium 2013, pp. 187–190. Communication University of China Press, Beijing (2013)
2. Shan, X.: Some thoughts on digital technology and museum technology. Popular Lit. Art **1**(22) (2021)
3. An, S.: Super-connected museums in the digital age. Tencent Cult. **3** (2018)
4. Tube specialist: design of new model of digital museum cultural relics display. Electron. World **2**(14) (2018)
5. He, G., Yang, K., Lin, J., et al.: Research on the interactive display technology of energy stations based on Unity3D. J. Syst. Simul. **1**(10), 2626–2631 (2016)
6. Li, L.: Research on virtual reality technology and its application. Chin. Sci. Technol. J. 30–31 (2019)
7. Zhang, S., Hou, W., Wang, X.: Research on the design of popular science knowledge learning method based on augmented reality interaction. Packag. Eng. **38**(20), 48–55 (2017)
8. Huang, Q., Yin, J., Wu, Y.: Research on exhibition construction of economic digital museum——taking 360-degree panoramic virtual exhibition of Wuxi Museum as an example. Decoration **5**, 102–104 (2015)
9. Kun, Y.: Research on digital exhibition design mode of museum. In: The Road to Digitalization of Museum in 2015, pp. 341–345. 2015 Beijing Digital Museum Seminar, Beijing (2015)
10. Yu, X.: Museum's Social Responsibility and Countermeasures in Post-epidemic Era. https://doi.org/10.16607/J.CNKI.1674-6708.2021.08.022
11. Figure 1 comes from: Huang, Q., Guo, W.: The new idea of "people-oriented" exhibition in modern museums guides design (2008). https://doi.org/10.16272/J.cnki.cn11-1392/J.2008.004
12. Xia, S.: Research on the Application of information visualization online museum app. Beijing Institute of Fashion Technology, Beijing (2016)
13. Wang, X.: Application and research of digital display in museums-taking Shanxi Museum as an example. Identif. Appreciation Cult. Relics **22**, 111–113 (2022)
14. Liu, Y.: Research on experiential interior space of museum based on architectural phenomenology, vol. 2. South China University of Technology, Guangzhou (2016)
15. Hao, C.: Research on the experience design of preschool children's dining utensils based on emotion. Xi'an Polytechnic University, Xi'an (2016)
16. Liu, N., Nan, Z.: A summary of space design research from narrative perspective. Huazhong Archit. **33**(10), 23–26 (2015)

Cross-Cultural Virtual Reality and Games

A Semiotic Framework for the Analysis of Virtual Architecture in Digital Games

Gabriele Aroni[✉]

Xi'an Jiaotong-Liverpool University, Suzhou, China
Gabriele.Aroni@xjtlu.edu.cn

Abstract. This paper proposes a semiotic framework for the analysis of architecture in digital games that combines the theory of Umberto Eco of denotation and connotation in architecture with the concept of "anticipatory play" devised by Brian Upton. Virtual architecture is a central signifier in digital games, and its design heavily influences the gameplay as well as the narrative. In 3D games players interact with virtual environments that closely resemble our real architecture, and as such many of the tools we use to analyse real architecture can be successfully applied to virtual architecture as well. Through a series of examples this paper will illustrate how architectural signs in games communicate to players and how they can be used to enhance gameplay, narration, and immersion.

Keywords: Semiotics · Architecture · Digital games · Space

1 Introduction

Digital games have come a long way in their fifty years of history, so much so that even the definition of "games" can now be seen as restrictive. Players are interested in games for factors that go well beyond the simple action or competition, but now inhabit proper virtual worlds. Fortes Tondello et al.'s neurobiological enquiry into why people play games resulted in three main motivations: 1. Action orientation: players who seek competition and risk-taking; 2. Aesthetic orientation: players who enjoy exploration, the visuals of the game world and socialization; and 3. Goal orientation: players who favours the completion of activities, solving puzzles, and physically engaging experiences, such as fear [1]. As we can see from the aesthetic orientation, the interest in the visual aspect and the virtual worlds is motivation enough for players to be interested in a game. As with much of our real world, virtual worlds are made of architectural constructs. Obviously, even the *natural* part of any digital game, such as a lush forest or a grassy valley, is man-made, but many environments are inevitably populated with buildings of some sort, for gameplay or narrative reasons. How do digital game environments communicate to players? How can they allow and enhance gameplay, narration, and immersion? This paper proposes a semiotic framework for the analysis of digital games architecture, in order to understand how players decode and react to architectural signs within games, as well as offer developers a system that helps them in the design of digital games environments. This framework is based on the semiotic theories developed by Umberto Eco in regard to architecture [2], and Brian Upton as concerns digital games [3].

P.-L. P. Rau (Ed.): HCII 2022, LNCS 13312, pp. 459–467, 2022.
https://doi.org/10.1007/978-3-031-06047-2_34

2 The Aesthetics of Digital Games

Philosopher Grant Tavinor affirms that the artistic status of digital games is due to their visual qualities, as "they do have perceptual and formal structures that are the object of an aesthetic and interpretive engagement in much the same way as other artworks" and "employ much of the same aesthetic vocabulary" [4]. Reaching a similar conclusion as Fortes Tondello et al., but from an aesthetics point of view, Tavinor affirms that players are attracted to digital games by the same interests as traditional art appreciators. Indeed, the artistic component of digital games is often a cardinal element of their success, and in fact visual artists and designers usually account for almost half of the development cost of games – second only to programmers – [5–7] demonstrating the importance of the visual, and arguably architectural, aspect of digital games.

This approach to the analysis of digital games is also known as "Prop Theory", which affirms that games are not a unique medium separated from other arts due to its interactive nature, but rather a medium that shares many traits with other representative arts. For instance, in a painting we can identify oils on a canvas as a landscape or a person; papier-mâché on a theatre stage can be crafted to reproduce a building or a landscape. These are the "props", the elements of visual arts that prompt specific imagery to the viewer. Digital games are no different, not only we interpret the pixels on screens as characters, buildings, and objects, but these objects are themselves 3D or 2D models, textures, and sounds designed, crafted, and placed by the developers within the game world.

Unlike the "props" of most other media, in digital games players can interact with the environment, and as such, virtual architecture is much closer to real architecture, since it can be experienced in a way close to its real counterpart. Unlike a static photograph, we can move around a building and change our point of view as we would in real life. Even without considering the possibilities allowed by virtual reality, such as the perception of depth, we interpret the perspective representation on screen as a close representation of real architecture. Moreover, the interaction in digital games is not limited to walking and looking around, but the form of spaces, their size and shape all influence how the game is played, and as such the design of virtual architecture is rather close to the one of real architecture.

Here we can draw a parallel with the concept of *utilitas*, brought forth by Roman architect Vitruvius in his *De architectura*, the only surviving Western architectural treatise of the ancient world, written in the 1st century BCE. Vitruvius recommends that all buildings be built in a way that is appropriate to their use, location, and occupants. In digital games, virtual architecture has to be equally designed to be appropriate to the gameplay style, players and level type. The architectural design of a level of a third-person action-adventure game such as *Shadow of the Tomb Raider* [8] (see Fig. 1), where players have to jump, climb, and fight, will be different from a first-person horror game such as *Layers of Fear* [9] (see Fig. 2), where there is no combat, but rather exploration aimed at building tension. Furthermore, virtual architecture is not limited to satisfy gameplay needs, but it also determines the characterization of the environment and the tone of the game. The aforementioned *Layers of Fear* is set in a haunted mansion, which characterizes the game as horror, and would of course have been a completely different experience if the architectural background was, for instance, a colourful shopping centre.

Fig. 1. A scene from *Shadow of the Tomb Raider* © Eidos-Montréal 2018.

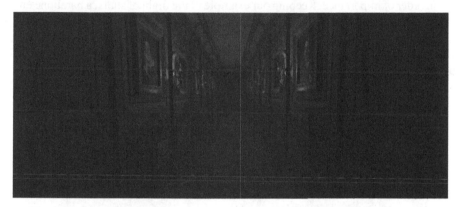

Fig. 2. A corridor of the haunted mansion in *Layers of Fear* © Blooper Team 2018.

Semiotically, we can consider virtual architecture as composed of *iconic signs*, signs that resemble their original counterpart in virtue of their formal qualities, i.e. a door in a game will look like a door in the real world since its aim is convey the message of "door". Moreover, virtual architecture, given its nature as part of a game, is always created with a meaning in mind related to players. In digital games, any prop has a dual function: one representational, similar to the oil on a canvas, and another functional to the gameplay. As much as the scenography of an opera must primarily allow for the singers to perform their role as singers, architectural elements in digital games must serve the function of gameplay. In other words, architectural signs that in the real world might be involuntary or incidental, such as deterioration or destruction, are instead planned and deliberate in virtual architecture in order to produce meaning, thus a semiotic framework of analysis is most appropriate [10].

3   The Semiotics of Virtual Architecture

3.1   Denotation and Connotation in Architecture

Based on the observations made hitherto, Umberto Eco's architectural semiotic theory of denotation and connotation is most appropriate for the analysis of virtual architecture. Eco affirms that architectural objects denote a primary function and connote a secondary "certain ideology of the function" [2]. The denotation of the function is based on the intrinsic physical properties of an object. For instance, a flight of stairs tells us that we can use it to ascend and descend by virtue of its shape, and our understanding of gravity and the space around us. An architectural sign can also connote a symbolic, additional meaning. Eco considers the symbolic aspect of architecture a function in and of itself, and the denomination of "primary" and "secondary" must be understood in the fact that the connotative function "rest[s] on the denotation of the primary function" [2], rather than in order of importance. Keeping our example of the flight of stairs, a barebone emergency staircase in a high-rise condo denotes the same function as the highly elaborate monumental staircase in Palazzo Barberini in Rome, designed by Francesco Borromini in 1633: they are both composed of a series of steps in a shape and size that allows for humans to easily climb or descend between floors of a building (see Fig. 3).

Fig. 3. The monumental staircase in Palazzo Barberini, Rome, designed by Francesco Borromini in 1633 (left), and an emergency staircase in a high-rise building (right) (photos by the author).

However, it is not hard to notice how the appearance of the two staircases differs. Evidently, while the primary denotative function is the same in both, the secondary connotative function led to visually very different designs: a monumental, colonnaded, spiral staircase in Palazzo Barberini, and a simply painted straight staircase in the high-rise condo. Naturally, this difference is also due to their primary denotative function. Borromini's staircase is one of the two main staircases in the palace, and the principal way of moving between floors, whereas the emergency staircase is designed to be used only in exceptional circumstances. As such, the secondary connotative function is a consequence of the primary one: firstly, the staircase is shaped as such for the necessity of fulfilling the function of a staircase, and secondly it is designed in a certain way based on its use and the image it wants to convey.

The connotative aspect of architecture is often used in corporate buildings to communicate their ideology. Let us take for instance banks, often some of the most notable buildings in many cities. In the city of Toronto, Canada, we can witness the changes in styles related to what the banks wanted to communicate in the span of a few blocks. From the opulently decorated neoclassical Bank of Montreal designed by Frank Darling and Samuel George Curry in 1886, displaying the wealth of the institution to its clients; to the massive and sparsely decorated tower of the Canadian Bank of Commerce, designed by York & Sawyer and Darling & Pearson in 1931, right after the Wall Street financial crash, aiming at demonstrating solidity and security, signs of a reliable institution that can be trusted, rather than extravagant expenditure; to finally the glass high-rise of the First Canadian Place, designed by B+H Architects in 1975, which, in line with the current trend, aims to represent a transparent, clear, and honest institution. Naturally, we can see the same techniques used in digital games to connote narrative clues to the players. For instance, in the cyberpunk RPG *Deus Ex: Mankind Divided* [11], the corporations of the dystopian future when the game is set manifest their power with impenetrable monolithic structures (see Fig. 4).

Fig. 4. The Palisade Blade data-archiving facility building dominates the skyline of Prague in *Deus Ex: Mankind Divided* © Eidos-Montréal 2016.

3.2 Anticipatory Play

Brian Upton was the lead designer of the first *Rainbow Six* [12], a tactical first-person shooter considered a classic, and which spurred a very popular franchise still alive today. He bases his semiotic theory of digital games in his experience as a level and game designer, and brings forth the concept of "anticipatory play" to examine how virtual game spaces communicate to players. Upton affirms that in both digital and non-digital games, the planning, expectation, and anticipation of events is as important as the action itself. In his opinion "Anticipatory play gives us a model for talking about the non-interactive beats of a game such as *Rainbow Six* – those moments when the player stops, looks, and thinks about what he is doing. Instead of defining a play experience entirely by what the player is allowed to do, anticipatory play allows us to focus instead on what opportunities any play experience provides for elaborated analysis, contemplation, and reflection." [3] Anticipatory play is thus expressed mostly through the architectural design in the game: "For example, if you are playing a shooter, a blank corridor is less exciting than a corridor with an open door on one side, even if there are no enemies beyond the door. The anticipatory chain triggered by the open door ("Is there an ambush ahead? I have to move carefully. I can't see anything. Can I peek around the corner?") is an interesting experience even though the play is taking place entirely inside your head." [3].

Hence, anticipatory play is particularly apt to analyse how architectural spaces in digital games are read by players, and constitutes a useful instrument in the planning of game levels. Architectural cues in games can be instructions for the player on how to play, they give indications on where to go next, or which areas might be dangerous and which ones are safe. In a role-playing-game the sight of a city is usually interpreted as a sign of a safe space, such as the city of Lestallum in *Final Fantasy XV* [13], where the players can expect safety from the dangers of the wilderness, and points of interest where to communicate with other characters and acquire items in shops. The looks of the city itself express its role as a safe hub, the squares are lined with shops and cafes, and only humans populate its streets (see Fig. 5). Conversely, in a first-person shooter, where the interaction is usually limited to shooting and being shot at, a city can be a dangerous place, full of hideouts for the enemy, but also a location that offers numerous covers and gameplay possibilities.

Fig. 5. The city of Lestallum in *Final Fantasy XV* © Square Enix 2016.

3.3   The Semiotics of Architecture in Digital Games

We have established in Sect. 3.1 that architecture has a primary denotative function, the utilitarian function of the architectural object in virtue of its forms and material properties. Similarly, architecture in digital games has a denotative function as well. It might differ from the one of its real counterparts, but architectural elements in digital games are functional to the gameplay. We can thus parallel the primary denotative function of real architecture to the ludic function of virtual architecture.

The secondary connotative function of architecture, which can be incidental or absent in real architecture, is all the more present in virtual architecture, as every architectural element is deliberately created and placed in the game by the designers. It is the connotative function that allows for anticipatory play, and that communicates to players through architectural signs information about the gameplay, the narrative, or instructions on how to play and proceed in the game.

For instance, seemingly secondary architectural elements can be important for anticipatory play, and as such carefully planned and placed. To wit, air vents can be used as hidden passages in *Deus Ex: Mankind Divided* [11], in order to sneak past enemies unseen, or to reach hidden locations. In the game *Alien: Isolation* [14], on the contrary, the air vents are used by the titular alien to travel through the space station and ambush the player. In this case the architectural element of the air vent is visually rather similar in the two games, both 3D first-person games with realistic graphic styles, but its semiosis is different if not opposite. The anticipatory play it allows is also different, where in *Deux Ex: Mankind Divided* the sight of an air vent will be interpreted by players as a sign of various gameplay possibilities, or even of safety in case they are pursued by an enemy, it is a sign of danger in *Alien: Isolation*, leading to an opposite planning and strategy.

Moreover, the connotative function of architecture influences the narrative of the game, and not just its ludic aspect. A certain design of architectural elements can give players indication and context of the game world. We can observe the use of connotation in architecture in 古剑奇谭三 (*Gujian3*) [15]. *Gujian 3* pertains to the *xuanhuan* genre, an offshoot of the *xianxia* tradition of fantasy fiction based on Chinese mythology, but with elements borrowed from Western conventions. While the visual style is for the most part based on Chinese elements, there are visual inspirations from both the West and Japan for some of their aspects.

In *Gujian 3* the "mortal" realm, as in, our normal world, is traditionally represented with vernacular Chinese architecture, as we can find in reality (see Fig. 6). The "spiritual" realm instead, in order to be clearly differentiated from the mortal one, takes architectural cues from a mix of Western architectural and Japanese digital games tradition. The buildings of the city of Skyelk (see Fig. 7) are designed in a whimsical art nouveau styles mixed with Nordic elements, which more than accurately resembling real examples of these architectural styles – such as the works of architect Hector Guimard, who designed the Paris Metro entrances in 1900 – takes inspiration from the reinterpretations we can see in Japanese role-playing games, especially in the *Final Fantasy* series [16].

Fig. 6. The city of Yangping in 古劍奇譚三 (*Gujian3*) © Aurogon Shanghai 2018.

Fig. 7. The spiritual realm city of Skyelk in 古劍奇譚三 (*Gujian3*) © Aurogon Shanghai 2018.

The dichotomy between the two worlds, the mortal and the spiritual, is thus highlighted through the connotation of their architectural design. In order for the players to understand that they are in a world radically different from the normal one, the choice of an unusual architectural style is a most effective way to achieve this effect. Naturally other elements help players understand the narrative and situate themselves within the game world, there are characters who are dressed differently, as well as dialogues explaining the context, but the effectiveness of architecture communicates the otherworldliness of the location without even the need of additional explanations.

4 Conclusions

Architecture is a central signifier in digital games. Players constantly interact and traverse digital game spaces, and understating how the virtual environment communicates with them is of paramount importance for the development of effective digital game environments, but also for a deeper understanding of how we perceive the space around us, virtual or otherwise. We have seen in the examples how a semiotic analysis of digital games architecture can be appropriate for various genres of games to help us understand how they are developed and how architectural design impacts both narration and the gameplay.

References

1. Fortes Tondello, G., Valtchanov, D., Reetz, A., Wehbe, R.R., Orji, R., Nacke, L.E.: Towards a trait model of video game preferences. Int. J. Hum.-Comput. Interact. **34**, 732–748 (2018). https://doi.org/10.1080/10447318.2018.1461765
2. Eco, U.: Function and sign: the semiotics of architecture. In: Leach, N. (ed.) Rethinking Architecture: A Reader in Cultural Theory, pp. 173–193. Routledge, London (1997)
3. Upton, B.: The Aesthetic of Play. MIT Press, Cambridge (2015)
4. Tavinor, G.: The Art of Videogames. Wiley, Malden (2009)
5. Reimer, J.: Why next-gen games have next-gen prices. In: Ars Technica (2006). https://arstechnica.com/gaming/2006/12/8479/. Accessed 9 Nov 2019
6. Leafy Games: Kickstarter Conversations: It Takes More Than Just the Captain to Control a Starship! PULSAR: Lost Colony (2013)
7. Ars Technica: How Much Everyone Working On a $250 Million Video Game Earns (2017)
8. Eidos-Montréal: Shadow of the Tomb Raider. Square Enix, Canada (2018)
9. Blooper Team: Layers of Fear. Aspyr, Poland (2016)
10. D'Armenio, E.: Mondi paralleli. Ripensare l'interattività nei videogiochi. Edizioni Unicopli, Milan (2014)
11. Eidos-Montréal: Deus Ex: Mankind Divided. Square Enix, Canada (2016)
12. Red Storm Entertainment: Tom Clancy's Rainbow Six. Red Storm Entertainment, United States (1998)
13. Square Enix: Final Fantasy XV. Square Enix, Japan (2016)
14. Creative Assembly: Alien: Isolation. Sega, United Kingdom (2014)
15. Aurogon Shanghai: 古剑奇谭三 (Gujian 3). Wangyuan Shengtang, China (2018)
16. Square, Square Enix: Final Fantasy (series). Square Enix, Japan (1987–2020)

How Do Narrative Features Affect a Player's Immersion in Computer Games? The Analytical Hierarchy Process Approach

Zixuan Guo and Cheng-Hung Lo[✉]

Xi'an Jiaotong-Liverpool University, Suzhou, China
ch.lo@xjtlu.edu.cn

Abstract. Video games have become an important narrative medium to convey stories, but previous studies lack of research on the relationship between immersion and narrative characteristics. With 2D side-scrolling puzzle games as the example, we utilize the method of Analytic Hierarchy Process (AHP) to reveal how the immersion as a whole are modulated by different narrative features through a set of immersive factors. We adopt an immersion model composed of six dimensions, and conducted a quantitative survey to collect players' reactions to the selected game. According to the results of AHP analysis, the three narrative features arouse mostly the players' curiosity when engaging them in the games. Both the spatial and interactive features contribute the least in invoking the players' empathy, whilst the structural features invoke the least concentration. The AHP method provides strong data support in understanding game narratives and the related immersive effects at a more elaborated level.

Keywords: Video game · Game narratives · Player immersion · Analytical Hierarchy Process · 2D side-scrolling puzzle games

1 Introduction

Video game has been an important application of computer technology in the field of entertainment. With the rise of role-playing games in 1980s, a growing number of video games began to build more comprehensive narrative systems to engage their players [1]. Game narratives could manifest through the scenes, character profiles, scripts, and inter-active mechanisms. They not only define the basis and framework of video games, but also make gaming experience a logically-connected sequence of events [2]. However, controversies exist in whether the traditional narrative theory is applicable in the analysis of video games [3, 4]. Some scholars put forward new narrative theories, which provided the lens for looking analytically and critically into the narrative design in games. Our study considers the narrative features discussed in Jenkins [5]. According to Jenkins, the stories conveyed in video games have several unique characteristics in comparison with traditional stories [5, 6]. The first characteristic is space, in which the characters explore, act, and reveal the plots. The second one is structure, which is normally non-linear and relatively more diversified to form a personalized experience. The third one is interactivity, with which the players can alter the narrative flows and effectively contribute in creating the overall gaming experience. Among these three characteristics, the space creates the prerequisites for an immersive narrative experience, while the structure and interactivity are the methods to allow the space to achieve narrative effects [5].

Immersion is a psychological state, which is characterized by perceiving and interacting with an environment that provides continuous stimulation. [7]. Game designers, like traditional artists, need to draw inspiration from literatures or artefacts to build attractive virtual worlds and engaging narrated experience for the game. However, in terms of game experience, only when the players get a better immersion can the game achieve a better narrative effect. Therefore, players' immersion is a critical measure for studying the narratives in games. Game researchers often looked at how immersion happens and develops in the playing process, rather than its contribution to the understanding and experience of game narratives [8]. This research aims to study and analyze players' immersion with the consideration of narrative features in a game. Because of the diversity of game genres, the narrative strategies may vary significantly from genre to genre. Our work selects 2D side-scrolling puzzle games as the target of study. There are two main reasons for such selection. Firstly, the narrative structure is fixed and similar to the traditional, literally-based storytelling approach. Secondly, 2D side-scrolling puzzle games have long been a popular format in video game history. The two more recent games, <Limbo> [9] and <Inside> [10], are popular games with the same style, which have induced many conversations among the players and game critics. This research uses <Limbo> and <Inside> as the study cases to analyze how narrative features influence the players' immersion. Specifically, we utilize the *Analytical Hierarchy Process* (AHP) method to reveal how the immersion as a whole are modulated by different narrative features through a set of immersive factors. It is worth noting that this research method can be applied to other genres of games or some specified games.

2 Review

Narratives can be used as the structure to give significance and order to a created virtual world [11]. Most traditional narratives have linear and fixed structures defined by the authors, while the narratives of game are often less linear and varied through the game mechanisms [3]. Games with linear narratives may limits the freedom of the player's actions, thus making the player's control passive [4]. However, Jenkins [5] suggested that these definitions simplified narratives into story forms but considered whether narrative elements might play a role at a more localized level. With the continuous challenges encountered in the game, players can experience and even create their own story flows. In this research, we consider the game narrative as the mode, method or style to tell game stories. On the other hand, we deem the story as the collected and ordered plots that the game designers and developers have produced in advance.

Video games have some narrative characteristics similar to those appeared in traditional media. However, there are some fundamental differences. Game narratives are not based on representation but simulation [12], which means that the game narrative may rely on and manifest through the simulated virtual features. In most video games, narratives are closely related to the passing of game time and the trigger mode of key events during game progression [13]. Based on the relevant literatures, we summarise the three key characteristics of game narratives as follows:

- **Space.** Traditional narratives is generally based on time, while the video game is a narrative form based on space [5]. The video games have strengthened the spatial elements of narration, which provides players a virtual space with various beautiful stories. A game's scene is the most intuitive embodiment of narrative space that induces a players' immersion. The transition of scenes can play a vital role in the presentation of the plots, and most plot triggers are set around the space.
- **Structure.** According to Jenkins [5], there are two structures for the narrative components of a game: the embedded narrative and the emergent narrative. The embedded narrative is pre-generated content that exists before the players interact with the game. Game designers need to distribute the information in the space to control the narrative process. In this structure, the game world becomes an information space or a memory palace. The emergent narrative generates stories by controlling the interaction between the game system and players. The stories in the emergent narrative are not pre-generated. Modern video games may implement both the embedded and emergent narratives. In our selected cases, <Limbo> and <Inside>, the narrative structure mainly uses the embedded approach.
- **Interactivity.** The third important characteristic of game narratives is that it involves players' choices and behaviors, which intervene the progress and endings of the story. Without the interaction between the players and games, the narratives cannot be formulate [6]. The interactions in a game may diversify its storylines but the encountered goals, conflicts, and uncertainties can help convey the narrative more completely [14].

Side-scrolling games require a player to control the movements of a character across the screen. When the player moves to the edge of the screen (usually from left to right), the game field moves or scrolls in an opposite direction adapting to the character's movements. In most side scrollers, the player moves horizontally and mostly around the center of the screen [15]. In the late '80s and early '90s, side scrollers reached their height of popularity, which declined after the rise of 3D games. However, the format still allows the construction of compelling stories for it has elements similar to fictional literatures: a protagonist, goals to be achieved, conflicts, and an orderly progression. A player's immersion depends on the time density and successive pattern of discrete events. Among these discrete events, puzzles are one of the often-used elements for planting plot transitions in game narratives. As an effective tool to test problem-solving skills, including logic, pattern and recognition [16], it helps maintain a player's concentration and expand the variety of game tasks. Indeed, the attraction of entertainment games largely comes from the players' sense of immersion and the satisfaction arise from achieving certain tasks [17]. Side-scrollers usually excel at these aspects, therefore providing a good sense of immersion [18].

Jennett et al. [19] suggested that immersion can be measured objectively as well as subjectively. Objective measures are aimed at the natural response and behavior of users. In general, these reactions are generated automatically without much conscious consideration. Subjective measures usually use survey questionnaires to collect the subjective opinions of participants. Calleja [20] suggested that immersion is not a stand-alone experience but a mixed result of various experiential phenomena generated through participation in the game. Qin et al. [2] proposed a model to measure a player's immersion in game narratives. The model includes seven dimensions: (1) Curiosity, (2) Concentration, (3) Challenge, (4) Control, (5) Comprehension, (6) Empathy and (7) Familiarity (see Appendix 1). Our study adopts this model to with two reasons: (1) this model focuses on players' psychological responses, which are the natural source for studying immersive feelings. (2) This model was developed in the context of game narration.

Analytic Hierarchy Process (AHP) is a structured method based on mathematics and psychology to organize and analyze complex information [21]. AHP can accurately quantify the weight of different criteria and estimate the relative size of each factor by comparing the data. It is thus practical and effective in dealing with complex projects, especially for weight analysis and ranking. Saaty [22] first introduced AHP to rank different criteria based on pairwise comparison. Ngai and Chan [23] suggested that AHP provided a multi-criteria approach suitable for analyzing and comparing influencing factors. They then applied it to evaluate knowledge management tools in the software market. Akaa et al. [24] obtained the ratings through the relative comparison of AHP-based in the structuralfire design decision criteria, and finally evaluate four application schemes of fire protection to steel structures.

3 Methods

3.1 Narrative Feature Analysis of <Limbo> and <Inside>

In order to establish the hierarchical influences of narrative features on players' immersion. We need to first identify and analyze the narrative features in the two game cases. <Limbo> and <Inside> are both 2D side-scroller puzzle games, which have similar gameplay mechanisms and visual layout. In <Limbo>, the player guides an unnamed boy to travel through a place called "Limbo" embedded with hazards and threats to find his sister (Fig. 3). In <Inside>, the player needs to control an unnamed boy to escape from a mysterious place embedded with fearful experiments (Fig. 4). Players need to use their logical thinking and creative imagination to solve the puzzles and unravel the mysterious events. Based on the three characteristics of the game narrative: Space, Structure and Interactivity, we analyze the narrative features in the two games as follows.

The two games are known for their unique construction of space. <Limbo> uses only black and white colors. The well-designed lightings, film grain effects and ambient sounds all contribute in creating the horrifying atmosphere (Fig. 1). <Inside> creates a 3D spatial texture in the form of 2D. The game also has a relatively darker tone but with sparingly-used colors to highlight both the player and certain parts of the environment (Fig. 2). Black, gray and white are all neutral colors. When combined harmoniously with other colors, they can strengthen or weaken a particular feeling [25]. The strong artistic style of the two games attracts and engages the players in the game space.

Fig. 1. Screenshot from <Limbo>: Encountering the big spider

Fig. 2. Screenshot from <Inside>: Exploring the game space

In terms of structure, both games use the embedded narrative approach. The players will gradually understand the structure and mechanisms of the game by controlling the protagonist and the props, which in turn achieves the understanding of the game stories. Meanwhile, the narrative structure of the two side-scrolling games is not completely linear. While exploring spatially in the game space, the players collect the clues related to the game narrative and splice these clues to progressively assemble the complete story.

Regarding interactivity, both games use simple control mechanisms. The player controls the basic actions of the protagonist, such as running, jumping, and moving objects. This style of play was termed by the developer as "trial and death", which uses terrifying imagery to signify the boy's deaths and warn the player away from failing actions [26]. When the players solve puzzles, they are interacting with the game environments. The interactions help reveal the plot details and steer the development of the story.

3.2 Questionnaire Design

As stated in the review section, this study refers to the player experience model proposed by Qin et al. [2] to design the questionnaire. Among the seven dimensions of the model, "Familiarity" is added by researchers on the basis of Curiosity. In comparison with the other six dimensions, "Familiarity" lacks references, and the validity of "Familiarity" is yet to be fully verified and therefore disregarded in this study.

The questionnaire is, therefore, designed according to the six dimensions, including (1) Curiosity, (2) Concentration, (3) Challenge, (4) Control, (5) Comprehension, and (6) Empathy. The questionnaire contains a list of statements about players' involvement and immersion in video games narratives. Each statement is followed by a Likert-type of scale with five options: "strongly disagree" (0), "disagree" (1), "no opinion" (2), "agree" (3) and "strongly agree" (4).

The original questionnaire designed by Qin et al. [2] is for all genres of games narratives. The contained statements do not have a strong pertinence to a specific type of game. We re-designed he questionnaire by rephrasing the statements more specifically towards the narrative characteristics (space, structure and interactivity) in the two selected games. Some statements have a strong directivity and connection to one characteristic, while some others have a more comprehensive directivity pertaining to more than one characteristics. We also added questions about personal background and the general experience of playing video games.

The final version of the questionnaire contained 26 statements. There are 14 questions related to space, 9 questions related to structure and 15 questions related to interactivity. The statements are also clustered with their corresponding dimensions. It is worth mentioning here that "Challenge" and "Control" are clustered with relatively more statements for they are associated stronger with interactivity, instead of space and structure.

3.3 Data Collection

The questionnaires were distributed online, and the target respondents were the players who had played <Limbo> or <Inside>. We used snowball and convenient sampling to recruit participants through four internet-based channels in China:

1. *Social Messaging/Chatting platforms (Wechat and QQ)*: We invited known contacts to introduce or recommend people who had played the two games (snowball sampling)
2. *Public social Network platforms (Weibo and Baidu Post Bar)*: We searched the keywords "Limbo", "Inside" and "Playdead" to find users who had posted relevant content. After explaining the purpose of the study to these users, we shared the questionnaire link through comments or private messages (convenient sampling – associate with user's feedback).

3. *Comment section of the relevant video-sharing website (Bilibili)*: Several game blog-gers recorded their own gaming process and shared the videos online. The viewers who commented might have relevant experience (snowball sampling - via bloggers).
4. *Game forums (Taptap, Keylol, 3DMGAME and Heybox)*: These forums also had designated sections for the two games (convenient sampling - relevant thematic communities).

The final number of responses was 78, of which 70 were valid. The gender ratio of participants was 57% for male and 43% for female. 80% of the participants aged from 19 to 30 and 17% of the participants were under 18 years old. 57% of participants had played both <Limbo> and <Inside>, while 26% of participants had played only <Inside> and 17% of participants had played only <Limbo>. Because of the releasing times of the two games, about 36% of the participants played the two games a year ago and only 11% of participants played the two games within this month. About 70% of the participants had completed the games. About 34% of the participants have a total game time of 4–8 h; the proportion of participants who have a game time of 3–4 h and 8–12 h is approximately the same, accounting for 25% respectively.

3.4 Analytic Hierarchy Process (AHP)

The first step of AHP is to establish the hierarchy model that decomposes the targeted problem into several related influential factors [21]. In our case, the effects of narra-tive features on players' immersion would be described as a hierarchy model consisting of the narrative features of the game and the factor is the 6 dimensions of immersion (Fig. 3). After the hierarchy model has been built, the factors' descriptive data (usually the average values) are collated into the AHP comparison matrix to make a series of pairwise comparison between each index [21]. Because there are three narrative char-acteristics of the game, we are to build three AHP comparison matrices. The questions concerning the three different narrative characteristics were designed into the corre-sponding statements in the questionnaire. There are 16 statements related to space: 2 in Curiosity, 4 in "Concentration", 3 in "Empathy", 3 in "Challenge", 1 in "Control" and 3 in "Comprehension". For structure, there are 12 related statements: 2 in Curios-ity, 2 in "Concentration", 2 in "Empathy", 1 in "Challenge", 2 in "Control" and 3 in "Comprehension". For interactivity, there are 16 related statements: 1 in Curiosity, 3 in "Concentration", 2 in "Empathy", 3 in "Challenge", 4 in "Control" and 3 in "Compre-hension". The participants' responses to the statements were aggregated and averaged

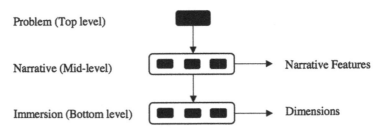

Fig. 3. AHP hierarchical structure

according to the dimensional classification. The three APH comparison matrices were thus obtained and to be discussed in detail in the following section.

4 Results and Discussion

Figure 4 shows the weights of the three narrative features and their influences on the dimensional factors of immersion. It can be seen that the space and interactivity are relatively higher than the structure. More detailed analysis and discussion are presented in the following sections.

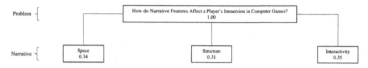

Fig. 4. AHP-narrative features hierarchical model

4.1 Space

The AHP analysis of space is shown in Table 1. One can see from the table that Curiosity accounts for the highest proportion, which is about 19%; while Empathy accounts for the lowest proportion, which is about 14%. Each of the other four dimensions accounts for about the same proportion, 16%. This indicates that the influence of space on the six dimensions of players' immersion is more evenly distributed on Concentration, Challenge, Control, and Comprehension.

Table 1. AHP analysis of space

	Cu	CC	EP	CH	CT	CP	Priority	Weight	Rank
CU	1	1.151	1.359	1.138	1.131	1.143	1.145	19.076%	1
CC	0.869	1	1.181	0.988	1.009	0.994	0.999	16.650%	4
EP	0.736	0.847	1	0.837	0.855	0.842	0.846	14.101%	6
CH	0.879	1.012	1.195	1	1.02	1.005	1.011	16.844%	2
CT	0.884	0.991	1.17	0.98	1	0.984	0.994	16.572%	5
CP	0.875	1.006	1.188	0.995	1.016	1	1.005	16.758%	3

CU: Curiosity CC: Concentration EP: Empathy CH: Challenge CT: Control CP: Comprehension

<Limbo> and <Inside> share similar construction styles in their game spaces. They also use primarily shades of a single color to render the spaces. To create an atmosphere is necessary for players to involve in the narrative, which is also frequently used in traditional media. For instance, both games are laying the groundwork for creating an

atmosphere at the beginning. With the black-and-white screen and the suspenseful sound, players can quickly enter the lonely and gloomy atmosphere.

The two games do not focus on the details of the game world, but this does not affect the players' sense of immersion. The reason might be that the two games used parallax layers to create a profound and rich environment. Parallax layers refers to the use of color tones to achieve environmental stratification [27]. For example, in <Limbo>, the little boy and front platform are the darkest, while the background is brighter. The contrast can highlight specific parts of the environment, the key clues to solve puzzles, and some important narrative elements. Therefore, <Limbo> and <Inside> can create playable game space even though they only use simple tones.

4.2 Structure

As shown in the AHP analysis of structure (Table 2), the ranking of the dimensions is similar to that of space. In terms of the proportional weights, the dimensions can be generally divided into three levels. The proportion of Curiosity is the highest (18.8%), followed by Challenge (18.2%), and the next is Comprehension, which is about 17%. Empathy and Control account for about the same proportion, which is about 15% respectively. Concentration accounts for the lowest proportion, which is about 14.9%.

Table 2. AHP analysis of structure

	Cu	CC	EP	CH	CT	CP	Priority	Weight	Rank
CU	1	1.256	1.212	1.03	1.23	1.087	1.126	18.772%	1
CC	0.796	1	0.964	0.82	0.977	0.866	0.897	14.942%	6
EP	0.825	1.037	1	0.85	1.012	0.898	0.929	15.491%	4
CH	0.971	1.22	1.177	1	1.192	1.056	1.094	18.231%	2
CT	0.815	1.024	0.988	0.839	1	0.887	0.918	15.301%	5
CP	0.92	1.155	1.114	0.947	1.128	1	1.036	17.262%	3

CU: Curiosity CC: Concentration EP: Empathy CH: Challenge CT: Control CP: Comprehension

As the 2D side-scrolling puzzle games, the narrative structure of <Limbo> and <Inside> inherently has a linear progression. This type of narrative structure can guide players invisibly in moving forward to the next scene. Players' anticipation of the next scene will result in a sense of Curiosity. Moreover, the uncertainty and newly-revealed elements in the next scene will induce a sense of Challenge. However, the linear structure may cause a player's frustration for not having a clear timeline of when the scene can be completed. In this case, the two games employ emergent narrative strategies to enhance the experience. As discussed in the review section, emergent narratives refer to the story developed through the game mechanism and players' interactions. As the mechanisms and scenes are completely written by game designers in these two games, the narrative should be embedded rather than emergent. However, what if the story that emerges does not exist in the game, but in the player's mind? For example, in the early scenes of

<Inside>, there are a little boy, a pile of dead pigs, a damaged fence and a waste factory building (Fig. 5). As long as the players get familiar with these elements, the story can be formed in their minds. As every player has his or her own imagination, there will be personalized stories developed throughout the play process.

As for why this structure has the least effect on Concentration, the reason might be that there are no clearly-segmented chapters in the two games. This structure could be played with strong continuity if a player has a high level of game skills. One can complete the game within 4–5 h and have a strong sense of immersion. However, for some players who spend a lot of time solving puzzles, the elongated and uncertain game process may decrease the level of engagement. As the data showed in the earlier section, about 30% of the players did not complete the game.

Fig. 5. The factory scene in <Inside>

4.3 Interactivity

In the AHP analysis of Interactivity, the overall proportion and ranking are different from those of space and structure (see Table 3). Curiosity still accounts for the highest proportion, which is about 18.4%. What follows next is Concentration, which is about 17%. The proportions of Challenge, Control and Comprehension are approximately the same, which is about 16%. Empathy has the lowest proportion of weight, 14%. Based on the similar connotations, there should be a strong association between interactivity and Control. However, according to the data, Control is only at the fourth place in the ranking.

Table 3. AHP analysis of interactivity

	Cu	CC	EP	CH	CT	CP	Priority	Weight	Rank
CU	1	1.063	1.289	1.085	1.115	1.112	1.105	18.420%	1
CC	0.941	1	1.212	1.02	1.048	1.053	1.04	17.326%	2
EP	0.776	0.825	1	0.842	0.865	1.87	0.858	14.296%	6
CH	0.922	0.98	1.188	1	1.028	1.033	1.019	16.984%	3
CT	0.897	0.954	1.156	0.973	1	1.005	0.992	16.527%	4
CP	0.893	0.95	1.15	0.968	0.995	1	0.987	16.447%	5

CU: Curiosity CC: Concentration EP: Empathy CH: Challenge CT: Control CP: Comprehension

There are two possible explanations for the low ranking of Control. First of all, it is difficult to control the characters in <Limbo> and <Inside>. In the puzzle games, the interactive part is simpler than some action games. However, since there is no text description, it is difficult for players to understand how to operate boys and how to use props at the beginning of the game. Moreover, although these two games are puzzle games, some puzzles in the game require the players to have strong operation ability, and the difficulty is equivalent to some action games. In addition, in some negative comments of <Limbo> and <Inside> on Steam, players mentioned that the extensive use of "Trial-and-Error" method is a problem. Some puzzles can only be passed after deaths, which will be considered as damaging the game experience.

The final integrated AHP model is illustrated below (Fig. 6). This figure gives an overview of how the immersion as a whole are modulated by different narrative features through a set of immersive factors.

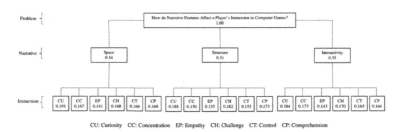

CU: Curiosity CC: Concentration EP: Empathy CH: Challenge CT: Control CP: Comprehension

Fig. 6. The complete AHP hierarchical model

4.4   Remarks on Curiosity and Empathy

On the whole, Curiosity accounts for the largest proportion of the three narrative characteristics. For puzzle games, Curiosity is the core to attract players in exploring the game and immersing into the game narrative. From the AHP analysis of the three characteristics, especially that of the structure, we can see that the key to make the players curious is to utilize their own imaginations. In some role-playing games, the story is clearly conveyed through the dialogues among the characters. The Curiosity aroused by that genre of game comes from the plots of the story, which is similar to a novel. However, the curiosity is aroused by the two game cases for their scenes and environments. The narratives are formed along the exploration of the game spaces.

There are three possible reasons for the low intensity of Empathy. First, the game length of both games is relatively short. According to the questionnaires, most of the players have less than 8 h of game time. Compared with games that take longer time to get through, it might be difficult for a short game to truly induce a player's empathetic affections. Second, because of the uncertainties in the story, the players may experience frustrations or confusions in playing the games. However, this does not represent empathetic responses for the protagonist. Finally, there are certain difficulties in solving puzzles in both games. When players are immersed in solving puzzles, they may ignore the narrative elements in the game, resulting in a low epithetical understanding of the story.

4.5 Consistency, Reliability and Validity

To check the consistency, Saaty [22] proposed Consistency Ratio (CR), which is a comparison between Consistency Index (CI) and Random Consistency Index (RI), or in formula: CR = CI/RI. If the value of CR is smaller or equal to 0.1, the inconsistency is acceptable. In the AHP, CI is defined as the quotient of this difference divided by $(n-1)$ and RI is a random index. According to the consistency check results, the value of CI in the three APH matrices are all 0.000, and the value of RI are all 1.650, so the calculated value of CR is 0.000 < 0.1. To conclude, the three AHP matrices satisfy the consistency check, and the calculated weights are consistent.

Reliability is defined as the extent to which an instrument yields the same results on repeated measurements [28]. Cronbach's alpha [29] is widely used in the test and an alpha (a) value of 0.70 or above is considered to indicate strong internal consistency [28]. The result of this measuring instrument is 0.857 > 0.70, which indicates that the reliability of the research data is acceptable.

We also perform a validity analysis to see whether the questionnaire items are reasonable and meaningful [30]. As shown in Table 4, the commonality values of the items are all higher than 0.4, which indicates that the desired information can be effectively extracted with this questionnaire. In addition, the Kaiser-Meyer-Olkin (KMO) value is 0.605 (>0.6) i.e. confirming the validity of the instrument for this research. A KMO test is used in research to determine the sampling adequacy of data that are to be used for Factor Analysis.

Table 4. Validity analysis

Item	Factor loadings					
	Factor 1	Factor 2	Factor 3	Factor 4	Factor 5	Factor 6
Featured root value (before) rotation)	7.25	2.418	1.981	1.937	1.697	1.385
Variance interpretation rate (before rotation)	27.88%	9.30%	7.62%	7.45%	6.53%	5.33%
Cumulative variance interpretation rate (before rotation)	27.88%	37.18%	44.80%	52.25%	58.78%	64.11%
Featured root value (after) rotation)	3.946	3.604	2.988	2.502	1.982	1.645
Variance interpretation rate (after rotation)	15.18%	13.86%	11.49%	9.62%	7.62%	6.33%
Cumulative variance interpretation rate(after rotation)	15.18%	29.04%	40.53%	50.16%	57.78%	64.11%
KMO value	0.605					
Bartlett's spherical value	903.764					
df value	325					
p value	0					

5   Conclusion

With the AHP approach, we have identified the impact of different narrative characteristics on the player's immersion on 2D Side-Scrolling games such as the selected two cases. In general, the narrative of these two games does not follow the conventional approach, e.g. cause-climax-result. Instead, they utilize the characteristics of game narrative to create the immersive game experience. In terms of the space feature, the overall environments are filled with elements that induce a player's Curiosity and reveal new Challenging tasks. Regarding the structure, the explorations of game scenes generate emergent narratives guided by individual player's Curiosity and immerse him or her in a personalized game experience. About interactivity, the puzzle-solving activities associated with the plots can engage the players at their Focus and Control. However, some narrative characteristics and modes may have a negative impact on the player's immersion. Regarding the structure, a strong game continuity may reduce the player's Concentration; In terms of interactivity, the difficulty of controlling the protagonist and the repetitive use of "Trial-and-Error' may reduce the player's sense of Control. This type of games has a strong influence on the player's Curiosity for they anticipate the player's active imagination. It is worth noting that some of these characteristics will lead to lower Empathy. Possible reasons include the short game length, uncertain plot and difficulty in solving puzzles. This work shows that the AHP approach effectively connect narrative features with immersion factors. It remains the objectivity of data analysis and elaborate the influencing factors and their extents. The proposed approach is not limited to 2D side-scrolling puzzle games. It can also be applied to other game genres in the future. In addition, researchers can use more objective measures to measure players' immersion, such as biosensors and human motion analysis. The data obtained from the combination of subjective measurement and objective measurement will be beneficial for further research in this direction.

Appendix

(1) Curiosity

Curiosity can stimulate players' senses and cognition to explore the game narrative. Attractive content makes players have desire to discover new things and explore new environments.

(2) Concentration

Concentration means that players focus on the game narrative. When players are immersed, they need to concentrate first and then keep their attention. The immersion level of players is directly proportional to the attention and energy they put in.

(3) Comprehension

Comprehension refers to the understanding of the structure and content of the game. Only when players understand the nature and content of the game can they begin to feel immersed.

(4) Control

Players can feel a sense of control characters and the game world. If players can control over the game characters and play games freely, they may feel like exploring a real environment and have a sense of immersion.

(5) Challenge

Challenge is the difficulty that players encounter in the game narrative. Challenge helps to focus the player's attention. In general, the difficulty of the game has different levels and gradually increases, which can attract players to continue the game.

(6) Empathy

Empathy means that players enter the imaginary game world mentally. When the players are immersed in the game story, they will invest the real emotion. For example, the players have a sense of cognition to the game characters and the game world.

(7) Familiarity

Familiarity means that players are familiar with the game background and content. The players who are familiar with the game have different game experiences to some extent.

References

1. Taylor, L.N.: Video Games: Perspective, Point-of-View, and Immersion (2002)
2. Qin, H., Patrick Rau, P.-L., Salvendy, G.: Measuring player immersion in the computer game narrative. Int. J. Hum.-Comput. Interact. **25**, 107–133 (2009)
3. Adams, E.: Three problems for interactive storytellers. In: Designer's Notebook Column, Gamasutra, p. 144 (1999)
4. Costikyan, G.: Where stories end and games begin (2000)
5. Jenkins, H.: Game design as narrative architecture. Computer **44**, 118–130 (2004)
6. Pearce, C.: Towards a game theory of game. In: First Person: New Media as Story, Performance, and Game, vol. 1, pp. 143–153 (2004)
7. Witmer, B.G., Singer, M.J.: Measuring presence in virtual environments: a presence questionnaire. Presence **7**, 225–240 (1998)
8. Sweetser, P., Johnson, D.: Player-centered game environments: assessing player opinions, experiences, and issues. In: Rauterberg, M. (ed.) ICEC 2004. LNCS, vol. 3166, pp. 321–332. Springer, Heidelberg (2004). https://doi.org/10.1007/978-3-540-28643-1_40
9. Studios, P.: Limbo. Denmark (2010)
10. Studios, P.: Inside. Denmark (2016)
11. Neitzel, B.: Narrativity of computer games. In: Handbook of Narratology, pp. 608–622. De Gruyter (2014)
12. Frasca, G.: Simulation Versus Narrative: Introduction to Ludology (2003)
13. Ip, B.: Narrative structures in computer and video games: part 1: context, definitions, and initial findings. Games Cult. **6**, 103–134 (2011)
14. Salen, K., Tekinbaş, K.S., Zimmerman, E.: Rules of Play: Game Design Fundamentals. MIT Press, Cambridge (2004)
15. Tong, M.: Side Scrollers: A Planar Odyssey (2001). https://web.stanford.edu/group/htgg/cgi-bin/drupal/sites/default/files2/mtong_2001_2.pdf
16. Grace, L.: Game type and game genre (2005). http://aii.lgracegames.com/documents/Game_types_and_genres.pdf. Accessed 22 Feb 8
17. Boyle, E., Connolly, T.M., Hainey, T.: The role of psychology in understanding the impact of computer games. Entertain. Comput. **2**, 69–74 (2011)
18. Nakevska, M., van der Sanden, A., Funk, M., Hu, J., Rauterberg, M.: Interactive storytelling in a mixed reality environment: the effects of interactivity on user experiences. Entertain. Comput. **21**, 97–104 (2017)
19. Jennett, C., et al.: Measuring and defining the experience of immersion in games. Int. J. Hum. Comput. Stud. **66**, 641–661 (2008)
20. Calleja, G.: Digital game involvement: a conceptual model. Games Cult. **2**, 236–260 (2007)
21. Podvezko, V.: Application of AHP technique. J. Bus. Econ. Manag. **10**(2), 181–189 (2009)
22. Saaty, R.W.: The analytic hierarchy process—what it is and how it is used. Math. Model. **9**, 161–176 (1987)
23. Ngai, E.W.T., Chan, E.W.C.: Evaluation of knowledge management tools using AHP. Expert Syst. Appl. **29**, 889–899 (2005)
24. Akaa, O.U., Abu, A., Spearpoint, M., Giovinazzi, S.: A group-AHP decision analysis for the selection of applied fire protection to steel structures. Fire Saf. J. **86**, 95–105 (2016)
25. Roohi, S., Forouzandeh, A.: Regarding color psychology principles in adventure games to enhance the sense of immersion. Entertain. Comput. **30**, 100298 (2019)
26. Brown, J.J., Jr.: Limbo and the Edge of the Literary (2013)
27. Study, V.G.A.: How Limbo & Inside Use Tone to Create Space (2018)
28. Nunnally, J.C.: Psychometric theory—25 years ago and now. Educ. Res. **4**, 7–21 (1975)

29. Cronbach, L.J.: Coefficient alpha and the internal structure of tests. Psychometrika **16**, 297–334 (1951)
30. Thorndike, R.M., Cunningham, G.K., Thorndike, R.L., Hagen, E.P.: Measurement and Evaluation in Psychology and Education. Macmillan Publishing Co, Inc., New York (1991)

From "Extension" to "Amputation": Technological Constructions and Digital Anxiety of Bodies in Cyberspace–A Critical Perspective Based on Design Philosophy

Hua Mi[✉]

College of Design, Shandong University of Arts, Jinan, China
mh_design666@163.com

Abstract. From 5G to IoT, from VR to AI, digital media technology is reshaping the design ecology. On one hand, technology intervenes in all aspects of design, even realizing the transformation of the designer from natural human to cyborg. Technology and human form a mutually constructive relationship. On the other hand, technology has a tendency to alienate, algorithmism and digital anxiety lead to the suspension of the body in design, which generates a new design logic in the digital state of existence. From the "extension" of the human body to the "amputation", the connotation of the key word "technology" has fundamentally changed over time. In this paper, we will examine the evolutionary path of the conceptual history of technology, consider the representation of technological amputation in the post-human context. Meanwhile we will discuss how to deal with the generation of design in the digital age from the critical perspective of the technical philosophy, think the "body turning" in contemporary design research.

Keywords: Embodiment · Cyborg · Digital survival · Technological anxiety

1 The Introduction of the Problem: From the Perspective of Design Philosophy

The dichotomy between art and technology has existed throughout the design history. Along with the explosion of new technologies, design has to face the impact of a technology-driven society actively or passively. As the metaverse is coming, the world has entered a technology-oriented phase, where the definition of design has been broadened and the multidimensional relationship between design and technology is being reshaped. At the same time, the relationship is becoming a core issues in academic community.

If 2016 was called the year of VR, it seems that 2021 could also be called the year of the Metaverse. The development of digital media has set off waves of technology. From the widespread use of smartphone, the arriving of the 5G era, the promotion of wearable devices in daily life, the continuous breakthrough of VR/AR/MR and XR technologies, to the disruptive revolution brought by the four technologies of NBIC

P.-L. P. Rau (Ed.): HCII 2022, LNCS 13312, pp. 484–496, 2022.
https://doi.org/10.1007/978-3-031-06047-2_36

(Nano, Bio, Information and Cognition) and the new exploration of artificial intelligence in various fields, we can know that information technology is kicking off the era of great changes and media technology and smart devices are also accelerating the Cyborgization of humanity.

The success of the BML VR holographic concert proved once again its influence among the young people of the Z-generation. When both real and virtual people become idols on the stage, virtual reality seems to be more realistic than the reality in daily life. The immortalized cyborgs have appeared in Sci-Fi movies and novels, such as in the movie Her, an artificial intelligence operating system Samantha falls in love with a real person. The novel Snow Crash describes a half-virtual, half-real info world, where everything (including persons) is becoming the transmission of information. In this novel both humans and computers exist on the basis of coding and the whole world is driven by a super-powerful metaphor that "humans are computers". The media ecology has changed dramatically in the real or future picture constructed by digital technology when the material body is disappearing and is presented as a kind of "fluid and changing symbol". In the era of Cyborg, the issue of "body" has been highlighted as a keyword and an important perspective for thinking about the relationship between human and machine in the era of intelligent design.

2 Cyborgs in Cyberspace

British physicist J.D. Bernard published a pamphlet entitled "The World, the Flesh and the Devil - An Enquiry into the Future of the Three Enemies of the Rational Soul" in 1929, which introduced the term "transformable cyborg" and inaugurated the study of cyborgs. In the 1960s, scientists M. E. Clynes and N. S. Kline proposed the word "cyborg" in their article "Cyber and Space" for the first time. They defined it in the context of interstellar travel in the field of space. Subsequently, the American scholar N. Katherine Hayles explained the term as a control organism, a mixture of machine and organism, a social reality creature, and a science fiction character [1]. "Cyberspace" is derived from the novelist William Gibson's science fiction novel *Necromancer*, which was written in 1984. In the book *An introduction to cybercultures,* David Bell defines cyberspace clearly, "The word 'Cyberspace' is a complex term to define; indeed, its definition can be refracted through our three story-telling tropes to give us different (though often overlapping) definitions. We can define cyberspace in terms of hard-ware, for example– as a global network of computers, linked through communications infrastructures, that facilitate forms of interaction between remote actors. Cyberspace is here the sum of all those nodes and networks" [2].

Although the concepts of cyborgs and cyberspace have been proposed for decades, they have mostly been discussed in film and literature. With the rapid development of digital smart devices in recent years, these concepts have been supported to a more realistic level. The rise of VR/AR/MR technology, smartphones, the Internet of Things and wearable devices has accelerated the cyborgization, that is to say, the existence of digital virtualization. Users can obtain a variety of information, such as visual and audible information with the help of various smart devices. They gain a sense of physical presence and get the feeling of orientation and distance in the virtual space, as well as have an immersive experience from a first-person perspective. As a kind of social reality, Cyberspace is gradually establishing the link between technology and human body, changing the modern way of living and accelerating the Cyborgization of people.

What does Cyborgization mean? Some researchers have defined it from four dimensions– From the perspective of ideology, the body becomes a fashionable symbol; from an epistemological point of view, the body, whose existence is guaranteed by consciousness according to Descartes, begins to disintegrate; from a semiotics point of view, the body becomes a tattoo or a fluid symbol; from a technical point of view, the body becomes "ultra refuse" and "hyper-functionality" [3]. The cyborgization reveals a certain adaptation of the human being under the impact of the technological waves, either actively or passively. In other words, there is some kind of body steering under the intelligent technology: on one hand, the human being realize the extension of human body by the helping of media as pointed out by Marshall McLuhan in his theory of media extension; on the other hand, the digital media technology has brought about a particulate distribution of society and a kind of data existence. It has achieved two kinds of transcendence of human beings by recreating "digital bodies": one is internal, that is the transcendence of human beings to the limits of their own bodies; the other is external, which means the expansion of human beings in Cyberspace. The two kinds of transcendence is accompanied by the emergence of the post-human, which is a result of the amputation and technology embedding of the physical body of a natural person. As the concept of Metaverse describes, a virtual world paralleling to the real world emerges, where real people acquire a cyber-identity 'Avatar', in addition to their physical bodies, and they can live with virtual people in the Metaverse by using smart devices. Because the metaverse activates people's vision of the future of Internet, this concept immediately attracted a lot of attention. When we take a closer look at the concepts of Cyberspace and Metaverse, it is easy to see that they have similarities in nature.

Some scholars summarize the characteristics of cyberspace as four points—the first one is that people's intuition can be freed from the bondage of material bodies and exist and move independently in cyberspace. The second point is that cyberspace can break through the limitations of the physical world and travel through space-time. The third one is cyberspace consists of information. The last one is that cyborgs gain immortality in cyberspace. These four points, which emphasize the freedom from the material body, the breakthrough of the physical world, the existence of information and cyborgs, are precisely the basis for the realization of the metaverse [4]. Because "meta" means beyond or super, and 'meta + universe' means the integration of the Internet, Internet of things, block chain, cloud computing, virtual reality and other elements. It means a new kind of world form which can transcend the existing world and link the real and the virtual world together technical solidity and discourse conceptuality. The "posthuman" does not simply mean an interface with an intelligent machine, but rather a broader one, in which the distinction between biological organic intelligence and biological information circuits becomes less recognizable. "This change is accompanied by a corresponding shift in the way how the ideation is understood and experienced" [5]. The emergence of cyborgs, metaverse and posthumans has not only triggered dramatic changes in the design industry, but also brought about profound changes in social structures and human-social relations. It lies a breakthrough of technology on the human body and a challenge to the way of human existence, which characterized by the transformation of technology from diffuse to embedded in everyday life.

3   From Extension to Amputation: The Evolutionary Path of the History of Technological Ideas

As Harold Innis has emphasized, changes in technologies invariably produce three kinds of results: they change the structure of human interests (what people think about), the type of symbols (the tools people use to think), and the nature of community (where ideas originate) [6].

The Greek etymology of the word "technology" is "tekhne", which originally appeared as a general term referring to technique, skill or craft. Aristotle clearly distinguished the differences between natural things and manufactured things in his book The Poetics. He pointed out that natural things come into being by their own power, embodying the principle of autonomy and the principle of immanence. For example, if one sows a seed, the seed will take root, then sprout, and grow spontaneously. In contrast, human beings create things by "technology" (techne), which is the essence of making things, embodying the principles of "externality" and "self-regulation" [7]. In short, "technology" refers to a logical artifact, which is created from nature by the Logos. In the Middle Ages, technology was seen as the use of reason, and St. Augustine, in The City of God, states that "the skill of man has advanced and reached perfection" [8]. The word "technique" also refers to the ability to manipulate objects with the hands, which is interpreted as "skills" as well. "Technique" is interpreted as "Tao" in the book Guangya. The word technique, refers both to methods and strategies in a general sense in the classical technical context. It refers to an ability related to experience in a special sense. It is particularly important to point out that the word "experience" emphasizes on-site. It is associated with the field of human feeling, which is the experience of passing.

Of course, to understand the rich semantics of the word "technology", it is necessary for us to return to a specific interaction of time, space and events from a chronological perspective, so as to identify the differences between modern technology and the classical technology of the agrarian era. In the first chapter of the book "Treatise on Architectural Methods", a book on ancient building techniques, for example, the construction of a "palace" is described as follows "In ancient times people lived in caves and wilderness, later great people changed into houses with beams above and walls below to cope with the wind and rain." The Poem said, "When the camp star shone in the sky, the king of Chu began to build the Chu Palace. The craftsmen measured by virtue of the shadow and the palace was built in the capital of the country." The Rites: "The Confucian had a house of one acre, and lived in a room of one square around, a gate made of bamboo, a small side door, a room made of poncho, and a round window made of an urn as a border" [9]. This section focuses on the extensive relationship between the palace and other things such as the wilderness, wind and rain, auspicious days, light and shadow, as well as how the palace developed from the cave dwelling, how the palace related to Confucianism, and how the palace related to the day it was built. As a classical technical book, "Building Style" does not explain what a "palace" is, but shows the relevance of a "palace" to all natural things. What was nature in that time? In nature, everything is connected. Nature contains nature, people and the whole universe. In nature, man has a place to place himself and his mind, and the purpose of nature is unified with the purpose of man's origin.

The greatest ancient Chinese treatise on science and technology, Kao Gong Ji, came out during the Spring and Autumn and Warring States period. The whole book is shy of ink, with a total of 7,000 words, but its content covers a rich variety of production techniques and specifications for houses, buildings, military vehicles, bronze technology, ceramics and musical instruments. The book emphasizes the interrelationship among four elements - heaven, earth, material and work. The work is closely related to heaven, earth and material, so the technology of making artifacts must follow the harmony and unity of heaven, earth and man. As the ancients used to say "the great music is in harmony with heaven and earth......and so a hundred things will not be lost" The thinking of the unity of heaven and man integrates heavenly and artificial work into one. It is because that classical technology is a highly sensual technology, based on the human senses of sight, hearing, and touch, classical technology has, to some extent, extended the human body (Fig. 1).

Fig. 1. The Marquis Yi set-bells unearthed in 1978 from the tomb of the Marquis Yi. The largest bell weighs 203.6 kg with a height of 153.4 cm, and the smallest weighs 2.4 kg with a height of 20.4 cm. Photo courtesy of Hubei Provincial Museum.

As Zong Baihua said in his book "*Aesthetic Walk*", "placing the tiger and the leopard under the drum, people hear the sound of the drum, at the same time, they see the shape of the tiger and the leopard. The two aspects are fictitiously combined in the mind, as if the tiger and the leopard were roaring. The image created by the artist is 'real' and the imagination caused to us is 'imaginary, so it is the combination of the real and the imaginary'" [10]. Insects, fish, birds and animals from the natural world, the sun, moon and stars, mountains and rivers, flowers and plants were used as decorative elements in the bronze works of the pre-Qin period. The aesthetic idea emphasizes the combination of functional utility and decorative artistry, as well as the combination of reality and emptiness, reflects the philosophy that "man follows the laws of heaven, heaven follows the laws of earth, earth follows the laws of Tao, and Tao follows the laws of nature". The classical conception of technology places classical technology in nature, in other words, classical technology itself is an integral part of nature (Fig. 2).

Fig. 2. Reconstruction of a hanging drum, with the bird-shaped rack and tiger-shaped base, unearthed in 2002 from the Chu tomb no. 2, the late Warring States period, in Jiuliandun, Wudian, Zaoyang, Hubei province. Photo courtesy of Hubei Provincial Museum.

Thus, nature and classical technology were linked inextricably. In a natural world of life where natural things and manual things were dominant, classical technology was able to achieve an extension of the human body by relying on great sensuality. The act of making things in the classical era was a kind of craft or an imitation, which was in harmony with the natural world of human life. This was the case in classical Greece, and it was the same in classical China.

We may recognize that throughout the classical technological era, the process of shaping people by technology has always existed. The interactivity between technology and people has also formed the basis of human actions, perceptions and lifestyles. Just as the invention of printing not only changed the mode of human reading, it also affected human communication habits. The emergence of telegraph broke the limits of time and space, the inventions of radio and television extended human vision and hearing, and the Internet changed our understanding of space and time, where time seemed to become faster and faster and the distance seemed to become smaller and smaller. In short, the extension of technology to the human body in the age of classical technology has a basic premise, that is, technology is dependent on human beings, and the human body is a subjective and ontological existence. In daily life technology participates in the process of man's construction of the real world and the process is based on material corporeal existence. As the Aesthetics Richard ShustermanS states, "The body is an important and fundamental dimension of our identity. It forms the initial perspective from which we perceive the world, or rather, it forms the mode of our integration with the world" [11].

The cyborg and cyborgization present a new challenge to the relationship between human and technology in the act of design. The body's tendency to be data-driven is slowly stripping away the biological attributes of the body. It is reengineering the "body" by preserving or enhancing the digital attributes of the individual. This reengineering process is precisely the process from diffusion to embeddedness in the human body and daily life. From the Internet of Things, artificial intelligence, virtual reality to wearable devices, the structure and logic of technology are embedded in the digital "body". Under the dual logic of technology and body, Cybog can walk between the real world and the virtual world without hindrance. Immanuel Kant pointed out in the Critique of Pure Reason that time and space are the most basic abilities of the subject's innate integrated unity, and this unity allows the subject's thinking and perception to have a certain order. The break of the order is accompanied by the transformation of technology from diffuse to embedded. The ccn temporary technology enables the regulation of the body and generates a new kind of technologized texture of daily life.

Although Marshall McLuhan predicted as early as the 1960s that he speed of electrons would make time and space disappear from human consciousness, in Cyberspace, the clear line between the human body and technology is becoming increasingly blurred. The expression "technology is an extension of the human body" is gradually transforming towards "the human body is an extension of technology" This direction is evolving. The transformation is multifaceted. From the perspective of physical existence, the technologized body can wander in the real space of the physical world and the virtual space created by digital technology; from the viewpoint of social structure existence, the fragmented senses of body are integrated into the data body, and the digital way of existence gives Cybog a new sense of existence, reflecting and generating a new social texture in reality; from the perspective of physical sensations, digital technology breaks through the limitations of the physical body in terms of vision, hearing and touching with an immersive experience, and constructs an intelligent body and digital individual with human-computer integration.

A young man named James Young, who lost an arm and a leg in a railroad accident in 2012. He received a bionic arm through a video game competition. Young planed to improve it by using crowdfunding to obtain a bone implant that can be controlled naturally with brain signals, achieving a bionic arm with brain nerve signals. Another computer science researcher, Tiana Sinclair, is working on brainwave technology, inventing a device that captures the brain's attention to control external objects through a helmet.

A German company designed the Eyesect helmet to enable the wearer to experience the visual perception of the other species in the world, like the rotating eyes of a chameleon, or the compound eyes of a dragonfly. In 2019 the brain-computer interface succussed and several products based on BMI technology are gradually achieving the ability to read human cognition, emotion, consciousness and memory. Technology has moved from being in the body to being in the mind. The boundary between living and non-living creatures is increasingly blurred and the embeddedness of digital technology in the human body has been pushed further [12]. Unlike the technology of the classical era, modern technology has somehow lost or is losing its connection with nature and technology can no longer be clearly perceived through human senses such as hearing, sight, and touch. The result of the independence of technology is the incomprehensibility of technology in the post-human era and this incomprehensibility is to some extent the amputation of technology to to people. Francis Fukuyama, who once proposed the "end of history" began to admit that: "History will not end without the end of modern science and technology" [13] (Fig. 3).

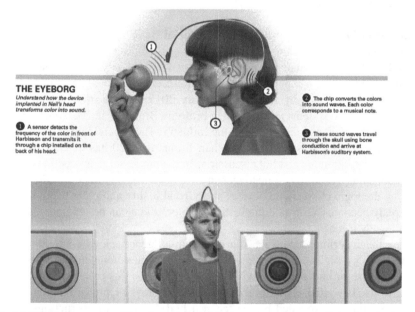

Fig. 3. Neil Harbisson, who suffers from colour blindness, has become a Cyborg and colour blind artist through wireless sensors implanted in his skull.

What kind of future will design create when the elements of natural human and cyborgs, physical reality and virtual reality are superimposed together? The cases that have happened or will happen prove to us again and again that in the process of the body experiencing the "world" through digital technology, the previously insurmountable boundary between technology and the body dissolves, and the body becomes an extension of digital technology. The Cyber Age has dramatically intensified the degree to which technology is embedded in the human body, and when the Cyborgs emerge as a new kind of subject, scholars are forced to rethink the meaning of the human body and the boundaries of technology in the practice of design.

4 Design in the Anthropocene Era: Rethinking the Relationship Between Human-Technology

Every change in technology brings about a change in social and cultural forms. "The medium of communication in a certain culture has a decisive influence on the formation of the spiritual and material center of the country." The accelerated escalation of digital technology in the future means dramatic changes in the social form of Cyberspace from both the material and the spiritual world. Many uncontroversial consensus and ideas will begin to encounter challenges. While reshaping the human body, the new technological landscape also reminds us to reexamine the body in the social picture. The focus on the body as a key element from the perspective of design is a fundamental shift in the Anthropocene era: the body is included into the study of design, which means design begins a body turning [14].

(1) The Extension and Alienation of the Material Body

Alpha Go played the first white chess on March 9, 2016 after "thinking" for a moment and finally defeated the human player Lee Sedol 4:1. If it only caused a sigh of relief in the human-computer game, however, the announcement of the latest brain-computer interface system invented by Nerualink in July 2019 and the official launch of two intelligent operating systems for the human brain by Brain OS in 2020 quickly became the focus of attention and discussion in the industry. The official launch of Brain OS's two intelligent operating systems for human brains in 2020 has quickly become the focus of industry attention and hot discussion. In the mode of reconstructing the natural human being, the human body is no longer an integrated existence in the traditional sense. Following the logic of wearable devices and virtual reality and other technologies, the human body becomes a sort of combination of blocks that can be separated, assembled and put together.

When the superimposed effect of artificial intelligence, cloud computing, convergence technology, big data and other technologies becomes more and more obvious, the traditional sense of human subjectivity will overturn. "In this process, the category of our 'body' also beyond the definition of the classical category, physical humans become the 'central body', surrounded by the 'central body' that gives instructions, there are 'extended body' composed of various intelligent devices, and the 'remote sensing body' beyond the super-visual distance" [15]. There are different opinions on whether the human body under the Cyborg metaphor makes people more human, or whether they lose their human nature and become more like machines. Fukuyama regards posthumanism as "the most dangerous idea in the world", and he believes that the uncertainty "X" brought by augmentation will destroy the dignity and the equal foundation of freedom and democracy in human society [16]. Take virtual reality technology as an example, the exploration of virtual worlds is precisely achieved by forgetting the real material body, because this exploration and experience is free from the limitations of the body's available visual and perceptual perception (Fig. 4).

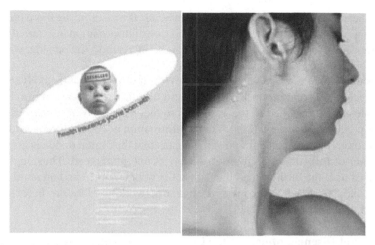

Fig. 4. Neugenics birthmark TM health insurance advertisement, 2002. Designer: Heather Frank.

Heather Frank's project Neugenics posits a not-too-distant future where genetic modification and re-engineering are so common that newborns are having pre-modified DNA samples implanted under their skin so that they can later have access to their 'original' self's genetic inheritance, should they wish to reset their genetic dials.

When the scenario referred by the concept of metaverse is really realized, when the real world and the virtual world form the future metaverse together, will the connection between human-human become much weaker than the strong human-machine connection, and will it lead to the neglect of one's own body and the alienation of real human relationships? "In the practice of intelligent daily life, the characteristics of the intelligent technology will make individuals become transparent people. The phenomena such as intelligent communication dependence and addiction have gradually revealed the loss of subjectivity." [17] Although the human body itself is not a static black box, the boundaries of the material body become blurred with the intervention of the digital body and the virtual body. It comes an interesting paradox here: while the human body and its functions extend outward in the Cyber Age, the body is constrained and checked by a counterforce. In other words, the extension of the body leads precisely to the alienation and disappearance of the subjectivity of the human body.

(2) The Rights and Regulations of Digital Subjects

In 1995, the American futurist Negroponte once wrote on the cover of his famous book Digital Survival: "Computing is no longer only about computing, it will determine our survival." The digitalization of people in the Cyber Age means that people's conscious or even unconscious behavior will be recorded in the form of data, from web browsing, video watching, shopping records to driving routes, the massive data records will depict a digital person who is even more real than himself. As the digitization of the body continues to deepen, on one hand, the digital subject will counteract the material subject and play an important role on design behaviors and choices. On the other hand, the physical person is fully exposed to the monitoring mechanism, and the person has to face the regulation of the body digitization while gaining the right. "Becoming a 'human terminal' means that the attributes of the human being as a medium are more prominent, a medium that not only participates in the transmission of information in external networks, but also transmits various data about the human being itself to the outside, which was a resource for companies to analyze or utilize" [18].

For example, while wearable devices achieve controllability of the body through the power of technology and produce a set of health discourse, the body in turn becomes a tool. People can be matched to the accurate product they need from various products, while this precision in turn gives birth to an information cocoon. Moreover, when technology becomes the new center of power, it means that the digital divide is growing. The digital power of marginalized groups in society is not guaranteed. Thus, in the context of the digital age, the birth of the outer subject is both a poison and an antidote, which can either make us attach to the invisible digital network and lose our inner soul, or let us discover an overflowing ME [19].

(3) Sanity and Disenchantment in the Context of the Anthropocene

The concept of "Anthropocene" was first introduced by Paul Crutzen and Eugene Stoermer in 2000 in Mexico at the International Geosphere-Biosphere Program (IGBP) meeting in Mexico. They argued that the human beings' impact on the Earth's environment has escalated over the past two hundred years. They used the term Anthropocene to refer specifically to the geological period when humans dominated climatic, geological and ecological changes. This concept warns us to go beyond the traditional view of space and time and rethink human beings. The holistic thinking of the earth as an organic living organism will certainly influence the design thinking and practice in the Cyber Age (Fig. 5).

Fig. 5. (left) Hydrogen energy future, 2004. Designers: Anthony Dunne and Fiona Raby. (right) Blood/meat energy future, 2004. Designers: Anthony Dunne and Fiona Raby.

The installation entitled Is this your Future? at the Science Museum in London illustrates the potential tensions between our current energy crises and the potentials for distributed energy production in the future. Like a project for Popular Science gone slightly mad, they prototype a future everyday in which children do their part to contribute to our shared energy needs.

The broadened perspective offered by the Anthropocene makes us, immersed in a technological delusion, realize that human beings and the technological world it has created are in a broader ecosystem. Global warming, resource scarcity, melting glaciers, species extinction and the spread of epidemics, as more and more problems emerge in this era, humanity has to reconsider returning to the holistic world. The thinking about the relationship between human and technology in the Cyber Age should be incorporated into the time-space view of the Anthropocene. We have to look towards a more open planetary space, and to analysis from the macro dimension about the impact of technology on people, on the natural environment, and on the ecosystem. After all, human beings have co-evolved with the technologies and the environment around them. "To be human…… means to be in a network where our humanity can only be articulated through our environment, tools, artifacts, and the networks of human and non-human life" [20].

5 Conclusion

Along with the explosion of a new technological revolution, cyborg is becoming a reality progressively. The interaction between technology and people, technology and human society is becoming more and more frequent. The evolution of mobile media, virtual reality, Internet of Things, artificial intelligence and other emerging technologies has redefined the body in the act of design. In the cyberspace, the technological construction of design theory and practice become a "cocoon" that humans make for themselves, in which we are often unaware. As a result, people are increasingly accustomed to assigning themselves to the digital world and running faster and faster on the road of digitalization, while ignoring the most precious emotional characteristics of human beings in design; people are increasingly seeking stronger sensory capabilities and self-binding in the name of technological evolution, while ignoring face-to-face communication, physical embrace and eye contact; people are increasingly adapting to the algorithmic model, obsessed with virtual space and time, using super-efficient society as the indicator of civilization, while neglecting the emotions that are designed to be carried beyond data, the original dependence of human beings on natural ecology and moral purification. The key to breaking the cocoon into a butterfly is never outside of human subjectivity, not in avoiding the coming of the Cyber Age, not in excessive concern about the subversion of human nature by cyborgs. In the epic change of digital civilization, the cyborg, as a part of the human civilization schema, is overturning the way we think about design. It may be an interesting point to take a critical perspective of design philosophy, to re-gaze the body, to construct an ethical system of design based on non-anthropocentrism, and to open a new perspective design research with a bodily turn in order to achieve the construction of a well-ordered society.

References

1. Katherine Hayles, N.: How We Became Posthuman: Virtual Bodies in Cybernetics, Literature, and Informatics, p. 135. University of Chicago Press, Chicago (1999)
2. Bell, D.: An Introduction to Cyberculture, pp. 50–51. Routledge, London (2001)
3. Katherine Hayles, N.: How We Became Posthuman: Virtual Bodies in Cybernetics, Literature, and Informatics, p. 124. University of Chicago Press, Chicago (1999)
4. Ran, D.: Cyberspace, disembodiment and embodiment. Philos. Dyn. **6**, 67–69 (2013)
5. Katherine Hayles, N.: How We Became Posthuman: Virtual Bodies in Cybernetics, Literature, and Informatics, p. 46. University of Chicago Press, Chicago (1999)
6. Postman, N.: The Disappearance of Childhood, p. 16. CITIC Press, Beijing (2015)
7. Aristotle: Poetics, p. 69. Shanghai People's Publishing House, Shanghai (2016)
8. Augustine, Wang, X.: The City of God, p. 103. People's Publishing House, Beijing (2018)
9. Jin, L.: Treatise on Architectural Methods, p. 5. Chongqing Publishing House, Chongqing (2017)
10. Zong, B.: Aesthetic Walk, p. 53. People's Publishing House, Beijing (2001)
11. Schuster, R.: Body Consciousness and Body Aesthetics. Cheng Xiangzhan, pp. 13–20. The Commercial Press, Beijing (2011)
12. Sun, Z.: Philosophy of the Anthropocene, p. 99. The Commercial Press, Beijing (2020)
13. Fukuyama, F.: Our Posthuman Future: Consequences of the Biotechnology Revolution, p. 18. Guangxi Normal University Press, Guilin (2017)
14. Zhu, Y.: The interconstruction and inter-embedding of communication and body: a study of body triad in the act of "listening". Modern Commun. **8**, 46 (2021)
15. Jane, S.Y.: Aesthetics of the body in the post humanist context. J. Guangzhou Univ. (Soc. Sci. Edn.) **5**, 31 (2020)
16. Fukuyama, F.: Our Posthuman Future: Consequences of the Biotechnology Revolution, p. 58. Guangxi Normal University Press, Guilin (2017)
17. Zhang, S.: Technology, Communication and the Individual: Participatory Risks and Adaptation Strategies for Intelligent Communication. China Editorial, vol. 12, p. 29 (2021)
18. Peng, L.: Digital technology opens up unlimited imagination of media. China Soc. Sci. J. **11**, 5 (2021)
19. Lan, J.: The birth of the external subject: the flux of subject formation in the digital age. Seeking **5**, 19 (2021)
20. Graham, E.L.: Post/human conditions. Theol. Sexuality **10**, 32 (2004)

Image Behavior: Re-examining Design Games from the Perspective of Design Anthropology

Yan Wang[✉]

Academy of Art and Design, Tsinghua University, Beijing, China
wyan13happyday@163.com

Abstract. This paper discusses how design games play a role in design anthropology historical research and serve the operation method of image behavior. Through game design in design anthropology, on the one hand, it focuses on how to promote group cooperation and help design researchers understand the relationship among image, space and behavior. On the other hand, it aims to help researchers empathize with the fuzzy roles and cultural cognition of stakeholders in participatory design. In the specific operation, we select Roy Arne Lennart Andersson's "En duva satt på en gren och funderade på tillvaron", through image extraction and annotation, illustration and collage, design and game and other means, to randomly combine the performance of objects and spatial subjectivity, changing people's perspective of observation, and expanding the game to the fields of art design and design anthropology. To show the reproduction of cultural cognition in the expression of image space, the ultimate purpose is to explore the process of design research methods and the reconstruction of logical thinking training.

Keywords: Design research method · Image behavior · Design games · Cultural cognition · Design anthropology

1 Introduction

When designing games is often used in a social or participatory design, we should not only focus on research problems but also the method's logic. The game proposed in this paper is different from the traditional game. It is a research method based on design anthropology. It is also a fragmented space of different visual images of the same film constructed based on the cultural cognition of users or stakeholders on the game design. The key point is to analyze and explain the dialogue between the participants in the design game and the actors themselves, so that the participants and stakeholders can re-understand the image operation and behavior. While implementing our research methodology centered around game design in design anthropology, we need to pay attention to how to promote cooperation during the game and how to help researchers understand image behavior again. Subsequently we should connect design, users, context, relationships, practices, and forms to achieve the key points of social design. The research should not only pay attention to the actors themselves, but also adopt the design game as a practical research method of design anthropology.

© The Author(s), under exclusive license to Springer Nature Switzerland AG 2022
P.-L. P. Rau (Ed.): HCII 2022, LNCS 13312, pp. 497–509, 2022.
https://doi.org/10.1007/978-3-031-06047-2_37

While there has been extensive research on game design, there is little focus on the question: how can game design help stakeholders understand their own roles, quickly achieve cooperation, rapidly change their research perspectives and participate in the same design research project creatively? To tackle this question, this study adopts the perspective of design anthropology with researchers participating in observation and designing a card game. As design researchers with different roles, they practically participate in it and reoperate and understand the research process. When we design games from the perspective of design anthropology, meta-narration and participation are different through the construction of game elements. For example, when the design assignment is different from design practice, the design researcher will carry out a series of social current investigations to check the design process and events. Re-examining the design game from the perspective of design anthropology, we can find that the design game is a research method, in order to unify the design process with the previous concepts and enable stakeholders to observe things from different perspectives and understand the design intention.

This paper takes the design game of cultural cognition as the main research object, and creatively discusses the purpose, significance and value of the subject by using the findings of design anthropology and the methods of existing literature and group discussion. Firstly, in the theoretical sense, this paper enriches and improves the theoretical knowledge system and provides a research perspective on the general development law governing people, games, and cognition. Secondly, in a practical sense, this study attempts to discover the relationship between cultural cognition, human behavior, and game design. Thirdly, in the practical sense, it attempts to demonstrate the problem consciousness in project practice, and study the cognition of design games under design anthropology by enumerating relevant theories and studying design game cases, to guide the utilization, development, renewal, and continuation of design education in the future. This paper takes the design game of cultural cognition as the main research object, and creatively discusses the purpose, significance, values of the subject by using the findings of design anthropology and the methods of existing literature and group discussion. First, in the theoretical sense, the article enriches and improves the theoretical knowledge system and provides a research perspective on the general development law among people, games, and cognition. Second, in a practical sense, this study attempts to answer the relationship between cultural cognition, human behavior, and game design. Third, in the practical sense, it attempts to demonstrate the problem consciousness in project practice, and study the cognition of design games under design anthropology by enumerating relevant theories and studying design game cases, to guide the utilization, development, renewal, and continuation of design education in the future.

2   Literature Review: Re-examining Game Design

The origin of design games can be traced back to nine urban environment design games [1], and the game is used as a research tool to provide a method to explore various concepts, to study design theories and methods. Design games are often associated with participatory design and social design [2, 3], showing the ideas of participatory education, game design elements, collaborative cooperation, and social design respectively [4–7], which can be understood from the aspects of composition system and complexity design experience. Therefore, the design game in some project work can enable design researchers and stakeholders to better show their ideas, narration, expressions, and comments. Taking the design game as a place for the public scientific experiment is conducive to the construction of collective imagination [8]. It is important to use design games to achieve cooperation among users, stakeholders, and designers and to strive to achieve a common goal.

Since the 1980s, practical theory has been constructed in the field of anthropology to solve the relationship between society and the individual. The theoretical problem concerned by anthropology is the relationship between man and structure, which aims to explore the dialectical relationship and bring into play man's initiative. At the same time, the design also drew lessons from anthropological methods and gradually incorporated practice and individual action into the research system. Design researchers believe that design research should "design by doing" [9, 10]. There is a space planning case that studies the views of single residents on shared space. It is based on a design game in action, determining and weighing family-related space functions and services, collecting user knowledge and resident files, guiding participants to explain their preferences, and negotiating the boundary between shared space and private space [11]. This project provides a new research direction for developing new housing concepts or re-planning existing spaces. In fact, a design game can be understood as a language game with practical action, which can enhance the dialogue relationship among users, stakeholders, and designers [12]. In the whole process of design participation, game design can also be understood as a metaphor [13]. Metaphors can not only blur the boundaries between roles to a certain extent but also enhance the cognitive experience between roles. However, some scholars gradually appeared critical reflection in the role of early participatory design researchers, combining teaching process, experience, critical events, individual and society [14–16]. Design researchers pay more attention to their values, agenda, views, social response, and other content. These critical reflections are gradually applied to a participatory and expressive design game research method [17, 18], and the social and humanized design research is also carried out. Design anthropologists also involve designers through anthropology, ethnography, and other research methods, and improve the depth and breadth of design problems. They think that design needs to have a humanistic spirit, advocate a new ethnographic research method involving design in the anthropological turn, and move towards social design, social practice, and social collaborative research [19–22]. In addition, the research of design needs the involuntary participation of designers, and the research is the combination of purpose and method [18]. When designing games is used as a kind of participation or sociality, it focuses on the study of combinatorial problems, which is also a logical method and a solution with problem consciousness. Its cognitive culture and cognitive practice, reflexivity are often used in participatory design, and it is a topic for designers to formulate research methods [23, 24]. It is to provide opportunities for consumption experience by cultivating the continuity of practice, that is, immersion, adaptation, and innovation [25].

Therefore, reflexivity needs not only the conceptual design of objective objects but also the process of design practice. Anthropologist Braudel believes that "for the present, the past is also a way to distance ourselves" [26]. In the past, human beings can reflexively think about the present. This is not only a critical attitude towards social problems but also the premise of social design and participatory design.

So what is the relationship between design games and design anthropology, and how to intervene in the research problem as a form or method in the research process of design Anthropology? The design game in the context of design anthropology focuses on the relationship between design practices and contexts of design [23]. The practice of research must undergo profound changes, so that action is a kind of becoming, not getting, reshaping motivation and action [27]. It is necessary to pull away from the design process, appropriately intervene in research problems, and find the construction method to establish and expand the research process. Anthropology emphasizes the data of natives in fieldwork and observes the dialogue between natives and researchers. The design game of design anthropology does not need to provide the basic data of users but does practical research and process research through traditional ethnography to reconstruct the internal relationship between things in different cultural situations.

3   Methodology

3.1   Daily Behavior Cognition in Culture

How do humans recognize themselves in daily life? This study discusses the design game through the art film "En duva satt på en gren och funderade på tillvaron" directed by Roy Arne Lennart Anderson in Sweden. The film has no linear narrative in the general sense. It consists of 39 fixed silent scenes about human nature, depicts a surrealist picture full of artistic and philosophical speculation, and deeply implies the significance of modern human daily life behavior and cognition (see Fig. 1).

Fig. 1. 39 scene images in the movie.

There are two main aspects of daily behavior cognition. One is image behavior generation. Starting from the phenomena of scrape together, discontinuity, and disorder in modern society, this method uses a seemingly meaningless random card game to deny the existing order and generate and create new space. According to the previous research part, this method discusses a new narrative space story. During the game operation stage, the team members upgraded the card game and continued to explore new spatial forms. The other is to explore new spatial forms in the way of random games. The film restores the elements of life scenes and uses cold jokes of human self-cognition to describe the cultural phenomena of depth, emotion, and history [28]. In his early anthropological studies, Boas described cultural phenomena as a unique way of existence and understood their respective cultures in their respective fields [29, 30]. Malinowski believes that in-depth field investigation is needed to understand social and cultural phenomena [31, 32]. In the 1950s, the change of cultural definition was marked by the cultural definition of gathering influence proposed by the American anthropologist Ward H. Goodenough and related their respective cultures and social cultures to the cognition of daily behavior. He believes that social cultural cognition consists of what people must know or believe [33]. Culture is not a material phenomenon, nor does it contain things, behaviors, or motives. It is an organization, a series of things recognized by people's minds, and a model of their perception, correlation, and interpretation [34, 35]. Whether in movies, photos, or paintings, the plot of each frame can extract space and character fragment elements to show the complete cultural life story to the audience or users. The reason why the film is selected as the basis of game design is to deepen life's understanding through the daily human behavior operation in the film. This method attempts to separate the relationship and plot between space and action, objects and objects in game design. It tries to make participants use random game behavior to get different design image results, to form relatively independent fragment elements. Finally, we extract the spatial elements of modern society from the film, combine the relevant elements of discontinuous and complex images, and use a seemingly meaningless random card game to deny the existing order and generate and create new spatial images. The ultimate goal is to explore people's cognitive behavior and find a pleasant and relaxed design research method through design means. The game can be used as a dialogue tool to understand human daily behavior through design practice. It is a process of discussing the internal objective image of space and participatory observation experience.

3.2 Game Card Scene and Design Assumptions

The project has produced a board game playing method similar to Chinese Mahjong (see Fig. 2), including ten black-and-white dice (points from 1 to 10), a coordinate map (10 multiply by 10 as a unit), card list, card game playing instructions, form cards (object cards, role cards, space cards, operation cards, form cards), etc. (see Fig. 3) The object cards, character cards, and space cards are extracted from the fragments of space scene elements in the film; Operation cards represent the operation means of design behavior, including intersection, union, difference, amplification, reduction, distortion, and rotation; Shape card is another image effect expressed by design behavior, including the form and content of plane, elevation, axis side, and perspective

CARD GAME

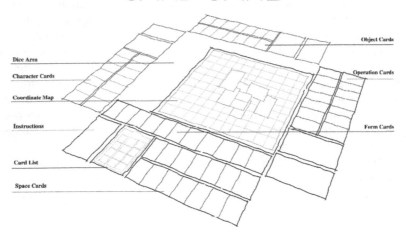

Object Cards

Dice Area

Character Cards

Operation Cards

Coordinate Map

Instructions

Form Cards

Card List

Space Cards

Fig. 2. Schematic diagram of board game playing method of card game

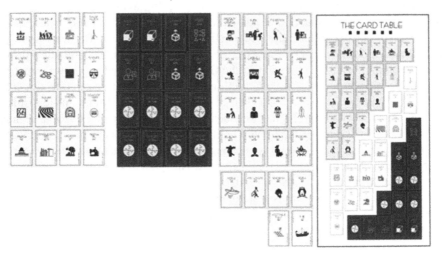

Fig. 3. Five card forms: object, role, space, operation and form

In terms of the overall operation, the design assumption of the card game is mainly divided into six steps (see Fig. 4, Fig. 5). Firstly, we look for the content of 39 scene elements about human nature in the film and intercept the picture. The elements in the scene are divided into three categories: objects, a character moving lines, and space, corresponding to object cards, character cards, and space cards respectively. Secondly, select and draw element cards from object, character, and space in order, and extract two cards in each round. Thirdly, it extracts different form cards for each card obtained before carrying out form operations (such as plane, elevation, axis side, and perspective).

Fourthly, the abscissa and ordinate points are established successively by rolling dice twice, and the position of the card is determined by taking the lower-left corner of the image as the coordinate base point. Fifthly, after determining the image coordinates, it is necessary to extract operation cards for each picture in turn, and determine the relationship with the next card by determining intersection, union, difference, amplification, reduction, distortion, rotation, and other means. Sixthly, we need to fuse to generate images. Finally, all elements are organized together by drawing to get the final spatial image result.

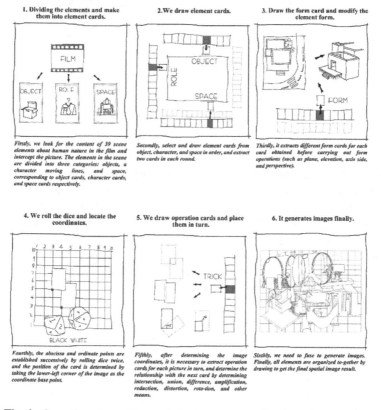

Fig. 4. Operation steps of image behavior reconstruction in card game space

The game design has a certain law of randomness. For participants to recognize the things themselves in the process of the experiment, a total of four participants need to complete the game design together, and all four participants need to make choices under the social background of unified understanding. Such a game process can not only enhance cooperation, but also experience and participate in human behavior and cognition in the design of games. Randomness is not static and abstract, but a dynamic system process with continuous change and development. In terms of statistical law, a large number of random events reflect the distribution of repeated probability in the process [36]. A large number of random phenomena in the game design must be a kind

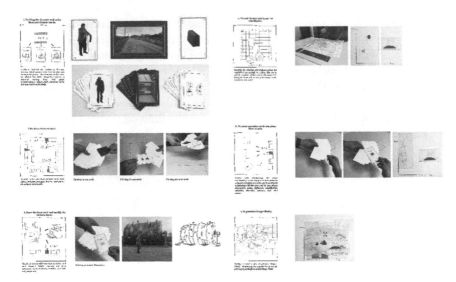

Fig. 5. Exploded view of card game steps

of systematic relevance as a whole. In the game, each stakeholder will be responsible for the production of an image type superposition, in which the randomness probability produces the relationship between interaction and communication. Through the behavior operation of card games, people get the design presentation of image script and the self-existence of authenticity. Finally, a new narrative will be born after the 9 rounds of game alternation of repeated card crossing and replacement (see Fig. 6, Fig. 7). We use games to generate new stories from random probability events. The events generated by probability are collaged and reorganized to generate a new image space. The process of designing game strategy itself is the result of spatial behavior, and it is also another way out of the cultural metaphor of card game, random probability, and crazy artistic imagination.

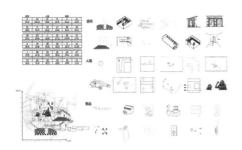

Fig. 6. Example of card game space, person and object conversion

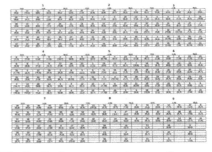

Fig. 7. Card game operation coordinate point record

3.3 Cognitive Process of Card Games: How to Understand Image Space

The process of game participation in image space is the process of human writing meta-narrative space. The stitching and composition of different element images is a deterministic random event, and it is also a design behavior composition mode integrating space, people, and things. When studying the spatial narrative of artworks, the French Immigration Museum reorganized the design behavior through the image and form of a single object to awaken the sensitivity and attention of the audience [37]. Therefore, each object space presented is an event clue. The object space is spliced and combined independently through images and forms to form a spatial order, and reorganized by designing game behavior operations. Each real social space image extracted from it is abstractly described, which represents the objective material existence under the social and cultural background. The visual image element in the film is not only the premise of narrative space construction but also the reinterpretation of image space. Through the reconstruction of game design, it is transformed into a spatial model. Image-space is expressed and presented through the experimental imagination and reasoning process of design research. This study takes the visual elements of the film "En duva satt på en gren och funderade på tillvaron" as the starting point, discusses the cooperation mode between users through the card game behavior operation mode, edits and collages the

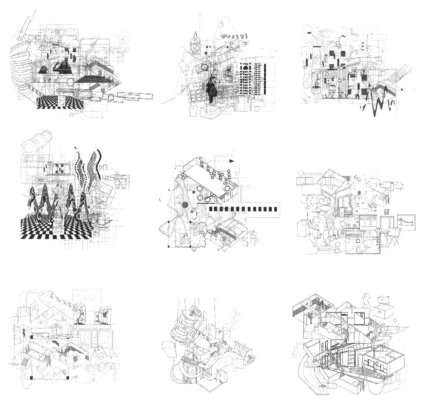

Fig. 8. Card game image space rendering results

image information, and then interprets it through the image visual method to express the relationship between the antagonistic and contradictory elements of space (see Fig. 8) The understanding reached by the British philosopher John Locke by referring to objects and the concept of these objects are used to describe the seemingly perfect natural imagination in reality [38]. In the process of designing research methods, card games, designers, users, and image elements overlap each other, which leads to the discussion of spatial imagination. By adding the reconstruction and reinterpretation of spatial images in the design of games, we can observe the constituent relationship of practice. Designing games as a means to promote and develop an early conceptual design or research methods can stimulate critical reflection between vision, image, and imagination in daily life.

Image behavior consists of events and plots. All event elements are behaviors, and narrative text is also the result of narrative behavior. Graphic image behavior can combine the images, devices, characters, stories, and other facts of the film, which is a strong structural tendency [39]. Graphic image behavior can combine the image, device, character, story, and other facts of the film. These image elements are also active because of human behavior itself and object form. The image itself is a presentation of visual cognition, and image behavior is the presentation of facts in human behavior activities.

4   Results

Design games is the reconstruction of cultural cognitive language. The purpose of this project is to reconstruct the cultural cognitive language by using a design game in the form of cards. The purpose/nature of cultural cognitive language is to simplify, classify, and abstract experience to form new design concepts and design contexts through the design practice means in design anthropology. Edward Sapir, an American anthropologist, and academician of the Academy of Arts and Sciences, compares cultural cognitive language to the form and structure of arbitrary symbol systems, and believes that language is a tool and thinking is a product [40]. The process of cognition is also a process of language re-memory, which mainly includes vocabulary, such as memory, perception, imagination, language, graphics, images, insight, unconsciousness, consciousness, stimulation, and so on. The processing method of information in the memory system consists of three processes: acquisition, retention, and extraction, and previous experience have an impact on the current behavior [41], which will be reflected in some task operations. Card games connect individual meaningful concept symbols through game design and establish the relationship between things through a priori subjective feelings.

The process of game design generates image space and uses the way of design behavior to preview the future. By exploring the "what", "why" and "possibility" to deal with complex design research problems, users can experience the process of design and gameplay. Intervening in practice through design games can be regarded as a field investigation method of design anthropology. On the one hand, we can understand the relationship between people, on the other hand, we can reproduce the metaphorical objective objects and ideas through practice.

5 Discussion

Design games is not only a way to re-recognize culture, but also a reconstruction of language. Designers discuss design games in the design practice and design context of anthropological research, which is a process of design research methods and thinking training. This paper generally discusses the following questions. How will human beings recognize themselves in their daily life in the future? How to re-examine game design from the perspective of anthropology? How can design games help stakeholders understand their own roles, quickly achieve cooperation, quickly change their research perspectives and participate in the same design and research project creatively?

Some of the questions have been answered. Next, designers participate more in design practice through design research methods, so that we can rethink the meaning of "field". The "field" of design anthropology is not only a real field or user observation but also takes design games as a practical way of current research. The splicing, deconstruction, and reorganization of visual elements are regarded as a behavioral operation means of design anthropology, and a random narrative space is reconstructed by setting card game rules, types, quantities, and participants. Telling the interactive relationship between man and space makes the spatial cognitive image visualized and forms distinctive cultural stories. The new space story narrative is like a game, showing a new view of the world, reality, and standard eyes.

6 Conclusion and Future Work

In this work, based on image research methods and game means of design anthropology, random probability events become more interesting. After six rounds of card changes, a new story will be generated, the probability occurrence standard will be determined, and deterministic random events will be found. The events generated by probability are reorganized and collaged to produce a new image behavior space. It is found that the process of the game is not only a means of image behavior operation but also a process of transformation and presentation of narrative space. We emphasize the use of game design elements when users participate in team cooperation, and provide a set of card game design methods that can be used to identify or recognize social culture. Through the design practice in design anthropology, cultural cognitive language simplifies, classifies, and abstracts experience to form new design concepts and design contexts. In future work, the design of game education can use game cards as the carrier to reconstruct the cultural cognitive language. We will also further demonstrate the social value of a cultural cognitive game according to this research work, and deploy and evaluate it to obtain further insights.

References

1. Habraken, N.J., Gross, M.D.: Concept design games. Des. Stud. **9**(3), 150–158 (1988). https://doi.org/10.1016/0142-694X(88)90044-0
2. Ampatzidou, C., Gugerell, K.: Participatory game prototyping ? Balancing domain content and playability in a serious game design for the energy transition. Codes. Int. J. Cocreat. Des. Arts **15**(4), 345–360 (2019). https://doi.org/10.1080/15710882.2018.1504084

3. Wanick, V., Bitelo, C.: Exploring the use of participatory design in game design: a Brazilian perspective. Int. J. Serious Games **7**(3), 3–20 (2020). https://doi.org/10.17083/ijsg.v7i3.358

4. Budde, M., Oexler, R., Beigl, M., Holopainen, J.: Sensified gaming - design patterns and game design elements for gameful environmental sensing. In: 13th International Conference on Advances in Computer Entertainment Technology (ACE), Osaka, Japan, 09–12 November 2016. ACM (2016). https://doi.org/10.1145/3001773.3001832

5. Ismail, R., Ibrahim, R., Yaacob, S.: Participatory design method to unfold educational game design issues: a systematic review of trends and outcome. In: 5th International Conference on Information Management (ICIM), Univ. Cambridge, Cambridge, England, 24–27 March 2019, pp. 134–138. IEEE (2019)

6. Voulgari, I., Vouvousira, S., Fakou, A.: A game about our neighbourhood: a case study of participatory game design with pre-school children. In: FDG 2020: International Conference on the Foundations of Digital Games (2020). https://doi.org/10.1145/3402942.3409612

7. Young, K.C.: 김기영A study on using urban design games in participatory planning and design workshops (마을만들기를 위한 주민참여워크샵에서 디자인게임의 활용 특성에 관한 연구). J. Urban Des. Inst. Korea **15**(2), 5–25 (2014)

8. Pollio, A., Magee, L., Salazar, J.F.: The making of Antarctic futures: participatory game design at the interface between science and policy. Futures **125** (2021). https://doi.org/10.1016/j.futures.2020.102662

9. Ehn, P.: Scandinavian design: on participation and skill. In: Participatory Design, pp. 41–77. CRC Press (2017)

10. Toralla, M.S.P., Falzon, P., Morais, A.: Participatory design in lean production: which contribution from employees? For what end? Work J. Prev. Assess. Rehabil. **41**, 2706–2712 (2012). https://doi.org/10.3233/wor-2012-0514-2706

11. Pirinen, A., Tervo, A.: What can we share? A design game for developing the shared spaces in housing. Des. Stud. **69** (2020). https://doi.org/10.1016/j.destud.2020.04.001

12. Brandt, E., Messeter, J.: Facilitating collaboration through design games. In: Proceedings of the Eighth Conference on Participatory Design: Artful Integration: Interweaving Media, Materials and Practices-Volume 1, pp. 121–131 (2004)

13. Brandt, E., Binder, T., Sanders, E.B.-N.: Tools and techniques: ways to engage telling, making and enacting. In: Routledge international Handbook of Participatory Design, pp. 165–201. Routledge (2012)

14. Ali, A.: Critically reflective practice in visual communication design teaching for higher education undergraduate program. Int. J. Technol. Des. Educ. (2020). https://doi.org/10.1007/s10798-020-09626-6

15. Carrington, S., Selva, G.: Critical social theory and transformative learning: evidence in pre-service teachers' service-learning reflection logs. High. Educ. Res. Dev. **29**(1), 45–57 (2010). https://doi.org/10.1080/07294360903421384

16. Dittmar, A.: Experience spaces for critical co-reflection on artefact use. Behav. Inf. Technol. **40**(5), 454–463 (2021). https://doi.org/10.1080/0144929x.2021.1912183

17. Eriksen, M.A., Brandt, E., Mattelmäki, T., Vaajakallio, K.: Taking design games seriously: re-connecting situated power relations of people and materials. In: Proceedings of the 13th Participatory Design Conference: Research Papers-Volume 1, pp. 101–110 (2014)

18. Vines, J., Clarke, R., Wright, P., McCarthy, J., Olivier, P.: Configuring participation: on how we involve people in design. In: Proceedings of the SIGCHI Conference on Human Factors in Computing Systems, pp. 429–438 (2013)

19. Garvey, P., Drazin, A.: Design dispersed: design history, design practice and anthropology. J. Des. Hist. **29**(1), 1–7 (2016). https://doi.org/10.1093/jdh/epv054

20. Murphy, K.M.: Design and anthropology. In: Brenneis, D., Strier, K.B. (eds.) Annual Review of Anthropology, vol. 45. pp. 433–449 (2016). https://doi.org/10.1146/annurev-anthro-102215-100224

21. Stuedahl, D.: Future orientation in design, participation and learning. Interact. Des. Archit. (26), 149–161 (2015)
22. Ventura, J., Bichard, A.: Design anthropology or anthropological design? Towards 'social design'. Int. J. Des. Creat. Innov. **5**(3–4), 222–234 (2017). https://doi.org/10.1080/21650349. 2016.1246205
23. Kjaersgaard, M.G., Knutz, E., Markussen, T.: Design games as fieldwork: re-visiting design games from a design anthropological perspective. Des. Stud. **73**, 100994 (2021)
24. Pihkala, S., Karasti, H.: Reflexive engagement: enacting reflexivity in design and for 'participation in plural'. In: Proceedings of the 14th Participatory Design Conference: Full papers-Volume 1, pp. 21–30 (2016)
25. Akaka, M.A., Schau, H.J.: Value creation in consumption journeys: recursive reflexivity and practice continuity. J. Acad. Mark. Sci. **47**(3), 499–515 (2019)
26. Ohnuki-Tierney, E.: Culture Through Time: Anthropological Approaches. Stanford University Press (1990)
27. Ortner, S.B.: Theory in anthropology since the sixties. Comp. Stud. Soc. Hist. **26**(1), 126–166 (1984)
28. Andersson, R.: En duva satt på en gren och funderade på tillvaron. TriArt Film (2015)
29. Boas, F.: The mind of primitive man. Science **13**, 281–289 (1901)
30. Boas, F.: Race, language and culture. J. Nerv. Ment. Dis. **94**(4), 513–514 (1941)
31. Malinowski, B.: Freedom and Civilization. Routledge (2015)
32. Young, M.W.: Malinowski: Odyssey of an Anthropologist, 1884–1920. Yale University Press (2004)
33. Casson, R.W.: Schemata in cognitive anthropology. Ann. Rev. Anthropol. **12**(1), 429–462 (1983)
34. Gahrn-Andersen, R., Cowley, S.J.: Autonomous technologies in human ecologies: enlanguaged cognition, practices and technology. AI Soc., 1–13 (2021)
35. Geeraerts, D.: Cognitive semantics. In: The Routledge Handbook of Cognitive Linguistics, pp. 19–29. Routledge (2021)
36. Gnedenko, B.V., Ushakov, I.A.: Theory of Probability. Routledge (2018)
37. Sherman, D.J.: The perils of patrimoine: art, history, and narrative in the immigration history museum, Paris. Oxford Art J. **39**(3), 457–480 (2016)
38. Locke, J.: An Essay Concerning Human Understanding. Kay & Troutman (1847)
39. Downs, R.M., Stea, D.: Image and Environment: Cognitive Mapping and Spatial Behavior. Transaction Publishers (2017)
40. Sapir, E.: Conceptual categories in primitive languages. Science **74**, 578 (1931)
41. Lorenc, E.S., Mallett, R., Lewis-Peacock, J.A.: Distraction in visual working memory: resistance is not futile. Trends Cognit. Sci. **25**, 228–239 (2021)

Design of Virtual Reality Scenes on Horticultural Therapy Treatment

Jielin Xu[1,2], Dan Liao[1,2(✉)], Xiaojun Peng[1], Guodong Liang[2], Yafei Li[1],
and Xiangqing Zheng[3]

[1] School of Design, South China University of Technology, Guangzhou, Guangdong, China
danl@scut.edu.cn
[2] School of Electronic and Information Engineering, South China University of Technology,
Guangzhou, Guangdong, China
[3] School of Architecture, South China University of Technology, Guangzhou, Guangdong,
China

Abstract. The prevalence of depression and anxiety disorders has increased dramatically in the last two years due to the global COVID-19 epidemic, which leads to a shortage of traditional mental health care resources. To address these issues, we propose to use the digital, immersive, and private features of virtual reality technology to assist in the treatment of mental illness. We designed and completed a garden scene for virtual reality horticultural therapy based on the basic principles of traditional horticultural therapy. In order to study the effectiveness of the gardening scenario, we recruited 30 subjects to explore the effectiveness of mood regulation. A survey of a PANAS scale was conducted before and after the garden scene, and a user experience scale was presented to the subjects after the experiment. The ANOVA results showed that there were significant differences between anxious, distressed and self-loathing before and after the experiment. This demonstrates that virtual reality horticulture therapy has a mood-improving effect. In future works, we will improve the design of VR gardening scenarios and conduct more in-depth research on virtual reality horticulture therapy.

Keywords: Virtual reality · Scenes design · Horticultural therapy

1 Introduction

Since 2020, Covid-19 has been in the global outbreak and has gradually coexisted with mankind for a long time. Research shows that the global cases of major depression and anxiety disorder have increased by 28% and 26% respectively in 2020, and rates have risen the most in the worst-hit countries. Among the new patients with major depression, more than 35 million are female, and 18 million are male [1].

During this period, people including medical staff, bereaved families, isolated people at home, etc., are affected by the epidemic. All of them faced anxiety, helplessness, pessimism and depression in varying degrees. Traditional psychological interventions such as cognitive behavioral therapy (CBT), supportive psychotherapy, cognitive therapy, relaxation training, etc., are effective means to relieve people's negative emotions

P.-L. P. Rau (Ed.): HCII 2022, LNCS 13312, pp. 510–519, 2022.
https://doi.org/10.1007/978-3-031-06047-2_38

which need professionals' conducting guidance [2]. Although these treatment methods are helpful, they rely highly on the face-to-face and long-time treatment process of professional psychological counselors. In addition, during the epidemic, most medical staff need to wear a full set of protective clothing in the medical front-line, so they rarely have face-to-face emotional communication with patients, which also poses a challenge to conventional psychological intervention methods. According to the statistics of the World Health Organization on 130 countries in six regions, many important mental health services have been interrupted on a broad range [3] in some countries, and mental medical resources are obviously insufficient.

In view of the situation above, we digitally reconstructed traditional horticultural therapy and designed a virtual reality-based horticultural healing scenario. Moreover, Taking advantage of the immersive and multisensory interaction of virtual reality technology, we provide a more private and efficient way for patients to self-regulation and promote the alleviation of negative emotions. This project is divided into three parts: the first part is the fundamental and design principles of horticultural therapy, the second part is the tour design of VR garden, and the third part is the experiment of emotion regulation effect. In the third part, the positive and negative emotion scale (PANAS) and User Experience Scale are used to measure and evaluate the emotion of the experimental subjects.

2 Horticultural Therapy Research

2.1 The Fundamental of Horticultural Therapy

Horticultural therapy is to use gardening as a means to improve the physical and mental state, which is characterized by being able to apply to treat almost all obstacles and all problems faced by people. In a broader sense, horticultural therapy refers to the therapy that uses plants or activities around plants to promote people's physical and mental health, including gardening activities, forest bath, color therapy, landscape therapy, phototherapy and garden work, etc. [4]. Previous studies have shown that gardening increases individual's life satisfaction, vigor, psychological wellbeing, positive affects, sense of community, and cognitive function [5].

The principle of horticulture therapy on human beings include visual stimulation, olfactory stimulation, auditory stimulation, etc. In traditional horticultural therapy, the stimulation of plants on people's vision, hearing, smell and taste can relieve people's anxiety, improve their vitality and promote their recovery.

Visual Stimulation: People receive information from the environment through five senses, and studies have shown that more than 70% of the information comes from visual perception [6]. The energy and vitality of plants can relieve people's internal pressure, and plants with different colors and shapes can have different influences on people. Ulrich used natural and urban landscapes as independent variables to observe the physiological and psychological responses of the subjects so as to assess the benefits of visual contact with the natural environment. The results showed that natural landscapes with predominantly green vegetation and waterscape had a better effect on the psychological state [7]. A study by Kaplan illustrates that workers in environments with greenery showed more enthusiasm and patience for their work, with less frustration, increased work ethic, and fewer health problems [8]. Adachi studied the impacts of plant color on people and concluded that yellow flowers were pleasant and blue flowers were calming [9]. Understanding the physiological functions of various colors and using colors correctly and can have the effects of eliminating fatigue, controlling emotions and improving people's physical functions.

Auditory Stimulation: In nature, cicadas and birds sing, and plants hit each other in the wind and rain can make a pleasant sound. Research shows that by listening to comfortable sounds, petients' preoperative anxiety will be reduced [10].

2.2 Design Principles of Horticultural Therapeutic Landscape

After studying and analyzing the cases of rehabilitation gardens in the United States, the United Kingdom, Canada and Australia, Marcus found that its design should follow the following key points to achieve the maximum healing effect of rehabilitation garden: knowability, accessibility, affinity, quietness, physical and psychological comfort, positive artistry, explorability, easy maintainability and target point, panorama [11].

In addition to the above principles, considering the immersive and interactive features of VR technology, we believe that VR horticultural therapy should follow the following principles:

Humanization: Considering the height of the users, the design of the road in VR garden scene should follow the principles of ergonomics, so that the users can visit in a comfortable perspective in the virtual environment. The garden should be used in a way that allows users to find their way easily with clear directions. Ulric et al. proposed the "supportive garden Theory" based on the Stress Education Theory (SRT), emphasizing that recovery gardens need sense of control and privacy [12]. Therefore, more attention should be paid to details in design section, such as for sensitive and vulnerable users, the shaded area should be increased while reduce the stimulation they receive; For users who lack sense of security, a more private space in the layout should be created to reduce the possibility of being concerned.

Personalization: The design of the garden should be in line with the living habits and preferences of users, and put them in a intimate and familiar space environment and the plant configuration that matches daily life, so as to develop sense of security and affinity.

Comfort: Comfortable garden design should pay attention to the psychological needs of users and to provide users with a safe, away from the hustle and bustle of the environment. American environmental psychologists Kaplan and Steven put forward the theory of attention recovery, that people will feel tired if they consciously focus on one thing for a long time. Therefore, people need to immerse in the natural environment regularly to generate unconscious attention and relieve pressure [13, 14]. Exposure to a soft natural environment has a powerful effect on restoring attention. In terms of sound effects, simulating clear birds song, gurgling spring water, rustling leaves and other natural notes can arouse users' good feelings for the natural environment and making the whole scene more immersive to users.

Authenticity: Since users are walking in VR space, the scene design should consider the integration of real and virtual landscape, and follow a reasonable scale and tourism logic. For example, a proper eye level should be set for users when walking in the garden. At the same time, certain target points should be std, such as pavilions, benches, low walls, etc., to provide space for users to rest.

3 VR Garden Design

Based on above principles, we carried out the interactive design of the virtual reality garden scene. It is mainly divided into following three steps. The first step is the research and design of horticultural scene elements, including style establishment, plant design, color design, architectural landscape design and sound design. Then we create the garden scene in unity 3D. Finally, we use VR equipment to test and adjust the scene of the tour process. The process is shown as Fig. 1.

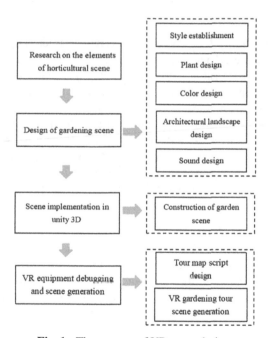

Fig. 1. The process of VR scene design.

3.1 Research on Elements of Garden Scene

Style: The overall garden scene should be designed in open and natural style. According to the biological hypothesis, open, vegetation-rich, watery landscapes are often more favored by people. More natural vegetation coverage can make people closer to the gardening environment and reduce users' feeling of rejection. It is precisely because such environmental features meet the basic needs of defense, food and water for early humans [15].

Plant Design: Research found that compared with spherical trees and conical trees, viewing umbrella trees can cause more positive psychological changes [16]. Therefore, we decide to use more ways of mixing umbrella trees with other trees in gardening scenes, so as to broaden and stretch our horizons and help users generate positive psychological states.

Color Design: Green is a natural color, which can make people feel alive and energetic; Green leaves can absorb ultraviolet rays from sunlight and reduce irritation to eyes, so they can protect eyes and improve eyesight. For people who use their eyes and brains for a long time, facing a bunch of green bonsai will achieve the effect of alleviating mental and physical fatigue. Therefore, the garden color design can make people feel calm and relaxed, and the whole light source can simulate sunny days. The light source can be warm in color, planted with flowers which has warm and cold colors, which makes the garden more colorful.

Landscape Design: Proper design of the pavilion in the garden can also provide patients privacy and safety spaces. Therefore, the architectural landscape in the scene can be composed of pavilions, corridors, mountains, paths and water bodies. Pavilions and corridors can adopt Chinese architectural style to improve the sense of cultural belonging of local users, and the main wooden structure, which brings more friendly and closing feelings. In the scene, undulating mountains can also be arranged to make the terrain more fun to explore. In terms of path design, a multi-directional walking path is set, giving consideration to safety, privacy and exploration interest. The lake is designed to go down the mountain, then surround the viewing road, and finally accumulate into an irregularly shaped pond, which reflects the natural interest and allows people to fully feel the vitality of water.

Sound Design: Research shows that the signal and frequency of natural sound are usually referring to the sound like waterfalls cascading down hills, breeze blowing through trees [17], and the effect is similar to white noise [18], which can make people relax and calm down physically and mentally. Therefore, based on the natural scene of the garden, we set up natural sounds that apposite to the scene, including birdsong, running water, white noise, etc., to increase the sense of immersion.

3.2 Unity3D Design

Firstly, by using Unity's own terrain creation toolkit, regions of mountain, flat field were created, and the sense of scattered terrain was created, and the materials of the terrain were edited accordingly through the unity basic material package. Then, with the self-built Chinese garden building models and various plant models such as umbrella trees and flowers which were previously made in Rhino, 3dmax, and the layout is designed reasonably according to the design principles.

Next, some modifications of the details of the building and the scale parameters of the characters are processed. Objects such as cobblestone and stone road in local areas were built to decorate the scene. After the final test, the scene was finally completed, as shown in Fig. 2.

(a)   (b)

Fig. 2. Snapshots of unity3D design process.

3.3 Tour Route Planning and Comprehensive Debugging

The tour route mainly starts from the gazebo, arrives at the corridor after a huge rockery, crosses a winding path to the pavilion, and finally end at a flower bush. From the line of sight, we need to comprehensively consider the depth of foreground, midground, background and the scene switching between the overall landscape and the local landscape.

A detailed description of the scenes during the tour are as follows:

Initially, accompanied with natural birdsong, the subjects came to a Chinese garden, and the scene that caught their eyes was a rockery, green plants around it and a pavilion behind it (Fig. 3a). Following the movement of the camera, the subjects walked to the pavilion on the lake (Fig. 3b). The pavilion is shaded by shadows. Walking out of the pavilion, the subjects came to a waterscape (Fig. 3c). At this time, as the camera looked around, they could see the surrounding umbrella trees, rockeries and lotus flowers, and the gurgling sound of water appeared in my ears (Fig. 3d). Then the subjects followed the camera to reach a small forest, with small white flowers under their feet (Fig. 3e), and finally stopped in front of a rockery pool (Fig. 3f).

Design Summary: In the aspect of garden design, with the design principles of comfort, humanization, individuality and rationality, we draw modeling elements from Chinese classical garden design, and make use of pavilions, corridors and other elements in gardens to design sightseeing and standing and watching routes. Comprehensive design of shape, color and sound was considered to create a natural and relaxed garden landscape.

Fig. 3. Snapshots of the tour scenes.

4   Horticultural Therapy Research

4.1   Experiment

We conducted an experiment on the effect of emotion regulation. Thirty-five subjects were recruited, and after screening by the SCL-90 scale, five positive subjects were excluded, resulting in 30 valid subjects, with an average age of 22 years and a gender ratio of 1:1. Then we asked the subjects to wear the test equipment and enter the resting state (eyes closed for 30 s, then opened for 10 s for rest) before starting the test. During the test, the subjects were asked to watch the VR video of the gardening tour, and after watching, they finished filling the PANAS scale and the user experience scale again. The experimental procedure is shown in Fig. 4.

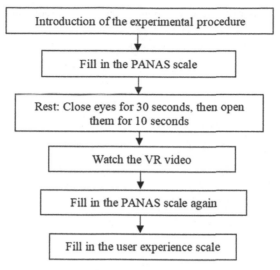

Fig. 4. Flowchart of the experimental process.

4.2 The Result

The ANOVA analysis in Fig. 5 shows that there are significant differences between anxious, distressed and self-loathing before and after the experiment (anxious P = 0.024, distressed P = 0.046, self-loathing P = 0.020), indicating that the scenario has a more obvious effect on relieving anxiety, stress and reducing the emotion of self-loathing.

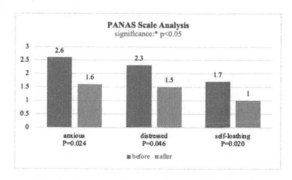

Fig. 5. The significance scores of PANS scale.

The experimental results prove that the overall user experience is good with all satisfaction scores above 4. The highest score is for sound pleasure, and the lowest score is for VR vertigo. Specific contents are shown in Table 1.

Table 1. The user experience questionnaire and average scores of each index.

User experience self-assessment	Average
Comfortable	4.4
Freshness	4.8
Natural feeling	4.6
Sense of space	5.3
Sense of security	4.5
Color feeling	4.7
Relax feeling	5.0
Transparency of sight	4.6
Pleasant of sound	5.4
VR sickness	3.5

5   Conclusion

The experimental results showed that after watching the gardening scene, the subjects' negative emotions were significantly lower than before. In terms of user experience, the feedback from subjects illustrate that the trees, water patterns and other VR stereoscopic visual presentation is preferable, the white noise shows the advantage of natural therapy with a better immersion experience, and the relaxing effect of music is more effective than the picture. However, probably due to unity3D rendering speed problems, which leads to a shortage of fluency and the immersive tour rhythm is slightly faster, the overall emotional improvement is not that obvious, and the design of the scene put too much emphasis on Chinese garden which is rather solemn and the relaxing feeling is relatively weakened.

In the future, we will continue to deepen the design of the scene, providing a more fluency VR experiment, reducing the sense of vertigo, adding more affinity scenes such as water interaction to enhance the positive emotional experience of users. Also we will add psychophysiological sensors to assist in the study of the effect of horticultural therapy's impact on the alleviation of negative emotions.

Acknowledgement. This work is supported by "Guangdong Education Science Planning Project" (2018GXJK003), "Guangdong Philosophy and Social Sciences Planning Project in 2020" (GD20CYS33) and "The Fundamental Research Funds for the Central Universities in 2019" (XYMS202006).

References

1. Santomauro, D.F., Herrera, A.M.M., Shadid, J., Zheng, P., et al.: Global prevalence and burden of depressive and anxiety disorders in 204 countries and territories in 2020 due to the COVID-19 pandemic. Lancet **398**(10312), 1200–1712 (2021). https://doi.org/10.1016/S0140-6736(21)02143-7

2. Wei, H., Li, T.: Impact of Epidemic of corona virus disease 2019 on Different Populations and Suggestions for Psychological Intervention. J. Pediatric Pharm. **26**(04), 6–7 (2020). (in Chinese)
3. Pulse survey on continuity of essential health services during the COVID-19 pandemic: interim report, 27 August 2020
4. https://www.who.int/publications/i/item/WHO-2019-nCoV-EHS_continuity-survey-2020.1
5. Li, S.: Introduction to Horticultural Therapy, pp. 8–9. China Forestry Publishing House. (2011). (in Chinese)
6. Soga, M., Gaston, K.J., Yamaura, Y.: Gardening is beneficial for health: a meta-analysis. Prev. Med. Rep. **5**, 92–99 (2016). https://doi.org/10.1016/j.pmedr.2016.11.007
7. Song, J.-E.: Effect of interior plantscape in office on psycho-physiological improvement and stress alleviation of indoor workers. Korean Society of Horticultural Society academic presentation summary, p. 150, Seoul, South Korea (2004)
8. Ulrich, R.S.: Natural versus urban scenes: some psychophysiological effects. Environ. Behav. **13**(5), 523–556 (1981). https://doi.org/10.1177/0013916581135001
9. Kaplan, R.: The role of nature in the context of the workplace. Landsc. Urban Plan. **26**(1–4), 193–201 (1993). https://doi.org/10.1016/0169-2046(93)90016-7
10. Adachi, M.: Psychological effect and preference of flower color. Agric. Hortic. **77**(1), 11–16 (2002)
11. Uğraş, G.A., Yıldırım, G., Yüksel, S., Öztürkçü, Y., Kuzdere, M., Öztekin, S.D.: The effect of different types of music on patients' preoperative anxiety: a randomized controlled trial. Complement. Ther. Clin. Pract. **31**, 158–163 (2018). https://doi.org/10.1016/j.ctcp.2018.02.012
12. (USA) Clare Cooper Marcus, Translated by Luo, H., Jin, H.: Healing gardens in hospitals. Chinese Lanscape Archit. **07**(1), 01–06 (2009). (in Chinese)
13. Ulrich, R.S., Simons, R.F., Losito, B.D., et al.: Stress recovery during exposure to natural and urban environments. J. Environ. Psychol. **11**(3), 201–230 (1991). https://doi.org/10.1016/S0272-4944(05)80184-7
14. Kaplan, S.: The restorative benefits of nature: toward an integrative framework. J. Environ. Psychol. **15**(3), 169–182 (1995). https://doi.org/10.1016/0272-4944(95)90001-2
15. Kaplan, R., Kaplan, S.: The Experience of Nature: A Psychological Perspective. Cambridge University Press, New York (1989)
16. Frumkin, H.: Beyond toxicity: human health and the natural environment. Am. J. Prev. Med. **20**(3), 234–240 (2001). https://doi.org/10.1016/S0749-3797(00)00317-2
17. Lohr, V.I., Pearson-Mims, C.H.: Responses to scenes with spreading, rounded, and conical tree forms. Environ. Behav. **38**(5), 667–688 (2006). https://doi.org/10.1177/0013916506287355
18. Chang, H., Liang, L., Zhang, M., Zhu, T., Hu, X.: Influence of white noise intervention on the sedative effect of ICU patients. Med. Res. Educ. **38**(02), 61–65 (2021). (in Chinese)
19. Kucukoglu, S., Aytekin, A., Celebioglu, A., et al.: Effect of white noise in relieving vaccination pain in premature infants. Pain Manag. Nurs. **17**(6), 392–400 (2016). https://doi.org/10.1016/j.pmn.2016.08.006

Sound-Guided Framing in Cinematic Virtual Reality – an Eye-Tracking Study

Wenbai Xue and Cheng-Hung Lo[✉]

Xi'an Jiaotong-Liverpool University, Suzhou, China
Wenbai.Xue20@student.xjtlu.edu.cn, CH.Lo@xjtlu.edu.cn

Abstract. When watching films made and displayed with Virtual Reality approaches, the viewers can freely move the visual field, resulting in possible disruptions in the narratives designed by the directors. This phenomenon demands novel narrative strategies in Cinematic Virtual Reality (CVR) to effectively guide a viewer's attention in following important plots. In this study, we evaluate the effect of using sound as a guiding mechanism in CVR. We conduct experiments to analyze the participants' responses to the sound cues outside the field of view with the eye-tracking technique. Statistical methods are then used to infer the significance of the differences among the responses. The experiments are conducted in a virtual scene with low complexity, reducing the possible confounding effects of the variety of visual elements. The results show that the viewer's visual attention can be guided by sounds sourced at the range outside the field of view. More specifically, the viewers react significantly better to sound stimuli varying in horizontal directions than those in vertical directions. Furthermore, different types of sounds also significantly affect the viewers' attention in the virtual scene.

Keywords: Cinematic virtual reality · Sound-guided framing · Visual attention · 3D sound · Eye-tracking

1 Introduction

1.1 Background

Unlike traditional 2D films, those produced and delivered through Virtual Reality (VR) technologies innovate visual storytelling in immersion and interactivity. In immersive virtual environments, the audience is surrounded by a spherical field of view. They are usually free to look at all the provided locations in the virtual scene if wearing a typical Head-Mounted Display (HMD). In this case, the control of "framing" in Cinematic Virtual Reality (CVR) is effectively handed over to the viewer from the director or cinematographer. In CVR experiences, all views can be deemed as being "voluntarily" sought by the audience. The viewing mode thus changes from passively accepting the imagery to actively seeking the imagery. This phenomenon may result in the loss of viewing goals when the narrative plots are implicit. Because it is too "free" to view, it disrupts the continuity of film narratives and impacts the immersive experience unique

© The Author(s), under exclusive license to Springer Nature Switzerland AG 2022
P.-L. P. Rau (Ed.): HCII 2022, LNCS 13312, pp. 520–535, 2022.
https://doi.org/10.1007/978-3-031-06047-2_39

to CVR [29]. This phenomenon becomes more evident when the scenes of plots appear outside the audience's visual range. Our work is initiated to investigate whether other sensory information such as sounds can be used to guide a viewer's attention to effectively follow the planned narratives. With the eye-tracking approach, this paper presents a foundation study that evaluates how the locations and types of sound attract the viewer in moving his/her visual field in a virtual scene.

1.2 Related Works

In traditional screen films, directors use various methods to tell the story, thereby directing the audience's attention and triggering curiosity and suspense [6]. Even as filmmakers and their audiences explore new aspects of the medium, visual storytelling in CVR is still experimental [11]. These traditional narrative techniques are used repeatedly in CVR production. However, since the director does not have absolute control over the camera and the picture, the filmmaker can no longer rely on readily framed views to show the components of the plot [2]. Therefore, traditional editing techniques may not fully apply in CVR [20]. Furthermore, the viewer's ability to explore freely in the film scene is also likely to hinder the development of the narrative and experience in VR films [10]. Nevertheless, whether the film is in a VR environment or not, its primary purpose is still to convey a good story [17].

Shafer [27] compared how the viewers watched the same films in an actual theatre and a VR movie theatre. The results suggested that there was no significant difference between those two ways of watching films. However, according to Mater [22], CVR is different from the projection-based VR experience. CVR allows the user's free control of HMD to choose the framings but less interaction with the elements in the virtual world. Moreover, most immersive VR experiences are triggered and processed through real-time rendering to make user interactions possible, while CVR content is not necessarily generated on the fly.

Many studies in classic films can provide insights for making VR films and support the development of VR video technology [15]. For example, short video sequences and transitional techniques are very useful assets in interactive visual storytelling. Specific guides such as interactable elements can be designed into the films without jeopardizing the sense of immersion and presence [7, 8, 21]. Moreover, when monitoring and analyzing the Region of Interest (ROI) [26, 32], the use of control mechanisms (forcing the audience's perspective to shift to the narrative point) and gaze-leading elements such as a firefly (using moving points of interest to guide the viewer) are also effective ways to attract the audience's attention in VR videos [20, 26].

However, these techniques work more effectively if they appear within the visual field that the user chooses to explore [24]. According to Masia [21], directional sound cues can be a critical element that strongly influences the user's attention when watching film content in VR during editing. Moreover, the proper embedment of audio cues in the virtual environment can evoke emotional responses to fit the storytelling needs and enhance presence and immersion [4].

In addition, off-screen things in CVR are explored by the viewers moving their fields of view [17]. Some researchers found that sound cues in CVR worked effectively in guiding a viewer's attention [3] [19]. According to the research project, Orpheus, Vosmeer [31] used an HMD to study 3D audio for audience attention guidance in a 360-video. Rothe et al. conducted a similar study [24]. These studies have confirmed that audio or audible cues can guide the viewer's gaze in CVR. However, to our knowledge, little exploration has been done in consideration of different sound types. [5]. At the same time, new narrative strategies may arise in VR as a new expressive medium. In the context of VR, time-based narratives may not work as effectively as space-based ones [17].

This study evaluates the effect of the audience's attention and framing guidance in CVR scenes with different sound cues outside the audience's field of view. Most previous research on CVR is usually based on readily-made 360 videos. However, most 360 videos inevitably have much eye-catching visual information. These visual cues have a certain degree of interference with the audience's attention, and technical processing can only weaken but not eliminate that interference. Our research plan is to test audio guidance by building a virtual space with no visual distractions as an experimental environment based on a game engine.

Our research responds to the following research questions:

First, do the sound cues direct the audience's attention to a specific location outside their range of sight?

Second, can the location of the sound cue be visually attended by the viewer after the sound is activated?

Third, how will the viewers change their visual fields when the sound sources vary in horizontal and vertical directions?

Fourth, will different types of sounds impact the viewer's judgment of the sound's location?

2   Method

2.1   Apparatus and Materials

We used the HTC VIVE Pro Eye as the experimental equipment. The game engine, Unreal Engine 4 (UE4), was utilized to design and render the VR environments and sound cues. UE4's Blueprint function allowed the engine to interact well with HMD via Steam VR (see Fig. 1). Moreover, scripting techniques were used for random selection, random generation, and recording of the experimental data.

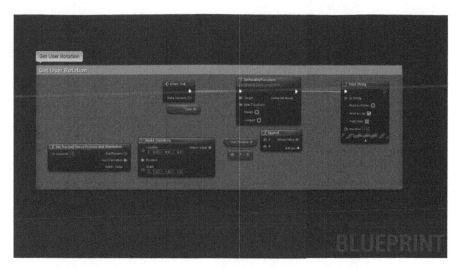

Fig. 1. Blueprint scripting to connect the HMD and get the user's head movement data.

2.2 Participants

We recruited 35 adults who voluntarily enrolled to participate in the experiment. However, due to the withdrawal of 2 participants, the number of participants who finally participated in the experiment was 33. The average age of the participants was 22.7 years old. There were 16 males and 17 females. Before the investigation, all participants answered questions about their conditions of vision, auditory, and direction judgement. None of them reported any defects in those sensory or perceptual functions. All of the participants had signed the consent forms before the experiment.

2.3 Test Scene

The purpose of this study was to explore the guiding effects of sound cues to the viewer's range of sight. To minimize the impact of visual information on the viewer and enhance the reliability of the experimental results, we chose to build a blank virtual room in UE4 as the test scene instead of using off-the-shelf 360 videos. We created a cylindrical virtual room in UE4 with a radius of 5 m and a height of 3.5 m. The wall texture of the cylindrical room was the stripe pattern set by default in the engine. (see Fig. 2 and 3).

The viewing position of the HMD is set at the centre of the room. It is located at 1.25 m above the ground (coordinates 0, 0, 0), which approximated the average height of the eye position in the human sitting position. From the HMD position, each block's size and aspect ratio on the wall in the space is consistent. At the same time, we placed a 0.05 m × 0.05 m red square on the wall directly opposite from the initial position of the HMD as the initial focal guide (coordinates 0, 5, 0, see Fig. 4).

Fig. 2. Overlook the virtual room.

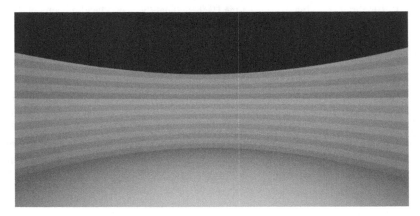

Fig. 3. Inside the virtual room.

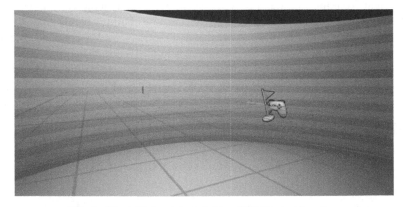

Fig. 4. The initial point of sight and HMD start location.

2.4   Sound Types

Due to the different expressiveness and meaning, sound elements are often more difficult to classify than visual elements [9]. Artists used various methods to organize sound in sound design. The standard classification method divides sound into speech, sound, and music [1, 25]. However, this classification is limited. For example, the methods mentioned by Sander in the article do not distinguish between background sounds and foreground sounds with coherent logic [25]. Foreman considered background and foreground sounds and produced four categories: sound, sound effects (foreground), atmosphere (background), and music [13]. However, this classification only reveals the relative relationship of sound in the scene and does not highlight the difference between sound and sound.

In reality, people use the events associated with sound expressions the actual events [16]. Moreover, in film art, the type to which sound belongs can reflect the expressive potential of the sound [14]. Sonnenschein classified sounds based on their sources and functions [28]. This classification method can promote the perceptual relationship between sound and sound potential and play a role in facilitating auditory information exchange.

The primary function of cinematic storytelling is to add meaning or value to images [18]. Considering this practical significance, we refer to Sonnenschein's classification that coincides better with the different purposes of sound. The sound cues in the experiment were, therefore, divided into five categories: *cultural sounds*, *natural sounds*, *human voices*, *mechanical sounds*, and *signal sounds*.

2.5   Sound Processing

We selected ten different sound clips from each of the five sound categories. Each sound clip was captured by us in the real world with a Sony PCM-D100 audio recorder. To ensure that each audio clip had a similar playback volume, we imported the sound clips into the Digital Audio Workstation (DAW) for further processing. We then used the iZotope Ozone 7 plug-in for noise reduction and de-reverb processing of the audio. PAZ-Meters plug-in was used to examine the final volume of each clip. The maximum volume per audio clip was around −6dB (±0.1dB).

We imported all the processed sounds into the UE4 scene. These sound clips worked as audible cues and needed to be consistent in reaching the human ears. Therefore, we set the playback volume value of all sound cues as '1', the diffusion range as '360°', and the distance as 3.5 m in the spherical area diffusion. All sounds are spatialized; each sound cue would be presented in a binaural manner, which means that when the sound cues appeared in different locations, the changes could be perceived. In the test scene, the duration of each sound lasted 6 s, and the attenuation time was set as the default value given by the UE4 engine. Each piece of audio has a similar direct-to-reverberation-to-energy ratio, with the proportion varying in time. In terms of the location, we control through the Blueprint scripts that generated sound cues randomly at 3 m outside the participant's field of view. (see Fig. 5).

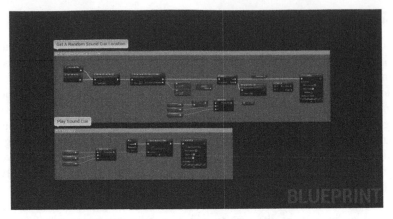

Fig. 5. Blueprint script of random location.

2.6 Experimental Procedures and Data Collection

The participants sat in a chair that could rotate 360° during the experiment. Before each trial, the participants were required to look at the initial focal position (the red square). Each participant was given 1 min prior to the formal trial to familiarize themselves with the virtual environment. When each sound cue was played, the participants determined the location of the sound and moved their heads with the HMD to look directly at the recognized sound location. The same trial process was repeated five times to go through each one of the five sound types. Controlled by a Blueprint script, the system randomly selected one sound clip and played it at a random position outside the participant's sight range. Each time the audio was played, the Blueprint script recorded the sound cue's type and the 3D coordinates. The participants were required to perform positional judgment on each of the five randomly-generated sound cues. Each sound cue was played after the participant had fixated at the initial point to avoid mutual influence between trials.

When the trial started, the Blueprint script would record the type of sound cues and their occurring 3D coordinates in real-time. At the same time, the script would also record the deflection angle of the HMD worn on the participants. The recording frequency is 5 Hz (sampled every 0.2 s). We set up two keys on the computer keyboard to accurately record the deflection angle of the participant's initial and final viewing locations. These two keys helped in placing a marker between the deflection angle data recorded in real-time and labelling the start and final positions, respectively. The researchers pressed the start button to confirm that the participants looked directly at the initial focal point. The researcher pressed the final key after the participant had completed the view movement to the identified sound location (see Fig. 6). The experimental data were then saved in the log file generated by the UE4 engine.

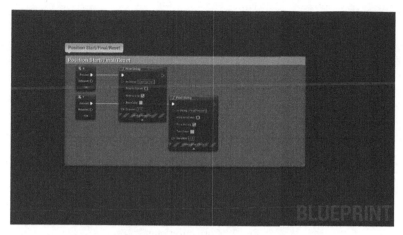

Fig. 6. Blueprint script set "R" for a start, "T" for final.

2.7 Data Processing

We recorded the coordinates of the sound cue in each trial. We then calculated how the participant moved his/her views horizontally and vertically in relation to the initial focal point (red square). By doing this, we obtained the horizontal and vertical displacements between the participant's view location and the sound cue position. The deflection angle was then computed with the inverse-cosine function. The horizontal angular range is between ±180° (use "−" for left and " + " for right), and the vertical angular range is between ± 90° (use " + " for up and "-" for down). The HTC VIVE Pro EYE HMD is known to have a field of view of nearly 106° horizontally and almost 110° vertically [30]. When the horizontal deflection is within 106° (±53°) and the vertical deflection is within 110° (±55°), it is considered as the participant having attended to both horizontally and vertically a visual field that "correctly" cover the sound cue; otherwise it is considered as making either or both the horizontal and vertical errors. All correct results are marked as "1", and the errors are marked as "0".

3 Result

3.1 Correction Rate of Visual Attendance

We have summed up the participants' correction rate at the vertical, the horizontal, and both directions. Note we use "sight range" to represent the participants attending correctly in both directions (see Fig. 7).

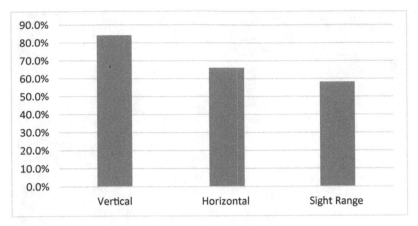

Fig. 7. Correction rate

In Fig. 7, the x-axis is denoted with directions, and the y-axis is the correction rate. The result shows that the rate of the participants correctly judging the location of the sound cue in the vertical direction is 84.2% (139 in 165 valid case data). The correction rate in the horizontal direction is 66.1% (109/165). The participants judged the position of the sound cue correctly in both directions 96 times, and the accuracy rate is 58.2%.

We have tested and found no significant correlation between the deflection angles made by the participants in the horizontal and vertical directions. That is to say, the participants' judgments on the sound cue positions are relatively independent in both directions. We follow the conventions used in statistical analysis [12] and adopt the p-value of 0.05 to determine statistical significance.

In the correlation test between the participant's horizontal deflection angle and the sound cue's horizontal position angle (see Table 1), the Pearson correlation coefficient is 0.425 ($p = 0$, $p < 0.05$). That is, the participant's judgment of the position of the sound cue in the horizontal direction is correlated with their horizontal deflection.

Table 1. Correlations between sound angle and participant angle on the horizontal plane

		Horizontal angel of sound cues	Horizontal turn angle of participants
Horizontal angel of sound cues	Pearson correlation	1	.425
	Sig. (2-tailed)		.000
	N	165	165
Horizontal turn angle of partcipants	Pearson correlation	.425	1
	Sig. (2-tailed)	.000	
	N	165	165

In the correlation test between the vertical deflection angle and the vertical position angle of the sound cue (see Table. 2), the correlation coefficient is 0.021 (p = 0.788, p > 0.05). The result shows that the two data sets do not exhibit a significant correlation. That is, the participants' deflection in the vertical direction is not significantly correlated with their judgment of the vertical position of the sound cue.

Table 2. Correlations between sound angle and participant angle on the vertical plane

		Vertical angel of sound cues	Vertical turn angle of participants
Vertical angel of sound cues	Pearson correlation	1	.021
	Sig. (2-tailed)		.788
	N	165	165
Vertical turn angle of participants	Pearson correlation	.021	1
	Sig. (2-tailed)	.788	
	N	165	165

We are concerned with the displacements of the actual deflection angle produced by the participants' head movements, disregarding the positive (right, up) or negative (left, down) differences. Therefore, we analyze the data of the participant's deflection angle and the sound cue's position angle by taking the absolute value. As shown in Fig. 8, the participants' deflection magnitude as a whole in the vertical direction is more concentrated. The average deflection angle is 4.82°, and the median is 2.31°.

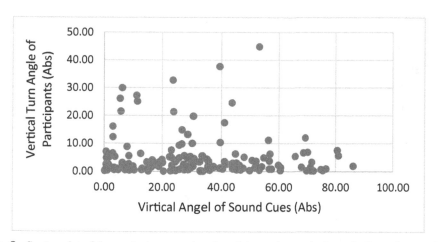

Fig. 8. Scatter plot of the vertical turn angle of participants by vertical angel of sound cues after taking the absolute value

On the other hand, the magnitude of the deflection made horizontally is more scattered. The average deflection angle is 105.09°, and the median is 106.92°.

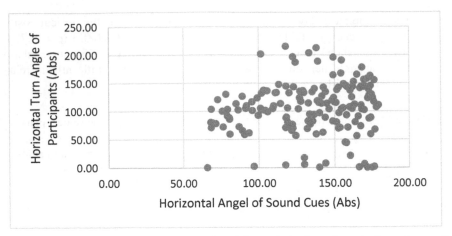

Fig. 9. Scatter plot of horizontal turn angle of participants by horizontal angel of sound cues after taking the absolute value

3.2 Influence of Sound Types

We further analyzed the correction rates by clustering the data with the sound types. Among them, in the vertical direction (see Fig. 10), the highest rate appears when the participants judge the positions of "cultural sound" and "mechanical sound", both of which is 90.9%. The lowest rate appears when they judge the positions of "sound of the signal", which is 72.7%. The inter-group range is 18.2.

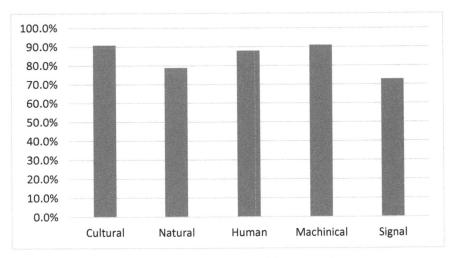

Fig. 10. Vertical correction rate on different sound groups

In terms of horizontal direction (see Fig. 11), the highest rate is of "mechanical sound", 81.8%. The lowest is of "voice of culture", the correction rate is 48.5%. The range is 33.3.

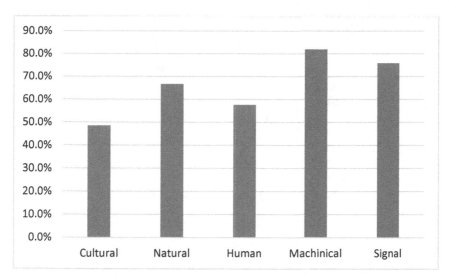

Fig. 11. Horizontal correction rate on different sound groups

To explore whether there are statistically significant differences in the correction rates among the sound types, we performed a correlation test and a chi-square test, respectively. This helps in determining whether the sound types could independently and/or interactively have a significant effect on changing participants' judgments about where the sound cues are located.

In the correlation test between the different sound types and the participants' vertical judgment of the sound cue (see Table. 3), the correlation coefficient is 0.094 ($p = 0.229$, and $p > 0.05$). The result indicates that the sound types are not significantly correlated with participants' vertical judgment. For the horizontal judgment, the correlation coefficient is 0.20 ($p = 0.007$, $p < 0.05$). That is, the participants' horizontal judgment of the sound cue is correlated with the changes of sound types.

Table 3. Correlations among sound groups and horizontal and vertical plane

		Sound groups	Horizontal judgement	Vertical judgement
Sound groups	Pearson correlation	1	.208	−.094
	Sig. (2-tailed)		.007	.229
	N	165	165	165
Horizontal judgement	Pearson correlation	.208	1	.041
	Sig. (2-tailed)	.007		.598
	N	165	165	165
Vertical judgement	Pearson correlation	−.094	.041	1
	Sig. (2-tailed)	.229	.598	
	N	165	165	165

The result of Chi-square analysis (see Table. 4) shows that the difference in sound types does not significantly affect the participant's vertical judgment (p = 0.16, p > 0.05).

Table 4. Chi-square test between Vertical judgement and Sound groups

	Value	def.	Asymptotic significance (2-sided)
Pearson Chi-Square	6.574	4	.160
Likelihood ratio	6.391	4	.172
Linear-by-linear association	1.452	1	.228
N of valid cases	165		

However, for the horizontal judgment (see Table. 5), the result shows that the different sound types do significantly impact the participants' judgment on the horizontal positions of the sound cues (p = 0.031, p < 0.05).

Table 5. Chi-square test between Horizontal judgement and Sound groups

	Value	def.	Asymptotic significance (2-sided)
Pearson Chi-Square	10.650	4	.031
Likelihood ratio	10.846	4	.028
Linear-by-linear association	7.106	1	.008
N of valid cases	165		

4 Discussion

This study evaluates the effect of sound cues and types on a viewer's visual attendance in a CVR scene. According to the results, we found that the sound cues outside the field of view in CVR are feasible for guiding the audience's framing, and the correction rate is generally greater than 50%. Even with minimum visual information provided in the virtual scene, the sound's guiding effect supports the findings in the previous studies [3, 19]. We have also found that such a guiding effect operates more prominently in the horizontal direction. The participants are not equally sensitive to the vertical changes of sound positions. The vertical field of view that the viewer can see in a VR environment is about 110° [30]. And the visual fields generated by vertical head movements usually overlap each other with large portions. So, in general, the viewer does not need to make drastic movements in the vertical direction to locate the sound source. The viewer reacts to the vertical position of the target only when a sound cue is located at an extreme position change from the centre axis [23]. One may regard the design of HMD in the vertical field of view reduces the loss of plot points in the vertical plane when the audience watches VR films. In comparison with the vertical judgment, the field of view in the horizontal direction is only 106°. Therefore, when using sound as the guiding element, the variance in the horizontal position of a sound source will have a significant impact on a viewer's visual attendance to the desired framings.

In addition, by analyzing the influence of different sound types on the participants' visual attendance, we have found that the sound types can significantly affect their judgments. This seems to coincide with the contextual importance of a sound in a film. For example, if there is a related object near the location of the sound, the object becomes salient to the audience [24]. Even though the difference in the guiding effects among sound types needs to be further examined, it seems that in the absence of a relevant object or visual information, different sounds still affect how the viewer moves his/her range of sight.

5 Conclusion

This research is the first step towards understanding how sounds can be used to guide a viewer's active framing in CVR. We have confirmed that a sound cue can attract the viewer from a location outside the field of view in VR environments. However, the appeal of sound to the audience only changes when the position of the sound source changes horizontally. Moreover, the viewer is less sensitive to the vertical changes of the sound cue. Finally, different types of sounds significantly influence the viewers' judgment of sound locations.

Our experiment was conducted in a low-visual information environment, mainly focusing on the attractiveness of sound. In our study, we also proposed a way to measure the participants' responses by adapting the eye-tracking approach. We evaluated differences in deflection angles to replace previous studies that used Euclidean distances. We believe that our approach can align better with the audience's head movements when watching VR films.

In films produced with CVR, visual narratives are still the primary storytelling method. The audience can be attracted by a variety of visual elements when watching the film. The results of our research provide important insights to the relevant practitioners when integrating sounds to facilitate visual narrations. The findings also suggest further research into the interrelationship between different sound cues and how they interactively function with potential visual elements.

References

1. Brandon, A.: Audio for Games: Planning, Process, and Production. (New Riders Games). New Riders Games (2004)
2. Aylett, R., Louchart, S.: Towards a narrative theory of virtual reality. Virtual Reality 7(1), 2–9 (2003)
3. Bala, P., et al.: When the elephant trumps: a comparative study on spatial audio for orientation in 360° videos. In: Conference on Human Factors in Computing Systems - Proceedings (2019)
4. Bhide, S., Goins, E., Geigel, J.: Experimental analysis of spatial sound for storytelling in virtual reality. Lecture notes in computer science, p. 3 (2019)
5. Langkjær, B.: 'Making fictions sound real - On film sound, perceptual realism and genre'. MedieKultur J. Media Commun. Res. 26(48) (2010)
6. Bordwell, D., Thompson, K.: Film Art: An Introduction, 10 ed. McGraw-Hill Education, New York (2012)
7. Sheikh, A., Brown, A., Watson, Z., Evans, M.: Directing attention in 360-degree video. The language of storytelling in immersive experiences. In: IBC 2016 Conference (2016). https://doi.org/10.1049/ibc.2016.0029
8. Cao, R., et al.: 'A preliminary exploration of montage transitions in cinematic virtual reality'. In: 2019 IEEE International Symposium on Mixed and Augmented Reality Adjunct (ISMAR-Adjunct), Mixed and Augmented Reality Adjunct (ISMAR-Adjunct), 2019 IEEE International Symposium on, ISMAR-ADJUNCT, pp. 65–70 (2019)
9. Chion, M, Gorbman, C., Murch, W.: Audio-Vision: Sound on Screen. Columbia University Press, New York (1994)
10. Fearghail, C.O., Ozcinar, C., Knorr, S., Smolic, A.: Director's cut - analysis of aspects of interactive storytelling for VR films. In: Rouse, R., Koenitz, H., Haahr, M. (eds.) ICIDS 2018. LNCS, vol. 11318, pp. 308–322. Springer, Cham (2018). https://doi.org/10.1007/978-3-030-04028-4_34
11. Fearghail, C.O., et al. :'Director's cut-Analysis of VR film cuts for interactive storytelling. In: 2018 International Conference on 3D Immersion, IC3D 2018 – Proceedings (2018)
12. Field, A.: Discovering Statistics Using SPSS. Second edn. Sage Publications Ltd, New York (2005)

13. Huiberts, S., Van Tol, R.: IEZA: a framework for game audio. Gamasutra. The Art & Business of Making Games (2008)
14. Knight-Hill, A.: Sonic Diegesis: reality and the expressive potential of sound in narrative film. Quart. Rev. Film Video **36**(8), 643–665 (2019)
15. Nielsen, L.T., et al.: 'Missing the point : an exploration of how to guide users' attention during cinematic virtual reality', Virtual Reality Software and Technology. (Virtual Reality Software and Technology), pp. 229–232 (2016)
16. Lemaitre, G., Houix, O., Misdariis, N., Susini, P.: Listener expertise and sound identification influence the categorization of environmental sounds. J. Exp. Psychol. Appl. **16**(1), 16–32 (2010)
17. Lescop, L.: 'Narrative grammar in 360'. In: 2017 IEEE International Symposium on Mixed and Augmented Reality (ISMAR-Adjunct), Mixed and Augmented Reality (ISMAR-Adjunct), ISMAR-ADJUNCT, pp. 254–257 (2017)
18. Lund, A.V.: 'Sound and music in narrative multimedia: a macroscopic discussion of audio-visual relations and auditory narrative functions in film, television and video games' (2012)
19. Manolas, C., Pauletto, S.: Designing the stereoscopic 3D media soundscape: an exploration of the perceptual effects of auditory cues alteration on stereoscopic 3D presentations. In: EuroMedia 2019, 12–13 July 2019, Brighton, United Kingdom (2019)
20. Maranes, C., Gutierrez, D., Serrano, A.: 'Exploring the impact of 360° movie cuts in users' attention'. In: Proceedings - 2020 IEEE Conference on Virtual Reality and 3D User Interfaces, VR 2020, pp. 73–82 (2020)
21. Masia, B., et al.: 'Influence of directional sound cues on users exploration across 360 movie cuts. IEEE Comput. Graph. Appl. (2021). https://doi.org/10.1109/MCG.2021.3064688
22. Mateer, J.: Directing for cinematic virtual reality: how the traditional film director's craft applies to immersive environments and notions of presence. J. Media Pract. **18**(1), 14–25 (2017)
23. Roffler, S.K., Butler, R.A., n.d.: 'Factors that influence the localization of sound in the vertical plane'. J. Acoust. Soc. Am. 43(6), pp. 1255–1259
24. Rothe, S., Hu, mann, H.: Guiding the viewer in cinematic virtual reality by diegetic cues. Lecture notes in computer science, p. 101 (2018)
25. Huiberts, S.: Captivating sound the role of audio for immersion in computer games. University of Portsmouth (2010)
26. Knorr, S., et al.: 'Director's cut: a combined dataset for visual attention analysis in cinematic VR content', Visual Media Production. In: International Conference on Visual Media Production, pp. 1–10 (2018)
27. Shafer, D.M., Carbonara, C.P., Korpi, M.F.: Exploring enjoyment of cinematic narratives in virtual reality: a comparison study. Int. J. Virtual Real. **18**(1), 1–18 (2018)
28. Sonnenschein, D., n.d.: Sound design. Studio City: Michael Wiese Productions (2001)
29. Syrett, H, Calvi, L., van Gisbergen, M.: The oculus rift film experience: a case study on understanding films in a head mounted display, vol 178. Lecture Notes of the Institute for Computer Sciences, Social-Informatics and Telecommunications Engineering, LNICST, Springer, Cham (2016). https://doi.org/10.1007/978-3-319-49616-0_19
30. VIVE: Configuration of FOV of HTC VIVE Pro Eye. https://forum.vive.com/topic/8550-configuration-of-fov-of-htc-vive-pro-eye/. Accessed 28 Oct 2021
31. Vosmeer, M., Schouten, B.: Project Orpheus A research study into 360° Cinematic VR. In: Proceedings of the 2017 ACM International Conference on Interactive Experiences for TV and Online Video, pp. 85–90 (2017)
32. Lin, Y.C., et al.: Tell me where to look: investigating ways for assisting focus in 360° Video. In: Human Factors in Computing Systems. (Conference on Human Factors in Computing Systems), pp. 2535–2545 (2017)

Author Index

Printed in the United States
by Baker & Taylor Publisher Services